Community-Based Landslide Risk Reduction

Community-Based Landslide Risk Reduction

Managing Disasters in Small Steps

Malcolm G. Anderson

Elizabeth Holcombe

THE WORLD BANK

Washington, DC

ISBN (paper): 978-0-8213-9456-4
ISBN (electronic): 978-0-8213-9491-5
DOI: 10.1596/978-0-8213-9456-4

Cover photo: © iStockphotocom/luoman; *cover design:* Drew Fasick

Library of Congress Cataloging-in-Publication Data

Anderson, M. G.
 Community-based landslide risk reduction : managing disasters in small steps / Malcolm G. Anderson, Elizabeth Holcombe.
   p. cm.
 Includes bibliographical references and index.
 ISBN 978-0-8213-9456-4 — ISBN 978-0-8213-9491-5 (electronic)
 1. Landslide hazard analysis. 2. Landslides—Risk assessment. I. Holcombe, Elizabeth. II. Title.
 QE599.2.A53 2013 363.34'9—dc23
                                        2012030220

Contents

FIGURES

TABLES

Preface

ABOUT MOSSAIC

MoSSaiC (Management of Slope Stability in Communities) is an integrated method for engaging policy makers, project managers, practitioners, and vulnerable communities in reducing urban landslide risk in developing countries.

MoSSaiC was begun with the idea of combining research, policy, and humanitarian interests to address rainfall-triggered landslide hazards through community-based implementation of surface water management measures in vulnerable urban communities. The vision was to lay sustainable foundations for community-based landslide risk reduction.

This vision was driven by the following premises:

- *Disaster risk mitigation pays*, and investment in reducing rainfall-triggered landslide hazards in vulnerable communities can often be justified.

- *Engaging existing government expertise* for implementing risk reduction measures can build capacity, embed good practice, and change policy.

- *Ensuring community engagement* from start to finish can establish ownership of solutions.

To achieve the vision and demonstrate the validity of these premises, three foundations need to be established: the *scientific base*, the *community base*, and the *evidence base* for landslide risk reduction in this setting.

1. From a *scientific* standpoint, the root causes of many landslides in urban communities are aggravated by human activities that can addressed in relatively simple and practical ways. A commonly observed situation is the negative effect of poor drainage on the stability of slopes comprised of weathered materials. This situation can often be remedied through the construction of a strategically aligned network of surface drains. Intercepting and conveying surface water runoff, household gray water, and roof runoff to ravines and main drains can significantly improve the stability of such slopes.

2. *Community* residents have detailed knowledge of the slopes in their immediate vicinity—where there have been minor landslides, where surface water runs, how the topography and vegetation have been changed. This information on slope features is frequently the scale at which landslide-triggering processes operate and the scale at which solutions can be found. Vulnerable communities are also where there is the greatest need for short-term employ-

ment (in constructing landslide mitigation measures) and for embedding good slope management practices. Generally, governments have sufficient technical and managerial skills that can be harnessed to design and deliver appropriate landslide risk reduction measures in communities. By creating a cross-disciplinary management unit from such a skill base, it is possible to embed MoSSaiC in government practice and policy.

3. An *evidence base* for the effectiveness of such targeted landslide risk reduction measures was needed. MoSSaiC was started small, with a pilot intervention in one community, a catalytic advocate in government, and a small team of in-house project managers and practitioners. On the evidence of its success, further government funding and demand for more interventions followed. This evidence was in the form of finished construction works, improved stability of slopes, community endorsement and ownership of the project, and demonstration of the combined skills of the government team. Savings in terms of avoided losses to the community and costs to the government were also estimated. Decision makers require such evidence in order to endorse expenditure on landslide risk reduction and to adopt ex ante policies.

CONTEXT FOR MoSSaiC

The MoSSaiC approach was researched and developed in a selection of Eastern Caribbean small island developing states with the support and funding of governments and international development agencies. Implementation of the hazard reduction measures was undertaken by government agencies and community residents in conjunction with contractors from the community.

This book offers a flexible blueprint for countries that want to use the MoSSaiC approach to reduce landslide risk in communi-

ties. It provides guidance on how to implement MoSSaiC, evidence of what has worked (and of potential risks and challenges), and guidance on options that should be considered to make it work within a specific country. It may be necessary to adapt the methodology for environments outside the Eastern Caribbean—in terms of both general approach and specific implementation—to take into account local landslide risk conditions and institutional contexts.

This is not intended to be a book detailing construction methods. Specific solutions are not offered; rather the book presents a summary of our experience, observations, and research. In that regard, two broad issues deserve emphasis: ensuring the long-term feasibility of the approach, and being sensitive to the scale and extent of the landslide risk problem.

- To ensure long-term sustainability of MoSSaiC projects requires the identification of localized landslide-triggering processes. The structural cause of landslide risk in many vulnerable urban communities is the absence of regulation regarding construction, infrastructure, and land use, resulting in increased exposure to landslides and increased landslide hazard. Changes in the natural stability conditions of slopes are mainly a consequence of changes in natural slope form, drainage, loading, and surface cover. In urban settings, the dominant destabilizing factors can often be attributed to insufficient drainage and sanitation infrastructure, cutting and filling of slope material, removal of vegetation, and high-density construction of houses. Therefore, from a public policy perspective, landslide risk management is strongly linked to the feasibility of addressing these unauthorized conditions in a politically, financially, and technically coordinated manner. If a coordinated strategy is adopted, the appropriate community-based landslide mitigation works can be implemented in accord with other policies to address both the immediate and underlying causes of the landslide risk. However, if an ad hoc approach to landslide mitigation is taken, the root causes of the landslide problem may remain. This can result in inefficient, unsustainable projects that create a false sense of security, provide incentives for new unauthorized occupation, bring conflicts into communities and/or with the government, and potentially lose any short-term landslide risk reduction benefits over the medium and long term.

- There are large numbers of cities in the humid tropics with very similar problems, but that are very different in terms of the spatial scale to which MoSSaiC projects have, to date, been implemented. The same problem (vulnerable communities at risk from landslides) in medium or large cities is likely to require that the approach to landslide mitigation be adjusted to reflect broader issues. For instance, in larger cities (those whose populations exceed 1 million), disaster risk management policies are typically more complex and demand strategic integration and consideration in the context of wider development policies. This does not mean that communities do not play a key role in delivering the solution, but rather that their vision and understanding of landslide risk are not unique elements in the process.

Success of community-based disaster risk management programs is conditioned by local cultural and social systems. Arguably this is best undertaken through careful learning by doing, as opposed to a wholesale application of best practices from projects that were successful in other contexts (Mansuri and Rao 2003).

ABOUT THIS BOOK

This book has two main aims:

- To demonstrate to international development agencies, governments, policy makers, project managers, practitioners, and community residents that landslide hazard

can often be reduced in vulnerable urban communities in the developing world

- To provide practical guidance for those in charge of delivering MoSSaiC on the ground.

In reflecting on and seeking to communicate our experience of landslide hazard mitigation, this is neither a conventional policy book nor an explicit field manual.

The purpose of the book is to take readers into the most vulnerable communities in order to understand and address rainfall-triggered landslide hazards in these areas. Community residents are not just seen as those at risk, but as the people with the best practical knowledge of the slopes in their neighborhood. As used here, "community based" means engaging and working with communities to find and deliver solutions to landslide risk together. This approach leads governments to develop new practices and policies for tackling landslide risk.

The book is directed at those responsible for initiating, delivering, and sustaining MoSSaiC in a particular country or city:

- **Funders and policy makers**, typically government officials and international development agency staff

- **MoSSaiC core unit (MCU) personnel** (MoSSaiC project managers), typically senior government personnel responsible for managing government agencies, departments, or projects; and leading local experts in disaster risk management, landslide hazard assessment, and community development

- **Government task teams**, comprising experts and practitioners responsible for designing and implementing physical works or directly coordinating with communities; these are typically engineers, community development workers, and technical staff

- **Community task teams** with responsibilities at the community level; these are typically comprised of community residents, community representatives, and community-based contractors.

In addressing these four audiences, the book is intended to

- assist in securing the political will to undertake community-based landslide risk reduction,
- illustrate how that objective might be realized by engaging the community,
- provide a scientific grounding in landslide hazard processes and solutions,
- demonstrate the steps involved in on-the-ground delivery, and
- emphasize the importance of evaluating project outcomes.

To these ends, the book contains several standard sections in each chapter:

- The *"Getting started" section* is aimed at helping the reader quickly and clearly understand the chapter's rationale and how to apply MoSSaiC to the local context.
- *Guiding principles* associated with each of the major activities of the program help the policy maker, project manager, or practitioner advocate for the methodology with stakeholders and demonstrate the central role played by community residents.
- The *capacity assessment exercise* (chapters 2–9) enables the MoSSaiC blueprint to be adapted depending on institutional structures, protocols, strengths, and weaknesses; the nature of the communities; local construction practices; and the degree to which the local context allows replication of MoSSaiC.

This book standardizes those elements of MoSSaiC that have led to its successful implementation in the Eastern Caribbean, and that are essential to the overall objectives (such as community engagement, mapping localized slope features, and broad drainage design principles). In providing a flexible blueprint for MoSSaiC, this book aims to balance the respective benefits of low and high levels of process standardization:

- Low levels of standardization can promote motivation of those charged with delivering the project and adaptation to local issues, but can jeopardize the consistency and quality of risk reduction measures.
- High levels of standardization can promote high levels of quality and speed of delivery, but can suppress innovation and lead to inflexibility in the local context.

ORGANIZATION AND CONTENTS OF THIS BOOK

The book's nine chapters provide guidance to project managers and practitioners on the entire end-to-end process of community-based landslide risk reduction. While certain chapters are more directly relevant to one audience than another, it is helpful for all audiences to read the "Getting started" section of each chapter and be alerted to the nine project milestones. The shared knowledge of milestones assists in achieving project ownership and encourages the likelihood of successful project continuity, implementation, and post-project outcome assessment.

Policy makers and MoSSaiC project managers should note that chapters 1 (MoSSaiC foundations), 2 (project inception), 4 (community selection), and 9 (project evaluation) give guidance in areas that predominantly fall within the remit of policy makers to ensure the existence of a suitable framework. However, it may fall to project managers to alert the relevant policy maker if local policies are incomplete or require refinement in order to fully allow project implementation.

An overview of the book follows.

Chapter 1. Foundations: Reducing Landslide Risk in Communities

The more socially, economically, and physically vulnerable people are, the more disastrous a landslide event will be. While there is growing recognition of the increased occurrence of natural disasters, there is equal recognition of the lack of on-the-ground implementation of ex ante landslide risk reduction measures.

This chapter provides an introduction to the MoSSaiC approach, which is focused on delivering landslide risk reduction measures in vulnerable urban communities in developing countries. Specifically, MoSSaiC identifies and, where appropriate, addresses some of the physical causes of landslide hazard.

The chapter's aim is to both inform the reader of the context within which the MoSSaiC approach is designed to work and to impart something of the vision behind the approach. The message is that the rainfall-triggered landslide hazard faced by the poorest urban communities can often be reduced using relatively simple measures—namely, the construction of surface drains in appropriate locations. This can be achieved if there is cooperation between government technicians and community residents; hands-on application of science and local knowledge; and proactive support from managers, politicians, and donor agencies.

In introducing MoSSaiC, the chapter provides the following:

- A framework for understanding disaster risk and, more specifically, landslide risk

- An overview of trends and lessons learned in disaster risk management

- Advocacy for taking a proactive approach to tackling landslide risk in communities

- An introduction to MoSSaiC and who should be involved

- An overview of how to start a MoSSaiC landslide risk reduction project.

This chapter should be read by all stakeholders and should be used by practitioners, project managers, and policy makers alike when explaining the project basis and advocating the MoSSaiC methodology.

Milestone 1: Key catalytic staff briefed on MoSSaiC methodology

Chapter 2. Project Inception: Teams and Steps

This chapter provides guidelines for the formation of the MCU which will manage the project, and of the task teams of practitioners who will be responsible for project implementation. The typical project steps, roles, and responsibilities are illustrated. While this process of configuring the teams and project steps may be led by policy makers, established project managers and expert practitioners may provide significant assistance.

To achieve the MoSSaiC vision of laying sustainable foundations for community-based landslide risk reduction, project managers will need to

- build local capacity in the broad area of landslide hazard reduction while seeking cost-effective solutions;

- identify community projects that can be undertaken by existing government-based staff and local communities; and

- establish team structures to deliver the vision: an MCU that can develop and communicate the vision, and task teams to develop project strategies and implement specific project steps.

To deliver landslide risk reduction measures in vulnerable communities requires the coordination of a diverse team including community residents, field and mapping technicians, landslide experts, engineers, contractors, and social development practitioners. This calls for a strong multidisciplinary MCU to configure and manage specific project steps, roles, and responsibilities.

Milestone 2: MoSSaiC core unit formed; key responsibilities agreed on and defined

Chapter 3. Understanding Landslide Hazard

This chapter provides project managers and practitioners with an introduction to landslide processes and illustrates ways of analyzing landslide hazard. A core feature of the MoSSaiC approach is that it seeks to ensure that all those participating in the program have as clear an understanding of the fundamental science of landslide processes as possible. Shared technical understanding encourages ownership of landslide mitigation solutions by both government and community.

The first step in the management of landslide risk is to define the scope of the project and correctly identify the form of the landslide risk. The landslide risk reduction and management process will only be successful if landslides are understood in terms of their underlying mechanisms and triggers.

Understanding landslide processes and potential triggering mechanisms

- ensures that any landslide risk assessment is scientifically informed,

- ensures that any proposed landslide hazard management strategies are appropriate to the specific local landslide hazard,

- determines if a MoSSaiC-style drainage intervention will actually address the landslide hazard,

- increases the ability of those implementing the project to justify the landslide hazard reduction measures,

- helps build confidence within the community that the fundamental causes of the landslide hazard are being tackled, and

- encourages a holistic and strategic approach to delivering effective landslide hazard reduction measures.

The content of this chapter is designed to be accessible to policy makers, project managers, practitioners, community contractors, and community members; however, it is likely to be project managers and expert practitioners who take the lead in communicating the science.

Milestone 3: Presentation made to MoSSaiC teams on landslide processes and slope stability software

Chapter 4. Selecting Communities

This chapter describes the community selection process and provides a framework for identifying areas where slopes are susceptible to landslides, the exposure and vulnerability of communities to these potential landslide events, and hence the overall landslide risk. The aim is to develop a prioritized list of communities for the implementation of landslide hazard reduction measures using the MoSSaiC approach.

Policy makers and project managers need to coordinate on community selection to ensure that there is a transparent process the MCU can endorse. Failure in this regard can lead to unintended consequences such as nonselected communities seeking political redress, vocal individuals being given a platform to promote related agendas, and in extreme cases, the demotivation of the MCU due to the lack of a robust decision-making process. This chapter is designed to help the MCU avoid these issues to the extent possible.

The sophistication of the methods used will depend on local data and software availability, and the level of expertise of the government task team involved. Practitioners with knowledge of local landslide issues, of digital mapping methods, or of assessing community vulnerability will be able to provide valuable guidance in this task. The outputs could range from a simple prioritized list of communities to a detailed landslide risk map for a region or country. Whatever the method used, community selection should be justifiable in terms of the science and rationale underpinning the landslide susceptibility assessment and vulnerability of the communities.

After the communities have been selected, the mapping task team seeks to assemble the most detailed maps available for these communities. These maps form the basis for the community-based landslide hazard and drainage mapping exercise described in chapter 5.

Milestone 4: Process for community selection agreed upon and communities selected

Chapter 5. Community-Based Mapping for Landslide Hazard Assessment

This chapter provides guidance on the community-based process to map localized slope stability features and identify the dominant causes of the landslide hazard in different zones of the slope. This is a central chapter for project managers and practitioners in the fields of mapping, community development, and engineering. The construction of such a community slope feature map and subsequent slope process zone map is the basis for assessing whether interventions that manage surface water would be likely to reduce the landslide hazard. Quantitative methods are introduced that can be used to investigate the physical slope stability processes and confirm the landslide hazard and effective solutions. The final stage described in this chapter is the production of an initial drainage plan and intervention prioritization matrix for the community.

Community members need to be fully engaged in the mapping process, not just as providers of the information, but as active participants in the development of the maps. The motivation for community member engagement at this level will vary locally. In some cases, there will already be formal community groups able to mobilize the rest of the community; in others, policy makers and project managers may need to take a much more active role in establishing suitable frameworks and approaches to facilitate community engagement.

The contents of this chapter are primarily directed to the project manager and those team members with engineering or other technical expertise; however, it is expected that key community members would use this chapter to develop local awareness of urban landslide processes and acquire landslide hazard mapping skills.

The chapter emphasizes that community-based slope stability mapping is a central element of the MoSSaiC program. As such, it is important that the project manager, in particular, ensures that all residents participate in the mapping process. This helps create community ownership and gives recognition to the fact that residents can be involved in the immediate solutions to landslide risk and longer-term improvement in slope management practices.

Milestone 5: Sign-off on prioritized zones and initial drainage plan

Chapter 6. Design and Good Practice for Slope Drainage

This chapter is concerned with the detailed design of drains and other surface water management strategies in communities where surface water has been identified as the main contributor to landslide hazard. The aim is to design an integrated drainage intervention plan against a fixed budget that has been approved by all stakeholders.

The products of the community-based mapping process detailed in chapter 5 are a community slope feature map, a slope process zone map identifying relative landslide hazard, and an initial drainage plan. Having identified surface water management as an appropriate measure for landslide hazard reduction, government engineers and technicians should find the steps outlined in this chapter helpful in developing the final drain alignments and detailed construction specifications.

Project managers and engineers will find useful resources and methods for estimating surface water and household water discharge into drains, designing the alignment and dimensions of drains, and estimating construction costs.

Milestone 6: Sign-off on final drainage plan

Chapter 7. Implementing the Planned Works

This chapter outlines the major issues to be addressed when undertaking drain construction. The aim is to provide guidance on the contracting process (tendering and letting of contracts to community contractors), construction (implementing the works and good construction practice), and the need to achieve high quality in both (supervision of works is central to project success). Project managers and practitioners in charge of construction should use and adapt these resources to local practices and standards and ensure good-quality works.

The proposed drainage plan agreed upon in chapter 6 is the document that forms the basis for all the activities relating to the construction and delivery of the intervention outlined in this chapter.

The construction phase of the project is of particular interest to policy makers, project managers, practitioners, community members, and the media. It is the point of project delivery as far as construction of landslide hazard reduction measures is concerned. Seeing that this process is successfully managed within time and budgetary constraints not only maximizes the likelihood of sound construction but also lays the foundation for community ownership postcompletion. A successfully managed project enhances the likelihood of the community becoming a powerful advocate for additional interventions and of influencing future policy. Poor construction and subsequent rejection of the intervention by the community has the reverse effect—and the potential of making landslide and flooding issues worse. This chapter provides guidance on how to run the implementation process in recognition of these potential challenges.

Milestone 7: Sign-off on completed construction

Chapter 8. Encouraging Behavioral Change

This chapter is concerned with developing communication and capacity-building strategies that encourage the adoption of good landslide hazard reduction practices and policies by communities and governments.

The strategies that work best are likely to be highly dependent on local situations. The aim of this chapter is to review behavior change processes and principles, and potential communication and capacity-building methods, in order to guide the development of locally relevant strategies. This chapter gives an indication of some such approaches that have been used for MoSSaiC programs.

Guidance is provided on who should be told what and when—identifying and understanding project audiences, developing appropriate project messages, and using different forms of communication. Formal and informal dialogue and community participation are emphasized as the basis for communication throughout the project. Ways of building local capacity are identified for different stakeholder groups, and learning by doing is highlighted as a fundamental part of the MoSSaiC capacity-building process.

Milestone 8: Communication and capacity-building strategies agreed upon and implemented

Chapter 9. Project Evaluation

This chapter stresses the importance of evaluating project outputs and outcomes. It provides a rationale for undertaking an evaluation and a blueprint for an evaluation strategy.

Monitoring and evaluation are widely spoken of in the context of project management, yet in many disaster risk reduction initiatives adequate baseline data are not collected. Consequently, it can be difficult to find adequate measures of success on which a project may be evaluated after just two or three years postproject. This in turn gives rise to the recognition that longer-term project impact evaluations are rarely, if ever, instigated (Benson and Twigg 2004). Landslide risk reduction evidence faces the challenge of counterfactual analysis—how to demonstrate conclusively what would have happened if a different action had been taken.

The MCU should therefore understand and communicate the following:

- The need to secure relevant data both during and after the project to support project impact

- How the immediate benefits (outputs) and longer-term benefits (outcomes) relate to the overall program objectives

- That delivering effective landslide hazard reduction measures provides evidence that ex ante landslide risk reduction can both work and pay.

This evidence base is important if the perceptions, practices, and policies of individuals, governments, and international funding agencies are to be changed regarding community-based landslide risk reduction.

Milestone 9: Evaluation framework agreed upon and implemented

HOW TO USE THIS BOOK

Note to funders and policy makers

It is important to provide a context when advocating for policy change. Globally, the amount of aid given to the developing world is increasing and represents only a small fraction of that needed with regard to natural disasters (Mills 2004)—the number of which continues to rise despite efforts to date. Mitigation measures are widely recommended but rarely implemented (Holmes 2008) because the benefits are not tangible; they are disasters that did not happen. Not surprisingly, there is clear evidence of the continued accumulation of urban disaster risk (Bull-Kamanga et al. 2003), driven largely by the speed of societal change, as the vulnerable move to urban areas, the hillsides of which are so often already prone to landslides. Thus, as Yunus (2011) comments, "The more time spent with poor people, the more one realizes that their circumstances are dictated by the systems society has constructed."

As a funder or policy maker, you should anticipate various stakeholder interests arising within community-based interventions. Issues that might need to be reconciled include political priorities, seeking objectivity in community selection, landowner interests, and

governance of the MoSSaiC project management structure.

You may be responsible for working with MoSSaiC project managers and managing their reporting line to the government. This book provides guidance on how to undertake that process, evidence of what has worked, and information on options to consider.

Of the entire delivery process, chapters 1 (MoSSaiC foundations), 2 (project inception), 4 (community selection), and 9 (project evaluation) are perhaps the most significant in policy terms. They represent areas that demand clear policy frameworks within which the more technical aspects of mitigation measure delivery can be undertaken. Lack of clarity in these areas can lead to inefficiency, delay, and failure to align stakeholder expectations.

Funders and policy makers play a key role in promoting structures that guide the transfer of project funds to the relevant implementing and community agencies in an efficient and timely manner. Project funds are finite, and governments can therefore fund only limited construction efforts. Funders and policy makers can seek to ensure that policies are in place to harmonize disaster risk reduction expenditure arising from different sources within a single community.

Funders and policy makers can encourage the use of this book within government and by other national agencies, nongovernmental organizations, and civil society organizations to communicate the vision of community-based landslide risk reduction and to encourage feedback so as to further refine the approach and provide additional content. You thus have an important role in creating a culture of commitment and delivery efficiency, and ultimately in driving changes in ex ante landslide risk mitigation practice and policy.

Note to the MoSSaiC core unit

The MoSSaiC process begins with a series of decisions that have to be made almost immediately to configure the MCU (the project management team). MCU personnel typically comprise senior government personnel responsible for managing government agencies, departments, or projects; and/or with expertise in a particular field such as disaster risk management, landslide hazard assessment, engineering, or community development.

Your role as a MoSSaiC project manager or expert advisor means that you should be familiar with the entire contents of this book. You will be responsible for implementing the policy decisions and for ensuring delivery of the appropriate measures on the ground in communities. You will need to apply the resources in this book according to local factors.

Replication should not be considered an automatic process. Sometimes things work for idiosyncratic reasons—a charismatic and literally irreplaceable leader or a particular and unrepeatable crisis that solidifies support for a politically difficult innovation. One-time successes thus may not be replicable (World Bank 2004, 108).

This book explains the project steps, teams, and supervision levels that are necessary to deliver appropriate construction of hazard reduction measures on the ground. It emphasizes the importance of basing the entire program in the community. It provides a logical description of how to configure teams and design physical measures to reduce landslide hazard in vulnerable communities. The book does not tell you exactly what to do, but it should improve the likelihood of good project outcomes and of delivering a strategic and holistic community-based landslide risk reduction program. Managing and delivering community-based projects is hard work, but working with the community empowers both residents and government teams to contribute their knowledge and skills.

Note to government task teams

Government task teams (typically government engineers, community development workers, and technical staff) are responsible for specific tasks related to implementing physical works on the ground or directly coordinating with communities.

If you are a task team leader, you will need to work closely with the MCU to adapt each project step according to local capacity, ensure that the tasks required to complete each step are appropriately assigned to a task team, and identify and build your team. As a practitioner—and since this book is a blueprint—you will be responsible for capturing and incorporating local good practice insofar as it relates to your area of expertise and the MoSSaiC methodology. Under the guidance of the MCU, you will be responsible for implementing specific project steps and tasks, and for ensuring delivery of the appropriate landslide mitigation measures on the ground in communities.

Note to community task teams

Community task teams comprise community residents and those with responsibilities at the community level, such as community representatives and community-based contractors.

Community residents are the most critical partners in the program; they are

- participants in the entire process,

- those to whom the initiative is directed,

- those who will "own" the implementation long after construction has finished,

- an important source of knowledge of local slope stability and drainage features in the community, and

- catalytic in making the project happen.

Each chapter begins with a "Getting started" section; these are intended to provide an accessible overview to allow communities to understand key project concepts. If you are a community representative, you may find it helpful to read these in depth. Other particularly relevant book sections to refer to are chapter 5, which describes the community-based mapping process; and chapter 8, which provides guidance on formal and informal community meetings, written and visual resources (e.g., leaflets and posters), and the use of the media. You will need to work with the government task teams to understand and communicate important project messages to community residents and facilitate their participation. You should also help the government task teams understand the community context.

If you are a construction contractor or a worker living in a community where MoSSaiC is being implemented, you will have specialist local knowledge that is vital to the success of the project. You may have useful information to share during the community-based mapping process. You may also have the opportunity to use your skills in the design and construction of landslide mitigation measures (see sections 6.4 and 6.5 on drain design, and sections 7.5–7.8 on good drain construction practices).

Helpful questions

Table P.1 presents some typical questions about MoSSaiC and where guidance can be found in this book.

TABLE P.1 Critical questions and decisions addressed in this book

CRITICAL QUESTION/DECISION	WHERE TO LOOK FOR HELP
Why should landslide risk reduction be community based?	Chapter 1. Foundations: Reducing Landslide Risk in Communities
What are the unique features of the MoSSaiC approach?	
Where can MoSSaiC be applied?	
What teams are needed?	Chapter 2. Project Inception: Teams and Steps
What are the project steps?	
What are the roles and responsibilities of the teams?	
What forms of slope failure does the MoSSaiC approach address?	Chapter 3. Understanding Landslide Hazard
What is the relevant spatial scale for MoSSaiC interventions?	
How is landslide hazard assessed?	
How can the most landslide-prone areas be identified?	Chapter 4. Selecting Communities
How can the most vulnerable communities be identified?	
How are communities selected for a MoSSaiC intervention?	
How can landslide hazard be mapped in a community?	Chapter 5. Community-Based Mapping for Landslide Hazard Assessment
How effective will surface water management be in reducing the landslide hazard?	
How is the initial drainage plan developed?	
Where should drains be built to improve slope stability?	Chapter 6. Design and Good Practice for Slope Drainage
How can surface water runoff, household gray water discharge, and required drain sizes be estimated?	
What are the most appropriate types of drain design and construction?	
What construction practices should be promoted?	Chapter 7. Implementing the Planned Works
Why is site supervision so important?	
How do communities and governments adopt new landslide mitigation practices and policies?	Chapter 8. Encouraging Behavioral Change
What are the components of a communication strategy?	
What are the components of a capacity-building strategy?	
How can landslide risk reduction measures be evaluated?	Chapter 9. Project Evaluation
What are the MoSSaiC key performance indicators?	
What evidence is needed to support ex ante landslide mitigation policies?	
Where can additional resources be found?	At the end of each chapter

REFERENCES

Benson, C., and J. Twigg. 2004. "Measuring Mitigation Methodologies for Assessing Natural Hazard Risks and the Net Benefits of Mitigation—A Scoping Study." ProVention Consortium, Geneva.

Bull-Kamanga, L., K. Diagne, A. Lavell, E. Leon, F. Lerise, H. MacGregor, A. Maskrey, M. Meshack, M. Pelling, H. Reid, D. Satterthwaite, J. Songsore, K. Westgate, and A. Yitambe. 2003. "From Everyday Hazards to Disasters: The Accumulation of Risk in Urban Areas." *Environment and Urbanization* 15 (1): 193–203.

Holmes, J. 2008. "More Help Now Please." *The Economist* November 19.

Mansuri, G., and V. Rao. 2003. *Evaluating Community-Based and Community-Driven Development: A Critical Review of the Evidence.* Development Research Group. Washington, DC: World Bank.

Mills, E. 2004. "Insurance in a Climate of Change." *Science* 309 (5737): 1040–44.

——. 2004. *Making Services Work for Poor People. World Development Report.* Washington, DC: World Bank.

Yunus, M. 2011. Blog post August 28. https://plus.google.com/114848435876861502546/posts/9SwwVFedo9P.

Acknowledgments

This book was written while the authors were working in the Latin America and the Caribbean Disaster Risk Management team at the World Bank, Washington, D.C. Colleagues in that team deserve our thanks for supporting and resourcing our continued commitment to deliver MoSSaiC (Management of Slope Stability in Communities) to communities more widely in the region and beyond.

In particular, we thank Francis Ghesquiere and Niels Holm-Nielsen for their continued support of initiatives that led to this book. Discussions with other World Bank team members, including Joaquin Toro, Maricarman Esquivel, Tiguist Fisseha, and Rossella Della Monica were enormously helpful throughout.

Review comments received from colleagues in the Latin America and the Caribbean Region's Disaster Risk Management and Urban Unit and Water Supply and Sanitation Unit at the World Bank, Washington, D.C., Kirk Frankson (Office of Disaster Preparedness and Emergency Management, Jamaica), Chamberlain Emmanuel (government of St. Lucia), Abhas K. Jha (East Asia and Pacific Infrastructure Unit, World Bank) and M. Yaa Pokua Afriyie Oppong (Social Development Department, World Bank), as part of the World Bank review process chaired by Francis Ghesquiere, are acknowledged with grateful thanks.

The Office of the Publisher provided editorial, design, composition, and printing services under the supervision of Patricia Katayama, Andrés Meneses, and Dina Towbin; and Nita Congress undertook copyediting, typesetting, and proofreading of the manuscript.

This book is based on a community-focused approach and has involved the authors spending many months working in communities with residents who are among the most vulnerable. We are grateful to members of communities in Bequia, Dominica, St. Lucia, and St. Vincent and the Grenadines with whom we have spent so much time, and from whom we have learned so much. We especially acknowledge the support and friendship of Robert Charles, McArthur Edwards, and Ruben Leon in St. Lucia.

Our vision for MoSSaiC would not have been realized had it not received support from Calixte George, Ignatius Jean, and Kenny Anthony as then-members of the government of St. Lucia. Equally accepting of the vision, Donovan Williams, then-Director of the Poverty Reduction Fund in St. Lucia, facilitated us in undertaking a pilot program in St. Lucia. This support was continued by his successor, Joachim Henry. We acknowledge with thanks the technical support for program delivery we have received from government of St. Lucia personnel: David Alphonse, Chamberlain Emmanuel, Peter Gustave, and Cheryl Mathurin. Within the Eastern Caribbean subregion, David Popo of the Organisation of Eastern Caribbean States helped facilitate pilot projects in Dominica and St. Vincent and the Grenadines.

During our time working overseas in communities and in writing this book in Washington, D.C., and Bristol, United Kingdom, we received support from many colleagues at the University of Bristol, especially Neil Bradshaw and Eric Thomas.

Funding for the work undertaken by the authors that provided the context for much of this book was provided by the World Bank, the governments of St. Lucia and Dominica, the United Nations Development Programme, the U.S. Agency for International Development, the University of Bristol, SETsquared Partnership UK, and the British High Commission, St. Lucia.

About the Authors

Malcolm Anderson is Visiting Fellow at Brasenose College and Visiting Professor of Hydrology at the University of Oxford, a Senior Landslide Risk Management Specialist Consultant in the World Bank's Latin America and the Caribbean Disaster Risk Management Team in Washington, D.C., and Professor at the University of Bristol, United Kingdom, where he was Pro Vice-Chancellor (Research) from 2005 to 2009. He holds a PhD from the University of Cambridge, and was elected to a Research Fellowship at Sidney Sussex College, Cambridge. He is the author of over 200 papers, as well as of industry standard software, and Founder and Editor-in-Chief of the journal *Hydrological Processes*. He has worked on many government research projects worldwide, principally in the Far East (Hong Kong SAR, China; Indonesia; and Malaysia), the United States, and the Caribbean. He is an elected Fellow of the Institution of Civil Engineers, London, and was a Council Member of the U.K. Natural Environment Research Council (2001–07), and a Board Member of the U.K. Engineering and Physical Sciences Research Council's Technology Strategy Board (2009–11).

Elizabeth Holcombe holds a PhD and an MSci from the University of Bristol, where she is a Lecturer in Civil Engineering. She is a Landslide Risk Management Specialist Consultant in the World Bank's Latin America and the Caribbean Disaster Risk Management Team in Washington, D.C. Her background is in environmental science and the numerical modeling of hillslope hydrology and stability. She has had extensive overseas experience in research, project management, and implementation of landslide risk reduction projects in vulnerable communities in the Eastern Caribbean. She has presented invited papers at international conferences in the Caribbean, Europe, and the Far East, and is the author of numerous papers and book chapters in the field of landslide risk reduction. Her research on MoSSaiC was highlighted in the 2010 *World Development Report* and profiled at the Aid Effectiveness Showcase hosted at the World Bank in 2011. She received the 2007 Trevithick Award from the Institution of Civil Engineers, London, and managed the team that was awarded the Grand Prize at the 2010 Random Hacks of Kindness hackathon in Washington, D.C.

Abbreviations

cf	cubic foot
CHASM	Combined Hydrology and Slope Stability Model
DRM	disaster risk management
DRR	disaster risk reduction
ft	foot
gal	gallon
GDP	gross domestic product
GIS	geographic information system
GPS	global positioning system
h	hour
in	inch
km	kilometer
kPa	kilopascal
KPI	key performance indicator
L	liter
m	meter
MCU	MoSSaiC core unit
min	minute
mm	millimeter
MoSSaiC	Management of Slope Stability in Communities
NGO	nongovernmental organization
RFT	request for tender
SAR	special administrative region
s	second
SIDS	small island developing states
UN	United Nations

All dollar amounts are U.S. dollars unless otherwise indicated.

"We're still to some extent sleepwalking our way into disasters for the future which we know are going to happen, and not enough is being done to mitigate the damage."

—John Holmes, UN Under-Secretary-General for Humanitarian Affairs (Lynn 2009)

CHAPTER 1

Foundations: Reducing Landslide Risk in Communities

1.1 KEY CHAPTER ELEMENTS

1.1.1 Coverage

This chapter outlines the foundations for delivery of MoSSaiC (Management of Slope Stability in Communities) landslide risk reduction measures in vulnerable communities. The listed groups should read the indicated chapter sections.

AUDIENCE				LEARNING	CHAPTER SECTION
F	M	G	C		
✓	✓	✓	✓	MoSSaiC vision and rationale	1.2
✓	✓	✓		Trends in disaster and landslide risk; components of disaster risk management	1.3
✓	✓	✓		MoSSaiC foundations: scientific basis, community base, and evidence base	1.4
✓	✓	✓		MoSSaiC components: book structure and chapter outputs	1.4.5
✓	✓	✓		How to start a MoSSaiC project and who to brief	1.5

F = funders and policy makers   **M** = MoSSaiC core unit: government project managers and experts   **G** = government task teams: experts and practitioners   **C** = community task teams: residents, leaders, contractors

1.1.2 Documents

DOCUMENT TO BE PRODUCED	CHAPTER SECTION
List of senior policy makers who will champion and endorse the project	1.2; 1.5.2
List of staff to be considered for inclusion in the MoSSaiC core unit	1.5.2

1.1.3 Steps and outputs

STEP	OUTPUT
1. Understand the disaster risk context with respect to landslides	Relevance of MoSSaiC approach to local landslide risk context identified
2. Understand the innovative features and foundations of MoSSaiC	
3. Identify general in-house expertise and the appropriate institutional structures for codifying a local approach toward landslide risk reduction	
4. Brief key individuals on MoSSaiC (politicians, relevant ministries, in-house experts)	Core unit of team members identified

1.1.4 Community-based aspects

The chapter introduces MoSSaiC as an integrated method for engaging policy makers, project managers, practitioners, and vulnerable communities in reducing urban landslide risk in developing countries. Community residents are not just seen as those at risk, but as the people with the best practical knowledge of the slopes in their area. By engaging and working with communities to find and deliver solutions to landslide risk, governments will develop new practices and policies.

1.2 GETTING STARTED

1.2.1 Briefing note

A practical approach to reducing landslide risk

In introducing MoSSaiC, the chapter provides

- a framework for understanding disaster risk, specifically landslide risk;

- an overview of recent influences on disaster risk management (DRM);

- advocacy for a proactive approach in tackling landslide risk in communities;

- an introduction to MoSSaiC's three foundations; and

- an overview on starting a MoSSaiC landslide risk reduction project.

Many areas of the world are at risk from landslides and their consequences (figure 1.1). Rainfall-triggered landslides particularly affect developing countries in the humid trop-

ics. Rapid urbanization and the associated growth of unauthorized and densely populated communities in hazardous locations (such as steep slopes) are powerful drivers in a cycle of disaster risk accumulation. Frequently, it is the most socioeconomically vulnerable who inhabit marginal landslide-prone slopes—thus increasing their exposure to landslide hazards and often increasing the hazard itself.

The more socially, economically, and physically vulnerable people are, the more disastrous a landslide event will be. While recognition is growing of the increased occurrence of landslide disasters, there is equal recognition that on-the-ground implementation of landslide risk reduction measures is lacking.

MoSSaiC aims to address these issues. Its key premises follow.

- ***Disaster risk mitigation pays***, and investment in reducing rainfall-triggered landslide hazards in vulnerable communities can often be justified.

- ***Engaging existing government expertise*** for implementing risk reduction measures can build capacity, embed good practice, and change policy.

- ***Ensuring community engagement*** from start to finish can establish ownership of solutions.

Specifically, construction of relatively simple measures such as surface water drains can often improve slope stability, reduce the landslide risk to communities, and reduce future disaster management costs to governments. Landslide mitigation can be achieved through cooperation between government technicians

FIGURE 1.1 Global landslide risk

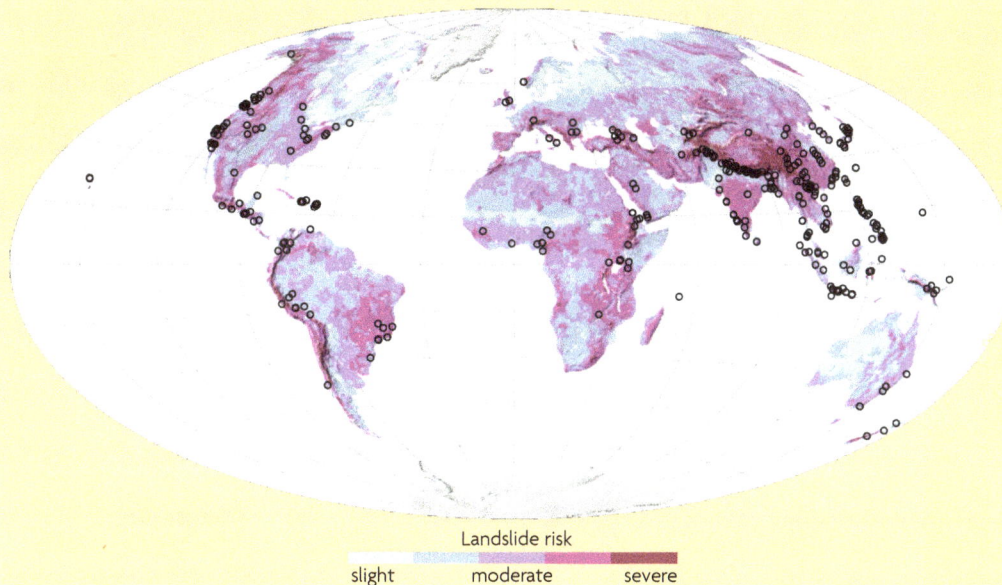

Landslide risk

slight   moderate   severe

Source: National Aeronautics and Space Administration (NASA) map adapted from Hong, Adler, and Huffman 2006.

Note: NASA scientists assembled the risk map from topographic data, land cover classifications, and soil types. Black dots identify the locations of landslides that occurred from 2003 to 2006. Light blue indicates areas of low risk; purple and dark red indicate areas at the highest risk.

and community residents; hands-on application of science and local knowledge; and proactive support from managers, politicians, and donor agencies.

MoSSaiC vision and foundations

The MoSSaiC vision is to lay sustainable foundations for community-based landslide risk reduction. These foundations are a ***scientific basis*** for reducing landslide hazard, a ***community-based*** approach for delivery of mitigation measures on the ground, and an ***evidence base*** demonstrating that such an investment both pays and works (figure 1.2).

These foundations govern the way in which MoSSaiC should be understood, implemented, and integrated into wider policy and practice.

- ***Foundation 1: MoSSaiC is science based.***

  - Localized physical causes (often poor drainage) of landslide hazard are identified.

  - Appropriate mitigation measures that address the causes of landslide hazard are identified and implemented.

  - Scientific methods are used to justify solutions to both communities and governments.

- ***Foundation 2: MoSSaiC is community based.***

  - Community residents are engaged in identifying landslide risk causes and solutions.

  - Contractors and workers from the community are employed in constructing drainage solutions.

  - Government managers and practitioners form teams with the necessary expertise to work with communities and deliver mitigation measures.

  - The vision is shared and championed in communities and by governments.

- ***Foundation 3: MoSSaiC is evidence based.***

  - Appropriate physical works are delivered to reduce landslide hazard.

  - The majority of project funding and time is spent in the communities.

FIGURE 1.2 MoSSaiC premises, vision, and foundations

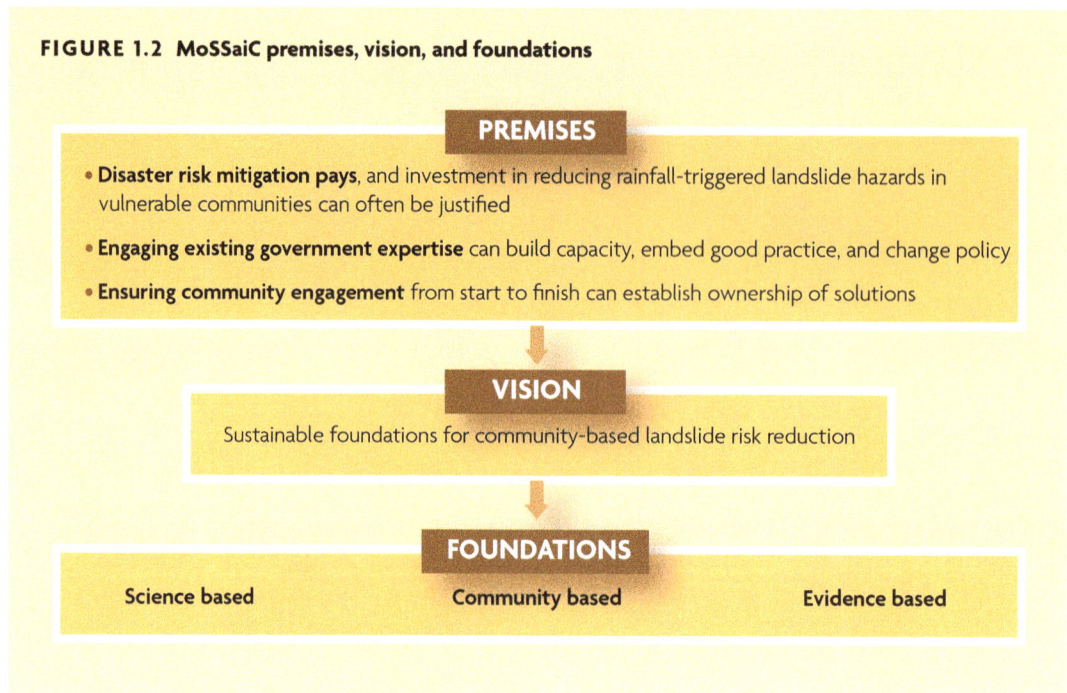

PREMISES

- **Disaster risk mitigation pays**, and investment in reducing rainfall-triggered landslide hazards in vulnerable communities can often be justified
- **Engaging existing government expertise** can build capacity, embed good practice, and change policy
- **Ensuring community engagement** from start to finish can establish ownership of solutions

VISION

Sustainable foundations for community-based landslide risk reduction

FOUNDATIONS

| Science based | Community based | Evidence based |

— The cost-effectiveness of landslide risk reduction is demonstrated.

— The benefits of community-based landslide risk reduction are demonstrated so that behavior and policy are changed.

Management and community in MoSSaiC

MoSSaiC recognizes that landslides are both a management issue and a community issue.

- ***Landslides are a management issue.*** Actions can be taken to reduce or manage landslide hazards or their consequences. Slope stability management must involve communities that may inadvertently be adding to the risk and will almost certainly be affected by it. This management must also involve governments. A government can choose to take a proactive approach to landslides in communities by identifying and enacting appropriate landslide risk management policies. Governments will often have experts with the combined skills necessary for reducing landslide risk in communities. Engaging existing government expertise for implementing risk reduction measures can build capacity, embed good practice, and change policy.

- ***Landslides are a community issue.*** Slope stability in communities is a community-scale issue in that landslides are spatially discrete events caused by localized slope stability mechanisms. Each community and the corresponding hillside it occupies will have its own unique landslide hazard and vulnerability profile. Thus, determining how to manage slope stability in a particular community requires application of community knowledge of the slope and scientific/engineering diagnosis of landslide mechanisms at the community scale. This community-based approach continues with the construction of drainage by community members, and with the support of government (table 1.1). Ensuring community engagement from start to finish can establish ownership of solutions.

Communicating the vision and establishing MoSSaiC in your country

The vision outlined above and detailed in this chapter may resonate with certain catalytic individuals in a particular country, be they community leaders, engineers, civil servants, or politicians. These leaders in turn will need to communicate the vision to decision makers

TABLE 1.1 The key teams and tasks in MoSSaiC

TEAM	TASK	
	Diagnose landslide hazard and design intervention	Implement physical measures to reduce landslide hazard
Community: residents, leaders, and contractors	Contribute local knowledge of slope, hazard, and vulnerability	Construct physical measures, change slope management practices
Government: policy makers, project managers, and practitioners	Apply in-house scientific, engineering, and development expertise	Issue and supervise contracts, build in-house capacity
	Manage project and teams	

and other influential individuals in order to initiate a MoSSaiC project.

Government approval is a prerequisite for initiating MoSSaiC, developing the financial basis for its implementation, and establishing a core unit of in-house experts and project managers. Securing government approval relies on a clear exposition of MoSSaiC. One of the primary functions of this book is to serve as a resource for this purpose.

Once there is a clear mandate for the establishment of a MoSSaiC project, it is vital to engage at-risk communities as early as possible, set realistic expectations within those communities, and ensure timely project delivery. It is often pragmatic to start small, and then build upon each success as the core unit and community adapt the MoSSaiC blueprint to fit the local context. It is easier to embrace a vision if there is evidence of success on the ground.

1.2.2 What is unique about MoSSaiC?

Taking an approach focused on community residents means

> ...integrating tasks into a long-term programme covering all phases of disaster and incorporating hazard mitigation into wider development planning. The methodology of working is necessarily slow, small scale, long term, multidisciplinary, and multisectoral. Because of its complexity, its incremental planning, and its dependence on political negotiation, this approach must seem like a recipe for chaos to many experts accustomed to working in conventional programs.

However, within it, scientific knowledge of hazards and their effects and technological alternatives for mitigation take on a completely new meaning, transforming themselves into vital instruments at the service of development (Maskrey 1992, 5).

Designed as explicitly community based, MoSSaiC provides a new method for delivering landslide risk reduction in the most vulnerable communities. The combination of features highlighted below is what makes this approach unique.

- It develops sustainable foundations for the delivery of landslide risk reduction measures in communities (chapter 1).

- It identifies, uses, and builds existing capacity for risk reduction (chapter 2).

- It identifies the risk drivers so that mitigation measures can be justified (chapter 3).

- It provides a method for prioritizing the most vulnerable (chapter 4).

- Community residents are active participants throughout the entire process (chapter 5).

- It delivers landslide hazard reduction measures on the ground (chapter 6).

- It emphasizes the critical role of site supervision in partnership with community contractors (chapter 7).

- It encourages behavioral change at the community level and within government (chapter 8).

- It promotes the importance of providing evidence of risk reduction achieved (chapter 9).

1.2.3 Guiding principles

- Develop a "mitigation mindset" with respect to urban landslide risk.

- Understand that there is no "one size fits all" solution to landslide risk reduction—each country and community will have its own landslide risk profile.

- Recognize that there is often something that can be done to reduce the risk—learn from other approaches and adapt the MoSSaiC blueprint.

- Learn the value of community knowledge and the importance of community involvement throughout.

- Realize that the government may already have the skills and know-how to tackle landslide risk in communities.

- Look for key individuals in government and communities who see the big picture and can drive behavioral change.

1.2.4 Risks and challenges

Getting commitment from all key stakeholders

Securing a mandate for MoSSaiC from government is necessary for establishing and managing the requisite teams, procuring services and resources, and implementing landslide mitigation measures in communities. The multidisciplinary nature of MoSSaiC means that its components may fall between or across the purview of different ministries, or that ministries may not wish to collaborate. A political champion may be able to overcome this, but energetic individuals from different agencies will also need to join forces.

In addition to requiring top-down government action, MoSSaiC is a bottom-up approach to landslide mitigation and needs to have a secure grounding in communities. This grounding can only be achieved through substantial interaction with communities, necessitating clear communication and a major time commitment. In the MoSSaiC approach, community residents are seen not as passive recipients of information, but as agents contributing both to the landslide hazard and to the solutions. The challenge is to ensure that individuals are major participants at every stage in the process so that everyone can own the project. Only in this manner can behavioral change be achieved.

Similarly, government field teams, technicians, and construction supervisors should be treated as contributors and their extensive field experience seen as a valuable resource. These team members are the interface with the community. If they are not well informed and involved by their managers, their ownership of the project cannot be ensured.

Sound project management delivers quality interventions. Conversely, poor management can actually make a landslide problem worse, alienate communities and field teams, result in budget overruns, and prevent the MoSSaiC approach from being established in a country. The project management and technical teams are responsible for designing and supervising construction, and for achieving a sufficiently high level of engagement with all stakeholders, so that the intervention meets the required goals, complies with necessary standards and safeguards, and encourages replication.

Securing evidence that risk reduction is working

Many disaster risk reduction (DRR) projects lack analysis of medium-term impacts. The challenge is to keep project engagement by all stakeholders sufficiently strong so that evidence of postproject performance is kept, analyzed, and communicated. Only with such evidence can policy be changed or existing DRR policy measures reinforced. Evidence of risk reduction is also important, since evaluations of mitigation measures have to respond to the counterfactual argument of what would have happened in the absence of the intervention.

Psychological and situational barriers

There are several reasons why relatively few people, communities, and governments are prepared or able to invest in landslide mitigation measures (Kunreuther, Meyer, and Kerjan forthcoming):

- **Lack of risk awareness.** Communities may not be aware that they live in a high-landslide-risk area, and governments may not have an adequate basis for identifying the most at-risk communities.

- **Helplessness in the face of landslide risk.** Communities and governments may be all too aware of the risk but have little realization of the potential for relatively low-cost, in-house solutions.

- **"Samaritan's dilemma."** Communities may avoid investing in good slope management practices and risk reduction measures on the assumption that a government (the "good Samaritan") will assist them in case of disaster.

- **Procrastination.** There is a natural tendency to postpone taking actions that require investments of time and money.

- **Budget constraints.** Communities may not be able to afford to invest in landslide risk reduction measures. Governments may not have sufficient understanding of the potential solutions and associated benefit-cost ratios, and therefore are unable to justify the expenditure.

- **Short-term planning horizons and hyperbolic discounting.** People in the most vulnerable communities may be living hand to mouth and consequently be unwilling to consider putting money toward low-cost slope management solutions that will not provide for their daily needs. Governments might place more value on projects that show immediate benefits rather than on investing to offset a future loss that may or may not occur.

- **Learning from failures.** People often do not seem to learn from past experiences of disaster. Following a landslide, people may rebuild their homes in the same or similar location. Governments also tend to repeat their reactions to disasters and may relocate communities to unsuitable locations.

1.3 DISASTER RISK: CONTEXT AND CONCEPTS

1.3.1 Global disaster risk

This subsection briefly reviews the evidence for the increasing number and consequences of disasters caused by natural hazards. It provides both the broad context for DRM and the specific context for the management of slope stability in communities.

Increases in the number of disasters

Reports from international development agencies and from the geoscience and engineering communities point to an increase in the occurrence of natural hazards and their consequences (figure 1.3), especially with respect to countries with low to medium levels of development (AGS 2000; Alcántara-Ayala 2002; UNDP 2004, 2008). See IFRC (2004) for a comprehensive discussion of this trend.

This apparent increase has many possible explanations (IEG 2006; IFRC 2004), including the following:

- **Increase in the reporting and recording of disasters.** Improved communication and the development of international and local disaster databases have enabled the systematic recording of disasters.

- **Development activities.** Construction, mining, and agriculture affect the natural environment and can increase some hydrometerological hazards (such as landslides, erosion, flooding, and drought).

- **Global anthropogenic effects such as climate change.** For example, a rise in tropical sea temperatures of approximately 1 degree Celsius over the past century may have contributed to an increase in weather-related disasters.

- **Socioeconomic and environmental drivers leading to increased exposure and** vulnerability. Poverty, drought, and famine can result in people moving to deltas, floodplains, the steep slopes on the fringes of urban areas, and other marginal areas exposed to natural hazards.

Such evidence further supports arguments for DRR that have been advanced in the international development policy community in recent years (DFID 2004; Pelling and Uitto 2001; Twigg 2004).

Increases in the cost of disasters

Paralleling the increase in the number of disasters has been the rise in their consequences with regard to direct and indirect impacts, and insured and uninsured losses (figure 1.3). It is widely recognized that the incidence and impact of disasters caused by natural hazards disproportionately affects developing countries. Numerous studies have documented evidence of the human, economic, and environmental losses experienced by developing countries at the local and national levels (e.g., Charveriat 2000; Rasmussen 2004; UNDP 2004). Such losses can affect the gross domestic product (GDP) of developing countries in a

catastrophic way, especially in small island developing states (SIDS) (World Bank 2010b). For example, Granada lost 200 percent of its GDP to Hurricane Ivan (World Bank 2005a).

Observed trends in disaster risk are not simply a physical phenomenon, but are closely related to the process of human development: "the development choices of individuals, communities and nations can generate new disaster risk" (UNDP 2004, 1). Analysis of time-series data has provided insight into the causative factors of the increased losses associated with disasters. A study of mainland U.S. hurricane damage from 1900 to 2005 shows that if damage data are normalized (with 2005 as the datum) with respect to changes in inflation and wealth at the national level, and changes in population and housing units at the coastal county level, there is no trend in damage over time (figure 1.4) (Crompton et al. 2010; Crompton and McAneney 2008; Pielke et al. 2008). The absence of a trend in normalized loss data suggests that increased observed losses are attributable to increases in the number of buildings over time; thus, it matters greatly what is built, where it is built, and how it is built.

FIGURE 1.3 **Number of great natural catastrophes and associated economic losses worldwide, 1950–2010**

a. Number of events with trend

b. Overall and insured losses with trend

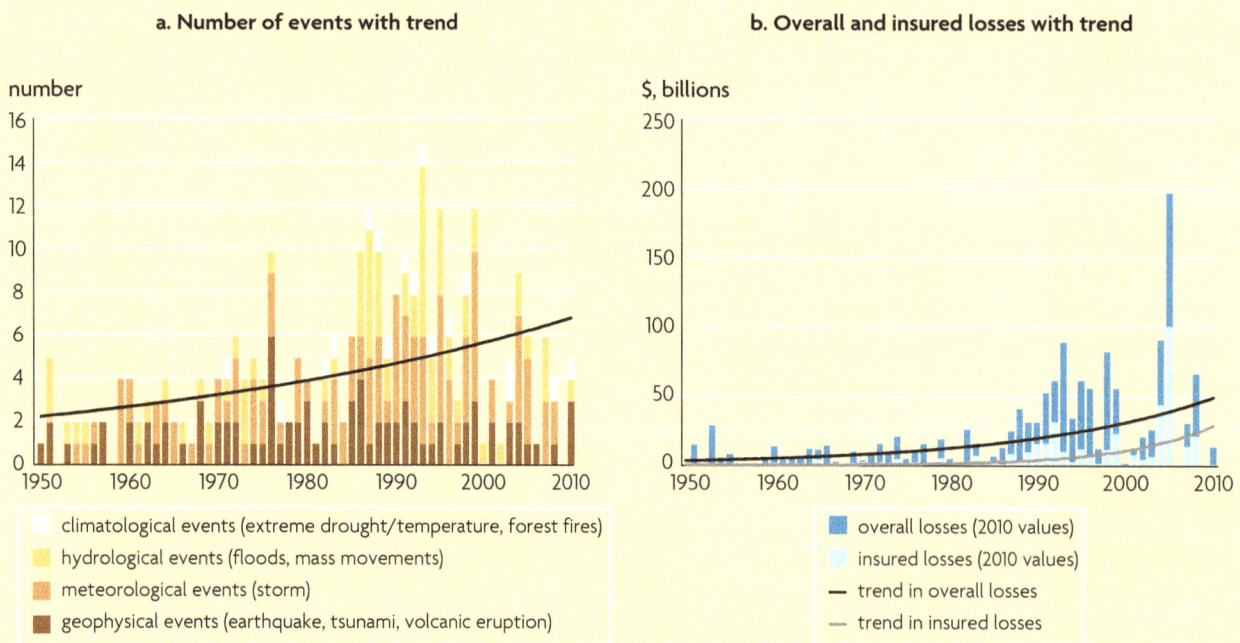

- climatological events (extreme drought/temperature, forest fires)
- hydrological events (floods, mass movements)
- meteorological events (storm)
- geophysical events (earthquake, tsunami, volcanic eruption)

- overall losses (2010 values)
- insured losses (2010 values)
- — trend in overall losses
- — trend in insured losses

Source: © Münchener Rückversicherungs-Gesellschaft, Geo Risks Research, NatCatSERVICE 2011.

FIGURE 1.4 Normalized losses from U.S. Gulf and Atlantic hurricane damage, 1900–2005

$, billions

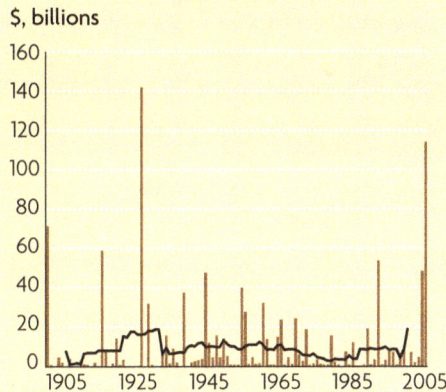

Source: Pielke et al. 2008.

Note: Data are normalized to 2005 by adjusting for changes in inflation, wealth, and housing units. The black line is an 11-year centered moving average.

Recording disasters

To assist in the analysis and management of risk, disasters are recorded and categorized by various agencies. For example, the Emergency Events Database (EM-DAT) is maintained by the World Health Organization Collaborating Centre for Research on the Epidemiology of Disasters (CRED). In EM-DAT a disaster is defined as an event in which 10 or more people are killed, 100 or more are injured, or where damage is sufficient to call in international agencies (UNDP 2004). Munich Re classifies disaster risk in terms of categories of catastrophe (table 1.2). The catastrophes in each category are likely to have different return periods,

spatial and temporal scales, affected parties, and methods of risk assessment and risk management.

Studies by regional networks such as La Red (Latin America) and Periperi (southern Africa) provide evidence that smaller-scale and "everyday" disasters (categories 0–2) have been increasing in developing countries in recent years (Bull-Kamanga et al. 2003). The landslide risk reduction approach described in this book has been built on experiences generally relating to categories 0–2. MoSSaiC may also be applicable to the higher categories of landslide catastrophe.

Global landslide risk

Rainfall-triggered landslides represent a significant but underreported threat to lives, property, and development, particularly in Southeast Asia and Latin America and the Caribbean (UNU 2006). Available data indicate that the majority of fatalities occur in lower-middle- and low-income countries (figures 1.5 and 1.6), and that in excess of 2 million people are exposed to landslide hazards worldwide (UNISDR 2009). However, the full impact of landslides is masked by broader statistics relating to the precipitation events that trigger them and the concurrent wind damage, floods, and storm surges. For a particular rainfall-triggered disaster, it is possible that "losses from landslides may exceed losses from the overall disaster" (USGS 2003, 7).

In the humid tropics, high-intensity and high-duration rainfall events act as the main

TABLE 1.2 Categories of catastrophe

CATEGORY	DEFINITION
0 Extreme natural event	No fatalities, no property damage
1 Small-scale loss event	> 1 fatality and/or small-scale damage
2 Moderate loss event	> 10 fatalities and/or damage to buildings and property
3 Severe catastrophe	> 20 fatalities, overall losses > $50 million
4 Major catastrophe	> 100 fatalities, overall losses > $200m
5 Devastating catastrophe	> 500 fatalities, overall losses > $500 million
6 Great natural catastrophe	Thousands of fatalities, economy severely affected, extreme insured losses

Source: © Münchener Rückversicherungs-Gesellschaft, Geo Risks Research, NatCatSERVICE 2011.

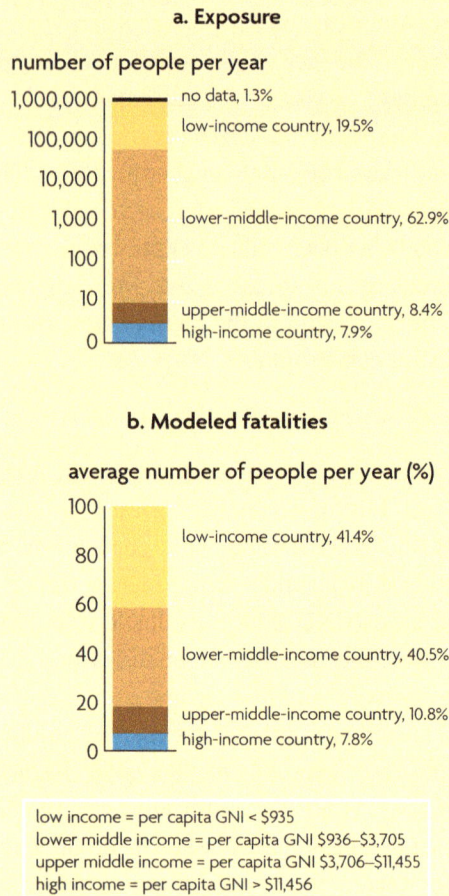

impact of rainfall-triggered landslides in areas of unauthorized housing is well recognized:

> Poverty can compel people to migrate to larger cities in search of employment opportunities. Without the economic means to participate and integrate into town and city societies, the poor create shantytowns often on the outskirts of cities in areas with high hazard exposure risks. For instance, in the case of the major rain-induced landslide in Venezuela in 1999, which affected between 80–100 thousand people, most of the thirty thousand disaster deaths can be traced back to an informal settlement that was washed away during the event (OAS 2004, 2).

As well as causing major landslide disasters, a single rainfall event can trigger numerous small- to medium-size landslides (AGS 2000)—a scale not recognized in most international records of disasters. The frequent occurrence of highly localized disasters anticipates the potential for much larger disasters.

To address landslide-related losses, and the interaction of development activities with slope stability, this **accumulation** of risk must be tackled. The ability to mitigate small events effectively, or to limit their impact, could result in an increased capacity to manage the risks associated with larger events (Bull-Kamanga et al. 2003).

Landslide risk and MoSSaiC

With respect to rainfall-triggered landslide risk, the Caribbean (where MoSSaiC has been developed) is typical of many developing regions in the humid tropics. The steep slopes and deep soils that characterize much of this region are naturally prone to landslides, which are triggered by high-intensity or high-duration rainfall (Lumb 1975).

A combination of poverty and increasing levels of urbanization is resulting in the construction of unauthorized settlements on such slopes, as they are often the only available location for the poor (Board on Natural Disasters 1999). Like many other developing countries, urban areas in Latin America and the Caribbean suffer from low-quality housing, inadequate (or unenforced) urban planning

trigger for landslides by reducing the shear strength of the slope materials. Some climate change predictions suggest an increase in the number and intensity of extreme rainfall events in these regions. However, even without climate change, the susceptibility of slopes to landslides is being increased by development activities involving earthworks (cuts and fills) and construction—whether planned or unauthorized. These activities change slope geometry, strength, loading, vegetation cover, and surface water and groundwater regimes. Thus, the process of development can increase the physical landslide hazard while exposing more of the most vulnerable people and structures to these hazards. The occurrence and

FIGURE 1.6 Global rainfall-triggered landslide fatalities

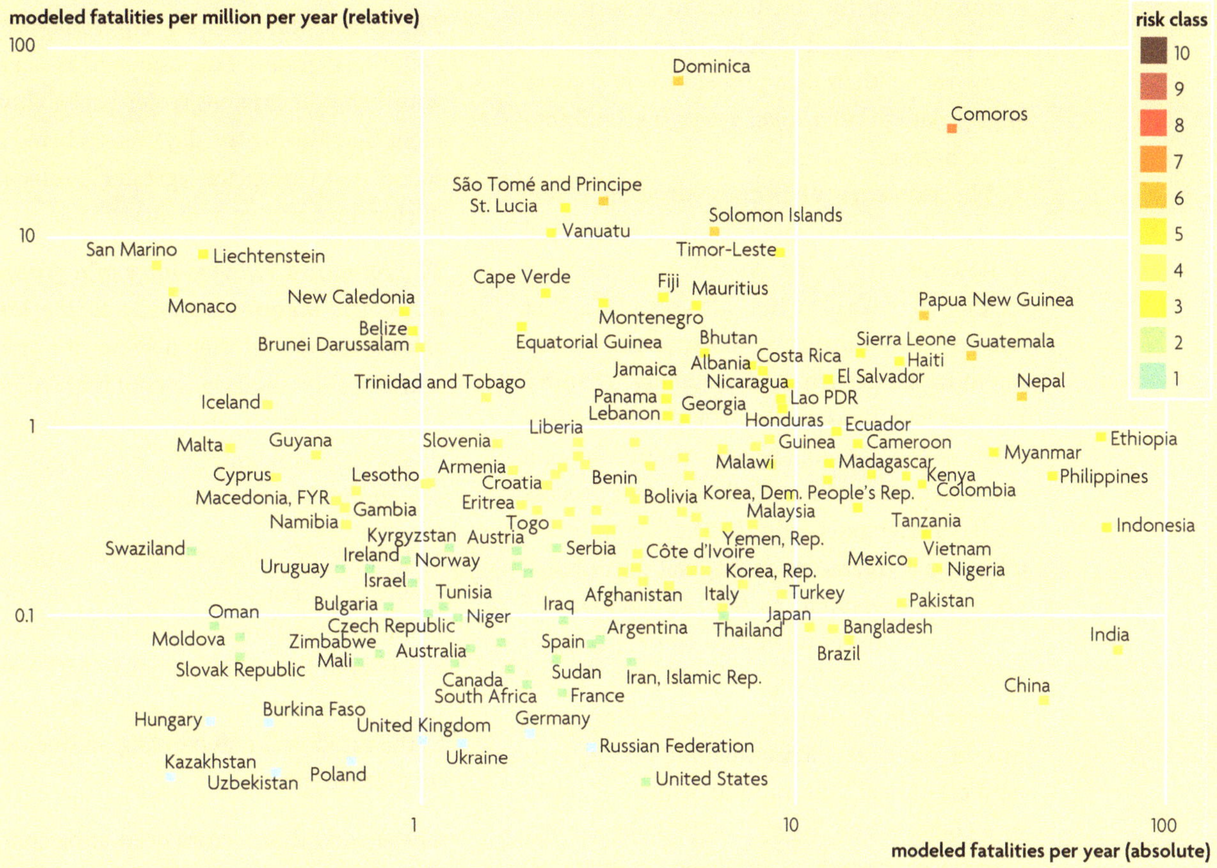

modeled fatalities per million per year (relative)

risk class
10, 9, 8, 7, 6, 5, 4, 3, 2, 1

(scatter plot of countries including Dominica, Comoros, São Tomé and Principe, St. Lucia, Solomon Islands, San Marino, Liechtenstein, Vanuatu, Timor-Leste, Monaco, New Caledonia, Cape Verde, Fiji, Mauritius, Papua New Guinea, Belize, Montenegro, Bhutan, Sierra Leone, Guatemala, Brunei Darussalam, Equatorial Guinea, Costa Rica, Haiti, Jamaica, Albania, El Salvador, Nepal, Trinidad and Tobago, Nicaragua, Iceland, Panama, Georgia, Lao PDR, Lebanon, Honduras, Ecuador, Liberia, Malta, Guyana, Slovenia, Guinea, Cameroon, Myanmar, Ethiopia, Cyprus, Armenia, Malawi, Madagascar, Kenya, Philippines, Lesotho, Croatia, Benin, Bolivia, Korea, Dem. People's Rep., Colombia, Macedonia, FYR, Eritrea, Malaysia, Tanzania, Indonesia, Namibia, Gambia, Togo, Yemen, Rep., Swaziland, Kyrgyzstan, Austria, Serbia, Côte d'Ivoire, Vietnam, Uruguay, Ireland, Norway, Korea, Rep., Mexico, Nigeria, Israel, Afghanistan, Italy, Turkey, Pakistan, Oman, Bulgaria, Tunisia, Iraq, Japan, Moldova, Czech Republic, Niger, Argentina, Thailand, Bangladesh, India, Zimbabwe, Australia, Spain, Brazil, Slovak Republic, Mali, Sudan, Iran, Islamic Rep., China, Canada, South Africa, France, Burkina Faso, Germany, Hungary, United Kingdom, Russian Federation, Kazakhstan, Ukraine, Uzbekistan, Poland, United States)

modeled fatalities per year (absolute)

Source: UNISDR 2009.

Note: Approximately 2.2 million people are exposed to landslides worldwide, but many small landslide events causing deaths are not internationally reported.

controls, and insufficient investment in infrastructure (Charveriat 2000).

The resulting landslide risk is the product of complex interactions between the inherent susceptibility of slopes to landslides (related to their soils and geology, topography, hydrology, and vegetation), the influence of human activities in affecting these factors at a highly localized scale, and the vulnerability of communities to the impact of landslides.

1.3.2 Disaster risk management

Defining risk

DRM requires an understanding of what is driving the risk. This can be broken down into three components: the physical **hazard**, the **exposure** of different elements (such as people, buildings, public utilities, economic infra-

> MoSSaiC is specifically targeted to reduce the frequent small- to medium-size rainfall-triggered landslides that occur in weathered soils and that are exacerbated by human influences on slope drainage and geometry. It is designed for application in the most economically, socially, and physically vulnerable communities.

structure, or the environment) to that hazard, and the **vulnerability** of those elements to damage by the hazard. Risk is commonly expressed as a function of hazard, exposure, and vulnerability.

A natural **hazard** (such as a landslide, flood, storm, volcanic eruption, or earthquake) is defined in terms of its frequency (annual probability or return period), magnitude, and type at a particular location or within a wider region. Where the likelihood of a particular hazard is expressed in relative or qualitative terms rather than as a probability, it is more appropriate to refer to an area's susceptibility to the hazard.

The **exposure** of people, structures, services, or the environment to a specific hazard is determined by the spatial and temporal location of those elements with respect to that hazard. **Vulnerability** is an expression of the potential of the exposed elements to suffer harm or loss. Thus, exposure and vulnerability relate to the consequences or the results of a natural force, and not to the natural process itself (Crozier and Glade 2005). In many cases, exposure is treated as an implicit part of vulnerability assessment, as described below.

Vulnerability is related to the capacity to anticipate a hazard, cope with it, resist it, and recover from its impact. It is determined by a mix of physical, environmental, social, economic, political, cultural, and institutional factors (Benson and Twigg 2007). Vulnerability may be expressed qualitatively or quantitatively, in terms of direct or indirect damage and tangible or intangible damage. The damage can be physical, environmental, social, or economic and have an impact at a range of local and national scales. The degree of direct physical or economic damage is often expressed in cost terms or on a scale of 0–1 (from no damage to total loss). Indirect and intangible damage is usually more difficult to quantify. The opposite of vulnerability is resilience (of people) or reliability (of structures).

Vulnerability assessment is especially complex for landslides since a wide range of effects have to be considered, such as the following:

- **The location, type, magnitude, and velocity of the landslide hazard.** These will directly determine its spatial impact and the exposure of elements at risk.

- **The physical and socioeconomic vulnerability of groups.** Children and the elderly or disabled will be able to respond less quickly than others; poorer households and communities will find economic recovery harder than richer communities.

- **The temporal exposure of different groups.** Differing degrees of exposure are associated with being at home (greater probability at night than during the day) versus being in a school or workplace (greater probability during the day than at night).

- **The temporal vulnerability of a group in a specific location exposed to the landslide hazard.** Differing degrees of physical vulnerability (injury or loss of life) will pertain depending on whether someone is outdoors, in a wooden house, or in a concrete structure when a landslide occurs.

- **Variation of vulnerability for different elements.** A house may have the same vulnerability to a slow or rapid landslide event, but people living in the house will have a lower vulnerability to the slower event than to the rapid event, depending on their ability to leave the house.

These and other factors need to be considered to assess vulnerability to landslides. Because of the wide range of factors involved, it has been noted that "vulnerability assessment is a complex issue, which is regularly not considered in an appropriate and thoughtful manner" (Crozier and Glade 2005, 27).

The disaster risk management process

A typical DRM process will include the following steps.

Step 1: Disaster risk assessment

- Analyze the risk. Identify and measure the frequency, magnitude, and type of hazard; and the vulnerability and exposure of the elements at risk.

- Understand the risk. Identify the underlying hazard and vulnerability processes, causes, and effects.

- Evaluate the risk. Compare with other risks and decide whether to accept or treat the risk.

Step 2: Disaster risk reduction

- Identify DRR options.

  - Avoid the hazard. Reduce exposure by enforcing planning controls, emergency evacuation, or permanent relocation.

  - Reduce the hazard, usually through some form of engineering measures.

  - Reduce the vulnerability and/or exposure. Increase the reliability of structures using engineering and building controls; or the resilience of people through public awareness, early warning, and planning for disaster response and recovery.

  - Transfer the risk, using disaster funds and insurance.

- Plan the risk treatment. Design the selected risk treatment option.

- Implement the risk treatment.

- Monitor the risk.

Taken together, DRR measures are often referred to as *mitigation*. Mitigation encompasses any structural (engineering) or nonstructural (planning, policy, public awareness) measures "undertaken to minimise the adverse impact of potential natural hazard events" (Benson and Twigg 2007, 16). Table 1.3 defines some of the terms commonly used to describe DRM components and gives examples of the activities typically involved.

The ultimate goal of DRM is to reduce disaster risk to an acceptable level. Figure 1.7 illustrates how this can be achieved via different DRR options (corresponding to those listed in Step 2 above): reducing the consequences, directly reducing the hazard, or redesigning to reduce both hazard and consequences.

The concept of acceptable risk

Elimination of risk is rarely feasible; however, mitigation measures can reduce risk. Risk reduction is thus undertaken in the context of seeking to achieve what society and the community regard as "acceptable risk" (or "tolerable risk"). According to the International Union of Geological Sciences Working Group on Landslides, acceptable risk can be defined as "a risk that society is willing to live with...in the confidence that it is being properly controlled, kept under review, and further reduced as and when possible" (Dai, Lee, and Ngai 2002, 78). When considering acceptable risk criteria for landslides, the following general principles, defined by the International Union of Geological Sciences, could be applied:

TABLE 1.3 Disaster risk management components

COMPONENT		EXAMPLE ACTIVITY
Risk assessment	Risk identification, analysis and evaluation	• Hazard mapping, prediction and monitoring • Community vulnerability assessment • Social risk perception analysis • Risk mapping
Ex ante risk reduction	Risk prevention and mitigation	• Planning controls • Building codes • Structural hazard reduction measures • Risk financing: risk transfer (insurance), risk retention (funds)
	Disaster preparedness	• Public awareness • Early warning • Institutional strengthening
Ex post disaster management	Disaster response	• Emergency management • Humanitarian relief
	Disaster recovery	• Postdisaster needs assessment • Reconstruction and rehabilitation

FIGURE 1.7 Disaster risk management options

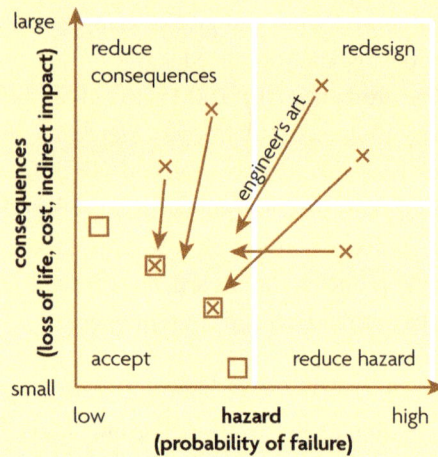

Source: International Center for Geohazards, Norway.

- The incremental risk from a hazard to an individual should not be significant compared to other risks to which a person is exposed in everyday life;

- The incremental risk from a hazard should, wherever reasonably practicable, be reduced i.e., the As Low As Reasonably Practicable (ALARP) principle should apply;

- If the possible loss of life from a landslide incident is high, the risk that the incident might actually occur should be low. This accounts for the particular intolerance of a society to incidents that cause many simultaneous casualties;

- Persons in the society will tolerate higher risks than they regard as acceptable when they are unable to control or reduce the risk because of financial or other limitations;

- Higher risks are likely to be tolerated for existing slopes than for planned projects, and for workers in industries with hazardous slopes, e.g., mines, than for society as a whole;

- Tolerable risks are higher for naturally occurring landslides than those from engineered slopes;

- Once a natural slope has been placed under monitoring or risk mitigation measures have been executed, the tolerable risks approach those of engineered slopes;

- Tolerable risks may vary from country to country and within countries, depending on historic exposure to landslide hazard, and the system of ownership and control of slopes and natural landslide hazards (Dai, Lee, and Ngai 2002, 78).

Defining acceptable risk is complex, and only in the most data-rich circumstances can it be seriously attempted in a quantitative manner. Figure 1.8 illustrates the definitions developed in Hong Kong SAR, China. Figure 1.8a illustrates a preferred definition, in that there is no acceptable risk zone defined; figure 1.8b illustrates an alternative definition where it is considered reasonable for society to accept a certain level of risk.

Such numerical formulations, and associated representations, of risk are only a guide to what a given society might accept. More commonly, social and political judgments are made on a case-by-case basis to help determine acceptable risk (Bunce, Cruden, and Morgenstern 1995; Dai, Lee, and Ngai 2002) and guide measures that are actually implemented.

1.3.3 Recent influences on disaster risk management policy and implications for MoSSaiC

Shift from ex post to ex ante policies

The increase in disaster risk described above has been recognized and responded to by policy makers, governments, and development agencies. DRM and DRR are now an established part of the extensive development literature, and are increasingly being mainstreamed in policy—often in conjunction with climate change adaptation and poverty reduction programs. This recognition has been the product of, and has contributed to, the complexity of the DRR advocacy and disaster response landscapes (figures 1.9 and 1.10). Notwithstanding, experts maintain that there is still insufficient global focus on and commitment to DRR (Sweikar et al. 2006). As a long-term, low-visibility process that offers no guarantee of tangible rewards, disaster mitigation is often overlooked by both sustainable development projects and the more immedi-

FIGURE 1.8 Societal landslide risk in Hong Kong SAR, China

a. Preferred definition

frequency per year

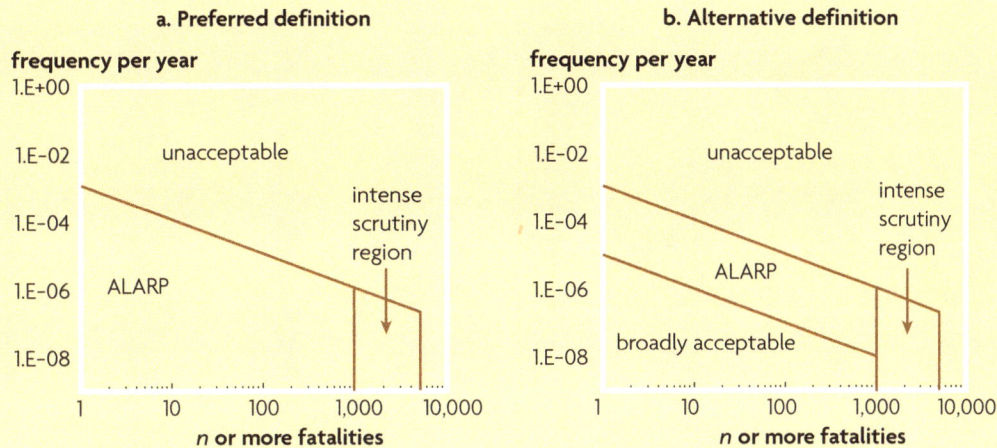

b. Alternative definition

frequency per year

Source: Dai, Lee, and Ngai 2002.

Note: ALARP = as low as reasonably practicable.

ate concerns of humanitarian aid responses to disasters. Even though it is acknowledged that ex ante risk reduction is likely to be preferable from both humanitarian and economic perspectives (Blaikie et al. 1994), 90 percent of bilateral and multilateral disaster-related funding is still spent on relief and recovery

after the event (Mechler, Linnerooth-Bayer, and Peppiatt 2006).

The emergence of new policy and funding trends generally occurs over a decadal cycle, which makes recording and reporting on project impact very important, given the lagged response between funding and project feed-

FIGURE 1.9 International advocacy landscape for disaster risk reduction

COALITION	NONGOVERNMENTAL ORGANIZATION	BILATERAL	MULTILATERAL
BOND Group (UK)		AusAID (Australia)	ECHO
IWG/ECB Project	Action Aid (UK)	BMZ (Germany)	DIPECHO
GDIN	Christian Aid (UK)	CIDA (Canada)	IASC Steering Committee
IAWG (Nairobi)	Catholic Relief Services	DFID (UK)	UNDP
ICVA	IFRC	DMFA (Denmark)	UN ISDR
InterAction	Lutheran World Relief	FFO (Germany)	UN OCHA
ProVention Consortium	Mercy Corps (UK/USA)	GMZ (Germany)	UN Special Envoy
Sphere Project	Oxfam (UK/USA)	MOFA (Japan)	
VOICE	PHREE-WAY	NMFA (Norway)	
	Plan International (UK)	SIDA (Sweden)	
	Practical Action (UK)	SDC (Switzerland)	INTERNATIONAL FINANCE
RESEARCH	Red Cross (UK/USA)	USAID (USA)	
	RiskRED	US State Department	African Development Bank
ADPC (Thailand)	Save the Children (UK/USA)		Asian Development Bank
ADRC (Japan)	Tearfund (UK)		Caribbean Development Bank
BHRC (UK)	World Vision (UK/USA)		Inter-American Development Bank
CRED (Belgium)			International Monetary Fund
ODI (UK)			The World Bank

Source: Sweikar et al. 2006.

Note: Organizations listed in italics play an identifiable role in advocacy; those listed in boldface are involved in coordination.

FIGURE 1.10 UN disaster response organizational framework

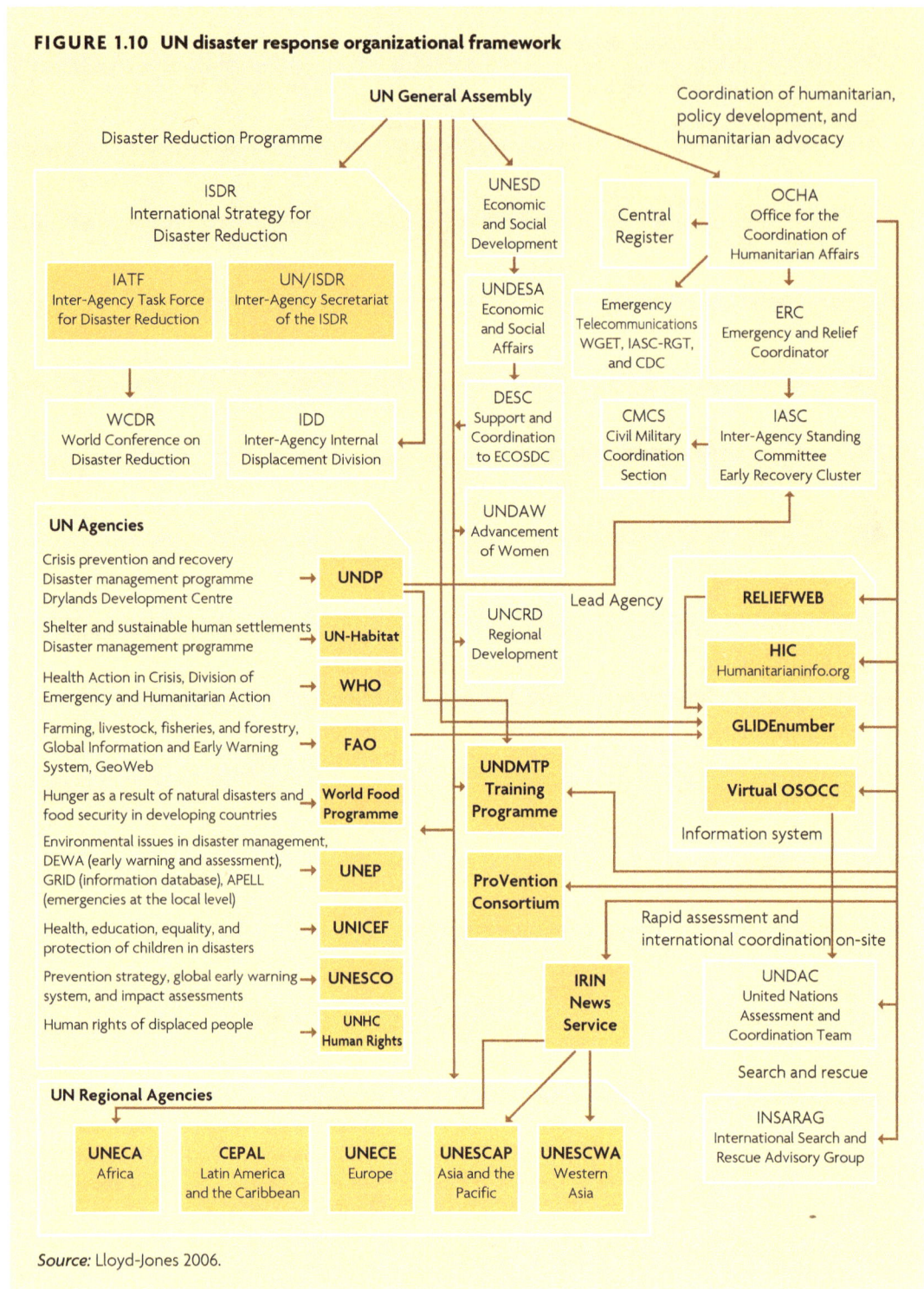

Source: Lloyd-Jones 2006.

back. If something works, evidence needs to be given, since this is the driver for further policy change and funding. The shift of emphasis from an ex post (response and recovery) to an ex ante (mitigation and preparedness) approach to disasters has been reflected in the portfolio of projects funded by development banks for a number of years (IDB 2005). How-ever, on-the-ground delivery has not material-ized in a correspondingly significant way. Wamsler (2006, 159) notes:

> During the past three decades policy state-ments by all major agencies have included risk reduction as a pre-condition and an integrated aspect of sustainable develop-ment... but when it comes to practical imple-

mentation, comparatively little has been done.

A recent World Bank project evaluation study provides clear evidence that disaster preparedness and mitigation need to be addressed as a priority (table 1.4).

Despite the seeming shift to ex ante DRM policy, there is an apparent lag in funding and consequently in the delivery of that policy on the ground. With respect to landslide risk reduction, the following appear to be the key issues:

- Decision makers will not naturally choose to invest in a project with unseen benefits (the main benefits of DRR are in the future in terms of losses avoided).

- A top-down policy approach to DRR can, in some cases, actually make it difficult to identify local physical risk drivers and thereby find a practical solution to the hazard.

- The top-down approach often fails to engage with the most vulnerable, who will therefore not be motivated to adopt new practices or own the mitigation measures.

Thus, practical implementation of landslide mitigation measures in vulnerable communities is rare, and so is evidence of the effectiveness of mitigation.

Three interrelated areas need strengthening—the evidence base for investment in risk reduction, the scientific basis for reducing the hazard, and the community basis for delivery on the ground. The following discussion explores recent influences on ex ante DRM policy in relation to these three areas, with particular reference to landslide risk and the importance of the government-community relationship. This discussion provides the policy context for MoSSaiC.

Need for evidence that mitigation pays

Studies undertaken with respect to specific DRM projects have consistently indicated that mitigation pays (World Bank 2010b): in general, for every dollar invested, between two and four dollars are returned in terms of avoided or reduced disaster impacts (Mechler 2005; Moench, Mechler, and Stapleton 2007). On the other hand,

> Building a culture of prevention is not easy, however. While the costs of prevention have to be paid in the present, its benefits lie in the distant future. Moreover, the benefits are not tangible; they are the wars and disasters that do not happen. So we should not be surprised that preventive policies receive support that is more often rhetorical than substantive (Annan 1999).

Evidence suggests that an individual's decision-making process will be biased against the activities and costs involved in reducing the risk of low-probability, high-consequence events. Meyer (2005) argues that our ability to make optimal mitigation decisions is hindered by three deep-rooted biases:

TABLE 1.4 Lessons learned from World Bank natural disaster projects

RANK	LESSON LEARNED	MENTIONS IN IEG DATABASE
1	Disaster management, preparedness, and mitigation need to be addressed	49
2	Simple and flexible procurement is fundamental to expeditious implementation	40
3	Lessons regarding project coordination units and/or working with existing agencies (pros and cons)	31
4	Maintenance is critical for sustainability	25
5	Simple project design is more important when activities to be implemented are urgent	25
6	Community participation produces several identifiable benefits	25

Source: IEG 2006.

Note: Lessons are from 303 completed World Bank natural disaster projects as identified by the World Bank's Independent Evaluation Group (IEG).

- How we learn from the past—We tend to learn by focusing on short-term feedback.

- How we see the future—We tend to see the future as a simple extension of the present rather than anticipating low-probability events such as disasters.

- How we make the trade-off between immediate capital investment in risk reduction compared with future savings in avoided losses—We tend to overly discount the value of ambiguous future rewards compared to short-term costs.

Taken together, Meyer argues, these limitations seem to explain many of the biases that have been observed in real-world DRM decisions—and, most critically, why we seem to have such difficulty correcting them. To overcome these biases, it is even more urgent that physical evidence be provided for the effectiveness of DRR—not just on the basis of economic investment, but also in terms of the social and indirect benefits to those most at risk.

An example showing that mitigation pays is provided by a series of studies conducted by the Wharton School of the University of Pennsylvania. These studies used catastrophe risk models to enable cost-benefit assessments to be made of mitigation measures. The four basic components of a catastrophe model—hazard, inventory, vulnerability, and loss—enable risk to be quantified in terms of cost (Wharton School 2008). In the case of a hurricane, the four components can be defined as follows:

- *Hazard*, quantified by the frequency, magnitude, and path of the hurricane

- *Inventory*, the list (or portfolio) of properties exposed to the predicted hurricane

- *Vulnerability*, the susceptibility to damage of the exposed structures

- *Loss*, the resulting direct or indirect financial loss to the property inventory

For a given hazard, catastrophe modeling allows the costs and benefits of different DRM investments to be compared. For example, modeling the costs and benefits of preventing hurricane damage to properties (by protecting windows and doors and upgrading roofs) in two villages in St. Lucia demonstrated attractive benefit-cost ratios for a wide range of potential discount rates (Hochrainer-Stigler et al. 2010) (figure 1.11).

Cost-benefit analysis uses a discount rate to compare economic effects occurring at different times. Discounting converts future economic impacts to their present-day value. The discount rate is usually positive because resources invested today can, on average, be transformed into more resources later. If hurricane mitigation is viewed as an investment, the return on that investment can be used to decide how much should be spent on mitigation. Assuming a 25-year project lifetime and a 12 percent discount rate, the example in figure 1.11 shows such an intervention yields a benefit-cost ratio of 1.5:1—in other words, it pays; but with an assumed project lifetime of only five years, cost exceeds benefit (benefit-cost ratio of 0.75:1).

The application of catastrophe modeling to wooden homes in Canaries, St. Lucia, illustrates how the effect of climate change on the benefits of hurricane mitigation measures can be assessed (Ou-Yang 2010). Figure 1.12 shows the change in benefit-cost ratios for different mitigation measures over different time scales

FIGURE 1.11 Benefit-cost ratio for hurricane-proofing prevention measures for houses in Canaries and Patience, St. Lucia

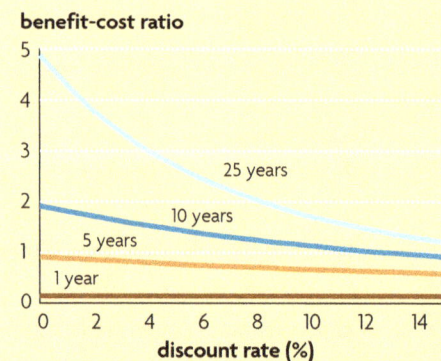

Source: Hochrainer-Stigler et al. 2010.

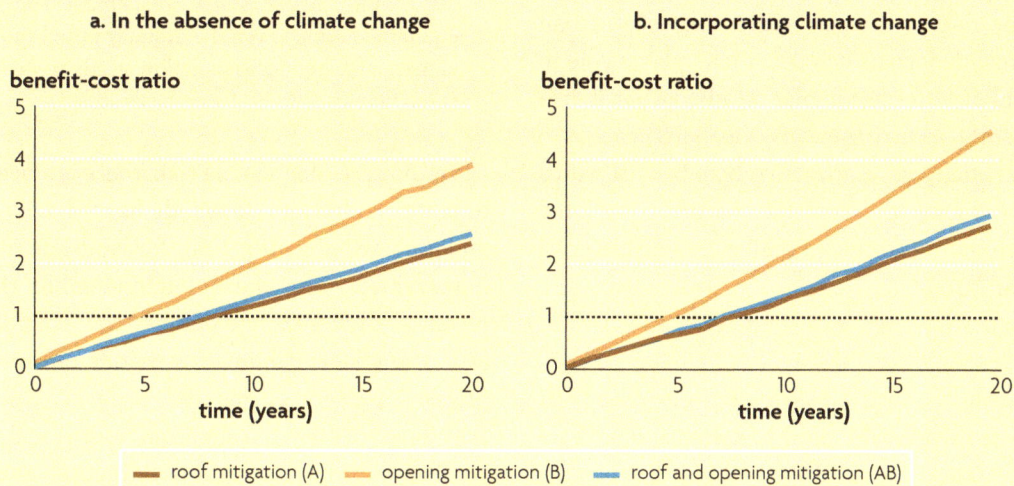

in the absence and presence of climate change. As expected, benefit-cost ratios increase with time in both cases, but grow faster in the presence of climate change. This phenomenon is more significant for longer time scales. After 20 years, the benefit-cost ratio is above 4.5:1 in the presence of climate change, but slightly below 4:1 in the absence of climate change.

The role of disaster risk insurance

How much to invest in risk reduction and how much to invest in insurance is a complex question. For risk reduction, investments are likely to have a better benefit-cost ratio for relatively frequent events than for infrequent low-probability events. Risk insurance, on the other hand, is seemingly less economically rational for frequent low-loss events that may be covered domestically or where the risk may be reduced (Mechler et al. 2010) (figure 1.13).

There has been growing interest in potential insurance vehicles for the relatively more extreme disaster risks (Kunreuther 2009). An example of one such vehicle is the Caribbean Catastrophe Risk Insurance Facility:

CCRIF is a risk pooling facility, owned, operated and registered in the Caribbean for

Caribbean governments. It is designed to limit the financial impact of catastrophic hurricanes and earthquakes to Caribbean governments by quickly providing short term liquidity when a policy is triggered. It is the world's first and, to date, only regional fund utilising parametric insurance, giving Caribbean governments the unique opportunity to purchase earthquake and hurricane catastrophe coverage with lowest-possible pricing (CCRIF 2012).

Consensus in this field suggests that insurance by governments is not appropriate for

FIGURE 1.13 Efficiency of risk management instruments and occurrence probability

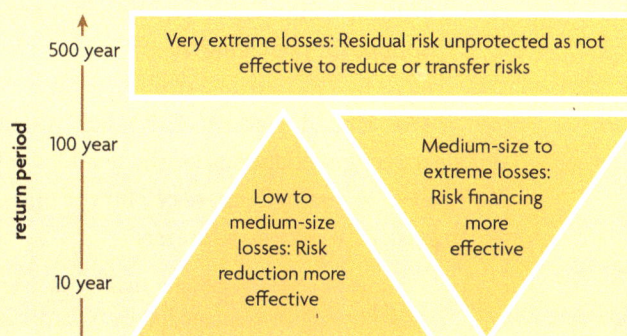

Source: Mechler et al. 2010.

frequently occurring risks; rather, expenditure on risk reduction is relevant in such circumstances. Since MoSSaiC seeks to reduce landslide risk by directly addressing local urban landslide hazard drivers, it may play a role in reducing the accumulation of just such frequently occurring events. MoSSaiC could also potentially have attractive benefit-cost ratios in reducing the landslide hazard associated with more extreme rainfall events (Holcombe et al. 2011).

Need for science-based risk assessment

The move toward investment in ex ante DRR carries with it the need to assess and address the underlying risk drivers—hazard, exposure, and vulnerability (defined in section 1.3.2). Risk assessment provides the basis for effective DRM by answering the following questions and identifying what risk management options will be most effective (Ho, Leroi, and Roberds 2000; Lee and Jones 2004):

- *Hazard identification.* What are the likely types of hazards?

- *Hazard assessment.* What is causing each hazard, and what is the frequency and magnitude of that hazard?

- *Identification of elements at risk.* What are the elements exposed to each hazard?

- *Vulnerability assessment.* What might be the degree of damage to these elements?

- *Risk quantification/estimation.* What is the risk associated with each hazard?

- *Risk evaluation.* What is the significance of these estimated risks, and what are the options for managing them?

The United Nations (UN) has provided clear recommendations on the need for effective risk assessment; these call for the underlying risk drivers to be addressed:

A failure to address the underlying risk drivers will result in dramatic increases in disaster risk and associated poverty outcomes. In contrast, *if addressing these drivers is given priority, risk can be reduced*, human

development protected and adaptation to climate change facilitated. Rather than a cost, this should be seen as an investment in building a more secure, stable, sustainable and equitable future. Given the urgency posed by climate change, decisive action needs to be taken now (UN 2009, 4; emphasis added).

In the case of landslide risk, there is a need to better understand landslide hazard drivers and provide a scientific basis for landslide risk management. This means understanding the physical processes affecting slope stability (and the effect of human activities on those physical processes) and the scale at which they operate (the hillside/community scale), so that appropriate hazard reduction measures can be identified and implemented. Relevant landslide hazard drivers and assessment methods are introduced in chapters 2, 3, and 4.

The need for the geoscience disciplines to inform an integrated approach to landslide risk reduction has been widely voiced:

While all regions experience landslide disasters, the harm they cause is most acute in developing countries, where the knowledge base required to identify landslide prone areas is often either nonexistent or fragmentary (UNU 2006).

In order to mitigate landslide hazard effectively, new methodologies are required to develop a better understanding of landslide hazard and make rational decisions on the allocation of funds for management of landslide risk... this relies crucially on a better understanding and on greater sophistication, transparency and rigour in the application of science (Dai, Lee, and Ngai 2002, 65, 82).

Scientific methods for assessing landslide hazard (location, frequency, magnitude) should be combined with an assessment of the vulnerability of those communities exposed to the hazard, so that the most at-risk communities are identified. The UN's specific recommendations are as follows:

- Shift the emphasis of social protection from an exclusive focus on response to including pre-disaster mechanisms and more *effective targeting of the most vulnerable groups*; [and]

- Promote a culture of planning and implementation of disaster risk reduction that builds on **government–civil society partnerships** and cooperation and is supportive of local initiative, in order to dramatically reduce the costs of risk reduction, ensure local acceptance, and build social capital (UN 2009, 5; emphasis added).

Commentaries by Maskrey (1989), Pelling and High (2005), and Twigg (2001) all bear on the community potential in this context. Social funds are perhaps one example of the formalization of this type of government–civil society partnership, in that such agencies might be well placed to contribute to MoSSaiC landslide risk reduction implementation projects.

Need to complement national risk maps with local studies

In the context of international and national DRM policies, a natural first step is to attempt to carry out a disaster risk assessment at a regional or national scale. This often involves using geographic information system (GIS) software to generate maps delineating broad zones of hazard, vulnerability, and risk. The accuracy and spatial resolution of risk maps are determined by the quality and resolution of the underlying layers of data—multiple digital maps of the different variables that affect hazard, exposure, and vulnerability. For example, landslide hazard may be expressed qualitatively, and at low spatial resolution, as landslide "susceptibility" according to general maps of slope angle, soil type, and land use.

In the last decade, there have been significant advances in spatially distributed landslide analysis. Glade and Crozier (2005) review current qualitative and quantitative approaches to the analysis of landslides at scales ranging from less than 1:10,000 to greater than 1:750,000. However, even at the most detailed spatial scales, GIS-based mapping methods are not able to identify detailed slope properties and local landslide mechanisms. National landslide susceptibility or hazard maps developed in this way are effectively decoupled from the dominant local landslide processes.

The scale of the map is incompatible with the scale of the physical processes.

Ideally, the most appropriate use of these maps would be to enable the identification of planning control zones—preventing occupation or development of the most landslide-prone areas and thereby avoiding exposure to the hazard altogether. However, in developing countries, there is often limited capacity for enforcing planning controls or for removing people from such areas.

If exposure of communities to landslide hazards cannot be easily reduced, the next question is whether the hazard or its consequences can be reduced. Unfortunately, wide-area landslide susceptibility/hazard maps will not yield answers about what is actually **causing** slope instability on a particular hillside or when a landslide might happen. Without such an understanding, an appropriate mitigation approach cannot readily be identified. This mismatch of scales may be one factor leading to the observation that, despite numerous major regional approaches, the uptake of hazard maps has been minimal (Opadeyi, Ali, and Chin 2005; Zaitchik and van Es 2003).

As noted, wide-area landslide hazard mapping represents the first step in the risk assessment process. Having identified broad zones of landslide hazard, the next step is to move to a more detailed scale—to go on site to identify the local hazard drivers. In this way, MoSSaiC involves communities and government teams combining local knowledge and scientific expertise to understand the local slope processes and identify potential landslide mitigation measures. Complementing existing wide-area landslide risk maps with this bottom-up approach can enable national DRM policies to be translated into the delivery of effective mitigation measures.

The role of social funds

In seeking to assist the most vulnerable communities, social funds have had a major role in many developing countries and have become increasingly focused on vulnerability reduction as part of DRM. Such funds are often assimilated into government as institutions and, in certain cases, are better integrated with related regional funding agencies. The mainstreaming of social funds over recent years (figure 1.14), combined with their focus on the neediest, makes them a potentially important partner in addressing the physical and social drivers of landslide risk.

Social funds can assist in DRM and contribute to elements of disaster risk insurance in the following ways (Siri 2006):

- Setting standards of best practice in infrastructure construction

- Setting an example by not promoting rebuilding in hazard-prone zones

- Delivering training activities aimed at strengthening technical capacity to mitigate the potential impact of natural disasters

- Broadening their portfolios to include damage mitigation projects for landslides

- Promoting microcredit programs

- Generating employment to low-income groups, thereby reducing the vulnerability of the poor to disasters.

While the MoSSaiC approach is essentially focused on addressing the physical landslide *hazard drivers* in the most vulnerable communities, it is important to couple such an approach with any existing local initiatives aimed at assessing and addressing the *vulner-*

ability drivers of landslide risk (such as poverty reduction or risk preparedness projects).

A flexible blueprint for landslide risk reduction policy and practice

MoSSaiC is designed to deliver effective landslide risk reduction measures by

- applying appropriate scientific methods (at the correct physical scale) for understanding the *physical risk drivers* and hence reducing the landslide hazard;

- doing so within the *context of the community*, while encouraging a government-community partnership for both the delivery of the measures and ongoing management of slope stability; and thereby

- providing a basis for development of an *evidence base* that mitigation can pay—socially and economically, directly and indirectly.

MoSSaiC assesses the specific landslide risk faced by vulnerable communities in two stages: (1) by using basic risk indicators to identify the most at-risk communities (utilizing any available wide-area landslide susceptibility or hazard maps and community vulnerability assessments); and (2) by undertaking detailed slope feature mapping at the community scale so as to understand the precise landslide mechanisms. In densely populated vulnerable communities, infiltration of surface water is often a significant factor in causing

---

FIGURE 1.14 Evolution of social fund objectives and activities

Late 1980s	1990	Late 1990s	2000	Late 2000s
Employment/crisis response	Centrally driven infrastructure/ social service development	CDD approaches	Support for decentralization/ CDD/microfinance	Agencies take on added responsibilities (such as CCT/ disaster management)

Temporary funds ⟶ Increased integration into country's poverty reduction efforts and mainstreaming as legitimate institutions of government

Source: de Silva and Sum 2008.

Note: CCT = conditional cash transfer; CDD = community-driven development.

landslides. Treatment of this hazard involves designing and constructing drains in key locations to capture surface water; this is undertaken by government teams and community contractors. Evidence of the effectiveness of the hazard reduction measures is evaluated. The role of the government in addressing both the physical and social risk drivers, and at the correct scale (hillside/community level), is vital.

This approach to community-based landslide risk reduction is discussed more fully in section 1.4. Indeed, this book as a whole aims to provide a flexible blueprint for this form of landslide risk management.

1.3.4 Landslide risk and other development policy issues

A range of development policy issues and processes can result in intensified landslide occurrence, including climate change, urbanization, land-use practices (deforestation, cutting of slopes for housing construction), and inadequate management of water and sewage systems. Two such issues are useful to introduce at this stage because of their connection to the predominant landslide risk drivers MoSSaiC seeks to mitigate.

- Some predictions (e.g., UNISDR 2009) maintain that *climate change* may cause an increase in the intensity of rainfall events in the humid tropics. Knutson et al. (2010, 157) additionally comment that "it must be acknowledged that trend detection is hampered by the substantial limitations in the availability and quality of globally available data." Because rainfall is one of the physical drivers of landslide hazard, it is possible that climate change could increase the frequency of rainfall-triggered landslides in this region.

- *Urbanization* is a major socioeconomic driver with respect to landslide risk. As noted above, the activity of developing landslide-prone slopes can increase landslide hazard, while those living on the slopes tend to be the most vulnerable to such disasters.

Many developing tropical and subtropical regions are subject to rainfall events that trigger landslides on steep slopes. Certain current climate change predictions point to the likelihood of an increase in the intensity of hurricanes and other extreme rainfall events in those regions, which could be expected to result in an increase in the number and magnitude of landslides (Mann and Kerry 2006).

The links between climate change, development, and DRR are strongly emphasized by international development agencies. For example, the United Nations International Strategy for Disaster Reduction notes that "Disaster risk reduction and climate change mitigation and adaptation share common goals. Both fields aim to reduce the vulnerability of communities and achieve sustainable development" (UNISDR 2012). This bolsters an earlier statement that "the impact of any increases in weather-related hazards will be highly asymmetric. Poorer countries that concentrate most existing risk will be disproportionately affected by climate change" (UNISDR 2009, 20).

Where possible, predicted changes in the recurrence intervals of landslide-triggering rainfall events should be incorporated in landslide hazard assessment. The risk of not doing so may leave a significant public liability, either because the private sector will no longer bear the risk or due to the increased costs of disaster recovery (UNISDR 2009). In some cases, even relatively simple structural measures could yield both short- and long-term benefits to climate change. Because such measures could include landslide mitigation, MoSSaiC is consistent with this policy agenda.

Urbanization

Societal change is more rapid than climate change. Four important societal drivers provide a critical context for the accumulation of landslide risk: a significant rise in the global population (figure 1.15a), accompanied by increased urbanization (figure 1.15b) and poor housing (figure 1.15c), which results in the

FIGURE 1.15 Population growth and urbanization drivers of landslide risk

a. Global population growth

billions

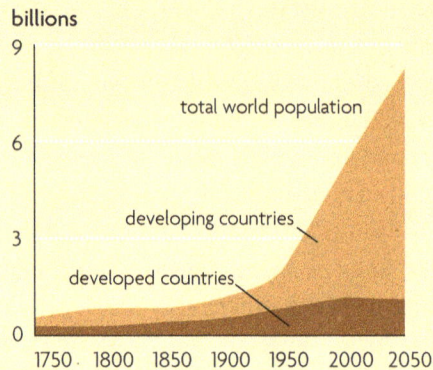

total world population

developing countries

developed countries

b. Urban/rural population shift

percent

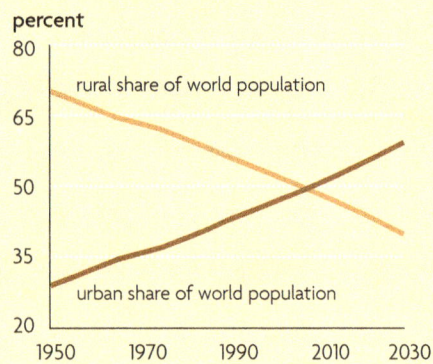

rural share of world population

urban share of world population

c. Growth in slum population

billions

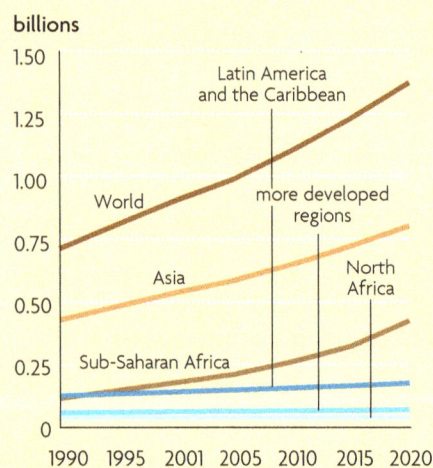

Latin America and the Caribbean

World

more developed regions

Asia

North Africa

Sub-Saharan Africa

Sources: a—Soubbotina 2004; b—UN 2007; c—UN-Habitat 2005.

Note: In c, figures for 1995 are interpolated using estimates for 1990 and 2001. Figures for 2005 are projections. Australia, New Zealand, and Japan are included in the more developed regions.

most vulnerable having the greatest exposure to landslide risk (figure 1.5).

Slums will grow on marginal urban land because the speed of economic growth in urban centers is not keeping pace with the combined impact of increasing population and rural-to-urban migration. People move to urban centers hoping to capture a place in the new economy. But this urban inflow outruns the capacity of private employment generation and government capacity to create infrastructure (Spence 2011).

Housing tenure is also relevant in this context. The World Bank (2009) reports that for low-income countries, the predominant housing tenure is unauthorized (defined by Angel 2000 as not in compliance with current regulations concerning landownership, land-use and planning zones, or construction), with small amounts of squatter housing (table 1.5).

The following urbanization factors serve to increase landslide risk:

- In many locations, the amount of unauthorized housing (approximately 60 percent in areas of the Eastern Caribbean, e.g.) exceeds that of authorized housing. Planning and associated zoning policies can be expected to have a limited impact in such circumstances.

- Unauthorized or informal housing is often located on already landslide-prone slopes. While typical slope zoning requirements for a landslide-prone area suggest that no houses should be built on slopes that exceed 14 degrees (Schuster and Highland 2007), informal housing settlements are invariably on hill slopes that are considerably steeper.

- Unauthorized housing may contribute to slope instability if residents

  — cut slopes at steep angles to provide benched slopes for additional housing;

  — redirect storm runoff so flows are concentrated onto portions of slopes that are not prepared to receive them;

  — add water to slopes from septic systems; or

TABLE 1.5 Percentage of owner occupancy, unauthorized housing, and squatter housing by country income group, 1990

HOUSING TENURE	LOW INCOME	LOWER-MIDDLE INCOME	UPPER-MIDDLE INCOME	HIGH INCOME
Owner occupancy	33	59	57	59
Unauthorized housing	64	27	9	0
Squatter housing	17	16	4	0

Source: World Bank 2009.

— remove trees, shrubs, and other woody vegetation (Olshansky 1996).

- The numbers of people living in unauthorized housing areas have grown very rapidly. In Caracas, República Bolivariana de Venezuela, it has been estimated that about 40 percent of the population lives in low-income districts (*barrios*) that grow at an annual rate of about 20 percent (Schuster and Highland 2007).

The trends in increasing unauthorized urban development and landslide risk will continue unless effective mitigation measures are delivered on the ground. An attendant issue for governments to consider is the degree to which they would regard the construction of landslide mitigation measures as legitimizing unauthorized communities in such circumstances. This is an issue that would need to be reviewed when any such project is considered for implementation.

1.4 MOSSAIC

1.4.1 Overview

The 2010 *World Development Report* provides this overview of MoSSaiC:

A new way of delivering real landslide-risk reduction to vulnerable communities was piloted by MoSSaiC, a program aimed at improving the management of slopes in communities in the Eastern Caribbean. MoSSaiC identifies and implements low-cost, community-based approaches to land-slide-risk reduction, in which community residents indicate areas of perceived drainage problems before assessing options for reducing landslide risk by managing surface water.

The activities? Managing surface water in all forms (roof water, gray water, and overland flow of rainfall water), monitoring shallow groundwater conditions, and constructing low-cost drain systems. All the work is bid out to contractors in the community. This end-to-end community engagement encourages participation in planning, executing, and maintaining surface water management on high-risk slopes. It produces a program owned by the community rather than imposed by the agency or government.

MoSSaiC has lowered landslide risk by offering the community employment and risk awareness—and has taken a participatory approach to rolling out the program to other communities. The program shows that changing community views of hazard mitigation can enhance community perceptions about climate risks. It also establishes a feedback loop between project inputs and outputs, with more than 80 percent of funds spent in the communities, allowing communities and governments to establish a clear link between risk perceptions, inputs, and tangible outputs (World Bank 2010a, 327).

In contrast to more top-down approaches, MoSSaiC has been developed at the scale of communities and hillsides, thus accessing community information and slope parameters at a process-relevant scale. This approach enables engagement with residents and government experts (including engineers, surveyors, planners, and community development officers) in order to develop a comprehensive assessment of likely landslide triggers, the level of hazard, and potential impact. Typically, the dominant instability mechanism in these densely constructed communities is the infiltration of rainfall and household water into the slope material—and the concentration of such flows at landslide-prone locations due to altered surface water runoff and slope drainage patterns. Landslide hazard mitigation measures therefore consist of appropriately located drains to intercept and control surface water, the capture of roof water, and the connection of households to the drainage network.

As introduced in section 1.2, MoSSaiC is based on three key foundations (table 1.6)—a **scientific** base that, combined with a **community** base, delivers the **evidence** base for landslide mitigation. Management and clear communication of this approach, within government and in partnership with the community, can result in **behavioral change** regarding slope stability practices and **policies**.

These three foundations—combining research, policy, and humanitarian interests to deliver evidence for undertaking mitigation and for establishing postmitigation outcomes—require a functional holistic structure (figure 1.16). The following chapters detail the various elements within this structure.

1.4.2 MoSSaiC: The science basis

A landslide risk assessment with an appropriate scientific basis provides the foundation for designing an intervention and allows those advocating the measures to justify their recommendations. An understanding of the mechanisms that trigger landslides and the scale at which they operate is thus essential.

The drivers of landslide risk can be summarized as follows.

- **Physical drivers.** Landslide hazard results from a combination of preparatory factors relating to slope geometry, soil and geology,

TABLE 1.6 The foundations of MoSSaiC

FOUNDATION	EXPLANATION	MoSSaiC
Science base	Need to understand the physical drivers for landslide hazard in order to design appropriate mitigation measures	• Identifies localized physical causes of landslide hazard at the correct physical scale (this coincides with the community scale and slope management practices) • Addresses physical causes of landslides at this scale • Provides scientifically based justification for community selection and mitigation measures
Community base	Need to understand the human risk drivers (as they relate to both the physical hazard and to vulnerability) and balance government policy approaches with community-based participatory solutions	• Focuses on the most vulnerable communities • Engages with the community to identify landslide hazard causes and solutions, often related to drainage • Employs contractors and workers from the community to construct the drainage measures • Recognizes the role of individuals in reducing landslide risk • Builds in-house teams of managers and expert practitioners to work with communities and deliver the mitigation measures • Encourages government-community partnerships
Evidence base	Need to provide evidence that landslide mitigation pays	• Delivers appropriate physical works to reduce landslide hazard • Delivers the majority of project funding and time in the most vulnerable communities • Demonstrates the benefits and cost-effectiveness of community-based landslide risk reduction to decision makers • Changes the local risk perception and encourages behavioral change with respect to sustainable management of slope stability in communities

FIGURE 1.16 MoSSaiC architecture—integrating science, communities, and evidence

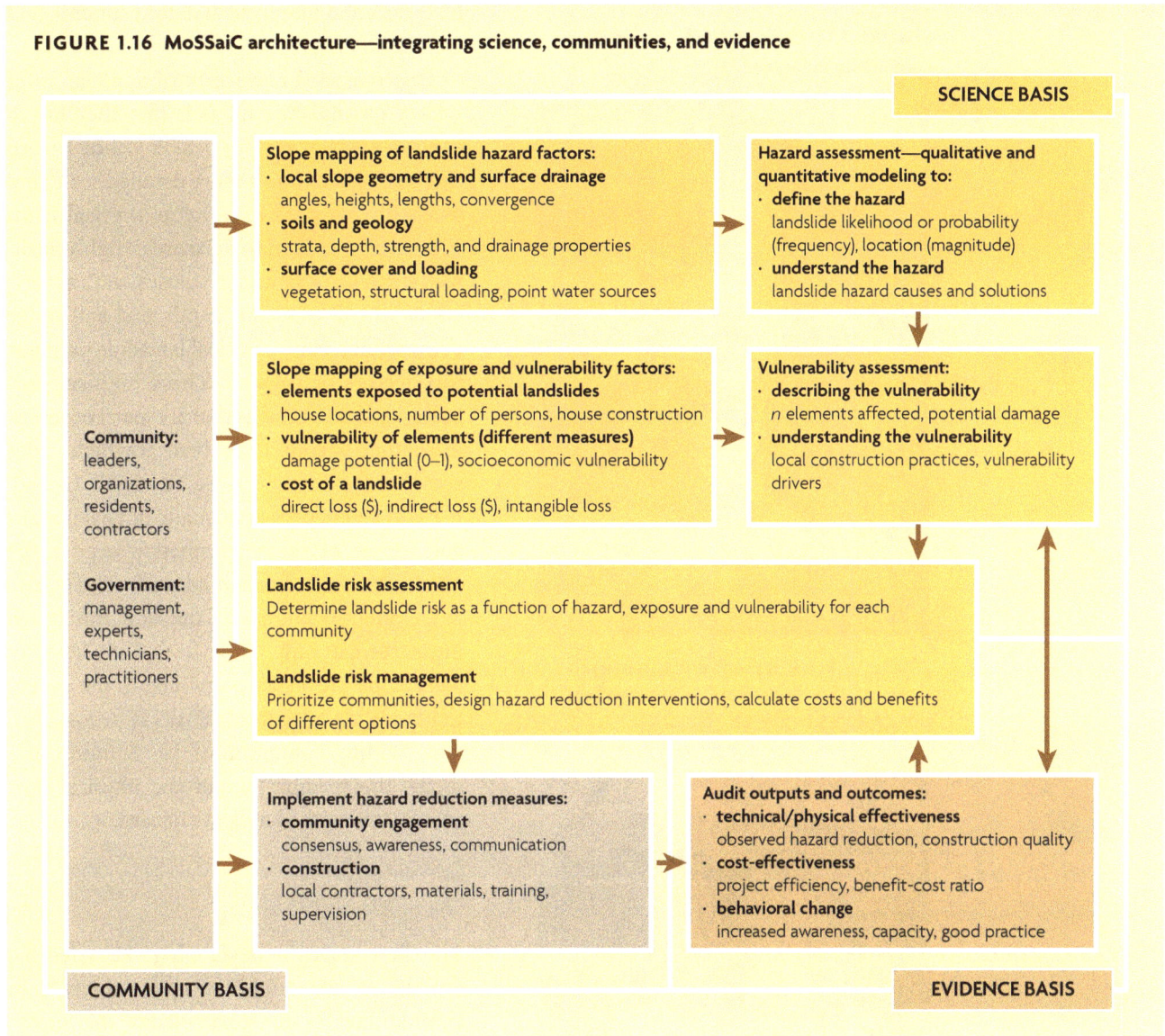

vegetation, surface water and groundwater regimes, and triggering mechanisms such as rainfall and seismic events. Tropical regions are especially susceptible to landslides because of high-intensity and -duration rainfall in the context of the deep soils (often on steep slopes) in such environments.

- **Anthropogenic contributors.** Even without climate change, anthropogenic activities are increasing landslide risk in some of the most vulnerable urban communities in developing countries. These activities include altering slope geometry with earthworks (cut and fill at the scale of household plots), loading slopes with buildings and infrastructure, changing the vegetation, and consequential changes in slope surface water and groundwater regimes. The pressure of development and population growth on available land means that the poorer, most vulnerable sections of society are living on the most-marginal, landslide-prone hillsides (figure 1.17).

> MoSSaiC is designed to address a very significant subset of landslide types: rotational and translational slides in predominately fine materials (soil) that are principally triggered by rainfall.

FIGURE 1.17 Housing stock can reflect community vulnerability

a. Because properties such as this can essentially be built in a weekend, effective urbanization of slopes can be very rapid.

b. Property abandonment can further complicate the issue of land and property titles in vulnerable communities.

Understanding the risk drivers at the local scale

Conventional top-down risk reduction initiatives typically focus on wide-area (100–1,000 m^2) mapping techniques which can be used to identify zones of landslide susceptibility based on the overlay and indexing of topographic, soil/geology, and vegetation maps. However, "management-oriented hazard models have been applied in the developing world only rarely and with mixed success...in large part because of the limitations of relevant

historical and biophysical data" (Zaitchik and van Es 2003, 267).

One reason for the lack of application of wide-area landslide maps is that they fail to capture many of the physical landslide hazard drivers that occur at a more detailed scale, and so cannot be used to develop physical landslide hazard reduction measures. Highly localized slope features and processes, such as variations in soil type and depth, and soil water convergence, can be critical landslide preparatory factors or triggers. These physical processes operate at scales that are many orders of magnitude smaller than those at which wide-area hazard maps can be resolved. Indeed, maps of soil depths are usually not even available. Some of these parameters need to be resolved at the household scale (1–50 m^2). Since identification of landslide mitigation measures can only come from knowledge of local slope processes pertaining to the potential landslide trigger, MoSSaiC is designed to look within communities to examine and model the specific human and physical processes driving the landslide hazard.

Landslide risk reduction measures must have a scientific basis

The first stage in developing the scientific foundation for landslide risk reduction in communities is to acknowledge the highly localized scale of the physical and human hazard drivers. MoSSaiC therefore takes landslide hazard mapping into the communities. Chapter 5 provides guidance on how to do this. The objective of community-based mapping is to observe and scientifically interpret slope features and processes, and to consider how they vary over both time and space. This analysis should be done at a scale that is capable of revealing the precise mechanisms determining the stability of the slope; this will enable identification of the potential mechanisms by which slope stability can be improved.

In densely populated unauthorized housing communities, it is essential to identify the effects of highly localized surface water regimes, built structures, and cut slopes. Slope hydrology is one such landslide hazard driver with a high spatial and temporal variability. The surface and groundwater regimes in such locations will vary over short time scales in response to rainfall events and the addition of household water to the slope. Slope instability is often increased where metered water is supplied to households in the absence of any surface water drainage. In the Caribbean, where housing density can approach 70 percent of the slope surface cover, the effect is to nearly double the amount of surface water going onto the slope compared with that of annual rainfall (Anderson and Holcombe 2006).

MoSSaiC employs a different approach to that used in generating wide-area hazard maps. Landslide hazard mapping is carried out at a much more detailed scale (1:500 or more) so that specific locations of landslide hazard can be identified and the physical drivers understood. This understanding of physical landslide drivers underpins design and implementation of appropriate hazard reduction measures.

So, while large-scale landslide hazard maps generated as a result of top-down government policies may provide an indication of approximate landslide zones, MoSSaiC practitioners must work at the highly resolved spatial scales coincident with the dominant slope process controls. This requires observation and interpretation of slope processes on the ground, with the support of appropriate scientific tools, in order to provide a scientific basis for delivering landslide risk reduction measures in communities.

> The MoSSaiC methodology is intended to reduce existing landslide risk and not to encourage, and provide for, the construction of houses on slopes deemed landslide prone.

1.4.3 MoSSaiC: The community basis

With top-down advocacy and managerial support, local-scale landslide risk reduction can have tangible benefits in terms of project delivery time, benefit-cost ratios, scientific basis, and sustainable policy uptake. The approach goes a long way to reconciling the scale issues and risk drivers (discussed above) encountered in delivering effective landslide risk reduction.

The aim of MoSSaiC is to engage with the community, recognize its vital role in understanding and managing slope stability, and build its capacity to do so. Simultaneously, the community becomes the classroom for the government teams to exercise their own expertise, develop partnerships with the community, and establish good technical and managerial practices with respect to landslide risk.

All too often, "aid flows from those who happen to be strong, to those who happen to be weak, reflecting an inherently unbalanced power relationship" (Curtis 2004, 422). An example of such an imbalance was identified by Green, Miles, and Svekla (2009) in an analysis of the institutions involved in DRR in the most vulnerable settlements in Guatemala City. The relationship among the stakeholders, shown in figure 1.18, suggests that

> [T]here are minimal opportunities provided by external actors to precarious settlement residents to influence the allocation of funds used in improving the settlements...quite literally, money flows around the precarious settlements, but not directly into them (Green, Miles, and Svekla 2009, 53).

Such imbalances are within a context of potential network instability, with a small change in that context (e.g., political turnover) potentially causing the network to collapse.

MoSSaiC aims to redress such imbalances affecting vulnerable communities by affirming and strengthening the community focus for risk reduction. For MoSSaiC, "community based" means engaging and working with communities to jointly find and deliver solutions to landslide risk.

Learning from communities

Residents influence the key variables underlying the complex system of landslide risk and disaster occurrence. A San Salvador slum dweller acknowledged the constant efforts

FIGURE 1.18 Stakeholder connections in Guatemala City's precarious settlements, showing how money flows around, but not into, the settlements

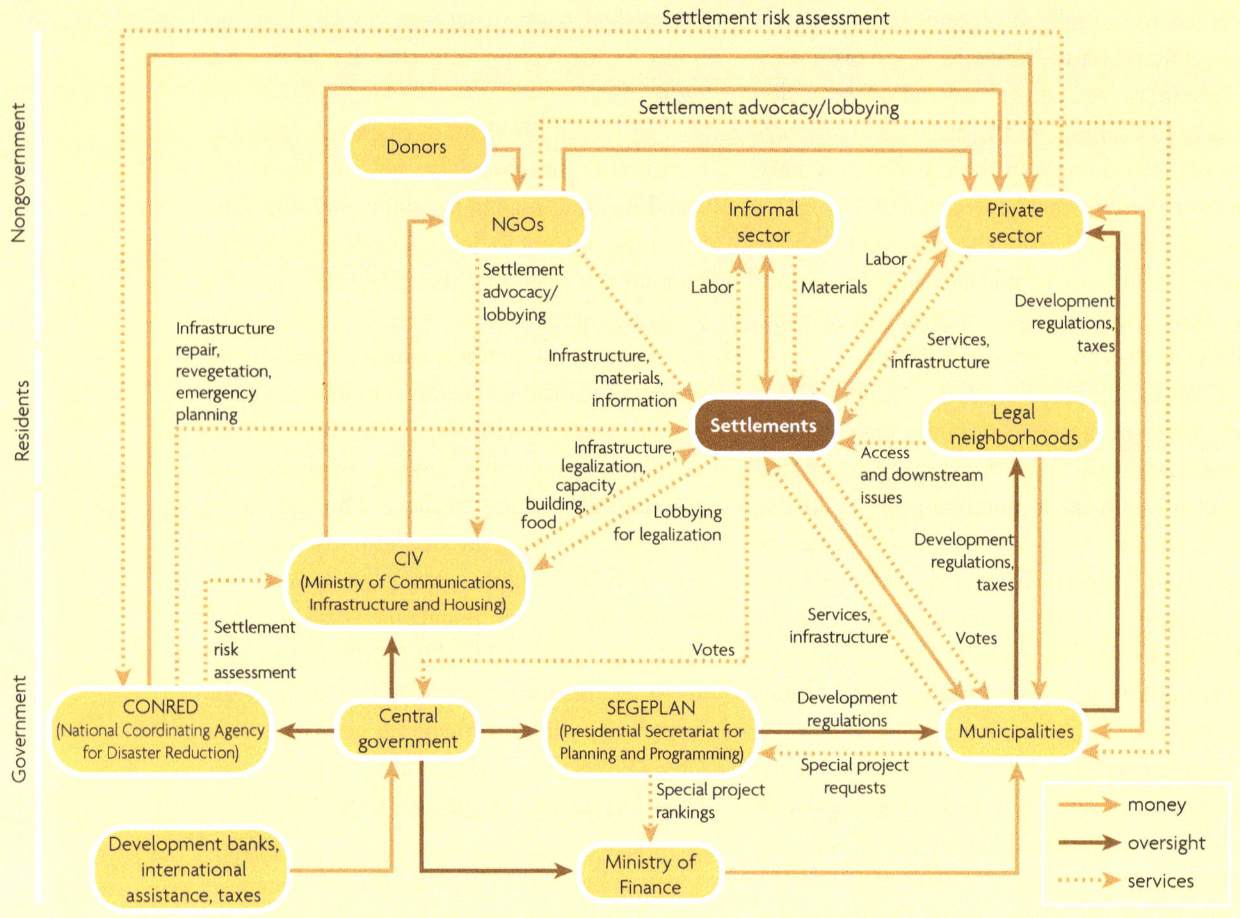

Source: Green, Miles, and Svekla 2009.

individuals make in coping with disasters and disaster risk: "We are always trying to improve, little by little, step by step, in order to become more secure" (Wamsler 2007, 118).

Household strategies to reduce risk are diverse and include physical/technological, environmental, economic, social/cultural, organizational, and institutional measures (table 1.7).

Because such DRR activity may be taking place in a vulnerable community at the household level, it is important to establish the degree of this activity and build on it through MoSSaiC. As Rayner and Malone (1997, 332) note, "adaptation is a bottom-up strategy that starts with changes and pressures experienced in people's daily lives." Whether a community is adapting to climate change or to existing

(and increasing) risks such as landslides, understanding the concerns of the residents is critical. In this respect, identification of the landslide hazard and appropriate landslide risk reduction measures properly begins with learning from communities (figure 1.19).

This learning process must extend to understanding the way in which the community functions and how MoSSaiC can best be applied in that context. The guidance and methods presented in this book should serve as a flexible blueprint toward this end.

Identifying the most sensitive and effective means for engaging with each community will also provide the best opportunity for residents to "own" the project and adopt good slope management practices for themselves (figure 1.20):

TABLE 1.7 Coping mechanisms deployed by individual residents in vulnerable communities to reduce landslide risk

FOCUS/AIM	ACTIVITY IDENTIFIED
Constructive structural house improvements	• Increasing inclination of roofs (for better runoff without damaging roof constructions) • Prolonging roof projections/eaves (to protect houses and pathways from damage/erosion) • Changing direction of roof inclination (so rainwater is discharged without causing damage/landslides) • Installing provisional gutters as roof eaves (so rainwater is discharged without causing damage/landslides) • Replacing mud walls with brick walls, wooden pillars with metallic ones, and corrugated iron with more durable materials (to better withstand earthquakes, rain, and/or floodwater) • Regularly replacing corrugated iron, wooden pillars, and beams (to better withstand rain or earthquakes) • Improving roof fittings (to better withstand earthquakes and windstorms) • Regularly covering walls and floors with (additional) cement (for better runoff without causing damage/erosion) • Filling cracks with cement (for better runoff without causing damage/erosion) • Closing holes in corrugated iron sheets using special fillings or patches on top of or under sheets (to prevent water entering the house) • Changing the locations of latrines and wash places (to mitigate landslides)
Nonconstructive nonstructural house improvements	• Blocking wastewater pipes with stones and other objects when river levels rise (to avoid flooding and/or related contamination) • Putting wood or bricks on the roof (to hold it in place during high winds) • Putting plastic sheets on the roof, on the inside walls, or over the bed (to prevent water entering or damaging the house) • Building water barriers in front of the house (to prevent water entering the house) • Digging water channels in earth floors inside the house (for better runoff without causing damage/erosion) • Putting pots under roofs with holes (to catch water, preventing damage/erosion) • Strengthening pathways by covering them with (additional) cement and filling cracks (to mitigate landslides and minimize damage caused by rain and earthquakes) • Filling in former latrine holes with earth, stones, and/or cement (to mitigate landslides and minimize damage caused by rain and earthquakes)
Constructive structural improvement of the surrounding living environment	• Repairing public infrastructure that passes through the settlement, such as wastewater pipes (to avoid flooding and related contamination) • Building provisional water channels with corrugated iron or cement (to discharge rainwater without causing damage/landslides) • Building fences to hold back soil (mitigating landslides) and/or to prevent children from falling (fences are made of corrugated iron, mattress springs, wooden pillars, and wire netting) • Compacting soil (to mitigate landslides and minimize damage caused by rain and earthquakes) • Building retaining walls or embankments from old tires, stones, and cement; old tires and soil; bricks and cement; stones only; nylon bags filled with soil and cement; and other materials (to mitigate landslides and minimize damage caused by earthquakes)
Nonconstructive nonstructural improvement of the surrounding living environment	• Putting plastic sheets on slopes, often during entire year (to mitigate landslides) • Digging water channels in earth outside the house (to discharge rainwater without causing damage/landslides) • Avoiding obvious flood- or landslide-prone locations for house expansion • Replacing eroded earth with new earth (to mitigate landslides and minimize damage caused by rain and earthquakes) • Cleaning water gutters (to mitigate flooding)
Use of natural resources to reduce risk	• Planting vegetation to prevent landslides
Removal of natural resources representing risk	• Cutting down bigger branches and trees located close to houses (to minimize the risk of them falling down and causing damage during earthquakes and landslides)
Cleanup of natural environment	• Cleaning waste from slopes (to mitigate flooding caused by blocked water gutters) • Replacing eroded earth with new earth (to mitigate landslides and minimize damage caused by rain and earthquakes)

Source: Wamsler 2007.

FIGURE 1.19 Learning from community residents

It is important to spend time in communities talking with residents and learning from them about their perceptions of risk and of any landslide occurrences within the community, however minor.

FIGURE 1.20 Effects of prompt and informed action

Prompt drainage action by the owner, taken while a major landslide rose halfway up the house's rear wall, undoubtedly saved this property from being lost. The resident had reported earlier minor slides in the same location.

A community-based approach aims to reduce their socially constructed vulnerability by involving communities as active participants in a disaster program. There is also a broadening consensus that it is cost-effective to train and educate communities about risks they face, provide them access to resources and knowledge, and to develop community-based preparedness and mitigation programs (World Bank 2007).

Such considerations are important in understanding the precise physical and social causality of landslide risk, which is intrinsically linked to the activity of individual households in terms of water and slope management practices. There is no blanket solution, as top-down hazard mapping approaches so often implicitly suggest. For this reason, the knowledge of all community members is vital in gaining an understanding of the highly localized slope processes leading to landslides.

Working toward community-owned solutions

A critical component of the MoSSaiC methodology is to discuss with residents why landslide risk drivers can vary over short distances, and therefore why they should expect that different hazard reduction measures may be needed on different parts of the hillside. Understandably, householders are anxious that they will tangibly benefit from such measures and will need reassurance, for instance, that a drain built upslope of their house will actually help them even if it is not on their property. That such a decision (the design of the community drainage system) is not an imposed solution, but one that the community has taken ownership of from the beginning is important—not least for residents in vulnerable communities who are too often the subjects of development rather than active participants in the process.

Numerous methods exist for community participation, but they need to be adapted to the local context; nearly all require facilitation and other forms of support from the government or from nongovernmental organizations (NGOs). Transparency and effective communication are essential to maintaining engagement and credibility with and within the community during the reconstruction process.

Engaging the community

A good risk reduction strategy engages communities and helps people work together to minimize risk. Participation should be by the *entire* community, particularly women, young people, and all livelihood groups—a point that should be clearly communicated to the community. Community engagement is valuable for the reasons given in table 1.8.

TABLE 1.8 Value of community engagement

VALUE	EXPLANATION
Allows community knowledge and scientific understanding of hazard and vulnerabilities to be combined	Community-based approaches require a somewhat different programming flow that begins with mobilizing social groups and communities and having them fully involved in the risk assessment process
Reveals community subgroups	"The community" is not a monolith, but a complex organism with many alliances and subgroups; it needs to be engaged in order to identify concerns, goals, and abilities, but there may not be consensus on these items
Provides high-resolution information	The scale at which community engagement is most effective may be quite small—for example, as few as 10 families; individuals may contribute valuable information on landslide processes at the scale of 1–50 m^2
Can reveal different perceptions to those of government	Engagement of the community may bring out different preferences and expectations, so agencies involved must be open to altering their preconceived vision of the landslide risk management process
Builds skills within the community	Strengthens community skills and capacity for assessing landslide risk, constructing drainage measures, maintaining the intervention, and developing sustainable slope management practices; training can play an important role in building a community's capacity to take on project responsibilities
Delivers social outcomes	Empowers individuals, increases local capacity, strengthens democratic processes, and gives voice to marginalized groups
Assists program effectiveness	Creates a sense of ownership, improves program quality, mobilizes resources, and stimulates community involvement in execution

Source: World Bank 2010c.

Participation empowers communities; however, the outcomes of that participation can be unpredictable. The participatory process may

- give rise to new actors and stakeholders;

- create conflicts among organizations that had previously worked together harmoniously;

- give a platform to vocal individuals whose views are not shared by the majority;

- inflame preexisting, but hitherto dormant, tensions within the community;

- raise expectations beyond delivery possibilities, insofar as community perceptions may differ from information residents are actually given;

- engender "mirror politics," with communities potentially feigning agreement in order to divert opportunities to other ends; and

- infuse political issues at the national level into the proposed community project.

Other behaviors possibly arising during discussions with community residents are that community members may not be immediately forthcoming with their perspectives, may downplay the significance of threats, or may reserve judgment until they see something tangible (UNDP 2008).

Communities participate in MoSSaiC projects through five activities:

- Provision of information on slope features and landslide hazard

- Organization of community meetings and coordination with government teams

- Involvement in identifying the landslide hazard reduction measures

- Construction (possibly also including contracting and procurement)

- Monitoring and maintenance of landslide mitigation measures

Building government capacity

Governments often have sufficient technical and managerial skills that can be harnessed to design and deliver landslide risk reduction measures in communities. By creating a cross-disciplinary management unit from such a skill base, it is possible to embed MoSSaiC in government practice and policy. Chapter 2 is focused on how such a management team—here referred to as the MoSSaiC core unit (MCU)—can be built. It identifies the types of in-house expert practitioners needed for implementing the various tasks. The methods and tools provided in this book can be adapted to suit the government's structures, protocols, and practices. The aim is that governments adapt and adopt MoSSaiC in a way that can be sustained and embedded in local practice and policy.

Clear communication in government-community partnerships

Organizing and facilitating community participation should not be done on an ad hoc basis. "Unless risk analysis and communication are adequately factored in, major differences in perceptions of risk can impede successful policy design and implementation" (World Bank 2010a, 325). It is important to guide the participation process and make sure that people's expectations are realistic, especially if they believe that large amounts of funding are available. Community-based projects require thoughtful engagement on the part of the government:

> Information, education, and awareness-raising as carried out so far, are at best not enough to spur people into action and at worst counter-productive... This calls for a different approach, where the individual is considered not merely the passive receiver of information but an agent in both causes and solutions (World Bank 2010a, 327).

When a government-community partnership is well configured, there can be a multiplier effect as the community realizes its capabilities, and new ideas for activities and projects emerge. Trained facilitators and other experts in community participation should be part of the MCU to ensure such synergies.

1.4.4 MoSSaiC: The evidence base

Decision makers need an evidence base in order to endorse expenditure on landslide risk reduction and adopt a proactive ex ante policy approach. A typical MoSSaiC project that tackles the root causes of landslide hazard will have measurable short-term outputs and longer-term outcomes (table 1.9).

Types of evidence

This book emphasizes the need to identify evidence of longer-term benefits of landslide risk reduction in communities—the actual reduction in the hazard, and the direct and indirect benefits (financial and social). The delivery of physical landslide risk reduction measures provides the opportunity to observe the benefits in terms of potentially avoided landslide occurrence and losses. This form of evidence is counterfactual and often anecdotal, since it is not know what would have happened if the physical measures had not been in place. However, it is still a powerful means of demonstrating the benefits of the intervention. Slope stability modeling can provide a means for quantifying the reduction in the frequency or magnitude of landslides. These model predictions can then be related to the value of the losses avoided (a project benefit) and compared with project costs. Less-tangible social benefits and changes in slope management practice should also be captured. Chapter 9 presents some potential methods for developing this evidence base and identifying the extent of behavioral change.

MoSSaiC project outcomes from sample interventions completed in St. Lucia and Dominica are outlined in table 1.10.

1.4.5 MoSSaiC project components

There are nine principle MoSSaiC project components, as reflected in the chapters in this book. While seven are sequential (figure 1.21), two (encouraging behavioral

TABLE 1.9 Basic MoSSaiC outputs and outcomes providing evidence for ex ante landslide mitigation

BASIC OUTPUTS AND OUTCOMES		MEASURE (EVIDENCE BASE)
Project outputs	Quantities	Quantity of physical measures constructed, funds disbursed, persons employed, etc.
	Direct physical benefits: landslide hazard reduced	Observation and local knowledge relating to the effect of heavy rainfall events post-intervention (qualitative)
		Modeled/predicted stability of slope for before and after scenarios (quantitative)
	Additional physical and social benefits to community: reduced localized flooding, less mud on paths, improved water supply through rainwater harvesting, improved environment	Observation and local knowledge relating to the effect of heavy rainfall events post-intervention (qualitative)
		Cost-benefit analysis of project
Longer-term project outcomes	Evidence of behavioral change	Institutional uptake of ex ante approach to managing slope stability in communities based on scientific understanding, community focus, and evidence of effectiveness
		Community uptake of good slope management practices based on understanding of local slope processes and demonstration of tangible benefits

change and project evaluation) are crosscutting components relevant from the start of any proposed MoSSaiC intervention and continuing through to the postproject period.

The nine components can be subdivided into a series of steps that deliver MoSSaiC.

These provide the framework for each chapter and are outlined in table 1.11.

1.4.6 MoSSaiC pilots

MoSSaiC was initially developed and applied in the Eastern Caribbean (table 1.12). Fig-

TABLE 1.10 Broad impacts of community-based landslide risk reduction program in St. Lucia and Dominica, 2005–10

CATEGORY	INDICATOR	IMPACT (IN 11 COMMUNITIES)
Physical	Hazard reduction	Pre-MoSSaiC: Minor and major failures during low-recurrence-interval events (~1 in 3–5 year 24 hour) with loss of houses in some communities
		Post-MoSSaiC: No reported failures from Hurricane Tomas (~1 in 500-year 24-hour rainfall event)
Economic	Project expenditure profile	~80% of funds spent on materials and community labor
		Intervention cost equates with approximately 2.3% of community relocation costs should a major landslide occur
		Average cost per community resident ~$250
		~1,000 person-weeks employment for community members
	Benefit-cost ratio	>2.7:1 in a selected community
Community	Persons involved	Number of households ~750, number of residents ~4,000
	Community construction partnerships	Residents share with government in terms of design, construction, and, in some cases, cost
	Water supply continuity	450-gallon water tanks supplied to most-deserving residents in selected communities
	Certification of key community members	A MoSSaiC certification system, resulting in award to three members from different communities for their commitment, leadership, and understanding of the MoSSaiC vision
Public awareness	Media recognition	St. Lucia, Dominica, St. Vincent and the Grenadines: TV/radio interviews, news coverage
	St. Lucia TV	30-minute MoSSaiC documentary commissioned by government

Source: Anderson et al. 2010.

FIGURE 1.21 MoSSaiC components

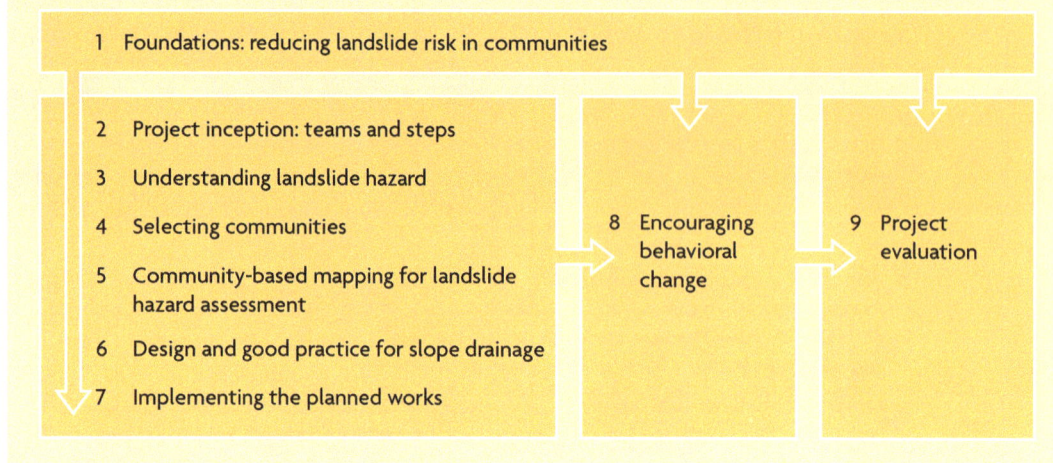

1 Foundations: reducing landslide risk in communities	

2 Project inception: teams and steps	
3 Understanding landslide hazard	
4 Selecting communities	8 Encouraging behavioral change
5 Community-based mapping for landslide hazard assessment	9 Project evaluation
6 Design and good practice for slope drainage	
7 Implementing the planned works	

ure 1.22 provides an indication of typical vulnerable urban communities and landslide risk drivers in this region.

Many of the countries in the region are particularly vulnerable to natural disasters (figure 1.23). To enable country comparisons, the World Bank (2010b) has assessed the impact of disasters on GDP over a 40-year period. For many countries, this impact exceeds 1 percent of GDP; notably, many SIDS fall into this category.

The vulnerability of this region is confirmed by the United Nations:

TABLE 1.11 MoSSaiC framework

CHAPTER	COVERAGE	OUTPUT
1. Foundations: Reducing Landslide Risk in Communities	1. Understand the disaster risk context with respect to landslides	Relevance of MoSSaiC approach to local landslide risk context identified
	2. Understand the innovative features and foundations of MoSSaiC	
	3. Identify general in-house expertise and the appropriate institutional structures for codifying a local approach toward landslide risk reduction	
	4. Brief key individuals on MoSSaiC (politicians, relevant ministries, in-house experts)	Core unit of team members identified
2. Project Inception: Teams and Steps	1. Establish the MCU; define and agree on key responsibilities • Identify available experts in government • Form the MCU and establish communication lines with government	MCU formed
	2. Identify and establish government task teams; define and agree on key responsibilities • MCU to identify individuals from relevant ministries to form government task teams (mapping, community liaison, engineering, technical support, communications, advocacy) • Define roles and responsibilities of the teams	Government task teams formed
	3. Identify and establish community task teams; define and agree on key responsibilities • MCU to identify individuals from selected communities to form community task teams (residents, representatives, construction teams) • Define roles and responsibilities of the teams	Community task teams formed
	4. Agree on a general template for project steps • Review project step template and amend as necessary • Assign team responsibilities to relevant project steps; confirm project milestones	Project steps determined and responsibilities assigned

(continued)

TABLE 1.11 MoSSaiC framework *(continued)*

CHAPTER	COVERAGE	OUTPUT
3. Understanding Landslide Hazard	1. Gain familiarity of different landslide types and how to identify those which may be addressed by MoSSaiC • Review landslide process introductory material in this book and other sources	MCU and task teams understand the types of landslide risk for which MoSSaiC is applicable
	2. Gain familiarity with slope processes and slope stability variables • Review landslide process variables as introduced in this book	MCU and task teams can identify different levels of landslide hazard and underlying physical causes
	3. Gain familiarity with methods for analyzing slope stability • Review slope stability software as introduced in this book and other sources	MCU and task teams can provide scientific rationale for landslide mitigation measures
4. Selecting Communities	1. Define the community selection process • Identify available experts in government • Determine availability of software and data • Request permission to use data if necessary • Design appropriate method for selecting communities	Agreed-upon selection method and criteria, roles and responsibilities, timeline
	2. Assess landslide hazard • Data acquisition: topography, soils, geology, land use, past landslides • Data analysis: landslide susceptibility or hazard within the study area	List or map of relative landslide susceptibility of different areas
	3. Assess exposure and vulnerability • Data acquisition: community locations, building footprints, housing/population density, census data or poverty data • Data analysis: vulnerability of exposed communities to landslide impacts in terms of physical damage, poverty, or other criteria	List or map of relative vulnerability of exposed communities
	4. Assess landslide risk • Data analysis: landslide susceptibility/hazard, exposure, and vulnerability data combined to determine overall landslide risk for study area • Data analysis: identify communities exposed to highest levels of landslide risk	List or map plus list of most-at-risk communities for possible risk reduction measures
	5. Select communities • Conduct brief site visits of short-listed communities to confirm results • Consult community liaison task team and other relevant local stakeholders to review list • Confirm prioritized community short list according to selection criteria	Prioritized community short list
	6. Prepare site map information for selected communities • Data acquisition: most detailed maps and aerial photos of selected communities • Map preparation: assemble community maps/photos and print hard copies	Hard-copy map and aerial photo for use on site
5. Community-Based Mapping for Landslide Hazard Assessment	1. Identify the best form of community participation and mobilization • Review and determine the most suitable form of community participation • Identify available community liaison experts in government	MCU agrees on appropriate community participation strategy
	2. Include key community members in the project team • Identify existing or new community representatives • Hold initial discussions with community representatives to brief them on mapping and project rationale	Key community members included

(continued)

TABLE 1.11 MoSSaiC framework (continued)

CHAPTER	COVERAGE	OUTPUT
	3. Plan and hold a community meeting	First community meeting held
	• Take advice from government and community representatives on location and style of meeting	
	• Compile a community base map from existing maps, plans, and aerial photos (see section 4.7) to bring to the meeting	
	4. Conduct the community-based mapping exercise; this will entail a considerable amount of time in the community	Community slope feature map
	• Talk with residents in each house to begin the process of engagement, knowledge sharing, and project ownership	
	• Observe and discuss wide-scale and localized slope features and landslide hazard	
	• Add local knowledge and slope feature information to the base map	
5. Community-Based Mapping for Landslide Hazard Assessment	5. Qualitatively assess the landslide hazard and potential causes	Slope process zone map (relative landslide hazard)
	• Use the community slope feature map to identify zones with different slope processes and landslide hazard	
	• Evaluate the role of surface water infiltration in contributing to the landslide hazard	
	6. Quantitatively assess the landslide hazard and the effectiveness of surface water management to reduce the hazard	Determination of viability of MoSSaiC approach
	• Use physically based software or simpler means to assess the likely contribution of surface water to landslide hazard	
	• Assess whether reducing surface water is likely to reduce landslide hazard	
	7. Identify possible locations for drains	Initial drainage plan and prioritization matrix
	• For each slope process zone, determine the most appropriate surface water management approach	
	• Prioritize the zones according to relative landslide hazard	
	8. Sign off on the initial drainage plan: organize a combined MCU-community walk-through and meeting to agree on the initial drainage plan	Initial drainage plan sign-off
	1. Identify the location and alignment of drains	Proposed drainage plan (drain alignments and dimensions)
	• Use the slope process zone map and initial drainage plan as a starting point; apply drainage alignment principles to identify potential drain network alignment	
	• Refine alignment details on site	
	2. Estimate drain discharge and dimensions	
	• Calculate surface water runoff and household water discharge into proposed drains	
	• Calculate required drain size	
	3. Specify drain construction and design details	Full drain specification
6. Design and Good Practice for Slope Drainage	4. Incorporate houses into the drainage plan	List of quantities needed for household connections
	• Identify houses to receive roof guttering, gray water pipes, water tanks, and hurricane straps	
	• Determine how household water will be directed to the drains (via pipes connected by concrete chambers or small drains)	
	5. Produce final drainage plan	Final drainage plan and cost estimate
	• Include all drain alignment and household connection details on the plan	
	• Estimate total project cost from unit costs	
	6. Stakeholder agreement on plan	Sign-off on the final drainage plan
	• Meet with the community and refine the plan	
	• Complete checks regarding relevant safeguards	
	• Submit plan for formal approval	

(continued)

TABLE 1.11 MoSSaiC framework *(continued)*

CHAPTER	COVERAGE	OUTPUT
7. Implementing the Planned Works	1. Prepare work package and request for tender documentation • Prepare a bill of quantities for the planned works • Incorporate appropriate contingency and any double-handling costs (i.e., where material has to be delivered to sites where access is difficult and requires the establishment of a storage site between delivery and construction site locations) • Decide on work package size that maximizes community engagement and meets procurement requirements • Prepare design drawings and plans to accompany each work package • Identify an appropriate plan for procuring materials depending on the community contracting approach, community capacity, and project procurement requirements	Work packages for implementation of drainage intervention to reduce landslide hazard
	2. Conduct the agreed-upon community contracting tendering process • Identify potential contractors from the community and provide briefing on proposed works and work packages, emphasizing the need for good construction practice • Invite tenders from contractors, providing assistance or training on how to submit a tender document • Evaluate tenders, award contracts, and brief contractors on safeguards	Briefing meeting for contractors held; community contracts awarded
	3. Implement construction • Select experienced site supervisors • Authorize start of construction and meet with the community to discuss the construction process and introduce site supervisors • Closely supervise the works to ensure good construction practices; clear communication among contractors, supervisors, community, and the MoSSaiC core unit; and timely disbursement of funds for procurement of materials and payment of contractors/laborers	Briefing meeting for community held; construction under way
	4. Sign off on completed construction • Identify outstanding works • Arrange for any necessary repairs or minor modifications • Sign off on completed construction and pay withholding payments to contractors	Construction completed and signed off on
8. Encouraging Behavioral Change	1. Understand how new practices are adopted • Use the steps in the ladder of adoption and behavioral change model to identify communication and capacity-building needs in each community and in government • Understand stakeholder perceptions and the role of community participation	Assessment of aspects of behavioral change to be addressed by communication and capacity-building activities
	2. Design a communication strategy • Review existing resources and methodologies for designing a communication strategy • Identify communication purposes and audiences • Select forms of communication and design messages	Communication strategy
	3. Design a capacity-building strategy • Review knowledge into action approaches • Identify levels of capacity, capacity requirements, and activities for building capacity	Capacity-building strategy
	4. Plan for postproject maintenance • Understand the need for incorporating maintenance into drain design and project planning	Project maintenance options
	5. Map out the complete behavioral change strategy • Map the agreed-upon behavioral change strategies and associated actions	Map of capacity-building strategies

(continued)

TABLE 1.11 MoSSaiC *(continued)*

CHAPTER	COVERAGE	OUTPUT
9. Project Evaluation	1. Agree on key performance indicators (KPIs) for immediate project outputs • Develop and agree on a list of KPIs that comply with donor/government needs and MoSSaiC output measures	List of project output KPIs for evaluation
	2. Agree on KPIs for medium-term project outcomes • Develop and agree on a list of project outcome measures that allow evaluation of landslide hazard reduction, project costs, and behavioral change	List of project outcome KPIs for evaluation
	3. Undertake project evaluation • Agree on responsibilities for short- and medium-term data collection and the project evaluation process • Carry out the evaluation	Project evaluation report

Countries with small and vulnerable economies, such as many SIDS and land-locked developing countries (LLDCs), have seen their economic development set back decades by disaster impacts. The countries with the highest ratio of economic losses in disasters with respect to their capital stock are all SIDS and LLDCs, such as Samoa and St. Lucia (UN 2009, 9).

Figure 1.24 shows the impact Hurricane Allen (1980) had on the economy of St. Lucia.

TABLE 1.12 Characteristics of MoSSaiC project locations in the Eastern Caribbean, 2004–10

FACTOR	DESCRIPTION
Region	Eastern Caribbean—SIDS with high vulnerability to natural disasters (UNISDR 2009)
Countries	St. Lucia, Dominica, and St. Vincent and the Grenadines
Slopes	Slopes of 25–50 degrees, which had previously exhibited instability at low rainfall intensities (typically as low as 1 in 1 year 24-hour events)
Slope material	Often comprising deep residual soils over highly weathered volcanic bedrocks or conglomerates
Communities	Unauthorized urban communities—unregulated development, densely built, with poor construction quality; each community typically comprising 20–100+ houses
Risk drivers	Rainfall events triggering landslides on slopes with increased susceptibility to landslides due to natural and anthropogenic influences

FIGURE 1.22 Typical communities and risk drivers for MoSSaiC interventions

a. Hillsides prone to landslides and populated by unauthorized housing.

b. Housing stock typical of vulnerable communities.

c. Density of unauthorized housing increases likelihood of property loss.

FIGURE 1.23 Countries with damages from disasters exceeding 1 percent of GDP

share of GDP (%)

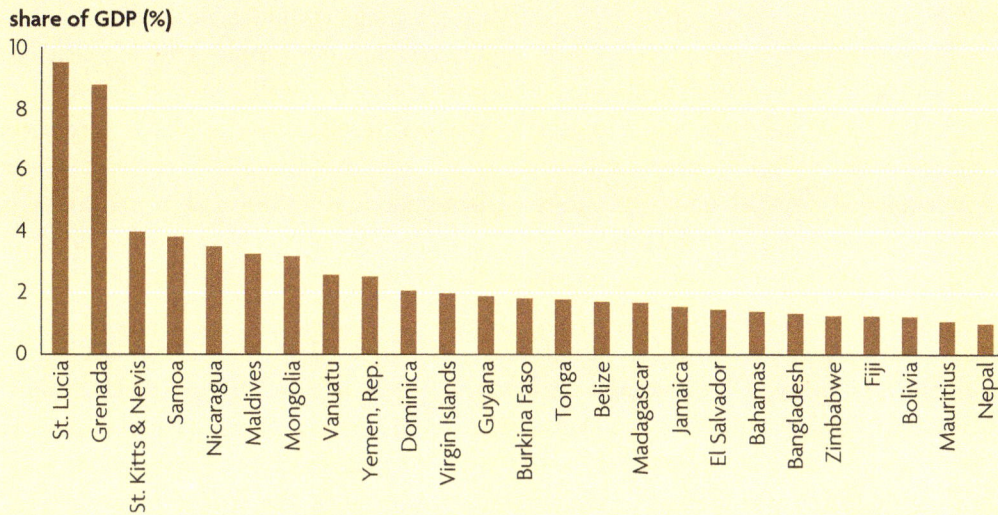

Source: World Bank 2010b.

FIGURE 1.24 Impact of Hurricane Allen (1980) on the economy of St. Lucia

constant 2000 $, millions

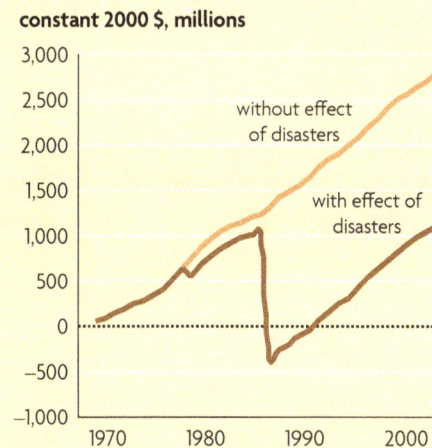

without effect of disasters

with effect of disasters

Source: UNISDR 2009.

The dark brown line shows the actual cumulative net capital formation for 1970–2006; the light brown line shows the projected cumulative net formation without economic losses from disasters.

The main MoSSaiC principles and methods developed in the Eastern Caribbean context are applicable in other parts of the humid tropics with comparable landslide risk drivers. The potential breadth of MoSSaiC applicability is illustrated by figure 1.25, which shows a community in Dumsi Pakha, a small village located in the Darjeeling Hills, in the Lesser Himalaya. It is a hillside with high-density housing and no provision for surface water management. With an average elevation of 2,050 m, the area has steep slopes and loose topsoil, giving rise to frequent landslides over recent years. In spite of strict rules and regulations, homes continue to be constructed in the area (Savethehills 2011). This environment is thus very similar to those of the Eastern Caribbean.

FIGURE 1.25 MoSSaiC is applicable to many locations outside the Eastern Caribbean

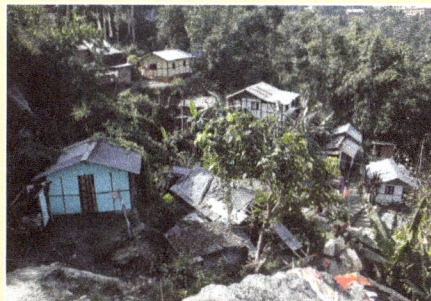

Source: Praful Rao, Savethehills, Kalimpong, India.

1.5 STARTING A MOSSAIC INTERVENTION

Starting a MoSSaiC intervention requires identification of the scale and scope of the project, creation of teams to deliver the program, selection of communities in which interventions are to be made, generation of a project logframe, and understanding of the issues involved in making the project sustainable.

This book is designed to provide a flexible blueprint for establishing a MoSSaiC intervention. While the majority of the text is, of necessity, devoted to the details of delivering on-the-ground mitigation measures, equal weight should be given by the MCU to evidence of performance of the measures (physical and cost-effectiveness, introduced in section 1.4.4), and to the longer-term outcomes and behavioral change achieved as a result (table 1.9 and figure 1.21).

1.5.1 Define the project scale

Initiating a new form of community-based project can rarely be done in one fell swoop at the national level; the numbers are just too daunting (table 1.13). Rather, starting with a few pilot projects should result in a locally relevant set of logistics, operational and training books, materials, and tools that can then be used to support a wider program.

Thus far, MoSSaiC has been applied at the small scale (section 1.4.6), using the definitions of Binswanger-Mkhize, de Regt, and Spector (2009) shown in table 1.13. MoSSaiC may potentially be scaled up to national and regional levels, while retaining community-scale effectiveness and innovation. Several potential issues need to be recognized when considering such scale-up (table 1.14), and Easterly's "test" should be taken into account:

> The sad part is that the poor have had so little power to hold agencies accountable that the aid agencies have not had enough incentive to find out what works and what the poor actually want. The most important suggestion is to search for small improvements, then brutally scrutinize and test whether the poor get what they wanted and were better off and then repeat the process (Easterly 2006, 180).

1.5.2 Define the project teams and stakeholders

Three types of team

To build the necessary teams involves identifying colleagues from all relevant stakeholder groups with a keen interest in promoting MoSSaiC and who have the requisite expertise. Three types of team need to be built:

TABLE 1.13 Magnitudes of scale-up

SMALL-SCALE LCDD SUCCESS	PILOT PHASE OF SCALE-UP	SCALED UP
1 district/administrative center	1–4 districts/administrative centers	All districts/administrative centers
1–4 subdistricts	6–24 subdistricts	All subdistricts
5–20 community groups	100–1,000 community groups	Tens of thousands–hundreds of thousands of community groups
< 50 community projects	100–2,000 projects	Hundreds of thousands of projects
< 50,000 people	100,000–1 million people	Many million people

Source: Binswanger-Mkhize, de Regt, and Spector 2009.
Note: LCDD = local- and community-driven development.

TABLE 1.14 Issues to consider when scaling up MoSSaiC

ISSUE	COMMENT
Replication may not be possible	"Sometimes things work for idiosyncratic reasons—a charismatic (and literally irreplaceable) leader or a particular (and unrepeatable) crisis that solidifies support for a politically difficult innovation. So one-time successes may not be replicable" (World Bank 2004, 108).
Experimentation may be necessary	While certain elements of the approach may provide sound guidance, there are limits to the standardization of any approach. "Experimentation, with real learning from the experiments, is the only way to match appropriate policies with each country's circumstances" (World Bank 2004, 108).
Adopting a recognized approach to scale-up may give value added	A social franchise model is recognized as a possible suitable scaling-up approach in which a close dialogue is maintained between countries undertaking the approach (franchisee) and the originators (franchisors). This aims to capture the advantage of standardization and experimentation referred to above. To that end, the franchisees (whose role is to implement the approach locally) are decentralized and largely autonomous. "A pilot project that is developed by the franchisor is replicated by a number of franchisees subject to defined guidelines. These are usually laid down in the form of a book and communicated to the franchisees through training offered by the franchisor" (Ahlert et al. 2008, 23).

- **MoSSaiC core unit.** This typically comprises local government agency expert practitioners and project managers in the fields of civil engineering, social development and community outreach, emergency management, financial management, water resource management, and agriculture. The MCU acts as the bridge between regional and national initiatives for risk reduction, the government technical and field task teams, and the communities. To be effective in its role, the MCU must have an understanding of the relational nature of the community—its key players, leaders, groups, and elected representatives; and its relationships with government, especially in terms of previous social intervention activities.

- **Government task teams.** Teams will include a number of groups of specialists and practitioners such as GIS technicians, field survey technicians, community liaison officers, local engineers, and planning officers. The leaders of the various government task teams are likely to be MCU members.

- **Community task teams.** The three main constituents from the community will be residents, contractors, and community leaders. Community leaders can play a catalytic part in projects: conveying the vision to other residents and coordinating with government teams. In some cases, an individual with particular skills and an understanding of the project's technical aspects can act as a catalyst and raise awareness of slope management issues in his or her own and other communities. Such understanding establishes appropriate consultative channels at the start of the intervention, and ensures that expectations are appropriately set in terms of outcomes and likely beneficiaries.

The teams, together with their roles and responsibilities, are fully defined in chapter 2.

Teams require an organizational structure to both manage a process and deliver outputs and outcomes. Structuring an MCU, and capturing existing government and community individuals within country, is a deliberate attempt to recognize that

> ...a Bureaucracy works best where there is high feedback from beneficiaries, high incentives for the bureaucracy to respond to such feedback, easily observable outcomes, high probability that bureaucratic effort will translate into favourable outcomes, and com-

petitive pressure from other bureaucracies and agencies (Easterly 2002, 4).

Stakeholder involvement

MoSSaiC requires a broad and cohesive stakeholder base, and one that deliberately encourages community participation. The MCU should identify all potential stakeholder groups and shape the management structure according to the local context. Table 1.15 indicates the likely stakeholders and their respective involvement.

Given the community basis of MoSSaiC, it is important for the MCU to

- be clear on the purpose of participation,

- know the value offered by community engagement,

- understand how the community can participate, and

- anticipate any unintended consequences of participation.

Participation allows stakeholders to collaboratively carry out a number of activities in the program cycle, including the following (World Bank 1998):

- **Analyzing**—identifying the strengths and weaknesses of existing policies and service and support systems

- **Setting objectives**—deciding and articulating what is needed

- **Creating strategy**—deciding, in pragmatic terms, directions, priorities, and institutional responsibilities

- **Formulating tactics**—developing or overseeing the development of project policies, specifications, blueprints, budgets, and technologies needed to move from the present to the future

- **Monitoring**—conducting social assessments or other forms of monitoring of project expenditures and outputs

Community selection

Communities can be prioritized and selected by addressing the following questions using available data:

- Which communities have suspected landslide problems?

- Are these communities vulnerable in poverty terms?

TABLE 1.15 Likely stakeholders and their potential involvement in a MoSSaiC intervention

STAKEHOLDER	INVOLVEMENT
Householders	• May be directly at risk from landslides and/or contribute to the hazard due to adverse slope management practices • May have important knowledge of localized slope processes and slope history • May have skills in drain construction
Landowners	Will need to be consulted if drainage structures are to be built and access rights required
Community representatives	May represent a community project committee and become advocates for the project
Government agency representatives	May have a formal role in project initiation and implementation
Residents of other potential communities	May perceive that their needs are greater or have skills or experiences to share
NGOs or similar agencies working in the same community	May be coordinating with the same government and community representatives on a different, but potentially related, project
Donors	May have instigated the approach but whose representatives may be seen as remote partners
Elected parliamentary representatives	May have lobbied in the community selection process and subsequently become advocates for the approach
Media representatives	Will cover project roll-out and can choose how they portray the delivery, purpose, and impact

- Can the landslide hazard be confirmed?

- Is the intervention likely to be cost-effective, and does it fit the project scope?

Typically, there will be a range of data and political factors that need to be assimilated by the MCU in prioritizing and selecting communities. Chapter 4 details a process that can be used for community selection.

1.5.3 Adhere to safeguard policies

Implementation of risk reduction itself carries potential risks. Safeguard policies seek to prevent and mitigate undue harm to people and their environment by providing guidelines for the identification, preparation, and implementation of programs and projects. The effectiveness and development impact of DRR projects can be substantially increased as a result of attention to such policies. These policies have often provided a platform for the participation of stakeholders in project design and have been an important instrument for building ownership among local populations.

Once teams are in place, stakeholders identified, and a project logframe developed (section 1.5.4), safeguard policies should be sourced, developed, and adapted as necessary for the local context; they should then be agreed upon and disseminated. While all those involved in a MoSSaiC intervention should be aware of safeguard policies, they are of special relevance to the MCU (in its managerial role; see section 2.3.2) and to those involved in construction (see section 7.7.1).

Practices for safeguards will vary depending on the country, donor agency, and government context. A useful starting point is the Safeguard Policies of the World Bank (2011). The MCU must ensure that the project complies with any relevant safeguards and protocols stipulated by a donor or the government, or dictated by good practice, although it is recognized that formal responsibility for compliance may well lie elsewhere. Table 1.16 illustrates some typical safeguards that might apply. This list should not be viewed as comprehensive and is not intended as a substitute for binding policies and procedures.

1.5.4 Establish a project logframe

Establishing a project framework at inception is an important starting point for the MCU in preparing the overall project design. A logframe is a widely used document that provides such a structure; it is essentially a project design checklist, and is a recognized framework among donor agency and government stakeholders. The MCU should create a MoSSaiC logframe at the start of the project and refer to it throughout.

> The logframe analysis can be used as an iterative, dynamic tool throughout the project cycle, rather than as a one-off exercise. It can be used for identifying and assessing activities, preparing the project design, appraising project designs, implementing approved projects and monitoring, reviewing and evaluating project progress and performance (AusAID 2000). In the words of DFID (c. 2003, 3), "it is a living document: it should be reviewed regularly during approach and project implementation" (Benson and Twigg 2004, 87).

The best logframes are designed with stakeholder involvement to ensure that everyone concerned understands the relationship between inputs and the desired outputs, outcomes, and impact. Both direct beneficiaries (primary stakeholders) and project partners (secondary stakeholders) should be involved in formulation of the project logframe.

The logframe should be simple and concise with the project goal, purpose, and outputs specified in full and anticipated activities summarized. It should be a stand-alone document explaining the intentions of the project comprehensively and at a glance, and should be no more than four pages long. Table 1.17 details a sample project logframe, presented in the form of a matrix.

In this book, the detailed steps and outputs identified in section 1.4.5 (and replicated at the beginning of each chapter) will be helpful in creating a logframe. Chapter 9 identifies typical key performance indicators, overall project outputs, and longer-term outcomes that might be included in a MoSSaiC project logframe.

TABLE 1.16 Typical safeguard policy considerations

SAFEGUARD	DESCRIPTION
Environmental assessment	Evaluates a project's potential environmental risks and impacts in its area of influence; examines project alternatives; identifies ways of improving project selection, siting, planning, design, and implementation by preventing, minimizing, mitigating, or compensating for adverse environmental impacts and enhancing positive impacts; and includes the process of mitigating and managing adverse environmental impacts throughout project implementation.
Natural habitats	Is there the potential to cause significant conversion (loss) or degradation of natural habitats? It must be expected that donors would not support projects that would lead to the significant loss or degradation of any critical natural habitats, i.e., natural habitats that are • legally protected, • officially proposed for protection, or • unprotected but of known high conservation value. In other (noncritical) natural habitats, projects might be allowed to cause significant loss or degradation only when • there are no feasible alternatives to achieve the project's substantial overall net benefits; and • acceptable mitigation measures, such as compensatory protected areas, are included in the project.
Disputed areas	Is the project situated in a disputed area? Has landownership been established and permission granted in writing if required? Projects in disputed areas may affect the relations between a wide range of stakeholders and claimants to the disputed area. Therefore, it is likely that donors and governments would only finance projects in disputed areas when there is no objection from the other claimant to the disputed area. It is possible that special circumstances of the case support financing, notwithstanding the objection. In this case it is to be expected that a transparent policy details the precise nature of such special circumstances.
Involuntary resettlement	Involuntary resettlement can be defined not only as physical relocation, but any loss of land or other assets resulting in (1) relocation or loss of shelter; (2) loss of assets or access to assets; (3) loss of income sources or means of livelihood, whether or not the affected people must move to another location. Involuntary resettlement is triggered in situations involving involuntary taking of land and involuntary restrictions of access to legally designated parks and protected areas. A safeguard policy would aim to avoid involuntary resettlement to the extent feasible, or to minimize and mitigate its adverse social and economic impacts. • A safeguard policy would promote participation of displaced people in resettlement planning and implementation, and its key economic objective would be to assist displaced persons in their efforts to improve or at least restore their incomes and standards of living after displacement. • A safeguard policy would prescribe compensation and other resettlement measures to achieve its objectives and require that borrowers prepare adequate resettlement planning instruments prior to donor appraisal of proposed projects.
Physical cultural resources	Cultural resources are important as sources of valuable historical and scientific information, as assets for economic and social development, and as integral parts of a people's cultural identity and practices. The loss of such resources is irreversible, but fortunately, it is often avoidable.

Source: World Bank 2011.

TABLE 1.17 Example of a logframe format

PROJECT SUMMARY	MEASURABLE INDICATOR	MEANS OF VERIFICATION	IMPORTANT RISKS AND ASSUMPTIONS
GOAL: Higher-level goal to which the project will contribute (such as Millennium Development Goals, poverty reduction). Note that the goal is not intended to be achieved through the project alone.			What external conditions are essential for the project to make its expected contribution to the goal
PURPOSE: What will be achieved? Consider what will change, who will benefit and how, and the impact the project will have in relation to the aims. This should be one statement.	The quantitative measures or qualitative evidence by which achievement of the purpose will be judged; these should be numbered.	Sources of information that will be used to assess the indicator(s). These should be numbered to correspond with indicator numbering.	Risks and external conditions on which the success of the project depends
OUTPUTS: Identify the set of realistic measurable outputs (outcomes/results) that will be needed to work together to ensure the achievement of the purpose. (Outputs are not simply completed activities—if training is the activity, then a completed training session is simply a completed activity; behavioral change as a result of receiving the training would be an output.) Normally, projects have four or five outputs. These should be numbered.	SMART (specific, measurable, achievable, relevant, and time-bound) indicators must be included for each output. Preparing useful and time-bound indicators is an essential element for effective monitoring and reporting. These should be numbered to correspond to output numbering.	Sources of information to be used to identify whether the indicators have been met. These should be numbered to correspond with indicator numbering.	Risks—factors not within the control of the project that may restrict the achievement of the outputs or of the purpose, even if all the outputs were achieved
ACTIVITIES: These are the tasks to be completed to produce the outputs. They should be given numbered to correspond to the relevant output.	A summary of the project budget and other key inputs and resources to complete the activities		

Source: DFID n.d.

1.5.5 Brief key leaders

Readers should use the information in this chapter to initiate discussions and brief strategically placed policy makers, senior project managers, and local experts. Effective communication of the MoSSaiC vision and foundations will help establish potential membership of the MCU, and thus help secure the support of people to champion the approach. This is the starting point for chapter 2.

> **MILESTONE 1:**
> **Key catalytic staff briefed on MoSSaiC methodology**

1.6 RESOURCES

1.6.1 Who does what

TEAM	RESPONSIBILITY	ACTIONS AND HELPFUL HINTS	CHAPTER SECTION
Policy/decision makers, funding agency	Understand DRM	• Become familiar with ex ante DRR approach **Helpful hint:** Be aware of recent influences on DRM policy (section 1.3.3).	1.3
	Understand MoSSaiC	• Become familiar with MoSSaiC approach **Helpful hint:** Be aware of unique aspects of MoSSaiC (section 1.2.1).	1.4
	Understand local institutional DRM context	• Identify government departments, agencies and other organizations that could contribute to community-based landslide risk reduction	1.5.2
	Identify individuals who have the potential to contribute to MoSSaiC	• Brief key individuals on MoSSaiC	1.5.5
MCU	Upon appointment, understand DRM and the MoSSaiC approach	• Become familiar with MoSSaiC approach **Helpful hint:** Be aware of unique aspects of MoSSaiC (section 1.2.1).	1.3; 1.4
Government task teams	Upon appointment, understand DRM and the MoSSaiC approach	• Become familiar with MoSSaiC approach **Helpful hint:** Be aware of unique aspects of MoSSaiC (section 1.2.1).	1.3; 1.4
	When community task teams have been appointed, inform the team members of MoSSaiC	• Communicate the MoSSaiC vision to community task teams	1.4
Community task teams	Upon appointment, understand DRM and the MoSSaiC approach	• Become familiar with MoSSaiC approach **Helpful hint:** Be aware of unique aspects of MoSSaiC (section 1.2.1).	1.3; 1.4

1.6.2 Chapter checklist

CHECK THAT:	TEAM	PERSON	SIGN-OFF	CHAPTER SECTION
✓ Existing local landslide risk reduction activities identified				1.3
✓ MoSSaiC approach understood				1.2.1; 1.4
✓ Relevant stakeholder groups and individuals identified and briefed				1.5.2
✓ All necessary safeguards complied with				1.5.3
✓ **Milestone 1:** Key catalytic staff briefed on MoSSaiC methodology				1.5.5

1.6.3 References

AGS (Australian Geomechanics Society). 2000. "Landslide Risk Management Concepts and Guidelines." http://australiangeomechanics. org/resources/downloads/.

Ahlert, D., M. Ahlert, H. V. D. Dinh, H. Fleisch, T. Heußler, L. Kilee, and J. Meuter. 2008. *Social Franchising: A Way of Systematic Replication to Increase Social Impact*. Munich: Bundesverband Deutscher Stiftungen.

Alcántara-Ayala, I. 2002. "Geomorphology, Natural Hazards, Vulnerability and Prevention of Natural Disasters in Developing Countries." *Geomorphology* 47: 107–24.

Anderson, M. G., and E. A. Holcombe. 2006. "Sustainable Landslide Risk Reduction in Poorer Countries." *Proceedings of the Institution of Civil Engineers—Engineering Sustainability* 159: 23–30.

Anderson, M. G., E. A. Holcombe, M. Esquivel, J. Toro, and F. Ghesquiere. 2010. "The Efficacy of a Programme of Landslide Risk Reduction in Areas of Unplanned Housing in the Eastern Caribbean." *Environmental Management* 45 (4): 807–21.

Angel, S. 2000. *Housing Policy Matters*. Oxford: Oxford University Press.

Annan, K. A. 1999. "UN Report of the Secretary-General on the Work of the Organization General." Assembly Official Records Fifty-Fourth Session Supplement No. 1 (A/54/1). http://www.un.org/Docs/SG/Report99/intro99.htm.

AusAID (Australian Agency for International Development). 2000. "The Logical Framework Approach." *AusGUIDElines* 1, AusAID. Cited in Benson and Twigg (2004).

Benson, C., and J. Twigg. 2004. "Measuring Mitigation Methodologies for Assessing Natural Hazard Risks and the Net Benefits of Mitigation—A Scoping Study." ProVention Consortium, Geneva.

———. 2007. "Tools for Mainstreaming Disaster Risk Reduction: Guidance Notes for Development Organisations." ProVention Consortium, Geneva.

Binswanger-Mkhize, H. P., J. P. de Regt, and S. Spector, eds. 2009. *Scaling Up Local & Community Driven Development (LCDD): A Real World Guide to Its Theory and Practice*. Washington, DC: World Bank.

Blaikie, P., T. Cannon, I. Davis, and B. Wisner. 1994. *At Risk: Natural Hazards, People's Vulnerability, and Disasters*. 1st ed. London: Routledge.

Bloom, D. E., and T. Khanna. 2007. "The Urban Revolution." *Finance & Development* 9. http://www.imf.org/external/pubs/ft/fandd/2007/09/pdf/bloom.pdf.

Board on Natural Disasters. 1999. "Mitigation Emerges as Major Strategy for Reducing Losses Caused by Natural Disasters." *Science* 284: 1943–47.

Bull-Kamanga, L., K. Diagne, A. Lavell, E. Leon, F. Lerise, H. MacGregor, A. Maskrey, M. Meshack, M. Pelling, H. Reid, D. Satterthwaite, J. Songsore, K. Westgate, and A. Yitambe. 2003. "From Everyday Hazards to Disasters: The Accumulation of Risk in Urban Areas." *Environment and Urbanization* 15 (1): 193–203.

Bunce, C. M., D. M. Cruden, and N. R. Morgenstern. 1995. "Hazard Assessment for Rock Fall on a Highway." In *Proceedings of the 48th Canadian Geotechnical Conference*, 449–508. Vancouver.

CCRIF (Caribbean Catastrophe Risk Insurance Facility). 2012. "The Caribbean Catastrophe Risk Insurance Facility." http://www.ccrif.org/content/about-us.

Charveriat, C. 2000. "Natural Disasters in Latin America and the Caribbean: An Overview of Risk." Working Paper No. 434, Inter-American Development Bank, Washington, DC.

Crompton, R. P., and K. J. McAneney. 2008. "Normalised Australian Insured Losses from Meteorological Hazards: 1967–2006." *Environmental Science & Policy* 11: 371–78.

Crompton, R. P., K. J. McAneney, K. Chen, R. A. Pielke Jr., and K. Haynes. 2010. "Influence of Location, Population and Climate on Building Damage and Fatalities due to Australian Bushfire: 1925–2009." *Weather, Climate and Society* 2: 300–10.

Crozier, M., and T. Glade. 2005. "Landslide Hazard and Risk: Issues, Concepts and Approach." In *Landslide Hazard and Risk*, ed. T. Glade, M. G. Anderson, and M. Crozier, 1–40. Chichester, UK: Wiley.

Curtis, D. 2004. "How We Think They Think: Thought Styles in the Management of International Aid." *Policy Administration and Development* 24: 415–23.

Dai, F. C., C. F. Lee, and Y. Y. Ngai. 2002. "Landslide Risk Assessment and Management: An Overview." *Engineering Geology* 64: 65–87.

de Silva, S., and J. W. Sum. 2008. "Social Funds as an Instrument of Social Protection: Analysis of Lending Trends." HNPSP Paper, World Bank, Washington, DC. http://documents.worldbank.org/curated/en/2008/07/9806577/social-funds-instrument-social-protection-analysis-lending-trends-fy2000-2007.

DFID (Department for International Development). n.d. "CSCF Monitoring, Evaluation and Lesson Learning Guidelines." http://www.dfid.gov.uk/Documents/funding/civilsocietycf-lesson-guidelines.pdf.

——. 2003. "Logical Frameworks." In *Tools for Development: A Handbook for Those Engaged in Development Activity*. London: DFID. Cited in Benson and Twigg (2004).

——. 2004. *Disaster Risk Reduction: A Development Concern*. London: DFID.

Easterly, W. 2002. "The Cartel of Good Intentions: The Problem of Bureaucracy in Foreign Aid Cartel of Good intentions." Working Paper 4, Center for Global Development, Washington, DC. http://papers.ssrn.com/sol3/papers.cfm?abstract_id=999981.

——. 2006. *The White Man's Burden*. Oxford: Oxford University Press.

Glade, T., and M. J. Crozier. 2005. "A Review of Scale Dependency in Landslide Hazard and Risk Analysis." In *Landslide Hazard and Risk*, ed. T. Glade, M. G. Anderson, and M. J. Crozier, 75–138. Chichester, UK: Wiley.

Green, R., S. Miles, and W. Svekla. 2009. "Situation Assessment in Villa Nueva Prospects for an Urban Disaster Risk Reduction Program in Guatemala City's Precarious Settlements." Institute Working Paper 2009, 1, Western Washington University, Bellingham, WA.

Ho, K. K. S., E. Leroi, and W. J. Roberds. 2000. "Quantitative Risk Assessment—Application, Myths and Future Directions. In *Proceedings of the International Conference on Geotechnical & Geological Engineering* (GeoEng 2000), vol. 1, 269–312. Melbourne.

Hochrainer-Stigler, S., H. Kunreuther, J. Linnerooth-Bayer, R. Mechler, E. Michel-Kerjan, R. Muir-Wood, N. Ranger, P. Vaziri, and M. Young. 2010. "The Costs and Benefits of Reducing Risk from Natural Hazards to Residential Structures in Developing Countries." Working Paper 2011-01, Wharton Risk Management and Decision Process Center, University of Pennsylvania, Philadelphia.

Holcombe, E. A., S. Smith, E. Wright, and M. G. Anderson. 2011. "An Integrated Approach for Evaluating the Effectiveness of Landslide Hazard Reduction in Vulnerable Communities in the Caribbean." *Natural Hazards*. doi:10.1007/s11069-011-9920-7.

Hong, Y., R. Adler, and G. Huffman. 2006. "Evaluation of the Potential of NASA Multi-Satellite Precipitation Analysis in Global Landslide Hazard Assessment." *Geophysical Research Letters* 33: L22402. doi:10.1029/2006GL028010.

IDB (Inter-American Development Bank). 2005. "Preliminary Companion Paper to the Draft Disaster Risk Management Policy." IDB, Washington, DC.

IEG (Independent Evaluation Group). 2006. *Hazards of Nature, Risks to Development: World Bank Assistance for Natural Disasters*. Washington, DC: World Bank.

IFRC (International Federation of Red Cross and Red Crescent Societies). 2004. *World Disasters Report*. http://www.ifrc.org/en/publications-and-reports/world-disasters-report/previous-issues/.

Knutson, T. R., J. L. McBride, J. Chan, K. Emanuel, G. Holland, C. Landsea, I. Held, J. P. Kossin, A. K. Srivastava, and M. Sugi. 2010. "Tropical Cyclones and Climate Change." *Nature Geosciences* 3: 157–63.

Kunreuther, H. 2009. "At War with the Weather and Other Extreme Events: Managing Large-Scale Risks in a New Era of Catastrophes." Presentation made at the London School of Economics. http://www.cccep.ac.uk/Events/Past/2009/MunichReEvents2009/Seminar_Kunreuther_Oct10.pdf.

Kunreuther, H., R. Meyer, and M. E. Kerjan. Forthcoming. "Overcoming Decision Biases to Reduce Losses from Natural Catastrophes." In *Behavioral Foundations of Policy*, ed. E. Shafir. Princeton: Princeton University Press.

Lee, E. M., and D. K. C. Jones. 2004. *Landslide Risk Assessment*. London: Thomas Telford Publishing.

Lloyd-Jones, T. 2006. *Mind the Gap! Post-Disaster Reconstruction and the Transition from Humanitarian Relief*. London: Royal Institute of Chartered Surveyors. http://www.rics.org/site/download_feed.aspx?fileID=2263&fileExtension=PDF.

Lumb, P. 1975. "Slope Failures in Hong Kong." *Quarterly Journal of Engineering Geology* 8: 31–65.

Lynn, Jonathan. 2009. "World 'Sleepwalking' into Disasters: U.N. Aid Chief." Reuters. http://www.reuters.com/article/worldNews/idUSTRE55F3Z320090616.

Mann, M. E., and A. E. Kerry. 2006. "Atlantic Hurricane Trends Linked to Climate Change." *EOS* 87: 233–44.

Maskrey, A. 1989. *Disaster Mitigation: A Community Based Approach*. Development Guidelines No. 3. Oxford: Oxfam.

———. 1992. "Defining the Community's Role in Disaster Mitigation." *Appropriate Technology Magazine* 19 (3). http://practicalaction.org/practicalanswers/product_info.php?products_id=214.

Mechler, R., J. Linnerooth-Bayer, and D. Peppiatt. 2006. *Disaster Insurance for the Poor? A Review of Microinsurance for Natural Disaster Risk in Developing Countries*. Geneva: ProVention Consortium/International Institute for Applied Systems Analysis.

Mechler, R., S. Hochrainer, G. Pflug, A. Lotsch, and K. Williges. 2010. "Assessing the Financial Vulnerability to Climate-Related Natural Hazards: Background Paper for the World Development Report 2010 'Development and Climate Change.'" Policy Research Working Paper 5232, World Bank, Washington, DC.

Meyer, R. J. 2005. "Why We Under-Prepare for Hazards." The Wharton School, University of Pennsylvania, Philadelphia.

Moench, M., R. Mechler, and S. Stapleton. 2007. "Guidance Note on the Costs and Benefits of Disaster Risk Reduction." Prepared for UNISDR Global Platform on Disaster Risk Reduction High Level Dialogue, June 4–7.

OAS (Organization of American States). 2004. "Managing Natural Hazard Risk." Policy Series #4. OAS, Washington, DC.

Olshansky, R. B. 1996. "Planning for Hillside Development." Planning Advisory Service Report 466, American Planning Association.

Opadeyi, S., S. Ali, and F. Chin. 2005. "Status of Hazard Maps, Vulnerability Assessments and Digital Maps in the Caribbean." Final report. Caribbean Disaster Emergency Response Agency.

Ostrom, E., C. Gibson, S. Shivakumar, and K. Andersson. 2001. "Aid, Incentives, and Sustainability: An Institutional Analysis of Development Cooperation." Sida Studies in Evaluation Report 02/01, Stockholm.

Ou-Yang, C. 2010. "Mitigating Losses from Climate Change through Insurance." The Wharton School, University of Pennsylvania, Philadelphia. http://rmi.gsu.edu/Research/downloads/2010/Chieh_Mitigating_Losses_Climate_Change_070810.pdf.

Pelling, M., and C. High. 2005. "Understanding Adaptation: What Can Social Capital Offer Assessments of Adaptive Capacity?" *Global Environmental Change* 15 (4): 308–19.

Pelling, M., and J. L. Uitto. 2001. "Small Island Developing States: Natural Disaster Vulnerability and Global Change." *Global Environmental Change Part B: Environmental Hazards* 3: 49–62.

Pielke Jr., R. A., J. Gratz, C. W. Landsea, D. Collins, M. Saunders, and R. Musulin. 2008. "Normalized Hurricane Damages in the United States: 1900–2005." *Natural Hazards Review* 9 (1): 29–42.

Rasmussen, T. N. 2004. "Macro Economic Impacts of Natural Disasters in the Caribbean." Working Paper WP/04/224, International Monetary Fund, Washington, DC.

Savethehills. 2011. "Working with the Communities 2011—Dumsi Pakha Village, Kalimpong." Blog entry January 9. http://savethehills.blogspot.com/2011/01/working-with-communities-2011-dumsi.html.

Schuster, R. L., and L. M. Highland. 2007. "The Third Hans Cloos Lecture. Urban Landslides: Socioeconomic Impacts and Overview of Mitigative Strategies." *Bulletin of Engineering Geology and the Environment* 66: 1–27.

Siri, G. 2006. "Targeting Assistance toward Those Most Affected by Disasters: The Role of Social Investment Funds." Draft, Disaster Management Facility, World Bank, Washington, DC.

Soubbotina, T. P. 2004. *Beyond Economic Growth: Meeting the Challenges of Global Development*. WBI Learning Resources Series. Washington, DC: World Bank.

Spence, M. 2011. *The Next Convergence: The Future of Economic Growth in a Multispeed World*. New York: Farrar, Straus and Giroux.

Sweikar, M., I. Mandadjiev, K. McCann, and G. Wikel. 2006. "Disaster Risk Reduction: Mapping the Advocacy Landscape." Center for Public Policy Research, College of William and Mary, Williamsburg, VA. http://www.wm.edu/as/publicpolicy/documents/prs/care.pdf.

Twigg, J. 2001. *Corporate Social Responsibility and Disaster Reduction: A Global Overview*. London: Hazard Research Centre, University College.

———. 2004. "Disaster Risk Reduction: Mitigation and Preparedness." *Development and Emergency Programming Good Practice Review* 9.

UN (United Nations). 2007. *World Population Prospects: The 2006 Revision*. New York: UN. Cited in Bloom and Khanna (2007).

UN (United Nations). 2009. "Summary and Recommendations: Global Assessment Report on Disaster Risk Reduction: Risk and Poverty in a Changing Climate." http://www.preventionweb. net/files/9414_GARsummary.pdf.

UN-Habitat. 2005. Global Urban Observatory database. Cited in Bloom and Khanna (2007).

UNDP (United Nations Development Programme). 2004. *Reducing Disaster Risk: A Challenge for Development*. New York: UNDP Bureau for Crisis Prevention and Recovery.

———. 2008. "A Guide to the Vulnerability Reduction Assessment." UNDP Working Paper.

UNISDR (United Nations Office for Disaster Risk Reduction). 2009. "Chapter 2. Global Disaster Risk: Patterns, Trends and Drivers." *In Global Assessment Report on Disaster Risk Reduction.* http://www.preventionweb.net/english/hyogo/ gar/report/documents/GAR_Chapter_2_2009_ eng.pdf.

———. 2012. "United Nations International Strategy for Disaster Reduction, Climate Change." www. unisdr.org/we/advocate/climate-change.

UNU (United Nations University). 2006. "Landslides. Asia Has the Most; Americas, the Deadliest; Europe, the Costliest; Experts Seek Ways to Mitigate Landslide Losses; Danger Said Growing Due To Climate Change, Other Causes." News Release MR/E01/06/rev1.

USGS (U.S. Geological Survey). 2003. *National Landslide Hazards Mitigation Strategy—A Framework for Loss Reduction*. Washington, DC: USGS.

Wamsler, C. 2006. "Mainstreaming Risk Reduction in Urban Planning and Housing: A Challenge for International Aid Organizations." *Disaster* 30: 151–77.

———. 2007. "Bridging the Gaps: Stakeholder-Based Strategies for Risk Reduction and Financing for the Urban Poor." *Environment and Urbanization* 19: 115.

Wharton School. 2008. *Managing Large-Scale Risks in a New Era of Catastrophes: Insuring, Mitigating and Financing Recovery from Natural Disasters in the United States.* http:// opim.wharton.upenn.edu/risk/library/ Wharton_LargeScaleRisks_FullReport_2008. pdf.

World Bank. 1998. *Participation and Social Assessment: Tools and Techniques.* Washington, DC: World Bank.

———. 2004. *Making Services Work for Poor People. World Development Report.* Washington, DC: World Bank.

———. 2005. *Grenada: A Nation Rebuilding. An Assessment of Reconstruction and Economic Recovery One Year after Hurricane Ivan.* Washington, DC: World Bank.

———. 2007. *Community Based Disaster Risk Management, India.* http://go.worldbank. org/0A4B712DW0.

———. 2009. *Urbanization and Growth: Commission on Growth and Development.* Washington, DC: World Bank.

———. 2010a. *Development and Climate Change. World Development Report.* Washington, DC: World Bank.

———. 2010b. *Natural Hazards Unnatural Disasters: The Economics of Effective Prevention.* Washington, DC: World Bank.

———. 2010c. *Safer Homes, Stronger Communities. A Handbook for Reconstructing after Natural Disasters.* Washington, DC: World Bank.

———. 2011. "Safeguard Policies." http://go. worldbank.org/WTA1ODE7T0.

Zaitchik, B. F., and H. M. van Es. 2003. "Applying a GIS Slope-Stability Model to Site-Specific Landslide Prevention in Honduras." *Journal of Soil and Water Conservation* 58: 45–53.

"...faced with a multi-faceted daily disaster, local people and their organisations develop their own strategies for improving living conditions, obtaining greater access to resources and changing the character of social relations with other groups, particularly with the state."

—A. Maskrey, "Defining the Community's Role in Disaster Mitigation" (1992, 4)

CHAPTER 2

Project Inception: Teams and Steps

2.1 KEY CHAPTER ELEMENTS

2.1.1 Coverage

This chapter identifies existing within-country capacity to build the MoSSaiC (Management of Slope Stability in Communities) teams responsible for project implementation and defines typical project steps. The listed groups should read the indicated chapter sections.

AUDIENCE				LEARNING	CHAPTER SECTION
F	M	G	C		
✓	✓	✓		How to start the project with the MoSSaiC core unit: mission, members, roles, responsibilities	2.2, 2.3
✓	✓	✓		How to select the government task teams; their roles and responsibilities	2.4
	✓	✓	✓	How to select the community task teams; their roles and responsibilities	2.5
	✓	✓	✓	Main MoSSaiC project steps for each team	2.6, 2.7

F = funders and policy makers   **M** = MoSSaiC core unit: government project managers and experts   **G** = government task teams: experts and practitioners   **C** = community task teams: residents, leaders, contractors

2.1.2 Documents

DOCUMENT TO BE PRODUCED	CHAPTER SECTION
Documents specifying team structures and personnel, and defining roles and responsibilities, with sign-off by representatives from the relevant government agencies	2.6
Project operations manual or equivalent specifying steps and associated milestones for implementation	2.6, 2.7

2.1.3 Steps and outputs

STEP	OUTPUT
1. Establish the MoSSaiC core unit (MCU); define and agree on key responsibilities • Identify available experts in government • Form the MCU and establish communication lines with government	MCU formed
2. Identify and establish government task teams; define and agree on key responsibilities • MCU to identify individuals from relevant ministries to form government task teams (mapping, community liaison, engineering, technical support, communications, advocacy) • Define roles and responsibilities of the teams	Government task teams formed
3. Identify and establish community task teams; define and agree on key responsibilities* • MCU to identify individuals from selected communities to form community task teams (residents, representatives, construction teams) • Define roles and responsibilities of the teams	Community task teams formed
4. Agree on a general template for project steps • Review project step template and amend as necessary • Assign team responsibilities to relevant project steps; confirm project milestones	Project steps determined and responsibilities assigned

*This can only be done once communities have been selected for a MoSSaiC project; see chapters 4 and 5.

2.1.4 Community-based aspects

An important part of this chapter is the identification of the members of community-based task teams (community residents, representatives, contractors, and landowners), which are an integral part of the wider MoSSaiC team. Without the full recognition and involvement of these teams, the project would have no grounding in the communities, the community-based mapping process and landslide hazard assessment would be incomplete (or incorrect), and there would be no sustainable delivery mechanism for appropriate landslide hazard reduction measures.

2.2 GETTING STARTED

2.2.1 Briefing note

An integrated approach to landslide risk management

To deliver landslide risk reduction measures in vulnerable communities requires the coordination of a diverse team including community residents, field and mapping technicians, engineers, contractors, and social development officers. A strong, multidisciplinary MoSSaiC core unit (MCU) needs to configure and manage specific project steps, roles, and responsibilities and thereby attempt to reproduce the success factors outlined in table 2.1.

The role of the MoSSaiC core unit

A central element of MoSSaiC is the development of a cross-ministry team of government managers and expert practitioners. This book refers to this team as the MCU; different countries may chose to give the team another name. The MCU will perform the following:

• Identify clear project steps that will effectively deliver on-the-ground landslide hazard reduction measures in communities in the form of surface water drainage

• Identify and draw on local expertise to implement project steps by establishing

TABLE 2.1 Key characteristics of highly successful social development projects

CHARACTERISTIC
Quality participation from all stakeholders
Participants given responsibility for structuring their project involvement
Participants, especially beneficiaries, involved in project design
Project team composition and team continuity
Integrated attention to social development themes affecting project implementation
Analysis of socially relevant aspects of the project

Source: IEG 2005.

appropriate task teams at the government and community levels

- Ensure that government and donor protocols are followed at every step

- Ensure that appropriate landslide assessment, community selection and engagement, and contracting procedures are followed

- Clearly communicate task team roles and responsibilities so each individual understands his or her specific tasks and contribution within the wider project

- Develop and convey the vision (and potential) for reducing landslide risk in vulnerable communities in a way that is relevant to the teams and wider audiences.

The breadth of activities involved in MoSSaiC demands that roles and responsibilities be very clearly identified and agreed upon. This chapter is designed so the MCU can be built and equipped to complement existing government structures.

2.2.2 Guiding principles

The following guiding principles apply in starting up the MoSSaiC project:

- An MCU should comprise a membership that is approved of and respected by government and within communities.

- Clear, widely known responsibilities should be established for the MCU and each MoSSaiC task team.

- Project steps and milestones should be agreed upon.

2.2.3 Risks and challenges

Appropriate objectives

The concepts contained in this book should be adapted by each country to reflect the local risk profile and government and community contexts. In particular, objectives should not be either overly ambitious or open-ended since this can weaken accountability, prevent the delivery of appropriate mitigation measures, and reduce the likelihood of adoption of good slope management practices by government and communities alike.

Taking time to identify MCU membership

The cross-disciplinary MCU is the core managerial structure of MoSSaiC. Identifying individuals within government and related agencies who are committed to the concept of formulating a community-based approach to landslide risk reduction is the starting point for any MoSSaiC project. Sufficient time should be spent talking to a broad range of interested parties and individuals to identify MCU team members who share the MoSSaiC vision and have relevant positions, skills, or expertise.

Avoiding parallel structures

The establishment of the MCU and its associated task teams should not create parallel structures that compete with or undermine existing institutional structures or democratically elected local or national governments (Mansuri and Rao 2003).

Fully developing and engaging with all task teams

Task teams should be identified and appropriately staffed for each project step to ensure that no individual or group is overburdened or required to take on tasks exceeding expertise.

Clear, consistent, and frequent communication will maintain momentum and commitment from individuals who may have other responsibilities. The form this communication takes needs to be agreed upon at the start of the project. Whether regular communication is by e-mail or briefing meetings, for example, will very much depend on local practices.

Realistic project time frames

Project initiators are frequently overly optimistic about the schedule for implementing multidisciplinary projects (see, e.g., IEG 2000). Because MoSSaiC integrates government and community, and focuses on delivery of physical landslide reduction measures in communities, it is particularly important that expectations of project timing and outcomes are set realistically. This is not just to avoid unrealized expectations and having to deal with the consequences (particularly in communities), but for the more positive reason that being seen to deliver the project on time and on budget is likely to encourage behavioral change. Small successes build confidence and lead to wider uptake.

Quality of project management

A lack good quality project management can lead to a variety of poor outcomes:

- Inadequate project conceptualization and design (potentially resulting in loss of financial or decision-making transparency, poor scientific justification of hazard reduction measures, and inadequate design or construction of hazard reduction measures)

- Poor quality construction (if site supervision is not scheduled sufficiently frequently)

- Project interruptions and contractors not getting paid on time (if the funding stream is not adequately managed)

- Inadequate attention to project safeguards (especially if there are issues of landowner-ship relevant to any proposed construction or required access)

Relevance of project documents

Avoid producing documents that are unlikely to be used and read. Instead, focus on developing a suite of documents that provide sound records for subsequent project impact analysis, enable teams to undertake their tasks, and serve public awareness and media initiatives.

Creating a platform for behavioral change

Urban development can generate landslide risk; conversely, landslide risk can affect development. At a community level, each household can inadvertently contribute to landslide risk or, with good slope management practices, play an important role in its mitigation. Government projects and policies can also either increase or reduce landslide risk at the community, municipal, or national scale. Creating a platform for behavioral change in communities and governments is an important part of the MoSSaiC vision, and it is best achieved by engaging with the community from start to finish and by using existing government staff to form the MCU. In this way, landslide hazard reduction measures can be delivered on the ground, and behavioral changes be achieved as the community and government teams learn by doing.

2.2.4 Adapting the chapter blueprint to existing capacity

This chapter provides a flexible blueprint for MoSSaiC project inception. Funders and policy makers, in conjunction with the MCU, should adapt this blueprint to suit local capacity and institutional structures.

Use the matrix opposite to determine existing capacity to configure multidisciplinary community-based projects, and hence the likely capacity for forming MoSSaiC teams.

1. Assign a capacity score from 1 to 3 (low to high) to reflect existing capacity for each element in the matrix's left-hand column.

| | EXISTING CAPACITY | | |
CAPACITY ELEMENT	1 = LOW	2 = MODERATE	3 = HIGH
Community organization and representation by leaders	Communities generally lack structures and leadership	Some community organizational or leadership structures	Functioning community-based organizations and leadership
Government-community liaison role	Role nonexistent	Government-community liaison on informal/unstructured basis	Well-developed government-community liaison role
Previous community-based projects	Little history of community-based projects	Some previous community-based projects, but outcomes not sustained	Good track record of delivering successful community-based projects
Government experience in implementing community-based works (construction)	Little or no experience in implementing community-based works	Some community-based works implemented by one or more government agencies	One or more agencies with proven experience in implementing community-based works with a range of donor/government funding models
Government experience in implementing community-based disaster risk management projects	Little or no experience in implementing community-based disaster risk management	Some community-based disaster risk management projects, with main focus on disaster preparedness or vulnerability reduction	Experience in community-based disaster risk management projects, including hazard assessment and mitigation
Coordination of multidisciplinary community-based projects	Community-based projects undertaken by a single implementing agency	Some cross-ministry coordination on a project-by-project basis	Well-integrated structures across government to facilitate cross-ministry coordination
Project safeguards	Documented safeguards need to be located; no previous experience in interpreting and operating safeguard policies	Documents exist for some safeguards	Documented safeguards available from all relevant agencies

CAPACITY LEVEL	HOW TO ADAPT THE BLUEPRINT
1: Use this chapter in depth and as a catalyst to secure support from other agencies as appropriate	The country needs to strengthen its capacity in order to initiate a MoSSaiC project and form the required teams. This might involve the following: • Actively searching for a policy entrepreneur to start the process by which an MCU is formed • Organizing cross-agency and cross-government department meetings to explain the MoSSaiC vision and the need to create an MCU
2: Some elements of this chapter will reflect current practice; read the remaining elements in depth and use them to further strengthen capacity	The country has strength in some areas, but not all. Elements that are perceived to be Level 1 need to be addressed as above. Elements that are Level 2 will need to be strengthened, such as the following: • If the government has experience in hazard mitigation using multidisciplinary teams but not at the community level, it should identify agencies already working in communities that could be partners in a MoSSaiC project.
3: Use this chapter as a checklist	The country is likely to be able to form an MCU based on existing proven capacity. The following would nonetheless be good practice: • Document relevant government experience in community-based hazard mitigation, project management, and related safeguards

2. Identify the most common capacity score as an indicator of the overall capacity level.

3. Adapt the blueprint in this chapter in accordance with the overall capacity level (see guide at the bottom of the previous page).

A review of selected capacity assessment methodologies can be found in UNDP (2006), and Venture Philanthropy Partners (2001, 84) provides an example of a detailed capacity assessment framework for nonprofit organizations.

2.3 ESTABLISHING THE MoSSaiC CORE UNIT

2.3.1 Rationale

Integrated approach to a multidisciplinary problem

Typically, the management of landslide risk involves assessment of the risk, evaluation of risk reduction options, and then treatment of the risk. This requires the coordination of experts in the areas (and order) shown in table 2.2.

A new way of building capacity

Forming the MCU from *existing* staff within governments and agencies is a sound way of seeking to build capacity within government. Initially, capacity is enhanced simply by providing the opportunity for government staff to exercise their expertise in an innovative way and as part of a multidisciplinary team. This expertise is developed and increased through hands-on experience as the project progresses. Successful implementation of landslide risk reduction measures in the first few communities encourages behavioral and policy changes within government.

The MCU thus becomes both a focus for building capacity and the means of building capacity in other teams, as it can provide the following:

TABLE 2.2 Typical landslide risk management project cycle

	TYPICAL PHASE	REQUIRED SKILLS/EXPERTISE
Landslide risk management project preparation	**Identify the project:** Determine the need for and interest in a landslide risk reduction project	Management, financial, donor agency, engineering/scientific
	Formulate the project: Define the project scope, budget, aims, objectives, and feasibility	
Landslide risk assessment	**Identify the broad landslide risk:** Identify the relative landslide susceptibility or hazard of different areas to different landslide types, and the relative vulnerability of the exposed communities	Local community knowledge, mapping, data management, engineering/scientific
	Understand and estimate the specific landslide risk: For a specific community and hillside, identify the underlying landslide hazard drivers and confirm the level of the hazard; confirm the relative exposure and vulnerability of the community	Mapping, engineering/scientific, social science, economic
	Evaluate the risk: Compare with other risks and decide whether to accept or treat the risk	Management, financial, engineering/scientific
Landslide risk reduction	**Identify disaster risk reduction options:** Typical options are to avoid or reduce the hazard, reduce vulnerability, or transfer the risk	
	Plan the risk mitigation: Design the landslide hazard reduction measures (drainage to capture surface water and household water)	Engineering/scientific
	Implement risk mitigation: Issue and manage contracts and construction, raise public awareness	Financial/contracting, community liaison, engineering, supervision, construction
	Monitor and evaluate: Check project progress, problems, solutions, sustainability, impact	Management, community liaison, engineering

- Project vision, in that it is distinctive and designed to deliver physical outputs in communities

- Task team coordination, to ensure that appropriate within-government and government-community linkages are forged

- Encouragement of capacity building and increased resilience at the community level, by engaging and involving communities from the outset and in a transparent manner

- Focal point for collating and managing information relating to landslides; such data are often dispersed across different ministries, agencies, and consultants

Sustaining good landslide management practice in-country

Certain projects may need high-level expertise to be brought into a country to supply specialized engineering or scientific knowledge, usually in terms of design but sometimes in site investigation as well. Such external expert input should supplement rather than replace in-country project management and task teams. Focusing on a government-based MCU and local task teams is the best approach to ensuring sustainable landslide risk management by

- creating a learning organization dynamic,

- promoting cost-efficiency,

- providing secure and sustainable government-community links,

- providing for a coherent connection with social development funds that can deliver projects at the community level, and

- ensuring the optimal assimilation of appropriate background data.

Avoiding the "Samaritan's dilemma"

A within-country MCU is a potentially sound way of avoiding the well-documented Samaritan's dilemma. This problem, posed by Buchanan (1977), revolves around the fact that a donor, faced with a circumstance that poten-

tially requires assistance, has the choice of helping or not helping. The aid recipient then has the choice of expending high or low effort in return. If the donor extends help and the recipient contributes high effort, both donor and recipient benefit significantly. However, from the recipient's perspective, it could be even better off by expending low effort (table 2.3).

Although the donor would prefer a situation in which the recipient expended high effort, most cases result in a low effort (Ostrom et al. 2001)—and consequent poor levels of sustainability. Ostrom et al. (2001, 32) conclude that "it is the recipient whose actions make the difference in outcomes between sustainable and non-sustainable," adding that a more sophisticated donor would condition aid on participation by the recipient and make efforts to give the recipient a sense of ownership. It is expressly these two features that MoSSaiC seeks to capture through its team structure.

MCU and the policy entrepreneur role

Policy entrepreneurs "introduce, translate, and help implement new ideas into public practice" (Roberts and King 1991). Given the issues observed by Prater and Londell (2000) and summarized in table 2.4, it is important to identify a policy entrepreneur to champion MoSSaiC and support, or be part of, the MCU.

MoSSaiC core unit mission

The MCU balances two elements that drive and contribute to MoSSaiC project success:

TABLE 2.3 The active Samaritan's Dilemma

		RECIPIENT	
		HIGH EFFORT	LOW EFFORT
DONOR (SAMARITAN)	NO HELP	2,2	1,1
	HELP	4,3	3,4

Source: Raschky and Schwindt 2009.

Note: Subject preference (payoff) ranked from high (4) to low (1). The first number in each pair is the donor preference, the second is the recipient preference.

TABLE 2.4 Landslide risk reduction issues that need to be offset by a policy entrepreneur

ISSUE	ROLE OF POLICY ENTREPRENEUR
Political agendas are unstable over time	Help keep disaster risk reduction on the agenda by being versed in the technical aspects of risk reduction, be a political expert, and have strong personal commitment
Prevailing view of landslide risk may be that there is nothing that can be done about it	Can counter this view with evidence that landslide risk reduction can work and pay
Hazard mitigation and socioeconomic development are complex issues; simplistic policies can have unintended consequences, while complex policies are difficult to develop	Understand and promote a scientific and socio-economic framework for landslide hazard mitigation policies

- **Top-down drivers and processes**—such as the social, economic, and political imperative to arrest landslide risk accumulation; and the requirements of project management and financing

- **Bottom-up drivers and processes**—such as the community imperative to reduce landslide risk and improve livelihoods, community participation in project design, and engaging workers from the communities to implement the intervention

2.3.2 MCU roles and responsibilities

The responsibilities of the MCU are prescribed by its five core missions (figure 2.1).

1. Establish project scope and teams

The first mission of the MCU is to establish the vision, scope, and cross-disciplinary basis of the project, and to identify task teams in the government and the community.

The MoSSaiC methodology needs to be understood and correctly applied if the goal of reducing landslide risk in communities is to be achieved. Each chapter in this book relates to a different phase of MoSSaiC implementation. The MCU should be aware of what is involved in each of these project phases (encapsulated in the "Getting started" section in each module) so as to correctly configure the project and establish the task teams.

Forming the MCU within-country delivers cost-effective project management. The MCU and government task teams should be comprised of existing government staff; the community task teams will include both unpaid volunteers (community leaders and residents) and paid contractors from within the community. Cultural norms and a lack of incentives may constrain effective management of task teams, and there will usually be limitations in the power of a single agency to influence behavioral change among a broader government base. The MCU should devise a communication and engagement strategy that combines formal government protocols with a culturally sensitive approach to achieve project acceptance, staff and team integration, and consensual ownership (World Bank 2003).

MCU roles and responsibilities in this regard are as follows:

- Be familiar with MoSSaiC aims and scope

- Define local project scope in terms of landslide risk management needs with respect to the appropriate application of MoSSaiC

- Adapt the MoSSaiC blueprint for building task teams and defining project steps, roles, and responsibilities

- Own and champion the vision, and lead and encourage the task teams

- Develop an effective strategy to facilitate the task teams in their roles

2. Stay community focused

From the outset, the MCU will need to focus on delivering landslide risk reduction mea-

FIGURE 2.1 Five missions of the MoSSaiC core unit

a. **Mission 1:** Establish the vision, scope, and cross-disciplinary basis of the project and identify task teams in government and communities.

b. **Mission 2:** Ground the project in communities throughout the process to create a platform for behavioral change in both government and communities.

c. **Mission 3:** Ensure good design of landslide hazard reduction measures, and the quality and completion of construction.

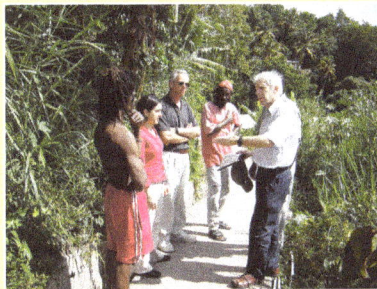

d. **Mission 4:** Create a culture of good slope management practice, and evaluate project impact and sustainability in partnership with communities and funding agencies.

e. **Mission 5:** Identify project safeguard requirements (relating to issues such as the potential for involuntary resettlement following slope failure and house destruction or for resolving landownership for drainage lines).

sures in vulnerable communities. This focus will require the development of strategies to engage the community from the start and to maintain that engagement during landslide hazard mapping and assessment, through the design process, during implementation, and in the follow-up phases.

The government task teams should be encouraged to work with community members both formally and informally in order to benefit from community knowledge of local slope processes and relevant community social structures. The community thus becomes the locus both of activities and of hands-on experience for the government and community task teams.

The MCU roles and responsibilities in this regard are as follows:

• Develop a community selection process that is justifiable in terms of susceptibility of slopes to landslides and vulnerability of communities to the impact of landslides

• Ensure that the selected communities are consulted on their priorities and the potential for implementing landslide hazard reduction measures

• Ensure that appropriate community participation approaches are used in selecting community task teams, mapping landslide hazards and drainage issues, designing a drainage intervention, and conducting liaison with residents during and after the project

• Establish a realistic community contracting process by which contracting and procurement are undertaken on behalf of or by the community

• Ensure that contractors from the community are engaged and supervised in the construction of the landslide hazard reduction measures

- Encourage horizontal and vertical learning through the hands-on involvement of task teams in the communities

3. Maintain quality control

The effectiveness of any engineering or physical measures constructed to reduce landslide hazard depends on sound design, specifications, and construction. MoSSaiC involves developing surface water drainage plans to reduce landslide hazard and construction by community-based contractors to achieve that goal. The MCU must therefore create strategies for quality control and monitoring of the drainage design and implementation process; this responsibility is pivotal to the success of the measures.

MCU roles and responsibilities in this regard are as follows:

- Select appropriately skilled task teams for mapping, landslide hazard assessment, and drainage design

- Select experienced site supervisors

- Establish an appropriate community contracting process and oversee the supervision of contractors

4. Evaluate the project and develop sustainable practices

The success of the MoSSaiC project should not be measured simply in terms of the quality and quantity of immediate outputs (such as the length of drains built, number of households benefiting, or money spent on employing local contractors), but in terms of medium-term impact and sustainability (outcomes). The MCU should thus monitor and evaluate the project beyond its immediate outputs. The observations and experiences of the community are a vital resource in this regard.

The sustainability of the project is reflected in the degree of uptake by community and government teams—the creation of a culture of good slope management prac-

tices and the structures to enable them. The MCU is the core enabler in seeding project sustainability.

The MCU's horizontal connection within government, and its vertical integration with communities, provides the opportunity to develop a sustainable mechanism for embedding landslide risk reduction in practice and policy. Building a team of senior civil servants and technical officers in this way has a potential longevity that is generally not matched by elected political representatives.

MCU roles and responsibilities in this regard are as follows:

- Create strong horizontal and vertical integration among senior civil servants, task teams, and communities

- Evaluate project outcomes (medium-term impacts and sustainability) as well as the standard outputs required by donors

- Engage the community in assessing project successes and failures, in developing new approaches and solutions, and in sharing experiences and expertise

- Promote the approach based on physical demonstration of good slope management practices, using project evaluations to develop an evidence base for raising awareness and for leveraging further funding

- Provide regular updates to key senior civil servants and engineers, using photos, site visits, and short presentations or reports

- Find a niche for the approach within the most appropriate government ministry or agency

5. Adhere to safeguards

The MCU must ensure that the project complies with relevant safeguards and protocols stipulated by a donor or by the government or dictated by good practice (section 1.5.3), although it is recognized that formal responsibility for compliance may well lie elsewhere. Table 1.16 (chapter 1) illustrates some typical safeguards that might apply. These should not be viewed as comprehensive and are not intended to be a substitute for binding policies and procedures.

MCU roles and responsibilities in this regard are as follows:

- Be fully conversant with the safeguards that apply to the project

- Communicate safeguards and processes for compliance to relevant stakeholders

- Keep a record of compliance

2.3.3 MCU membership

MCUs will vary in structure from country to country. Typically, members might be drawn from the following government departments, ministries, and agencies:

- Public works
- Social development
- Planning
- Finance
- National emergency organization
- Statistics and census
- Agriculture
- Water and sewerage company

Higher education and community colleges (where there is relevant technical expertise that would be of value) may also contribute MCU members.

Members selected should be fully conversant with and supportive of the MCU missions, roles, and responsibilities as outlined above. They should be committed to delivering landslide risk reduction measures using an interdisciplinary, community-based approach. MCU members need to be able to command respect from the communities, government, donors, and media (Anderson and Holcombe 2004, 2006a, 2006b; Anderson, Holcombe, and Williams 2007).

MCU members need to stay fully engaged throughout the project; if they do not, believing that the project has been established and is to some degree running itself, project outputs will suffer as a consequence.

Qualitative evidence suggests that the role of project facilitators (MCU members in this case) is key to the success of community-based projects. In a survey of the World Bank Development Research Group, Mansuri and Rao (2003) found that projects are often undertaken with young, inexperienced facilitators whose incentives are not aligned with the best interests of the community. This finding reinforces the critical role of the MCU and the nature of its membership.

> **MILESTONE 2:**
> MoSSaiC core unit formed; key responsibilities agreed on and defined

2.4 IDENTIFYING THE GOVERNMENT TASK TEAMS

Part of the MCU's first mission is to develop teams dedicated to specific project tasks that will ensure the delivery of appropriate physical measures to reduce the landslide hazard.

Identification and initial engagement of task team members will probably be an iterative and consultative process in conjunction with the development of specific project steps. In many cases, MCU members themselves may be the most appropriate people to contribute to or lead a particular task team.

Each MCU member will need to identify and consult with expert practitioners (engineers, officials, and technicians) in their respective ministries to

- identify motivated, knowledgeable, and skilled individuals who want to contribute to the overall vision of achieving landslide hazard reduction in communities; and

- consult with these individuals to identify cross-ministry collaborations and specific steps that they (as part of the ministry or agency) would need to undertake for project success.

Table 2.5 provides guidance on factors relevant to the team selection process.

TABLE 2.5 Government task team selection factors

FACTOR	COMMENT
Team size	Typically, each government task team consists of about three individuals who display commitment to the vision. With six task teams, this totals about 18 government task team members in all. Team leaders may also be part of the MCU.
Financial compensation	Experience has shown that it is not necessary for the respective government departments/agencies from which the team members were drawn to receive financial compensation. Such a circumstance can be seen as increasing ownership of the vision.
Time commitment	Depending on the scale of the intervention, it is unlikely that any team member role will, on average, be full time. However, there may be periods when the individual is working full time for a few days.
Convening of team members	MCU members, having been chosen with regard to their respective specialization (section 2.3.3), search for and identify potential task team members. This process will entail both taking advice on suitable members as well as discussing opportunities with potential individuals.
Membership composition	In establishing the teams, it may be useful to achieve a mix of middle-management members (to deliver skills) combined with a modest number of more senior officials to drive policy acceptance.
Housing of the MCU	It is appropriate to seek an office location for the MCU (perhaps a ministry office or a relevant agency in which there is administrative support and in which there may be a top-level advocate for MoSSaiC). This helps demonstrate government support for the MCU and assists in project implementation.

This section identifies typical areas of project activity for which motivated and experienced task team leaders will need to take responsibility (table 2.6). The task team leader

TABLE 2.6 Task teams and guidance notes

	TEAM	MAIN TASK	TYPICAL EXPERIENCE/POSITION OF TASK TEAM LEADER	CHAPTER SECTION
GOVERNMENT-BASED	Mapping	Produce high-resolution maps for landslide hazard assessment	Geographic information system (GIS), planning, and census officials	2.4.1
	Community liaison	Develop community prioritization method with mapping team	Community development	2.4.2
	Landslide assessment and engineering	Map landslide and drainage hazard, advising the MCU of the appropriateness of the MoSSaiC approach and overseeing the preparation and letting of work packages	Scientists or engineers with expertise in landslide risk assessment and hydrology Civil engineers, especially with expertise in drainage, environmental engineering, bioengineering, design, and contract management	2.4.3
	Technical support	Site survey work and site supervision	GIS, census, computing, surveying, materials laboratory technicians, supervision of works	2.4.4
	Communications	Support the MCU in raising public awareness	Media, public relations	2.4.5
	Advocacy	Engage with other decision makers and the media to explain the MoSSaiC vision and its practical implementation	Elected officials, funding agency representatives	2.4.6
COMMUNITY-BASED	Residents	Assist all government teams on the ground in their community	Residents, community leaders, and groups	2.5.1
	Community representatives	Provide detailed community context to the MCU and other task teams	Community-elected officials	2.5.1
	Construction	Community contractors provide knowledge of local practices and undertake the works	Contractors	2.5.2

will need to work closely with the MCU to design the project steps and build the team. Each task team may comprise individuals from other ministries with the necessary skills to undertake the assigned tasks. This information is provided as guidance only; specific circumstances may dictate variations depending on the local roles held by individuals in a particular country.

2.4.1 Mapping task team

The key responsibilities of the mapping task team are as follows:

- Integrate any available spatial data on poverty and landslide susceptibility to support the process of identifying and prioritizing communities for landslide risk reduction

- Produce high-resolution maps of selected communities to serve as the basis for the community-based mapping of slope features, landslide hazard, and proposed drain locations.

There may be many government departments that make use of geographic information system (GIS) technology (figure 2.2). It is important to identify the ministry with the most skilled individual(s) and the main repository of digital maps (such as topography, soils, geology, housing/landownership, and land use) and aerial images. The ministry responsible for planning is often the most appropriate host agency for this team. However, other ministries may be able to contribute data and expertise in specific areas such as census information relating to poverty and the vulnerability of communities. Consider including representatives from such groups on the team to ensure optimal coordination of both data assimilation and presentation.

2.4.2 Community liaison task team

The key responsibilities of the community liaison task team are as follows:

- Coordinate with the mapping team to develop a transparent method for prioritizing vulnerable communities

- Identify for the mapping team any social surveys or other data that would be helpful in the prioritization process

- Coordinate with communities to identify community representatives

- Act to moderate political or other motives for selecting certain communities, community representatives, or contractors

- Coordinate with community residents and representatives throughout the project (figure 2.3)—organizing informal and formal meetings and any public awareness materials that might be relevant

- Bring knowledge of how the community works to the MCU

- Ensure that the other teams engage with the community at each project stage.

The role of the community liaison team is to ensure that communities are represented and engaged in the community selection process, mapping and intervention design, implementation of measures, and any subsequent follow-up. This team may need to be part of other task team activities as the project progresses.

FIGURE 2.2 Mapping team from a national disaster management agency demonstrates GIS software to MCU team leader

FIGURE 2.3 Coordinating with Social Development Ministry and community residents on site

2.4.3 Landslide assessment and engineering task team

The key responsibilities of the landslide assessment and engineering task team are as follows (figure 2.4):

- Direct the mapping team in the analysis of available data on landslide susceptibility and hazard to assist in community selection

- Undertake community-based mapping of slope features; landslide hazard and drainage issues; and assessment of the location, magnitude, and cause of the hazard

- Appraise the MCU of the relevance and potential cost-effectiveness of MoSSaiC in reducing landslide hazard in the community

- Engage and coordinate with additional specialists (such as ground and quantity surveyors)

- Design surface drainage measures, generate work packages, and manage the contracting process to engage contractors from the community in construction

- Ensure the quality of the works (to be managed by an experienced site supervisor).

Successful reduction of landslide hazard depends on correct identification and assessment of the hazard, and design of appropriate mitigation measures (surface drainage, in the case of MoSSaiC). The landslide assessment and engineering task team should include at least one civil or environmental engineer and any other government staff member with a background in and working knowledge of the physical, geotechnical, and hydrological sciences.

In many countries, residents and government agencies will report landslide and drainage issues to a specific government ministry. This ministry, which is often responsible for civil works, is likely to be the most appropriate one for fulfilling the key responsibilities outlined above. It will also have the necessary processes and personnel to implement construction of landslide hazard reduction measures.

FIGURE 2.4 Examples of landslide assessment and engineering task team responsibilities

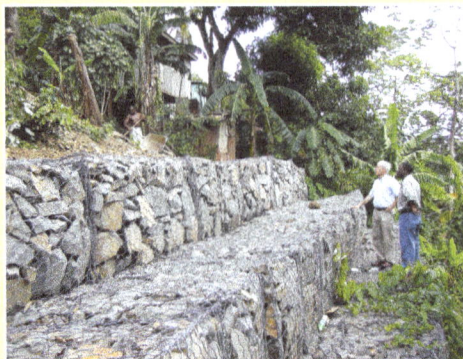

a. Assess different slope stabilization options.

b. Design drain dimensions and alignment in complex topography.

2.4.4 Technical support task team

The key responsibilities of the technical support task team (figure 2.5) are as follows:

- Provide technical support to other teams in data acquisition, processing, and presentation

- Provide field support to other teams—e.g., undertaking ground or quantity surveys, or assisting in monitoring and evaluation

- Provide site supervision during implementation of works

- Suggest ways of working that would improve on-the-ground implementation.

Generally, skilled government technicians stay in a given role for long periods. Therefore, investment in their skills and inclusion in the wider MoSSaiC project can encourage good slope management practices to be embedded in government beyond the end of the project.

FIGURE 2.5 Technical team training course attendees: Sharing and developing expertise across ministries

2.4.5 Communications task team

The key responsibilities of the communications task team are as follows:

- Support the MCU with regard to public awareness of the project

- Produce leaflets, posters, invitations to community meetings, and other appropriate communications for use within the communities

- Communicate project aims and progress to the wider public

- Engage and manage media interest—from newspapers, radio, television—in the form of interviews of team and community members, press releases, information on good slope management practices, and other coverage of the project.

The appropriate communication of landslide issues, good slope management practices, and project aims and progress can encourage MoSSaiC uptake and sustainability. In many communities, the main form of communication is word of mouth, often informed by some combination of community meetings, radio, and television (figure 2.6).

The MCU should decide on the message it wishes to convey to the selected communities and the public, and how that message is to be conveyed. The communications task team may consist of existing government information service personnel who will engage the media at different stages of the project.

In some cases, it may be possible to secure the services of either the government or a private production company to make a short documentary on the project. The project will thus receive coverage in a professional manner, thereby lengthening the "shelf life" of public awareness of good slope management practices.

2.4.6 Advocacy task team

Political advocacy

Elected officials would most likely have been party to the original decisions to undertake the MoSSaiC project; they should be kept informed at all project stages. A policy entrepreneur may emerge as an advocate for MoSSaiC—keeping landslide risk reduction on the political agenda and helping streamline funding and political processes for the initiative.

FIGURE 2.6 Aspects of communication

a. Have a clear and agreed-upon message to communicate at the start of a project.

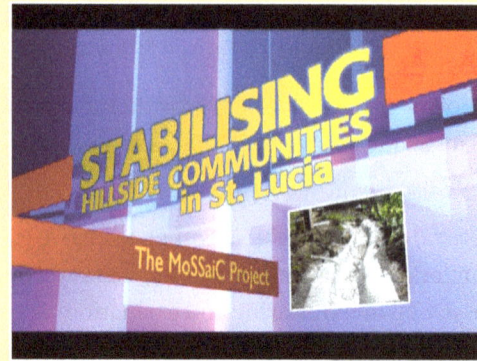

b. Consider commissioning a documentary in which community residents tell the project's story (source: Government of Saint Lucia).

The MCU has a key role to play in developing a strategy of engagement with politicians, which could include the following:

- Presenting progress documents at cabinet/government committee meetings

- Maintaining a one-to-one dialogue with government ministers who have adopted the vision to reduce landslide risk

- Organizing site visits when work is under way, including receiving feedback from community residents

- Conducting on-site briefings at which completed works are presented to government ministers; this can be a powerful tool in encouraging policy change (figure 2.7).

FIGURE 2.7 On-site briefing

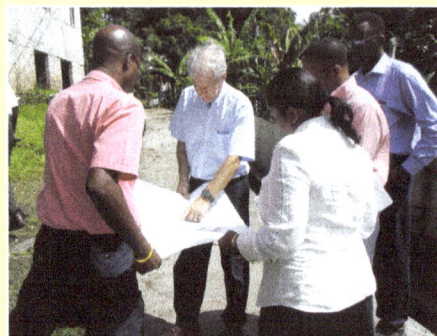

A change in government may mean that what was once perceived as innovative policy (such as undertaking MoSSaiC projects) may be less attractive politically. Thus, connecting the MCU with senior civil servants and technical officers is central to achieving a sustained and sustainable landslide mitigation policy.

Politicians and the media

Politicians may take ownership of the project and promote it—although sometimes this will be to achieve a political agenda not necessarily in accord with the technical aspects of community prioritization.

Combining the media and elected officials can be a very powerful vehicle for project promotion, especially in the early to mid-stages of a project cycle. The MCU has a key role in briefing politicians so that they own the key messages (figure 2.8), and should develop specific plans for coordinated media opportunities.

Funding agency advocates

It should be assumed that it is a formal requirement to keep the funding agency appraised of project progress; this reporting is usually standardized. There is additional benefit in maintaining less formal communications with both current funders and similar agencies to publicize project innovation, success in delivering landslide hazard reduction measures on the ground, and lessons learned. Informal visits,

FIGURE 2.8 Media film elected officials during a MoSSaiC project

possibly with a media component (figure 2.9), can help maintain a funding agency's advocacy of MoSSaiC, especially if funding agency staff turnover is significant.

The MCU should create and encourage links with funding agency staff in order to

- raise international awareness of a country program,

- potentially provide links to other funding sources,

- provide an opportunity to exchange best practices, and

- build self-esteem among those engaged in MoSSaiC at the community level—residents and team members alike would not otherwise gain exposure to such groups or be able to express their perceptions and firsthand project knowledge to them.

FIGURE 2.9 Funding agency staff on site at initial stage of MoSSaiC project

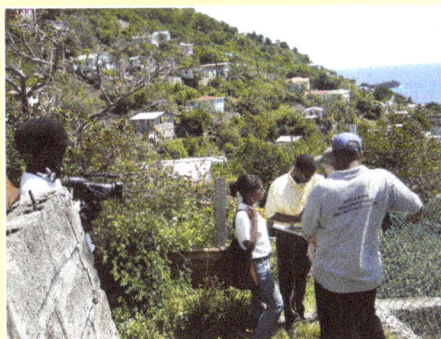

2.5 IDENTIFYING THE COMMUNITY TASK TEAMS

2.5.1 Community residents

The key responsibilities of community residents with regard to MoSSaiC are as follows:

- Discuss and influence project conceptual design—the specific form of community participation and community contracting processes will vary depending on local community structures

- Provide detailed local knowledge on past landslides, slope features and processes, rainfall impacts, and drainage issues

- Select representatives from the community to interface with the government task teams

- Make in-kind contributions to project implementation, or earn money as part of a contractors' team

- Learn about good slope management practices and put them in use wherever possible.

Frequently, the first engagement of community residents in the project will be informal as part of initial government task team site visits to confirm the selection of communities for the project. These initial visits are good for opening up discussions with residents in a nonthreatening way, but formal communication with the community should also occur early on. It is important to identify existing community-based organizations and formal community leadership structures that may be required to endorse (or facilitate) a MoSSaiC project. Having established an appropriate means for engaging with the community, a meeting should be held to present and discuss the proposed project (figure 2.10a). This meeting will often be a multipurpose event, with media and local government representatives also in attendance. These formal and informal occasions give residents the opportunity to express their views and begin to select a group of community representatives for the project.

Informal opportunities should be created for community residents to contribute to the project on an individual or small-group basis. Meetings should literally be taken to the community in the form of walk-throughs and impromptu discussions. Gathering at a visible site in the community encourages others to join the group out of curiosity as they pass (figure 2.10b). In this way, residents effectively become a task team, contributing their knowledge of slope features and drainage issues.

Both informal and formal engagements allow community members to provide a significant amount of detailed local knowledge throughout the project, such as the height the flow in a drain might have reached in a particular rainfall event (figure 2.10c). This engagement should continue throughout the mapping, design, and implementation phases so that local knowledge is captured and acted upon where relevant in the construction phase, and the intervention is owned by residents. Continued community engagement also provides the best foundation for ongoing drain cleaning and maintenance.

Community representatives

• directly interface with government task teams as spokespersons for the community;

• assist in the mapping of landslide hazard and drainage issues;

• collaborate with the community liaison team to organize informal and formal community meetings (figure 2.10d);

• collaborate with the engineering task team to identify potential contractors and work-

FIGURE 2.10 Aspects of community resident involvement in MoSSaiC

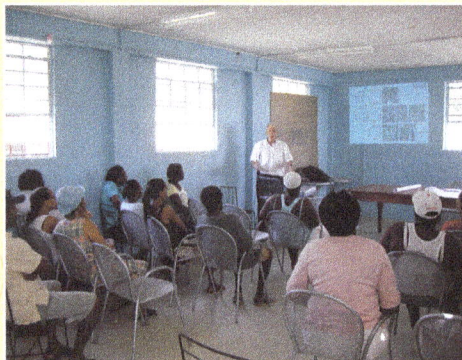

a. Meeting with residents at the start of a project can produce enthusiasm from members of the community to actively participate in the project.

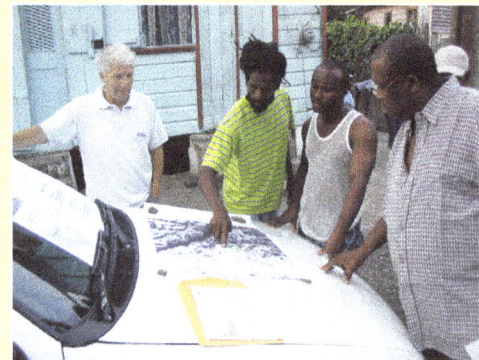

b. An informal community focus meeting is often the best way to begin a project.

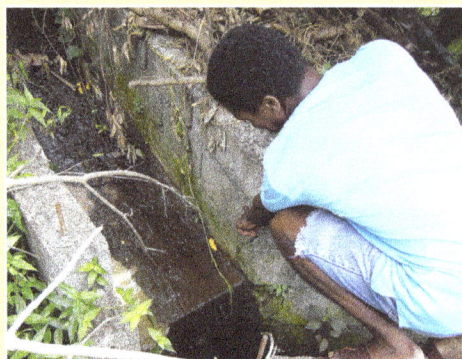

c. Residents can help postproject impact assessment by indicating maximum observed water levels in completed drains after heavy rainfall.

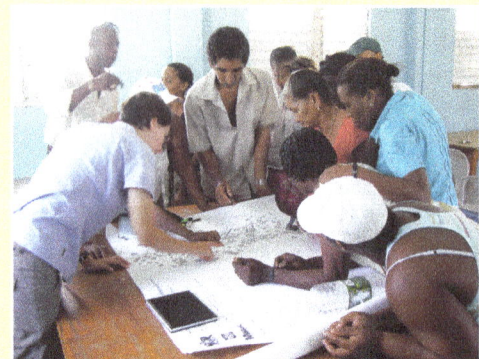

d. A formal community meeting is often most effective when held after initial informal on-site meetings.

ers from the area, monitor the works, and report any problems; and

- communicate and demonstrate good slope management practices to residents.

Community-elected leaders can provide useful information when communities are in the process of being selected for interventions, as well as at the start of a potential project. Such individuals can play a key role in championing the project, given their strong community engagement and links with government and agency officials.

If appropriate, the community contracting process may involve a selected (and trained) group of community leaders and residents managing the contracting and procurement process with support from the government task teams. Alternatively, if the government handles this process, community leaders and residents should be included as fully as possible.

2.5.2 Construction task team

The key responsibilities of the construction task team are as follows:

- Provide local knowledge as part of the community mapping process

- Provide insight into local construction practices and designs, and how they could potentially be used in the engineering task team's design

- Assist in the consideration of transport and safe storage of materials, and advise on approximate implementation times

- Undertake specific works (construction of drains, installation of household gray water and roof water connections) as detailed in contracts

- Coordinate with engineering and technical task teams (especially the site supervisor) to ensure correct implementation and quality

- Employ workers from within the community.

Locally based contractors can make a vital contribution to the design of works, as well as

potentially bidding on the final work packages. A list of contractors from within or near the community should be compiled; they may have attended a community meeting or have been recommended. They should be invited to participate in the bid process, as part of an agreed-upon community contracting process (figure 2.11).

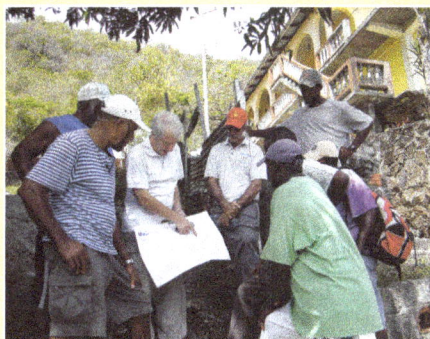

FIGURE 2.11 Briefing potential contractors on site after calling for expressions of interest from within the community

Contractors should be supervised by the engineering and technical task teams during implementation of the works; they may also have a role in training government technicians and demonstrating good practices to other contractors or communities (figure 2.12). Time should be invested in community-based contractors because of the vital role they play in vulnerable communities.

2.5.3 Landowners

Building drains and related interventions on slopes demands that landownership be known to the MCU and that adequate safeguards be put in place to ensure that there will be no disputes before, during, or after construction. In unauthorized housing areas, the following landownership possibilities are likely to exist:

- Single landowner (who possibly resides overseas) who rents out houses, or plots of land for building on, to individual households

- Government-owned land

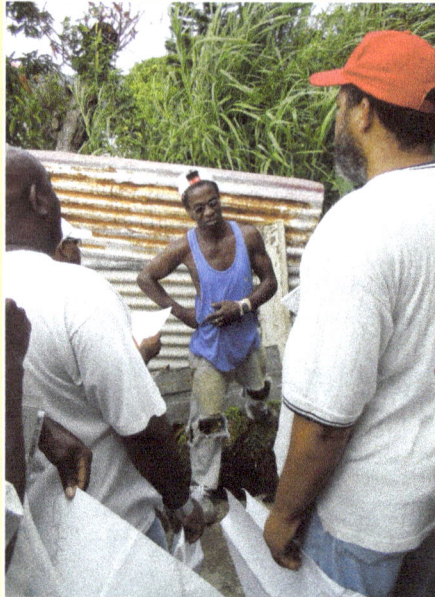

FIGURE 2.12 Contractor briefs government technical officers on project implemented in his community

- Multiple landowners with family land partitioned as families grow and houses are built on subdivided land parcels.

The MCU should take particular care to obtain, review, agree on, and implement relevant safeguard policies (sections 1.5.3 and 2.3.2).

2.6 INTEGRATION OF MoSSaiC TEAMS AND PROJECT STEPS

2.6.1 Team structure and reporting lines

Once the task teams have been established, the MCU should prepare a summary document listing the selected teams, naming team members, and assigning broad roles and responsibilities; table 2.6 could be used as a template.

Defining roles and responsibilities is important in ensuring that project safeguards are owned by the relevant task team or the MCU as appropriate. It also helps prevent mission drift.

The MCU should have a reporting line to the government. The exact nature of this reporting line will depend on local government and agency structures. The MCU could, for example, be hosted by a ministry through which it reports. Conversely, in cases where MoSSaiC is adopted as a national program, the MCU may report directly to the government. MoSSaiC should not create parallel structures within the government; rather, it should create a management structure that **works with existing roles of accountability** wherever possible. Individual MCU members can be delegated to manage the government task team, reflecting their interest and adding value to their existing roles.

The government teams should work with the community, within the broad roles defined above, to allow the most marginalized and vulnerable communities to

- have ownership, as they are explicitly engaged in the initial landslide risk mapping exercise;

- provide project guidance, as they are involved in the prioritization of works in their own community;

- undertake construction, as contracting workers from within the community is an integral part of implementation;

- export the methodology, as community members provide guidance and support to neighboring communities; and

- gain self-esteem, as they participate in providing on-site community training to government community officials and deliver presentations at relevant international conferences.

The broad team management structure in figure 2.13 highlights the central role of the MCU in the management process.

2.6.2 Integrating teams with project steps

Once all the teams are in place, the MCU can create a template that sequences the necessary steps for project implementation. The nine components of MoSSaiC (section 1.4.5) can be used as the basis for the template.

Each of the project steps needs to be assigned to one or more task team. The par-

FIGURE 2.13 Typical MoSSaiC team reporting structure

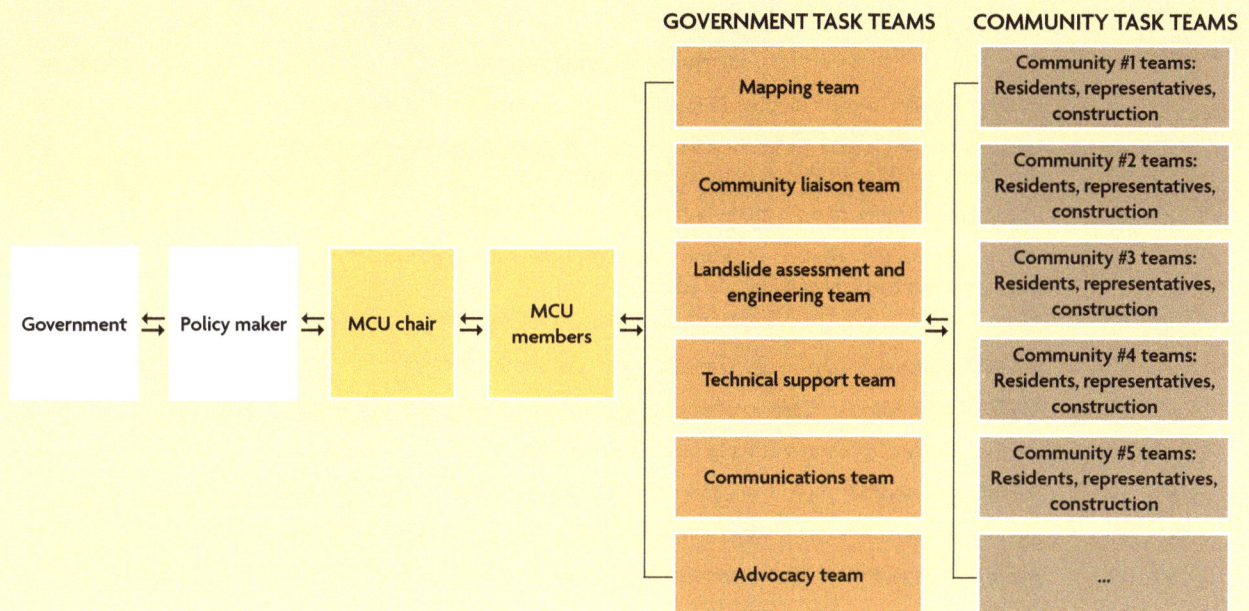

| | | | | GOVERNMENT TASK TEAMS | COMMUNITY TASK TEAMS |

Government ⇆ Policy maker ⇆ MCU chair ⇆ MCU members ⇆

GOVERNMENT TASK TEAMS:
- Mapping team
- Community liaison team
- Landslide assessment and engineering team
- Technical support team
- Communications team
- Advocacy team

COMMUNITY TASK TEAMS:
- Community #1 teams: Residents, representatives, construction
- Community #2 teams: Residents, representatives, construction
- Community #3 teams: Residents, representatives, construction
- Community #4 teams: Residents, representatives, construction
- Community #5 teams: Residents, representatives, construction
- ...

ticular government and community task team to take responsibility of relevant steps will depend on local conditions. A central role for the MCU is to design, consult on, agree to, and communicate the project steps. The steps shown in table 2.7 (on the following pages) are illustrative of those that have been used in MoSSaiC programs in the Eastern Caribbean; these should be discussed and adapted as local conditions dictate.

It is good practice to identify milestones for the project and assimilate them into the agreed-upon project steps.

Table 2.7 integrates summary information on MoSSaiC teams (sections 2.3 and 2.4), project steps (section 1.4.5), and milestones.

2.6.3 Establishing a user group community

Establishing a user group forum might be useful in enabling MoSSaiC to improve slope management practices (achieve behavioral change) as a medium-term outcome. Both local and regional workshops have proved to be a powerful vehicle for senior politicians, contractors, residents, and the media from different countries to share experiences and develop best practices (figure 2.14).

FIGURE 2.14 User group forum activities

a. A regional workshop captures project outcomes and identifies potential process improvements.

b. Community contractors address a workshop attended by community residents and other stakeholders.

TABLE 2.7 Summary template of MoSSaiC project teams, steps, and milestones

TEAM				**ACTIVITY/STEP/MILESTONE**	**CHAPTER**
F	**M**	**G**	**C**		
✓				Funding for pilot, project, or phase 2 (carried over or levered from existing projects)	1
✓	✓	✓	✓	Understand the disaster risk context with respect to landslides; relevance of MoSSaiC approach to local landslide risk context identified	
✓	✓	✓	✓	Understand the innovative features and foundations of MoSSaiC	
✓		✓		Identify general in-house expertise and the appropriate institutional structures for codifying a local approach toward landslide risk reduction	
✓	✓	✓		Brief key individuals on MoSSaiC (politicians, relevant ministries, in-house experts)	
✓	✓	✓		**MILESTONE 1:** Key catalytic staff briefed on MoSSaiC methodology	
	✓	✓	✓	**MILESTONE 2:** MoSSaiC core unit formed: key responsibilities agreed and defined	
✓				Establish the MCU; define and agree on key responsibilities	2
	✓	✓		Identify and establish government task teams; define and agree on key responsibilities	
	✓	✓	✓	Identify and establish community task teams; define and agree on key responsibilities	
	✓	✓		Agree on a general template for project steps	
✓	✓	✓		Gain familiarity with different landslide types and how to identify those that may be addressed by MoSSaiC	3
	✓	✓	✓	Gain familiarity with slope processes and slope stability variables	
	✓	✓		Gain familiarity with methods for analyzing slope stability	
	✓	✓	✓	**MILESTONE 3:** Presentation made to MoSSaiC teams on landslide processes and slope stability software	
✓	✓			Define the community selection process	4
		✓		Assess landslide hazard	
		✓		Assess exposure and vulnerability	
		✓		Assess landslide risk	
	✓	✓		Select communities	
	✓	✓		Prepare site map information for selected communities	
✓	✓	✓		**MILESTONE 4:** Process for community selection agreed and communities selected	
✓	✓	✓		Identify the best form of community participation and mobilization	5
		✓		Include key community members in the project team	
		✓		Plan and hold a community meeting	
		✓	✓	Conduct the community-based mapping exercise; this will entail a considerable amount of time in the community	
	✓	✓		Qualitatively assess the landslide hazard and potential causes	
	✓	✓		Quantitatively assess the landslide hazard and the effectiveness of surface water management to reduce the hazard	
		✓		Identify possible locations for drains	
	✓		✓	Sign off on the initial drainage plan: organize a combined MCU-community walk-through and meeting to agree on the initial drainage plan	
				MILESTONE 5: Sign-off on prioritized zones and initial drainage plan	

(continued)

TABLE 2.7 Summary template of MoSSaiC project teams, steps, and milestones *(continued)*

	TEAM			ACTIVITY/STEP/MILESTONE	CHAPTER
F	**M**	**G**	**C**		
	✓	✓		Identify the location and alignment of drains	6
		✓		Estimate drain discharge and dimensions	
		✓	✓	Specify drain construction and design details	
		✓		Incorporate houses into the drainage plan	
	✓	✓		Produce final drainage plan	
	✓	✓	✓	Stakeholder agreement on plan	
	✓	✓	✓	**MILESTONE 6:** Sign-off on final drainage plan	
	✓	✓		Prepare work package and request for tender documentation	7
		✓	✓	Conduct the agreed-upon community contracting tendering process	
		✓	✓	Implement construction	
		✓		Sign off on completed construction	
	✓	✓	✓	**MILESTONE 7:** Sign-off on completed construction	
✓	✓	✓		Understand how new practices are adopted	8
	✓			Design a communication strategy	
	✓	✓		Design a capacity-building strategy	
	✓	✓	✓	Plan for postproject maintenance	
	✓			Map out the complete behavioral change strategy	
	✓	✓	✓	**MILESTONE 8:** Communication and capacity-building strategies agreed on and implemented	
	✓			Agree on key performance indicators (KPIs) for immediate project outputs	9
	✓			Agree on KPIs for medium-term project outcomes	
	✓	✓		Undertake project evaluation	
				MILESTONE 9: Evaluation framework agreed upon and implemented	

F = funders and policy makers   **M** = MoSSaiC core unit: government project managers and experts   **G** = government task teams: experts and practitioners   **C** = community task teams: residents, leaders, contractors

Note: The steps listed for chapters 8 and 9 are relevant throughout the project.

2.7   RESOURCES

2.7.1   Who does what

TEAM	RESPONSIBILITY	ACTIONS AND HELPFUL HINTS	CHAPTER SECTION
Funders and policy makers	Establish the MCU	• Understand MCU missions, roles, and responsibilities • Identify MCU team members from relevant government ministries and other agencies **Helpful hint:** Look for potential members who will command respect and be advocates of MoSSaiC, rather than simply represent particular interests.	2.2; 2.2.4; 2.3.3; 2.6
	Coordinate with the MCU		
MCU	Own and communicate the MoSSaiC vision	• Understand MCU missions, roles, and responsibilities	2.2
	Identify and form government task teams	• Identify task team members from relevant government ministries and other agencies	2.4
	Once community selected (chapter 4), identify community task team members	• Initiate community participation process; engage with community residents and representatives	2.5
	Establish project step template	• Review MoSSaiC components with respect to task team capacity and resources • Modify project step template **Helpful hint:** This is a vital step in the process of project inception. Organize a meeting to review the template and encourage the modification of the template to fit local conditions and protocols.	2.2.4; 2.6
	Coordinate with new task teams		
Government task teams	Provide the MCU with assessment of task team capacity for each project step	• Become familiar with MoSSaiC approach and local context • Identify specific team skills and resources for project delivery	2.2; 2.2.4
	Coordinate with the MCU		
Community task teams	Once community selected (chapter 4), coordinate with relevant government task teams and the MCU to identify appropriate form of community participation	• Become familiar with MoSSaiC approach with respect to community context • Advise on existing community-based leadership structures and organizations • Identify specific community-based skills and resources • Attend community meetings	2.5
	Coordinate with government task teams		

2.7.2 Chapter checklist

CHECK THAT:	TEAM	PERSON	SIGN-OFF	CHAPTER SECTION
✓ List compiled of individuals supportive of MoSSaiC across government/agencies				2.3.3
✓ **Milestone 2:** MCU formed				
✓ MCU has identified individuals for government task teams				2.4
✓ MCU and appropriate government task teams have identified individuals for community task teams				2.5
✓ MCU has established clear line of responsibility to a specific government entity				2.6
✓ All necessary safeguards complied with				1.5.3; 2.3.2

2.7.3 References

Anderson, M. G., and E. A. Holcombe. 2004. "Management of Slope Stability in Communities." *Insight* 1: 15–17.

——. 2006a. "Purpose Driven Public Sector Reform: The Need for within-Government Capacity Build for the Management of Slope Stability in Communities (MoSSaiC) in the Caribbean." *Environmental Management* 37: 5–29.

——. 2006b. "Sustainable Landslide Risk Reduction in Poorer Countries." *Proceedings of the Institution of Civil Engineers—Engineering Sustainability* 159: 23–30.

Anderson, M. G., E. A. Holcombe, and D. Williams. 2007. "Reducing Landslide Risk in Poor Housing Areas of the Caribbean—Developing a New Government-Community Partnership Model." *Journal of International Development* 19: 205–21.

Buchanan, J. M. 1977. "The Samaritans' Dilemma." In *Freedom in Constitutional Contract*, ed. J. M. Buchanan. College Station, TX: Texas A & M University Press.

IEG (Independent Evaluation Group). 2000. "IEG Report on Project ID P003985 Indonesia." World Bank, Washington, DC.

——. 2005. *Putting Social Development to Work for the Poor: An OED Review of World Bank Activities.* Washington, DC: World Bank.

Mansuri, G., and V. Rao. 2003. *Evaluating Community-Based and Community-Driven Development: A Critical Review of the Evidence.* Development Research Group. Washington, DC: World Bank.

Maskrey, A. 1992. "Defining the Community's Role in Disaster Mitigation." *Appropriate Technology Magazine* 19 (3). http://practicalaction.org/practicalanswers/product_info.php?products_id=214.

Ostrom, E., C. Gibson, S. Shivakumar, and K. Andersson. 2001. "Aid, Incentives, and Sustainability: An Institutional Analysis of Development Cooperation." Sida Studies in Evaluation Report 02/01, Stockholm.

Prater, C. S., and M. K. Londell. 2000. "Politics of Natural Hazards." *Natural Hazards Review* 1 (2): 73–82.

Raschky, P. A., and M. Schwindt. 2009. "Aid, Natural Disasters and the Samaritan's Dilemma." Policy Research Working Paper 4952, World Bank, Washington, DC.

Roberts, N. C., and P. J. King. 1991. "Policy Entrepreneurs: Their Activity Structure and Function in the Policy Process." *Journal of Public Administration Research and Theory* 1 (2): 147–75.

UNDP (United Nations Development Programme). 2006. "A Review of Selected Capacity Assessment Methodologies." http://lencd.com/data/docs/242-A%20Review%20of%20Selected%20Capacity%20Assessment%20Methodologies.pdf.

Venture Philanthropy Partners. 2001. *Effective Capacity Building in Nonprofit Organizations.* http://www.vppartners.org/sites/default/files/reports/full_rpt.pdf.

——. 2003. *Strategic Communication for Development Projects: A Toolkit for Task Team Leaders.* http://siteresources.worldbank.org/EXTDEVCOMMENG/Resources/toolkitwebjan2004.pdf.

"A failure to address the underlying risk drivers will result in dramatic increases in disaster risk and associated poverty outcomes. In contrast, if addressing these drivers is given priority, risk can be reduced..."

—United Nations, "Global Assessment Report on Disaster Risk Reduction" (2009, 4)

CHAPTER 3

Understanding Landslide Hazard

3.1 KEY CHAPTER ELEMENTS

3.1.1 Coverage

This chapter identifies the physical and human drivers for landslide hazard. Understanding the scientific basis for assessing landslide hazard is one of the MoSSaiC (Management of Slope Stability in Communities) foundations. The listed groups should read the indicated chapter sections.

AUDIENCE				LEARNING	CHAPTER SECTION
F	M	G	C		
✓	✓	✓		How to identify types of landslides that can be addressed by MoSSaiC	3.3
	✓	✓		Slope stability factors and common landslide hazard assessment methods	3.4
	✓	✓	✓	Detailed localized factors that affect slope stability in communities	3.5
	✓	✓		Specific scientific landslide hazard assessment methods relevant to MoSSaiC	3.6

F = funders and policy makers   **M** = MoSSaiC core unit: government project managers and experts   **G** = government task teams: experts and practitioners   **C** = community task teams: residents, leaders, contractors

3.1.2 Documents

DOCUMENT TO BE PRODUCED	CHAPTER SECTION
Briefing by landslide assessment and engineering task team for the MoSSaiC core unit and all other task teams on (1) MoSSaiC applicability to local landslide types; (2) landslide preparatory, aggravating, and triggering factors; and (3) the scientific basis for assessing slope stability, especially with respect to locally available expertise and software	3.2–3.5

3.1.3 Steps and outputs

STEP	OUTPUT
1. Gain familiarity with different landslide types and how to identify those that may be addressed by MoSSaiC • Review landslide process introductory material in this book and other sources	MoSSaiC core unit (MCU) and task teams understand the types of landslide risk for which MoSSaiC is applicable
2. Gain familiarity with slope processes and slope stability variables • Review landslide process variables as introduced in this book	MCU and task teams can identify different levels of landslide hazard and underlying physical causes
3. Gain familiarity with methods for analyzing slope stability • Review slope stability software as introduced in this book and other sources	MCU and task teams can provide scientific rationale for landslide mitigation measures

Those on the MoSSaiC landslide assessment and engineering task team with the most experience in analysis of landslide risk could use the material in this chapter to organize a presentation to the MoSSaiC core unit (MCU) and other task teams to foster a common and shared understanding of landslide triggering processes, the relevance of MoSSaiC (chapter 1), and the associated project structure and implementation steps (chapter 2).

3.1.4 Community-based aspects

The chapter outlines the need to understand landslide triggering mechanisms at the household/local scale within communities.

3.2 GETTING STARTED

3.2.1 Briefing note

Importance of understanding landslide processes

Both the occurrence and the impact of landslides are increasing, especially in tropical developing countries (Charveriat 2000; UNDP 2004), with the majority of landslide fatalities occurring in urban areas (Petley 2009; UN 2006). Here, intense rainfall triggers landslides in highly weathered soils and rapid urbanization increases the susceptibility of slopes to failure, while socioeconomic vulnerability increases the damage caused. Even so,

there are few examples of effective physical landslide hazard reduction measures in such communities (Wamsler 2007).

Development agencies have mainstreamed disaster risk management policies, estimating that for every dollar spent in mitigation, two to four dollars will be saved in avoided costs (Mechler 2005). Landslide risk mitigation requires an understanding of the interactions between physical and human risk drivers, and how to assess the risk and deliver solutions at a scale that relates to these risk drivers. Community-scale landslide hazard reduction can only be successful if landslide hazard mechanisms and triggers are understood. Such an understanding

• ensures that any landslide risk assessment is scientifically informed,

• ensures that any proposed landslide risk management strategies are appropriate to the specific local landslide hazards,

• determines if a MoSSaiC-style drainage intervention will address the landslide hazard,

• increases the ability of those implementing the project to justify the risk reduction measures adopted,

• helps build confidence within the community that the fundamental causes of risk are being tackled, and

- encourages a holistic and strategic approach to implementation of landslide risk reduction measures among all stakeholders.

Landslide hazard as a component of landslide risk

Three components contribute to landslide risk: the physical landslide **hazard** (its likelihood, location, and magnitude), the **exposure** of different elements (such as people, buildings, public utilities, economic infrastructure, or the environment) to that hazard, and the **vulnerability** of those elements to damage by the hazard.

- Landslide hazard is defined in terms of its frequency (e.g., an annual probability of 0.1, meaning a 1-in-10-year landslide event), magnitude, and type at a particular location or within a wider region. When the likelihood of a particular landslide hazard is expressed in relative or qualitative terms rather than as a probability, it is more appropriate to refer to **susceptibility** (more versus less susceptible to landslides).

- The exposure of people, structures, services, or the environment to a specific landslide hazard is determined by the spatial and temporal location of those elements with respect to the landslide.

- Vulnerability is an expression of the potential of the exposed elements to suffer harm or loss. Thus, exposure and vulnerability relate to the consequences or results of the landslide, and not to the landslide process itself (Crozier and Glade 2005). In many cases, exposure is treated as an implicit part of vulnerability assessment. Vulnerability is related to the capacity to anticipate a landslide hazard, cope with it, resist it, and recover from its impact. A combination of physical, environmental, social, economic, political, cultural, and institutional factors determine vulnerability (Benson and Twigg 2007).

To understand landslide risk, it is necessary to understand the nature and causes of the hazard. Many development studies and programs focus on assessing vulnerability and exposure to landslide hazards; relatively few look at the physical causes of the hazard at the highly localized scales at which they occur. Various natural and human preparatory and aggravating factors can reduce slope stability and trigger landslides. By understanding these driving factors and identifying the dominant landslide mechanisms, it is often possible to address the root causes of landslides and thus reduce the hazard (the frequency or magnitude of the event).

One of the main premises of MoSSaiC is that rainfall-triggered landslide hazards can often be reduced in vulnerable communities in developing countries. This is because a common driver for such landslide hazards is poor slope drainage and surface water infiltration into weathered slope materials on densely populated urban slopes. Scientific principles and methods can be used to confirm the role of surface water infiltration and therefore indicate a potential solution—the construction of appropriately located surface water drains.

Science as part of the landslide risk management process

A typical disaster risk management process was introduced in section 1.3.2. Table 3.1 presents the scientific basis of each step in this process with particular reference to landslide risk management and the MoSSaiC approach.

3.2.2 Guiding principles

The following guiding principles apply in understanding landslide hazard:

- Develop a shared understanding of landslide processes within the MCU

- Identify and collate data on past, existing, or predicted landslide hazards in the project area and on physical and human factors relating to slope stability

- Explain and explore the scientific rationale for landslide hazard reduction in a way that is accessible to residents in vulnerable communities; assure residents that the local landslide processes are

TABLE 3.1 Typical landslide risk management project steps and associated scientific basis for MoSSaiC

STEP		MoSSaiC SCIENCE BASE
Landslide risk management project preparation	Identify and formulate the project	**Confirm the relevance of MoSSaiC.** A basic understanding of landslide types and triggers is needed in order to identify the dominant landslide hazard in the project area. MoSSaiC specifically addresses rainfall-triggered rotational/translational landslides in weathered materials.
Landslide risk assessment	Identify the broad landslide risk	**Identify communities most at risk from landslides.** This requires assessment of the relative rotational/translational landslide susceptibility or hazard in different areas. This hazard information is combined with an assessment of community exposure and vulnerability.
	Understand and estimate the specific landslide risk	**Identify the underlying landslide hazard drivers and confirm the level of the hazard.** For selected communities, the local slope features and slope stability processes must be identified, science-based methods used to confirm the hazard drivers, and the vulnerability of exposed households assessed.
	Evaluate the risk	**Compare the landslide risk with other risks.** Expert judgment and/or scientific methods should be applied to determine where investment in landslide risk reduction is a priority.
Landslide risk reduction	Identify disaster risk reduction options	**Determine whether the landslide hazard can be reduced.** Disaster risk reduction options include avoiding or reducing the hazard, reducing vulnerability, or transferring the risk. MoSSaiC focuses on landslide hazard reduction through appropriate surface water management measures. For each community, expert judgment and/or scientific methods should be applied to confirm whether this MoSSaiC approach will be effective.
	Plan the risk mitigation	**Design the landslide hazard reduction measures.** Engineers should design the physical measures to directly address the localized landslide hazard drivers. In the case of MoSSaiC, this requires appropriate alignment and design of a drainage network to capture surface water and reduce infiltration.
	Implement risk mitigation	**Construct landslide hazard reduction measures.** This involves issuing contracts for and managing construction, and raising public awareness. Knowledge of slope processes and construction of drainage works are vital in ensuring that hazard reduction measures are correctly implemented.
	Monitor and evaluate	**Assess project progress, sustainability, and impact.** Science-based methods should be used to determine the effectiveness of landslide hazard reduction measures.

understood and that the project is likely to be effective in addressing the causes of the problem

3.2.3 Risks and challenges

Regional policies and local landslide hazards

In international development, disaster risk reduction funding policies are often decided at a regional level and then translated into national programs to address multiple risk types. This top-down approach typically leads to the production of wide-area qualitative maps of landslide susceptibility that practitioners in developing countries may find difficult to apply (Zaitchik and van Es 2003). There are two possible reasons for the lack of uptake of such maps (Holcombe and Anderson 2010):

• Their inherent limitation in predicting specific landslide locations, timing, and causes due to the mismatch between coarse map scales and fine-scale variations in slope processes (Keefer and Larsen 2007)

• Their lack of utility in land-use planning for exposure reduction (Opadeyi, Ali, and Chin 2005), as high-density unauthorized housing often already occupies hazardous slopes.

Holistic awareness of slope processes

Several interrelated factors can affect the stability of a slope at a variety of spatial and temporal scales. These factors should be investigated at the relevant scale using either a qualitative or quantitative (modeling) approach or a mixture of both. Direct measurement of all slope parameters is not always possible; however, engineers or scientists will be able to make an expert judgment of the dominant causes of the landslide hazard based on their knowledge of the principles governing slope stability.

3.2.4 Adapting the chapter blueprint to existing capacity

This chapter provides an introduction to landslide processes and the various factors that can affect slope stability. It identifies the main forms of landslide hazard assessment appropriate at different spatial scales and for various levels of data and expertise.

Members of the MCU and task teams should understand basic slope stability processes in order to configure the landslide hazard reduction measures appropriately and share this knowledge with community residents and other stakeholders. The MCU and government task teams should have at least one civil, environmental, or geotechnical engineer, or an expert in physical, geotechnical, or hydrological sciences, who can lead the landslide hazard assessment process. The project should be scientifically justified and that justification understood by all involved.

The MCU should begin by assessing available capacity in this area. Use the matrix on the next page to help make that assessment.

1. Assign a capacity score from 1 to 3 (low to high) to reflect existing capacity for each element in the matrix's left-hand column.

2. Identify the most common capacity score as an indicator of the overall capacity level.

3. Adapt the blueprint in this chapter in accordance with the overall capacity level (see guide on the bottom of next page).

3.3 LANDSLIDE TYPES AND THOSE ADDRESSED BY MOSSAIC

The first step in the landslide risk management process is to define the scope of the project in terms of funding constraints, geographical extent, policy context, and type of landslide hazard to be mitigated.

Correctly identifying the type of landslide hazard affecting a particular area is vital. Different landslide types have very different physical mechanisms and consequences. Each type therefore requires a different hazard assessment approach and set of mitigation measures. This section presents a simple classification of landslide types and identifies those that may be mitigated by a MoSSaiC project—namely, rotational and translational rainfall-triggered slides in weathered slope materials affecting multiple households or entire urban communities.

MCU and task teams should use this section to identify the dominant landslide hazards in the project area in terms of

- types of movement and material involved,
- geometry,
- triggering mechanism, and
- slope stability over time.

3.3.1 Types of slope movement and landslide material

Although many types of mass movements are referred to as landslides, the technical use of the term applies only to mass movements where there is a distinct zone of weakness that separates the slide material from more stable underlying material. For a helpful, well-illustrated guide to different landslide types and geometries, see USGS (2004).

Varnes (1978) classified five principle types of mass movement in three types of slope material (table 3.2). As highlighted in the table, MoSSaiC is designed to address rotational and translational slides in predominately weathered materials (unconsolidated fine soils) that are principally triggered by rainfall.

- **Rotational slide.** The surface of rupture is curved concavely upward, and slide movement is roughly rotational (figure 3.1a).
- **Translational slide.** The landslide mass moves along a roughly planar surface with

CAPACITY ELEMENT	EXISTING CAPACITY		
	1 = LOW	2 = MODERATE	3 = HIGH
MCU member(s) familiar with landslide processes and hazard reduction measures	No major education in landslide processes or previous experience with landslide hazard reduction projects	Some MCU members have a basic grounding in landslide processes or some experience with landslide hazard reduction projects	Two or more MCU members have sound education in landslide processes and experience in implementing landslide hazard reduction projects
Training available on landslide processes and hazard reduction	No local provision for training	Courses on some aspects of landslide processes and hazard reduction locally available	Training courses on both landslide processes and hazard reduction locally available
Availability of slope stability analysis software and expertise	No slope stability analysis software or expertise available	Either slope stability analysis software or expertise available to government, but not both	Slope stability analysis software and expertise available within government and used on projects
Government capacity to support landslide mitigation (hazard reduction) projects	Limited government capacity to support and implement landslide mitigation projects	One-off landslide mitigation projects previously under-taken by government	Government department routinely handles landslide mitigation work
Project safeguards	Documented safeguards need to be located; no previous experience in interpreting and operating safeguard policies	Documents exist for some safeguards	Documented safeguards available from all relevant agencies

CAPACITY LEVEL	HOW TO ADAPT THE BLUEPRINT
1: Use this chapter in depth and as a catalyst to secure support from other agencies as appropriate	The MCU needs to strengthen its capacity in understanding landslide processes and using relevant analytical software. This might involve the following: • Working with local commercial or higher education partners to share and learn from their experience in slope stability analysis • Searching for colleagues in government with relevant slope stability experience and considering their appointment to the MCU • Approaching suitable materials laboratories and consultants for data on soil material properties
2: Some elements of this chapter will reflect current practice; read the remaining elements in depth and use them to further strengthen capacity	The MCU has strength in some areas, but not all. Elements that are perceived to be Level 1 need to be addressed as above. Elements that are Level 2 will need to be strengthened, such as the following: • Where there is no slope stability analysis software, seek training on the use and application of such software • Where there is limited existing government coordination of landslide hazard assessment, pool the relevant expertise and data from different ministries and agencies • Where there is limited or incomplete understanding of landslide causes, provide a technical briefing session for nonexperts based on material in this chapter
3: Use this chapter as a checklist	The MCU is likely to be able to proceed using existing proven capacity. The following would nonetheless be good practice: • Document relevant prior experience in landslide hazard assessment and related safeguard documents • Endorse such a document at an MCU meeting prior to commencement of works

TABLE 3.2 Slope instability classification

TYPE OF MOVEMENT		BEDROCK	TYPE OF MATERIAL	
			UNCONSOLIDATED SOIL	
			Coarse	Fine
Falls		Rock fall	Debris fall	Earth fall
Topples		Rock topple	Debris topple	Earth topple
Slides	Rotational	Rock slide	Debris slide	Earth slide—the landslide type relevant to MoSSaiC
	Translational			
Flows		Rock flow	Debris flow	Earth flow
Complex		Combination of two or more types		

Source: Cruden and Varnes 1996. © National Academy of Sciences, Washington, DC, 1996. Reproduced with permission of the Transportation Research Board.

Note: The types of slope movement and associated material that are addressed by MoSSaiC are highlighted.

little rotation or backward tilting (figure 3.1b). A block slide is a translational slide in which the moving mass consists of a single unit or a few closely related units that move downslope as a relatively coherent mass.

3.3.2 Landslide geometry and features

Different types of landslide can be recognized by their geometry and features (figure 3.2). The idealized forms shown in figures 3.1 and 3.2 are not always easy to identify in the field if vegetation cover obscures the landslide or if the landslide is old. Only comparatively recent landslides are likely to exhibit an identifiable failure zone at the head of the moved mass.

When mapping landslide locations, as many of these features as possible should be identi-

fied and plotted (in accordance with figure 3.2).

The scale of landslides in vulnerable communities in the tropics will generally be determined by soil depth, since the slip surface is often at the interface between the soil and the bedrock (or at a marked change of soil weathering grade). Typical depths to the slip surface may be in the range 1–10 m.

The lateral extent of landslides in such locations is often controlled by topographic features such as zones of drainage convergence and deeper soils. Where more localized factors are acting to destabilize the slope, the landslide may be less extensive. Typical maximum widths of the main body of the landslides (figure 3.2, feature 6) may be in the range 10–50 m or more.

Rotational landslides in soils are not as mobile as some other forms of landslide (such as debris slides). Typically, the surface of separation of rotational landslides (figure 3.2, feature 12) may be in the range of a few meters to about 100 m, depending on the volume of material involved and the slope angle.

3.3.3 Landslide triggering events: Rainfall and earthquakes

Every slope has stabilizing and destabilizing forces. The different preparatory and aggravating factors that determine the relative susceptibility of a slope to landslides are detailed in section 3.4. A slope that is relatively suscep-

FIGURE 3.1 Characteristics of rotational and translational slides in predominantly weathered materials

a. Rotational slide   b. Translational slide

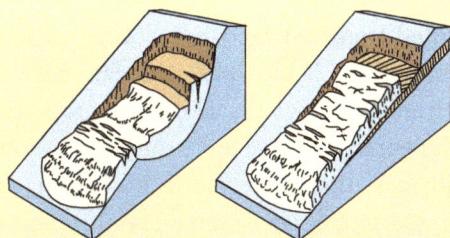

Source: USGS 2004; reproduced with permission.

FIGURE 3.2 Definitional features of a landslide

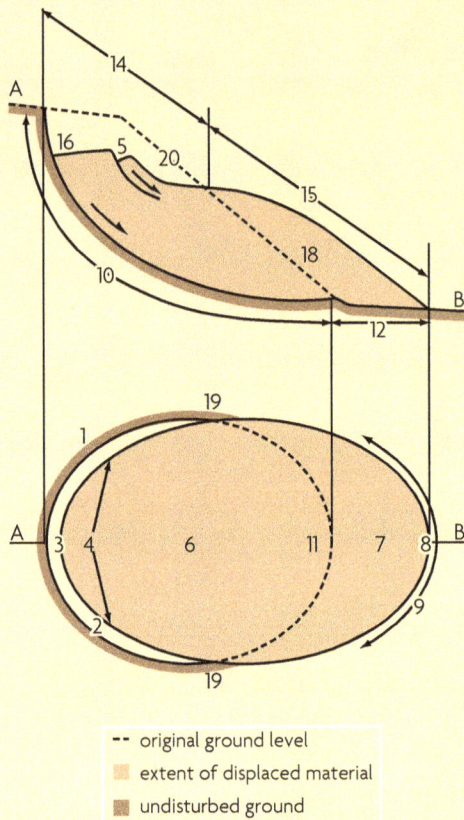

1. **Crown:** The undisplaced material adjacent to the highest parts of the main scarp.

2. **Main scarp:** A steep surface on the undisturbed ground at the upper edge of the landslide, caused by movement of the displaced material away from the undisturbed ground; the visible part of the surface of rupture.

3. **Top:** The highest point of contact between the displaced material and the main scarp.

4. **Head:** The upper parts of the landslide along the contact between the displaced material and the main scarp.

5. **Minor scarp:** A steep surface on the displaced material of the landslide produced by differential movements in the displaced material.

6. **Main body:** The part of the displaced material of the landslide that overlies the surface of rupture between the main scarp and the toe of the surface of rupture.

7. **Foot:** The portion of the landslide that has moved beyond the toe of the surface of rupture and overlies the original ground surface.

8. **Tip:** The point of the toe farthest from the top of the landslide.

9. **Toe:** The lower, usually curved, margin of the displaced material of a landslide; it is the most distant from the main scarp.

10. **Surface of rupture:** The surface that forms the lower boundary of the displaced material below the original ground surface.

11. **Toe of the surface of rupture:** The intersection (usually buried) between the lower part of the surface of rupture of a landslide and the original ground surface.

12. **Surface of separation:** The part of the original ground surface overlaid by the foot of the landslide.

13. **Displaced material:** Material displaced from its original position on the slope by movement in the landslide. It forms both the depleted mass and the accumulation.

14. **Zone of depletion:** The area of the landslide within which the displaced material lies below the original ground surface.

15. **Zone of accumulation:** The area of the landslide within which the displaced material lies above the original ground surface.

16. **Depletion:** The volume bounded by the main scarp, the depleted mass, and the original ground surface.

17. **Depleted mass:** The volume of the displaced material that overlies the rupture surface but underlies the original ground surface.

18. **Accumulation:** The volume of the displaced material that lies above the original ground surface.

19. **Flank:** The undisplaced material adjacent to the sides of the rupture surface. Compass directions are preferable in describing the flanks but if left and right are used, they refer to the flanks as viewed from the crown.

20. **Original ground surface:** The surface of the slope that existed before the landslide took place.

Source: International Geotechnical Societies UNESCO Working Party on World Landslide Inventory 1993.

---

tible to landslides may exist in a state of marginal stability for a long period until a particular event decreases the stabilizing forces and/or increases the destabilizing forces, triggering a landslide. The most common landslide triggers are rainfall events and seismic events (earthquakes). Because these triggers act on a slope in different ways, it is important to distinguish between those landslides that are rainfall triggered versus those that are seismically triggered so that appropriate risk mitigation measures can be identified.

The majority of landslides in the humid tropics are triggered by rainfall (Crosta 2004;

Lumb 1975). MoSSaiC is specifically targeted to address this form of landslide hazard through the construction of a network of surface water drains.

Rainfall, slope hydrology, and landslides

Rainfall-triggered landslides occur in most mountainous landscapes and can have an enormous effect on the landscape, properties, and people. Intense or prolonged rainfall infiltrates the slope surface, causing an increase in soil pore water pressure and an associated lowering of slope material strength. The forces that act to stabilize the slope are thus reduced, and the slope fails along the zone where the destabilizing forces (gravity and loading) overcome the stabilizing forces.

Urban development can alter the preparatory factors affecting slope stability, changing slope geometry, loading, surface cover, and slope hydrology. Significantly, urban development can increase the effectiveness of rainfall in triggering landslides by changing natural drainage routes, concentrating surface water flows, changing surface vegetation cover (which would normally intercept and store rainfall and remove water from the soil), increasing rainfall runoff from impermeable surfaces, and increasing surface water infiltration in other areas (figure 3.3). The most vulnerable communities in developing countries will probably not have sufficient surface water drainage, but may have publicly supplied piped water, which further increases the amount of water on the slope. Rainfall-triggered landslide hazard is thus often increased by urbanization.

As noted, in humid tropical developing countries, the majority of fatalities and physical losses occur in urban areas (Petley 2009). At the local scale, even small landslide events in densely populated areas can result in significant loss of life and property and stall economic development. Houses may be lost or made unsafe, and community infrastructure destroyed (figures 3.4a and b). Multiple landslides may be widespread throughout the area (figure 3.4c).

Shallow and deep-seated landslides alike can be triggered by rainfall. Records of landslides and associated rainfall triggers (characterized by intensity, duration, and frequency) can be used to predict the timing of future rainfall-triggered landslide events. Extensive research has been conducted to identify both landslide-prone terrains (Hansen 1984; Soeters and van Westen 1996) and the rainfall intensities and durations that cause slopes to fail (Larsen and Simon 1993). These two issues are discussed further in section 3.4; De Vita et al. (1997) provide an extensive bibliography on rainfall-triggered landslides.

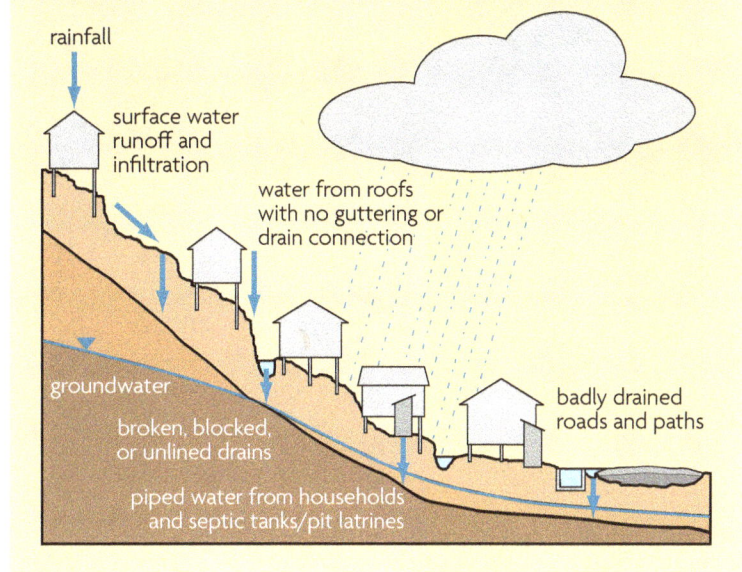

FIGURE 3.3 Typical surface and subsurface water sources and flow paths associated with unauthorized construction on hillslopes

Seismic events

Seismic activity can also affect the forces acting on a slope and trigger landslides. Currently, MoSSaiC does not address the landslide mechanisms associated with this triggering process. Nevertheless, the MCU should have some familiarity with seismic risk where it coexists with the potential for rainfall-triggered landslides. In such cases, a holistic approach to disaster risk reduction should be taken if possible. For example, the MoSSaiC approach to community-scale slope drainage networks, plus the house-by-house installation of roof guttering and gray water connections to the drains, could be coupled with guidelines on earthquake-resilient property design for such communities (Build Change 2011).

Globally, many locations have oversteepened and highly weathered hillsides, where large landslides could cause significant harm to local communities—many of which are already vulnerable in terms of housing structures and poverty. The 2001 earthquakes in El Salvador (figure 3.5) are a notable example in this regard, causing over 600 landslides and resulting in many hundreds of fatalities, with 585 deaths in the community of Las Colinas alone (figure 3.6).

FIGURE 3.4 **Rotational and translational landslides**

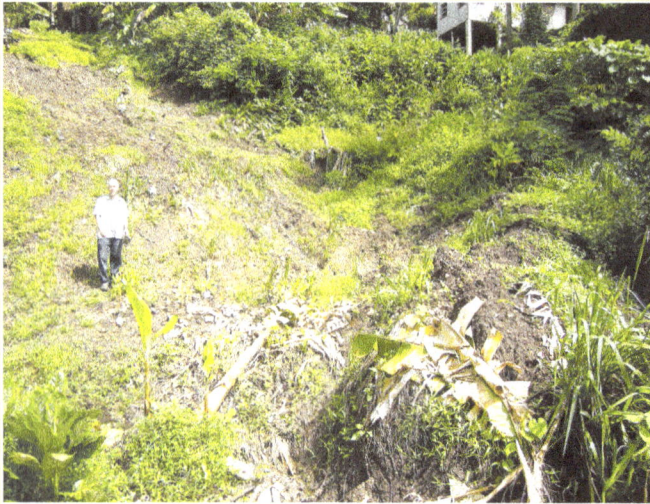

a. Rotational slide in St. Lucia triggered by rainfall during Hurricane Dean (2007) caused the loss of three houses.

b. Translational slide in St. Lucia triggered by ~500 mm of rainfall in 24 hours associated with Hurricane Tomas (2010); slide caused the loss of a road (center) and significantly damaged houses at the landslide crest.

c. Hillside-wide translational landslides St. Lucia triggered by Hurricane Tomas.

Empirical evidence linking seismic activity; preparatory factors such as slope angle, geology, and soils; and landslide events can be formalized by measures of seismic intensity. An instrument-based measure of seismic intensity developed by Arias (1970) was first used for analyzing the occurrence of landslides by Wilson and Keefer (1985), and its use has become relatively widespread for that purpose since. The Arias intensity, for any given strong-motion recording, is expressed as

$$I_a = \pi/2g \int_0^{Td} [a(t)^2]dt$$

Where:

I_a = Arias intensity in units of velocity
t = time
$a(t)$ = ground acceleration as a function of time
Td = total duration of the strong-motion record
g = acceleration due to gravity

Arias intensity is a ground motion parameter that captures the potential destructiveness of an earthquake as the integral of the square of the acceleration-time history. It correlates well with several commonly used demand measures of structural performance, liquefaction, and seismic slope stability (Travasarou, Bray, and Abrahamson 2003). Based on theoretical considerations, statistical analysis of strong-motion attenuation, and empirical data on landslide limits in historical earthquakes, the Arias intensity thresholds can be related to types of landslide (table 3.3) (Keefer 2002; Keefer and Wilson 1989; Wilson and Keefer 1985).

Keefer (2002, 504) notes that while earthquake-induced landslides have been documented for more than 3,700 years, it is clear that more seismic data are needed:

> ...the number of earthquakes with relatively complete data on landslide occurrence is still small, and one of the most pressing research needs is for complete landslide inventories for many more events in a wider variety of environments.

These empirical data, when coupled with analytical tools such as geographic informa-

FIGURE 3.5 Distribution of seismicity during the 2001 El Salvador earthquakes

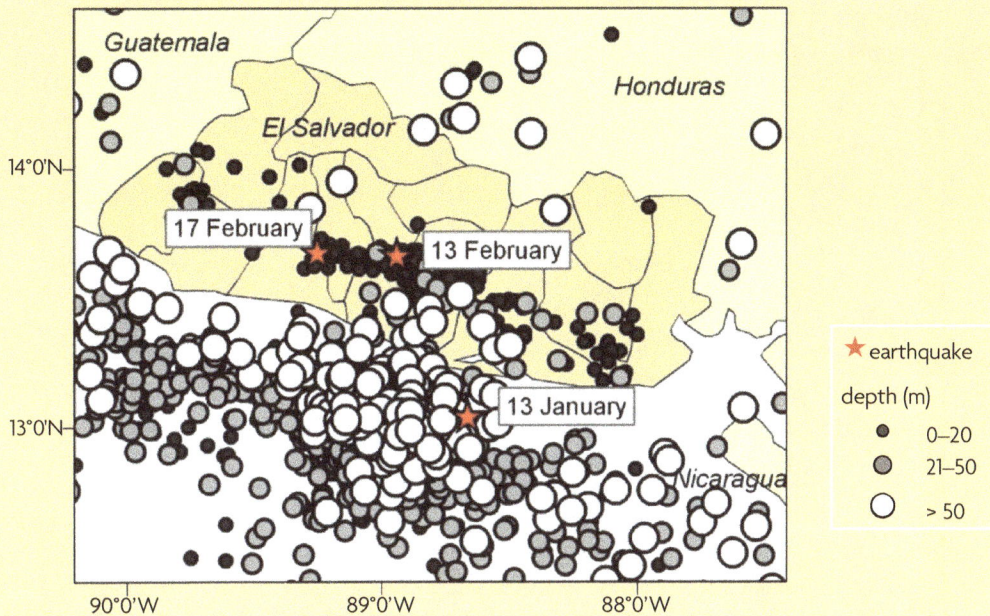

Source: Garcia-Rodriguez et al. 2008.

Note: Data were recorded and relocated by the Salvadoran Short-Period Network of the Center for Geotechnical Investigations. Shown are the main earthquakes on January 13, February 13, and February 17, 2001, and their aftershocks. The January 13 earthquake, which triggered over 600 landslides including in Las Colinas, was located in the subduction zone between the Cocos and Caribbean plates, with a magnitude of 7.7 (moment magnitude) and a focal depth of 40 km.

FIGURE 3.6 Aerial view of earthquake-triggered landslide in Las Colinas, El Salvador, January 13, 2001

Source: Garcia-Rodriguez et al. 2008.

TABLE 3.3 Arias intensity and associated landslide categories

ARIAS INTENSITY VALUE THRESHOLD	RESULTANT LANDSLIDE CATEGORY
0.11 ms^{-1}	Disrupted landslides
0.32 ms^{-1}	Coherent slides, lateral spreads, and flows
0.54 ms^{-1}	Lateral spreads and flows

Source: Keefer and Wilson 1989.

tion systems (GIS), could lead to substantial additional refinements in physically based models that relate seismic shaking and geologic conditions to slope failure.

3.3.4 Slope stability over time

Landslide velocities can vary significantly depending on type, material, trigger, and a range of other slope properties. Table 3.4

shows the landslide velocity scale proposed by Cruden and Varnes (1996).

In the tropics, rainfall-triggered landslide movement typically lasts anywhere from a few minutes to a few hours. Progressive slides and subsequent slope settlement can continue over periods as long as a year or more. Figure 3.7 shows a rotational landslide periodically moving over five years, causing increased damage to the property.

The magnitude of a landslide will determine the damage caused to people and property. Landslide magnitude is defined by the velocity of the slide and the size of the area

TABLE 3.4 Landslide velocity scale

VELOCITY CLASS	DESCRIPTION	VELOCITY (mm/s)	TYPICAL VELOCITY	PROBABLE DESTRUCTIVE SIGNIFICANCE
7	Extremely rapid			Catastrophe of major violence; buildings destroyed by impact of displaced material; many deaths; escape unlikely
		5×10^3	5 m/s	
6	Very rapid			Some lives lost; velocity too great to permit all persons to escape
		5×10^1	3 m/min	
5	Rapid			Escape evacuation possible; structures, possessions, and equipment destroyed
		5×10^1	1.8 m/h	
4	Moderate			Some temporary and insensitive structures can be temporarily maintained
		5×10^3	13 m/month	
3	Slow			Remedial construction can be undertaken during movement; insensitive structures can be maintained with frequent maintenance work if total movement is not large during a particular acceleration phase
		5×10^5	1.6 m/year	
2	Very slow			Some permanent structures undamaged by movement
		5×10^7	15 mm/year	
	Extremely slow			Imperceptible without instruments; construction possible with precautions

Source: Cruden and Varnes 1996. © National Academy of Sciences, Washington, DC, 1996. Reproduced with permission of the Transportation Research Board.

FIGURE 3.7 Progressive landslide

a. In 2005, rainfall triggered a progressive rotational landslide in a vulnerable community in St. Lucia.

b. The same house in 2008 shows the slow progressive movement of the rotational failure.

c. The same house in 2010 shows the structure's near collapse after five years of very slow progressive slope failure.

affected, in terms of both the actual failed area and the travel distance of the displaced material (the accumulation zone).

The slope's postfailure stability can also contribute to overall landslide impact. Depending on the geometry of the slide and the resulting geometry of the slope, there may be either a relative increase in overall stability (reduction in hazard) or a decrease in stability due to the slide's creating an unstable scarp (figure 3.8).

In an area of existing landslides, postfailure stability should be carefully assessed to identify possible future hazard, since this may be either increased or decreased by occurrence of a slope failure.

FIGURE 3.8 Postfailure slope stability

a. Landslide caused by soil water convergence at, and immediately above, the zone of failure, the impact of which serves to reduce subsequent landslide risk since the local slope angle has been reduced as a consequence of the failure.

b. Landslide below unauthorized houses triggered by the discharge of upslope water, causing oversteepening at the crest of the landslide, and subsequent increase in landslide hazard.

3.4 SLOPE STABILITY PROCESSES AND THEIR ASSESSMENT

This section introduces the different factors and variables that can determine the stability of a slope and some of the main methods for assessing slope stability. More information on slope stability processes and assessment is provided in the following two sections:

- Section 3.5 describes how each of the slope stability variables can be identified, measured, and interpreted in the field.

- Section 3.6 details the physically based slope stability assessment methods that are particularly relevant to MoSSaiC.

3.4.1 Landslide preparatory factors and triggering mechanisms

The factors that determine the stability of a slope can be categorized as

- *preparatory factors*, determining the stability of a slope over a period of time,

- *triggering mechanisms*, the dynamic events that result in a landslide, and

- *aggravating factors*, the many human activities that can reduce the stability of a slope without necessarily triggering a landslide (table 3.5).

These various factors will act and interact across a particular slope to determine its stability state at any point in time. Each factor must be taken into account and their combined influence assessed in order to understand the stability of a slope.

Factors that cause landslides are often quite localized in nature. Extensive work in Hong Kong SAR, China, has demonstrated that, for a large number of landslides, the main rainfall trigger works in conjunction with highly specific local preparatory factors (GCO 1984). Table 3.6 provides a summary of the range of scales over which the different preparatory and triggering factors could be expected to operate. To deliver landslide hazard reduction measures at the community scale (the MoSSaiC objective), the relevant slope processes must be assessed at the 1–100 m scale.

3.4.2 Overview of slope stability assessment methods

In discussing the methods and outputs of an assessment of slope stability, it is necessary to understand the difference between landslide susceptibility and landslide hazard:

TABLE 3.5 Factors determining slope stability and associated assessment methods

FACTOR DETERMINING SLOPE STABILITY		ASSESSMENT METHOD
Preparatory	**Aggravating**	
Slope angle	Construction—oversteepening of slopes	GIS, maps, survey, Abney level
Slope hydrology	Poor or altered slope drainage—leaking or incomplete drains; blocked drains and natural channels; saturated soils; water from house roofs, kitchens, and bathrooms	• Topographic convergence from maps/survey • Water table from piezometer records • Detailed on-site drainage survey
Slope material depth, structure, and type	Poorly compacted fill or previously failed material	Material grades, shear box direct measurement
Vegetation	Change or removal of vegetation due to cultivation or construction	Field observation
Loading	Overloading—dense, unplanned housing, water tanks, or infrastructure	Survey of housing density and construction material
Previous landslides	Ongoing or progressive movement of slope	Survey and records of known failures
DYNAMIC TRIGGERING MECHANISMS		
Rainfall events (e.g., storms, hurricanes, prolonged periods of rainfall)		Rainfall data and frequency analysis
Seismic events (not currently incorporated in MoSSaiC methodology)		Seismograph data and frequency analysis

TABLE 3.6 Spatial scales of landslide triggering mechanisms, preparatory factors and anthropogenic influences

MECHANISM/FACTOR/INFLUENCE	SPATIAL SCALE OVER WHICH VARIATION OCCURS				
	Local/household		Hillside		Region
	1 m	10 m	100 m	1,000 m	100 km
Triggering mechanisms					
Rainfall			■	■	■
Seismic activity				■	■
Preparatory factors					
Slope geometry		■	■	■	
Soils and geology	■	■	■	■	■
Slope hydrology	■	■	■	■	
Vegetation	■	■	■	■	■
Anthropogenic (aggravating) influences					
Surface water	■	■	■		
Groundwater level		■	■	■	
Slope angle (cut)		■	■	■	
Load (building)		■	■		
Vegetation	■	■	■	■	

Source: Holcombe and Anderson 2010.

- **Landslide susceptibility** relates to the type and spatial distribution of existing or potential landslides in an area. Susceptibility assessment is based on the qualitative or quantitative assessment of the role of **preparatory** factors in determining the relative stability of different slopes or zones. The magnitude and velocity of existing or potential landslides may be taken into account, but the frequency or timing will not be specified.

- **Landslide hazard** is the probability of a landslide (qualitatively or quantitatively assessed) of a certain type, magnitude, and velocity occurring at a specific location. Quantitative hazard assessment takes into account the role of the **triggering** event (of a known probability) causing the landslide.

Several different approaches can be used to assess landslide susceptibility and hazard, including direct geomorphologic mapping, index-based mapping and heuristic (expert) assessment, inventory-based empirical and statistical modeling of slope parameters, and deterministic (physically based) and probabilistic modeling of slope processes (Aleotti and Chowdhury 1999; Dai, Lee, and Ngai 2002; and Huabin et al. 2005; these also contain summaries of these methods). Table 3.7 outlines the respective advantages and disadvantages of the principal approaches.

Selection of the most suitable approach for a given study must consider the spatial scale for which it is most appropriate, the data requirements, and the level of quantification it affords (van Westen et al. 2006; van Westen et al. 2008). Four methods of relevance to MoSSaiC are briefly reviewed in sections 3.4.3–3.4.6:

- Spatially distributed landslide susceptibility mapping using GIS-based methods—useful for the initial identification and prioritization of areas with relatively high landslide susceptibility (as described in chapter 4)

- Direct landslide hazard mapping—also useful for identification of areas of existing slope instability and for confirmation of the type of landslide hazard

- Empirical rainfall threshold modeling—if sufficient empirical data are available, this method can be used in conjunction with susceptibility maps to indicate the potential timing and spatial distribution of multiple landslide events

- Physically based slope stability modeling—the most relevant approach for MoSSaiC, as it allows investigation of the slope stability processes and landslide trigger at a scale enabling the identification of appropriate hazard reduction measures (1–100 m^2).

3.4.3 GIS-based landslide susceptibility mapping

Many wide-area and spatially distributed landslide assessments use GIS software as the platform for assembling digital maps of preparatory variables such as topography, soils and geology, drainage patterns, and land use. The data can be augmented and the analysis extended if there is a record of the locations of past landslides. Landslide inventories allow the identification of precedents in which the influence of each preparatory variable is determined with respect to slope stability and assigned a weighting. Alternatively, experts may assign weights based on their judgment and experience. The resulting index overlay maps define the landslide susceptibility for each terrain unit. On their own, these GIS-based susceptibility maps cannot be used to predict the exact timing and location of individual landslides, but they do provide a vital tool for planning and management in terms of broad zones of relative landslide susceptibility.

An example of GIS capability for developing landslide susceptibility maps is given by Nandi and Shakoor (2010). They developed relationships between landslides and various instability factors contributing to their occurrence using GIS. A landslide inventory map was prepared using landslide locations identified from aerial photographs, field checks, and existing literature. Seven instability factors were then selected—slope angle, soil type, soil

TABLE 3.7 Advantages and disadvantages of different forms of landslide susceptibility and hazard assessment

METHOD	ADVANTAGE	DISADVANTAGE	S	M	L
Field geomorphologic analyses	• Allow rapid assessment taking into account a large number of factors	• Totally subjective methodology • Use of implicit rules that hinder critical analysis of results	R	Y	Y
Combination of index maps	• Solve the problem of hidden rules • Total automation of steps • Standardization of data management	• Subjectivity in attributing weighted values to single classes of each parameter	R	Y	Y
Logical analytical models	• Allow the comparison of different slopes • Mathematically rigorous and perfectible	• Require monitoring data, preferably from installed instruments applicable mainly to slow-speed landslides	R	R	Y
Statistical analyses (bivariate and multivariate)	• Objective methodology • Total automation of steps • Standardization of data management	• Systematic collection and analysis of data concerning different factors is quite cumbersome	Y	Y	R
Safety factor-deterministic approaches	• Objective scope and methodology • Quantitative scope • Encourages investigation and measurement of geotechnical parameters in detail	• Need for detailed knowledge of the area • Use of appropriate geotechnical model requires a lot of experience • Does not take various uncertainties into account	R	R	Y
Probabilistic approaches	• Allow consideration of different uncertainties • Quantitative scope • Objective scope and methodology • Provide new insight not possible in deterministic methods	• Require comprehensive data, otherwise subjective probabilities required • Probability distributions difficult especially for low level of hazard and risk	Y	R	R
Neural networks	• Objective methodology • Do not require theoretical knowledge of physical aspects of the problem	• Difficult to verify results when instrumental data are not available	R	Y	Y

Source: Aleotti and Chowdhury 1999.

Note: S = small; M = medium; L = large; R = restricted use; Y = yes.

erodibility, soil liquidity index, land cover pattern, precipitation, and proximity to stream—that were considered to be of significance in terms of landslide occurrence. These were imported into the GIS as raster data layers and ranked using a numerical scale corresponding to the physical conditions of the region. Figure 3.9 illustrates the spatial data for four of the presumed independent controlling variables.

Regression analysis was used to associate the occurrence of known landslides with the independent slope variables in a subarea of the watershed (a process known as model training). By assuming that similar slope instability–related conditions existed in the entire

watershed, the results from the training area could be extrapolated using the regression model. This process yielded a landslide susceptibility map (figure 3.10).

Basic regression methods for landslide susceptibility assessment can be refined by computing weight-based combinations of significant factors and excluding insignificant factors from consideration; GIS mapping of this type has been widely researched (Lee 2005; Nefeslioglu, Gokceoglu, and Sonmez 2008; Van Den Eeckhaut et al. 2006; Van Westen 2004).

A GIS environment can also be used as the platform for simplified deterministic modeling of landslide hazard zones or coupling with

FIGURE 3.9 Classified spatial factor data

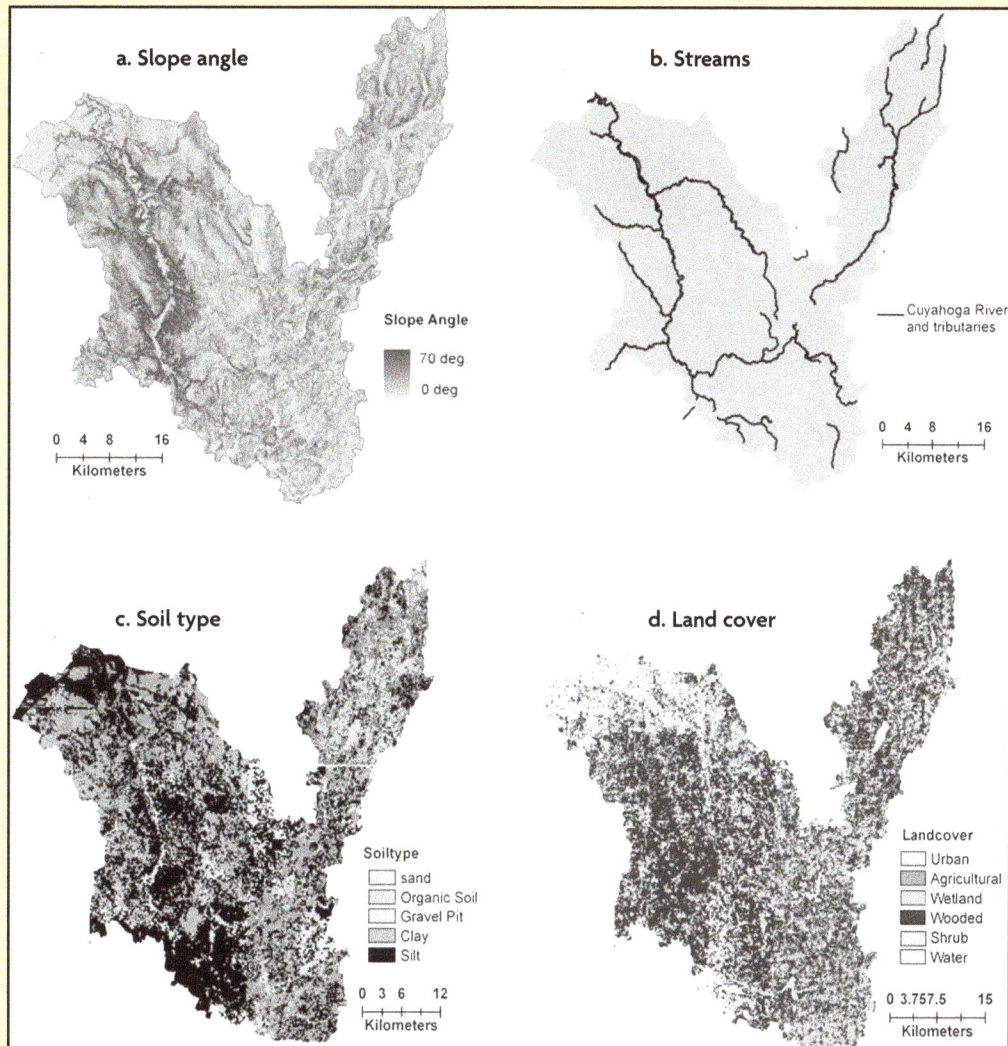

a. Slope angle

Slope Angle

70 deg

0 deg

0 4 8 16
Kilometers

b. Streams

Cuyahoga River and tributaries

0 4 8 16
Kilometers

c. Soil type

Soiltype
☐ sand
☐ Organic Soil
☐ Gravel Pit
☐ Clay
■ Silt

0 3 6 12
Kilometers

d. Land cover

Landcover
☐ Urban
☐ Agricultural
☐ Wetland
■ Wooded
☐ Shrub
☐ Water

0 3.757.5 15
Kilometers

Source: Nandi and Shakoor 2010.

rainfall forecasts. This form of modeling requires accurate and detailed spatially distributed data on slope parameters and a high level of expertise.

3.4.4 Direct landslide mapping

On-the-ground mapping of existing landslides in areas of known slope instability produces maps that can potentially be used for land-use planning, informing landslide risk management strategies, and creating landslide inventories that can be included in GIS-based landslide hazard analyses. An experienced mapping team can plot both visible landslide features and the possible locations of histori-

cal landslides—the relevant features of which might be masked by subsequent land-use change.

Even at the hillside and community scales, direct landslide hazard mapping can be prone to significant error. Ardizzoni et al. (2002) outline the potential extent of such errors by comparing hazard mapping results from three independent mapping teams in a landslide-prone area of Italy. They found large differences between the landslide hazard maps in the form of positional errors (55–65 percent); these increased significantly when all three maps were overlaid (~85 percent spatial mismatch). Figure 3.11 illustrates the differences

FIGURE 3.10 Landslide susceptibility map

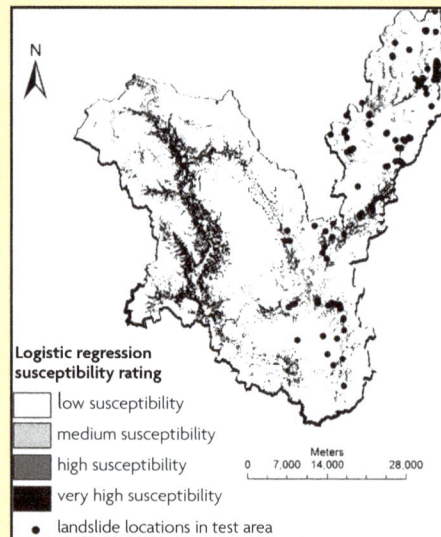

Logistic regression susceptibility rating

- [ ] low susceptibility
- medium susceptibility
- high susceptibility
- very high susceptibility
- • landslide locations in test area

0   7,000 14,000   28,000 Meters

Source: Nandi and Shakoor 2010.

Note: The landslides of the test area are overlaid on the map.

FIGURE 3.11 Three landslide inventory maps

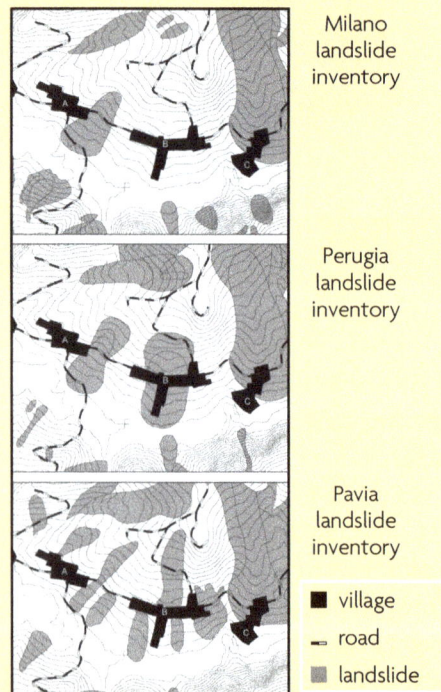

Milano landslide inventory

Perugia landslide inventory

Pavia landslide inventory

- ■ village
- ▬ road
- ▨ landslide

Source: Ardizzoni et al. 2002.

Note: Maps were surveyed by three independent teams in the Apennines, Italy. Mapped area comprises hillside surrounding three small villages. Overall errors in positional mismatch approximately 85 percent.

in the teams' interpretations of the location of existing landslides.

Information is lacking regarding the uncertainties associated with landslide inventory maps (Gallie et al. 2008). Rather than only mapping existing landslides, studies suggest that it may be appropriate for expert mapping teams to identify the topography and other preparatory factors likely to be associated with both existing and future slope failure. In this way, direct mapping of slope features could be used to inform the design of landslide mitigation measures to address the potential landslide causes.

3.4.5 Empirical rainfall threshold modeling

Historical data on landslides and associated rainfall events can be used to establish landslide probability based on the probability of the triggering rainfall. With sufficient data, the critical rainfall characteristics required to trigger landslides can be established for a particular region. This is referred to as ***threshold analysis***, and it can be used to predict the expected number of landslides for a particular rainfall forecast. Although this is a useful planning tool, it cannot be used on its own to identify the landslide hazard affecting a specific slope.

There are a number of forms that empirical threshold equations can take depending on the rainfall parameters selected (IRPI 2012). A common form is an intensity-duration equation, which is derived by plotting rainfall intensity (I) against rainfall duration (D) and identifying the threshold above which landslides will be triggered. *I-D* thresholds have the general form

$$I = c + \alpha D^{-\beta}$$

Where:

I = Rainfall intensity
D = Rainfall duration
c $\geq$ 0
α > 0
β > 0

Commonly, intensity lies between 1 and 100 mm s⁻¹, duration between 1 and 200 hours, β between 2.00 and 0.19, and $c = 0$ (Guzzetti et al. 2007; figure 3.12). When $c = 0$, the threshold relationship is a simple power law. This negative power law holds for four orders of magnitude of rainfall duration (up to durations of 500 hours), suggesting a self-similar scaling behavior of the rainfall that triggers landslides (Guzzetti et al. 2007).

Specific rainfall intensity-duration threshold relationships should be calculated for individual regions or countries. For example, for Puerto Rico, $I = 91.46D^{-0.82}$ (Larsen and Simon 1993).

3.4.6 Physically based slope stability modeling

To determine the landslide hazard affecting a specific slope, the preparatory and triggering mechanisms unique to that slope need to be taken into account. This can be undertaken by experts directly mapping slope features in the field (heuristic approach; see section 3.4.4). Conversely, a quantitative analytical or numerical modeling approach can be applied in which geotechnical equations are used to represent landslide processes.

Many such quantitative approaches express slope stability in terms of its factor of safety (F) which is the ratio between the total available shear strength of the slope (resisting forces) and the shear stresses (destabilizing forces).

$$F = \frac{available\ shear\ strength\ of\ slope}{shear\ stress\ acting\ to\ destabilize\ slope}$$

$F = 1$ Marginally stable slope
$F < 1$ Unstable slope
$F > 1$ Stable slope

There are three broad types of physically based modeling that may be used to determine slope stability; these are as follows, in order of increasing complexity:

- Analytical methods for calculating factor of safety (static limit equilibrium methods)

FIGURE 3.12 Global rainfall intensity-duration thresholds

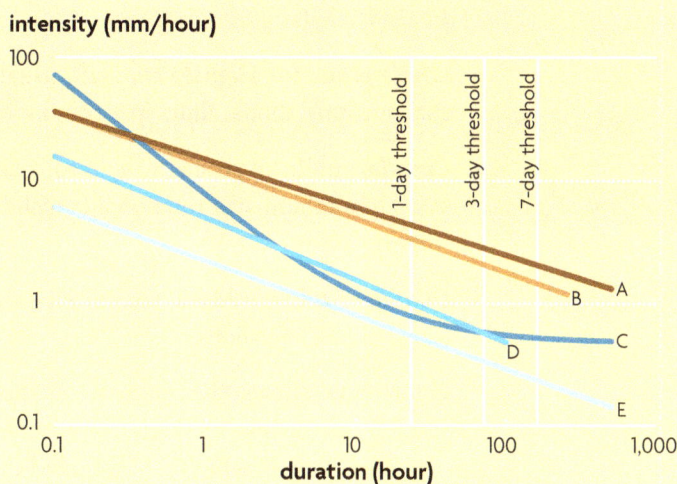

Source: Kirschbaum et al. 2009.

Note: A = Caine 1980; B = Hong, Adler, and Huffman 2006; C = Crosta and Frattini 2001; D = Innes 1983; E = Guzzetti et al. 2008.

- Numerical models that couple dynamic hydrology with limit equilibrium analysis

- Numerical models that represent slope material in terms of its stress-strain behavior (continuum models) or as particles (discrete element models)

Analytical methods for determining factor of safety

Static limit equilibrium methods (analytical or lumped mass approaches) evaluate the stabilizing and destabilizing forces affecting a mass of material on an observed or assumed potential failure surface (known as the slip surface or shear surface). The slope is analyzed as a two-dimensional cross-section, and the material above the slip surface is typically divided (discretized) into vertical slices. The stabilizing and destabilizing forces acting at the base of each slice (at the slip surface) are calculated for a single point in time and take into account the angle of the slip surface at the slice base, the weight of the slice material, loading on top of the slice (such as buildings or vegetation), the effect of pore water pressure, and the shear strength of the material (cohesion and angle of internal friction). F is then calculated for the entire slip surface.

Different limit equilibrium methods are employed according to the assumed geometry of the landslide failure surface:

- **Single plane (or slightly curved)**, usually shallow translational slides in steep slopes

- **Circular**, uniform strata or deep soils and small to medium-size rotational landslides (figure 3.13)

- **Double or triple wedges**, medium to large translational landslides.

Figure 3.13 shows the method of slices (Ordinary and Bishop methods) represented on a sample slope in which it is assumed that failure will occur by rotation of a block of soil on a cylindrical slip surface. (See Nash 1987 for a review of different limit equilibrium methods.)

Limit equilibrium analysis requires several simplifying assumptions to be made to calculate F:

- A slope will fail as a coherent mass of material sliding along a specific two-dimensional slip surface defined by the user (stress-strain relationships and three-dimensional effects involved in the mechanics of failure are not represented).

- Along the slip surface, the material will exhibit failure according to the specific criteria selected for representing shear strength (the Mohr-Coulomb criteria for elasto-plastic failure is typically used for soils).

- At the moment of failure, the shear strength is fully mobilized along the length of the slip surface.

- The water table location (and hence, the pore water pressure field) is static and is defined by the user.

- Different assumptions are made about the interslice forces, depending on the method.

- Behavior of the slope material once failure has occurred is not accounted for.

The results of the factor of safety analysis are of limited value in themselves, as they depend on the simplifying assumptions of the method adopted, the parameter values selected, the water table location, slip surface geometry and location, and the discretization of the slope. For example, in figure 3.13, the Bishop method gives an F of 1.52, while the Ordinary method of slices gives an F of 1.43. Note that a factor of safety of 1 does not necessarily indicate that failure of the slope is imminent. Moreover, the real factor of safety is influenced by many variables that are not necessarily represented in the slope stability model, such as minor geological or soil details, and progressive failure of the slope, among many others (Nash 1987).

Dynamic slope hydrology and limit equilibrium models

The second type of slope stability model significantly advances the static analysis methods by dynamically integrating external "forcing" variables (landslide triggering factors) such as rainfall and slope hydrology, so that slope stability can be analyzed over a period of time. Although there are fewer commercially available integrated dynamic hydrology and limit equilibrium models than static limit equilibrium models, they are an improvement over

FIGURE 3.13 Discretization of a slope into slices to facilitate slope stability calculations

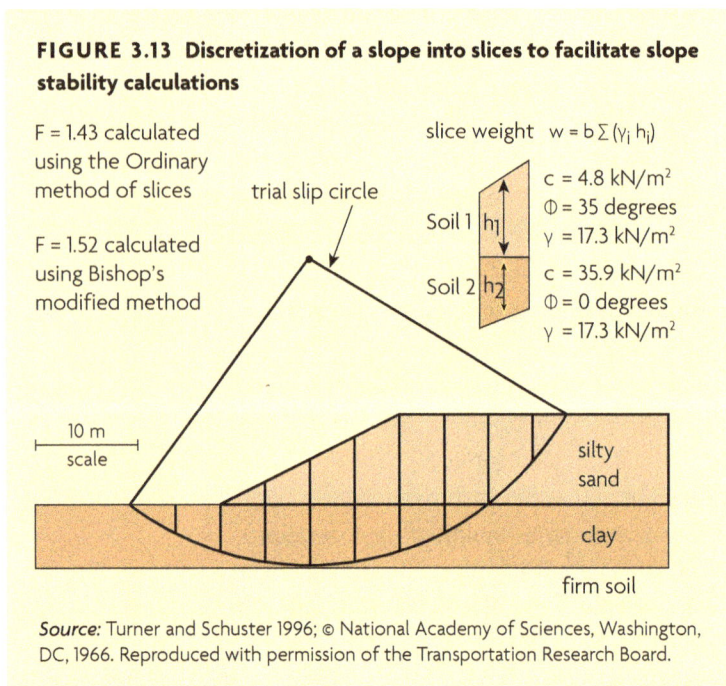

F = 1.43 calculated using the Ordinary method of slices

F = 1.52 calculated using Bishop's modified method

trial slip circle

slice weight $w = b \sum (\gamma_i h_i)$

Soil 1 h_1 c = 4.8 kN/m²   Φ = 35 degrees   γ = 17.3 kN/m²

Soil 2 h_2 c = 35.9 kN/m²   Φ = 0 degrees   γ = 17.3 kN/m²

10 m scale

silty sand

clay

firm soil

Source: Turner and Schuster 1996; © National Academy of Sciences, Washington, DC, 1966. Reproduced with permission of the Transportation Research Board.

the classic limit equilibrium method in the following ways:

- Groundwater conditions are dynamically modeled over time in terms of saturated and unsaturated flow, positive and negative pore water pressures, and rainfall. These dynamic processes are particularly influential in deep tropical residual soils.

- Limit equilibrium methods, such as Bishop and Janbu for circular or noncircular failure, are applied using a search method to identify the minimum F surface at specific times during the dynamic hydrology simulations.

Some limitations of dynamic hydrology models relate to the simplifying assumptions used in the calculation of groundwater flow, which means that these models cannot represent soils with complex or highly spatially variable flow patterns. Limitations in the stability component are related to those inherent in limit equilibrium analysis.

The value of this type of dynamic slope stability model is that it allows slope processes dominating the stability of a particular slope to be explored.

Continuum and discrete element models

Continuum models use distinct rheological formulas known as constitutive equations to describe the behavior of a particular soil type under dynamic stress and strain conditions. Therefore, in these models, the shear zone "evolves" (rather than being artificially imposed in terms of geometry or location) according to the geometry of the slope, the initial conditions applied, and the particular rheology of the material.

Related to the continuum approach are macroscale discontinuous deformation analysis models, which allow for the local deformation of shear zones and the overall slope while accounting for strong discontinuities and detachment of mesh elements. Conversely, distinct (or discrete) element methods represent the movement of rigid elements (on a

scale from blocks to grains) using a force-based approach.

Although some of these models are commercially available, their data requirements, model sensitivity, and complexity can pose significant challenges to their application.

3.5 SLOPE STABILITY VARIABLES

This section provides a more detailed description of the main slope stability variables introduced in section 3.4.1—preparatory factors, triggering mechanisms, and anthropogenic (aggravating) factors—in terms of their identification and measurement, and their influence on slope stability. This information is the basis for the process of community-based slope feature mapping, landslide hazard assessment, and design of landslide hazard reduction measures detailed in chapters 5 and 6.

Different slope variables may contribute to the shear strength of the slope (stabilizing forces) or to the shear stresses acting on the slope (destabilizing forces). Some variables may contribute to both shear strength and shear stress. The way in which each variable operates can be complex and may change over time with natural processes (such as hydrological variations) or human activities. For example, figure 3.14 shows preparatory factors that could have potential roles in slope instability, illustrating a variety of subsurface routes infiltrating surface water may take. Differences in soil water flow paths can lead to delayed or rapid slope instability responses to rainfall.

The role of these variables in affecting slope stability may be assessed qualitatively or measured and used as an input in a quantitative slope stability assessment.

3.5.1 Rainfall events

Rainfall-triggered landslides are the result of surface water infiltration, increased pore water pressure, and a reduction of the shear strength of the slope material. The particular combination of preparatory variables and

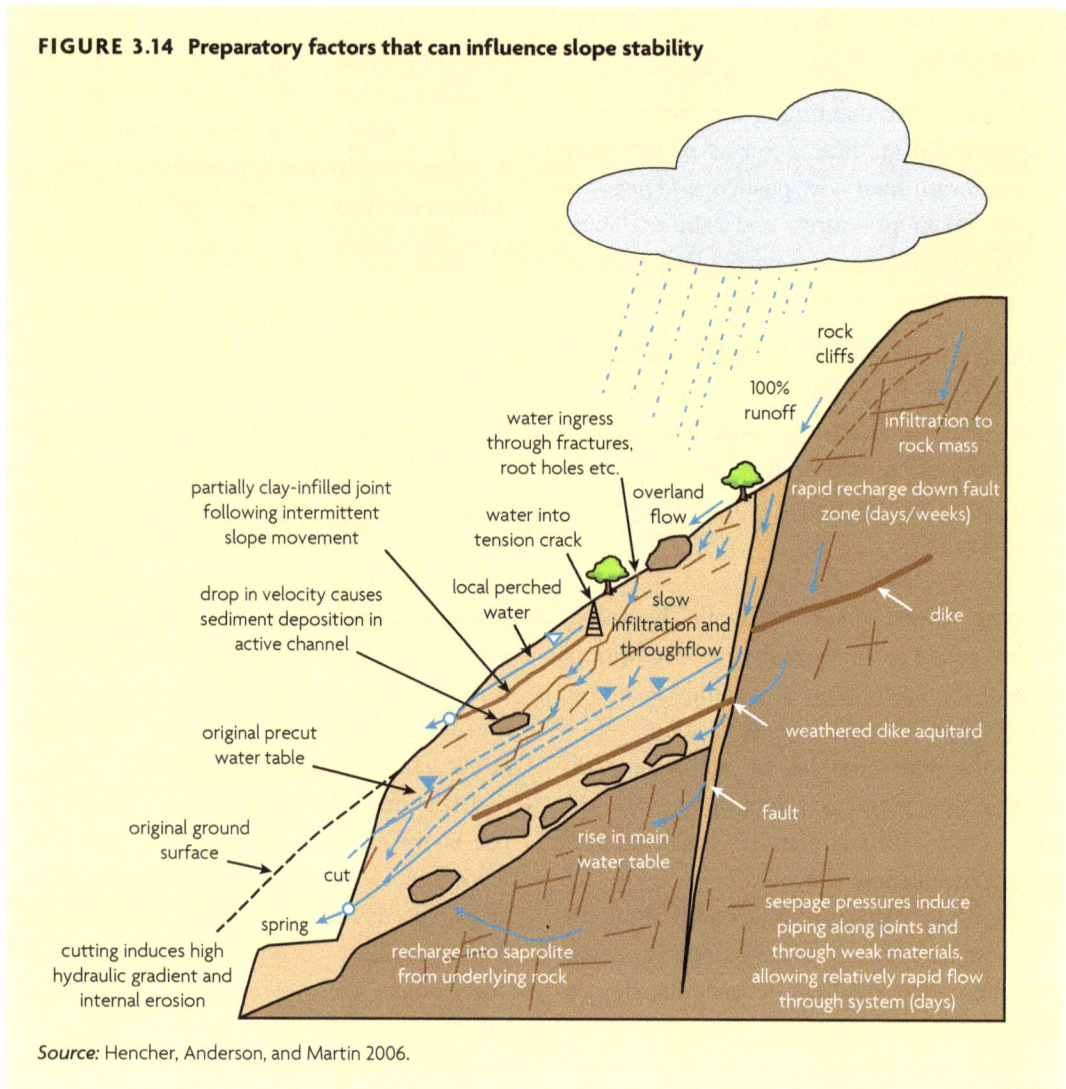

FIGURE 3.14 Preparatory factors that can influence slope stability

rock cliffs

100% runoff

infiltration to rock mass

water ingress through fractures, root holes etc.

rapid recharge down fault zone (days/weeks)

partially clay-infilled joint following intermittent slope movement

water into tension crack

overland flow

slow infiltration and throughflow

local perched water

dike

drop in velocity causes sediment deposition in active channel

weathered dike aquitard

original precut water table

fault

original ground surface

cut

rise in main water table

spring

cutting induces high hydraulic gradient and internal erosion

recharge into saprolite from underlying rock

seepage pressures induce piping along joints and through weak materials, allowing relatively rapid flow through system (days)

Source: Hencher, Anderson, and Martin 2006.

rainfall characteristics will determine which slopes fail.

Not all rainfall events will trigger landslides, and not all slopes will fail as a result of a particular event. The intensity and duration of the rainfall event will determine its effect on a specific slope. A short, intense rainfall event may have less impact than a longer-duration, less intense event if the hydraulic conductivity of the slope is low. It is the hydraulic conductivity of the slope that determines how much rain infiltrates and how much is retained as surface runoff. Conversely, prolonged very low–intensity rainfall may have little effect on a slope with a high hydraulic conductivity, since the infiltrated water will be rapidly conveyed through the subsurface without saturating the soil.

Summary: assessment of rainfall events

- Rainfall events should be described in terms of their intensity (mm/h) or total volume (mm), and their duration (h).

- Rainfall data may be recorded by manual or automatic rain gauges.

- Government ministries and meteorological organizations usually collect some form of daily or hourly rainfall data.

- Satellite and radar data can be interpreted to determine rainfall intensity.

Records should be obtained for all major rainfall events, in particular the generally heavy rainfalls that are associated with hurricanes, tropical storms, and tropical waves (figure 3.15).

FIGURE 3.15 Hurricane Tomas over the Eastern Caribbean, 2010

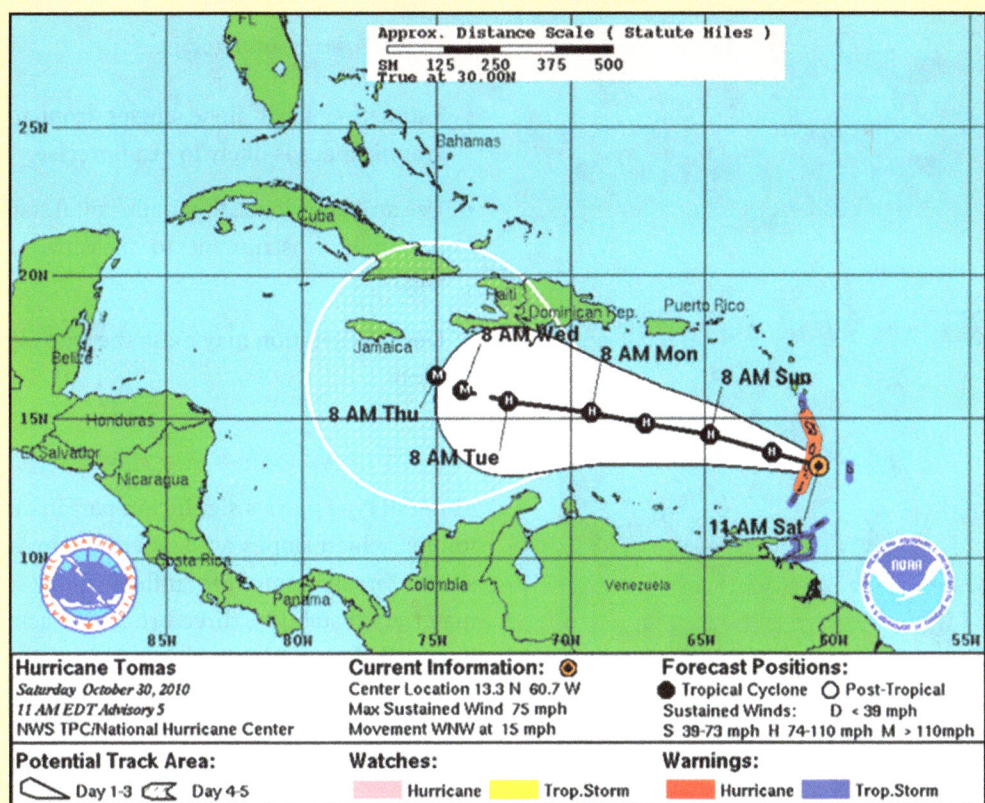

Source: National Oceanic and Atmospheric Administration.

3.5.2 Slope angle

Slope angle is one of the key determinants of slope stability. The greater the slope angle, the greater the shear stresses acting on the slope. However, the relationship between slope angle and slope stability is not straightforward, since the stabilizing forces (the shear strength of the slope) will be determined by variables such as material type and strength, water table height, and the influence of loading and vegetation. Thus, shallow slopes with deep, weak soils can be less stable than steeper slopes comprised of shallower soils or exposed bedrock.

When assessing slope angles from existing topographic maps, the accuracy and precision of the contours needs to be taken into account since the contours may

- be interpolated and therefore inaccurate with respect to the actual topography (particularly areas of slope plan convergence and divergence), and/or

- not be precise enough to determine slope angles over small distances.

Slope angle can be efficiently measured with a low-cost instrument such as an Abney level (figure 3.16a), which consists of a fixed sighting tube, a movable spirit level connected to a pointing arm, and a protractor scale. The instrument is held at eye level in order to "sight" a colleague of the same height either up- or downslope; alternatively, a ranging pole can be marked at eye height (figure 3.16b).

Accurate slope angle determination is more difficult in communities where there is high housing density or dense vegetation (figure 3.17), or where previous landslides (which can result in significant ground disturbance) have occurred. In such cases, ensuring that the steepest slope segments have been identified requires particular care. At a later stage in the project, a more comprehensive topographic survey may be required to confirm slope

FIGURE 3.16 An Abney level and its use

a. Abney level.

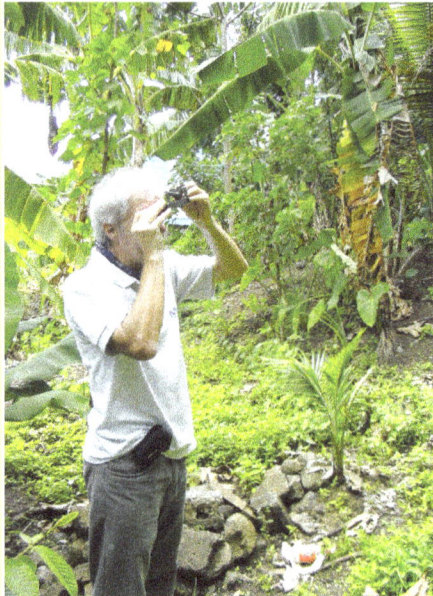

b. Abney level being used to measure slope angle.

FIGURE 3.17 Slope benched by resident to build a house

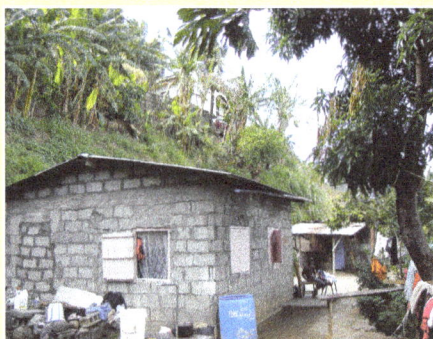

Dense vegetation above the benched slope and a major failure below the property can make it more difficult to estimate the hillslope segment slope angles.

angles, distances, and drain gradients (see chapter 6).

Summary: assessment of slope angle

- Estimating local slope angles from topographic maps is likely to be imprecise.

- Use an Abney level, theodolite, total station, or similar instrument to measure slope angles.

- Dense vegetation may mask the true topography.

3.5.3 Material type and properties

Material type plays a significant part in determining which slopes are susceptible to landslides. In assessing the influence of slope material on stability, three broad characteristics need to be determined:

- The depth and location (strata) of different material types on the slope

- The strength of the materials

- The hydrological properties of the materials

Soil formation

In the tropics, rock is weathered relatively rapidly due to the high temperatures and humidity; this can result in the formation of deep soils over weakened bedrock. The first stage in assessing the influence of materials on slope stability is therefore to estimate the approximate depth of soil and weathered material. The MoSSaiC methodology addresses slopes where the dominant surface material is residual soil.

Weathering and strength

The typical weathering profile of tropical soils is commonly expressed in terms of six weathering grades (figures 3.18 and 3.19).

The weathering grade of slope material can be considered a surrogate for strength: generally, the greater the weathering from rock to soil, the weaker the material. The strength of residual soils can vary greatly depending on its parent material (composition). Soils can be

FIGURE 3.18 Typical weathering profiles of tropical soils

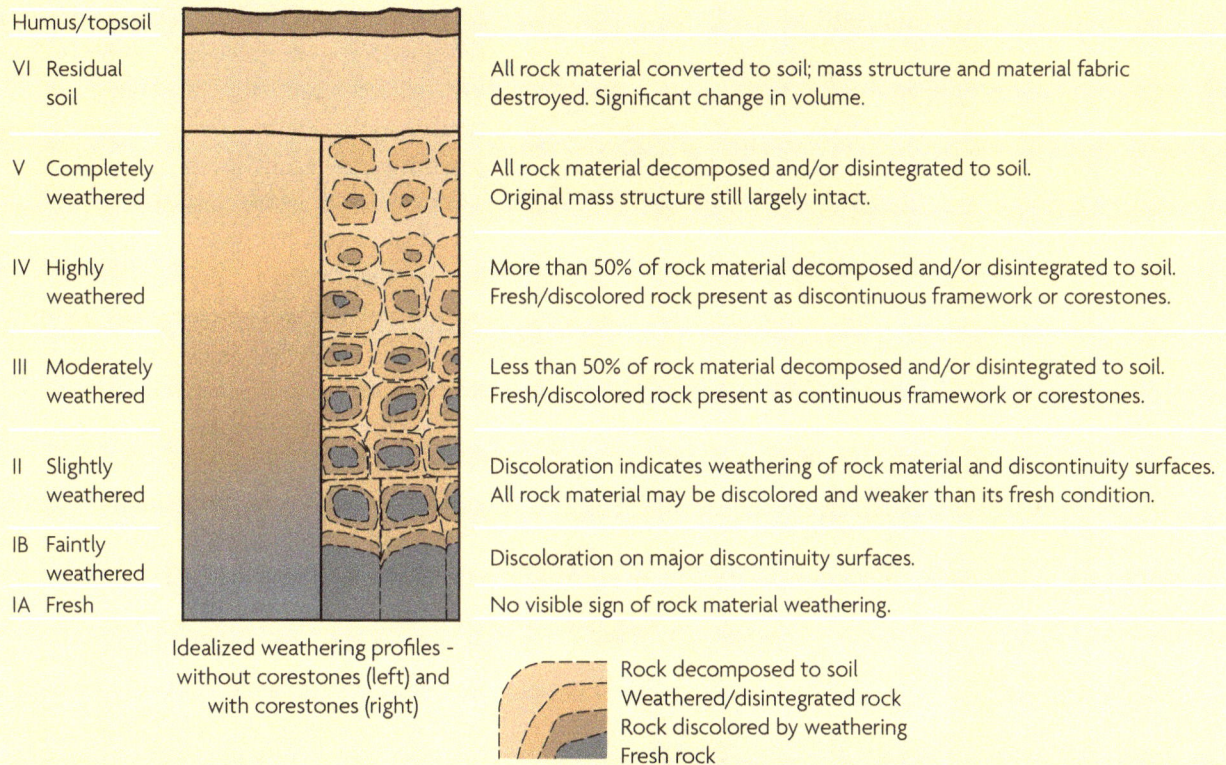

	Humus/topsoil	
VI	Residual soil	All rock material converted to soil; mass structure and material fabric destroyed. Significant change in volume.
V	Completely weathered	All rock material decomposed and/or disintegrated to soil. Original mass structure still largely intact.
IV	Highly weathered	More than 50% of rock material decomposed and/or disintegrated to soil. Fresh/discolored rock present as discontinuous framework or corestones.
III	Moderately weathered	Less than 50% of rock material decomposed and/or disintegrated to soil. Fresh/discolored rock present as continuous framework or corestones.
II	Slightly weathered	Discoloration indicates weathering of rock material and discontinuity surfaces. All rock material may be discolored and weaker than its fresh condition.
IB	Faintly weathered	Discoloration on major discontinuity surfaces.
IA	Fresh	No visible sign of rock material weathering.

Idealized weathering profiles – without corestones (left) and with corestones (right)

Rock decomposed to soil
Weathered/disintegrated rock
Rock discolored by weathering
Fresh rock

Source: Fookes 1997, reproduced with permission of the Geological Society, London. Weathering grades are based on the commonly used classification of Fookes 1997, Komoo and Mogana 1988, and Little 1969.

characterized in terms of particle size distribution and structure; bulk density; the ratio of sand, silt, and clays; and the chemical composition of the clay. These characteristics can be used as proxies for strength and hydrological properties based on empirical relationships (Carter and Bentley 1991).

For slope stability analysis, a more precise measure of soil strength entails laboratory assessment of the geotechnical properties of slope soil samples (figure 3.20). The shear strength of a specific soil can then be described in terms of soil cohesion (c, kPa) and angle of internal friction (Φ, degrees), which are the parameters that need to be specified in analytical and numerical slope stability models (Nash 1987).

In areas where landslides have already occurred, the slope material will have a much lower strength than its original intact strength; this is its residual strength.

Hydrological properties

The strength of soils and weathered materials will be affected by moisture content. Increased moisture content of slope material causes increases in pore pressure, which reduces shear strength. Conversely, the drying of slope material can cause negative pore pressures (matric suction), which increase shear strength (Fredlund 1980; Fredlund and Rahardjo 1993). The magnitude of pore pressures associated with wetting and drying are dictated by material properties such as pore size and chemistry. For instance, clay particles carry a negative charge, which influences the retention of moisture in the pores. Thus, sandy porous soils may experience little variation in strength, while the strength of clay soils can vary significantly with moisture content.

The deep residual soils of the humid tropics can often have relatively high hydraulic conductivities, allowing rainfall to infiltrate rap-

FIGURE 3.19 Weathering profiles

a. Grade II material transitioning to Grade III above.

b. Indication of abrupt change in weathering grade from V to VI above.

FIGURE 3.20 Shear box used to determine soil strength parameters

idly. Periods of rainfall can result in the formation of saturated zones within the soil strata nearer the ground surface. Different material types, when saturated, will exhibit different hydraulic conductivities depending on their structure and composition. In unsaturated conditions, hydraulic conductivity will vary as a function of moisture content.

Subsurface water flows within soil pores can be augmented by the development of a network of wider-diameter pipes within the soil (figure 3.21). Soil pipes can be a contributory factor to landslides by giving rise to locally high pore water pressures (Brand, Dale, and Nash 1986; Pierson 1983; Uchida 2004). The effect of pipe flow is also spatially complex—reducing pore pressures in the upslope area covered by the pipe network, while increasing pore pressures in downslope locations, especially if the pipe network is blocked. Sharma, Konietzky, and Kosugi (2009) report numerical model results summarizing this complex relationship.

FIGURE 3.21 Exposed soil pipe some 30 cm below the soil surface

Summary: assessment of slope material types and properties

- The dominant slope material type can often be determined by referring to soil and geological surveys available from government engineering departments or similar organizations.

- More precise assessments of material types and strata can be made in the field through direct observation, boreholes, or soil pits.

- Material strength can be inferred from weathering grades.

- Basic descriptions of material characteristics can be used to infer strength and hydrological properties, using the findings from numerous studies in the scientific and engineering literature.

- Areas where there have been previous landslides will have lower (residual) material strength.

- The specific geotechnical properties (c, Φ) of a material can be measured by triaxial or shear box testing.

- Material hydrological properties can be measured using equipment such as a permeameter or infiltrometer.

- Pore pressures and subsurface water levels can be measured in the field using a peizometer.

3.5.4 Slope hydrology and drainage

The dynamic nature of a slope's response to surface water infiltration and subsurface flows make an understanding of the overall hydrology of a slope essential for gaining insights into its stability.

Convergence zones

It is important to identify zones of topographic convergence—elements of the slope that are concave in plan. Convergence zones concentrate surface water flows and strongly influence subsurface water flows.

Water moves through soils according to the total potential of soil water, being the sum of the gravitational potential (the elevation of the point in the soil above some arbitrary datum) and the pressure potential (either positive or negative soil water pressure). Other than for the shallowest slopes, topographic contours can be considered an approximation of the lines of total potential (in that the gravitational potential dominates the equation—Anderson

and Kneale 1982). Since soil water flow takes place at right angles to the lines of total potential, soil water flow lines can—again as an approximation—be drawn at right angles to topographic contours. It is this logic that gives rise to the construction of potential zones of soil water convergence and divergence on a hillslope, as shown in figure 3.22. The two locations A and B depict zones of convergence and divergence, respectively; much higher pore water pressures will be anticipated in the former case (due to the concentration of flow), with lower pore water pressures (perhaps unsaturated conditions) in the zone of divergence.

Subtle topographic hillslope hollow features (zones of convergence) are important to locate since they represent areas of potential slope instability because of the relatively higher pore water pressures, which in turn serve to reduce soil shear strength. This means that failures can occur on relatively shallow slopes, triggered by soil water convergence taking place upslope. Figure 3.23 shows an example of such a failure on an 18-degree slope; slopes above, with slope angles as high as 45 degrees, remained stable since they lacked the same

FIGURE 3.22 Definition of the planimetric contributing area at two locations in a hypothetical landscape

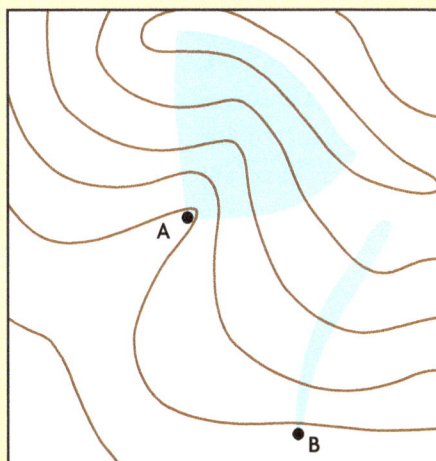

Source: Iverson 2000.

Note: Blue = planimetric contributing areas; brown lines = topographic contours, with lowest elevations at bottom left.

FIGURE 3.23 Shallow rotational slip on an 18-degree slope at the foot of an extensive hillside

degree of topographic convergence, and hence retained lower pore pressures.

Urban slope drainage

Population growth, urbanization, and poverty have led to the development of large vulnerable communities on steep slopes in many tropical areas. If there is a publicly provided piped water supply, but no drainage, the discharge of water from houses onto the slope can be significant, especially when housing density is high.

Sources of water from properties include gray water from kitchens and bathrooms, leakage from supply pipes, and septic tank discharges. The construction of houses, footpaths, and drains can change surface and subsurface water flow patterns on the slope—typically concentrating them at certain locations or resulting in zones of constant saturation. Figure 3.24 illustrates a range of common conditions that require identification and assessment of their impact. Surface water management measures can then be designed to improve slope stability. This process is explained in chapters 5–7.

Summary: Assessing slope hydrology and drainage

- Shallower slopes at the base of hillsides may be as, or even more, susceptible to landslides as the steeper slopes above because of the convergence of surface and subsurface water.

- High vegetation densities may disguise topographic features.

- Existing contour maps may incorrectly portray the detailed slope topography.

The following effects of vulnerable unauthorized communities on drainage should also be noted:

- Addition of water to the slope by households (point water sources)

- Altered drainage patterns, incomplete drains, or uncontrolled flows

- Zones of saturation created by housing structures, modified slope angles, and access alignments such as footpaths or roads

3.5.5 Vegetation

Although vegetation may generally have a positive effect on slope stability, it can reduce the stability of slopes in some cases.

Beneficial and adverse effects

Vegetation can influence hydrological and mechanical slope stability mechanisms (table 3.8).

In vulnerable urban communities, slope stability may be influenced by changes in slope vegetation, such as the following:

- Removal of deep-rooted vegetation that may have had a stabilizing effect on the slope material through root reinforcement and uptake of water from the soil

- Cultivation of water-demanding plants (such as dasheen; figure 3.25a) that require irrigation or the deliberate retention of water on the slope in trenches or terraces—this increases infiltration and soil pore water pressures, thus reducing soil shear strength

- Cultivation of shallow-rooted plants (such as banana and plantain) that add loading to the slope and disturb the soil structure (increasing soil permeability) without adding root tensile strength

- Planting certain vegetation species for the specific purpose of stabilizing slopes (bio-

FIGURE 3.24 Common drainage issues in unauthorized communities

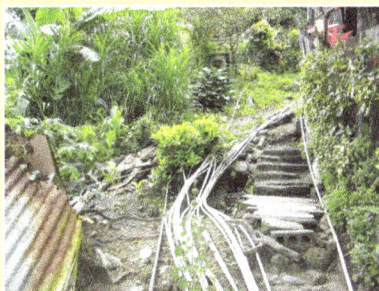

a. Unauthorized housing is often supplied with water delivered through plastic pipes.

b. Slope failure caused by lack of water management from upslope unauthorized housing.

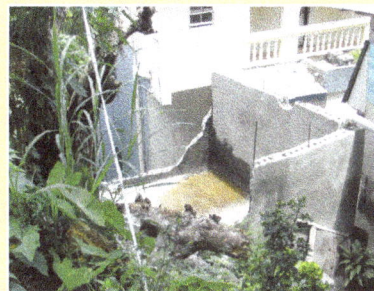

c. A water tank constructed of a single skin of blocks which failed and caused significant downslope damage. Such structures have the potential to trigger slope instability.

d. A drain that is incomplete and may thereby cause instability downslope.

e. Small footpath drain rendered completely ineffective by routing water supply pipes along its length.

f. Damaged roof guttering discharging to poorly configured drain at the foot of a retaining wall.

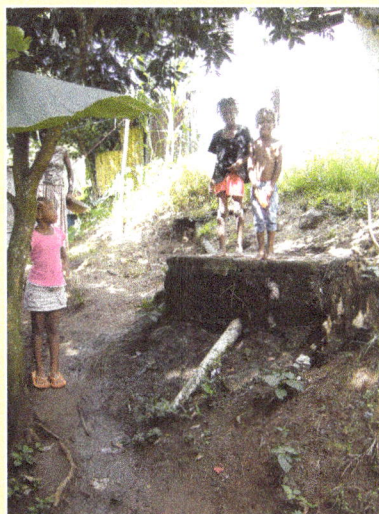

g. Household septic tank discharging directly into the slope.

h. High-volume discharges from washing machines.

i. Shower and hand-washing water discharging onto the slope, leading to saturated soil and stagnant water.

TABLE 3.8 Vegetation influences on slope stability

STABILITY MECHANISM	VEGETATION EFFECT	DESCRIPTION
Hydrological	Beneficial	Rainfall interception on foliage increases evaporative losses and reduces infiltration into the slope material
		Uptake of soil water by roots reduces the water content of slope material and therefore reduces pore water pressures
	Adverse	Roots increase soil permeability
		Soil moisture depletion may cause desiccation cracking and increase soil permeability
		Stem flow and live or decaying roots can generate preferential flow paths within the slope material (macropores and soil pipes), thus increasing the concentration of water in certain locations, particularly if the water is directed to the soil-rock interface, which is a common zone of weakness
Mechanical	Beneficial	Roots can provide soil reinforcement and increase soil shear strength
		Tree roots may anchor into firm material at depth and have a buttressing effect in resisting the shallow movement of soils
	Adverse	Trees are subject to "wind throw" which exerts a force on the slope during high winds
		Large trees will significantly increase the loading on the slope

engineering); for example, vetiver grass is widely used for its extensive root network and slope-stabilizing properties (figure 3.25b).

Vegetation effects on slope stability are thus complex, being dependent on the nature of the slope and vegetation species. For this reason, the relative influence of each of the factors in

FIGURE 3.25 Examples of adverse and beneficial effects of vegetation on slopes

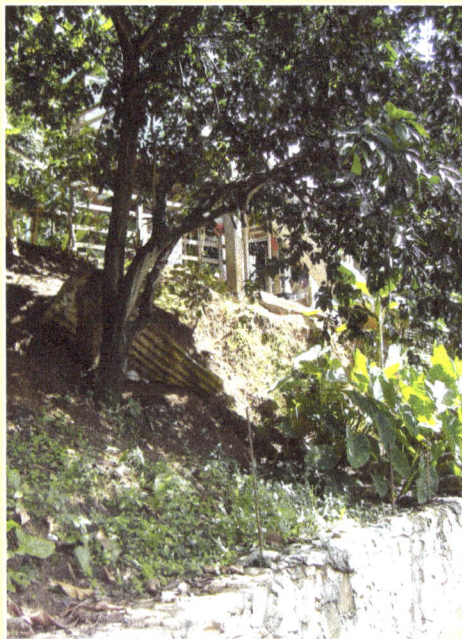

a. Water-demanding plants, such as dasheen, the large-leafed plants on the right, may be cultivated in naturally saturated areas, or water may be retained on slopes for this purpose.

b. Roots of vetiver grass can grow to some 3 m.

table 3.8 will vary from slope to slope. Consequently, "it is not sufficient simply to classify individual mechanisms, they must be quantified. Only then can the net influence of vegetation be clarified and its influence on stability be defined" (Greenway 1987, 192).

Vegetation as an indicator of past landslides

The succession of plants on a particular part of a slope can indicate the location of an earlier slope disturbance—an abandoned cultivated area, the site of a fire, or a landslide. In the tropics, landslide scars and debris will revegetate within a short time if the soil depth is sufficient and nutrients are available (for instance, from decomposition of the vegetation mixed into debris or from erosion). Figure 3.26 presents a model of post-landslide vegetation succession for the Caribbean showing the relationship between slope stability, soil organic matter, and slope revegetation.

Summary: Assessing vegetation cover

- Discussions with local botanical specialists may help establish the net influence of vegetation and local planting practices on slope stability.

- The presence of certain species on slopes can indicate either natural or manmade saturated conditions.

- The succession of plants on a particular part of a slope can indicate the location of a previous landslide.

3.5.6 Loading

Construction adds to slope loading, increases the shear stresses acting on the slope, and thus contributes to destabilizing forces.

Construction materials and loading

In vulnerable communities, unauthorized houses are typically enlarged in an incremental manner. Often, there is a progression from traditional wooden structures to heavier concrete construction (figure 3.27). This incremental construction increases slope loading in terms of the weight of the construction material.

Construction on former landslide zones

A landslide significantly reduces the strength of failed slope material—not just along the slip surface, but also within the failed mass. Construction on previously failed material is common in rapidly developing unauthorized urban areas in the tropics and may occur immediately after a landslide or several years later (figure 3.28). Rapid reconstruction on the site of a landslide reflects the severe pressure for housing that can lead to residents discounting the hazard, in full knowledge of past failure. In the case of historic landslides, the majority of

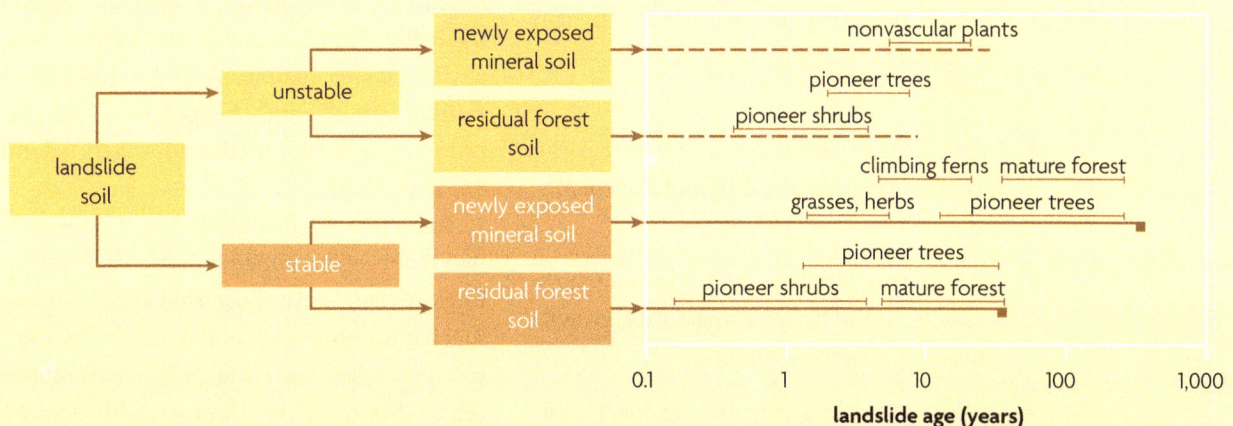

FIGURE 3.26 Model of post-landslide vegetation succession for the Caribbean

Source: Walker et al. 1996.

Note: Four plant succession pathways for landslides in a low-elevation forest in Puerto Rico. On unstable soils, erosion constantly resets succession (dotted lines). On stable soils, filled squares indicate age at which pre-landslide vegetation may reestablish.

FIGURE 3.27 Examples of incremental construction

a. Additional loading of a 55-degree slope with an already high housing density increases landslide risk.

b. Property enlarged by building outside the existing walls.

the community may be unaware of past slope history and the associated potential hazard. In both cases, the effect of construction in such locations is to reduce slope stability in all the ways discussed here, potentially reactivating a landslide or triggering new ones.

Summary: Assessing loading and former landslides

- Housing density and construction type can be rapidly assessed from aerial photographs.

- More detailed site surveys will reveal the interaction between loading and slope material.

- Areas of very old large landslides may have become masked by dense vegetation growth and subsequent construction.

- An integrated interpretation of local geology, topography, variations in soil depth, boulder locations, and vegetation can help identify landslides that occurred before living memory.

3.6 SCIENTIFIC METHODS FOR ASSESSING LANDSLIDE HAZARD

To assess the landslide hazard affecting a particular hillside community requires a method that can account for the roles of the different slope stability variables described in the previous section at the correct scale and over time. This assessment can indicate potential landslide hazard mitigation strategies such as surface water management for intercepting rainfall runoff and household water, and reducing infiltration (the approach taken by MoSSaiC).

In section 3.4, physically based slope stability models noted as being particularly relevant for MoSSaiC were those that represent slope mechanical processes and dynamic hydrological processes at local hillside/community scales. Many of the slope stability variables described in section 3.5 are used as inputs to physically based models, thus allowing their relative roles in determining slope stability to be analyzed. The community-based mapping

FIGURE 3.28 Examples of reconstruction on former landslide sites

a. Unauthorized housing built on a preexisting landslide within one year of the failure having taken place.

b. Houses built on the site of a landslide that affected the whole hillside approximately 90 years previously.

and measurement of these variables is described in chapter 5.

This section introduces three physically based (scientific) methods for assessing landslide hazard.

- *Coupled dynamic hydrology and slope stability models* to simulate physical processes affecting slope stability over time (including dynamic hydrology), identify dominant landslide causes, and predict landslide hazard (probability, magnitude, location)

- *Resistance envelope calculations* to determine whether negative pore pressures are required to maintain the stability of a slope

- *Static analysis of retaining walls* to determine the stability of retaining walls.

The above is not intended to be an exhaustive list of landslide hazard assessment methods, but rather demonstrates the level of process representation that is required and that can be realistically achieved in the context of MoSSaiC.

3.6.1 Coupled dynamic hydrology and slope stability models

Coupled dynamic hydrology and slope stability models can allow the identification of those processes that dominate the stability of

a particular slope. If surface water infiltration from rainfall and piped water supplies is the driving factor in slope failure, this form of simulation can allow the potential effectiveness of surface drainage to be investigated. The use of coupled hydrology-stability models is an important part of the design and scientific justification of any drainage measures aimed at reducing the landslide hazard. Estimating the impact of surface water infiltration—and thus the effectiveness of potential drainage measures—demands a numerical model that incorporates dynamic hydrology so the slope stability response can be simulated over time.

Several numerical models are available that would allow such an analysis (see http://www.ggsd.com). One example is CHASM (Combined Hydrology and Slope Stability Model) software, which has been developed by the authors and used in numerous research and practical applications to date, including MoSSaiC. The following overview of CHASM's structure and capabilities is based on this experience and is in no way intended as an endorsement. The overview may assist the MCU in discussions regarding the selection of appropriate slope stability models. It is beyond the scope of this text to review the suitability of all such potential models for particular applications. In any event, it is likely that local engineers will be familiar with, and have access to, other slope stability models that may be suitable for MoSSaiC interventions.

Model configuration

The main features of CHASM are described in Anderson et al. (1996, 1997) and Wilkinson, Brooks, and Anderson (1998, 2000), among others. Figure 3.29 shows how a slope cross-section is represented in CHASM; the principle equation set is given in section 3.7.4. The simulation is configured as follows:

- The slope is divided into regular columns and cells, the centers of which form computational points for the solution of equations for slope hydrology.

- Each cell is assigned a material type, and the strength and hydraulic properties of each material are specified (in this example, there are three material types).

- Vegetation, slope loading, and point water sources can be defined for specific surface cells.

- Hydrological boundary conditions are defined—the initial estimated position of the water table, the initial moisture content of each cell, the initial surface suction, and the dynamic rainfall conditions for each hour of the simulation.

- The slip surface search mode is also defined, searching for the location of either a circular or noncircular slip surface with the lowest factor of safety.

Dynamic hydrology component

Within CHASM, infiltration during rainfall is calculated using Darcy's Law; vertical flow in the unsaturated zone is computed using Richards' equation solved in explicit form inside vertical columns. Within the integrated model structure, the hydrology scheme represents slope plan curvature (convexity and concavity) by varying the breadth of the columns (figure 3.30). The pseudo-effect of the three-dimensional topography on water fluxes can thus be investigated and its impact on stability estimated (GCO 1984).

Slope stability component

At the end of each simulation hour, the pore pressure field generated by the hydrology component is used as input to standard two-dimensional stability analyses where the slip surface is located within the midplane of the three-dimensional structure. CHASM uses Bishop's (1955) simplified circular method with an automated search procedure (Wilkinson, Brooks, and Anderson 2000), or Janbu's noncircular method for estimation of the slope's factor of safety (Nash 1987). Pore pressures, both negative and positive, are incorporated directly into the effective stress determination of the Mohr-Coulomb equation for soil shear strength. This allows derivation of the minimum factor of safety with temporal variations arising from hydrodynamic responses and changes in the position of the critical slip surface (Wilkinson 2001).

Other useful features for identifying hazard drivers

CHASM's numerical scheme includes a surface cover model, which allows investigation of the hydrological and geotechnical effects of vegetation on slope stability. Vegetation

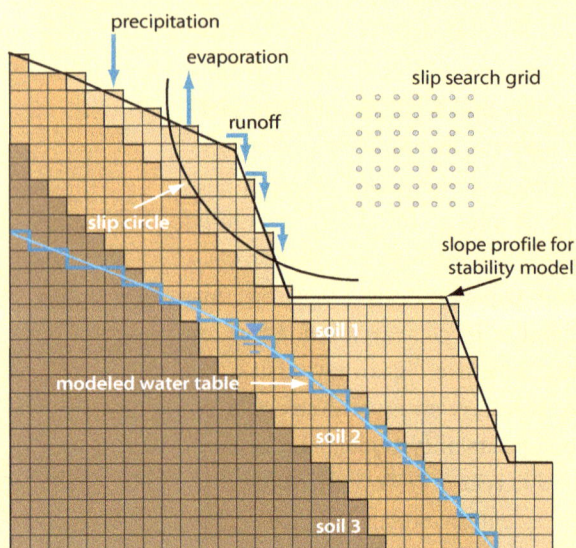

FIGURE 3.29 Representation of a slope cross-section for analysis in CHASM software

affects slope stability through rainfall interception, evapo-transpiration, changes in hydraulic conductivity, root reinforcement, and surface loading—all of which are included in the model (Collison 1993; Wilkinson, Brooks, and Anderson 1998; Wu, McKinnell, and Swanston 1979).

Piped water is often supplied to hillside communities. In unauthorized communities, there is usually no drainage or sewerage provision, so gray water from sinks and bathrooms is discharged directly to the slope. Foul water drainage goes to a septic tank or pit latrine usually within a few meters of the property, the outflow from which returns directly to the slope. It is possible within CHASM to assign leakage at defined points on the slope surface with specified flux rates by increasing the effective rainfall to the grid columns where water leakage into the slope has been identified.

Unauthorized housing density can approach 70 percent of the surface area of slopes—adding significant loading. Building loads need to be taken into account when establishing comparative influences on slope stability. In Bishop's method, loading is incorporated by increasing the weight of the slices on which the buildings are located.

Interpreting simulation results

For each computation time-step of the simulation, the typical outputs of models such as CHASM include

- predicted slip surface location,

- pore water pressure and soil moisture fields throughout the slope, and

- factor of safety.

These outputs can often be directly visualized in the model's graphic user interface or may simply be in the form of text files. Text file outputs can be graphically represented using standard software such as R, Matlab, or IDL. Figure 3.31 presents the graphical representation of CHASM outputs using open source software developed by volunteers at the Random Hacks of Kindness event in Washington,

FIGURE 3.30 CHASM representation of a natural hillslope

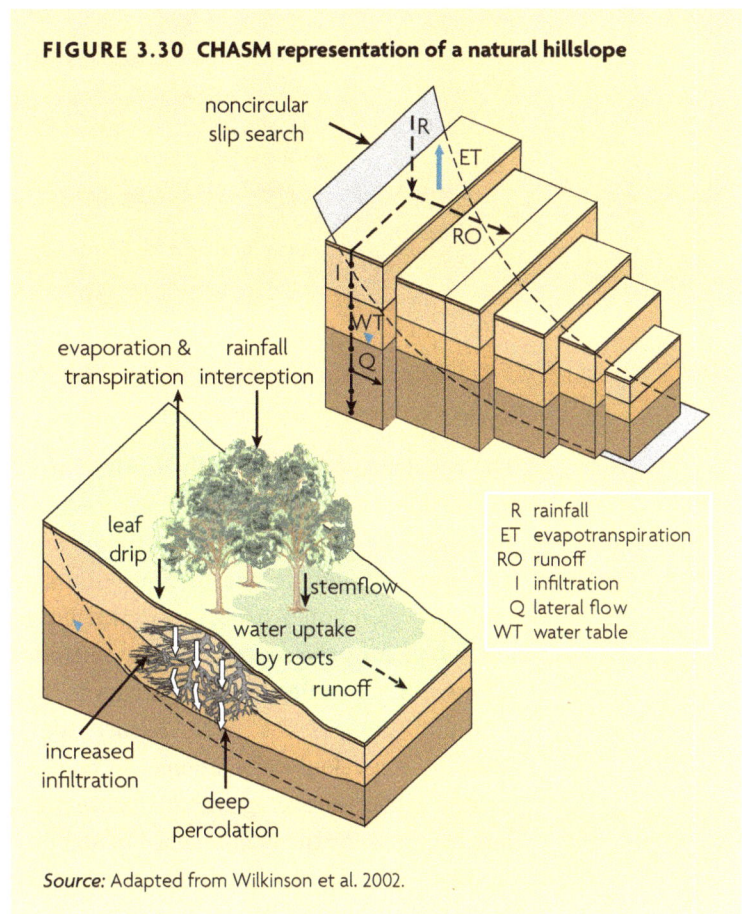

R rainfall
ET evapotranspiration
RO runoff
I infiltration
Q lateral flow
WT water table

Source: Adapted from Wilkinson et al. 2002.

D.C., in 2010. The simulation time-step shown here is toward the end of a 1-in-100-year, 24-hour rainfall event, in which the factor of safety has fallen from approximately 1.32 to 1.28. Perched water tables are visible at the interface between the upper two soil strata. By the end of the storm, F is predicted to be approximately 1.25 before recovering as the water table drops. Although a landslide is not predicted ($F > 1$), the weakest part of the slope can still be identified from the location of the slip circle.

Slope stability models with features similar to those outlined above, and that include the dynamic modeling of pore pressure conditions (both positive and negative), allow determination of the impact of rainfall as a landslide triggering mechanism. Using a model with these attributes, an assessment can be made of the likely impact of surface water management as a means of contributing to improving slope stability.

PHYSICALLY BASED SLOPE STABILITY MODELS	
USAGE	• Simulation of the physical processes affecting slope stability • Identification of dominant landslide causes • Landslide hazard prediction (probability, magnitude, location)
SOURCE	See http://www.ggsd.com for a comprehensive listing of slope stability software
FURTHER DISCUSSION	See section 5.6.3 for CHASM application

3.6.2 Resistance envelope method for determining suction control

The resistance envelope method can be used to determine whether negative pore pressures are required to maintain the stability of a slope. The apparent significance of slope drainage can be corroborated using resistance envelopes to identify the controls on slope stability (Chowdhury, Flentje, and Bhattacharya 2010; Fredlund 1980; Janbu 1977; Kenny 1967). Resistance envelope calculations can be used to show either the average negative pore pressure required for the maintenance of stability or, conversely, the saturated conditions under

which the slope may be expected to remain stable (Anderson, Kemp, and Shen 1987).

In the resistance envelope method, several slip surfaces are assumed and the average shear strength required for equilibrium is determined (using an appropriate method of analysis, such as Bishop 1955) along each of the surfaces, together with the corresponding average normal stress. The average mobilized shear strength is then plotted against the average effective normal stress, with each point on the plot representing a critical slip surface. Joining all these points together forms the resistance envelope, onto which the plot of the

FIGURE 3.31 Outputs from a CHASM simulation

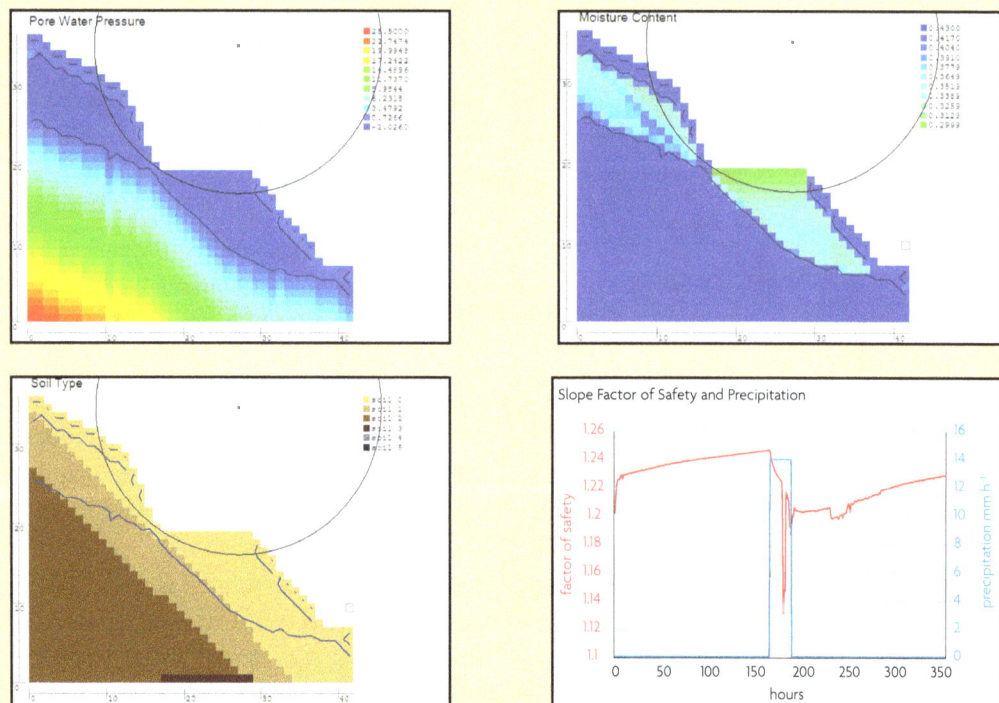

Source: Prototype visualization software created at Random Hacks of Kindness event 2010.

shear strength of the soil can be superimposed (Chowdhury, Flentje, and Bhattacharya 2010). The methodology assumes negative pore pressures act directly in effective stress terms. Figure 3.32 provides a generalized illustration of the superimposition of the resistance envelope and the laboratory-determined soil strength envelope for a case in which the slope is dependent upon soil suction (negative pore pressures) for stability.

Application of the method to a site in the Eastern Caribbean is illustrated in figure 3.33. Using two different pairs of values for the geotechnical properties (effective cohesion, c', and effective angle of internal friction, Φ'), obtained from two separate sites on the slope, the results suggest that the slope must be maintained at *either*

- marginal negative pore pressure (figure 3.33a; $c' = 10$ kPa, $\Phi' = 20$ kPa), since for normal loads in excess of 50 kPa, the resistance envelope shows marginally greater shear strength is required for stability than can be mobilized by the slope material (as indicated by the laboratory shear strength values used); or

- very low positive pressures (figure 3.33b; $c' = 10$ kPa, $\Phi' = 25$ kPa).

It is to be inferred that significant rainstorm events will, through lack of drainage provision on the slope, increase pore pressures beyond those limits, thus suggesting that instability can reasonably be attributed to infiltration controls.

3.6.3 Modeling the impact of small retaining walls

Many residents in vulnerable communities seek to reduce landslide risk by constructing single-skin, reinforced block retaining walls (figure 3.34). Such walls are common because they can be constructed at the household level, require no community consensus or government permission, and can be built progressively as the resident accumulates funds to purchase materials. But even if they are expe-

FIGURE 3.33 Resistance envelope plots

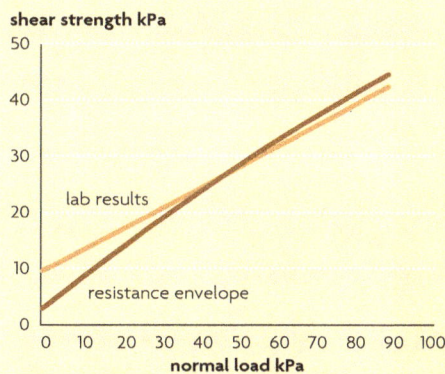

a. The graph shows negative suction is required to bring the mobilized shear strength equal with the resistance envelope (for normal loads > 50 kPa; for material properties $c' = 10$ kPa, $\Phi' = 20$ kPa).

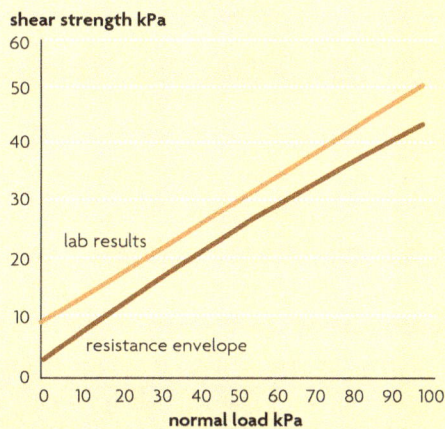

b. Only a modest increase in pore pressure is required to lower the mobilized shear strength to the resistance envelope (material properties, $c' = 10$ kPa, $\Phi' = 25$ kPa).

Source: Anderson, Kemp, and Shen 1987.

FIGURE 3.32 Superimposition of resistance and strength envelopes

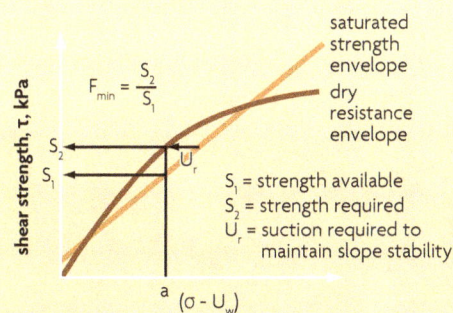

S_1 = strength available
S_2 = strength required
U_r = suction required to maintain slope stability

Source: Anderson, Kemp, and Shen 1987.

FIGURE 3.34 Inadequate retaining wall design

a. Typical failure of modest retaining wall built by resident.

b. Retaining wall built by resident failed, with lower part of wall displaced to rear of property.

unlikely to provide an effective landslide risk reduction measure. The essential general stability requirements for such structures would appear to be drainage to ensure the maintenance of unsaturated conditions behind the wall, and an avoidance of surcharging the slope immediately behind the wall. In reality, these two conditions are not likely to be met in such communities with unauthorized housing. Alternative retaining wall designs incorporating features to counteract overturning failure, such as wall backtilt and an extended wall toe, would also seem impractical in this context, given their increased costs over simple walls and the greater construction control required to ensure structural integrity.

Summary: landslide hazard assessment methods

- Review slope stability software available either locally or online.

- Use the resistance envelope method for assessing the role of negative pore pressures, only if there is adequate technical support for the analysis and interpretation and if circumstances warrant that discrimination.

- Use retaining wall analysis software to generate local case studies to affirm the type of structures that would be needed to enhance slope stability. Assess whether such structures would be affordable and desirable at the community scale.

MILESTONE 3:

Presentation made to MoSSaiC teams on landslide processes and slope stability software

dient, are such structures effective? Given the number of such retaining wall failures, it is important to assess the stability of a typical structure so clearer guidance can be given to community residents.

For this purpose, a standard static hydrology retaining wall stability analysis can be undertaken (see, e.g., BSI 1994; Craig 1997; and USACE 1989). The findings of such an analysis, outlined in section 3.7.5, suggest that simple single-skin structures of the type commonly constructed by residents are unlikely to meet the stability criteria—and are equally

3.7 RESOURCES

3.7.1 Who does what

TEAM	RESPONSIBILITY	ACTIONS AND HELPFUL HINTS	CHAPTER SECTION
Funders and policy makers	Know the types of landslides addressed by MoSSaiC	• Become familiar with the specific types of landslides that MoSSaiC seeks to address	3.3
	Coordinate with the MCU for any technical information required		
MCU	Understand the types of landslides addressed by MoSSaiC	• Become familiar with the specific types of landslides that MoSSaiC seeks to address	3.3
	Understand the factors that determine slope stability and the associated assessment methods		3.4; 3.5
	Coordinate with government task team for any technical information required		
Government task teams	Understand the types of landslides addressed by MoSSaiC	• Become familiar with the specific types of landslides that MoSSaiC seeks to address	3.3
	Understand the factors that determine slope stability and the associated assessment methods	• Look at this chapter, field sites, and local reports of landslides to appreciate all the possible triggering mechanisms **Helpful hint:** Undertake site visits to landslide sites and identify types and potential localized causes.	3.4; 3.5
	Be familiar with, and select appropriate, scientific methods for assessing local landslide hazards	• Review relevant slope stability assessment methods with respect to software, expertise, and data likely to be locally available	3.6
	Brief the MCU and all task teams on (1) the scope of MoSSaiC with respect to local landslide types; (2) landslide preparatory, aggravating, and triggering factors; and (3) the scientific basis for assessing slope stability, especially with respect to locally available expertise and software	• Landslide assessment and engineering task team should prepare and deliver presentation	Whole chapter
	Coordinate with community task teams when appointed		
Community task teams	When appointed, understand the variables that affect slope stability	• Look at this chapter, visit field sites (this is especially important), and review local reports of landslides to appreciate all the possible preparatory, aggravating, and triggering mechanisms	3.5
	Coordinate with government task teams		

3.7.2 Chapter checklist

CHECK THAT:	TEAM	PERSON	SIGN-OFF	CHAPTER SECTION
✓ Knowledge has been acquired of the subset of landslide types that MoSSaiC seeks to address				3.3
✓ Knowledge has been acquired of relevant slope stability processes				3.4; 3.5
✓ Site visits to known and potential landslide sites to examine potential triggering mechanisms and suitability for MoSSaiC approach have been undertaken				3.3; 3.4; 3.5
✓ Potential scientific tools for assessing landslide hazard have been examined				3.6
✓ **Milestone 3**: Presentation made to MoSSaiC teams on landslide processes and slope stability software				
✓ All necessary safeguards complied with				1.5.3; 2.3.2

3.7.3 Rainfall thresholds for triggering landslides

The website developed by the Italian Istituto di Ricerca per la Protezione Idrogeologica (IRPI) contains a comprehensive worldwide listing of rainfall threshold triggering relationships (http://wwwdb.gndci.cnr.it/php2/rainfall_thresholds/thresholds_all.php?lingua=it).

3.7.4 CHASM principle equation set

The following equation sets are from Wilkinson et al. (2002). See table 3.9.

Richards' equation (Richards 1931)

$$\frac{\partial \theta}{\partial t} = -\frac{\partial}{\partial z}\left(D\frac{\partial \theta}{\partial z} \right) - \frac{\partial K}{dz}$$

θ = volumetric moisture content (m³ m⁻³)
t = time (s)
z = vertical depth (m)
D = hydraulic diffusivity (m² s⁻¹)

Millington-Quirk equation (Millington and Quirk 1959)

$$K_i = K_s \left(\theta_i / \theta_s \right)^p \frac{\sum_{j=i}^{m}\left((2j+1-2i)\psi_j^{-2} \right)}{\sum_{j=1}^{m}\left((2j-1)\psi_j^{-2} \right)}$$

p = pore interaction term
K_i = unsaturated conductivity (m s⁻¹)
K_s = saturated conductivity (m s⁻¹)

θ_i = unsaturated moisture content (m³ m⁻³)
θ_s = saturated moisture content (m³ m⁻³)
ψ_i = suction value at moisture content θ_i (m)
m = number of equal increments of θ from $\theta = 0$ to $\theta = \theta_s$
j,i = summation indexes

Mohr-Coulomb equation (Coulomb 1776)

$$s = c' + (\sigma - u)\tan\phi'$$

s = soil shear strength (kPa)
c' = effective soil cohesion (kPa)
Φ' = effective angle of internal friction (degrees)
σ = total normal stress (kPa)
u = pore water pressure (kPa)

Bishop stability equations (Bishop 1955)

$$FS = \frac{\sum_{i=0}^{n}\left(c'l + (P - ul)\tan\phi' \right)}{\sum_{i=0}^{n} W\tan\alpha}$$

where

$$P = \left[W - \frac{1}{FS_0}(c'l\sin\alpha - ul\tan\phi'\sin\alpha) \right] / m_\alpha$$

and

$$m_\alpha = \cos\alpha\left(1 + \tan\alpha\frac{\tan\phi'}{FS_0} \right)$$

n = number of slices

TABLE 3.9 Units for the parameters used in CHASM

PARAMETER GROUP	PARAMETER NAME	SYMBOL/UNIT
Feature geometry	Slope height	H (m)
	Slope angle	α (degrees)
	Slope plan convergence/divergence radius	C (m)
Numerical	Mesh resolution (width, depth, breadth)[a]	w, d, b (m)
	Iteration period[a]	t (s)
Hydrological	Rainfall	p (m s^{-1})
	Saturated hydraulic conductivity	K_s (m s^{-1})
	Initial surface suction[b]	ψ_{t0} (m)
	Initial water table height[b]	wt (% slope height)
	Suction-moisture curve	ψ (m) $-\theta$ (m^3 m^{-3})
Geotechnical	Effective angle of internal friction	Φ' (degrees)
	Unsaturated/saturated bulk density	γ_{us}, γ_s (kN m^{-3})
	Effective cohesion	c' (kN m^{-2})
Vegetation	Root tensile strength	τ_r (kN m^{-2})
	Vegetation cover/spacing	v_c (%), v_s (m)
	Leaf area index	lai (m^2 m^{-2})
	Aerodynamic resistance[c]	r_a (s m^{-1})
	Canopy resistance[c]	r_c (s m^{-1})
	Canopy/trunk storage capacity	c_s, t_s (m)
	Root depth/lateral extent	R_d, R_l (m)
	Vegetation surcharge	S_w (kN m^{-2})
Atmospheric[c]	Net radiation	R_n (W m^{-2})
	Relative humidity	R_h (%)
	Temperature	T (^{0}C)

a. Determined according to Beven (1985) to maintain numerical stability in Richards' equation.

b. Initial surface suction and water table heights (defined as percentage of slope height measured to the toe of the slope) are assigned according to measured field conditions or hypothetical scenario. Richards' equation is then iterated until steady-state conditions are attained or the required soil moisture conditions are reached.

c. Atmospheric variables and canopy/aerodynamic resistance are required if the user wishes to determine soil evaporation and evapotranspiration using the Penman-Monteith equation. In the absence of this information, a sinusoidal function is used with the maximum evaporation rate defined at midday The sinusoidal function operates between 0600 and 1800 hours. During the remaining time, the respective evaporation rate is set to 1/100th of the midday maximum.

FS = factor of safety

c' = effective soil cohesion (kPa)

l = slice length (m)

α = slice angle (degrees)

u = pore water pressure (kPa)

Φ' = effective angle of internal friction (degrees)

W = weight of the soil (kPa)

Penman-Monteith equation (Monteith 1973)

$$E_p = \frac{R_n + \rho c_p VPD / r_a}{\lambda\left[\Delta + \gamma\left(1 + r_c / r_a\right)\right]}$$

E_p = potential evapotranspiration rate (m s^{-1})

r_a = aerodynamic resistance (s m^{-1})

r_c = canopy resistance (s m^{-1})

Δ = slope of the saturation vapor pressure—temperature curve (kg m^{-3} K^{-1})

λ = latent heat of vaporization of water ($\approx 2.47 \times 10^6$ J kg^{-1})

ρ = density of air (≈ 1.2 kg m^{-1})

γ = psychrometric constant ($\gamma \approx 66$ Pa K^{-1})

VPD = vapor pressure deficit (kg m^{-1} s^{-2})

c_p = specific heat of air (J kg^{-1} K^{-1})

R_n = net radiation (W m^{-2})

Root reinforcement equation (Wu, McKinnell, and Swanston 1979; Wu 1995)

$$\Delta c' = c'_R = t_R (\cos\theta \tan\Phi + \sin\theta)$$

c' = effective cohesion (kPa)

c'_R = effective cohesion attributed to the root network (kPa)

θ = angle of shear rotation (degrees)

Φ = angle of internal friction (degrees)

t_R = average tensile strength of the roots per unit area of soil (kPa)

3.7.5 Static hydrology retaining wall stability analysis

The following describes a simple retaining wall stability analysis by Anderson et al. (2011).

A simple wall geometry was defined (figure 3.35) with the following specifications: active earth pressure acting on the back of the

FIGURE 3.35 A simple retaining wall geometry used for the retaining wall analysis

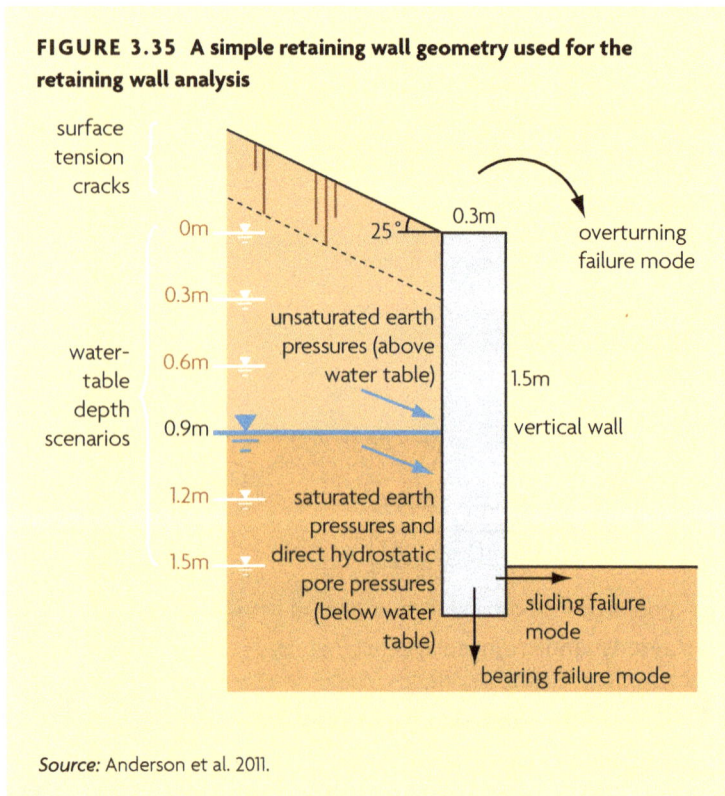

Source: Anderson et al. 2011.

wall, groundwater included as a specified horizontal water table position, unsaturated earth pressures acting above the saturated groundwater level, and saturated earth pressures and direct hydrostatic pore water pressures acting below. Details of the specific methodology may be found in Blake (2003).

No uplift water force on the base of the wall or at the front of the wall was considered. The active earth pressure was calculated using the Coulomb coefficient method. Factors of safety against sliding, overturning, and bearing-limit-state retaining wall stability failure modes were determined.

Earth pressures in front of retaining walls and the possibility of tension cracks in the retained material both need to be considered. No passive earth pressures acting in front of the wall were included in this analysis, which is a common conservative assumption. In reality, the wall stability will be increased slightly by this force although it cannot be relied upon due to unplanned excavations in front of the wall. Tension cracks resulting from the retained material cohesive properties were included in the analysis, with their depth calculated using the method given in Craig (1997). Their effect is to reduce the stability benefits of the cohesive element of the retained material. Similarly, no account was taken of any water filling these cracks and exerting detrimental additional hydrostatic pressure on the wall. Cohesion reduces the horizontal component of the total active earth pressure on the back of the wall (a stabilizing effect) while also resulting in adhesion between the wall and the retained material. Thus, the effect of cohesion is to reduce the effectiveness of the wall weight (a destabilizing effect).

Using these specifications, an analysis was undertaken for the following horizontal water table depths (with hydrostatic pore water pressure distribution) below the ground surface: 1.50 m (at base of wall—fully unsaturated retained material), 1.20 m, 0.90 m, 0.60 m, 0.30 m, 0.00 m (at top of wall—fully saturated retained material).

The stability analysis parameters and results are given in table 3.10. The results show

TABLE 3.10 Results of an illustrative standard static hydrology retaining wall stability analysis

WATER TABLE DEPTH BELOW SURFACE (m)	NO SURCHARGE			10 kN m^{-2} SURCHARGE		
	Overturning failure	Sliding failure[a]	Bearing failure	Overturning failure	Sliding failure	Bearing failure
1.50	1.79	−1.74	4.47	0.22	0.55	0.58
1.20	1.72	−1.90	4.38	0.22	0.54	0.58
0.90	1.39	−2.65	3.89	0.21	0.50	0.57
0.60	0.90	−8.13	3.00	0.20	0.44	0.55
0.30	0.51	4.03	2.09	0.17	0.38	0.51
0.00	0.28	1.33	1.40	0.15	0.32	0.45

Source: Anderson et al. 2011.

a. In the factor of safety calculation, while negative values are possible, such solutions have no physical meaning.

Note: Parameter values used for the analysis:

Wall unit weight:	23 kN m^{-3} (concrete blocks)
Retained material unsaturated unit weight:	15 kN m^{-3}
Retained material saturated unit weight:	19 kN m^{-3}
Effective cohesion:	10 kPa
Wall adhesion:	5 kPa (standard assumption of cohesion ÷2)
Effective angle of internal friction ($\emptyset$):	25°
Wall-backfill friction angle:	13° (standard assumption of $\emptyset$ ÷2)
Wall-foundation friction angle:	17° (standard assumption of 2 × $\emptyset$ ÷3)
Foundation bearing capacity:	400 kN m^{-2}
Surcharge:	0 or 10 kN m^{-2} (it is usual to have a conservative assumption of 10 kN m^{-2} minimum to provide a margin of safety against unplanned loads, vehicle movement, etc.)

that if there is a modest (10 kN m^{-2}) surcharge, the wall will be unstable for ***all*** failure modes and water table scenarios. Comparison with the Hong Kong SAR, China, Geotechnical Control Office (GCO 1984) critical stability threshold factor of safety values (overturning: 1.50, sliding: 1.25, bearing: 3.00) shows that the wall will meet these design thresholds providing the material behind the wall remains unsaturated. The overturning failure mode is critical, an observation in agreement with field evidence of overtilted retaining walls. This is explained partly by the fact that (beneficial) soil cohesion has a smaller effect on the wall overturning moment, since tension cracks reduce the height at which the force is assumed to act, and thus explains why the slope can be stable against sliding, but not against overturning.

In this static analysis, the modeled conditions are representative of groundwater rise events only, and the effect of soil moisture suc-

tion enhanced material shear strength is not accounted for. However, this is not considered material to the broad conclusions given in table 3.10.

3.7.6 References

Aleotti, P., and R. Chowdhury. 1999. "Landslide Hazard Assessment: Summary Review and New Perspectives." *Bulletin of Engineering Geology and the Environment* 58: 21–44.

Anderson, M. G., A. J. C. Collison, J. Hartshorne, D. M. Lloyd, and A. Park. 1996. "Developments in Slope Hydrology—Stability Modelling for Tropical Slopes." In *Advances in Hillslope Processes*, ed. M. G. Anderson and S. M. Brooks, 799–821. Chichester, UK: Wiley.

Anderson, M. G., E. A. Holcombe, J. Blake, F. Ghesquiere, N. Holm-Nielsen, and T. Fisseha. 2011. "Reducing Landslide Risk in Communities: Evidence from the Eastern Caribbean." *Applied Geography* 31 (2): 590–99.

Anderson, M. G., M. J. Kemp, and D. M. Lloyd. 1997. "Instruction 2.1: Procedure for the Construction of a Resistance Envelope for a Slope." In *Hydrological Design Manual for Slope Stability in the Tropics*, 14–20. Crowthorne, UK: Transport Research Laboratory. http://www.transport-links.org/transport_links/filearea/publications/1_711_ORN%2014.pdf.

Anderson, M. G., M. J. Kemp, and M. Shen. 1987. "On the Use of Resistance Envelopes to Identify the Controls on Slope Stability in the Tropics." *Earth Surface Processes and Landforms* 12 (6): 637–48.

Anderson, M. G., and P. E. Kneale. 1982. "The Influence of Low-Angled Topography on Hillslope Soil-Water Convergence and Stream Discharge." *Journal of Hydrology* 57 (1–2): 65–80

Ardizzone, F., M. Cardinali, A. Carrara, F. Guzzetti, and P. Reichenbach. 2002. "Impact of Mapping Errors on the Reliability of Landslide Hazard Maps." *Natural Hazards and Earth System Sciences* 2 (1–2): 3–14.

Arias, A. 1970. "A Measure of Earthquake Intensity." *Seismic Design for Nuclear Powerplants*, ed. R. J. Hansen, 438–83. Cambridge, MA: MIT Press.

Benson, C., and J. Twigg. 2007. "Tools for Mainstreaming Disaster Risk Reduction: Guidance Notes for Development Organisations." ProVention Consortium, Geneva.

Beven, K. J. 1985. "Distributed Models." In *Hydrological Forecasting*, ed. M. G. Anderson and T. B. Burt, 405–35. New York: Wiley.

Bishop, A. W. 1955. "The Use of the Slip Circle in the Stability analysis of Slopes." *Geotechnique* 5 (1): 7–77.

Blake, J. R. 2003. "Modelling the Dynamic Interaction between Hillslope Hydrology and Retaining Structures (Hydrology and Retaining Walls Model: HYDRET)." PhD thesis, University of Bristol.

Brand, E. W., M. J. Dale, and J. M. Nash. 1986. "Soil Pipes and Slope Stability in Hong Kong." *Quarterly Journal of Engineering Geology and Hydrogeology* 19 (3): 301–03.

BSI (British Standards Institution). 1994. *BS8002: Code of Practice for Earth Retaining Structures.* London: BSI.

Build Change. 2009. "You Can Keep Your Family Safe from Earthquakes—How to Build Strong and Sturdy Homes." http://www.buildchange.org/resources.php.

Caine, N. 1980. "The Rainfall Intensity Duration Control of Shallow Landslides and Debris Flows." *Geographisca Annaler* 62 (1): 23–27.

Carter, M., and S. P. Bentley. 1991. *Correlations of Soil Properties.* Chichester, UK: Wiley.

Charveriat, C. 2000. "Natural Disasters in Latin America and the Caribbean: An Overview of Risk." Working Paper No. 434, Inter-American Development Bank, Washington, DC.

Chowdhury, R., P. Flentje, and G. Bhattacharya. 2010. *Geotechnical Slope Analysis.* New York: CRC Press.

Collison, A. 1993. "Assessing the Influence of Vegetation on Slope Stability in the Tropics." PhD thesis, University of Bristol.

Cooper, R. G. 2007. *Mass Movements in Great Britain.* Geological Conservation Review Series 33. Peterborough, UK: Joint Nature Conservation Committee.

Coulomb, C. A. 1776. "Essai sur une application des règles des maximis à quelques problèmes de statique relatifs à l'architecture." *Memorandum Académie de Royal des Sciences par divers Savans* 7, 343–82.

Craig, R. F. 1997. *Soil Mechanics.* 6th ed. London: E & FN Spon.

Crosta, G. B. 2004. "Introduction to the Special Issue on Rainfall-Triggered Landslides and Debris Flows." *Engineering Geology* 73: 191–92.

Crosta, G. B., and P. Frattini. 2001. "Rainfall Thresholds for Triggering Soil Slips and Debris Flow." *Mediterranean Storms 2000*, ed. A. Mugnai, F. Guzzetti, and G. Roth. Proceedings of the 2nd EGS Plinius Conference on Mediterranean Storms, 2000. Siena, Italy.

Crozier, M., and T. Glade. 2005. "Landslide Hazard and Risk: Issues, Concepts and Approach." In *Landslide Hazard and Risk*, ed. T. Glade, M. G. Anderson, and M. Crozier, 1–40. Chichester, UK: Wiley.

Cruden, D. M., and D. J. Varnes. 1996. "Landslide Types and Processes." In *Landslides: Investigation and Mitigation*, Transportation Research Board Special Report 247, ed. A. K. Turner and R. L. Shuster, 36–75. Washington, DC: National Academies Press.

Dai, F. C., C. F. Lee, and Y. Y. Ngai. 2002. "Landslide Risk Assessment and Management: An Overview." *Engineering Geology* 64: 65–87.

De Vita, P., P. Reichenbach, J. C. Bathurst, M. Borga, G. Crosta, M. Crozier, T. F. Glade, A.

Hansen, and J. Wasowski. 1997. "Rainfall-Triggered Landslides: A Reference List." *Environmental Geology* 35: 219–33.

Fookes, P. G. 1997. *Tropical Residual Soils.* London: Geological Society.

Fredlund, D. G. 1980. "The Shear Strength of Unsaturated Soil and Its Relationship to Slope Stability Problems in Hong Kong." *Hong Kong Engineer* 8: 57–59.

Fredlund, D. G., and H. Rahardjo. 1993. *Soil Mechanics for Unsaturated Soils.* Chichester, UK: Wiley.

Galli, M., F. Ardizzone, M. Cardinali, F. Guzzetti, and P. Reichenbach. 2008. "Comparing Landslide Inventory Maps." *Geomorphology* 94: 268–89.

Garcia-Rodriguez, M. J., J. A. Malpica, B. Benito, and M. Diaz. 2008. "Susceptibility Assessment of Earthquake-Triggered Landslides in El Salvador Using Logistic Regression." *Geomorphology* 95 (3–4): 175–91.

GCO (Geotechnical Control Office). 1984. *Geotechnical Manual for Slopes.* 2nd ed. Government of Hong Kong Special Administrative Region.

Greenway, D. R. 1987. "Vegetation and Slope Stability." In *Slope Stability: Geotechnical Engineering and Geomorphology,* ed. M. G. Anderson and K. S. Richards, 187–230. Chichester: Wiley.

Guzzetti, F., S. Peruccacci, M. Rossi, and C. P. Stark. 2007. "Rainfall Thresholds for the Initiation of Landslides in Central and Southern Europe." *Meteorology and Atmospheric Physics* 98: 239–67.

———. 2008. "The Rainfall Intensity-Duration Control of Shallow Landslides and Debris Flows: An Update." *Landslides* 5: 3–8.

Hansen, A. 1984. "Landslide Hazard Analysis." In *Slope Instability,* ed. D. Brunsden and D. B. Prior, 523–604. New York: Wiley.

Hencher, S. R., M. G. Anderson, and R. P. Martin. 2006. "Hydrogeology of Landslides in Weathered Profiles." In *Proceedings of the International Conference on Slopes,* 463–74. Kuala Lumpur.

Holcombe, E. A., and M. G. Anderson. 2010. "Implementation of Community-Based Landslide Hazard Mitigation Measures: The Role of Stakeholder Engagement in Sustainable Project Scale-Up." *Sustainable Development* 18 (6): 331–49.

Hong, Y., R. Adler, and G. Huffman. 2006. "Evaluation of the Potential of NASA Multi-Satellite Precipitation Analysis in Global Landslide Hazard Assessment." *Geophysical Research Letters* 33: L22402. doi:10.1029/2006GL028010.

Huabin, W., L. Gangjun, X. Weiya, and W. Conghu. 2005. "GIS-Based Landslide Hazard Assessment: An Overview." *Progress in Physical Geography* 29: 548–67. doi:10.1191/0309133305pp462ra.

Innes, J. L. 1983. "Debris Flows." *Progress in Physical Geography* 7: 469–501.

International Geotechnical Societies UNESCO Working Party on World Landslide Inventory. 1993. "A Suggested Method for Describing the Activity of a Landslide." *Bulletin of the International Association of Engineering Geology* 47: 53–57.

IRPI (Istituto di Ricerca per la Protezione Idrogeologica). 2012. "Rainfall Thresholds for the Initiation of Landslides." http://rainfallthresholds.irpi.cnr.it/.

Iverson, R. M. 2000. "Landslide Triggering by Rain Infiltration." *Water Resources Research* 36 (7): 1897–1910.

Janbu, N. 1977. "Slope and Excavations in Normally and Lightly Consolidated Clays." In *Proceedings of the Ninth International Conference on Soil Mechanics and Foundation Engineering,* vol. 2, 549–66. Tokyo.

Keefer, D. K. 2002. "Investigating Landslides Caused by Earthquakes—A Historical Review." *Surveys in Geophysics* 23 (6): 473–510.

Keefer, D. K., and M. C. Larsen. 2007. "Assessing Landslide Hazards." *Science* 316: 1136–38.

Keefer, D. K., and R. C. Wilson. 1989. "Predicting Earthquake-induced Landslides, with Emphasis on Arid and Semi-Arid Environments." In *Landslides in a Semiarid Environment,* vol. 2, ed. P. M. Sadler and D. M. Morton, 118–49. Riverside, CA: Inland Geological Society of Southern California Publications.

Kenny, T. C. 1967. "Slide Behaviour and Shear Resistance of a Quick Clay Determined from a Study of the Landslide at Selnes, Norway." In *Proceedings of the Geotechnical Conference on Shear Strength Properties of Natural Soils and Rock,* vol. 1, 57–64. Oslo.

Kirschbaum, D. B., R. Adler, Y. Hong, and A. Lerner-Lam. 2009. "Evaluation of a Preliminary Satellite-Based Landslide Hazard Algorithm Using Global Landslide Inventories." *Natural Hazards Earth System Science* 9: 673–86.

Komoo, I., and S. N. Mogana. 1988. "Physical Characterization of Weathering Profiles of Clastic Metasediments in Peninsular Malaysia." In *Proceedings of the 2nd Conference on Geomechanics in Tropical Soils, Singapore 1*, 37–42.

Larsen, M. C., and A. Simon. 1993. "A Rainfall Intensity-Duration Threshold for Landslides in a Humid-Tropical Environment, Puerto Rico." *Geografiska Annaler Series A-Physical Geography* 75 (1–2): 13–23.

Lee, S. 2005. "Application of Logistic Regression Model and Its Validation for Landslide Susceptibility Mapping Using GIS and Remote Sensing Data." *International Journal of Remote Sensing* 26 (7): 1477–91.

Little, A. L. 1969. "The Engineering Classification of Residual Tropical Soils." In *Proceedings of the 7th International Conference on Soil Mechanics and Foundation Engineering, Mexico*. 1, 110.

Lumb, P. 1975. "Slope Failures in Hong Kong." *Quarterly Journal of Engineering Geology* 8: 31–65.

Mechler, R. 2005. *Cost-Benefit Analysis of Natural Disaster Risk Management in Developing Countries: Manual*. Bonn: Deutsche Gesellschaft fuer Technische Zusammenarbeit (GTZ) GmbH.

Millington, R. J., and J. P. Quirk. 1959. "Permeability of Porous Media." *Nature* 183: 387–88.

Monteith, J. L. 1973. *Principles of Environmental Physics*. London: Edward Arnold.

Nandi, A., and A. Shakoor. 2010. "A GIS-Based Landslide Susceptibility Evaluation Using Bivariate and Multivariate Statistical Analyses." *Engineering Geology* 110 (1–2): 11–20.

Nash, D. 1987. "A Comparative Review of Limit Equilibrium Methods of Stability Analysis." In *Slope Stability, Geotechnical Engineering and Geomorphology*, ed. M. G. Anderson and K. S. Richards, 11–73. Chichester, UK: Wiley.

Nefeslioglu, H. A., C. Gokceoglu, and H. Sonmez. 2008. "An Assessment on the Use of Logistic Regression and Artificial Neural Networks with Different Sampling Strategies for the Preparation of Landslide Susceptibility Maps." *Engineering Geology* 97: 171–91.

Opadeyi, S., S. Ali, and F. Chin. 2005. "Status of Hazard Maps, Vulnerability Assessments and Digital Maps in the Caribbean." Final report. Caribbean Disaster Emergency Response Agency.

Petley, D. N. 2009. "On the Impact of Urban Landslides." *Geological Society Engineering Geology Special Publications* 22: 83–99.

Pierson, T. C. 1983. "Soil Pipes and Slope Stability." *Quarterly Journal of Engineering Geology* 16: 1–11.

Richards, L. A. 1931. "Capillary Conduction of Liquids in Porous Mediums." *Physics* 1: 318–33.

Sharma, R. H., H. Konietzky, and K. Kosugi. 2009. "Numerical Analysis of Soil Pipe Effects on Hillslope Water Dynamics." *Acta Gepotechnica* 5 (1): 33–42.

Soeters, R., and C. J. van Westen. 1996. "Slope Instability Recognition, Analysis and Zonation." In *Landslides: Investigation and Mitigation*, Transportation Research Board Special Report 247, ed. A. K. Turner and R. L. Shuster, 129–77. Washington, DC: National Academies Press.

Travasarou, T., J. D. Bray, and N. A. Abrahamson. 2003. "Empirical Attenuation Relationship for Arias Intensity." *Earthquake Engineering and Structural Dynamics* 32: 1133–55.

Turner, A. K., and R. L. Schuster, eds. 1996. *Landslides: Investigation and Mitigation*, Transportation Research Board Special Report 247. Washington, DC: National Academies Press.

Uchida, T. 2004. "Clarifying the Role of Pipe Flow on Shallow Landslide Initiation." *Hydrological Processes* 18: 375–78.

United Nations. 2006. "State of the World's Cities 2006/7." United Nations Human Settlement Programme (UN-Habitat), Nairobi, Kenya.

——. 2009. "Making Disaster Risk Reduction Gender-Sensitive: Policy and Practical Guidelines." Geneva: UN.

UNDP (United Nations Development Programme). 2004. *Reducing Disaster Risk: A Challenge for Development*. New York: UNDP Bureau for Crisis Prevention and Recovery.

USACE (U.S. Army Corps of Engineers). 1989. *U.S. Army Corps of Engineers Engineering Manual: Engineering and Design - Retaining and Flood Walls*. http://140.194.76.129/publications/eng-manuals/em1110-2-2502/toc.htm.

USGS (U.S. Geological Survey). 2004. "Landslide Types and Processes." Fact sheet 2004-3072. http://pubs.usgs.gov/fs/2004/3072/.

Van Den Eeckhaut, M., T. Vanwalleghem, J. Poesen, G. Govers, G. Verstraeten, and L. Vanderkerckhove. 2006. "Prediction of Landslide Susceptibility Using Rare Events Logistic Regression: A Case-Study in Flemish Ardennes (Belgium)." *Geomorphology* 76: 392–410.

Van Westen, C. J. 2004. "Geo-Information Tools for Landslide Risk Assessment: An Overview of Recent Developments." In *Landslide Evaluation and Stabilization*, ed. W. A. Lacerda, M. Ehrlich, S. A. B. Fountoura, and A. S. F. Sayao, 39–56. Rotterdam: Balkema.

Varnes, D. J. 1978. "Slope Movement Types and Processes." In *Landslides: Analysis and Control*, Transportation Research Board Special Report 176, ed. R. L. Schuster and R. J. Krizek, 11–33. Washington, DC: National Academies Press.

Walker, L. R., D. J. Zarin, N. Fetcher, R. W. Myster, and A. H. Johnson. 1996. "Ecosystem Development and Plant Succession on Landslides in the Caribbean." *Biotropica* 28: 566–76.

Wamsler, C. 2007. "Bridging the Gaps: Stakeholder-Based Strategies for Risk Reduction and Financing for the Urban Poor." *Environment and Urbanization* 19: 115.

Wilkinson, P. L. 2001. "Investigating the Hydrological and Geotechnical Effects of Vegetation on Slope Stability: Development of a Fully Integrated Numerical Model." PhD thesis, University of Bristol.

Wilkinson, P. L., M. G. Anderson, D. M. Lloyd, and J. P. Renaud. 2002. "Landslide Hazard and Bioengineering: Towards Providing Improved Decision Support through Integrated Model Development." *Environmental Modelling and Software* 7: 333–44.

Wilkinson, P. L., S. M. Brooks, and M. G. Anderson. 1998. "Investigating the Effect of Moisture Extraction by Vegetation upon Slope Stability: Further Developments of a Combined Hydrology and Stability Model (CHASM)." In *Hydrology in a Changing Environment*, ed. H. Wheater and C. Kirby, 165–78. Proceedings of the British Hydrological Society International Symposium, Exeter, UK, July 6–10.

——. 2000. "Design and Application of an Automated Non-Circular Slip Surface Search within a Combined Hydrology and Stability Model (CHASM)." *Hydrological Processes* 14: 2003–17.

Wilson, R. C., and D. K. Keefer. 1985. "Predicting Areal Limits of Earthquake-Induced Landsliding." In *Earthquake Hazards in the Los Angeles Region—An Earth-Science Perspective*, U.S. Geological Survey Professional Paper 1360. Washington, DC: Government Printing Office.

Wu, W., and R. C. Sidle. 1995. "A Distributed Slope Stability Model for Steep Forested Basins." *Water Resources Research* 31: 2097–110.

Wu, T. H., W. P. McKinnell, and D. N. Swanston. 1979. "Strength of Tree Roots and Landslides on Prince of Wales Island, Alaska." *Canadian Geotechnical Journal* 16: 19–33.

Zaitchik, B. F., and H. M. van Es. 2003. "Applying a GIS Slope-Stability Model to Site-Specific Landslide Prevention in Honduras." *Journal of Soil and Water Conservation* 58: 45–53.

"How can we encourage developing countries to invest more in disaster risk reduction? We need to help governments make the choices of where to invest."

—Department for International Development,
"Frequently Asked Questions on Disaster Risk Reduction" (2006)

CHAPTER 4

Selecting Communities

4.1 KEY CHAPTER ELEMENTS

4.1.1 Coverage

This chapter outlines the process for identifying the communities most at risk from landslides so they can be prioritized for MoSSaiC (Management of Slope Stability in Communities) projects. The listed groups should read the indicated chapter sections.

AUDIENCE				LEARNING	CHAPTER SECTION
F	M	G	C		
✓	✓	✓		Principles for comparing landslide risk at various locations; data and expertise required; how to design an appropriate community prioritization process	4.1, 4.2, 4.3
	✓	✓		How to compare landslide susceptibility or hazard at multiple locations	4.4
	✓	✓	✓	How to compare the vulnerability of exposed communities	4.5
	✓	✓		How to create a prioritized list of at-risk communities	4.6
		✓		How to create a base map for each selected community	4.7

F = funders and policy makers   M = MoSSaiC core unit: government project managers and experts   G = government task teams: experts and practitioners   C = community task teams: residents, leaders, contractors

4.1.2 Documents

DOCUMENT TO BE PRODUCED	CHAPTER SECTION
Report on decision-making process, roles, and responsibilities for community selection	4.1, 4.2, 4.3
Report on outcomes of landslide susceptibility/hazard assessment and vulnerability assessment concluding with a prioritized list of communities for engagement in MoSSaiC project	4.4, 4.5, 4.6
Base maps for the selected communities	4.7

4.1.3 Steps and outputs

STEP	OUTPUT
1. Define the community selection process • Identify available experts in government • Determine availability of software and data • Request permission to use data if necessary • Design appropriate method for selecting communities	Agreed-upon selection method and criteria, roles and responsibilities, timeline
2. Assess landslide hazard • Data acquisition: topography, soils, geology, land use, past landslides • Data analysis: landslide susceptibility or hazard within the study area	List or map of relative landslide susceptibility of different areas
3. Assess exposure and vulnerability • Data acquisition: community locations, building footprints, housing/population density, census data or poverty data • Data analysis: vulnerability of exposed communities to landslide impacts in terms of physical damage, poverty, or other criteria	List or map of relative vulnerability of exposed communities
4. Assess landslide risk • Data analysis: landslide susceptibility/hazard, exposure, and vulnerability data combined to determine overall landslide risk for study area • Data analysis: identify communities exposed to highest levels of landslide risk	List or map plus list of most-at-risk communities for possible risk reduction measures
5. Select communities • Conduct brief site visits of short-listed communities to confirm results • Consult community liaison task team and other relevant local stakeholders to review list • Confirm prioritized community short list according to selection criteria	Prioritized community short list
6. Prepare site map information for selected communities • Data acquisition: most detailed maps and aerial photos of selected communities • Map preparation: assemble community maps/photos and print hard copies	Hard-copy map and aerial photo for use on site

4.1.4 Community-based aspects

A critical part of the selection process is for government task teams to visit short-listed communities to confirm the likely landslide risk and the suitability of a MoSSaiC project. Community representatives can provide information on local landslide history, socio-economic vulnerability, and community perceptions of the risk; they should be consulted during these visits.

4.2 GETTING STARTED

4.2.1 Briefing note

The aim of this chapter is to provide a framework for developing a prioritized list of com-

munities for implementation of landslide hazard reduction measures using MoSSaiC. This community selection process identifies (1) areas where slopes are susceptible to landslides, (2) the exposure and vulnerability of communities to these potential landslide events, (3) the overall landslide risk, and (4) the suitability of a MoSSaiC project for at-risk communities.

The sophistication of the methods used will depend on local data and software availability, and the level of expertise of the government task teams. Outputs could range from a simple prioritized list of communities to a detailed landslide risk map for a region or country. A variety of different approaches might be adopted in performing this task. Whatever method is used, community selection should be justifiable in terms of the scientific rationale underpinning the landslide risk assessment.

Once the communities have been selected, the mapping task team assembles the most-detailed maps available for these communities. These maps form the basis for the community-based landslide hazard and drainage mapping exercise (described in chapter 5) and subsequent implementation of appropriate hazard reduction measures.

Why a community selection process is needed

The aim of a MoSSaiC intervention is to reduce landslide hazard in the most vulnerable communities.

In any country or region, there may be many communities at risk, and government awareness of these communities will vary. The MoSSaiC core unit (MCU) should agree on a process by which communities are selected for this type of landslide risk reduction project.

Having a structured approach to community selection also ensures that community inclusion, exclusion, and prioritization can be justified to the communities, the government, and donor agencies. Therefore, the selection process should make use of any relevant quantitative data relating to landslide susceptibility/hazard and community vulnerability. It should also be able to incorporate qualitative data such as local knowledge, reports from communities, and information from government ministries (such as public works, social development, and emergency management).

Key activities, resources, and teams

The community selection process primarily involves data acquisition and analysis. Data may be in the form of maps and lists of known or suspected landslides; digital maps of land use, topography, drainage, soil, and geology; and data relating to vulnerability (such as census data at enumeration district level or better). Depending on the scope of the study and the available data and expertise, the analysis may be carried out using spreadsheet or database software (to compile and compare data on a list of communities), or a geographic information system (GIS) (for mapping and

spatially distributed analysis of risk over wide areas).

The MCU should oversee the development of the method for community selection and be responsible for deciding the final list of priority communities. A lead investigator should be selected to coordinate the multidisciplinary process of data acquisition and analysis. Different task teams should work together to combine their understanding of slope processes and landslide hazard, technical expertise in data management and/or GIS mapping, and experience in vulnerability or poverty assessment.

4.2.2 Guiding principles

The following guiding principles apply in selecting communities for MoSSaiC project interventions:

- Be realistic about the data, time, and expertise available for the community selection process. It is better to design a simple, low-tech, but achievable decision-making process than to attempt to use software and techniques for which there is insufficient expertise or poor quality data.

- The community selection process should be transparent, regardless of the quality of the data or the sophistication of the landslide hazard and vulnerability assessment methods, so that priorities and decisions can be justified to all stakeholders. This transparency assists in explaining decisions to residents in communities that may subsequently not be selected, avoiding bias toward particular individuals or agendas in decision making, and enabling the project to be more easily audited and evaluated.

4.2.3 Risks and challenges

Limited available data

The community selection process requires the comparison of the landslide risk affecting multiple communities. This may be done as a search for at-risk communities over a wide area (with no prior knowledge of which communities may be identified), or may involve comparing known at-risk communities. Both approaches require data—the type, quality, and availability of which will determine the community selection method used.

Whatever data are used in the community selection process, be transparent about their source and quality when presenting results to decision makers and communities.

Interpreting landslide hazard maps

When using preexisting landslide hazard maps be aware how they were generated because this affects how they should be interpreted.

As described in chapter 3, several different factors can act together to cause landslides. These factors can vary over very short distances and also over time. The best landslide hazard maps are based on a combination of accurate, high-resolution digital maps of these factors and records of past landslides. Developing such maps requires a good understanding of the processes that cause landslides and experience in using GIS and spatial data sets. A landslide hazard map based on inaccurate, incomplete, or low-resolution data, or on faulty scientific assumptions, can be misleading.

Assess the provenance and utility of preexisting landslide hazard maps in terms of the following:

- The data used to compile the map, and its quality and resolution—These data can include environmental (preparatory) factors, triggering factors, and past landslides

- The type of landslide represented—MoSSaiC is directed toward rotational and translational slides in weathered materials

- The expertise of the map maker and the method used—Methods include direct landslide mapping, semi-quantitative index overlay methods, and spatially distributed modeling of slope factor of safety

- The slope stability information conveyed by the map—Landslide susceptibility maps show the relative spatial likelihood of land-

slide initiation; hazard maps additionally convey the temporal probability of landslide initiation.

Test the provenance and utility of other types of data, such as community vulnerability information, in a similar manner before including it in the risk analysis.

4.2.4 Adapting the chapter blueprint to existing capacity

Use the matrix opposite below to determine the availability of physical data (relating to landslides), vulnerability data, software, and the expertise of the government team.

1. Assign a capacity score from 1 to 3 (low to high) to reflect existing capacity for each element in the matrix's left-hand column.

2. Identify the most common capacity score as an indicator of the overall capacity level.

3. Adapt the blueprint in this chapter in accordance with the overall capacity level (see guide at the bottom of the opposite page).

4.3 DEFINING THE COMMUNITY SELECTION PROCESS

The community selection process comprises two integrated methods—a landslide risk assessment at multiple locations and the application of decision-making criteria for selecting communities. The selection process will be constrained by the technical capacity for landslide risk assessment and the scope of the project as defined by funders and government.

For a given technical capacity and project scope, use the guidance in this section to identify the following:

- A suitable approach to comparing levels of landslide risk at multiple locations

- The criteria for community selection

- The data requirements for the community selection process

- The roles of the MCU and task teams

CAPACITY ELEMENT	EXISTING CAPACITY		
	1 = LOW	2 = MODERATE	3 = HIGH
Local geotechnical expertise	No local geotechnical experts and no local knowledge of landslide processes or hazard assessment	Geotechnical engineers or academics with some experience of landslide hazard assessment in the field or in using GIS	Geotechnical engineers or academics with expertise in landslide hazard assessment in the field and in using GIS
Digital map availability	No digital maps	Some digital maps available or at low resolution	High-resolution digital maps available
Preexisting landslide suscepti-bility, hazard, or risk maps	No (or poor quality) landslide susceptibility/hazard maps	Relevant landslide susceptibil-ity map available, sufficient resolution and quality	Good quality, high-resolution, relevant landslide susceptibil-ity/hazard map available
GIS software expertise	No software or trained staff	GIS software available and experience with simple GIS analysis	GIS software and experienced staff
Landslide records	No landslide records	Some landslide records kept separately by different agencies in different formats for different purposes	Comprehensive, geo-refer-enced landslide records integrated and accessible across multiple agencies
Vulnerability data availability	No data on community vulnerability	Data on proxies for vulnerabil-ity (e.g., census data for calculating poverty indicators)	Vulnerability assessment methods and data established
Project safeguards	Documented safeguards need to be located; no previous experience in interpreting and operating safeguard policies	Documents exist for some safeguards	Documented safeguards available from all relevant agencies

CAPACITY LEVEL	HOW TO ADAPT THE BLUEPRINT
1: Use this chapter in depth and as a catalyst to secure support from other agencies as appropriate	Unless outside GIS expertise and data can be obtained, the community selection process should be based on reports and local knowledge (word of mouth) of landslide-prone areas and vulnerable communities. The output will be a refined list of communities based on qualitative information sources only. The MCU needs to strengthen its capacity for community selection; this might involve the following: • Using this book/chapter to gain an understanding of types of available community selection methods • Identifying colleagues in government or higher education with knowledge of landslides and community vulnerability assessment and considering their appointment as the lead investigator in the community selection process • Working with local commercial or higher education partners to access digital maps or GIS expertise
2: Some elements of this chapter will reflect current practice; read the remaining elements in depth and use them to further strengthen capacity	It might be possible to use GIS data to indicate relative risk across a wide area; this can be refined with local knowledge. The expected output at this level will be a low-resolution risk map and a list of priority communities. The MCU has strength in some areas, but not all. Elements that are perceived to be Level 1 need to be addressed as above. Elements that are Level 2 will need to be strengthened, such as the following: • Receiving assistance or training in the use and application of GIS software • Integrating such data and knowledge across ministries
3: Use this chapter as a checklist	The MCU can likely produce and implement community selection using existing capacity. Detailed GIS-based landslide risk mapping is possible without any additional training and can be refined with data on past landslides. The expected output will be a high-resolution landslide risk map and a community short list verified through field visits. The following would nonetheless be good practice: • Document the community selection methodology for future reference • Establish a landslide risk database and risk management planning tool

4.3.1 Approaches to comparing levels of landslide risk at multiple locations

The community selection process is founded on data acquisition and analysis involving a combination of fieldwork and computer-based work to obtain a relative ranking of landslide risk. The aim is to undertake an appropriate form of landslide risk assessment to identify the communities with the highest risk. Two possible approaches to this risk assessment task are introduced below. The exact form the landslide risk assessment will take depends on local capacity and data. Sections 4.4–4.6 provide greater information on the specific landslide hazard, vulnerability, and risk assessment methods associated with these two approaches.

Field reconnaissance and risk ranking

A low-tech approach to landslide risk comparison among communities is to undertake a *qualitative* assessment of the relative hazard and vulnerability of an existing list of communities using rapid field reconnaissance methods. This approach entails having a team of landslide experts, engineers, or geotechnicians, and vulnerability assessment experts visit each community on the list. This team describes landslide hazard, exposure, vulnerability, and risk in relative terms or by using a numerical scoring system. An inventory of hazardous slopes is thus established, and the relative landslide risk to communities can be ranked.

Digital data and GIS analysis

A more technically demanding approach involves using digital spatial data and GIS. This approach can be useful when there are too many communities for field reconnaissance to be practical, and/or where is little prior knowledge about which communities are affected by landslides. If the digital spatial data are of sufficient quality, large areas can be assessed using this approach.

There are four main classes of GIS-based landslide hazard assessment:

- *Heuristic* (expert-based) methods for combining digital maps of potential landslide causal factors and identifying zones of relative landslide susceptibility

- *Probabilistic* methods (based on landslide inventories) for determining the likelihood of landslide occurrence derived from previous events

- *Bivariate and multivariate* statistical approaches (also requiring historical landslide data) for indirectly identifying landslide causal factors

- *Deterministic spatially distributed modeling* of physical slope stability processes (this is not the same as using site-specific models such as CHASM [Combined Hydrology and Slope Stability Model], section 3.6).

GIS may also be used to determine the exposure of different elements (people, houses, public buildings, utilities, etc.) to the landslide hazard and to assess the physical, economic, and social vulnerability of these elements. Sources of information on exposure and vulnerability include land-use maps, maps of land and asset values, and geo-referenced census data containing socioeconomic information.

Table 4.1 indicates the main types of spatially distributed data that may be used to assess and map landslide risk at different spatial scales—from information on past landslides, to environmental and triggering factors, to data relating to elements at risk. In many cases, comprehensive data on past landslides may not be available or may relate to types of landslide hazard not relevant to MoSSaiC (such as rock falls or debris flows). Similarly, not all the environmental and triggering factors and elements at risk in this table will necessarily be applicable (such as lithology, seismic data, and transportation network maps).

If hazard, exposure, vulnerability, and risk mapping exercises have been previously undertaken as part of another study or project, it may be appropriate to incorporate such maps into the community selection process. Review these maps to confirm that they have a sound basis and take into account the landslide hazard types relevant to MoSSaiC.

TABLE 4.1 Schematic representation of the basic data sets for landslide susceptibility, hazard, and risk assessment

DATA		IDEAL UPDATE FREQUENCY (YEARS) 10......1......0.002(DAY)	RS[a]	SCALE[b]				HAZARD MODEL[c]				RISK METHOD[d]	
Main type	**Layer**			S	M	L	D	H	S	D	P	S	Q
Landslide inventory	Landslide inventory	←——→											
	Landslide activity	←→											
	Landslide monitoring	←→											
Environmental factors	Digital elevation model	←→											
	Slope angle/aspects, etc.	←→											
	Internal relief	→											
	Flow accumulation	→											
	Lithology	→											
	Structure	→											
	Faults	→											
	Soil types	→											
	Soil depth	→											
	Slope hydrology	←→											
	Main geomorphology units	→											
	Detailed geomorphology units	→											
	Land-use types	←→											
	Land-use changes	←→											
Triggering factors	Rainfall	←											
	Temperature/evapotranspiration	←											
	Earthquake catalogues	←→											
	Ground acceleration	←→											
Elements at risk	Buildings	←→											
	Transportation networks	←→											
	Lifelines	←→											
	Essential facilities	←→											
	Population data	←→											
	Agriculture data	←→											
	Economic data	←→											
	Ecological data	←→											

Note: In the "RISK METHOD" columns, the S column is labeled "Requires results of probablistic hazard analysis" and the Q column is labeled "Requires results of heuristic, statistical, or deterministic hazard analysis."

Source: van Westen, Castellanos Abella, and Sekhar 2008.

Note: ■ = critical; ■ = highly important; ■ = moderately important; ■ = less important; □ = not relevant.

a. Usefulness of remote sensing for acquisition of data.

b. Importance of the data layer at small (S), medium (M), large (L), or detailed (D) scales, related to feasibility of obtaining data at that particular site.

c. Importance of the data set for heuristic (H), statistical (S), deterministic (D), or probablistic (P) models.

d. Importance of the data layer for (semi-)quantitative (S) or qualitative (Q) vulnerability and risk analysis.

Choosing a risk comparison approach

Be pragmatic when deciding which approach to use for analyzing and comparing landslide risk among communities. Use this section to identify the general data requirements for different approaches to landslide risk assessment. Sections 4.4–4.6 provide more detailed descriptions of specific methods and data requirements. The chosen method should be

- not overly ambitious—requiring skills, software, data, and time far beyond the reasonable capacity of the government task teams;

- designed to provide enough information for the purpose of the project, but not necessarily a comprehensive **quantitative** analysis of risk—in many cases, decision makers will simply need a screening process for identifying and prioritizing communities; and

- rigorous, in that, regardless of the government's technical capacity, there should be a transparent method for community selection that provides the basis for justifying selections.

4.3.2 Methods for community selection

To create an integrated community selection process, combine the chosen landslide risk assessment approach with project-specific criteria for selecting communities.

When choosing the landslide risk assessment approach and defining the community selection criteria, take the following influences into account:

- Obligations under the funding loan or grant contracts to work in specific locations or meet certain criteria and safeguards

- Community-driven demands for solutions to landslide issues

- Scientific/technical interest in using certain risk assessment methods

- Awareness and availability (or lack thereof) of digital data, GIS, or mapping methods

- Political agendas

Selection criteria

Begin by defining the questions that, when answered, will become the selection criteria. Each country will ask these questions and define their criteria differently depending on their expertise, priorities, and approach to the task. However, two broad criteria for community selection should always be met: the high level of landslide risk to a community (hazard, exposure, and vulnerability) relative to other communities, and the appropriateness of MoSSaiC as a means of addressing that risk.

If there is no regular use of wide-area data for landslide risk mapping, or if there is already a long list of communities requesting help, then a bottom-up or list-driven approach may be appropriate. This approach could be vulnerable to political agendas to include certain communities on the list. On the other hand, experienced users of wide-area digital maps and GIS software might formulate questions in a top-down manner to derive a list of communities. Such an approach is perhaps more politically objective, but requires considerable technical expertise and a good data set. In reality, a combination of the two methods may be used to confirm the communities on the list.

- ***Example 1: A priori list-driven questions for bottom-up selection***

  1. Where have landslides already occurred?

  2. How many houses are exposed, and is housing density moderate to high?

  3. Are the exposed households physically and socioeconomically vulnerable?

  4. Based on the above, which communities are at greatest risk from landslides?

  5. Would an intervention be cost-effective, and does it fit the project scope?

- ***Example 2: GIS-based approach for wide-area or top-down selection***

  1. Where are the areas with the highest landslide susceptibility or hazard?

  2. Within these landslide areas, where are the most-exposed communities?

  3. Within these exposed communities, where is the greatest physical and socio-economic vulnerability?

  4. Based on the above, which communities are at greatest risk from landslides?

  5. Where would an intervention be most cost-effective and appropriate?

Figure 4.1 illustrates how these two types of approach may be used individually or in conjunction.

FIGURE 4.1 Top-down and bottom-up community selection methods

Assessment criteria	Method: Top-down national search (wide area/GIS based)	Method: Bottom-up local search (list driven/reconnaisance based)
Hazard	Map of landslide susceptibility or hazard zonation based on • slope angle • soil types • drainage density • topography • previous rotational/translational rainfall-triggered landslides	Question: Where have landslides already occurred? • Known landslides • Areas of slope instability • Suspected future landslides • Occurring during or after rain • In soils not rock • Rotational or translational
Exposure	Map of locations of houses and density of settlements showing • house locations or footprints • housing density and clustering (footprint area of houses as a proportion of the ground surface) • population density	Question: How many houses are affected, and is housing density moderate to high? • More than 10 houses in potential landslide area • Houses clustered in potential landslide area (housing density comprising > 30% land cover)
Vulnerability	Map of socioeconomic vulnerability showing • settlement type (authorized, unauthorized, squatter) • building type (concrete/wooden, high/low rise, etc.) • poverty (indicators, proxies)	Question: Are the affected households low income? • Wooden or small concrete houses on small plots • Lack of infrastructure (metaled paths/roads, drainage, lighting, etc.) • High unemployment
Landslide risk to communities	**Create national list and refine using bottom-up local search**	**Confirm top-down search and/or create community short list**

MoSSaiC interventions involve the construction of strategically aligned networks of surface water drains. Thus, the greater the housing density within the drainage network area, the greater the cost-effectiveness will be in terms of the number of households benefiting from the intervention. To estimate the cost-effectiveness of a MoSSaiC intervention, take into account the number and density of houses exposed to the landslide hazard as well as the potential damage and costs that could be avoided by reducing the likelihood of landslide occurrence. Other cost factors to take into account might relate to the potential cost of construction at that location (determined by factors such as transportation of materials and ease of excavating slope material).

Regardless of the precise wording of the selection criteria, the aim should be to assess landslide susceptibility/hazard, the exposure and vulnerability of communities to that hazard, the overall landslide risk, and the appropriateness of MoSSaiC. Project-specific criteria may be used to refine and prioritize the community short list.

Data sources and methods of analysis

Once the general landslide risk assessment approach and community selection criteria have been identified, consider the specific sources of information that could help answer these questions. Confirm how the information will be analyzed—whether by simple qualitative field reconnaissance methods for ranking or scoring landslide risk in communities or with qualitative, semi-quantitative, or quantitative methods using digital maps and GIS software.

Table 4.2 provides a wide-ranging, although not exhaustive, list of potential data and analysis methods. Generally, the more data sources and the better the quality and analysis of the data, the more comprehensive the landslide risk assessment will be. However, it is not expected or required that every country have the complete suite of data listed here.

Agreeing on the community selection process

Each step in the community selection process should be defined and agreed upon by the

TABLE 4.2 Framework of potential data and analysis methods

INFORMATION SOURCE	FORMAT (LIST/HEURISTIC TO DIGITAL MAP)	POSSIBLE ANALYSIS METHOD (QUALITATIVE TO QUANTITATIVE)
Prior list of communities requesting assistance		
Residents reporting problems to government	List	Qualitative assessment
Government ministers or agencies reporting problems	List	Qualitative assessment
Landslide susceptibility and hazard assessment		
Records of previous landslide locations	List	Qualitative assessment
	Hard-copy map/aerial photos	Qualitative assessment
	Digital map	Incorporate within GIS-based qualitative or semi-quantitative landslide susceptibility or hazard analysis
Wide-area landslide preparatory factors (slope angles, soil types, land use, drainage, etc.)	Local expert knowledge	Qualitative assessment
	Hard-copy map	Qualitative assessment
	Digital map	GIS-based: landslide susceptibility analysis
		GIS plus infinite slope model: quantitative hazard analysis
Site-specific slope data and landslide expert or engineer[a]	Expert observations	Expert-based qualitative or semi-quantitative hazard assessment
	Physical parameters	Physics-based modeling (quantitative)
Exposure and vulnerability assessment		
Exposure: housing type and density information	Site visits by community officer and engineer[a]	Qualitative assessment
	Aerial photos and land-use maps	Qualitative assessment
	Landownership maps	Semi-quantitative assessment
Physical vulnerability of elements at risk to damage by landslide	Site visits by engineer[a]	Qualitative assessment
	Records of previous damage	Semi-quantitative assessment
	Value of elements at risk	Quantitative assessment
Socioeconomic vulnerability	Site visit by social scientist or community officer[a]	Qualitative assessment
	Census data	Semi-quantitative or quantitative assessment of poverty
	Geo-referenced census data	GIS-based semi-quantitative or quantitative assessment of poverty
	Poverty survey	Various methods
	Geo-referenced poverty survey	Map directly in GIS

a. These data may be collected in the field as part of the community short list review or to confirm a wider landslide risk assessment.

MCU. The timeline, roles, and responsibilities for undertaking the analysis should then be set.

For the examples given above, the main steps in the community selection process could be defined as follows.

- **Example 1: A priori list-driven process for bottom-up selection**

  — **Main data format:** Soft data comprising lists of known landslide hotspots and areas of concern (requiring input from engineers, field technicians, community development officers, census officers)

  — **Main steps:**

    1. Conduct reconnaissance of listed communities, completing slope inventory forms to capture landslide hazard, exposure, and vulnerability factors.

    2. Rank landslide hazard, exposure, and vulnerability qualitatively using terms such as low, medium, or high; or use a numerical scoring system.

    3. Confirm rankings using any available secondary sources of hazard data (knowledge of previous slides, aerial photos, maps relating to slope features), exposure (housing density and construction type), and vulnerability information (poverty surveys, census data).

    4. Prioritize communities on basis of risk ranking or score.

- **Example 2: GIS-based process for wide-area or top-down selection**

  — **Main data format:** Digital spatial data relating to landslide preparatory and triggering factors, past landslides, and exposure/vulnerability of communities

  — **Main steps:**

    1. Conduct GIS analysis of landslide risk:

       a. Using basic semi-quantitative GIS map analysis and index overlay to indicate areas of relative landslide susceptibility, exposure, vulnerability, and risk (undertaken by GIS technicians and engineers/geo-technicians) **or**

       b. Using advanced quantitative GIS map analysis in conjunction with spatially distributed numerical slope stability models to quantify landslide hazard, exposure, vulnerability, and risk affecting different areas (requiring experienced GIS analysts and specialists in numerical landslide modeling)

    2. Compare the results obtained with an ex ante list of at-risk communities, or generate a new list.

    3. Confirm the community short list and priorities for intervention using field-based reconnaissance methods as per Example 1, based on expert judgment.

Agree on the method by which relative landslide risk will be assessed, then agree on any further criteria for community selection. Such criteria should answer questions relating to whether a MoSSaiC-type intervention would be appropriate, whether it would fit the project scope or specific requirements from funders or the government, and whether it would be cost-effective. To make the decision-making process transparent, these criteria should be set before generating the prioritized list of communities.

Once the list of eligible communities has been generated and confirmed via brief reconnaissance of the sites, the task teams will need to carry out detailed mapping in each community to identify the specific causes of landslides. These specific slope processes cannot be identified remotely from maps since they typically occur on scales of 1–10 m, and are affected by human activity (construction, farming, etc.). The detailed community-based mapping method is the subject of chapter 5 and is the basis for the design of the physical landslide risk reduction measures in chapter 6.

4.3.3 Roles and responsibilities in community selection

The community selection process encompasses a wide range of disciplines and stakeholder interests. Use the following overviews of roles and responsibilities to ensure the process is scientifically grounded, rigorous, and transparent.

MoSSaiC core unit

The MCU has the following responsibilities:

- Agree on the process for community selection, who will be involved in decision making, and how the process will be run

- Agree on the criteria or thresholds for inclusion of communities

- Identify a lead investigator for the task of landslide risk data acquisition and analysis

- Ensure that existing government procedures and protocols are followed (e.g., with regard to access to and sharing of sensitive data)

- Review the outcomes of the data acquisition and landslide risk analysis process

- Agree on a prioritized list of communities for detailed mapping and MoSSaiC projects.

For the purposes of community selection, the MCU could be augmented to include landslide risk assessment experts from local higher education institutions, and representatives from ministries and agencies responsible for utilities (water, electricity) and census data. These stakeholders should perform the following:

- Advise on the technical aspects of landslide risk assessment

- Provide data held by their institutions or ministries

- Advise on the reliability of data

- Contribute to the decision-making process

Task teams

Members of the landslide hazard assessment and engineering team, mapping team, community liaison team, and technical support team may all be involved in landslide risk data acquisition and analysis. Typical tasks include the following:

- Review the data acquired and handle preliminary error checking

- Process data into appropriate formats

- Conduct field reconnaissance or data analysis to determine landslide hazard, and the exposure and vulnerability of communities

- Combine the results of hazard and vulnerability assessments to determine overall landslide risk

- Present the risk comparison results in a format that is accessible for decision-making purposes

- Maintain and update hazard, exposure, vulnerability, and risk data for future use (if required as part of the project)

- For selected communities, generate base maps for use in detailed community-based landslide hazard and drainage mapping (see chapter 5)

4.4 LANDSLIDE SUSCEPTIBILITY AND HAZARD ASSESSMENT METHODS

Different approaches can be used to assess relative landslide susceptibility or hazard depending on the data, expertise, and resources available (see above and section 3.4). Following is a brief overview of some commonly used assessment methods; these are presented in order of increasing data requirements, complexity, and level of quantification:

- Field-based reconnaissance and heuristic (expert) ranking/scoring of landslide hazard (qualitative results at a detailed scale)

- GIS-based index overlay of digital maps using a heuristic approach to give landslide susceptibility (qualitative results over medium to regional scales)

- GIS-based landslide susceptibility and hazard assessment using probabilistic, statistical, or deterministic methods (semi-quantitative and quantitative results particularly suited to large and medium scales).

Regardless of whether a simple qualitative or in-depth quantitative method is used, it is important to distinguish between landslide susceptibility and landslide hazard:

- **Landslide susceptibility** relates to the type and spatial distribution of existing or potential landslides in an area. Susceptibility assessment is based on the qualitative or quantitative assessment of the role of preparatory factors in determining the relative stability of different slopes or zones. The magnitude and velocity of existing or potential landslides may be taken into account, but the frequency or timing will not be specified.

- **Landslide hazard** is the probability of a landslide (qualitatively or quantitatively assessed) of a certain type, magnitude, and velocity occurring at a specific location. Quantitative hazard assessment takes into account the role of the triggering event (of a known probability) causing the landslide.

A comprehensive list of all the potential data on environmental factors related to slope stability is given in table 4.3. The relevance of these data to landslide susceptibility and hazard assessment is described, and their applicability at different scales is indicated. It is not expected that all of these data are available for—or even relevant to—the community selection process.

Most of the methods introduced in this section can be applied to both landslide susceptibility and landslide hazard assessment; the main difference is whether the landslide probability is estimated for a specific location.

4.4.1 Qualitative landslide hazard assessment: Field reconnaissance and hazard ranking methods

Qualitative slope stability assessment methods involve the systematic classification of slopes in relative terms such as high, medium, or low landslide hazard or using a relative rating derived from a numerical scoring system. These methods are usually based on a combination of expert judgment and empirical evidence (local knowledge or records of past landslides). They can be used as a means of initial assessment of slope stability in the field or in combination with remote sensing, GIS, and mapping methods.

Field reconnaissance and hazard ranking methods can be used for community selection in one of two ways:

- As the primary method in a bottom-up (list-driven) approach, where communities have been listed by government agencies and/or community representatives as requiring assistance, and where there are insufficient digital map data for a top-down/wide-area assessment of landslide susceptibility or hazard

- As the second stage in a top-down approach, as a means of verifying and prioritizing the communities identified via wide-area GIS-based susceptibility or hazard mapping.

Similar methods are used for detailed community-based slope feature mapping once a community has been selected for a MoSSaiC intervention. This in-depth mapping process is fully described in chapter 5.

These methods are usually applied in combination with an assessment of the exposure and vulnerability of the elements at risk (see section 4.5) in order to arrive at an overall landslide risk rating (section 4.6). Field reconnaissance and hazard ranking methods are also used in the development of a national slope stability database (or risk register) for use in landslide management.

One limitation of this type of approach is the difficulty in achieving consistent evalua-

TABLE 4.3 **Overview of environmental factors and their relevance to landslide susceptibility and hazard assessment**

GROUP	DATA LAYER AND TYPE	RELEVANCE	SCALE OF ANALYSIS			
			R	M	L	D
Digital elevation models	Slope gradient	Most important factor in gravitational movements	moderate	high	high	high
	Slope direction	Might reflect differences in soil moisture and vegetation	high	high	high	high
	Slope length/shape	Indicator for slope hydrology	moderate	high	high	high
	Flow direction	Used in slope hydrological modeling	less	moderate	high	high
	Flow accumulation	Used in slope hydrological modeling	less	moderate	high	high
	Internal relief	Used in small-scale assessment as indicator for type of terrain	high	moderate	less	less
	Drainage density	Used in small-scale assessment as indicator for type of terrain	high	moderate	less	less
Geology	Rock types	Lithological map based on engineering characteristics rather than stratigraphic classification	high	high	high	high
	Weathering	Depth of weathering profile is an important factor for landslides	less	moderate	high	high
	Discontinuities	Discontinuity sets and characteristics for rock slides	less	moderate	high	high
	Structural aspects	Geological structure in relation with slope angle and direction is relevant for predicting rock slides	high	high	high	high
	Faults	Distance from active faults or width of fault zones is important factor for predictive mapping	high	high	high	high
Soils	Soil types	Engineering soil types, based on genetic or geotechnical classification	moderate	high	high	high
	Soil depth	Soil depth based on boreholes, geophysics and outcrops, is crucial data layer in stability analysis	less	moderate	high	high
	Geotechnical properties	Grain size distribution, cohesion, friction angle, and bulk density are crucial parameters for slope stability analysis	less	moderate	high	high
	Hydrological properties	Pore volume, saturated conductivity, PF curve are main parameters used in groundwater modeling	less	moderate	high	high
Hydrology	Water table	Spatially and temporal varying depth to groundwater table	less	less	moderate	high
	Soil moisture	Spatially and temporal varying soil moisture content main component in stability analysis	less	less	moderate	high
	Hydrologic components	Interception, evapotranspiration, through fall, overland flow, infiltration, percolation, etc.	moderate	high	high	high
	Stream network	Buffer zones around first-order streams, or buffers around eroding rivers	high	high	high	less
Geomorphology	Physiographic units	Gives a first subdivision of terrain in zones, which is relevant for small-scale mapping	high	moderate	less	less
	Terrain mapping units	Homogeneous with respect to lithology, morphography, and processes	high	high	moderate	less
	Geomorphological units	Genetic classification of main landform building processes	high	high	moderate	less
	Geomorphological (sub)units	Geomorphological subdivision of the terrain in smallest units, also called slope facets	high	high	high	less
Land use	Land-use map	Type of land use/land cover is a main component in stability analysis	high	high	high	high
	Land-use changes	Temporal varying land use/land cover main component in stability analysis	moderate	high	high	high
	Vegetation characteristics	Vegetation type, canopy cover, rooting depths, root cohesion, weight, etc.	less	moderate	high	high
	Roads	Buffers around roads in sloping areas with road cuts often used as factor maps	moderate	high	high	high
	Buildings	Areas with slope cuts made for building construction are sometimes used as factor maps	moderate	high	high	high

Source: van Westen, Castellanos Abella, and Sekhar 2008.

Note: R = regional; M = medium; L = large; D = detailed; ■ = highly applicable; ▨ = moderately applicable; □ = less applicable.

tions of landslide hazard. Different practitioners will inevitably make different judgments of the same slope and will rank hazards differently across wide areas. In several countries, numerical scoring systems have been developed to enable even relatively inexperienced engineers and geologists to carry out consistent and repeatable slope assessments. Examples of numerical scoring systems are described at the end of this subsection.

General procedure for field reconnaissance of landslide hazard

1. Obtain any existing maps of the area and secure permission to access the site if necessary. Traverse the area on foot (figure 4.2) and identify any features that indicate a landslide hazard. Consider slope angle, material type and properties (soil formation, weathering and strength, permeability), slope hydrology and drainage (convergence zones, drainage routes), vegetation, loading, and existing or past landslides (as described in chapter 3).

2. Identify any elements exposed to the potential or existing landslide hazard and determine their vulnerability (degree of damage)

FIGURE 4.2 Field reconnaissance

from such an event (see section 4.5 on vulnerability assessment).

3. Record observations consistently and clearly, using a slope reconnaissance form designed for this purpose. Sketch or take photos of key slope features and, if the data are to be added to a digital map, use a handheld global positioning system (GPS) receiver to record their location. At this stage, detailed mapping of the community or measurement of slope parameters is not necessary; this will be carried out if the community is selected for a landslide mitigation intervention (see chapter 5).

4. Make a judgment as to the level of landslide susceptibility—high, medium, low—and the likelihood of the occurrence of the hazard, or use a numerical scoring system to derive a hazard score. Different methods for doing this are described below.

Frameworks for ranking landslide hazard

Due to the inherent subjectivity of qualitative methods, it is important to make the slope assessment process as transparent as possible by recording observations and the basis for judgments clearly and systematically. Basic forms simply act as a record of observations; more sophisticated methods allow different slope features to be numerically scored on the basis of their likely contribution to slope stability/instability. A standard slope reconnaissance form should be developed for this purpose (table 4.4). It could be adapted from existing forms used in other countries.

Once the slope features have been recorded in the agreed-upon format, landslide hazard should be assessed in terms of potential landslide type, likelihood, and magnitude. The likelihood of a landslide is usually described in terms of the expected frequency or return period, or in qualitative terms with respect to other slopes. An example of a landslide likelihood rating system is given in table 4.5.

The magnitude of the potential landslide consists of at least two components: an estimate of the potential size of the failed area (or volume of ground displaced; see the following

TABLE 4.4 Typical sections of a slope reconnaissance form

SLOPE FEATURE	DESCRIPTION
Slope angle	• Gently sloping (< 15°) to very steep (> 45°)
Topography	• Concave/convex/planar/hummocky/complex/terraced
Slope-forming material	• Degree of weathering as indicator of strength (from bedrock to residual soils and colluvium) • Depth of soil to bedrock
Erosion	• Type: indistinct/rill/gully/piping/washout • Extent: isolated or small areas/multiple features/almost continuous area
Geological features	• Outcropping of bedrock • Presence of joints • Joint spacing: wide (massive)/medium (blocky)/close (fractured)
Ground moisture	• Extent: isolated/substantial • Location: base of slope/midslope/convergence zone/strata interface/other • Occurrence: only after rainy/wet season/all year
Seepage	• Extent: isolated/substantial • Location: bedding planes/joints/shear zone/strata interface/other • Water: clear/muddy
Vegetation	• Type (%): grass/shrub/forested/cultivated/other • Density: sparse/moderate/dense
Site stability	• Known: past landslide activity/landslide-prone area • Indicators: tilting of trees or structures/hummocky ground/tension cracks/other
Adverse human impact	• Slope excavation/loading/removal of vegetation/irrigation/mining/water leakage/drainage failure
Sketch	• Slope cross-section indicating geometry, strata, geological features, seepage, ground moisture, vegetation, site stability indicators, adverse human impacts, and location of any elements at risk • Slope plan indicating the above features and location of previous landslides
Landslide hazard (see chapter 3)	• Landslide type: fall/topple/slide/flow/complex • Slope material: bedrock/unconsolidated material • Landslide likelihood (see table 4.5) • Landslide magnitude: estimate size of potential failure and potential distance of runout (Finlay, Mostyn, and Fell 1999) • Hazard score (if using numerical scoring system)

equation given by Cruden and Varnes 1996), and some description of what will happen to the failed material such as the distance/depth/speed/volume of runout.

Volume of ground displaced $= 1/6\pi \times D \times W \times L$

Where:

D = Maximum depth to slip surface below original ground surface

W = Maximum width between flanks of landslide perpendicular to length, L

L = Minimum distance from landslide crown to toe

Empirical methods for estimating the travel distance and depth of failed material require few measurable parameters. If the landslide type is properly identified and the relevant equations used, Wong and Ho (1996, 419)

TABLE 4.5 Example of a landslide likelihood rating system

TOTAL SCORE	DESCRIPTION OF LIKELIHOOD	INDICATIVE ANNUAL PROBABILITY	HAZARD LEVEL
5	The event is expected to occur and may be triggered by conditions expected within a 2-year period	0.5	Very high
4	The event is expected to occur and may be triggered by conditions expected within a 2- to 5-year period	0.5–0.2	High
3	The event will probably occur under adverse conditions expected over a 5- to 50-year period	0.2–0.02	Moderate
2	The event could possibly occur under adverse conditions expected over a 50- to 500-year period	0.02–0.002	Low
1	The event is unlikely to occur except under very adverse circumstances over a 500- to 5,000-year period	0.002–0.0002	Very low

Source: Indicative measures of landslide hazard based on Australian Geomechanics Society 2000 and Ko Ko, Flentje, and Chowdhury 2004.

assert that such an approach provides a "quick and realistic assessment of the likely range" of runout distances and depths. An approach such as that by Finlay, Mostyn, and Fell (1999) requires three parameters that can be readily estimated in the field or modeled: initial slope angle, the maximum depth to the potential slip surface, and the height of the landslide crest above the base of the slope. See section 3.3.2 for a definition of these landslide features.

If a numerical scoring system has been used, the values for landslide likelihood and magnitude should be summed to give a total hazard score. Otherwise, the level of hazard should be described relative to other slopes using terms such as high, moderate, or low, and provide the rationale for their assessment. Once community vulnerability to landslides has been assessed (section 4.5), the hazard score or ranking is combined with the vulnerability score or ranking to provide an indication of the overall landslide risk posed to each community.

Examples

The details of site-specific slope assessment methods and resulting slope inventories are rarely published by governments. In particular, there do not appear to be examples of systematic field-based methods for qualitative assessment of slope stability in urban commu-

nities in developing countries. However, three case studies are presented below to exemplify the general principles of this class of slope stability assessment. These principles are as follows:

- The aim of the field study should be clearly defined, primarily so as to develop a prioritized list of slopes in specific communities but also potentially to lead to the establishment of a national database of slopes, observed landslides, and slope stabilization works.

- The data requirements and assessment method should be tailored to local conditions (slope types, landslide types, local knowledge of landslides).

- The assessment method should be formalized to enable the training of field technicians and the consistency of data collection across field teams and over time.

The following three case studies exemplifying these principles are drawn from Hong Kong SAR, China; Australia; and the United States.

- ***Example 1: Geotechnical Engineering Office, Hong Kong SAR, China.*** Hong Kong SAR, China, is a world leader in terms of its establishment of a comprehensive slope and landslide database, the assessment of landslide hazard and risk, and management of manmade and natural slopes. The New Priority Ranking System is used for assessment of soil cut slopes, rock cut slopes, retaining walls, and fill slopes. For each slope type, a field team records the detailed slope geometry, exposed slope materials, slope protection and drainage, signs of instability, engineering judgment as to the hazard posed, and the location of facilities (buildings and roads) with respect to the slope. Technicians and engineers use computation sheets to assign numeric scores to each slope characteristic and derive instability and consequence scores. Slopes can then be prioritized for remediation measures, maintenance, or monitoring (Cheng 2009).

- *Example 2: University of Wollongong, Australia.* Ko Ko, Flentje, and Chowdhury (2004) report on a method for assessing the stability of four classes of slopes: natural slopes, embankments, rock slopes or rock cuttings, and soil cuttings. They include a sample field data sheet for recording the characteristics of natural slopes and assigning numeric scores to describe their influence on landslide hazard. Five categories of relative hazard are defined (from very high to very low) which relate to the total score. A nominal landslide probability is then identified based on the score and expert judgment. This hazard rating can then be combined with a consequence (vulnerability) score (also described in the paper) to give an indication of the relative landslide risk associated with a particular slope. The authors conclude that, by using this method, the careful observation and expert judgment of slope characteristics can provide a rapid means for prioritizing slopes for more detailed landslide assessment and risk reduction.

- *Example 3: U.S. Federal Highway Administration.* Several U.S. states have developed field-based slope assessment methods focusing on the risk to roads and road users.

Liang (2007) provides a helpful review of several of these methods, and of the slope management framework developed in Hong Kong SAR, China (see above). Included in the report's appendixes are landslide hazard reconnaissance forms used by the Ohio Department of Transportation. While not directly applicable to urban landslides in developing countries, this report demonstrates the principles of site-based assessment of slopes and the use of this information in prioritizing expenditure on landslide risk reduction.

4.4.2 Qualitative landslide susceptibility mapping: GIS index overlay methods

The stability of a slope is related to environmental factors such as slope angle, topography, drainage (on the surface and in the ground), soil type, geological characteristics, land use, and vegetation cover. In many countries, there are digitized maps of these environmental factors available at small (regional) scales of 1:250,000 to 1:100,000, medium scales of 1:50,000 to 1:25,000, and—sometimes—at large scales of 1:10,000. If GIS software and expertise are also available, it is possible to analyze digital maps and produce landslide susceptibility, hazard, or risk maps at these scales. The four main classes of GIS-based landslide assessment are heuristic (expert-based), probabilistic, statistical, and deterministic.

This subsection outlines the basic principles of GIS-based heuristic landslide susceptibility mapping methods and presents related case studies. These methods are closely related to the numerical scoring approach often used in field reconnaissance in that scores (an index) are assigned to different slope, soil, geology, drainage, and land cover characteristics. These layers are then overlaid, and the influence of the various environmental factors weighted to reflect their importance in determining slope stability. This procedure is commonly called index-overlay analysis. GIS mapping approaches enable the assessment of slope stability over continuous large areas, rather than just considering individual sites. Because the GIS environment allows many layers of information to be added, a landslide susceptibility/hazard map can be added to a vulnerability map to derive an overall risk map.

With heuristic mapping approaches, expert knowledge of the local environmental factors for landslides is essential. Ideally, if the locations and types of previous landslides are known and mapped, this information can be used directly to derive appropriate weights for the different environmental factors on each layer of the landslide hazard map. In many countries, a record of landslides is not always kept or may be incomplete. In the absence of a landslide inventory, the analyst must apply local knowledge and expert judgment in assigning weights to the various environmental factors. This results in a qualitative map indicating relative landslide susceptibility.

Limitations of GIS-based approaches are related to the availability, quality, and scale of the digital data and the expertise of the analyst. Keep in mind that landslide processes tend to be highly localized and cannot usually be captured at the wide-area scale.

Note that a **landslide susceptibility map** simply identifies the spatial variation of different ensembles of slope characteristics and how landslide prone these slopes are in relation to each other. A **landslide hazard map** contains more information by indicating both the spatial and temporal likelihood of landslide occurrence—that is, the location and timing of potential landslide events.

General procedure for GIS index overlay

1. Acquire any available digital data relating to the environmental factors associated with slope stability, including elevation data (e.g., contour maps), geology, soil, and land-use maps. If important data relating to a particular environmental factor are not available in a digital format but do exist in hard copy, these may need to be digitized. Numerous field-based and remote-sensing methods exist for generating digital spatial data;

these are not reviewed here, as they can represent a significant financial or time investment which may not be within the scope of the project.

2. Convert the digital data layers into the correct format for the chosen GIS platform. It may be necessary to geo-reference, transform, or reproject the data so that all the layers are in the same coordinate system and geographical projection. Verify the accuracy and completeness of the data, and make any necessary corrections.

3. Use the elevation data to generate a digital elevation model in raster or vector format (grid-based or triangular irregular network). Use tools within the GIS environment to derive key slope stability factors from the digital elevation model such as slope angle, aspect, and length; internal relief; and drainage routing.

4. Process other map layers to derive useful information. Geology maps can be reinterpreted in terms of engineering geological classifications (relating to rock composition and strength). Soil depths and strengths can sometimes be inferred or approximated from maps of soil erosion and soil type. Despite the importance of soil properties for predicting slope stability, there are often very little direct data on soil strength, hydrology, or depth over wide areas. In many cases, the limited data on soils will need to be augmented by local knowledge and by verifying soil characteristics at selected sites.

5. For each environmental factor, convert the range of values of the data in that layer into an index that describes the relative contribution to slope stability. Low index values may be assigned where the characteristic of the environmental variable is associated with stable slopes (such as a strong soil or bedrock); high index values indicate an association with less stable slopes (e.g., weak soils). Index each factor (GIS layer) in this way—from flat land to steep slopes, shallow soils to deep soils, strong soils to

weak soils, established deep-rooting vegetation to bare land, and so on. This process is similar to numerical scoring systems applied in slope reconnaissance methods. Within each environmental factor or layer, normalize the index values from 0 to 1.

6. Apply a weighting to each of the normalized indexed layers, and overlay them by combining them to derive an overall landslide susceptibility map. The higher the total score, the more susceptible the terrain unit or grid cell is to landslides. Use experience and local knowledge to determine how important each class of environmental factor is in influencing slope stability and to assign different weights to the layers accordingly. Various methods have been developed for systematically assigning weights; these include the following:

- *Direct methods*, based on expert opinion and field experience

- *Pair-wise*, using a comparison matrix in which each environmental factor is taken in turn and compared with each other factor to assess the most significant contributor to slope stability within each pair

- *Ranking*, ordering environmental factors according to their expected influence on slope stability and then normalizing the ranked list between 0 and 1

- *Indirect methods*, using statistical methods to give weights based on data for previous landslides and the inferred causal factors.

The resulting index overlay map presents the relative landslide susceptibility of different terrain units (in the case of vector maps), or grid cells (raster maps) at a resolution determined by that for the original digital data and any GIS transformation of that data.

Examples

The following examples, both from Cuba, illustrate GIS-based landslide susceptibility assessment.

- *Cuba: National Landslide Risk Assessment Project.* Cuba is recognized as having a more comprehensive national risk management strategy than many other countries in the Caribbean region. However, because losses from landslides remain high, in 2004 the National Civil Defense organization of Cuba and the Institute of Geology and Paleontology initiated a new national landslide risk assessment project. In the absence of a sufficient national landslide inventory, a qualitative approach was taken: the application of spatial multicriteria evaluation techniques, in a GIS environment, to develop a national landslide risk index map. Castellanos Abella and van Westen (2007) report the development and implementation of this approach, which is briefly summarized below.

Five landslide susceptibility and five vulnerability indicators were digitally mapped at a cell size of 90 × 90 m. Each indicator was standardized and weighted by experts according to its contribution to landslide susceptibility or vulnerability in order to produce a measure of landslide risk. Three weighting methods were used (direct weighting, pair-wise comparison, and rank ordering), and the weights combined to produce a landslide risk index. The resulting map is used by local authorities to target high-risk zones that require further detailed landslide investigation so as to identify appropriate landslide risk management strategies (figure 4.3).

- *Cuba: Medium-scale qualitative assessment of landslide susceptibility.* A second helpful example from Cuba is the qualitative assessment of landslide susceptibility in San Antonio del Sur, Guantánamo, at a scale of 1:50,000. The first stage of the analysis was the preparation of a geomorphological map from aerial photos and fieldwork. The project identified 603 terrain mapping units of homogenous geomorphological origin, physiography, lithology, morphometry, and soil type. The resulting

FIGURE 4.3 Method for developing a national landslide risk index map for Cuba

| Goal | Subgoals | Indicators |

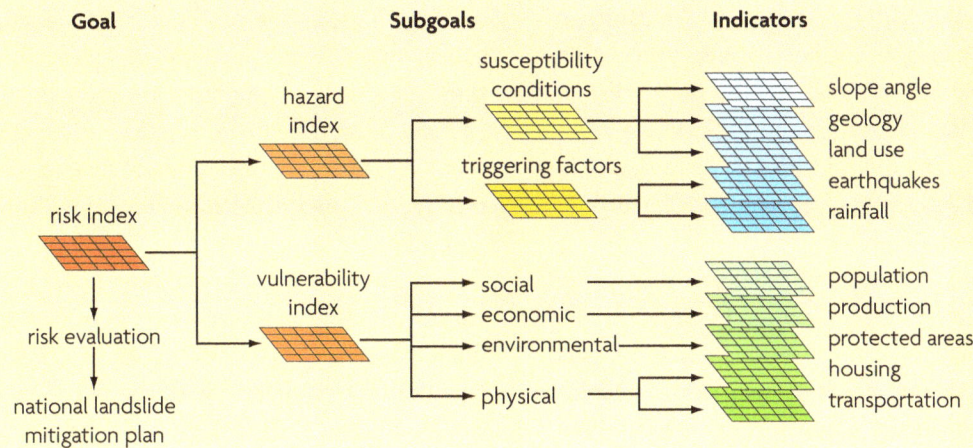

Source: Castellanos Abella and van Westen 2007.

insight into local factors contributing to landslides allowed for the development of weights for mapping landslide susceptibility. Again, three weighting methods were explored—direct weighting, pair-wise comparison, and rank ordering. This heuristic identification of local terrain mapping units and related observations on slope stability,enabled the generation of a qualitative landslide susceptibility map at a more detailed resolution than would have been possible with the conventional index-overlay method applied at the national scale (Castellanos Abella and van Westen 2008).

4.4.3 Semi-quantitative and quantitative landslide susceptibility and hazard mapping methods

The third group of GIS-based landslide hazard mapping methods are more data intensive and require higher levels of scientific expertise than the qualitative approaches described above. Probabilistic, statistical, and deterministic modeling methods can provide semiquantitative or quantitative measures of landslide hazard that include indicative or numerical predictions of landslide probability. These methods are briefly introduced here; teams with the requisite level of expertise are presumably already familiar with these methods and their data requirements.

Probabilistic approaches

Probabilistic approaches require a comprehensive inventory of past landslides—their location with respect to environmental factors (topography, geology, soils, drainage, etc.) and their timing with respect to triggering factors (such as rainfall events). In many cases, they also include information on the damage caused, thus allowing the vulnerability of elements at risk to be inferred. Some of the best examples of national landslide databases can be found in Canada; Colombia; France; Hong Kong SAR, China; Italy; and Switzerland. Analysis of these data within a GIS setting (and often in combination with heuristic methods) can allow the prediction and mapping of future landslides in terms of mean recurrence interval, landslide density, and exceedence probability.

Statistical methods

Statistical methods also require data on past landslides—in this case, the role of individual environmental factors, or combinations of factors, in contributing to slope failures is statistically evaluated. Thus, landslide susceptibility can be indirectly inferred by applying these causal relationships over wide areas. Bivariate statistical approaches, such as weights of evidence methods, consider each causal map in turn in order to derive weighting values for that environmental factor. These methods are widely employed in conjunction with heuristic methods. Multivariate approaches use methods such as logistic regression, artificial neural networks, and fuzzy logic to determine the relative contribution of all the causative environmental factors in determining the landslide hazard for a defined land unit.

Limitations of statistical methods include the inherent generalization of landslide causative factors—the assumption that the same combination of factors will cause landslides throughout the study area. This limitation is magnified if the data on past landslides do not differentiate between landslide types, if the landslide data are incomplete, or if the environmental factor maps are not sufficiently detailed to capture localized variations.

Deterministic approaches

Deterministic approaches address landslide hazard in terms of underlying physical processes. For engineering and geotechnical applications, deterministic modeling is usually undertaken at the scale of individual slope cross-sections. However, in a GIS environment, the ability to represent slope parameters over a wide area allows spatially distributed deterministic modeling of slope stability. These methods are most appropriately applied over small areas, such as river catchments or subcatchments; and at detailed scales, since they require large amounts of good quality spatially distributed data relating to topography, soil depth and strength, and hydrological properties. A digital elevation model is used to determine rainfall and surface water infiltration, groundwater levels, and pore water pressures. A typical distributed deterministic model uses a simple infinite slope stability equation in conjunction with the two-dimensional hillslope hydrology calculations to determine the factor of safety for each mapping unit or grid cell.

Examples of deterministic models include the shallow landsliding model (SHALSTAB) developed by Montgomery and Dietrich (1994) and available as an ArcScript for use in ArcView GIS; and the Stability Index Mapping (SINMAP) model developed by Pack, Tarboton, and Goodwin (1998), which is also available as an ArcView GIS extension.

Figure 4.4 shows the results of such an analysis for the assessment of debris flow hazard in Tegucigalpa, Honduras. The spatial data for this study by Harp et al. (2009) included a digital elevation model (for deriving slope angle),

FIGURE 4.4 Quantitative GIS-based hazard map for Tegucigalpa, Honduras

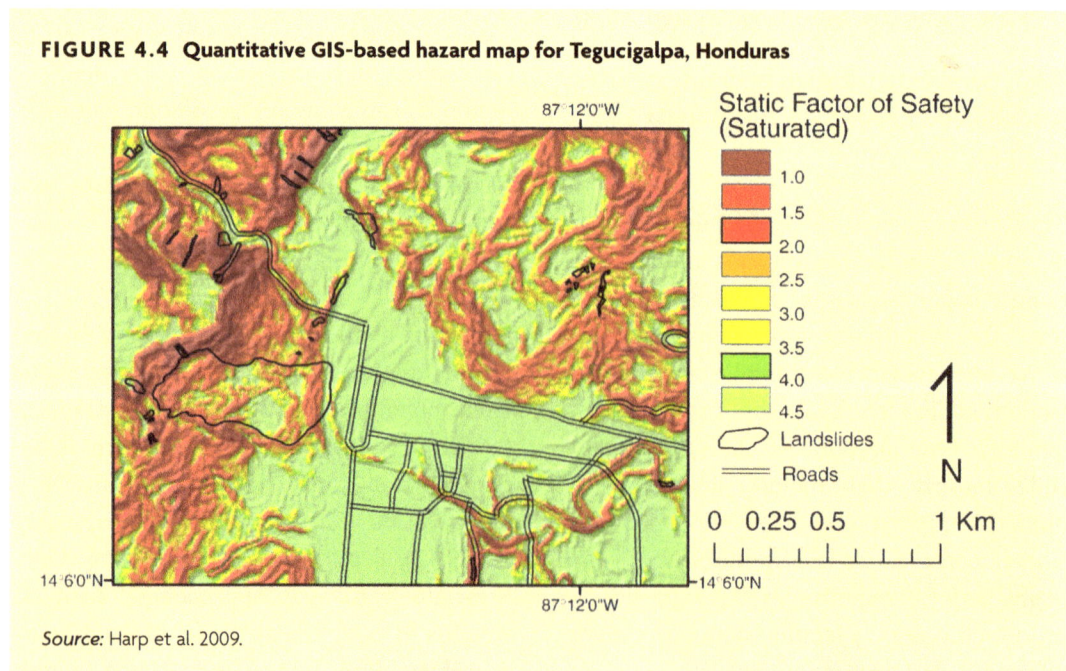

Source: Harp et al. 2009.

a geological map (for deriving material strength), and an inventory of debris flows triggered by Hurricane Mitch in 1998. An infinite slope stability model (based on the limit equilibrium approach described in chapter 3) was used to predict the slope factor of safety and hence determine the debris flow hazard for different hillslopes.

Deterministic methods can also be applied in the prediction of landslide runout—travel distance, velocity, and depth of landslide debris. The development and application of such approaches require extensive data and significant expertise, and are therefore not necessarily appropriate for use in community selection.

4.5 ASSESSING COMMUNITY VULNERABILITY TO LANDSLIDES

Having identified the landslide susceptibility or hazard for a list of communities, or on a wider spatial scale using GIS-based methods, the next stage is to consider what the consequences of a landslide event would be in terms of the exposure and vulnerability of different elements (people and property) to that hazard. The overall landslide risk is the combination of hazard, exposure, and vulnerability.

Exposure describes the location of a particular element with respect to the potential landslide—whether it is on the upper or side margins of the slide, within the failed mass, or in the path of the debris. In selecting communities for potential MoSSaiC interventions, both the number of houses exposed to each particular landslide hazard and the density of housing within that hazard zone (often expressed as the proportion of land coverage by houses) must be noted. Housing density is particularly significant, because MoSSaiC projects involve the construction of a network of surface water drains to improve slope stability and reduce the hazard to multiple households. The greater the housing density, the more households will benefit from the drainage intervention.

The *vulnerability* of exposed elements is expressed in terms of the potential degree of damage (or loss) with respect to the magnitude (or intensity) of a given landslide. MoSSaiC projects are intended for the most-physically and -socioeconomically vulnerable communities. As with landslide hazard assessment, the scale of this assessment can vary from regional to detailed household level, and the data requirements, methodology, and outputs will vary accordingly. Exposure is often considered in conjunction with, or as an integral part of, vulnerability (Crozier and Glade 2005).

Table 4.6 identifies the ways in which the exposure and vulnerability of different elements at risk may be represented at different spatial scales. Of particular relevance to MoSSaiC are data on buildings, population, and economic factors that describe the physical and socioeconomic exposure and vulnerability of urban communities to landslides.

At medium mapping scales, the *physical* exposure and vulnerability of the community can be described simply in terms of how many buildings (houses) might be affected by a landslide event. At a more detailed scale, for a given landslide location and magnitude, the physical exposure and vulnerability of a house may be described in terms of how easily it could be damaged. For example, if hit by a small landslide, a concrete house with good foundations may be less likely to collapse than a wooden structure with poor foundations. The physical vulnerability of people within a community relates to the level of injury or loss of life; this is a very difficult aspect of vulnerability to assess since it requires the combined spatial and temporal prediction of both the landslide event and the exposure of people to that event.

The *socioeconomic* vulnerability of a community to landslides is related to the ability of households to recover from a landslide. This recovery might involve rebuilding part or all of a house, replacing possessions, finding a different means of income (if tools or stock have been lost), or moving to a different location. While not synonymous with poverty, socio-

TABLE 4.6 Main elements at risk used in landslide risk assessment studies and their spatial representation at four mapping scales

ELEMENT	SCALE OF ANALYSIS			
	Small	Medium	Large	Detailed
Buildings	By municipality • Number of buildings	Mapping units • Predominant land use • Number of buildings	Building footprint • Generalized use • Height • Building types	Building footprints • Detailed use • Height • Building types • Construction types • Quality/age • Foundation
Transportation networks	General location of transportation networks	Road and railway networks, with general traffic density information	All transportation networks with detailed classification, including viaducts, etc., and traffic data	All transportation networks with detailed engineering work and detailed dynamic traffic data
Lifelines	Main power lines	Only main networks • Water supply • Electricity	Detailed networks • Water supply • Wastewater • Electricity • Communication • Gas	Detailed networks and related facilities • Water supply • Wastewater • Electricity • Communication • Gas
Essential facilities	By municipality • Number of essential facilities	As points • General characterization • Building as groups	Individual building footprints • Normal characterization • Buildings as groups	Individual building footprints • Detailed characterization • Each building separately
Population data	By municipality • Population density • Gender • Age	By ward • Population density • Gender • Age	By mapping unit • Population density • Daytime/nighttime • Gender • Age	People per building • Daytime/nighttime • Gender • Age • Education
Agriculture data	By municipality • Crop types • Yield information	By homogeneous unit • Crop types • Yield information	By cadastral parcel • Crop types • Crop rotation • Yield information • Agricultural buildings	By cadastral parcel, for a given period • Crop type • Crop rotation and time • Yield information
Economic data	By region • Economic production • Import/export • Type of economic activities	By municipality • Economic production • Import/export • Type of economic activities	By mapping unit • Employment rate • Socioeconomic level • Main income types plus larger-scale data	By building • Employment • Income • Type of business plus larger-scale data
Ecological data	Natural protected areas with international approval	Natural protected area with national relevance	General flora and fauna data per cadastral parcel	Detailed flora and fauna data per cadastral parcel

Source: van Westen, Castellanos Abella, and Sekhar 2008.

economic vulnerability is often related to the level of poverty: poorer households will find it more difficult to recover. In many ways too, socioeconomic vulnerability is closely related to the exposure and physical vulnerability of a community since poorer households are more likely to live in landslide-prone areas than wealthier households, and in houses that are less resilient to the physical impact of a landslide. Poverty assessments can sometimes provide an indication of a community's vulnerability.

The following subsections outline two broad approaches to assessing the potential consequences of landslides with a view to determining which communities have the greatest exposure and vulnerability.

- Field reconnaissance and heuristic (expert-based) ranking/scoring of community and household exposure and vulnerability to landslides

- GIS-based methods using land-use maps to determine community exposure, and census data to assess vulnerability (qualitative to semi-qualitative results over medium to regional scales).

Use these guidelines to identify a methodology compatible with available data and expertise, and that can be interfaced with landslide hazard information in terms of its format (list or map) and spatial scale.

4.5.1 Field reconnaissance and vulnerability ranking methods

Field reconnaissance and ranking methods were introduced in section 4.4.1 as a means for rapid assessment of landslide hazard by a team of experts. Similar methods can be applied to assess community exposure and vulnerability—either qualitatively (e.g., as high, moderate, or low), or quantitatively (using a numerical scoring system). Hazard, exposure, and vulnerability measures can be combined to rank overall landslide risk.

General procedure for field reconnaissance of vulnerability

Specific procedures relating to the assessment of community exposure and vulnerability to landslide hazards are highlighted here; see section 4.4.1 for the general procedure for field reconnaissance.

If a landslide hazard has been identified, the team should have already estimated the spatial extent of the landslide-prone area and the potential downslope extent of the failed material. On the basis of this assessment, estimate the physical exposure and vulnerability in terms of the following:

- The number of houses and people likely to be exposed to the landslide and debris

- The housing density (this helps with the assessment of the possible cost-effectiveness of constructing a drainage network)

- The potential physical damage to individual houses based on their construction type (if there is sufficient knowledge of past landslide impacts and the resilience of structures to such impacts; figure 4.5)

- The cost of the potential landslide damage (if the approximate value of the elements at risk is known).

FIGURE 4.5 Resilience of structures depending on construction type

a. Minor landslide where the impact of the debris has damaged a concrete home.

b. Minor landslide where the impact of the debris has destroyed a wooden home.

Consider the overall socioeconomic vulnerability of the community using locally relevant indicators such as

- the size of houses and plots, house construction type, and ownership of vehicles;

- the presence or absence of basic infrastructure such as publicly supplied piped water, provisions for sanitation and waste disposal, electricity, and paved roads and paths; and

- evidence of unemployment, low levels of educational attainment, overcrowded housing, and isolated or marginalized groups (such as the elderly or disabled).

Semi-quantitative measures of socioeconomic vulnerability (based on census data or community questionnaires) are outlined in section 4.5.2; at this stage, on-site application of such methods at the household level would be time consuming, and may be more appropriate once the selection of individual communities has been confirmed.

Frameworks for ranking vulnerability to landslides

Given the inherent subjectivity of qualitative methods, it is important to make the slope assessment process as transparent as possible by recording observations and the basis for judgments clearly and systematically. Basic forms can be used to record observations; more sophisticated tools allow different community and household characteristics to be numerically scored on the basis of their likely contribution to exposure and vulnerability. The task team should develop a standard community reconnaissance form for this purpose. The typical sections of a slope reconnaissance form that relate to vulnerability assessment are outlined in table 4.7.

Based on these observations, rank physical vulnerability to the potential landslide hazard, estimating how much physical damage could be caused. This can be done either qualitatively (high, moderate, or low), or quantitatively (from 0 to 1—no loss to total loss), using a scoring system such as that illustrated in table 4.8.

Similarly, for areas of the community potentially exposed to landslide hazard, develop a qualitative or quantitative scoring system to indicate the socioeconomic vulnerability.

TABLE 4.7 Typical sections of a slope reconnaissance form that relate to vulnerability assessment

VULNERABILITY COMPONENT	DESCRIPTION
Exposure of elements to landslide hazard	• Number of houses on landslide-prone area • Number of houses in potential landslide runout zone • Density of houses exposed to the landslide hazard
Physical vulnerability of elements to landslide hazard	• Number of houses likely to be lost • Number of houses likely to be significantly damaged • Number of houses likely to need minor repairs • Number of households likely to need relocating
Socioeconomic vulnerability	Various possible measures including: • Financial resources/level of poverty (quality of housing, ownership of possessions) • Presence/absence of basic infrastructure • Level of unemployment (adults not at work) • Level of education (children not at school) • Level of overcrowded housing • Existence of marginalized groups

TABLE 4.8 Example of a numerical scoring system for landslide damage to houses

SCALE OF LANDSLIDE (m³)	DISTANCE (m)		
	< 10	10–50	> 50
< 10^2	0.3	0.2	0.1
10^2–10^3	0.4	0.3	0.2
10^3–10^4	0.6	0.5	0.4
> 10^4	1.0	0.9	0.8

Source: Dai, Lee, and Ngai 2002.

Note: Damage is indicated on a scale of 0 (no loss) to 1 (total loss) depending on landslide scale and proximity.

4.5.2 GIS-based mapping methods for vulnerability assessment

GIS software is designed for the overlay of digital spatial data, the analysis of that data, and the generation of combined maps. Thus, if the location of communities is available as a digital map, this information can be used in conjunction with landslide susceptibility or hazard maps to determine exposure to landslides. The number or density of buildings within these landslide zones can be used as a proxy for the physical vulnerability of communities and the likely cost-effectiveness of a drainage intervention; the socioeconomic vulnerability (or resilience) of communities can be represented by some form of poverty measure.

Vulnerability may be expressed in qualitative terms (such as high, medium, or low), semi-quantitative terms (e.g., using a poverty index), or quantitative terms (such as the number of houses likely to be damaged and the estimated value of the damage). Quantitative measures are often used to indicate direct damage, but it is less easy to quantify indirect damage, such as the social, emotional, long-term economic damage to individuals and the wider community. Thus, semi-quantitative poverty indicators are often used as a proxy for vulnerability to direct and indirect damage.

It is helpful if the spatial scale and level of quantification of the vulnerability assessment is matched to the scale and output format of the hazard mapping exercise to enable calculation of the overall landslide risk.

Data sources

At regional and medium scales, the number of buildings per area may be derived from census information or from land-use maps (identifying urban or semi-urban residential areas); and at larger scales, individual building footprints may be indicated. Since the most vulnerable communities are often unauthorized or informal settlements, it is likely that maps of buildings will be out of date. In such cases, aerial photos may be used supplement this information. At the scales required for the community selection process, the physical vulnerability of communities may simply be derived as the likely number of buildings to be affected by a landslide (and assuming equal damage).

For the purpose of community selection it may be helpful to use poverty as an indicator for comparing the relative socioeconomic vulnerability of communities (although it is recognized that poverty and vulnerability are not synonymous). In many countries, poverty or welfare indicators have been derived that use information from surveys or the national census. Poverty surveys and census data are often geo-referenced to allow mapping of different levels of aggregation such as at the level of municipal and enumeration districts. It is sometimes possible to map this information at the community and street-level scales—the scale of the potential landslide hazard and mitigation measures.

Frameworks for assessing poverty

The most straightforward poverty measures simply consider household income and consumption expenditure as indicators of the level of welfare. More sophisticated measures incorporate other indicators. For example, Human Development Index (HDI) of the United Nations Development Programme is a composite of income, education, and health measures designed to facilitate comparison of deprivation and development levels nationally and globally. Locally derived poverty indicators may also be available that have been tailored to the specific characteristics of a particular region or country. Table 4.9 illustrates the typical components of a locally derived poverty index.

These measures can be applied both in the field (using a household questionnaire), or using GIS (by acquiring geo-referenced census data at the least aggregated, most detailed, level possible). The required census variables may initially be processed in the census database software using available search and query protocols. For more complex analysis, export the data to a spreadsheet. Finally, sort the list of communities according to socioeconomic vulnerability (poverty in this case)

and present either as a list or import into GIS to create a map.

4.6 ASSESSING LANDSLIDE RISK AND CONFIRMING COMMUNITY SELECTION

Landslide risk is a product of the level of landslide susceptibility or hazard and the vulnerability of the elements exposed to damage by that hazard (the potential landslide consequences). The previous two sections have outlined a range of methods for deriving landslide

TABLE 4.9 Typical components of a locally derived poverty index

ITEM	CLASSIFICATION	SCORE	MAXIMUM SCORE FOR ITEM
Wall type	Brick/block/concrete	3	
	Wood and concrete	2	3
	Wood	1	
	Wattle/tapia/makeshift	0	
Toilet type	WC to sewer/cess pit	1	1
	Pit latrine/none	0	
Light source	Electricity/gas	1	1
	Kerosene/none	0	
Possessions	TV, telephone, video, stove, refrigerator, washing machine	0.5 each	4
	Car/pick-up	1	
No. persons per bedroom	<1	3	
	1–1.99	2	3
	2–3	1	
	3.01 or more	0	
Education of head of household	Tertiary/university	5	
	Secondary complete	4	
	Secondary incomplete	3	5
	Primary complete	2	
	Primary incomplete	1	
	None	0	
No. of employed to total no. of persons	1	3	
	0.49–1	2	3
	0.25–0.5	1	
	< 0.25	0	
	Maximum total score:		**20**

Source: Government of St. Lucia 2004.

susceptibility or hazard, exposure and vulnerability in qualitative, semi-quantitative, and quantitative terms; in list or map-based formats; and using field reconnaissance or GIS processing of digital spatial data. This section brings these outputs together to derive an assessment of landslide risk to enable selection of the most appropriate communities in which to initiate MoSSaiC projects.

4.6.1 Combining the hazard and vulnerability information

Depending on the approach taken for assessing landslide hazard, expose and vulnerability, use one of the following methods to combine these assessments and derive the overall landslide risk to communities.

Field reconnaissance methods

Complete the reconnaissance forms and assess the overall landslide risk when on site in each community—assigning both hazard and vulnerability ratings in qualitative terms or according to a numerical scoring system. Combine these ratings or scores to give the landslide risk rating using a matrix such as that in table 4.10.

Once all the communities on the list have been visited and assessed in this way, review the completed reconnaissance forms and rank the communities in order of landslide risk.

GIS-based methods

An alternative to a risk rating matrix is to overlay GIS-generated hazard and vulnerability maps to produce a composite landslide risk map. Different weights may be assigned to the hazard and vulnerability maps according to the agreed-upon community selection criteria.

To identify a community short list, review the attributes of the risk map and sort the communities by overall risk. Compare the risk assessment with local knowledge, known landslides, and past events and ask whether the results are realistic and reasonable or whether the method needs refining. Abstract a short list of high-risk communities from the GIS for final verification.

TABLE 4.10 Example of a risk rating matrix

HAZARD RATING	OVERALL PHYSICAL AND SOCIOECONOMIC VULNERABILITY RATING				
	Very high	High	Medium	Low	Very low
Very high	5	5	4	3	2
High	5	4	4	3	2
Medium	4	4	3	2	1
Low	3	3	2	1	1
Very low	2	2	1	1	1

A team of landslide experts/engineers or geotechnicians and a social scientist or community development practitioner should visit each of the short-listed communities and use rapid field reconnaissance to confirm the selection.

4.6.2 Confirming selected communities

The task team should present the results of the risk comparison and analysis to the MCU along with the following information to support the decision-making process:

- Executive summary

  — A list or table of the communities in rank order of landslide risk together with the hazard, exposure, and vulnerability ratings or scores (derived from field reconnaissance results or GIS maps)

  — Maps of the landslide hazard, exposure, vulnerability, and risk assessments if GIS methods have been applied

- Appendixes

  — Supporting materials detailing the data acquisition and analysis process and providing the rationale behind qualitative heuristic (expert-based) judgments

  — Key reconnaissance data sheets or subsidiary maps developed as part of the risk assessment process

The MCU should review the list and decide how well each of the priority communities meets the selection criteria and whether they are within the scope of the project. Some of the more technical aspects of this review may require further discussion with experts on the task team. Other information (or pressures) from communities and their political representatives may need to be tested against the results of the risk analysis to justify the final list of prioritized communities.

For each of the communities on the priority list, the MCU should provide a short summary justifying its suitability for a MoSSaiC intervention against the criteria decided in section 4.3.2 (table 4.11).

Finally, the MCU should report, agree, and sign off on the community short list with the government and the project funding agency.

> **MILESTONE 4:**
> **Process for community selection agreed upon and communities selected**

TABLE 4.11 Sample justification for community selection

COMMUNITY	SUITABLE FOR MoSSaiC	COST-EFFECTIVE	NOTES
		JUSTIFICATION FOR DECISION	
A	Yes	Yes	Selected for MoSSaiC • A vulnerable community with multiple households exposed to landslide hazards (rotational or translational slides in weathered materials) • A community-based drainage intervention is potentially appropriate for reducing the hazard • Housing density is high giving a low drain length, and construction cost, per house
B	Yes, if combined with road drainage intervention	Yes	Selected for MoSSaiC • A vulnerable community exposed to landslide hazards (rotational or translational slides in weathered materials) as a result of surface water runoff from roads above the community and from households • A suitable location for a road drainage intervention that would protect adjacent houses and the road, combined with a community-wide drainage intervention • Per house cost could potentially be high, but this would be offset by preventing loss of road (a high-cost event)
C	Yes	No	Not selected for MoSSaiC • A moderately wealthy community exposed to multiple small landslide hazards (rotational or translational slides in weathered materials) in cut slopes behind houses • Low housing density, so a community-wide drainage intervention would have a high cost per house • A more cost-effective solution would be education and enforcement of regulations relating to cut slopes, drainage, and retaining structures at the household level
D	No	No	Not selected for MoSSaiC • Landslide hazard is caused by, and/or only affects, one house (low exposure) • The landslide hazard relates to physical processes not targeted by MoSSaiC approach • An appropriate risk reduction approach would be relocation of the household, or a localized engineering intervention such as a retaining wall; not a community-based or community-wide MoSSaiC drainage intervention

4.7 PREPARING A BASE MAP FOR DETAILED COMMUNITY MAPPING

Once the list of prioritized communities has been confirmed, the mapping task team should compile all the spatial data available to produce a composite base map for each community. These maps will be used to identify the precise localized slope processes and triggering mechanisms that contribute to the landslide hazard in each community. This detailed community mapping is undertaken in the next stage of the project (chapter 5).

The base map is used both as a guide in locating and understanding these slope processes, and as a template to which detailed observations can be added by the community mapping team and the residents. The annotated base map is thus a working document in the identification of landslide causes and potential solutions. It may be used as an input for physically based analysis of slope stability and to communicate slope stability concepts and project aims to the community. And, after many revisions, it will provide the template for the detailed drainage design and work packages for construction.

4.7.1 Useful features

It is useful to work from a geo-referenced map of the community. Such a map will make it easier to analyze the cause/effect relationships between slope features, processes, and landslide triggering mechanisms, and will allow measurements to be made, other maps to be overlaid, and GPS locations to be identified.

Base maps should be at the most detailed resolution possible to permit identification (or, later, addition) of individual features such as houses, paths, and drainage patterns (figure 4.6a). The area covered by each base map should encompass the topographic unit within which the community resides (i.e., the hillside or drainage subcatchment), since this is the greatest area over which potential landslide mechanisms and associated environmental factors may operate.

Topographic, or contour, maps provide a useful starting point for preparing the base map, since the scale and coordinate system are known and topographic units can be recognized. Many topographic maps also include land-use information and the locations of houses, roads, paths, and drainage lines—thus providing a head start in the detailed mapping of a community (figure 4.6b). A base map that includes these features as vectors (points, lines, and polygons) is usually quite clear and easy to interpret; such a document is also very easy to annotate.

4.7.2 Supporting data

Maps of geology, lithology, and soils can provide useful supplementary data in support of field observations and slope stability calculations. In general, however, they should not be included in the base map owing to the sheer volume of information they would add. Aerial and satellite photos can similarly supplement the base map, providing information on the location of houses, paths, and—sometimes—drainage routes; but the density of their information and the solid coloration of these raster images can make annotation difficult (figure 4.6c). On the other hand, aerial photos are a very useful tool for engaging residents in discussing landslide and drainage issues.

If field reconnaissance forms have been used in the rapid assessment of landslide hazard and vulnerability (as described in this chapter), this information should be added to the base map or included in the supplementary material.

4.7.3 Sources of spatial data

If field reconnaissance was the main methodology for community selection and there are no digital maps, photocopy and scale up any available hard-copy maps of each community as necessary.

Where GIS-based mapping was used in the community selection, print out a high-resolution base map of each community. Ideally, the base map should comprise GIS layers with vector data (points, lines, and polygons) showing contours, roads, paths, drains, and

FIGURE 4.6 Generating the base map from a topography map and an aerial photo

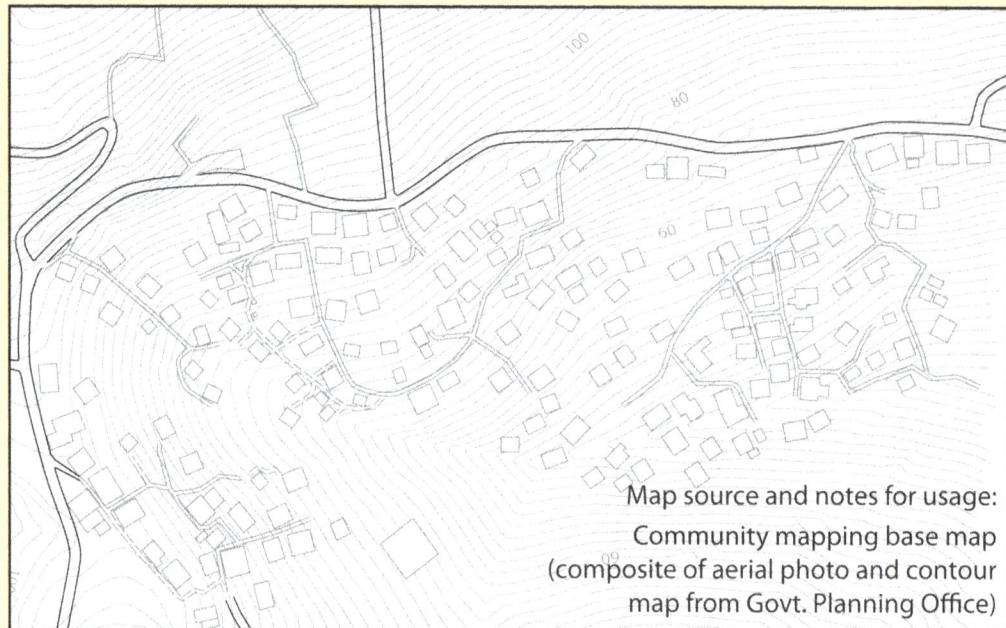

Map source and notes for usage:
Community mapping base map
(composite of aerial photo and contour
map from Govt. Planning Office)

a. A community base map prepared from the original topographic map (b) and updated using an aerial photo (c).

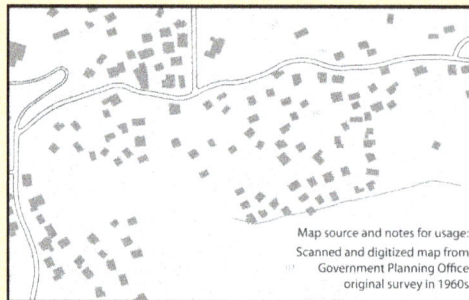

Map source and notes for usage:
Scanned and digitized map from
Government Planning Office
original survey in 1960s

b. A topographic map may be available. In this example, the main roads and some of the houses in the community are also shown.

c. An aerial photograph of the community can be used in updating existing digital maps to create the base map and as a supplementary resource for the community mapping process.

Source: Reproduced with permission of the Chief Surveyor, Ministry of Physical Planning, St. Lucia.

houses. Try not to include raster layers, such as aerial photographs or digital elevation models, or layers with soils, geology, and lithology; these data can be provided as supplementary maps.

A final source of information for the base map may be surveys and plans generated for previous community projects, such as the construction of paths and other infrastructure.

Depending on the quality of the survey conducted and whether the plans are geo-referenced, such information can be a useful part of the base map. However, maps and information consolidated from government or other sources may not be up to date. Before these can be added, significant on-site verification and further relevant detail may be needed; this process is outlined in section 5.4.

4.8 RESOURCES

4.8.1 Who does what

TEAM	RESPONSIBILITY	ACTIONS AND HELPFUL HINTS	CHAPTER SECTION
Funders and policy makers	Agree to the community selection process	• Become familiar with potential community selection criteria approaches	4.3.2; 4.6
	Coordinate with the MCU and government task team		
	Agree to the list of prioritized communities	• Review the report from the community selection team	
MCU	Build the community selection team	• Identify task team members from relevant government ministries and other agencies	4.2; 4.3
	Coordinate with the government task team Agree on and communicate the process for community selection	• Review available software and existing data on landslide susceptibility or hazard and community vulnerability • Identify an appropriate assessment method • Modify the project step template (section 2.6)	4.3
	Finalize the prioritized list of communities	• Review the task team report • Finalize community selection against agreed-on selection criteria and report to government and funders and policy makers	4.6
	Coordinate with funders and policy makers		
Government task teams	Agree on and communicate the process for community selection	• Review available software and existing data on landslide susceptibility or hazard and community vulnerability • Identify an appropriate assessment method • Modify the project step template (section 2.6)	4.4; 4.5
	Assess landslide susceptibility or hazard	• Data acquisition and application of selected methodology	4.4
	Assess community exposure and vulnerability	• Data acquisition and application of selected methodology	4.5
	Generate a prioritized list of at-risk communities	• Combine hazard and vulnerability data to indicate relative risk • Confirm list with site visit and rapid reconnaissance • Write report for the MCU	4.6
	Report to the MCU		
	Prepare the community base map	• Acquire all relevant spatial data to assist in the mapping within the selected communities	4.7

4.8.2 Chapter checklist

CHECK THAT:	TEAM	PERSON	SIGN-OFF	CHAPTER SECTION
✓ Capabilities, personnel, data, and software identified				4.3
✓ Appropriate method specified for selecting communities				4.3.2
✓ Areas of landslide hazard identified and ranked				4.4
✓ Most vulnerable communities identified and ranked				4.5
✓ Overall landslide risk to communities determined and priority communities identified				4.6
✓ **Milestone 4:** Process for community selection agreed upon and communities selected				4.3.2; 4.6.2
✓ Base maps for the short-listed communities prepared				4.7
✓ All necessary safeguards complied with				1.5.3; 2.3.2

4.8.3 References

Australian Geomechanics Society. 2000. "Landslide Risk Management Concepts and Guidelines." http://australiangeomechanics. org/admin/wp-content/uploads/2010/11/ LRM2000-Concepts.pdf.

Castellanos Abella, E. A., and C. J. van Westen. 2007. "Generation of a Landslide Risk Index Map for Cuba Using Spatial Multi-Criteria Evaluation." *Landslides* 4: 311–25.

———. 2008. "Qualitative Landslide Susceptibility Assessment by Multicriteria Analysis: A Case Study from San Antonio del Sur, Guantánamo, Cuba." *Geomorphology* 94 (3–4): 453–66.

Cheng, P. F. K. 2009. "The New Priority Ranking System for Man-Made Slopes and Retaining Walls." Special Project Report SPR4/2009, Geotechnical Engineering Office, Government of Hong Kong Special Administrative Region. http://hkss.cedd.gov.hk/hkss/eng/download/ SIS/cnprs/SPR%204_2009.pdf.

Crozier, M., and T. Glade. 2005. "Landslide Hazard and Risk: Issues, Concepts and Approach." In *Landslide Hazard and Risk*, ed. T. Glade, M. G. Anderson, and M. Crozier, 1–40. Chichester, UK: Wiley.

Cruden, D. M., and D. J. Varnes. 1996. "Landslide Types and Processes." In *Landslides: Investigation and Mitigation*, Transportation Research Board Special Report 247, ed. A. K. Turner and R. L. Shuster, 36–75. Washington, DC: National Academies Press.

Dai, F. C., C. F. Lee, and Y. Y. Ngai. 2002. "Landslide Risk Assessment and Management: An Overview." *Engineering Geology* 64: 65–87.

Department for International Development. 2006. "Frequently Asked Questions on Disaster Risk Reduction." http://webarchive.nationalarchives. gov.uk/+/http://www.dfid.gov.uk/Media-Room/ News-Stories/2006-to-do/Frequently-Asked- Questions-on-Disaster-Risk-Reduction-/.

Finlay, P. J., G. R. Mostyn, and R. Fell. 1999. "Landslide Risk Assessment: Prediction of Travel Distance." *Canadian Geotechnical Journal* 36 (3): 556–62.

Harp, E. L., M. E. Reid, J. P. McKenna, and J. A. Michael. 2009. "Mapping of Hazard from Rainfall-Triggered Landslides in Developing Countries: Examples from Honduras and Micronesia." *Engineering Geology* 104 (3–4): 295–311.

Ko Ko, C., P. Flentje, and F. Chowdhury. 2004. "Landslides Qualitative Hazard and Risk Assessment Method and Its Reliability." *Bulletin of Engineering Geology and the Environment* 63: 149–65. DOI 10.1007/s10064-004-0231-z http:// www.springerlink.com/content/ eqa4jf2jq95p7mfa/fulltext.pdf.

Liang, R. Y., 2007. "Landslide Hazard Rating Matrix and Database." Final report, FHWA/ OH-2007/18, U.S. Federal Highways Administration and Ohio Department of Transportation.

Montgomery, D. R., and W. E. Dietrich. 1994. "A Physically-Based Model for the Topographic Control on Shallow Landsliding." *Water Resources Research* 30: 1153–71.

Pack, R. T., D. G. Tarboton, and C. N. Goodwin. 1998. "The SINMAP Approach to Terrain Stability Mapping." Paper submitted to 8th Congress of the International Association of Engineering Geology, Vancouver, September 21–25. http://hydrology.usu.edu/sinmap/.

van Westen, C. J., E. A. Abella, and L. K. Sekhar. 2008. "Spatial Data for Landslide Susceptibility, Hazards and Vulnerability Assessment: An Overview." *Engineering Geology* 102 (3–4): 112–31.

Wong, H. N., and K. K. S. Ho. 1996. "Travel Distance of Landslide Debris." In *Landslides*, vol. 1, ed. K. Sennest, 417–22. Rotterdam: Balkema.

"Community participation has been recognized as the additional element in disaster management necessary to reverse the worldwide trend of exponential increase in disaster occurrence of and loss from small- and medium-scale disasters."

—Lorna P. Victoria, Director, Center for Disaster Preparedness, Philippines (2009, 1)

CHAPTER 5

Community-Based Mapping for Landslide Hazard Assessment

5.1 KEY CHAPTER ELEMENTS

5.1.1 Coverage

This chapter illustrates how to work with communities to develop a map of slope drainage and landslide hazard for use in the MoSSaiC (Management of Slope Stability in Communities) process. The listed groups should read the indicated chapter sections.

AUDIENCE				LEARNING	CHAPTER SECTION
F	M	G	C		
✓	✓	✓	✓	The community mapping process	5.4
	✓	✓		How to assess if a MoSSaiC intervention is suitable	5.5, 5.6
	✓	✓	✓	How to develop an initial drainage plan for landslide hazard reduction	5.7

F = funders and policy makers   **M** = MoSSaiC core unit: government project managers and experts   **G** = government task teams: experts and practitioners   **C** = community task teams: residents, leaders, contractors

5.1.2 Documents

DOCUMENT TO BE PRODUCED	CHAPTER SECTION
Community slope feature map	5.4
Slope process zone map	5.5
Initial drainage plan	5.7
Priority matrix of slope zones and proposed drainage interventions	5.7

5.1.3 Steps and outputs

STEP	OUTPUT
1. Identify the best form of community participation and mobilization • Review and determine the most suitable form of community participation • Identify available community liaison experts in government	MCU agrees on appropriate community participation strategy
2. Include key community members in the project team • Identify existing or new community representatives • Hold initial discussions with community representatives to brief them on mapping and project rationale	Key community members included
3. Plan and hold a community meeting • Take advice from government and community representatives on location and style of meeting • Compile a community base map from existing maps, plans, and aerial photos (see section 4.7) to bring to the meeting	First community meeting held
4. Conduct the community-based mapping exercise; this will entail a considerable amount of time in the community • Talk with residents in each house to begin the process of engagement, knowledge sharing, and project ownership • Observe and discuss wide-scale and localized slope features and landslide hazard • Add local knowledge and slope feature information to the base map	Community slope feature map
5. Qualitatively assess the landslide hazard and potential causes • Use the community slope feature map to identify zones with different slope processes and landslide hazard • Evaluate the role of surface water infiltration in contributing to the landslide hazard	Slope process zone map (relative landslide hazard)
6. Quantitatively assess the landslide hazard and the effectiveness of surface water management to reduce the hazard • Use physically based software or simpler means to assess the likely contribution of surface water to landslide hazard • Assess whether reducing surface water is likely to reduce landslide hazard	Determination of viability of MoSSaiC approach
7. Identify possible locations for drains • For each slope process zone, determine the most appropriate surface water management approach • Prioritize the zones according to relative landslide hazard	Initial drainage plan and prioritization matrix
8. Sign off on the initial drainage plan: organize a combined MCU-community walk-through and meeting to agree on the initial drainage plan	Initial drainage plan sign-off

This chapter provides guidelines for involving and engaging the community; a step-by-step description of how to develop a community slope feature map; principles for identifying slope process zones and assessing landslide hazard; and examples of quantitative, physically based methods for confirming landslide hazard and slope drainage processes. Milestone 5 is achieved at the end of this chapter with sign-off on the initial drainage plan. The final drainage plan for landslide hazard reduction is designed in chapter 6.

5.1.4 Community-based aspects

The chapter outlines different processes for community participation and how to work with community members to produce a map of slope drainage and landslide hazard.

5.2 GETTING STARTED

5.2.1 Briefing note

What is community-based mapping for landslide hazard assessment?

Community-based mapping is a central element of MoSSaiC. It allows identification of the natural and human causes of slope instability at a sufficiently detailed scale for potential landslide hazard reduction measures to be determined.

The starting point is the mapping of detailed slope features (at scales of 10–50 m) and stability history based on community residents' knowledge and careful observations by engineers or landslide experts. By mapping slope features at this scale, zones of different slope stability processes and relative landslide hazard can be identified. An initial assessment is then made of the role of surface water infiltration in contributing to the landslide hazard, allowing the potential effectiveness of surface water drainage in reducing the landslide hazard to be evaluated. Scientific methods are used to confirm and refine the landslide hazard assessment. Finally, possible locations of new surface drains are discussed with the community, and an authorized stakeholder signs off on the prioritized zones and initial drainage plan.

Community-based landslide hazard mapping is a two-way learning process. Engaging with individuals in the community enables the synthesis of their detailed local knowledge of the slope with scientific and engineering knowledge of slope processes. During these discussions, community awareness of slope processes and of good and bad slope management practices is also likely to be raised.

Why is such a detailed map necessary?

Mapping landslide hazard at the community level is a vital component of the overall landslide hazard reduction process described in section 1.2.

Community-based mapping is very much the start of the MoSSaiC process in a particular community, and an **input** to the development of landslide hazard reduction measures. The initial community slope feature map is eventually developed into a formal drainage plan (chapter 6) detailing drain alignments, household connections, and other related works for reducing landslide hazard.

In contrast, traditional community-based (participatory) landslide hazard mapping approaches are typically used to provide information to residents and authorities so that construction can be limited in hazardous locations, disaster preparedness improved, and vulnerability reduced. These landslide hazard maps are usually seen as an output from the exercise rather than an input for designing hazard reduction measures.

Similarly, wide-scale (regional or country-based) landslide hazard maps usually deliver information that provides only general guidance as to areas of landslide susceptibility or hazard. Such maps do have a role to play in MoSSaiC, and chapter 4 reviews how they can be generated and used in selecting communities where MoSSaiC projects might be relevant. However, the information contained in these maps is not resolved at a sufficiently fine scale to capture the detailed physical causes or triggers of potential landslides (as described in chapter 3). They thus cannot provide enough information to design physical landslide hazard mitigation measures in communities.

Landslide processes at the community scale

Understanding the mechanisms that trigger landslides, and the scale at which they operate, provides the scientific basis for mitigating landslide hazard. As outlined in chapter 3, landslide hazard results from a combination of preparatory factors relating to slope geometry, soil and geology, vegetation, surface water and groundwater regimes; and triggering mechanisms such as rainfall and seismic events. Tropical regions are especially susceptible to landslides because of high-intensity and high-duration rainfall events, the rapid rate of weathering, and resulting deep soils (often on steep slopes). Rainfall is the main landslide trigger in the tropics, and preliminary evidence suggests that climate change could produce more intense precipitation events in regions such as the Caribbean, thus increasing the probability of landslides (Knutson et al. 2010).

Even without climate change, anthropogenic activities are increasing landslide risk in some of the most vulnerable communities. These activities include altering slope geometry with earthworks (cut and fill), changing slope vegetation, loading slopes with buildings and infrastructure; all of which can cause variations in surface water and groundwater regimes. The pressure of development on both land and population results in the poorer, most vulnerable sections of society living on the most-marginal, landslide-prone hillsides.

The scales at which the preparatory and anthropogenic factors operate were summarized in chapter 3 (table 3.6). At the hillside scale (100–1,000 m), geographic information system– (GIS-) based mapping techniques can be used to *identify* zones of increased landslide hazard or susceptibility by overlaying and indexing topographic, soil/geology, and vegetation maps. But to *predict* landslide hazard so as to inform a community-based landslide risk reduction strategy requires that certain parameters be resolved at the household scale (1–10 m). In densely populated communities, it is vital to identify the effects of highly localized surface water regimes, manmade structures, and cut slopes. The surface- and groundwater regimes in such locations will vary over short time scales in response to rainfall events and the addition of household water to the slope. These physical parameters need to be modeled in a fully dynamic way (i.e., over time) to reveal the precise mechanisms determining the stability of the slope, and hence how slope stability can be improved.

What information should be on the map?

Detailed community-based mapping of slope features provides information for determining the local slope destabilizing mechanisms and the potential for rainfall-triggered landslides. A well-constructed community slope feature map will

- identify zones of past, present, and potential future landslide hazard;

- provide information about the local topography (~30 m scale) and mechanisms contributing to slope instability such as drainage and poor construction practices (~10 m scale);

- contain sufficient information to allow a scientific assessment of landslide hazard (using data such as slope angle, basic soil characteristics, vegetation cover, and sources of household water as inputs to slope stability models);

- be sufficiently accurate to allow the provisional alignment of new drains to be plotted;

- be comprehensive, incorporating information from residents and measurements made on the ground; and

- be clear, so that residents, engineers, and decision makers can understand and correctly interpret it.

To meet these criteria, community-based mapping and landslide hazard assessment must be carried out carefully and rigorously.

5.2.2 Guiding principles

The following guiding principles apply in community-based mapping and landslide hazard assessment:

- Recognize the importance of full and repeated consultation and discussion with community residents; recognize the value of their knowledge of slope features and processes, and be aware of different concerns, perceptions of risk, and competing agendas.

- Ensure that the wider topographic controls on drainage, soil depth, and slope stability are identified; be aware of potential connections between features in one part of the slope and the related landslide hazard in another.

- When considering small-scale instability affecting individual houses, be alert to potential pressure from owners to solve their specific problems; do not neglect looking for wider causes and solutions.

- Construct maps carefully and clearly to ensure all relevant information is captured and available for future reference. Each mapping stage builds on the information from the previous map to develop an accurate drainage plan and work packages for construction.

- Undertake repeated community walk-throughs to ensure adherence to all of the above principles.

- Ensure that all relevant safeguards are addressed.

5.2.3 Risks and challenges

Mapping topographic features at the necessary resolution

Identifying major topographic features is a critical element of the walk-through and field survey processes. It is likely that the existing plans and maps incorporated in the community base map (as described in section 4.7) will not be resolved at sufficient detail to reliably indicate zones of water convergence or divergence on the slope. Identification of topographic hollows at a scale of ~30 m is integral to the MoSSaiC mapping process, and time must be spent in carefully identifying such features, since they are likely to control soil water flow and pore pressure changes, and thus landslide hazard.

Spending sufficient time with the community

Community members can provide a significant amount of information regarding the drainage conditions that prevail on the slope during heavy rain. Repeated efforts should be made to talk to as many residents as possible. Choose times when the majority of residents are at home, such as early evenings, weekends, and public holidays. Try to visit the community during heavy rainfall to observe drainage patterns and issues, and to discuss these with residents.

Engage the community in the science of landslide risk reduction from the very beginning of the project, using illustrations to help explain slope processes and good slope management practices. This builds trust and encourages those within the community to bid on the possible works.

The slope feature map should be the product of several visits to the community, not just a single two- to three-day mission. Repeated visits test initial thoughts, encourage the maximum number of community residents to participate, and provide the best opportunity for securing information critical to the formulation of landslide mitigation measures.

Learning by doing

The community-based mapping process is an integral part of community and government training in good practice for landslide risk reduction. The government task teams will need to be open to what they can learn from community residents and from one another. Team members with technical or engineering backgrounds will have to adapt their typical data acquisition and mapping approaches to incorporate community knowledge. Project managers and supervisors of construction works might need to identify new ways to involve community residents and contractors. Conversely, team members with roles in community development will need to familiarize themselves with some of the more technical aspects of the mapping process.

Connecting with key community members

Spending time in the community throughout the process encourages key members of the community to own the project—and, more importantly, to own the methodology. Their engagement thus becomes a significant training opportunity, in that they may thus become advocates for MoSSaiC and potential trainers themselves. Identify respected residents in the community to champion MoSSaiC.

Challenges of community engagement

Communities should not be seen as idealized entities with homogenous views, abilities, or vulnerabilities. Recognize that some residents may have diverging agendas.

Residents' attitudes toward participating in a community-based hazard mapping exercise are likely to be influenced by their perception of risk (chapter 8). In communities where landslides have occurred, residents may sometimes be less receptive to mitigation measures than the general public since they are likely to have a sense of powerlessness (Lin et al. 2008).

Although residents may correctly identify slope surface processes and features, their interpretation of the importance of these in determining slope stability may be incomplete. Local knowledge thus must be integrated with scientific and expert knowledge.

5.2.4 Adapting the chapter blueprint to existing capacity

Use the matrix opposite to assess the quality of core mapping data (the base map) for each community, and government capacity to combine scientific and community-based knowledge of local landslide processes. This information will guide the process of community-based mapping for landslide hazard assessment.

1. Assign a capacity score from 1 to 3 (low to high) to reflect existing capacity for each element in the matrix's left-hand column.

2. Identify the most common capacity score as an indicator of the overall capacity level.

3. Adapt the blueprint in this chapter in accordance with the overall capacity level (see guide at the bottom of the opposite page).

5.3 DECIDING ON HOW TO WORK WITHIN A COMMUNITY

Before community engagement is instigated, the MoSSaiC core unit (MCU) and the government task teams should understand different forms of community participation and the community-based foundation for MoSSaiC projects (section 1.4.3).

This section introduces some general community participation principles and identifies specific principles and practices related to MoSSaiC. Comprehensive guidelines on community participation for development and disaster risk reduction are often available from international development agencies and practitioners such as nongovernmental organizations (NGOs).

5.3.1 Community participation: Principles

An important MoSSaiC project objective is to achieve behavioral change among all stakeholders regarding landslide risk reduction in communities. To this end, community residents should be enabled to participate in the complete process of mapping, drainage design, contracting, construction, and maintenance; and government task teams should be prepared to spend significant time on site with the community. MoSSaiC project steps and expenditure profiles should demonstrate government commitment to a high level of community engagement. Previous experience shows that the majority of total project expenditure can be within the community in the form of construction materials and labor costs.

Determine the most appropriate form of participation

Approaches to community participation can be defined as instrumental, collaborative, or supportive. The Active Learning Network for Accountability and Performance in Humanitarian Action describes these approaches as follows (ALNAP 2003):

- **Instrumental approaches** regard community participation as a means of achieving project objectives; while these approaches can build community capacity, this is not a project objective in itself.

- **Collaborative approaches** are based on exchange of resources throughout the project cycle in order to achieve a shared objective. With this type of approach, the govern-

CAPACITY ELEMENT	EXISTING CAPACITY		
	1 = LOW	2 = MODERATE	3 = HIGH
MoSSaiC core unit (MCU) and government resources for developing community base maps at the household scale	No existing plans or maps of the selected communities	Some plans or maps available, but with incomplete or low-resolution data	Geo-referenced digital plans or maps available with all necessary information (contours, house locations, paths, roads, drainage lines)
Government capacity for engagement with communities in development or disaster risk management	• Limited government activity in community development or disaster risk management • No government agency with mandate for working in/with communities	Significant number of community-based projects undertaken, but no formal agency has overall responsibility	Established community-government liaison and track record of successful projects
Capacity and structure of communities	No formal community structure or community-based organizations	Community-elected representatives or community-based organizations, but generally inactive or with limited influence	Active community-based organizations with elected members and good acceptance within community and by government
MCU and government task team experience in landslide hazard assessment and surface water management	No experience in direct mapping or assessment of slope processes related to landslide hazard	Some experience in direct mapping of slope processes but limited or no experience in landslide hazard assessment	Prior experience in direct mapping of slope processes and the use of scientific methods/models for assessing landslide hazard
Project safeguards	Documented safeguards need to be located; no previous experience in interpreting and operating safeguard policies	Documents exist for some safeguards	Documented safeguards available from all relevant agencies

CAPACITY LEVEL	HOW TO ADAPT THE BLUEPRINT
1: Use this chapter in depth and as a catalyst to secure support from other agencies as appropriate	The MoSSaiC core unit (MCU) needs to strengthen its resources prior to starting the community-based mapping and landslide hazard assessment process. This might involve the following: • Holding discussions with the community liaison task team to identify any previous community project in the area that may help in establishing a dialogue with the community • Talking with the community to see if there is a natural community spokesperson who could be a focus for engagement, but taking note of the risks and challenges in community engagement mentioned above • Talking with commercial or academic partners to ascertain their willingness to share in or collaborate on slope stability analysis • Approaching all relevant agencies to acquire their safeguard documents and distill them into a coherent working document for community engagement
2: Some elements of this chapter will reflect current practice; read the remaining elements in depth and use them to further strengthen capacity	The MCU has identified strength in some areas, but not all. Elements that are perceived to be Level 1 need to be addressed as above. Elements that are Level 2 will need to be strengthened, such as the following: • If there is limited expertise in map/plan production, advice could be sought from a commercial or academic partner or relevant agency • If relevant safeguard documents are available but not collated, the MCU should systematically integrate them • If there is limited expertise in community engagement, seek advice from nongovernmental organizations or other agencies with experience in this area
3: Use this chapter as a checklist	The MCU is likely to be able to proceed using existing proven capacity. It would nonetheless be good practice for it to document relevant experience in community-based projects and related safeguards.

ment or agency aims to build the capacity of the community and also to learn from it. There is no expectation of existing community structures (formal leadership or community-based organizations), and collaboration for specific tasks may be through informal delegation or development of formal partnerships.

- **Supportive approaches** recognize existing or potential capacity within a community—the government or agency provides technical, financial or material support for the community to initiate and undertake its own project.

MoSSaiC is most closely aligned with the collaborative approach, but the MCU and community liaison task team should also seek and support existing community capacity where possible.

Putting a particular participatory approach into practice involves a series of activities. The ladder of participation (table 5.1), originally developed by Arnstein (1969), is a helpful way of describing the type of participation and the role of community residents in project activities.

The MCU and the community liaison task team should decide on a participation strategy that allows an appropriate (and realistic) balance between

- community knowledge and expert knowledge,

- project scope and community perceptions of risk, and

- policy constraints and community decision-making powers.

Consider culture and social organization

The United Nations notes that "Disaster risk reduction projects, policies and programs will be meaningful and successful only if the interests of the whole community are taken into consideration" (UN 2008, v). Different cultures and communities will have different experiences and expectations of participation in community-based projects. Consider the potential effect on participation of local beliefs, language, and history; and aspects of social organization such as ethnic composition, gender relations, relationships between different generations, and social hierarchies.

Also consider the participation of less-prominent or vocal groups (which may include women, the elderly, children and youth, people with disabilities, and the poorest residents), and varying levels of participation within the community due to different levels of interest or knowledge.

Ensure that the participation strategy is culturally and socially appropriate, and that

TABLE 5.1 Types of community participation

TYPE OF PARTICIPATION	COMMUNITY ROLE
Local initiatives	Conceives, initiates, and runs project independently; agency participates in the community's projects
Interactive	Participates in the analysis of needs and in program conception, and has decision-making powers
Through the supply of materials, cash, or labor	Supplies materials and/or labor needed to operationalize an intervention or cofinances it; helps decide how these inputs are used
Through material incentives	Receives cash or in-kind payment from agency
By consultation	Asked for views on a given subject, but has no decision-making powers
Through the supply of information	Provides information to agency in response to questions, but has no influence over the process
Passive	Informed of what is going to happen
Manipulative	Participation is simply a pretense

Sources: Pretty 1995; World Bank 2010.

less-prominent groups are empowered and included in the project.

Consider gender relations

Genuine inclusion of gender considerations is likely to result in more sustainable projects (UNISDR 2008). More broadly, equality is widely regarded as essential in reaching the ultimate goal of development—the well-being of all people (Klasen 1999). In this regard, it is useful to understand and apply a strategy of gender mainstreaming. The United Nations Economic and Social Council defines gender mainstreaming as

> ...the process of assessing the implications for women and men of any planned action, including legislation, policies or programmes, in all areas and at all levels. It is a strategy for making women's as well as men's concerns and experiences an integral dimension of the design, implementation, monitoring and evaluation of policies and programmes in all political, economic and societal spheres so that women and men benefit equally and inequality is not perpetuated. The ultimate goal is to achieve gender equality (UNECOSOC 1997).

Women have a critical role to play in all aspects of community-based projects. Women bring different skills and expertise to the table, as a participant in a Pacific community case study observed:

> Women are great at implementing and organising and they advise the chiefs. The women are the very strong part of the village because they take care of their families. They make sure the kids are safe and the water is clean (Gero, Meheux, and Dominey-Howes 2010, 36).

Frequently, however, men dominate, given their control of nearly all resources available at the household level (University of Warwick 2002) (figure 5.1).

Experience has shown that gender mainstreaming is often difficult to realize (UN 2002) and cannot be achieved without explicit commitment to the strategy and systematic efforts to implement it.

The MCU and community liaison task team should incorporate into the participation strategy a sensitive and positive policy of inclusion and empowerment for all residents, including women. Such inclusion should go beyond a "token" approach that, for example, simply mandates a certain number of women serve on a particular committee.

Table 5.2 provides a practical gender-sensitive risk assessment checklist (UN 2009), much of which is relevant to MoSSaiC's community-based approach to landslide hazard

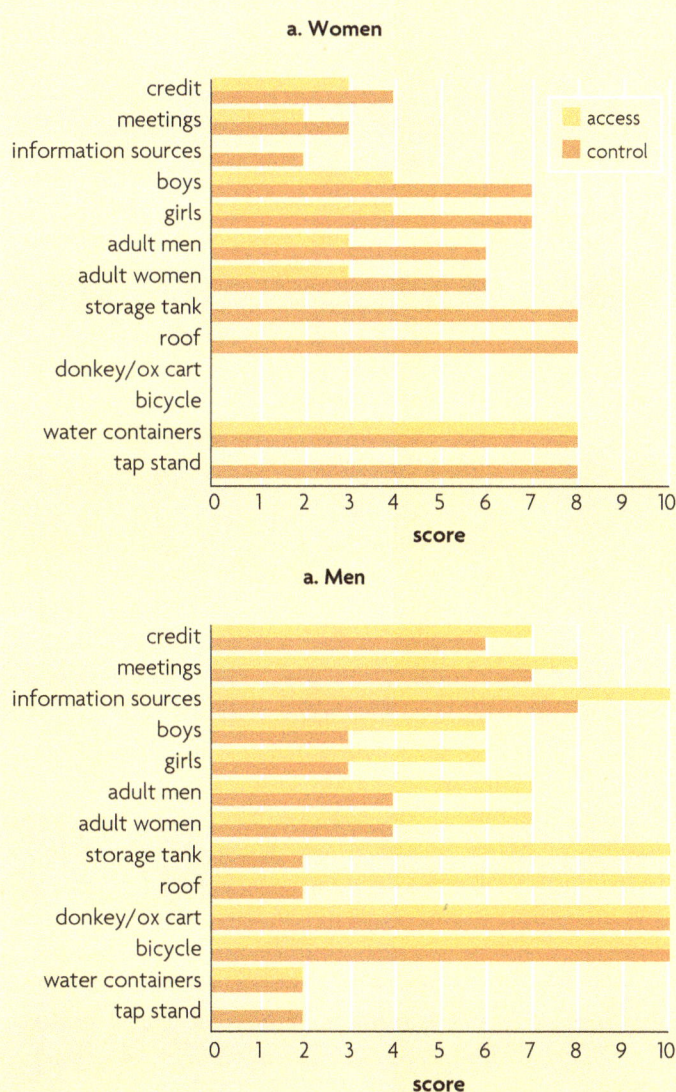

FIGURE 5.1 Access and control over resources in Ethiopia by women and men

Source: University of Warwick 2002.

Note: A maximum of 10 points was allocated between women and men to represent their relative access to, and control over, each resource listed. A score of 10 indicates that that sex has sole access to/control over a particular resource; a score of 5:5 would indicate that women and men enjoy equal access/control.

reduction. Consider adapting this list and incorporate it into the community-based mapping and landslide hazard assessment processes in this chapter.

5.3.2 Community participation: Practices

Typical practices for community participation in project initiation and design may include informal and formal communication such as meetings, focus groups, and interviews; and practical activities such as mapping, community walk-throughs, and construction of priority ranking matrixes.

This subsection describes some of the practices for initiating and sustaining community engagement in MoSSaiC projects. Section 5.3.3 describes specific points of engagement during the community-based mapping process.

The MCU and community liaison task team should use this guidance to translate their principles and strategies for community participation into practice. All government task

---

TABLE 5.2 Checklist for gender-sensitive risk assessment

STEP	GENDER-SENSITIVE ACTION
1. Identifying risks	• Identify and implement strategies that are socially and culturally sensitive to the context to actively engage women and men from the communities in local risk identification • Map the available community organizations that can ensure the participation of both men and women, and involve them in consultation on hazards, including collecting and sharing information and assessing risk • Determine the risks faced by men and women separately in each region or community • Include women's traditional knowledge and perception in the analysis and evaluation of the characteristics of key risks • Involve women and men equally in the process to review and update risk data each year, and include information on any new or emerging risks
2. Determining vulnerabilities	• Ensure the active engagement of men and women in vulnerability analysis (by engaging men's and women's organizations and setting schedules that enable the participation of both men and women) • Conduct gender analysis for the identification of gender-based inequalities between men and women • Map and document the gender-differentiated vulnerabilities (physical, social, economic, cultural, political, and environmental) • Ensure the inclusion of gender-based aspects of age, disability, access to information, mobility, and access to income and other resources that are key determinants of vulnerability identification • Identify and include women's needs, concerns, and knowledge in the community vulnerability assessments conducted for all relevant natural hazards
3. Identifying capacities	• Acknowledge and assess women's and men's traditional knowledge • Ensure the capacities of all women's groups, organizations, or institutions are assessed along with those of men • Identify the specific functions, roles, and responsibilities carried out by women and men and build these into the analysis • Identify the gender-specific support mechanisms for women to get involved in risk management programs and actions (e.g., mobility and child care issues) • Identify mechanisms to enhance the existing capacities of both men and women, and ensure that capacity-building programs incorporate measures to enable women's participation • Recognize the equal importance of the capacities and authority of women and men empowered to conduct risk assessment programs or train other members of the community • Actively engage women's organizations to assist with capacity building • Identify female role models to advocate for gender-sensitive risk assessment
4. Determine acceptable levels of risk	• Involve both women and men in the development of hazard and risk maps • Collect and analyze gender-differentiated data for assessing acceptable levels of risk • Ensure that hazard maps include the gender-differentiated impacts of risk • Ensure that hazard maps include gender-differentiated vulnerability and capacity

Source: UN 2009.

---

teams should be briefed on the participation principles and practices before engaging with the community.

Sensitize communities and government task teams

The MoSSaiC community-based mapping process starts with discussions between two lead government task teams (the community liaison task team and the landslide assessment and engineering task team) and community residents. The government teams need to listen to and understand residents' concerns regarding landslides, and learn what residents consider the main causes of the landslide risk (figure 5.2). They should allow residents to freely discuss issues related to maintenance of drains and the practice of discharging both rain and gray water onto slopes. In this way, they become sensitized to the specific characteristics of the community as well as to the landslide hazard.

FIGURE 5.2 Listening to community residents is important

Conversely, the mapping process allows the government task teams to raise community awareness about the potential causes of landslides and therefore what the possible solutions might be. This process should be undertaken in such a way that the resulting community slope feature map can be used to identify zones of relatively high landslide hazard and indicate major surface drainage lines in wet season conditions. Community residents are thereby sensitized to the highly

localized controls that exist with respect to landslide hazard.

Involve community leaders

Identify those residents with leadership roles in the community; this may require repeat visits to the community. While some leaders are elected and thus immediately known, others may have leadership roles that emanate solely from informal social networks within the community, which can take time to understand. Community engagement has very specific challenges. In some locations, communities may be relatively well organized with elected persons representing the community's interests to local social intervention funds, government agencies, and NGOs. Even with relatively clear structures, though, leadership roles—and those who fill those roles—can change as projects move from concept to implementation and delivery.

Understand community risk perception and agendas

Community representatives can greatly assist in providing information on slope features relating to landslide hazard. However, it can be a challenge to ensure that the advice received from such representatives is truly objective—particularly since landslide hazard reduction measures (such as drains), aimed at protecting the community as a whole, can seem to benefit certain individual properties more than others. Community information should be assessed and moderated through a number of mechanisms prior to any final decisions on drainage interventions being made.

To ensure that the interests of all groups within the community are heard and that information is triangulated, use a variety of participatory activities such as the following:

- Informal discussions with community residents while mapping, stopping for lunch breaks, or walking through the community

- Formal discussions by the whole community at community meetings

- Focus groups with separate constituencies (gender, age, ethnic group) or mixed constituencies

- Discussions with the community's government representatives (and other politicians)

Engage the community in understanding landslide hazard reduction

Maintaining community engagement throughout the project develops trust and is critical for developing residents' understanding of landslide hazard causes and solutions.

Ensure the mapping process is interactive and takes place over a number of visits to present residents with on-site access to the government task teams and the opportunity to understand—and contribute to—the following:

- Assessment of different zones of slope processes and landslide hazard

- Identification of different types of drainage intervention in different landslide hazard zones

- Installation of roof guttering and connection of wastewater pipes from houses to drains

5.3.3 Community knowledge and participation in the mapping process

Identify community members to guide the initial community walk-through

Gaining acceptance within communities is a very important process. At an early stage in community engagement identify one or two respected members of the community who are willing to accompany the government task teams during community mapping and act as guides (figure 5.3). Ask the guides to start by showing the task team the layout of the community and hillside, and point out any known areas of landslides and drainage issues.

Select people who have lived in the community for a while, who are familiar with its layout and history, and who are respected and trusted by other community members. A good starting point is to ask community leaders or

FIGURE 5.3 Engaging community representatives and guides in identifying slope features and landslide issues

leaders of community-based organizations whom they would recommend as a guide. Also, seek out community members who have had experience working alongside government ministries or agencies on other projects. Such individuals can be a critical link in facilitating rapid project acceptance and delivery.

Visit each house

With the assistance of the community representatives or guides, the next step is to have house-by-house discussions with as many residents as possible. The community base map (prepared in section 4.7) and any additional maps or aerial photos should be used to allow residents to add their knowledge of slope features and slope history. Aerial photos in particular are a useful focal point. The full technical details of the mapping process are presented in section 5.4.

House-by-house visits are a crucial part of the MoSSaiC mapping process for several reasons:

- Conversations allow residents to convey their priorities—explaining in their own words and in their own way the risks that they face from landslides.

- The science of the problem can be explained and discussed with residents (figure 5.4), with direct reference to visible slope features (as opposed to a meeting held at a remote venue).

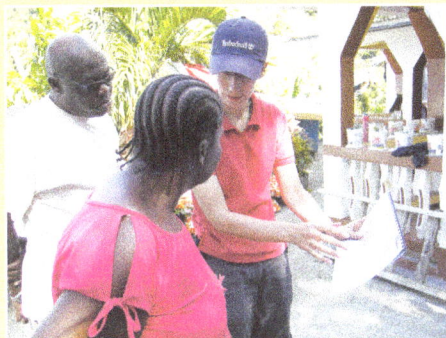

FIGURE 5.4 Discussing slope stability and drainage hazards around residents' houses

- Conversations build trust and allow the project to be fully explained and appreciated.

- Residents have the opportunity to express their desire to be involved in the project (or not) without community peer pressure dynamics that vulnerable groups could find inhibiting at a community or more formal meeting.

- Time taken with conversations allows contact details such as cell phone numbers to be exchanged when offered. Such information is valuable, as it allows follow-up for project management and accountability through a two-way flow of information.

- Informal conversations reveal the workings of the community and provide an important context for the MCU to consider with regard to how it undertakes the bid process and project implementation.

- Conversations provide a means of sensitizing residents to good practices regarding drainage, regardless of whether the particular interventions ultimately form part of the project.

- These interactions yield information on the best time to hold community meetings.

- Being invited into residents' homes allows team members to learn more about the real context of risk as it is perceived and experienced in the home.

The government task teams thus should spend a considerable amount of time in the community talking to residents. This part of the process may take at least two to three weeks and involve visits on weekends and evenings.

Create informal focus groups

Informal group discussions should be held in tandem with house-by-house visits (figure 5.5), perhaps with a group of residents who have expressed particular interest in the project or with community members who would otherwise be marginalized or less vocal at formal community meetings.

FIGURE 5.5 Informal group discussion held at an accessible location

For focus group meetings, assemble a selection of base maps and aerial photographs of the community. These materials will enable residents to identify their houses and to mark relevant surface water issues or indicate any areas of instability they can recall. A poster explaining the science of surface water management for landslide hazard reduction can aid in this discussion.

Hold formal meetings in or near the community

Community meetings should take place at several stages in the project (figure 5.6). These may be timed

- before the mapping process begins—to raise awareness of the project and what to expect;

- after the initial period of conversations with residents—once a preliminary version

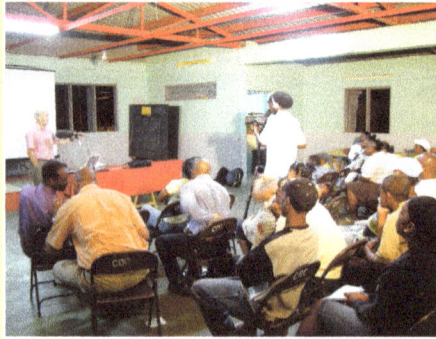

FIGURE 5.6 Local community hall used as venue for hearing residents' views

of the community slope feature map has been developed (using the method described in section 5.4);

- after the qualitative landslide hazard assessment, based on the interpretation of the slope process zones (section 5.5); and

- after the quantitative landslide hazard assessment, to discuss and agree on an initial drainage plan to reduce the landslide hazard (sections 5.6 and 5.7).

Community meetings provide an opportunity for everyone to express their views, for information to be shared, and for community dynamics to be appreciated more comprehensively. Elected representatives, community representatives, the MCU, the government task teams, and the media should all attend. Consider advertising meetings through a variety of approaches, including informal communication within the community (generally the most effective in vulnerable communities) and flyers.

The initial community meeting should include

- an appropriate welcome;

- a brief introduction to the project by the MCU or government task team leader outlining the scope of the project (i.e., landslide hazard reduction), the process, and the expected timeline for implementation;

- an opportunity to listen to community representatives' and residents' views; and

- a question and answer session.

During these meetings, be clear about the project process, what can and cannot be achieved, and provide any known timelines. Such information, and its accuracy, is critical, as it establishes appropriate expectations for project delivery. Often, the community will have had experience with past projects that failed in this aspect, with promises of delivery that were not met. MoSSaiC programs must set accurate expectations, given the level of community engagement that is sought.

5.4 COMMUNITY SLOPE FEATURE MAPPING

This section describes the technical aspects of the community mapping process—what questions to ask residents and the slope features to look for and record. Begin by identifying hillside scale slope processes, then walk from house to house to understand and map localized slope stability controls. Researching and understanding slope processes at the household scale is a central element in landslide hazard mapping and assessment.

Use the items in the following checklist to capture, and later augment, key slope features and the relative location of housing structures.

- Essential items
  — Base map (from section 4.7)
  — Marker pens and pencils
  — Camera
  — Magnetic compass
  — Surveyor's measuring tape

- Additional items if available
  — Abney level
  — Global positioning system (GPS) receiver
  — Aerial photo of community

5.4.1 Hillside scale: Mapping overall topography and drainage

The first stage of the mapping process is to determine the hillside scale controls on slope stability. With the assistance of a community representative, the mapping team should walk through the community to become familiar with the overall topography, main patterns of water movement, and any variations in slope angle and material. Mark these features on the base map (generated in section 4.7; see figure 5.7a) and add, confirm, or correct the positions of houses, paths, drainage lines, and other key structures. Use a compass to take bearings or a GPS receiver to record coordinates; if available, use an aerial photograph (figure 5.7b) to help with navigation and mapping.

Topography and natural drainage

Topography affects drainage, soil formation, and slope stability over scales as localized as 20–50 m. It can be difficult to recognize topographic features at this scale for several reasons:

- Vegetation can mask the view over even very short distances.

- Unauthorized housing can give a false impression of the topography.

- Contours on topographic maps may be interpolated from coarser resolution surveys, thus smoothing out these features (note the relatively straight and evenly spaced contours depicted in figure 5.7a).

The topography of a slope should be described in terms of its constituent convex, concave, or planar (straight) elements, in plan and section (figure 5.8) at a scale of ~20–50 m. In particular, the mapping team should be careful to identify concave topographic elements and associated slope processes.

- **Concave downslope profile (concave in section).** Soil depth is often related to topography. Where the slope profile is concave in section (types 7, 8, and 9 in figure 5.8), it is common for soil depth to increase downslope (figure 5.9). This is due to the erosion or mass wasting of soils from upper slope sections and the deposition of this material on lower slopes. The depth and relative lack of strength of accumulated soils (colluvium) makes them particularly prone to landslides (section 3.5.3).

FIGURE 5.7 Community base map and supplementary aerial photograph

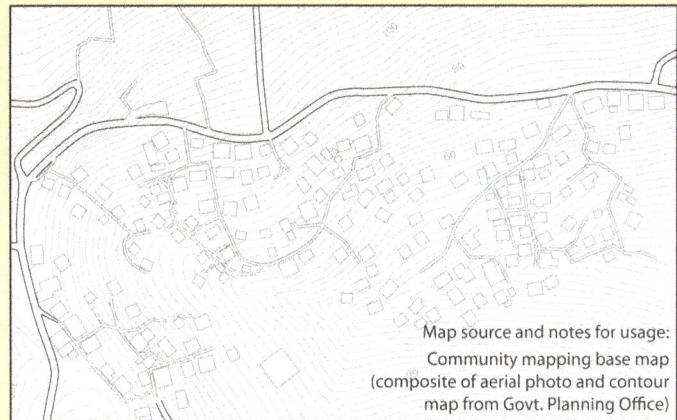

a. A typical community base map compiled from existing contour data and building footprints extracted from a recent aerial photo. Contours may be interpolated and are best used as a general guide to topographic variations (convergent/divergent zones and drainage patterns). See figure 5.18 for an example of this map with slope process features added.

b. An aerial photograph of the community can help with identifying structures and other landmarks.

Source: Reproduced with permission of the Chief Surveyor, Ministry of Physical Planning, St. Lucia.

A downslope increase in soil depth can have a broadly counterintuitive effect: steeper slopes, higher up the hillside, can exhibit stability because of their shallower soils or exposed rock (figure 5.10a), while relatively shallow slopes further downslope may, in certain circumstances, prove less stable due to the accumulation of deeper soils (figure 5.10b).

- **Topographic convergence zones (concave in plan).** Areas of the hillside that are con-

FIGURE 5.8 Topographic elements to be distinguished and identified in the field

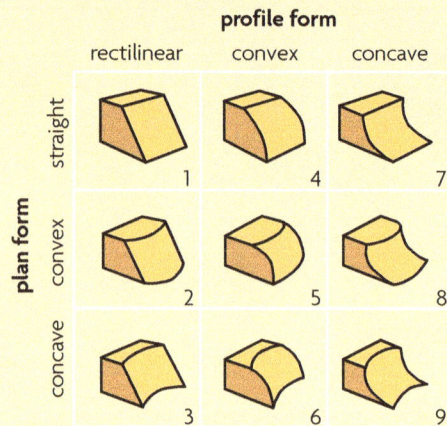

profile form

	rectilinear	convex	concave
straight	1	4	7
convex	2	5	8
concave	3	6	9

plan form

Source: Parsons 1988.

FIGURE 5.10 Soil depth and stability

a. Steep slopes can be stable if the depth to bedrock is very shallow.

b. Shallow slopes can be unstable if fed by significant subsurface water flow from upslope convergent topography.

cave in plan (types 3, 6, and 9 in figure 5.8) are especially important to identify since they serve to focus and concentrate both overland and subsurface flow, and lead to relatively higher pore water pressures in the soil. Convergence zones can also have relatively deep soil because of the accumulation of eroded material from the hillside above. This topographic control of pore water pressure and soil formation generates areas of increased landslide susceptibility that are often associated with hillside hollows.

FIGURE 5.9 Example of a tropical hillslope profile illustrating common weathering features

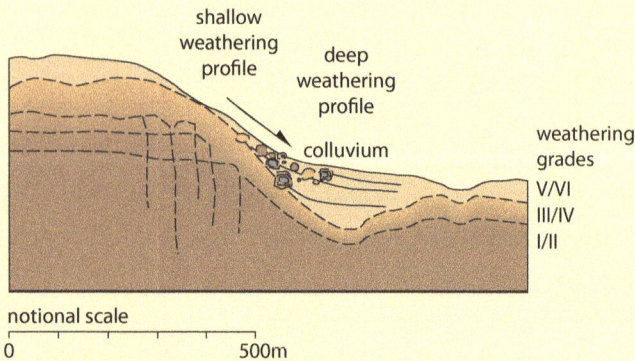

shallow weathering profile

deep weathering profile

colluvium

weathering grades

V/VI

III/IV

I/II

notional scale

0   500m

Source: Fookes 1997.

Although one or two specialized, algorithm-based approaches are available for determining topographic convergence (see, e.g., Quinn et al. 1991; and Quinn, Beven, and Lamb 1995), they are likely to be insufficiently resolved for the spatial scale of such features in dense urban communities.

Ask the community about soil depths—how deep house foundations are, whether they are on bedrock, and what soil conditions were encountered during construction. Look for evidence of erosion and accumulation such as exposed bedrock and loose, mixed, or washed soils and stones.

Look for seepage zones

The combination of deep soils and concentrated water flow in topographic convergence zones can mean that the ground is wet even in the absence of rain. Zones of saturation or seepage of water from the soil provide important evidence of how the slope drains. Sometimes seepage can be observed where there is no obvious topographic hollow (figure 5.11). The reasons for this may include a subsurface drainage pattern that differs from the surface drainage pattern; a change in slope material properties (an interface between soil or rock with differing hydraulic conductivities); or a point source of water such as a burst water pipe, septic tank, or household wastewater pipe. Ask residents if there are places where the soil is always wet even when it has not rained. Look for plants that like wet conditions, mossy or mildewed rocks and concrete, saturated soils, or running water emerging at a point in the soil surface.

Observe slope angles

Observe the shape of the slope in terms of slope angle, and how this varies across the slope and from top to bottom. Although contour maps may give an impression of slope angle, contours may be interpolated, or averaged over a hillside, and thus can be misleading. An Abney level will give a more accurate indication of slope angle changes (see figure 3.16).

Be careful: slope angles can be misleading in terms of landslide hazard. Residents can often associate landslide hazard with steeper slopes. While this may be true in many cases, it is important to ascertain whether shallow slopes may in fact pose a greater landslide risk.

As an example, the upper slopes in a community may comprise rock and could be as steep as 45 degrees, while the lower shallower slopes might be 20 degrees and comprise a significant amount of residual and colluvial (accumulated) soil overlying bedrock. If these shallow slopes lie within a hillslope hollow, water (both surface and subsurface) from the steeper slopes will be concentrated and will infiltrate the lower slopes. This circumstance may lead to increased pore pressures and a potentially greater landslide risk on the lower 20 degree slopes than on the higher 45 degree slopes.

Look carefully at lower, shallow slopes

Be sure to map all areas of the hillside with equal emphasis. Shallow slopes should be seen as areas of potential landslide risk for the reasons given above.

Look for alterations to natural drainage

The development of communities on slopes will inevitably alter the natural drainage pattern, either through the deliberate construction of drains or as an unintended consequence of human activities. Look for existing main drains (ones that affect more than one household plot) and determine whether they follow and augment natural drainage routes or change the drainage pattern. Note where drains start and finish, what condition they are in, and whether they connect to other drains or natural ravines. Ask the community how deep the water is in the drains when it rains heavily, and if the drains overflow or leak.

FIGURE 5.11 Seepage occurring in dry weather conditions where there is no sign of a zone of topographic convergence

It is common for unauthorized construction to cause concentrated water flows at specific locations. These point source discharges can cause erosion and flooding, and potentially increase landslide risk. When mapping existing drains, look for sections of drain that are unfinished, unconnected, or broken and to note the effect of the resulting point source discharges on slope drainage and stability.

Houses can create significant point water sources by discharging gray water (bathroom and kitchen wastewater) and black water (septic waste) onto the slope, and rainwater from roofs. Where there is a piped water supply to houses this can significantly increase the volume and impact of household water discharges. Note the presence of piped water and evidence of broken or leaking water supply pipes.

Other structures that change the flow of water on slopes are paths and steps (which can form a preferential flow path for surface water runoff, figure 5.12a), and retaining structures or walls that can block and divert surface and subsurface flow. Sometimes poorly constructed drains can act as a barrier to surface

runoff, causing water to flow alongside or under the drain instead of into it (figure 5.12b).

Table 5.3 summarizes hillside scale features to include in the community slope feature map.

5.4.2 Household scale: Mapping the detail

Once the broad slope characteristics have been captured, the mapping team should begin to investigate the household-scale influences on slope stability and evidence of any potential instability. This stage of the mapping process provides a vital opportunity to meet residents; discuss drainage and slope stability issues; and listen to concerns, priorities, and ideas. Do not rush this stage, as it is a significant opportunity to encourage community ownership of the project while ensuring that any landslide hazard reduction measures are appropriate both scientifically and socially.

Identify the location of each house

Identify each house on the community map and verify that its position is correctly mapped

FIGURE 5.12 Looking for natural and altered slope drainage

a. An eroded earth footpath also acts as a drainage route and causes the lower concrete path to flood.

b. A drain built in a natural drainage channel with high side walls prevents surface runoff entry.

TABLE 5.3 Hillside scale features to mark on slope feature map

LOOK FOR	ASK ABOUT	CAUTION	MAP
Hollows and ridges	Where the water flows when it rains, where the soil is wet even when there's no rain, if drains overflow, whether there is a piped water supply...	Vegetation, structures, and contour maps can be misleading. Human influence can change the natural slope and drainage	Zones of different topography; see figure 5.8
Water convergence, natural drainage routes, seepage			Drainage routes and convergence zones; see figure 5.8
Main drains, unfinished drains, flow along paths, barriers to drainage, point water sources			
Exposed rock, disturbed soils and stones, evidence of erosion and accumulation	How deep the soil is, what the soil is like (strong, soft, clayey, sandy, stony, disturbed, etc.)	The terms people use to describe slope materials and their properties will vary	Differences in soil and bedrock
Changes in slope angle and soil/rock evidence		Shallow slopes may be more landslide prone than steep ones	Zones of different slope angle

(using a GPS receiver, or by taking compass bearings from known fixed points). Take note of the location of the house relative to overall topographic and drainage features already mapped. Bear in mind the influences these features are likely to have at the household level, such as whether the household is likely to experience flooding or slope instability, or to contribute water to neighbors farther downslope.

It is sometimes helpful to use an aerial photograph for verification. If residents show an interest, the photo can be a good visual tool for initiating discussion on drainage or landslide issues.

Note local slope geometry and material

In constructing houses on steep slopes, residents may have altered the slope geometry by cutting into the slope or building and backfilling retaining structures (figure 5.13). Look for evidence of altered slope geometry in the form of steep cut slopes, flat terraced areas (like steps in the slope), and retaining walls. Is there any evidence of weakness or failure of these slopes and structures?

If there is an exposed (unvegetated) cut slope, ascertain if the material is soil or rock,

FIGURE 5.13 Potential landslide hazard driver: Cutting platforms to build houses

and if there are variations or strata. Homeowners can provide useful information about the nature of the slope material if they constructed the houses themselves. Ask how deep the foundations are, what the slope material is like at different depths, and how deep it is to the bedrock.

Map drainage at the household level

Having noted the location of a house with respect to the overall slope topography and drainage patterns, try to establish whether there is any evidence of how these factors may have an impact at the household scale. Incorporate into the map areas that exhibit

- saturation or seepage—evidenced by water-demanding plants, moss, mildewed concrete, saturated soil, water flowing from cut slopes, damp or flooded foundations;

- overland flow (surface runoff)—flattened vegetation and grasses, debris and rubbish carried and deposited by surface flows, eroded soils, undermined buildings and paths;

- natural, manmade, or diverted drainage routes—concrete and earth drains, enhanced flow paths such as footpaths, blocked drainage routes; and

- point water sources—leaking water pipes, household water.

Identify where the household gray water goes

Vulnerable unauthorized communities may have a piped water supply but typically no drainage provision. This situation represents a potentially significant landslide hazard driver that should be carefully reviewed throughout the community, since unmanaged surface water can be a major trigger for slope instability.

Some households may discharge gray water directly onto the slope (figure 5.14), while others will discharge water into a functional concrete block drain. Both cases should be indicated on the community slope feature map.

Potential drainage hazards

Households in vulnerable communities will often undertake unauthorized construction work—that is, works that do not comply with planning regulations, structural design practices, and building codes.

Map any evidence of such structures that could affect slope drainage or stability. For example, poorly constructed or single-skin

FIGURE 5.14 Potential landslide hazard driver: Household roof and gray water discharged directly onto slopes

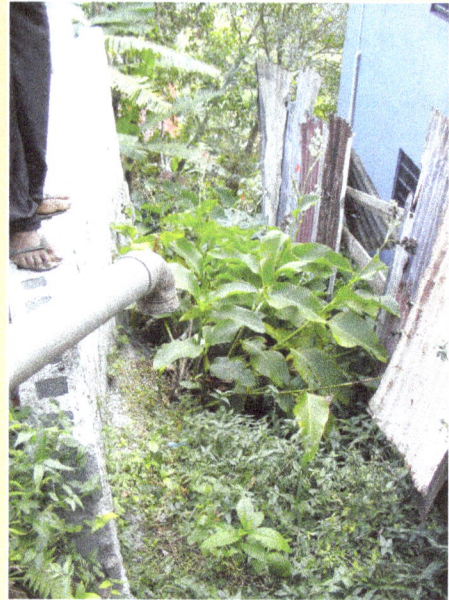

a. Water-demanding plants (dasheen, center) indicate saturated soil near gray water outflow.

b. Stagnant water on the lower slopes of a populated hillside indicates soil saturation.

c. Shower and laundry water goes straight into the ground.

Note: Map all sources of household water; a MoSSaiC intervention should capture as much of this water as possible.

(single-block-thick) water tanks that could easily fail, causing not only flood damage but also slope instability downslope (figure 5.15).

FIGURE 5.15 **Potential landslide hazard driver: Failure of poorly designed and constructed water storage structure**

Summary: Household-scale contributors to instability

Table 5.4 summarizes household-scale contributors to slope instability to include in the community slope feature map.

5.4.3 Indicators of slope stability issues

Local knowledge of past landslides

Talk to as many residents as possible—especially those who have lived in the community for a long time—as they will typically recall the timing, location, and impact of any past landslides and major rainfall events. Such events have a significant effect on residents, and first-hand recollections tend to be precise, making them particularly valuable.

Evidence of slope movement: Slope features

Typical indicators of slope movement include the following:

- Undulating or unusual slope profile indicative of previously disturbed material

- Cracks in the slope (tension cracks), which would indicate recent movement

- Unsorted slope materials—soils, stones, boulders, and debris mixed together

- Minor slope movement, which could precede a larger landslide event (figure 5.16).

Larger-scale indicators, such as unusual topography over a whole hillside, are not always discernible at ground level and can sometimes be identified on aerial photos and accurate topographic maps.

Evidence of slope movement: Structures

Identify and record significant cracks in structures that indicate slope movement. Try to dis-

TABLE 5.4 Household-scale contributors to slope instability to mark on slope feature map

LOOK FOR	ASK ABOUT	CAUTION	MAP
Steep-cut slopes, stepped or terraced slopes, retaining structures	How the homeowner has constructed the house, how deep the foundations are, whether bedrock was encountered, what the soil structure was like		Altered slope geometry
Exposed soil and rock		The terms people use to describe slope materials and their properties will vary	Evidence of deep or shallow soils
Main drains, unfinished drains, flow along paths, barriers to drainage, evidence of seepage	What happens when it rains, where the water flows from/to, if the ground is always wet even when it hasn't rained	Try to get residents to be precise about depths or quantities of water	Water coming from upslope
Household water sources, leaking pipes, flooding hazards		Be aware of disputes between neighbors about drainage	Point sources of water and drainage downslope

It is important to map such areas on the drainage hazard plan.

tinguish between poor construction and ground movement, since it is the latter that is of significance here.

Cracks in concrete structures (figure 5.17) may be caused by

- historic land movement;

- current land movement;

- past seismic events;

- poor construction, shallow foundations, or poorly compacted fill material; or

- a combination of all or some of the above.

It is important to distinguish between these causes when developing the slope feature map.

Look for evidence of structures (such as buildings, fences, and retaining walls), trees and utility poles having been displaced, or

FIGURE 5.17 Cracks in a wall: Past slope instability or poor construction?

leaning. Take note of ruined houses and try to find out why they were abandoned: were they damaged by previous slope movement?

Reported landslide problems

If a landslide problem is reported at a particular house, try to determine the cause and scale of the problem.

Use the evidence collected at the hillside and household scales (described in sections 5.4.1 and 5.4.2) to look for potential causes of instability such as

- topographic and drainage convergence,
- deep or weak soils,
- drainage and point sources of water,
- landslide problems on the same hillside,
- structural clues, and
- evidence of slope movement.

Try to ascertain the scale of the unstable zone:

- Is the problem localized to the house and augmented by local factors such as drainage from the house or from a point source farther up the slope?

- Is the problem part of a wider drainage or slope stability issue that could affect more than one house?

Determine whether this is truly a landslide issue or if it has another cause. For example, is the reported problem the result of

- undermining of structures through soil erosion or flooding due to uncontrolled surface water runoff; or

- poor construction practices such as cutting a slope too steeply, not compacting the fill/foundation material sufficiently, not constructing deep enough foundations, or not using enough cement or reinforcement.

Determine whether the cause is an acute (sudden onset) destabilizing event that should be immediately addressed at the source. For example, has there been a sudden change in conditions, such as a burst pipe or rapid excavation of the slope for construction?

Summary: Evidence of instability

Table 5.5 summarizes slope instability evidence that should be sought when constructing the community slope feature map.

5.4.4 Finalizing the community slope feature map

Improve map accuracy

Augment the map with detailed information on slope angles and topography (using Abney level or similar instrument) and the location of slope features and structures (using a compass for triangulation, or a GPS receiver). Try to make the map as accurate as possible in terms of the locations, orientation, and scale of the following (figure 5.18):

- Houses
- Paths and roads (concrete and unmetaled)
- Natural drainage channels and flow paths
- Existing drains
- Other key landmarks or features.

TABLE 5.5 Slope instability evidence to mark on slope feature map

LOOK FOR	ASK ABOUT	CAUTION	MAP
Undulating or uneven topography, cracks in the ground	Recollections of landslides, recent changes in the slope, when cracks appeared, have they changed, what did this coincide with (rainfall, earthquakes, construction...)	Try to obtain several corroborating accounts	Past landslides and evidence of movement
Cracks, leaning structures		Poor construction can also result in cracks or subsidence	Structural indicators of instability
Localized causes and wider causes—use the map for evidence	When, how this occurred	Erosion and flooding may be reported as landslides	Household-scale indicators of instability

FIGURE 5.18 Example of a community slope feature map showing household-level detail

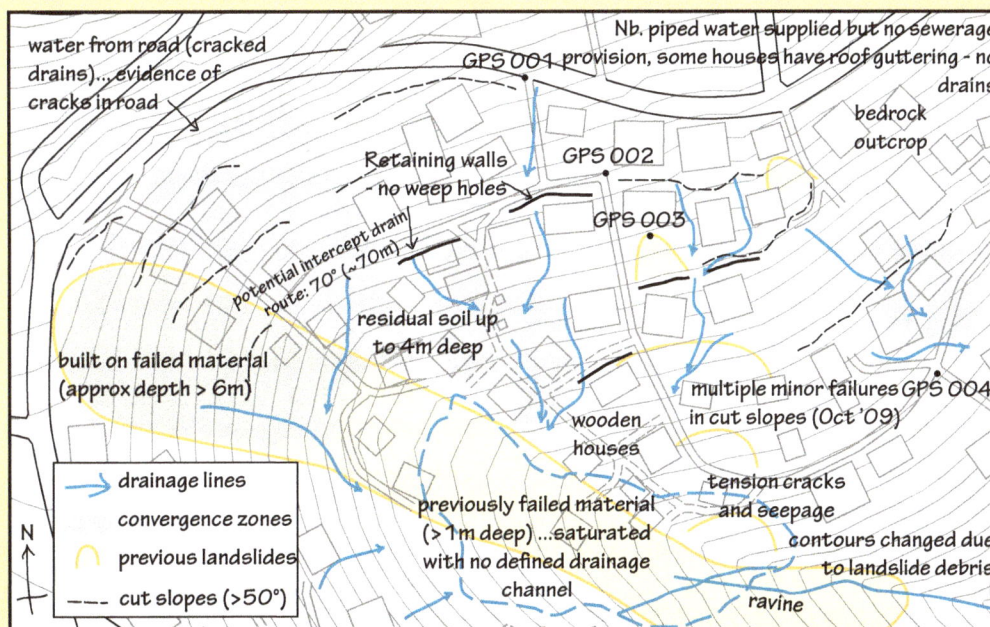

Note: See original base map (figures 4.6 and 5.7), subsequent slope process zone map (figure 5.21) and initial drainage plan (figure 5.32).

It is important that the slope feature map be accurate since it will form the basis of the initial drainage plan (section 5.7) and be used to indicate the scope of the construction works (e.g., potential drain lengths and alignments—chapters 6 and 7). Once this drainage concept has been agreed upon in principle, more precise measurements may be taken for the purpose of preparing work packages and contracts and for developing the final drainage plan for implementation.

Repeat the survey at least three times

Even for the most experienced mapping team, it will not be possible to identify or appreciate all the slope features relating to landslide hazard and drainage issues in a particular community in just one or two visits.

Undertake the mapping process over the course of at least three walk-through surveys. In particular, develop a comprehensive understanding of the relationship between the topography, soil water convergence, and other slope processes based on direct observations and information obtained from as many residents as possible.

Visit during rainfall

Rainfall events can reveal additional drainage features, providing important information for understanding potential landslide causes and configuring landslide hazard reduction measures. If at all possible, the mapping team should visit the community during or immediately after heavy rainfall to confirm that relevant drainage processes have been included in the map.

During rainfall events, observe whether surface water runoff follows the drainage lines that have already been mapped and/or whether there are additional flow routes. Look for the drains that are flowing (noting those that are flowing near, at, or over capacity) and areas of uncontrolled surface water flow or flooding. Also note the following:

- Flows along footpaths and roads

- Areas of flow convergence and concentration

- Additional evidence of seepage that was not previously visible

- Additional comments, recollections, and observations from residents that the rainfall event may prompt

Evaluate the effect of publicly supplied piped water

If houses are provided with an affordable (and reliable) piped water supply but no drains, this can significantly increase the volume of water infiltrating the slope and reduce slope stability. In densely populated urban areas, the total annual water supply to a community can sometimes equate to the total annual rainfall—effectively doubling the volume of water the slope receives.

Note whether there is a piped water supply and if households are discharging gray water directly onto the slope. Use an aerial photo or the community slope feature map (to which house locations should now have been added) to estimate the potential scale of the household gray water contribution—the denser the housing stock, the greater the proportion of surface water derived from households.

Other effects of piped water supply to include on the map include the following:

- Locations of burst or leaking water pipes

- Locations where water supply pipes have been laid in existing drainage routes affecting drain capacity or causing an obstruction (figure 5.19)

5.5 QUALITATIVE LANDSLIDE HAZARD ASSESSMENT

5.5.1 Landslide hazard assessment for MoSSaiC projects

The community slope feature map (figure 5.18) should now contain sufficient information to allow a qualitative assessment of the landslide hazard. This section provides guidelines for the initial assessment of the dominant slope

FIGURE 5.19 Piped water supplied to unauthorized communities

a. Water meters allow an estimation of the volume supplied to the community.

b. Water supply pipes may have been laid in drains for ease of installation, thus reducing drain capacity.

stability controls within a community. In particular, the landslide assessment and engineering task team should evaluate the extent to which slope instability is dominated by surface water infiltration. This will indicate whether a MoSSaiC project to improve surface water management might be effective in improving slope stability. Section 5.6 provides scientifically based tools and methods to assist in making this assessment.

Importance of justifiable measures

Providing a scientifically based justification for landslide hazard reduction measures is important for several reasons:

- Any physical works claiming to reduce landslide hazard (i.e., reduce the likelihood of landslide occurrence) should be targeted at the specific causes of the landslide hazard.

- To facilitate community participation, there should be an explanation of the science behind the proposed intervention.

- Engineers, works supervisors, and contractors will need a basis for understanding the design and specification of the works.

- Decision makers involved in funding projects and government agencies will have to be able to justify community activities and expenditures.

The qualitative landslide hazard assessment process

Figure 5.20 illustrates a typical workflow and related decisions in the interpretation of the community slope feature map. The aim is to evaluate the relative degree of landslide hazard and the potential causes and solutions, thus allowing identification of cases where MoSSaiC interventions are likely to be appropriate.

5.5.2 Identify landslide hazard zones

Begin by identifying the various slope processes, landslide hazards, and drainage zones within the community. From this, produce a

FIGURE 5.20 The qualitative landslide hazard assessment process

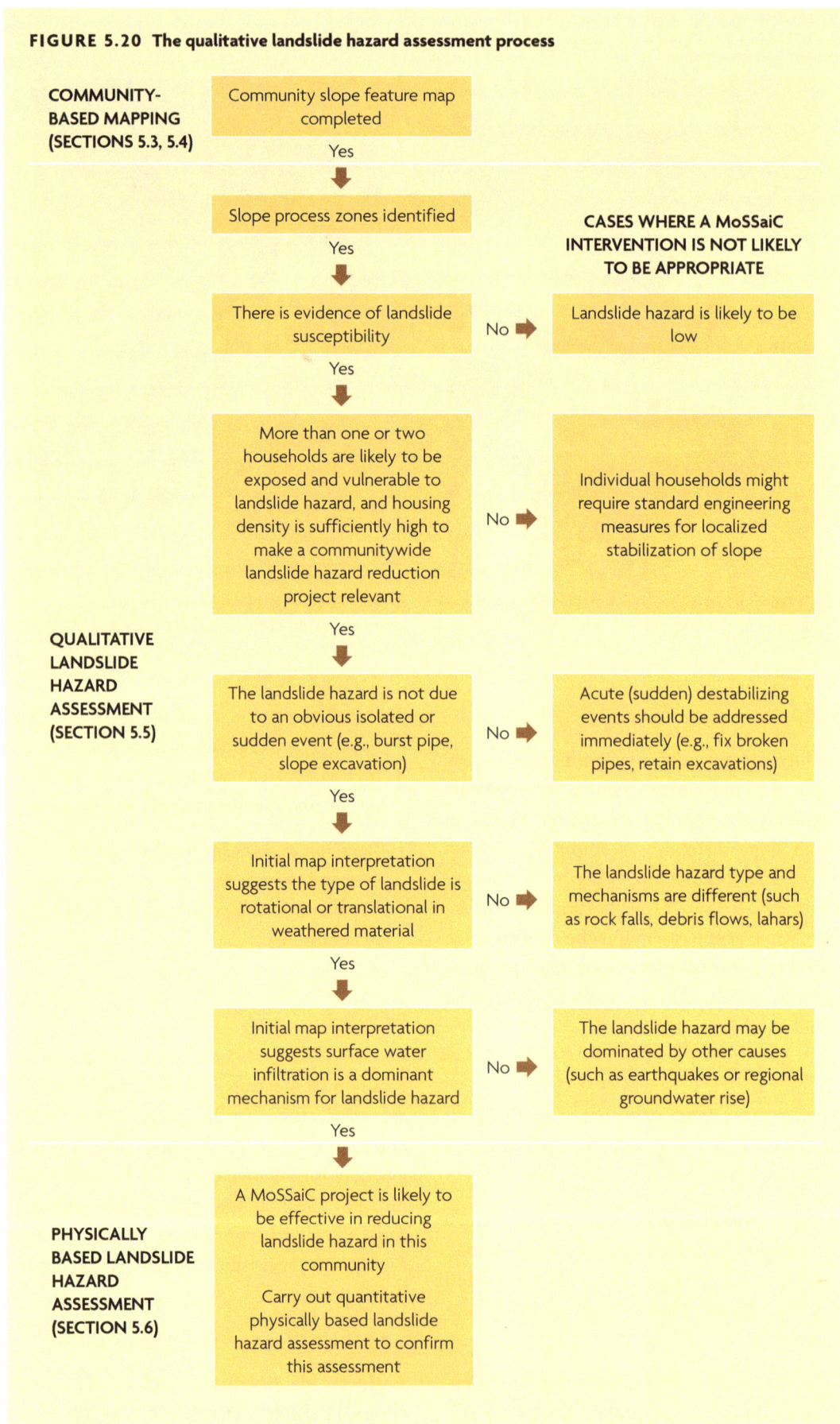

COMMUNITY-BASED MAPPING (SECTIONS 5.3, 5.4)

Community slope feature map completed

Yes ⬇

Slope process zones identified

Yes ⬇

There is evidence of landslide susceptibility

No ➡ **CASES WHERE A MoSSaiC INTERVENTION IS NOT LIKELY TO BE APPROPRIATE**

Landslide hazard is likely to be low

Yes ⬇

QUALITATIVE LANDSLIDE HAZARD ASSESSMENT (SECTION 5.5)

More than one or two households are likely to be exposed and vulnerable to landslide hazard, and housing density is sufficiently high to make a communitywide landslide hazard reduction project relevant

No ➡ Individual households might require standard engineering measures for localized stabilization of slope

Yes ⬇

The landslide hazard is not due to an obvious isolated or sudden event (e.g., burst pipe, slope excavation)

No ➡ Acute (sudden) destabilizing events should be addressed immediately (e.g., fix broken pipes, retain excavations)

Yes ⬇

Initial map interpretation suggests the type of landslide is rotational or translational in weathered material

No ➡ The landslide hazard type and mechanisms are different (such as rock falls, debris flows, lahars)

Yes ⬇

Initial map interpretation suggests surface water infiltration is a dominant mechanism for landslide hazard

No ➡ The landslide hazard may be dominated by other causes (such as earthquakes or regional groundwater rise)

Yes ⬇

PHYSICALLY BASED LANDSLIDE HAZARD ASSESSMENT (SECTION 5.6)

A MoSSaiC project is likely to be effective in reducing landslide hazard in this community

Carry out quantitative physically based landslide hazard assessment to confirm this assessment slope process zone map, based on the community slope feature map and confirmed by additional field observations.

Slope process zones typically take the following forms:

- Steep rocky slopes with no soil, relatively low landslide hazard, but significant generation of surface runoff to the slope below (from houses and during rainfall)

- Moderate slope angle, midslope position, receiving surface runoff from the slope above, with significant topographic convergence, deep soils, and high landslide hazard

- Lower slope locations, with shallower angles and deep soils, relatively low landslide hazard, but issues with saturated soils and flooding due to drainage from slopes above

- Known areas of previous instability

- Areas with no soil water convergence and perceived low landslide hazard

- Ravines and natural channels with steep banks prone to undercutting and landslides during heavy rainfall runoff events (potential for increased channel discharge if new drains are built farther up the slope).

Figure 5.21 presents a typical slope process zone map and an interpretation of the slope features shown in terms of the associated landslide hazard.

5.5.3 Identify the dominant landslide mechanisms

Many different and often highly localized processes can be involved in determining landslide hazard (chapter 3). Unauthorized construction of high-density housing on slopes changes local drainage and surface water infiltration processes and may increase the landslide hazard.

For each slope process zone, and for the slope as a whole, experts in the landslide assessment and engineering task team should have identified the physical processes likely to affect slope stability (figure 5.21). The team should

review observations of the influence of surface water infiltration including the following:

- Topographic controls on drainage

- Natural flow paths and alterations of these paths

- Seepage

- Condition and location of drains (good, broken, unconnected, poorly constructed, leaking, insufficient capacity, blocked)

- Household-scale influence on drainage patterns

- Piped water supply

- Previous rainfall-triggered landslides

- Observed effects of rainfall on the slope.

Interpret the influence of surface water infiltration on slope stability for each of the slope process zones and add to the zone description as shown in the right-hand column of table 5.6.

If the interpretation of the slope feature map and slope process zones is that surface water is a dominant mechanism for landslide hazard, this suggests a MoSSaiC drainage project would be appropriate. In table 5.6, every zone except Zone D would benefit from some form of improved surface water management to reduce landslide hazard.

The decision to implement a MoSSaiC project should only be taken if sufficient scientifically based justification can be provided. Therefore, this initial landslide hazard assessment should be tested using the tools described in section 5.6.

5.6 PHYSICALLY BASED LANDSLIDE HAZARD ASSESSMENT

5.6.1 Models

A range of quantitative, physically based models can be used to provide the scientific justification for a MoSSaiC project. It is important

FIGURE 5.21 Example of a slope process zone map with supporting observations and interpretations

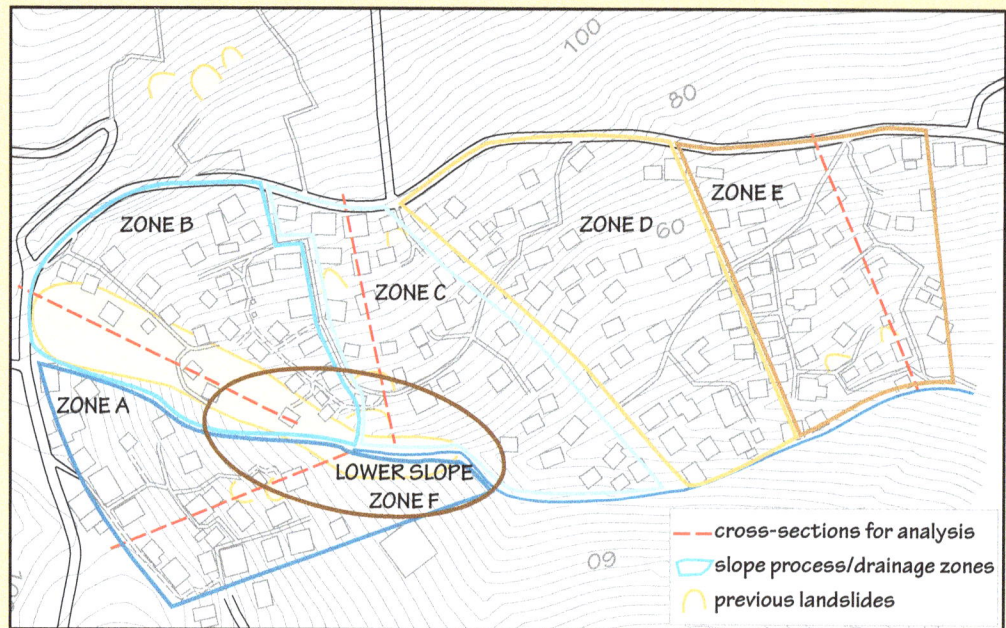

ZONE	FIELD OBSERVATIONS AND INTERPRETATION OF THE SLOPE FEATURE MAP	INITIAL INTERPRETATION OF RELATIVE LANDSLIDE HAZARD
A	Planar slope topography with multiple cut slopes and several associated minor slides Dense housing with incomplete or broken surface water drains	Moderate landslide hazard—potential for further cut slope failures
B	Highly convergent topography with previous major landslide and deep accumulation of debris. Some houses rebuilt on debris. Higher-density housing adjacent to debris—multiple cut slopes, incomplete or broken drains and retaining walls Significant surface runoff and seepage	High landslide hazard—likely reactivation of existing landslide debris by rainfall and surface runoff (several houses exposed); multiple smaller failures of cut slopes and retaining walls also likely
C	Small-scale convergent zones due to alteration of topography and drainage by house construction Multiple small slides and tension cracks Dense housing with incomplete drains and highly altered natural drainage pattern leading to convergence at multiple locations	Moderate landslide hazard—potential reactivation of failed material in multiple minor slides behind individual houses
D	Steep planar topography with very shallow soils/bedrock outcrops Significant surface runoff (including runoff from road and roofs) but relative stability	Relatively low landslide hazard
E	Small-scale convergent zones aggravated by cut slopes and altered drainage Minor cut slope failures exacerbated by discharge of roof water into soil and poorly designed drains	Moderate to high landslide hazard—in cut slopes and wider convergent zone adjacent to lower footpath
F	Lower slope—deep soils saturated by infiltration of water from upslope Tension cracks indicate instability	Moderate to high landslide hazard—likely triggering of new landslides at base of slope due to high pore pressures in saturated material

TABLE 5.6 Interpreting the influence of surface water infiltration on slope stability for different slope process zones

ZONE	FIELD OBSERVATION AND INTERPRETATION OF SLOPE FEATURE MAP	INFLUENCE OF SURFACE WATER INFILTRATION
A	Planar slope topography with multiple cut slopes and several associated minor slides Dense housing with incomplete or broken surface water drains	Household water and incomplete drainage network directly affecting slope stability at several locations
B	Highly convergent topography with previous major landslide and deep accumulation of debris. Some houses rebuilt on debris. Higher-density housing adjacent to debris—multiple cut slopes, incomplete or broken drains and retaining walls Significant surface runoff and seepage	Significant surface water runoff from upper slope area and road likely to be causing saturation of previous landslide debris Highly altered drainage network and household water causing localized instability and flooding
C	Small-scale convergent zones due to alteration of topography and drainage by house construction Multiple small slides and tension cracks Dense housing with incomplete drains and highly altered natural drainage pattern leading to convergence at multiple locations	Household water and incomplete drainage network directly affecting slope stability in areas of convergence
D	Steep planar topography with very shallow soils/bedrock outcrops Significant surface runoff (including runoff from road and roofs) but relative stability	Surface water infiltration probably not an issue for slope stability
E	Small-scale convergent zones aggravated by cut slopes and altered drainage Minor cut slope failures exacerbated by discharge of roof water into soil and poorly designed drains	Household water and incomplete drainage network directly affecting slope stability at several locations Partial reactivation of previous failures observed during rainfall
F	Lower slope—deep soils saturated by infiltration of water from upslope Tension cracks indicate instability	Surface water infiltrating upper slopes is likely to be a significant cause of instability

that the selected model can account for the roles of surface water infiltration and pore water pressure in slope stability, and be used to confirm whether improved surface water management is likely to reduce landslide hazard.

Table 5.7 identifies two types of scientific models that are relevant for assessing landslide hazard drivers. Chapter 6 introduces four additional calculations for the quantitative assessment of surface water runoff, piped water supply, roof water interception, and required drain dimensions.

The models outlined in this section will require some level of technical knowledge. The MCU should identify models that balance the need for scientific justification of a

MoSSaiC project with available expertise, data, and software.

It is worth noting that in the field of hydrology, many models are, as Lin et al. (2006) state, either "too good to be real" (the model is oversimplified and fails to reflect reality) or "too real to be good" (detailed input data requirements render the model impractical). Models are inevitably a compromise between the search for perfection, the complexity of real slopes, and the perennial availability of only at best partial data. The models identified in this book seek to achieve that balance but should be viewed alongside alternative quantitative procedures depending on local conditions of data availability and expertise.

TABLE 5.7 Quantitative physically based landslide hazard assessment models appropriate for use as part of MoSSaiC

MODEL	PURPOSE	EXAMPLE SOURCE	BOOK SECTION
Slope stability model	Simulation of the physical processes affecting slope stability Identification of dominant landslide causes Landslide hazard prediction (probability, magnitude, location)	See http://www.ggsd.com for a comprehensive listing of slope stability software	3.6.1; 5.6.3
Resistance envelope	Assessment of the role of negative pore water pressure (matric suction) in controlling slope stability	Resistance envelope calculation in Anderson, Kemp, and Lloyd (1997, 14–20)	3.6.2; 5.6.4

Note: For each purpose, many alternative tools may be applicable.

5.6.2 Data for slope stability models

Physically based slope stability software such as CHASM (Coupled Hydrology And slope Stability Model), which was introduced in section 3.6.1, is designed to enable assessment of the stability of a slope and to identify the underlying hydrological and geotechnical process controls.

Whatever form of slope stability analysis is used, it is likely that three groups of input data will be needed: slope cross-section configuration, soil and weathered slope material geotechnical and hydraulic properties, and sources of water added to the slope.

For each group of data, table 5.8 lists typical parameters required for slope stability analysis. These data will need to be estimated, collected, or measured in three ways:

- *Community mapping process*—e.g., slope angles and distances along the cross-section selected for analysis, evidence of soil and water table depths, weathering grades of exposed materials

- *Desk study*—review of previous reports and scientific or engineering texts; e.g., local rainfall records, water supply records, typical soil geotechnical and hydraulic characteristics for relevant weathering grades

- *Additional laboratory and field measurements*—e.g., detailed survey of slope cross-section using a total station or similar equipment, sampling and shear box testing of soils.

Figure 5.22 shows a typical slope selected for stability analysis. Note the density of vegetation and housing which obscures the slope features and ground surface. Engineers and technicians should not be deterred by this apparent complexity. Much of the initial data required for landslide hazard analysis is often readily estimated during the community mapping stage. For a more detailed discussion of each of these parameters, see section 3.5.

5.6.3 Using slope stability models

Various slope stability assessment methods were introduced in chapter 3. Deterministic models based on limit equilibrium methods were highlighted as an accessible and appropriate tool for use at the community scale. Such models can help engineers identify the current slope stability state, the dominant physical mechanisms causing instability, and the potential effectiveness of slope drainage measures. The following four steps (after Holcombe et al. 2011) have been successfully applied in using CHASM for this purpose:

TABLE 5.8 Typical input parameters and their measurement for slope stability analysis

PARAMETER		SIMPLE ESTIMATION METHOD	MORE PRECISE MEASUREMENT METHOD
SLOPE CROSS-SECTION CONFIGURATION	Slope profile geometry	Abney level measurement Contour maps	Detailed topographic survey Existing high-resolution digital elevation models (e.g., generated using LiDAR)
	Soil depths and strata	On-site inspection of any exposed soils and bedrock Talk with residents who may have knowledge of soil strata depths, especially if they have carried out excavations for house construction	Search for any previous detailed reports from geotechnical engineers that might give borehole data from the area Carry out bore-hole analysis
	Depth to water table	On-site inspection of any seepage from the slope Talk with residents who may have knowledge of depth to water table	Search for any previous reports that might contain field determinations of depth to water table
SOIL AND WEATHERED SLOPE MATERIAL GEOTECHNICAL AND HYDRAULIC PROPERTIES	Material strength	On-site inspection to identify material weathering grade as a guide to relative material strength. Comparison with grade-strength relationships in research or engineering reports/textbooks See Fookes (1997); GCO (1982)	Search for any previous reports of the area that might contain laboratory or field determinations of soil strength in terms of cohesion (c') and phi (Φ') (see figure 5.27) Take samples of the material and carry out shear box testing in a laboratory.
	Material hydraulic properties	On-site inspection to identify material weathering grade as a guide to relative material permeability Comparison with grade-permeability relationships in research or engineering reports/textbooks See Ahmad, Yahaya, and Farooqi (2006); Carter and Bentley (1991)	Search for any previous reports of the area that might contain laboratory or field determinations of hydraulic conductivity (K_{sat}) and suction-moisture curves Idealized curves can be found in many standard soil science or engineering textbooks (Anderson et al. 1985; van Genuchten 1980)
SOURCES OF WATER ADDED TO SLOPE	Piped water	On-site inspection and information from residents to estimate relative contribution of piped water compared with rainfall Aerial or satellite photographs to enable calculation of housing density, and hence potential contribution of piped water	Obtain water company data on average supply per household over a specific time period; multiply by the number of households in the community to obtain the total amount of water supplied to the slope for that period
	Rainfall	Use records of a specific rainfall event known to have caused landslides in the local area	Obtain rainfall intensity/duration/frequency data to allow design storms to be specified (e.g., 1-in-100-year 24-hour event with an intensity of 12 mm/h)

FIGURE 5.22 Typical slope selected for stability analysis

regardless of the software selected, the steps described here should assist in the model application.

Step 1: Build the input files for the simulation

On the plan, identify the location of slope cross-sections selected for analysis. Two sections have been identified in the example in figure 5.23. Section X_1-X_2 encompasses several houses in an area identified during the mapping process to be potentially susceptible to a single large landslide. Y_1-Y_2 represents part of the slope in which there was drainage conver-

FIGURE 5.23 Zone E of the example community with two slope cross-sections marked for analysis

concrete house
concrete + wooden house
wooden house
roads, paths, or steps
existing landslides
cross-sections for analysis

road

N

ravine

approx   50 m

Note: See figure 5.21.

gence and several cut slopes that showed signs of instability. The following considers the example of section X_1-X_2.

a. Draw the slope cross-section.

— Draw the slope cross-section to scale by reading contours from an accurate topography map or by using field measurements and applying trigonometry.

— Identify how many material types are present (ranging from weathering grade VI to grade I material—i.e., residual soils to bedrock, figure 3.18) based on observations, residents' knowledge, local expert knowledge, and previous reports.

— Estimate the depth and angle of the different material strata—again using observations, residents' knowledge, local expert knowledge, and previous reports. Draw the strata on the cross-section.

— Estimate the depth to the water table in a similar way and add to the cross-section.

— If CHASM software is used, these data are encapsulated in the geometry input file.

b. Define the material geotechnical and hydraulic properties.

— Define the properties required by the model for each of the material types identified in the slope cross-section.

— If CHASM software is used, the data requirements are as follows: saturated and unsaturated bulk density, saturated moisture content, cohesion, angle of internal friction, and suction-moisture curve coordinates. These data are encapsulated in the soil input file.

c. Define the boundary conditions.

— In dynamic hydrology models, the hydrological boundary conditions represent the initial conditions and the behavior of the water at the edge of the model domain. Boundary conditions can include initial surface suction conditions, rainfall, point water sources, evaporation rates, and groundwater flow.

— Rainfall conditions should be defined for each simulation time-step according to the particular scenario to be tested. Typically, the modeler will define an initial dry period to allow the model hydrology to become numerically stable, and then impose a design storm of a known intensity, duration, and return period.

See chapter 3 (section 3.6.1) for further guidance.

Step 2: Run the model to simulate current stability conditions

Simulate the effect of the chosen rainfall event on the stability of the slope. If possible, first run a rainfall scenario that is known to have caused previous landslides at this location. Verify that the model represents the slope processes realistically by carrying out a back analysis—examining water table changes, pore water pressure patterns, and factor of safety response. If the simulations do not appear physically realistic, check the input data and account for any uncertainties (see section 5.6.5).

Once satisfied with the model behavior, run a sequence of rainfall events of increasing intensity or duration to determine the associated factor of safety. A factor of safety of less than 1 implies potential slope failure. Record the minimum frequency rainfall event that is predicted to cause a landslide and the position of the resultant failure surfaces (figure 5.24).

Step 3: Plot predicted landslides on the map

If the analysis is carried out using CHASM or a similar limit equilibrium-based model, the slope and any landslides are likely to be represented in two dimensions (i.e., a cross-section of the slope). Mark the location of the crest and toe of any predicted landslides on the community map and estimate the width of the main body of the landslide (figure 5.25) using field observations of topographic or geological features that would constrain the landslide geometry.

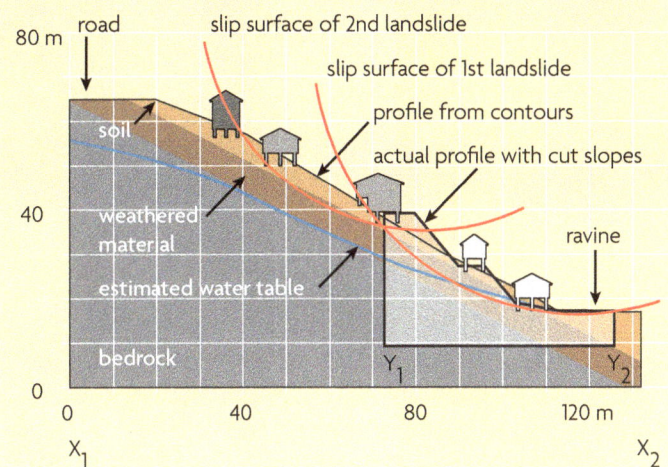

FIGURE 5.24 Model configuration and predicted location of landslides

Limit equilibrium slope stability models do not account for the dynamics of landslide runout. Landslide runout (travel distance) can be estimated using empirical relationships (see Finlay, Mostyn, and Fell 1999 for a simplified method for cut slope failures) or local expert knowledge.

Step 4: Run simulations for different drainage scenarios

If the model indicates that the slope has an unacceptable level of landslide hazard (in terms of probability or magnitude), the next step is to try to identify measures that might reduce this hazard.

Based on the earlier qualitative assessment of the role of surface water infiltration for the relevant zone of the community (table 5.6), run the model with different surface water management options:

- **Interception of rainfall runoff,** represented as a percentage reduction in rainfall—based on an estimation of how much runoff could be intercepted by new drains

- **Rainwater capture from roofs,** also represented as a percentage reduction in rainfall—based on the area of roofs covering the slope (e.g., if houses cover 50 percent of the slope, then assume that completely effective rainwater capture will reduce the rainfall reaching the slope surface by 50 percent)

FIGURE 5.25 Predicted landslide locations and estimated runout

- concrete house
- concrete + wooden house
- wooden house
- roads, paths, or steps
- existing landslides
- cross-sections for analysis
- predicted landslides X_1-X_2
- predicted houses lost
- predicted houses damaged and possessions lost

approx   50 m

Note: House construction types and locations allow very basic estimation of impact.

- *Capture of household gray water (piped water),* represented by a reduction in the volume of water discharged onto the slope from household point water sources.

Compare the change in the factor of safety for each of the surface water management scenarios. Figure 5.26 illustrates the effect of a

FIGURE 5.26 Predicted improvements in the factor of safety for different drainage interventions

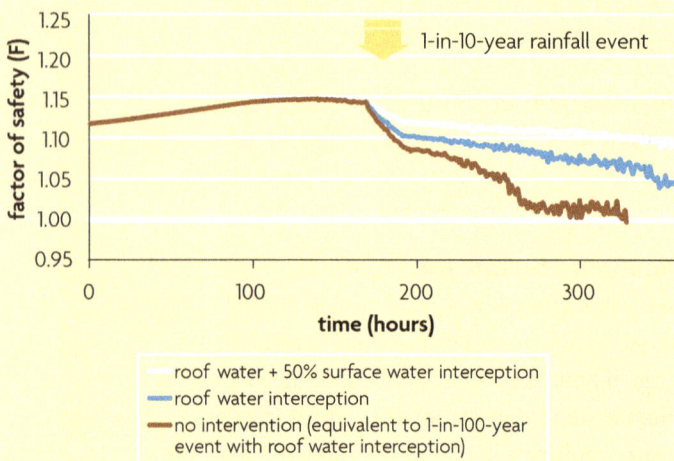

1-in-10-year rainfall event

roof water + 50% surface water interception
roof water interception
no intervention (equivalent to 1-in-100-year event with roof water interception)

1-in-10-year 24-hour rainfall on the factor of safety at cross-section X_1-X_2, where $F \leq 1$ indicates slope failure for the no intervention case. Surface water management in this example increases the factor of safety to 1.1 (marginally stable); that is, to make the slope fail would require a 1-in-100-year rainfall event.

5.6.4 Analyzing the role of pore water pressure

Negative soil pore water pressures can help maintain slope stability in certain soils found in the tropics. Loss of negative pore pressures due to rainfall infiltration can therefore potentially reduce slope stability. It is important to understand the response of a particular soil to infiltration to assess whether the stability of a slope requires the maintenance of negative pore pressures or whether the slope is stable for a certain level of positive pore pressures. Resistance envelopes allow such a determination to be made (for method, see section 3.6.2), thereby helping the team determine whether surface water management is an appropriate strategy for improving slope stability.

5.6.5 Uncertainty in physically based landslide hazard assessment

There are limitations and uncertainties associated with the application of slope stability models and resistance envelopes: "In soil mechanics the accuracy of computed results never exceeds that of a crude estimate, and the principle function of the theory exists in teaching us what and how to observe in the field" (Terzaghi 1936, 13). Some of these issues are described below (after Christian, Ladd, and Baecher 1994; Malkawi, Hassan, and Abdulla 2000; Sidle, Pearce, and O'Loughlin 1985).

- Representation of slope parameters (especially with respect to the slope material)

  — A high degree of natural anisotropy and heterogeneity in soil and weathered material properties (i.e., bulk density, strata depth and geometry, geotechnical and hydraulic parameters) means that the precise spatially distributed values for these properties cannot be fully known.

  — Each modeler will configure soil parameters differently given different methods of data collection, analysis, and interpretation.

- Representation of physical processes

  — Static slope stability analysis methods do not account for dynamic slope hydrology.

  — Temporal changes such as the effects of deforestation or downslope creep on soil strength are difficult to estimate and incorporate.

  — Detailed knowledge of the principle factors leading to failure may be lacking, especially with respect to local factors affecting pore water conditions.

  — Postfailure deformation, movement, and deposition of the failed material (runout) are difficult to represent.

  — Most landslide models represent three-dimensional phenomena in two dimensions.

  — The process of dividing a slope profile into a mesh of discrete elements and solving physics-based equations at discrete time-steps results in an approximation of physical reality.

  — Physics-based equations incorporated into a dynamic model will often exhibit rounding errors.

  — Interactions between model components and sensitivities to different parameters are not always known or predictable.

Acknowledging sources of uncertainty is a central element in correctly interpreting physically based numerical models. Be careful not to overinterpret simulation results. Physically based numerical models rely on spatial and temporal data that may be difficult to acquire, so assumptions of both data input and model structure have to be made. Thus, as Fellin et al. (2004, 14) note, "results from the most sophisticated contemporary models will remain 'crude estimates.'"

Two specific areas of uncertainty of which the landslide assessment and engineering task team should be aware are discussed below: uncertainty in soil parameters and uncertainty associated with model formulation.

Uncertainty in soil parameters

Soil properties lack uniformity, even within soils of the same type or weathering grade. Figure 5.27 shows variations in material strength properties (cohesion and angle of internal friction) which have been measured using a shear box and classified by weathering grade. This plot was derived by consolidating data from numerous materials reports from a small island state in the Caribbean, and shows the degree of variability that can exist within single material weathering grades.

The cohesion and angle of internal friction values throughout a slope can only be determined at a small number of locations compared to the number of potential cells a model is capable of representing (0.1 percent repre-

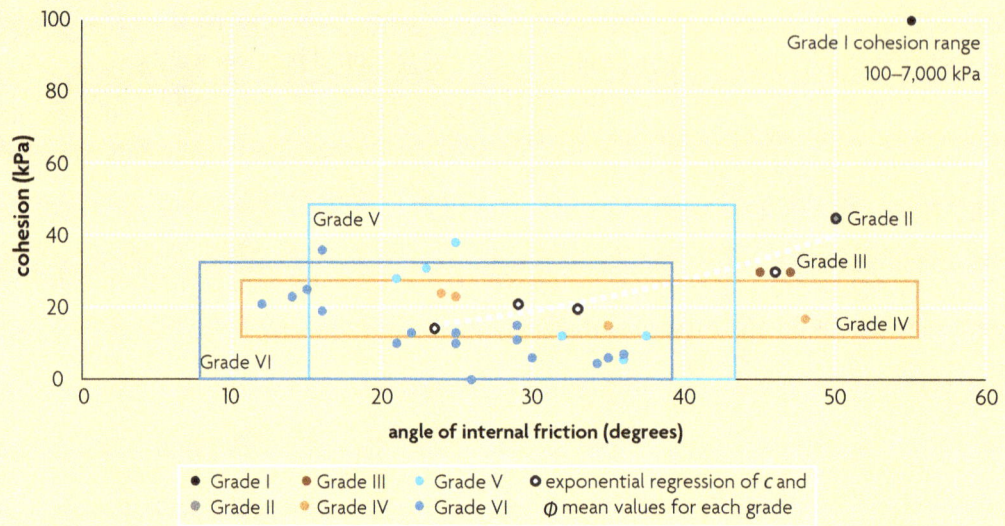

FIGURE 5.27 Example of heterogeneity in angle of internal friction and cohesion, classified by weathering grade

Note: For weathering Grades IV, V, and VI, the boxes represent 2 standard deviations from the respective grade means.

sentation would be a high value). Uncertainty in model parameters must be recognized if models are used for inferential purposes (see Anderson and Bates 2001 for a more substantive discussion on model validation).

A second source of uncertainty in soil properties derives from the fact that experts will interpret soil data differently when selecting parameters for stability analysis. In a study by Fellin et al. (2004), a set of four soil strength values, determined from four different samples of the same soil type and location, were given to 90 geotechnical engineers. Each engineer was asked to select the characteristic shear strength parameters to use in a stability analysis. The friction angle deemed to be characteristic ranged from 25 degrees to 35 degrees (figure 5.28), while the range in cohesion was from 0 to 27 kN m^{-2} (with a modal group of 10 kN m^{-2}). Thus, even with soil data available, the interpretation and final selection of a parameter value can differ quite appreciably among experts.

Uncertainty associated with model formulation

Increasingly complex models are being developed for geotechnical analysis. However complex a slope stability model is, it remains

FIGURE 5.28 Number of geotechnical engineers selecting various friction angles as characteristic for a given set of soil strength data

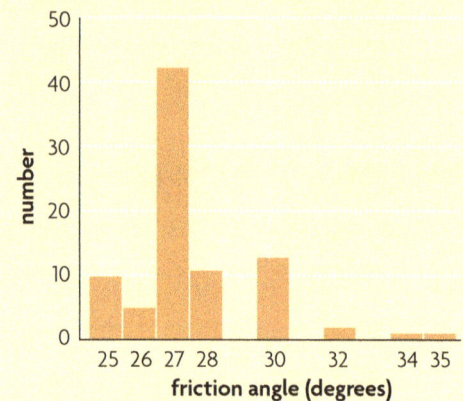

Source: Fellin et al. 2004.

a specific formulation and approximation of the processes it seeks to represent. Even if the input data for a slope stability model are specified exactly, the predictions of that model can be expected to deviate from reality for the reasons given at the beginning of this subsection.

There are many choices to be made in model design, including which failure mechanisms to employ, what space-time resolution to use, and how to represent unsaturated soil water conditions. There can thus be multiple feasible versions of reality (see Beven 2006 for a full discussion of this issue) and many models from which to choose. Moreover, modelers almost never declare a model to be invalidated, since most models have enough adjustable parameters to fit the available observed data. The modeler must then distinguish between an apparent fit, based on artificial manipulation of an overparameterized model, and one based on an accurate representation of process (NRC 1990).

Representing uncertainty

Data and model uncertainty can be represented in simulations by repeatedly running the model using a range of input parameters values to reflect parameter uncertainty. In slope stability modeling, such multiple realizations yield a distribution of factor of safety values and related outputs (figure 5.29).

For a given test slope and a sophisticated representation of uncertainty relating to all the model parameters, Rubio, Hall, and Anderson (2004) showed that CHASM yielded a factor of safety distribution in the range of 1.0– 1.8. Significantly, the variance in the effective angle of internal friction dominated the variance in factor of safety (accounting for 89 percent of the variance). Thus, while individual components of these models (such as the unsaturated zone water retention, or the Bishop slope stability submodels in CHASM) are generally well understood, their emergent behavior may be more difficult to diagnose.

The MCU, in general, and the landslide assessment and engineering task team, in particular, must be aware of the issues entailed in slope stability model selection, data uncertainty, and the associated model outcome interpretation. It might be useful to hold a workshop at which colleagues can contribute relevant data sources, understand data uncertainty, appreciate the consequential uncertainty in numerical modeling, and share experiences in running software (figure 5.30).

FIGURE 5.29 Effect of soil parameter variability on CHASM simulation results

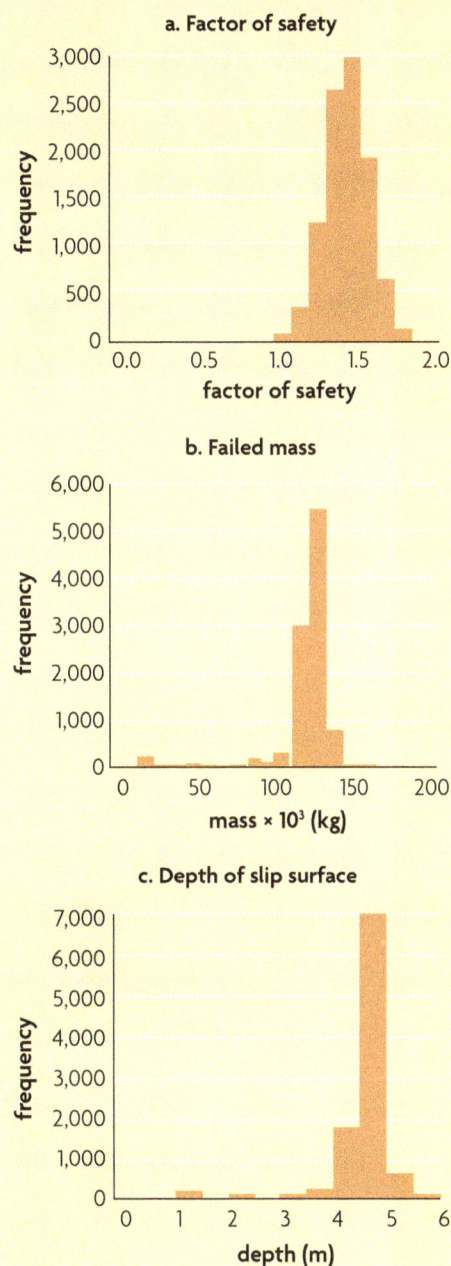

Source: Hamm, Hall, and Anderson 2006.

5.6.6 Interpreting physically based landslide hazard assessment results

For MoSSaiC, the objective of using physically based slope stability assessment methods is to confirm the degree of landslide hazard affecting a specific zone of the community and to investigate the main causes and potential solutions. In particular, these assessment methods should be used to confirm or reject the hypoth-

FIGURE 5.30 Slope stability modeling workshop for landslide assessment and engineering task team

esis that surface water infiltration is the dominant destabilizing influence, thereby demonstrating the potential effectiveness of rainfall interception and surface water management measures as a means of reducing that hazard. Table 5.9 summarizes this approach.

This landslide hazard assessment process is an iterative one. The simplest approach is to take a known major storm event, run the slope stability model for that event, and then again with 75 percent, and again with 50 percent, of recorded rainfall levels. Simply put, the resulting change (potential increase) in the factor of safety will provide a broad indication of whether such reductions in surface water infiltration would be likely to result in a significant reduction in landslide hazard. If the simulations indicate no apparent reduction in hazard (no increase in the factor of safety), this would suggest that a MoSSaiC intervention would probably not be appropriate. Conversely, a significant increase in the factor of safety when effective rainfall is reduced would

TABLE 5.9 Summary of the physically based landslide hazard assessment process

LOOK FOR	METHOD	CAUTION	UNCERTAINTY
Quantitative, physically based methods, models, and expertise already available locally	Ask government departments, agencies, consultants, and colleges or universities	Select a method that accounts for the relevant slope processes (landslide type, material type, hydrological processes)	Be aware of uncertainties due to the way the model represents (or omits) physical processes
Slope data that can realistically be acquired for the available methods and models	Acquire data on slope geometry, soil strata, water table, soil properties, water supply (see table 5.8)	Make sure that the method or model selected is realistic in terms of data availability and level of expertise	Be aware of natural parameter variability, sampling, and measurement errors (or biases) and differences in expert opinion
The current slope stability state and the physical processes that have the greatest influence on stability	Assess stability with respect to different conditions; use rainfall events ranging from those expected to occur every year to more intense or longer-duration events with lower return periods	Be aware of the effect that the results of this analysis could have when made known to local residents, landowners, government representatives, and the media; use appropriate safeguards.	Represent uncertainty by applying the method or model several times with varying input parameters; be honest in communicating the level of uncertainty in model results
The potential effectiveness of surface water management for reducing landslide hazard (look for improved slope stability, lower water table in the model)	Account for the likely effect of rainfall runoff interception (by drains and roof guttering) and reduction in household gray water added to the slope	To incorporate these surface water management approaches, it may be necessary to use a proxy (such as reducing rainfall input by a certain percentage)	Represent uncertainty in the effectiveness of surface water management measures by applying the method or model several times with varying reductions in rainfall and point water sources

indicate that a MoSSaiC intervention could be appropriate.

The landslide assessment and engineering task team should communicate the results of the quantitative landslide hazard assessment clearly to the MCU so that nonexperts can understand and make decisions about the project. Be transparent about uncertainties in the specific values of slope factor of safety or percentage changes in stability for different drainage interventions. Importantly, identify the overall trends in the model results to convey whether surface water infiltration is a significant driver for the landslide hazard, and whether drains would be likely to improve slope stability.

If physically based simulations support a MoSSaiC intervention, continue to use the model to determine the specific impact of surface water management. Chapter 6 details the components of such an intervention: the various configurations of contour (intercept) drains and downslope drains; and the installation of downpipes, guttering, gray water drain pipes, and related infrastructure. Once a detailed drainage design has been undertaken, the simulations can be rerun with more precise rainfall reduction figures that reflect anticipated rainfall capture data.

5.7 PRIORITIZE ZONES FOR DRAINAGE INTERVENTIONS

If the quantitative, physically based landslide hazard analysis indicates that a MoSSaiC project is appropriate, the next step is to prioritize zones of the community for specific drainage measures. The landslide assessment and engineering task team should integrate all the information generated by the mapping and modeling processes described in this chapter:

- Hillside-scale slope features and processes (topography, slope angles, locations of deeper soils versus bedrock, convergence zones, major natural and altered drainage lines, evidence of past or potential landslides)

- Household-scale features and influences on slope processes (local slope geometry—cuts, fills, and retaining structures, household-scale drainage lines and point water sources, evidence of previous or potential landslides)

- Quantitative landslide hazard assessments (slope stability modeling, analysis of the effect of piped water and rainfall, assessment of suction control).

Building on the initial qualitative landslide hazard assessment process outlined in figure 5.20, figure 5.31 consolidates and presents the complete landslide hazard assessment and decision-making process described in this chapter.

The final phase of the community-based landslide hazard mapping process described in this subsection entails the following:

- For each of the slope process and landslide hazard zones in the community, confirming the potential surface water management option likely to be most effective in improving the slope stability and drainage issues within each hillside zone

- Sketching potential new drain locations on an initial drainage plan and taking photos of these locations

- Assigning priorities to the various drainage interventions based on relative landslide hazard and likely effectiveness

- Gaining consensus from all stakeholders on the initial drainage plan.

5.7.1 Assign a potential drainage intervention to each zone

Each landslide hazard and drainage zone will require a slightly different intervention to reduce landslide hazard; some zones may not need any intervention at all.

The community needs to understand the rationale behind the identification of the different zones, and therefore the purpose and suitability of the different categories of intervention proposed for each zone. Some areas of

FIGURE 5.31 Complete community-based landslide hazard assessment process for MoSSaiC interventions

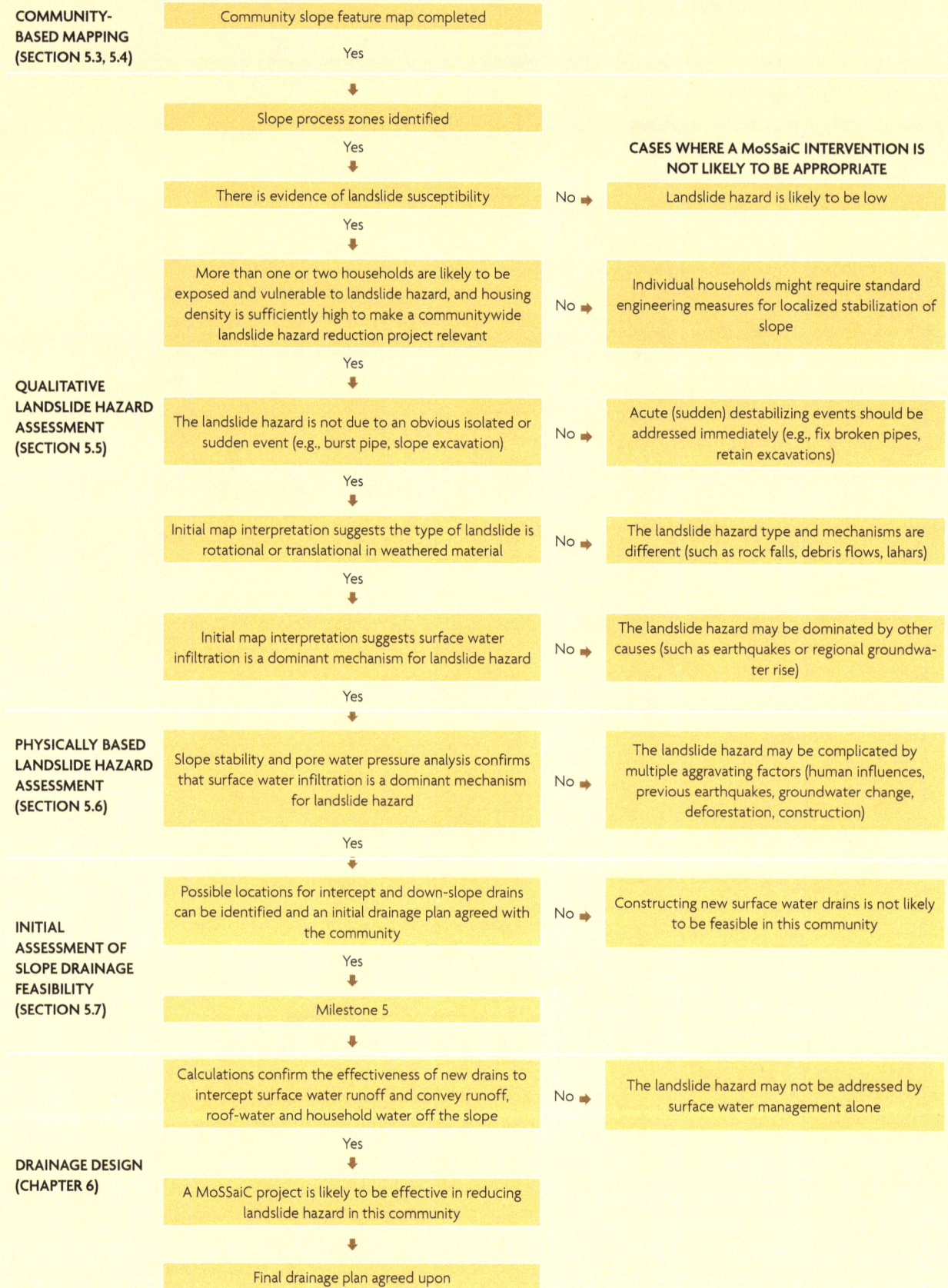

COMMUNITY-BASED MAPPING (SECTION 5.3, 5.4)	Community slope feature map completed	
	Yes ↓	
	Slope process zones identified	**CASES WHERE A MoSSaiC INTERVENTION IS NOT LIKELY TO BE APPROPRIATE**
	Yes ↓	
	There is evidence of landslide susceptibility — No →	Landslide hazard is likely to be low
	Yes ↓	
QUALITATIVE LANDSLIDE HAZARD ASSESSMENT (SECTION 5.5)	More than one or two households are likely to be exposed and vulnerable to landslide hazard, and housing density is sufficiently high to make a communitywide landslide hazard reduction project relevant — No →	Individual households might require standard engineering measures for localized stabilization of slope
	Yes ↓	
	The landslide hazard is not due to an obvious isolated or sudden event (e.g., burst pipe, slope excavation) — No →	Acute (sudden) destabilizing events should be addressed immediately (e.g., fix broken pipes, retain excavations)
	Yes ↓	
	Initial map interpretation suggests the type of landslide is rotational or translational in weathered material — No →	The landslide hazard type and mechanisms are different (such as rock falls, debris flows, lahars)
	Yes ↓	
	Initial map interpretation suggests surface water infiltration is a dominant mechanism for landslide hazard — No →	The landslide hazard may be dominated by other causes (such as earthquakes or regional groundwater rise)
	Yes ↓	
PHYSICALLY BASED LANDSLIDE HAZARD ASSESSMENT (SECTION 5.6)	Slope stability and pore water pressure analysis confirms that surface water infiltration is a dominant mechanism for landslide hazard — No →	The landslide hazard may be complicated by multiple aggravating factors (human influences, previous earthquakes, groundwater change, deforestation, construction)
	Yes ↓	
INITIAL ASSESSMENT OF SLOPE DRAINAGE FEASIBILITY (SECTION 5.7)	Possible locations for intercept and down-slope drains can be identified and an initial drainage plan agreed with the community — No →	Constructing new surface water drains is not likely to be feasible in this community
	Yes ↓	
	Milestone 5	
	↓	
DRAINAGE DESIGN (CHAPTER 6)	Calculations confirm the effectiveness of new drains to intercept surface water runoff and convey runoff, roof-water and household water off the slope — No →	The landslide hazard may not be addressed by surface water management alone
	Yes ↓	
	A MoSSaiC project is likely to be effective in reducing landslide hazard in this community	
	↓	
	Final drainage plan agreed upon	

the community will appear to benefit directly from large-scale interventions (e.g., construction of main drains); others will see less construction activity, even though they might still benefit from the overall reduction in surface water infiltration. The project rationale should thus be reiterated: the intervention is designed to improve drainage and reduce landslide hazard for the **whole community and slope**, rather than for individual houses.

It might be appropriate to consider several categories of intervention for a particular community. Be sure to describe these categories clearly and simply, so they are readily distinguishable from one another and easily understood by community residents. Following are some examples:

1. Construction of contour (intercept) drains to capture surface water runoff

2. Construction of downslope drains to convey water off the slope

3. Repair of existing drains

4. Installation of roof guttering and gray water pipes to capture water from houses

5. Construction of rip-rap to protect natural channels or gabion baskets to retain steep sections of slope

Referring to the above example categories, table 5.10 illustrates how different drainage interventions may be appropriate in different slope process zones for improving slope stability.

5.7.2 Draw an initial drainage plan

Go back into the community with the slope process zone map and summary of potential drainage measures and, in each zone, identify possible locations for any new drains. Draw these on a fresh plan of the community (figure 5.32) and take photographs of key locations to enable easy identification of the drainage routes or any potential problems. Be fully aware of safeguards regarding landownership, compensation for trees or land, and any other relevant issues.

Drawing potential drain locations on photographs is especially useful in fostering discussion with community residents and in presentations at community meetings. Figure 5.33 presents an annotated photo that should be

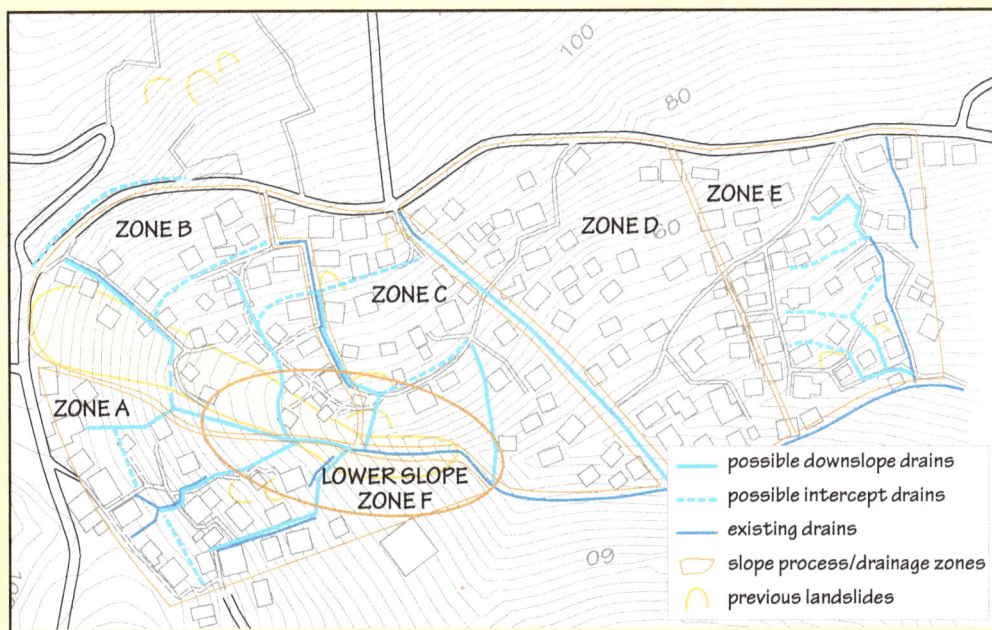

FIGURE 5.32 Example of an initial drainage plan

FIGURE 5.33 Proposed midslope intercept drain alignment

linked to the initial community drainage plan using GPS coordinates or descriptions of the precise location.

5.7.3 Assign priorities to the different zones

To assist in decision making and budgeting, each of the zones and interventions should be assigned a priority rank based on the relative landslide hazard and potential effectiveness of the proposed intervention. Table 5.11 illustrates a helpful way of summarizing this infor-

TABLE 5.10 Illustrative slope process zones and associated potential drainage measures

ZONE	FIELD OBSERVATION AND INTERPRETATION OF SLOPE FEATURE MAP	DESCRIPTION OF EFFECTIVE DRAINAGE INTERVENTIONS (CATEGORIES 1–5)
A	Planar slope topography with multiple cut slopes and several associated minor slides Dense housing with incomplete or broken surface water drains	Rationalization of household drainage network to prevent convergence at cut slope locations (1, 2, 3) Roof water capture (4).
B	Highly convergent topography with previous major landslide and deep accumulation of debris; some houses rebuilt on debris Higher-density housing adjacent to debris—multiple cut slopes, incomplete or broken drains and retaining walls Significant surface runoff and seepage	Fixing road drain (3); interception of surface water runoff on upper slope area (1) Rationalization of household drainage network to prevent convergence at cut slope locations (1, 2, 3, 4)
C	Small-scale convergent zones due to alteration of topography and drainage by house construction Multiple small slides and tension cracks Dense housing with incomplete drains and highly altered natural drainage pattern leading to convergence at multiple locations	Rationalization of household drainage and chaotic drainage network to prevent convergence at cut slope locations (1, 2, 3) Roof water capture (4)
D	Steep planar topography with very shallow soils/bedrock outcrops Significant surface runoff (including from road and roofs) but relative stability	Drainage would not significantly improve stability but could be implemented to reduce flooding (1, 2)
E	Small-scale convergent zones aggravated by cut slopes and altered drainage Minor cut slope failures exacerbated by discharge of roof water into soil and poorly designed drains	Rationalization of household drainage and chaotic drainage network to prevent convergence at cut slope locations (1, 2, 3) Roof water capture (4)
F	Lower slope—deep soils saturated by infiltration of water from upslope Tension cracks indicate instability	Interception of surface water in upper slopes is likely to lower the water table in this zone and hence improve stability; existing ravine channel subject to erosion, flooding, siltation, and meandering—requires channelization and protection due to projected increased discharge from new drains (5)

Note: See section 5.7.1 for descriptions of example drainage intervention categories 1–5

TABLE 5.11 Illustrative prioritization of different drainage interventions in each of the zones

CATEGORY OF INTERVENTION	ZONE					
	A	B	C	D	E	F
1. Construct intercept drains to capture surface water runoff	✓	✓	✓	✓	✓	
2. Construct downslope drains to convey the water off the slope	✓	✓	✓	✓	✓	
3. Mend or repair existing drains and connections	✓	✓	✓		✓	
4. Install roof guttering and gray water pipes to capture water from houses	✓	✓	✓			✓
5. Construct rip-rap to protect channels or gabion baskets to retain slopes						✓
Minor or no intervention needed				✓		
Priority	High	Very high	High	Low	Medium	Medium

Note: See figure 5.21 and tables 5.6 and 5.10 for descriptions of the zones.

mation as a matrix of zones, intervention types, and priorities (this is derived from information presented in figure 5.21 and tables 5.6 and 5.10). This priority matrix should be clearly communicated to the community and to the rest of the task teams and the MCU in the context of the slope process zone map, initial drainage plan, and landslide hazard assessment process.

Additional benefits to the community should be considered (such as potential for reduced flooding, short-term employment, or improved environmental health). These benefits may be deemed as, or more, important as the potential reduction in landslide hazard.

5.7.4 Sign-off on the map and the proposed intervention

Organize a community meeting to discuss and finalize the landslide hazard reduction and drainage prioritization plan with the commu-

nity, the implementing agency, and all stakeholders. This vital part of the process should be conducted in the same manner as the previous discussions. Because the map and the proposed intervention and priority matrix have been developed with the involvement of all stakeholders, there should at this point be no surprises. Be sure to include a community walk-through during this phase of the discussions so that details can be identified and the plan annotated or adjusted accordingly.

Once all stakeholders have agreed on the map and the intervention, the next stage is to formulate a detailed drainage design and to generate work packages; this is the subject of chapter 6.

MILESTONE 5:
Sign-off on prioritized zones and initial drainage plan

5.8 RESOURCES

5.8.1 Who does what

TEAM	RESPONSIBILITY	ACTIONS AND HELPFUL HINTS	CHAPTER SECTION
Funders and policy makers	Knowledge of community engagement principles and practices	• Become familiar with the process used for community engagement	5.3
	Coordinate with the MCU and government task teams		
MCU	Identify the best form of community participation and mobilization (principles, practices, and specialists)	• Review and determine the most suitable form of community participation • Identify community liaison experts; such individuals are already likely to be part of the community task team, but there may be other specialist colleagues or NGOs that can offer additional advice	5.3
	Coordinate with community liaison task team		
	Understand whether a MoSSaiC project is scientifically justified in a community	• Review a summary of the slope stability assessment • Review the slope process zone map and initial drainage plan	5.7
	Coordinate with landslide assessment and engineering task team		
	Sign off on initial drainage plan		
Government task teams	Include key community members in mapping team	• Identify key community residents to assist **Helpful hint:** Give time to residents who help in this way at the start of a project. They can become strong advocates of MoSSaiC and help ensure positive uptake.	5.3.2
	Hold community meetings to mobilize community	• Take advice from the community as to where they would like such meetings held and what venue is likely to attract the greatest number of attendees	5.3.3
	Undertake walk-through surveys	**Helpful hint:** Repeat this several times. New information is acquired on each visit perhaps from different residents, and new drainage details are observed. Repeat visits build trust and community ownership.	5.4
	Construct community slope feature map	• Construct the map on site so relevant details are captured	5.4.4
	Assess whether a MoSSaiC project is appropriate	**Helpful hint:** Speak to relevant geotechnical colleagues in other agencies to assist as required.	5.3; 5.6
	Assign different surface water management approaches as appropriate	• Identify hillside zones requiring different surface water management approaches **Helpful hint:** Communicate the zoning concept to residents to ensure expectations are correctly set.	5.7
	Coordinate with community task teams		
Community task teams	Contribute local knowledge to drainage hazard mapping	• Become familiar with MoSSaiC approach and local context	5.3.3
	Coordinate with government task teams		

5.8.2 Chapter checklist

CHECK THAT:	TEAM	PERSON	SIGN-OFF	CHAPTER SECTION
✓ Base map drawn				4.7
✓ Community representatives and community groups approached for an initial discussion				5.3
✓ Plans made for a community meeting, and all stakeholders, elected officials, and media invited; comments from the Q&A session recorded				5.3
✓ High percentage of residents visited during the community slope feature mapping process to gain as much local information as possible regarding drainage and landslide issues				5.4
✓ Main drainage lines, topographic convergence, evidence of instability, and previous landslides identified and incorporated into a slope process zone map; landslide hazard and role of surface water infiltration qualitatively assessed				5.5
✓ Quantitative or scientifically based methods applied to confirm landslide hazard and dominant slope mechanisms; surface water management identified as an effective way to reduce landslide hazard in the different slope process zones				5.6
✓ Appropriate drainage measures identified and prioritized, and an initial drainage plan drawn up				5.7
✓ **Milestone 5**: Sign-off on prioritized zones and initial drainage plan				5.7
✓ All necessary safeguards complied with				1.5.3; 2.3.2

5.8.3 References

Ahmad, F., A. Shukri Yahaya, and A. Farooqi. 2006. "Characterization and Geotechnical Properties of Penang Residual Soils with Emphasis on Landslides." *American Journal of Environmental Sciences* 2 (4): 121–28.

ALNAP (Active Learning Network for Accountability and Performance in Humanitarian Action). 2003. *Participation by Crisis-Affected Populations in Humanitarian Actions—A Handbook for Practitioners.* London: Overseas Development Institution. http://www.alnap.org/publications/gs_handbook/gs_handbook.pdf.

Anderson, M. G., and P. D. Bates. 2001. *Model Validation: Perspectives in Hydrological Sciences.* Chichester, UK: Wiley.

Anderson, M. G., S. Howes, P. E. Kneale, and J. M. Shen. 1985. "On Soil Retention Curves and Hydrological Forecasting in Ungauged Catchments." *Nordic Hydrology* 16 (1): 11–32.

Anderson, M. G., M. J. Kemp, and D. M. Lloyd. 1997. "Instruction 2.1: Procedure for the Construction of a Resistance Envelope for a Slope." In *Hydrological Design Manual for Slope Stability in the Tropics,* 14–20. Crowthorne, UK: Transport Research Laboratory. http://www.transport-links.org/transport_links/filearea/publications/1_711_ORN%2014.pdf.

Arnstein, S. R. 1969. "A Ladder of Citizen Participation." *Journal of the American Institute of Planners* 35: 216.

Beven, K. 2006. "A Manifesto for the Equifinality Thesis." *Journal of Hydrology* 320 (1–2): 18–36.

Carter, M., and S. P. Bentley. 1991. *Correlations of Soil Properties.* Chichester, UK: Wiley.

Christian, J. T., C. C. Ladd, and G. B. Baecher. 1994. "Reliability Applied to Slope Stability Analysis." *Journal of Geotechnical Engineering Division, ASCE* 120 (12): 2180–207.

Fellin, W., H. Lessmann, M. Oberguggernberger, and R. Vieider. 2004. *Analyzing Uncertainty in Civil Engineering.* Heidelberg: Springer.

Finlay, P. J., G. R. Mostyn, and R. Fell. 1999. "Landslide Risk Assessment: Prediction of Travel Distance." *Canadian Geotechnical Journal* 36 (3): 556–62.

Fookes, P. G. 1997. *Tropical Residual Soils.* London: Geological Society.

GCO (Geotechnical Control Office). 1982. "Mid-Levels Study: Report on Geology, Hydrology and Soil Properties." Government of Hong Kong Special Administrative Region.

Gero, A., K. Meheux, and D. Dominey-Howes. 2010. "Disaster Risk Reduction and Climate Change Adaptation in the Pacific: The

Challenge of Integration." Miscellaneous Report 4, Australia-Pacific Tsunami Research Centre Natural Hazards Research Laboratory, University of New South Wales.

Hamm, N. A. S., J. W. Hall, and M. G. Anderson. 2006. "Variance-Based Sensitivity Analysis of the Probability of Hydrologically Induced Slope Stability." *Computers and Geosciences* 32 (6): 803–17.

Klasen, S. 1999. *Does Gender Inequality Reduce Growth and Development? Evidence from Cross-Country Regressions.* Washington, DC: World Bank.

Knutson, T. R., J. L. McBride, J. Chan, K. Emanuel, G. Holland, C. Landsea, I. Held, J. P. Kossin, A. K. Srivastava, and M. Sugi. 2010. "Tropical Cyclones and Climate Change." *Nature Geosciences* 3: 157–63.

Lin, H., J. Bouma, Y. Pachepsky, A. Western, J. Thompson, R. van Genuchten, H.-J. Vogel, and A. Lilly. 2006. "Hydropedology: Synergistic Integration of Pedology and Hydrology." *Water Resources Research* 42: W05301.

Lin, S., D. Shaw, M.-C. Ho, and S. Lin. 2008. "Why Are Flood and Landslide Victims Less Willing to Take Mitigation Measures Than the Public? *Natural Hazards* 44: 305–14.

Malkawi, A. I., W. F. Hassan, and F. A. Abdulla. 2000. "Uncertainty and Reliability Analysis Applied to Slope Stability." *Structural Safety* 22 (2): 161–87.

National Research Council. 1990. *Groundwater Models, Scientific and Regulatory Applications.* Washington, DC: National Academy Press.

Parsons, A. J. 1988. *Hillslope Form and Process.* London: Routledge.

Pretty, J. 1995. "Participatory Learning for Sustainable Agriculture." *World Development* 23: 1247–263.

Quinn, P. F., K. Beven, P. Chevallier, and O. Planchon. 1991. "The Prediction of Hillslope Flow Paths for Distributed Hydrological Modeling Using Digital Terrain Models." *Hydrological Processes* 5: 59–79.

Quinn, P. F., K. J. Beven, and R. Lamb. 1995. "The ln (a/tan beta) Index: How to Calculate It and How to Use It within the TOPMODEL Framework." *Hydrological Processes* 9: 161–82.

Rubio, E., J. W. Hall, and M. G. Anderson. 2004. "Uncertainty Analysis in a Slope Hydrology and Stability Model Using Probabilistic and Imprecise Information." *Computers and Geotechnics* 31 (7): 529–36.

Sidle, R. C., A. J. Pearce, and C. L. O'Loughlin. 1985. "Hillslope Stability and Land Use." Water Resource Monograph 11, American Geophysical Union.

Terzaghi, K. 1936. "Relation between Soil Mechanics and Foundation Engineering." Presidential address. In *Proceedings of the First International Conference on Soil Mechanics and Foundation Engineering*, vol. 3, 13–18.

UN (United Nations). 2002. *Gender Mainstreaming: An Overview.* www.un.org/womenwatch/osagi/pdf/e65237.pdf.

———. 2008. "Gender Perspectives—Integrating Disaster Risk Reduction and Climate Change Adaptation. Good Practice and Lessons Learned." http://www.un.org/waterforlifedecade/pdf/2008_isdr_gender_perspectives_disaster_risk_reduction_cc_eng.pdf.

———. 2009. "Making Disaster Risk Reduction Gender-Sensitive: Policy and Practical Guidelines." http://www.preventionweb.net/files/9922_MakingDisasterRiskReductionGenderSe.pdf.

UNECOSOC (United Nations Economic and Social Council). 1997. *UN Economic and Social Council Resolution 1992/2: Agreed Conclusions 1997/2.* http://www.unhcr.org/refworld/docid/4652c9fc2.html.

UNISDR (United Nations Office for Disaster Risk Reduction). 2008. *Gender Perspectives: Integrating Disaster Risk Reduction into Climate Change Adaptation.* www.unisdr.org/we/inform/publications/3391.

University of Warwick. 2002. "Very Low-Cost Domestic Roofwater Harvesting in the Humid Tropics: Existing Practice." School of Engineering, University of Warwick, Warwick, UK.

van Genuchten, M. Th. 1980. "A Closed-Form Equation for Predicting the Hydraulic Conductivity of Unsaturated Soils." *Soil Science Society of America Journal* 44: 892–98.

Victoria, L. P. 2009. "Community Based Approaches to Disaster Mitigation." Document UNPAN009661, UN Public Administration Network. http://unpan1.un.org/intradoc/groups/public/documents/APCITY/UNPAN009661.pdf.

World Bank. 2010. *Safer Homes, Stronger Communities. A Handbook for Reconstructing after Natural Disasters.* Washington, DC: World Bank.

"During the past three decades policy statements by all major agencies have included risk reduction as a pre-condition and an integrated aspect of sustainable development... but when it comes to practical implementation, comparatively little has been done."

— C. Wamsler, "Mainstreaming Risk Reduction in Urban Planning and Housing: A Challenge for International Aid Organizations" (2006, 159)

CHAPTER 6

Design and Good Practice for Slope Drainage

6.1 KEY CHAPTER ELEMENTS

6.1.1 Coverage

This chapter discusses the delivery of MoSSaiC (Management of Slope Stability in Communities) landslide risk reduction measures on the ground. The listed groups should read the indicated chapter sections.

AUDIENCE				LEARNING	CHAPTER SECTION
F	M	G	C		
✓	✓	✓		Principles for general alignment of drains	6.3
	✓	✓		Methods for estimating drain discharge and designing drain size	6.3
	✓	✓	✓	Drain functions and locations affecting detailed drain alignment	6.4
	✓	✓		Drain construction specifications: materials and details	6.5
	✓	✓		Approaches to capturing household water	6.6
	✓	✓		Producing the final drainage plan and estimated cost	6.7

F = funders and policy makers   **M** = MoSSaiC core unit: government project managers and experts   **G** = government task teams: experts and practitioners   **C** = community task teams: residents, leaders, contractors

6.1.2 Documents

DOCUMENT TO BE PRODUCED	CHAPTER SECTION
Proposed and final drainage plans	6.3–6.7
Table of cost estimates for drainage construction	6.7

6.1.3 Steps and outputs

STEP	OUTPUT
1. Identify the location and alignment of drains • Use the slope process zone map and initial drainage plan as a starting point; apply drainage alignment principles to identify potential drain network alignment • Refine alignment details on site	Proposed drainage plan (drain alignments and dimensions)
2. Estimate drain discharge and dimensions • Calculate surface water runoff and household water discharge into proposed drains • Calculate required drain size	
3. Specify drain construction and design details	Full drain specification
4. Incorporate houses into the drainage plan • Identify houses to receive roof guttering, gray water pipes, water tanks, and hurricane straps • Determine how household water will be directed to the drains (via pipes connected by concrete chambers or small drains)	List of quantities needed for household connections
5. Produce final drainage plan • Include all drain alignment and household connection details on the plan • Estimate total project cost from unit costs	Final drainage plan and cost estimate
6. Stakeholder agreement on plan • Meet with the community and refine the plan • Complete checks regarding relevant safeguards • Submit plan for formal approval	Sign-off on the final drainage plan

6.1.4 Community-based aspects

This chapter takes the outputs of the community-based mapping process (slope process zone map and initial drainage plan) and develops a detailed drainage plan for implementation in the community. Residents with knowledge of the community, hillslope layout, and local construction practices can contribute valuable information and ideas at this stage. The community agrees to the final drainage plan before sign-off by the MoSSaiC core unit (MCU).

6.2 GETTING STARTED

6.2.1 Briefing note

Drainage design for landslide hazard reduction

Improving surface water drainage can increase slope stability in communities where rainfall and household water infiltration have been confirmed as the main contributors to landslide hazard. For such drainage interventions to be effective and stay within budget requires an understanding of the localized causes of the landslide hazard, and careful design and specification of the works. Drainage should be designed to intercept and control surface water flows generated by rainfall and domestic water usage, thus reducing the infiltration of water into the slope material and improving slope stability.

The community-based mapping process and landslide hazard assessment described in chapter 5 provides the foundation for this design process. Experienced engineers and technicians will need to refine or revise the initial drainage alignments, estimate the volume of water likely to be entering the new drains, define the required drain size and design for construction, identify household drainage measures, and estimate overall project cost.

The importance of good design

A good drainage design will achieve the following:

- Interception of rainfall runoff from the slope surface and roofs

- Capture of gray water from houses

- Controlled flow of all intercepted/captured surface water in a network of drains

- Reduced landslide hazard.

Good design will also minimize the need for land-take, the potential for drain obstruction by debris, and ongoing maintenance.

Even if the government has little experience in designing and implementing drainage works in vulnerable unauthorized communities, there are likely to be relevant local design and construction standards or specifications for drains. Entities such as nongovernmental organizations (NGOs), local contractors, and community residents with construction skills also may be able to identify examples of good practices in drainage design. These sources of information should be reviewed by the landslide assessment and engineering task team, and appropriate standards and specifications selected. Drain effectiveness in reducing landslide hazard depends on adhering to such standards and specifications. Accurate specification of these details also ensures accurate estimates of the total project budget for decision-making, financial, and management purposes. The final drainage plan will need to meet appropriate standards, provide adequate construction specifications and cost estimates, and be approved before work packages can be drawn up and contracts awarded.

Additional benefits

Besides reducing landslide hazard in a targeted and cost-effective manner, a community-based program of surface water management can

- reduce localized flooding and soil erosion;

- improve the community's environment;

- inform residents of good slope management and landslide hazard reduction practices;

- be the focal point of a holistic approach to landslide risk reduction for governments and international development agencies; and

- be included in broader poverty reduction, disaster risk reduction, and climate change adaptation programs.

6.2.2 Guiding principles

The following guiding principles apply in slope drainage design:

- Be as precise as possible in specifying drainage alignment and design in terms of type, size, and materials. Conduct supplementary surveys of any complicated drainage lines within the community as necessary.

- Apply relevant engineering and construction standards and protocols.

- Be as precise and realistic as possible in the initial estimate of quantities so the overall project budget can be estimated.

- Deliver a holistic presentation of the project (plan and budget) for approval by the MCU and the government agency in charge of implementation.

- Ensure that all relevant safeguards are addressed, especially regarding drain alignment, with both landowners and community residents.

6.2.3 Risks and challenges

Design for easy drain maintenance

Although the importance of drain maintenance is widely recognized by funders, governments, and communities, it is rarely undertaken. The need for cleaning and structural maintenance should be explicitly factored into drainage design and on-site construction decisions. Drains can, to some extent, be designed to be self-cleaning and therefore easier to maintain. In particular, shallow flow gradients should be avoided, and contour (intercept) drains should be designed to keep flow velocities generally high (to limit sediment deposition). Areas of drain constriction, such as narrow culverts or abrupt changes in alignment, should be avoided so debris does not accumulate and cause the drain to overflow. Well-designed drains that have been constructed and finished to a good standard, kept clear of debris, and regularly inspected for damage will afford a greater level of protection to communities and have a longer design life than poorly designed and constructed drains.

Prioritizing locations for drain construction to reduce landslide hazard

Donors and governments cannot build drains for all houses in all communities. Even in the vulnerable landslide-prone communities selected for MoSSaiC projects, it is not possible from a budgetary or political standpoint to fund every drainage intervention that might be beneficial. For each of these communities, the slope process zone map, initial drainage plan, and drainage prioritization matrix developed in chapter 5 should enable broad priorities to be established. Once the design and specification of the drainage plan is complete, the cost of these interventions can be estimated. Decision makers should use this information—along with the relevant local safeguards and protocols—to allocate the project budget in a transparent and justifiable way.

Household rainwater and gray water management

In unauthorized communities and among the wider public, there may be little awareness of how simple, low-cost improvements in household drainage can reduce landslide hazard. Yet the adoption of such drainage and slope management practices can ensure the sustainability of MoSSaiC projects and be highly cost-effective. One means of encouraging adoption is to demonstrate simple household-scale surface water management practices that can be used in conjunction with standard drain construction methods.

Throughout the project, residents should be made aware of the need for roof guttering and downpipes that should be connected directly to lined drains, or to properly covered containers for rainwater harvesting (with overflow pipes into drains). Gray water outlets (e.g., sinks and showers) should also be connected to the drainage network if there is no other provision for household drainage. Soak-aways should be avoided if possible since they act as a point water source by directly adding water to the slope material.

If there are no new drains adjacent to a house, connections can be made using readily available materials and appropriate technology, such as wide diameter plastic pipes connected by a sequence of concrete chambers. MoSSaiC has also developed a type of drain suitable for use in locations where a shallow trench can be excavated in the soil. The trench is lined with sturdy polythene sheeting (such as sunlight-stable greenhouse polythene sheeting) held in place by a wire mesh. The mesh is formed to the shape of the drain by hand and secured with U-shaped pegs made from steel reinforcing rods. These materials can be purchased for less than 10 percent the cost of similarly sized concrete drains; are much cheaper to transport and easy to carry; and, apart from some short instruction in their assembly, require no previous construction experience.

In some high-priority zones of the community, these household-level drainage measures may be included as part of the project. Because it is not feasible or affordable to provide such measures for every house, including examples of these methods in the final drainage plan will encourage residents to adopt low-cost or other appropriate technology solutions on a self-help basis. Such solutions offer certain technical, political, and financial advantages, and play a role in the overall improvement of surface water management.

6.2.4 Adapting the chapter blueprint to existing capacity

Use the matrix opposite to assess the capacity of the MCU and the government task teams (or collaborating government agency) to deliver a final drainage plan at a professional level in accordance with relevant engineering design standards. This plan will include a drainage design that affords best possible landslide hazard reduction, complete with construction specifications and cost estimates for the development of work packages.

1. Assign a capacity score from 1 to 3 (low to high) to reflect the existing capacity for each of the elements in the matrix's left-hand column.

2. Identify the most common capacity score as an indicator of the overall capacity level.

3. Adapt the blueprint in this chapter in accordance with the overall capacity level (see guide on next page).

6.3 PRINCIPLES AND TOOLS FOR GENERAL ALIGNMENT OF DRAINS

The initial drainage plan should already indicate potential drain locations, identified on the basis of slope zone processes, dominant surface water issues, and possible types of surface water management. The landslide assessment and engineering task team (assisted by an experienced engineer, if necessary) must develop this plan into a fully specified drainage design that will capture as much surface water as possible, given budget and site constraints.

This section provides guidance on principles for designing main drain alignments—intercept (contour) drains and downslope drains, methods for estimating the discharge of surface water runoff from specific slope sec-

CAPACITY ELEMENT	EXISTING CAPACITY		
	1 = LOW	2 = MODERATE	3 = HIGH
Experience in designing drainage networks on slopes, calculating slope surface water and drain capacity, applying engineering design standards, and writing specifications for drain construction	No practical experience in designing surface water drains for slopes	Some experience with drain construction on slopes or knowledge of drain design calculations	Sound experience in all aspects of designing drainage networks on slopes—engineering expertise and understanding of slope hydrology
Experience in developing accurate and detailed site plans at a large scale and high resolution, and in incorporating other mapped data (features such as drain alignment and design, paths, and houses) into these plans	No experience in drawing site plans at large scale/high resolution, or in incorporating other mapped data	Experience in drawing site plans at large scale/high resolution or in using geographic information system/computer-assisted design (GIS/CAD) software to combine spatial data and produce maps	Experience in drawing site plans at large scale/high resolution and in using GIS/CAD software to incorporate relevant mapped data
Guidelines available on local drain design and construction standards and specifications	No guidelines available, and few examples of good practices	Some guidelines and examples of good practices are available	Comprehensive guidelines and several examples of good practices are available
Information on unit costs of construction, procedures for quantity estimation, and expertise in estimating community-based project costs available	No information or procedures available, and limited experience in estimating community project costs	Some information and procedures for quantity estimation, and some experience in estimating community project costs	Standard unit costs for construction and quantity estimation procedures available, and sound experience in community-based project cost estimation
Project safeguards	Documented safeguards need to be located; no previous experience in interpreting and operating safeguard policies	Documents exist for some safeguards	Documented safeguards available from all relevant agencies

CAPACITY LEVEL	HOW TO ADAPT THE BLUEPRINT
1: Use this chapter in depth and as a catalyst to secure support from other agencies as appropriate	The MCU needs to strengthen its capacity before developing a final drainage plan. This might involve the following: • Hiring an experienced engineering technician from the commercial sector to estimate slope surface water flows and drain capacity • Hiring an experienced geographic information system/computer-assisted design (GIS/CAD) technician to develop the final drainage plan • Developing standard drain design, construction, and cost estimation practices from those documented in this book and from drain designs available in similar countries • Seeking advice from donors, the private sector, or other sources on project cost estimation practices • Approaching all relevant agencies to acquire their safeguard documents and distill them into a coherent working document for designing construction projects in communities
2: Some elements of this chapter will reflect current practice; read the remaining elements in depth and use them to further strengthen capacity	The MCU has strength in some areas, but not all. Elements that are perceived to be Level 1 need to be addressed as above. Elements that are Level 2 will need to be strengthened, such as the following: • If there is no substantive experience in community-based projects and generation of relevant unit costs (e.g., for double handling of materials), these could be acquired from similar projects undertaken by NGOs or in other countries, and this book used as a guide • If there is limited expertise in producing detailed site plans or using GIS/CAD, advice could be sought from a commercial partner or relevant agency • If relevant safeguard documents are available but not collated, the MCU should systematically integrate them into the implementation process
3: Use this chapter as a checklist	The MCU is likely to be able to proceed using existing proven capacity. It would be good practice nonetheless for the MCU to document relevant experience in developing drainage designs, estimating project costs, and applying related safeguards.

tions (for example, above a proposed intercept drain) and gray water from houses, and calculation of drain dimensions.

The design of the drainage network and drain alignments is an iterative process summarized in figure 6.1.

6.3.1 Drainage alignment patterns and principles

In identifying the overall drainage alignment pattern, adhere to the following general principles:

• **Capture.** Ensure that as much surface water, roof water, and gray water are captured by the drainage network as possible.

• **Connectivity.** Ensure that each drain section connects with and discharges into another drain, and that the entire drainage network discharges into an appropriate receiving water body (such as a river, retention basin, main drain, or the sea).

• **Channel slope.** Ensure that each drain section has a sufficient channel slope (grade) in the planned direction of flow (i.e., avoiding reverse flows), and that the elevation of the drainage network outflow is above that of the receiving water body.

• **Capacity.** Ensure that each drain section has sufficient capacity for calculated discharges from surface water runoff, household gray water, and subsidiary connecting drains; and that the combined drainage network discharge into the receiving water body will not cause flooding downstream.

The revised drainage alignment design should take into account actual on-site conditions, including the following:

• Conditions that may restrict drain construction or reduce drain effectiveness and functionality

• Existing drains that may need to be repaired, replaced, or eliminated

FIGURE 6.1 Iterative design process for developing final drainage plan

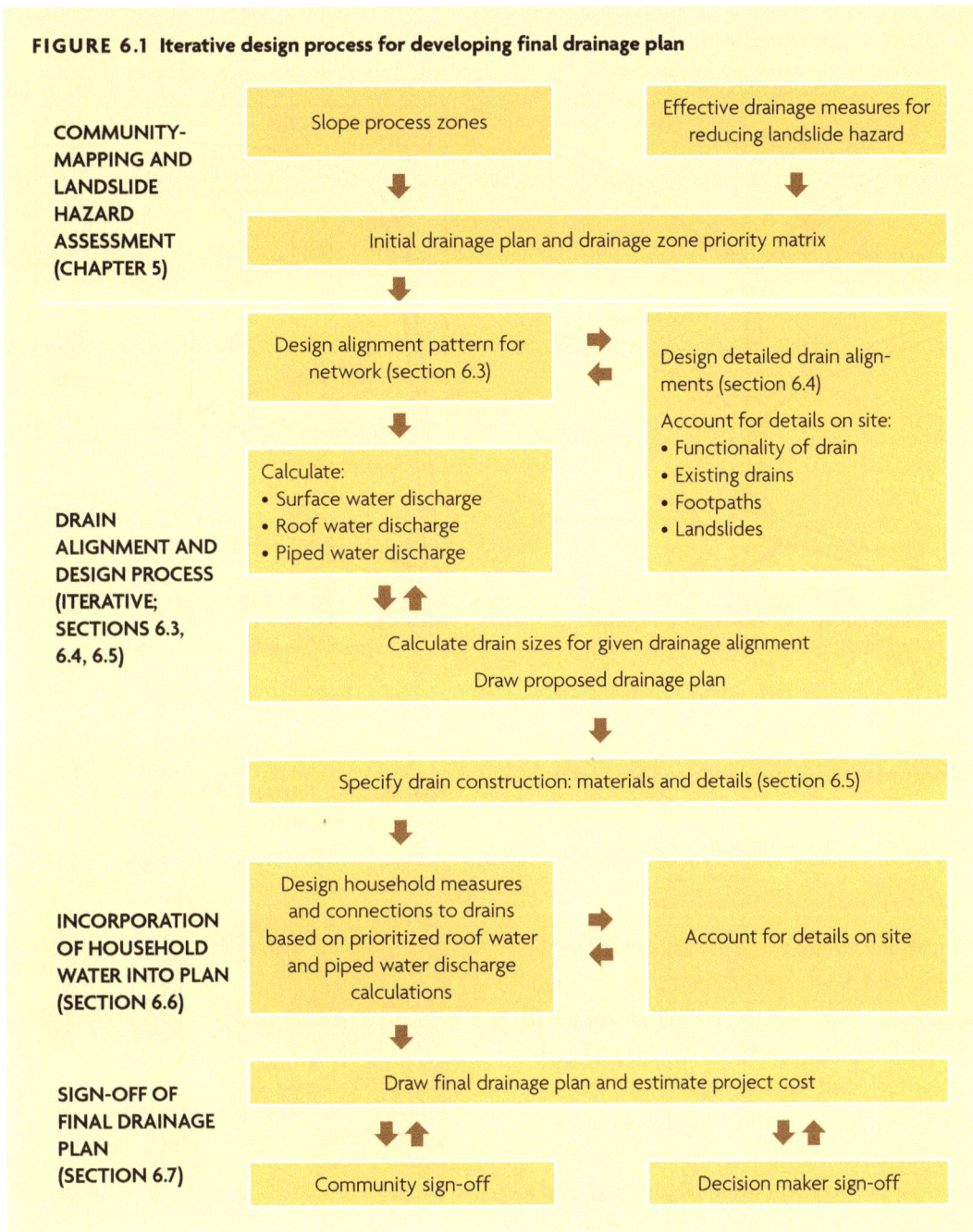

COMMUNITY-MAPPING AND LANDSLIDE HAZARD ASSESSMENT (CHAPTER 5)

| Slope process zones | | Effective drainage measures for reducing landslide hazard |

Initial drainage plan and drainage zone priority matrix

DRAIN ALIGNMENT AND DESIGN PROCESS (ITERATIVE; SECTIONS 6.3, 6.4, 6.5)

Design alignment pattern for network (section 6.3)

Design detailed drain alignments (section 6.4)

Account for details on site:
• Functionality of drain
• Existing drains
• Footpaths
• Landslides

Calculate:
• Surface water discharge
• Roof water discharge
• Piped water discharge

Calculate drain sizes for given drainage alignment

Draw proposed drainage plan

Specify drain construction: materials and details (section 6.5)

INCORPORATION OF HOUSEHOLD WATER INTO PLAN (SECTION 6.6)

Design household measures and connections to drains based on prioritized roof water and piped water discharge calculations

Account for details on site

Draw final drainage plan and estimate project cost

SIGN-OFF OF FINAL DRAINAGE PLAN (SECTION 6.7)

Community sign-off

Decision maker sign-off

• Existing footpaths with or without drains

• Proposed new footpaths to be included in the project

• Areas requiring additional protection such as existing landslides or channels prone to undercutting and bank failure.

More detailed alignment issues associated with different drain types are described in section 6.4.

Idealized drain alignment

An idealized surface water drainage network comprises regularly spaced intercept (contour) drains connecting with a downslope drain in a herringbone pattern (figure 6.2).

Local conditions, such as slope topography and the existing layout of houses and paths, are likely to make such an idealized configuration impractical. Use the following four examples of slope drainage patterns to help confirm, adjust, or augment the initial drainage plan

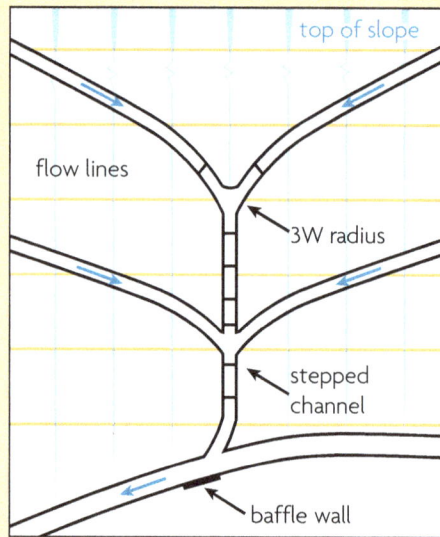

FIGURE 6.2 Idealized hillside drainage plan showing intercept and downslope drains

Note: Lines orthogonal to contours (flow lines) indicate likely surface and subsurface water flow paths.

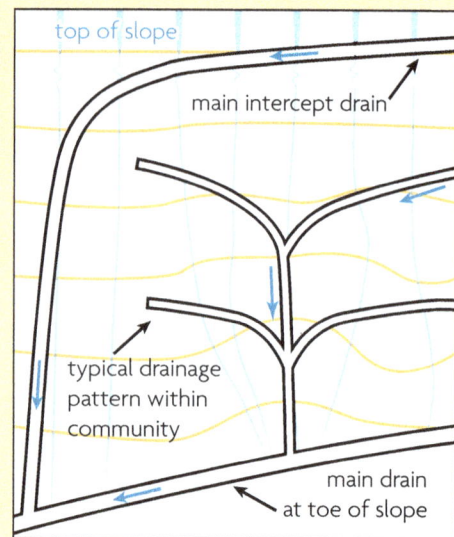

FIGURE 6.3 Generalized alignment for use with top-of-slope intercept drains

Note: Lines orthogonal to contours (flow lines) indicate likely surface and subsurface water flow paths.

and ensure that drains are aligned for best possible capture of surface water given the topography and on-site conditions.

Linear drain alignment and easy access

In locations where there is easy access to the hillside and few restrictions to drain alignment, a configuration similar to that shown in figure 6.2 may be possible. This design can be augmented with an intercept drain running across the upper section of the slope. Figure 6.3 shows such an alignment with a major top-of-slope intercept drain (figure 6.4), and a complementary herringbone drain alignment downslope. This configuration can be very effective in managing surface water on steep but otherwise accessible slopes.

Complex topography and difficult access

Vegetation, buildings, topography, landownership issues, boundaries, and other restrictions may prevent the alignment of a single uninterrupted intercept drain across the entire slope (figure 6.5).

In such cases, it may be appropriate to design several separate drains along a particular contour that each connect to a different

FIGURE 6.4 Intercept drain built on a slope with few restrictions to alignment

downslope drain and together create an intercept zone across the slope (figures 6.6 and 6.7).

Currently inactive landslide sites

In many unauthorized hillside communities, there may be sites where landslides have occurred and that subsequently appear to have stabilized. The community mapping process completed in chapter 5 should have identified such sites.

Even if there is no evidence of current movement, there is no assurance that—given reduced soil strength, post-landslide topogra-

FIGURE 6.5 Drain alignment complexities

a. Vegetation, a previously built footbath (with underdesigned slip drain) and topography restrict the alignment of a new intercept drain.

b. Undulating topography needs to be carefully surveyed, especially when aligning an intercept drain, so as to achieve self-cleaning gradients.

FIGURE 6.6 Network of small intercept drains intercepting surface water along entire uppermost contour of slope

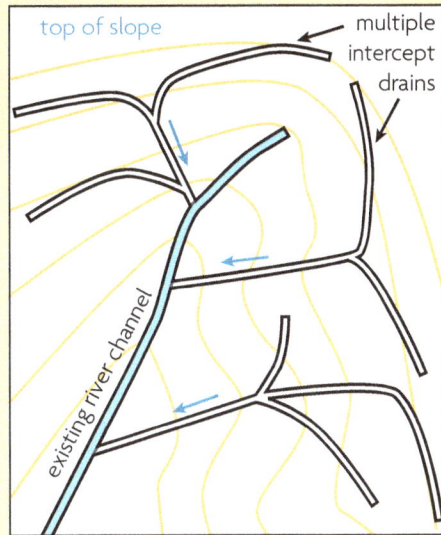

FIGURE 6.7 Downslope drain

This drain is designed to receive water from the main intercept drain, and a minor intercept drain (center right) under construction.

phy, and associated subsurface flow patterns (such as soil pipes)—the landslide will not be reactivated by future rainfall events. It is thus important to align drains to minimize water inflow to these failed sites. The alignment shown in figure 6.8 can be used to good effect in such circumstances (figure 6.9).

Currently active landslide sites (progressive failure)

Some hillsides exhibit progressive failures—the continued, imperceptibly slow movement of material following a landslide-triggering event. Progressive failures are commonly associated with, but not restricted to, slope materials with high clay content.

The community mapping process should have identified sites of progressive slope failure and noted observations from residents about periods of slope movement. Ascertaining that a landslide is still active is important, since this can affect the alignment of main drains around the unstable area and may also require well-maintained minor drains to drain the slide itself. Main drains should not be built on or across progressive landslides or unstable

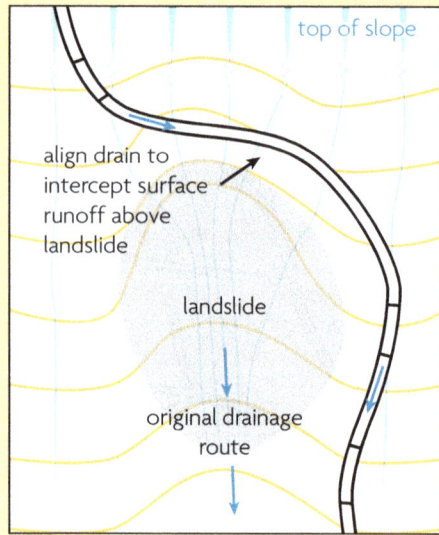

FIGURE 6.8 Drain alignment to minimize surface and immediate subsurface water flow into previously failed material

align drain to intercept surface runoff above landslide

landslide

original drainage route

top of slope

Note: Lines orthogonal to contours indicate likely surface and subsurface water flow paths and emphasize the importance of the drain in preventing increased pore water pressures within the landslide.

FIGURE 6.9 Drain aligned to intercept surface water and routed around a major preexisting landslide

Crest of preexisting landslide is toward upper center.

Figure 6.10 illustrates a drain alignment designed to prevent water flow into the slide area (to the left of the drain) from upslope, and drain the progressive slide material at the midpoint of the slide as well as immediately downslope.

FIGURE 6.10 Drain alignment for site of progressive failure

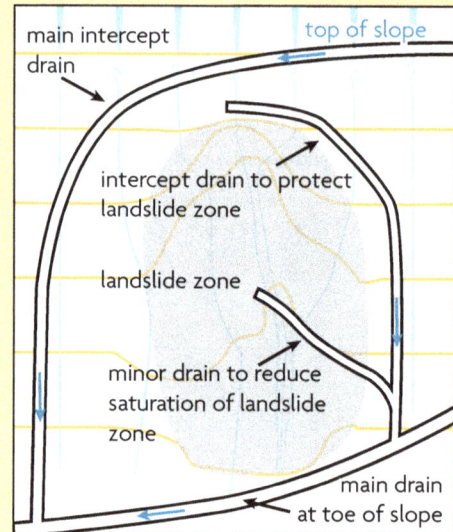

main intercept drain

top of slope

intercept drain to protect landslide zone

landslide zone

minor drain to reduce saturation of landslide zone

main drain at toe of slope

Note: Lines orthogonal to contours (flow lines) indicate likely surface and subsurface water flow paths. A comparatively high-density drain network can help prevent downslope water ingress to a failed site; consider aligning drains above, within, and immediately downslope of the failed material.

6.3.2 Calculating drain flow and drain dimensions

Estimate the potential volumes of surface water runoff, roof water, and gray water that will be discharged into the new drains. Use local engineering protocols to select an appropriate design rainfall intensity (i.e., with a specified probability or return period) to estimate surface water and roof water runoff. From these estimations, determine the required drain capacities and dimensions. This drain alignment-dimension design process is iterative and involves the steps described in figure 6.11.

Methods that may be used to calculate the discharge into drains, and hence the required drain size, are summarized in the following sections; see table 6.1.

material, since slope movement could cause cracking and leakage—potentially discharging drain water into the unstable material. However, minor drains that start within the failed mass and remove water from the area can be used to good effect. Low-cost drains made of flexible materials, such as those introduced in sections 6.5.2 and 6.5.3, might be appropriate.

FIGURE 6.11 Iterative process for designing drain alignments and dimensions

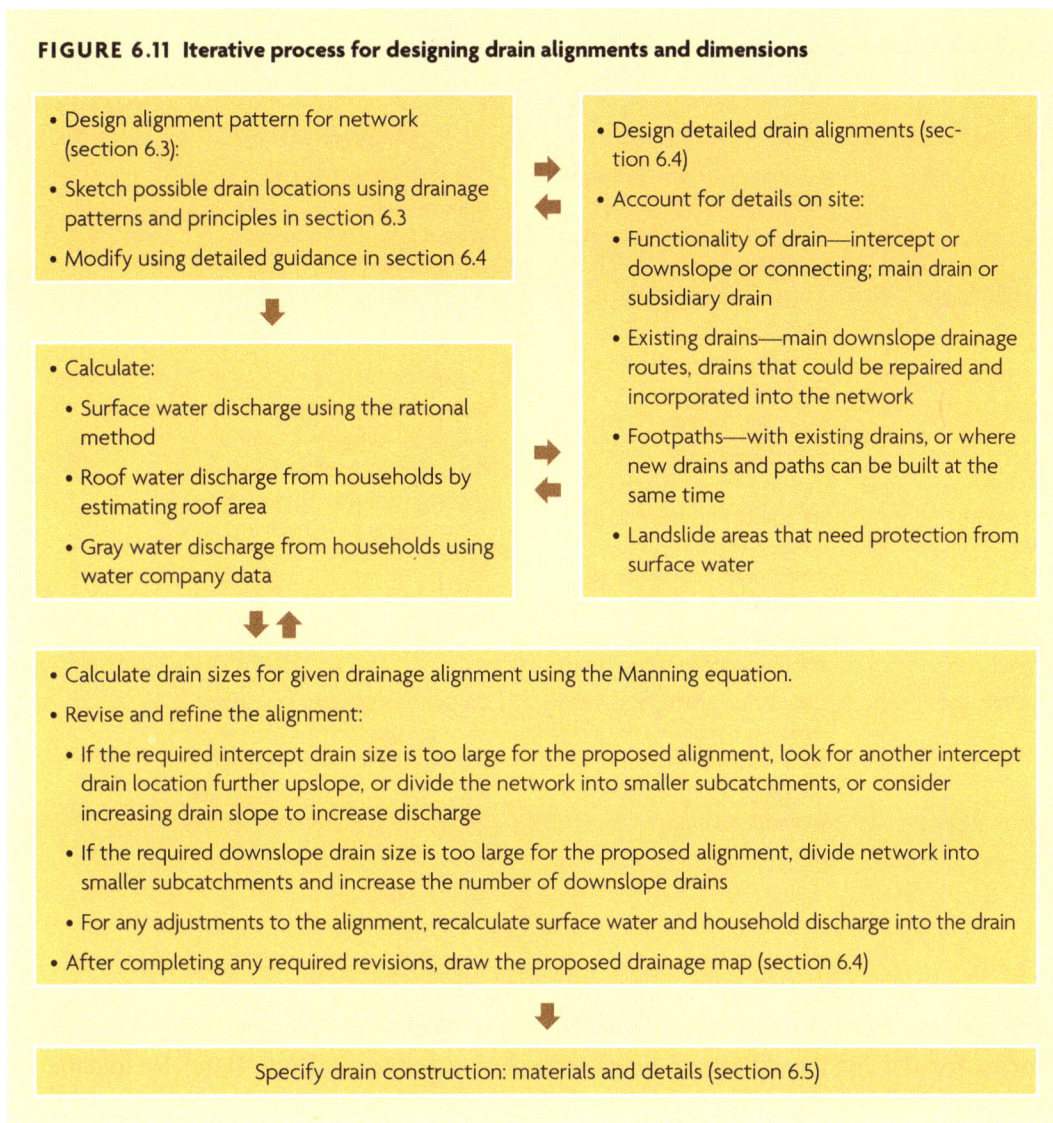

- Design alignment pattern for network (section 6.3):
- Sketch possible drain locations using drainage patterns and principles in section 6.3
- Modify using detailed guidance in section 6.4

- Design detailed drain alignments (section 6.4)
- Account for details on site:
  - Functionality of drain—intercept or downslope or connecting; main drain or subsidiary drain
  - Existing drains—main downslope drainage routes, drains that could be repaired and incorporated into the network
  - Footpaths—with existing drains, or where new drains and paths can be built at the same time
  - Landslide areas that need protection from surface water

- Calculate:
  - Surface water discharge using the rational method
  - Roof water discharge from households by estimating roof area
  - Gray water discharge from households using water company data

- Calculate drain sizes for given drainage alignment using the Manning equation.
- Revise and refine the alignment:
  - If the required intercept drain size is too large for the proposed alignment, look for another intercept drain location further upslope, or divide the network into smaller subcatchments, or consider increasing drain slope to increase discharge
  - If the required downslope drain size is too large for the proposed alignment, divide network into smaller subcatchments and increase the number of downslope drains
  - For any adjustments to the alignment, recalculate surface water and household discharge into the drain
- After completing any required revisions, draw the proposed drainage map (section 6.4)

Specify drain construction: materials and details (section 6.5)

6.3.3 Estimating surface water discharge

The amount of water flowing over a slope surface during rainfall (surface water discharge) depends on the intensity and duration of rainfall, rate of infiltration into the soil, slope steepness, and surface cover. The capacity of a drainage network should be designed to accommodate surface water discharge captured by intercept drains for a specified rainfall event. The optimal design rainfall return period should be chosen based on local engineering standards and expert engineering judgment on the following issues, among others:

- Designing large drains for a low-frequency, high-intensity rainfall event (e.g., with a return period of 1 in 100 years) will be more expensive than designing small drains for annual or high-frequency events.

- Designing large drains for low-frequency, high-duration rainfall events may efficiently remove surface water from a hillside community but cause flooding downstream unless the drain flow velocity is reduced or water is stored.

- The money spent in constructing a high-capacity drain might be otherwise spent on building a number of smaller drains (WHO 1991).

Surface water discharge can be estimated using the rational method; a simple approximation widely used for calculating peak dis-

TABLE 6.1 Calculations for estimating discharge into drains and drain size

CALCULATION	PURPOSE	IMPLEMENTATION	CHAPTER SECTION
Surface water runoff	Calculation of surface water runoff discharged (m³/s) from specific area of the slope for specific rainfall event	See the online calculator for the rational method, http://www.lmnoeng.com/Hydrology/rational.htm	6.3.3
Roof water	Calculation of percentage of rainfall intercepted by roofs; used to estimate the effectiveness of roof guttering for removing water from the slope and the discharge entering drains	Calculation can be developed as a simple spreadsheet model using equations to account for housing density, roof area, average piped water supply to houses, and rainfall intensity	6.3.4
Piped water supply	Calculation of piped water supplied to houses and discharged to slope; used to estimate effectiveness of household drains for removing gray water from the slope and the discharge entering drains		6.3.4
Drain size	Calculation of the required cross-sectional area for a drain to accommodate a specific discharge on a given slope gradient	Online calculators for prismatic channels are at http://onlinecalc.sdsu.edu/onlinechannel15.php and http://www.calculatoredge.com/new/manning.htm#velocity	6.3.5

charge in small urban drainage areas (< 80 hectares). The method uses a runoff coefficient to account for the difference between rainfall and the resulting surface water runoff due to variations in land use (table 6.2), which is a proxy for a number of processes including infiltration, temporary storage, and other losses (see Premchitt, Lam, and Shen 1986 for evidence of surface cover effects on slope discharge). Because these processes are not explicitly accounted for, the rational method (equation 6.1) does not allow calculation of the timing of peak discharge (also known as the time of concentration). It also assumes constant rainfall intensity across the drainage area and over time. These simplifying assumptions do not significantly affect discharge estimations for small, steeply sloping drainage areas with no flood storage; but for larger catchment areas (> 80 hectares), engineers should use other calculation methods.

$$Q = k\,C\,i\,A \qquad (6.1)$$

Where:

Q = Peak flow (cf/s or m³/s)

k = Conversion factor (1.008 for imperial or 0.00278 for metric)

C = Runoff coefficient (see table 6.2)

i = Rainfall intensity (in/h or mm/h)

A = Upslope contributing drainage area (acres or hectares)

Estimate the potential surface water discharge from areas of the slope above proposed intercept drains to determine the required capacities of intercept and downslope drains. Perform the following steps to apply the rational method:

Step 1: Contributing area (A)

• Calculate the area of the slope that will discharge surface water runoff into the proposed intercept drain (the contributing area).

• Use a contour map to estimate the boundaries of the contributing area. Assuming

TABLE 6.2 Values of runoff coefficient C for the rational method

LAND USE	C	LAND USE	C
Business:		**Lawns:**	
Downtown areas	0.70–0.95	Sandy soil, flat, 2%	0.05–0.10
Neighborhood areas	0.50–0.70	Sandy soil, average, 2–7%	0.10–0.15
		Sandy soil, steep, 7%	0.15–0.20
		Heavy soil, flat, 2%	0.13–0.17
		Heavy soil, average, 2–7%	0.18–0.22
		Heavy soil, steep, 7%	0.25–0.35
Residential:		**Agricultural land:**	
Single-family areas	0.30–0.50	Bare packed soil	
Multi units, detached	0.40–0.60	Smooth	0.30–0.60
Multi units, attached	0.60–0.75	Rough	0.20–0.50
Suburban	0.25–0.40	Cultivated rows	
		Heavy soil, no crop	0.30–0.60
		Heavy soil, with crop	0.20–0.50
		Sandy soil, no crop	0.20–0.40
		Sandy soil, with crop	0.10–0.25
		Pasture	
		Heavy soil	0.15–0.45
		Sandy soil	0.05–0.25
		Woodlands	0.05–0.25
Industrial:		**Streets:**	
Light areas	0.50–0.80	Asphaltic	0.70–0.95
Heavy areas	0.60–0.90	Concrete	0.80–0.95
		Brick	0.70–0.85
Parks, cemeteries	0.10–0.25	Unimproved areas	0.10–0.30
Playgrounds	0.20–0.35	Drives and walks	0.75–0.85
Railroad yard areas	0.20–0.40	Roofs	0.75–0.95

Source: http://water.me.vccs.edu/courses/CIV246/table2.htm.

Note: The designer must use judgment to select the appropriate coefficient value within the range. Generally, larger areas with permeable soils, flat slopes, and dense vegetation should have the lowest coefficient values. Smaller areas with dense soils, moderate to steep slopes, and sparse vegetation should be assigned the highest coefficient values.

surface water will run over the slope at 90 degrees to contours, sketch flow lines on the map to identify the area of slope above the drain that will contribute surface water runoff.

- Conduct a site visit to verify the boundaries of the contributing area.

- If calculating discharge from house roofs separately, be sure to subtract the roof area from the slope area so as not to double count roof water (see section 6.3.4).

Step 2: Rainfall intensity (*i*)

- Use past rainfall records to identify the intensity, duration, and frequency of different rainfall events.

- Select the maximum rainfall intensity for which the drains are to be designed.

Step 3: Runoff coefficient (*C*)

- Select a runoff coefficient from table 6.2 that best represents the contributing area land use.

- If there is more than one distinct type of land use, subdivide the area accordingly and assign appropriate values of C to each subarea.

- If the area has been subdivided according to different values of C, recalculate A for each area. Multiply A and C for each subarea, add the results together, and divide by the total area to obtain a weighted value of C for the entire contributing area.

Step 4: Peak discharge (Q)

Use the rational method to calculate peak surface water discharge from the contributing area.

6.3.4 Estimating the discharge from houses

Each household can affect the amount of surface water on a slope in two ways: (1) by intercepting rainfall on roofs and either discharging it directly onto the slope, collecting it, or directing it into drains; and (2) by discharging gray water and septic waste onto the slope.

If the housing density is high, the proportion of rainfall intercepted by roofs will be correspondingly high. If there is piped water supply, this can result in a significant increase in surface water discharge—in some cases, amounting to as much as that generated by rainfall.

If the project scope includes installing roof guttering, gray water pipes, and connections to the new drains, the resulting discharge should be accounted for in drain capacity calculations. The importance of household water capture also needs to be established both as part of the justification for the intervention and as a way of changing slope management perceptions and practices.

Use the following steps to estimate household water contributions to surface water. This method can be applied to the whole community to estimate an average discharge for the area or specific contributing area discharges into different drains.

Step 1: Proportion of rainfall intercepted by roofs

- Calculate the total contributing area of the slope that will discharge water into the proposed drain.

- Estimate the area of the slope covered by houses by using geographic information system/computer-assisted design (GIS/CAD) to directly measure the building footprints, or estimating the average house size and multiplying this by the number of houses on the slope.

- Divide the total house footprint area by the slope area to obtain the proportion of the slope over which houses directly intercept rainfall on their roofs.

- Multiply the result by the rainfall for the chosen design event (see section 6.3.3) to calculate the potential maximum roof water capture and subsequent discharge into drains.

- Be careful not to double count the roof water contribution in estimating surface water discharge (section 6.3.3).

Step 2: Water supply

- Obtain water company data on average supply per household over a specific time period.

- Multiply the average supply by the number of households in the community to obtain the total amount of water supplied to the slope for that period.

- Convert from volume to equivalent depth (e.g., mm/day), and compare with the average rainfall rate for the equivalent time period to determine the significance of piped water supply in adding water to the slope.

- Estimate how much water is lost from pipes through leakage and how much will be added to the slope as septic waste. (The water company should be able to provide an estimate of these figures.) The remaining supply represents the maximum volume that could be captured from houses as gray water and discharged into the drains.

6.3.5 Estimating dimensions for main drains

Use the predicted surface water discharge and, if relevant, the estimated household water discharge to determine appropriate dimensions (cross-sectional areas) for the main intercept and downslope drains. Typically, the dimensions of the smaller subsidiary or household drains can be determined by rule of thumb, experience, or local knowledge. However, if drain size calculations are needed in order to conform with local engineering design standards or building codes, then these protocols should be followed.

The Manning equation (6.2) is a semi-empirical equation that is the most commonly used to calculate uniform steady-state flow of water in open channels.

$$V = (k/n) \times R^{2/3} \times S^{1/2} \qquad (6.2)$$

Where:
V = Velocity (ft/s or m/s)
k = Constant (1.485 for imperial units, or 1.0 for metric)
R = Hydraulic radius (ft or m)
S = Channel slope (ft/ft or m/m)
n = Manning's constant defined for different channel materials

Drain discharge can be calculated using equation (6.3), in which flow velocity is estimated by the Manning equation (6.2).

$$Q = A \times V \qquad (6.3)$$

Where:
Q = Discharge ($ft^3 s^{-1}$ or $m^3 s^{-1}$)
A = Channel cross-sectional area (ft^2 or m^2)
V = Flow velocity ($ft\ s^{-1}$ or $m\ s^{-1}$)

This calculation can be applied iteratively to identify the drain cross-sectional area required to accommodate a specified discharge. A number of online calculators are available for this calculation. Alternatively, the sequence of calculations can be entered into a spreadsheet to allow multiple iterations to be carried out until the correct drain size is identified. A typical sequence of steps using an online calculator is as follows.

Step 1: Define an initial trial drain size and channel slope

- Select a channel width and flow depth and assume a vertical side slope for a typical open box drain.

- Define the channel slope based on the proposed drain alignment identified in the field (channel slope = vertical channel rise/ horizontal channel run).

Step 2: Select a value for Manning's constant (n)

Typical values of finished and unfinished concrete channels are 0.012 and 0.014, respectively.

Step 3: Use an online calculator to determine the maximum drain discharge

- Enter the values from Steps 1 and 2 into an online calculator.

- Calculate maximum drain discharge Q.

Step 4: Identify the required drain size

- Compare the maximum drain discharge with the estimated discharge from slope surface runoff and from households (sections 6.3.3 and 6.3.4) and the flow entering from any other drains.

- Repeat the process with different realistic drain sizes and gradients until the required discharge can be accommodated by the drain.

6.3.6 Example to demonstrate intercept drain effectiveness

In this example, the rational method was used to calculate surface water discharge upslope of a proposed intercept drain location. The drain was subsequently constructed (figure 6.12a). Several households adjacent to the drain then connected their downpipes and gray water to the drain. During a storm event, a resident noted the flow depth in the drain and observed the flow velocity (figure 6.12b). These observations enabled estimations to be made of the total drain discharge for the 12-hour storm and of the actual proportion of rainfall captured by the drain.

Step 1: Calculate the total rainfall delivered to the slope

- Total rainfall was 84 mm over 12 hours on an area of 20,000 m².

- Determine the rainfall delivered to the slope (before runoff):

$Q = 0.084$ m × 20,000 m²
$Q = 1,680$ m³ (1,680,000 L)

FIGURE 6.12 Estimating observed drain flows

a. Main downslope drain conveys flow from an intercept drain.

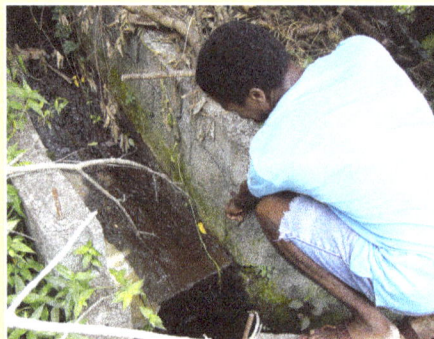

b. Resident indicates maximum flow depth reached during a previous day's storm.

Step 2: Estimate the total drain discharge

- Flow depth of 5 cm was observed in a 30 cm wide section of the intercept drain with a drain slope angle of approximately 4 degrees and Manning's n of 0.018 (unfinished concrete with minor debris)

- Using the Manning equation, estimate flow velocity and discharge: $V = 1.646$ m/s, and $Q = 0.024$ m³/s (24 L/s)

- Assuming constant rainfall, the total drain discharge for the 12-hour storm is approximately 1,036,800 L.

Step 3: Compare total drain discharge to total rainfall

The percentage of actual rainfall estimated to be captured by the drain is approximately $(1,036,800/1,680,000) \times 100 = 62$ percent.

Step 4: Estimate surface water runoff from the slope using the rational method

- Apply the rational method using an average rainfall intensity of 7 mm/h (84 mm over 12 hours), a slope area of 20,000 m², and a runoff coefficient of 0.6.

- Assuming constant rainfall intensity, the steady-state surface water discharge from the slope is estimated to be 0.023352 m³/s, and the estimated total surface runoff is 1,008,806 L in 12 hours.

- The percentage of rainfall estimated by the rational method to be converted into surface water runoff is $(1,008,806/1,680,000) \times 100 = 60$ percent.

This calculation allows two conclusions to be drawn: that the intercept drain is effective (capturing approximately 62 percent of total rainfall, Step 3), and that the rational method closely predicts the observed drain flow (comparing the results of Steps 2 and 4).

6.3.7 Example to demonstrate the impact of drain channel slope on flow capacity

Steeper channel slopes increase the flow conveyance of drains. Without proper design, drains with steep channel slopes are often overbuilt—too large for likely flow rates—and construction materials are wasted.

The impact of drain channel slope on flow velocity and discharge is accounted for in the Manning equation. The following example assumes a concrete drain with an internal dimension of 45 cm wide by 40 cm deep and Manning's n of 0.012. Figure 6.13 shows that for a 5 degree drain channel slope (typical of an intercept drain running across a slope), the maximum drain flow velocity is 6.78 m/s for a maximum discharge of 1.24 m³/s. On a slope of 45 degrees, a downslope drain of the same dimensions has much greater maximum flow velocity: 22.89 m/s and a maximum discharge of 4.12 m³/s—more than three times that of the same size intercept drain. The calculated flow velocities and drain discharges for each drain channel slope plotted in figure 6.13 appear below the figure.

6.3.8 Example to demonstrate the impact of household water

The potential impact of household water (and hence the effectiveness of comprehensive household water management) can be demonstrated using the example of a typical Eastern Caribbean hillside community with the following characteristics:

- Slope area = 7,000 m²

- Average house footprint = 60 m²

- Housing density = 30 percent of slope surface

- Annual average rainfall = 1,868 mm

- Daily average piped water consumption per house = 450 L

Calculating the total water supplied to the slope shows that the publicly supplied piped water effectively adds the equivalent of another 40 percent of annual average rainfall. However, if all the rainfall intercepted by roofs is captured, this reduces the effective rainfall volume by 30 percent; if, in addition to capturing roof water, 50 percent of household waste water is captured, the total surface water can

FIGURE 6.13 Impact of drain gradient on flow velocity and discharge

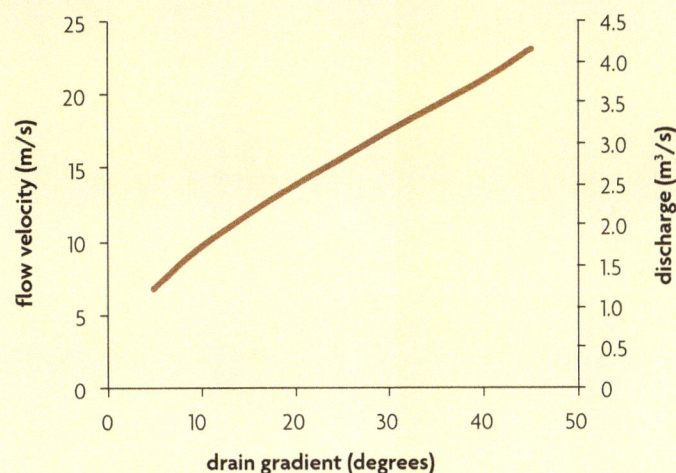

Drain channel slope				Drain discharge capacity compared
Degrees	Gradient	Velocity (m/s)	Drain discharge capacity (m³/s)	to 5° drain channel slope (%)
5	0.09	6.78	1.24	100
10	0.18	9.71	1.75	141
20	0.36	13.73	2.47	199
30	0.58	17.43	3.14	253
40	0.84	20.98	3.78	305
45	1.00	22.89	4.12	332

be reduced by approximately 45 percent. This example is illustrated in figure 6.14.

Figure 6.15 shows the impact of publicly supplied piped water on the amount of surface water added to the slope as the number of houses grows. As housing density increases, so does the effectiveness of roof guttering as a means of reducing surface water—the larger the roof area, the greater the percentage of rainfall intercepted.

6.4 DRAIN TYPES AND DETAILED ALIGNMENTS

Once the general alignment and provisional dimensions of the main drains have been determined, the next task is to confirm the exact alignment of each drain on site, taking into account different drain types and functions. In addition to the overall distinction

FIGURE 6.14 Effect of household water drainage in a typical community

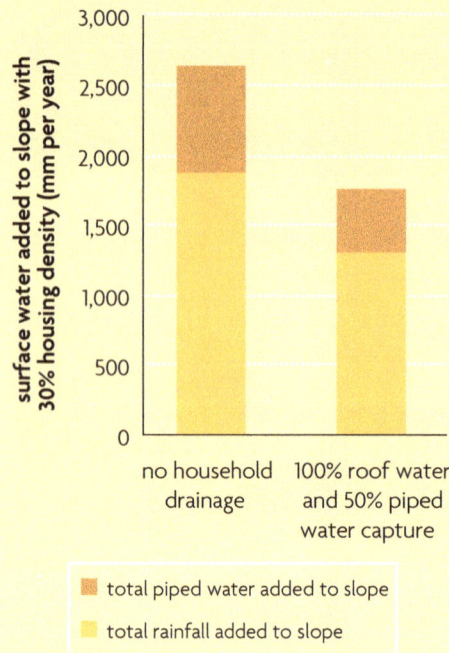

surface water added to slope with 30% housing density (mm per year)

- total piped water added to slope
- total rainfall added to slope

Note: See text for values of input parameters.

between intercept and downslope drains, this section considers detailed alignment issues associated with drains beside footpaths, existing drainage lines that might require repair, and drains across or above landslides. Drains connecting households to the main drains will

often involve several of the detailed alignment issues described in this section. Finally, in designing the detailed drain alignment, wider, accessible drain sections may need to be incorporated to allow for the installation of debris traps.

The following questions apply to the alignment of all types of drains:

- Is there enough space between houses, paths, and other structures or obstacles to safely build a drain with adequate capacity?

- Can the ground be excavated to a sufficient depth or constructed in such a way that the top of the drain walls will be flush with the slope surface, thus allowing surface water runoff to enter the drain? If this is not possible, the drain may cause flooding and slope instability by blocking or concentrating surface water flows.

- Does the proposed alignment have smooth bends, or will structures or obstacles mean that the drain alignment has abrupt changes in direction? Sharp bends can result in turbulent flow, accumulation of debris, or overtopping during high flows.

- Does the drain alignment capture significant sources of water from surface runoff and from tributary drains?

FIGURE 6.15 Potential effectiveness of household drainage measures

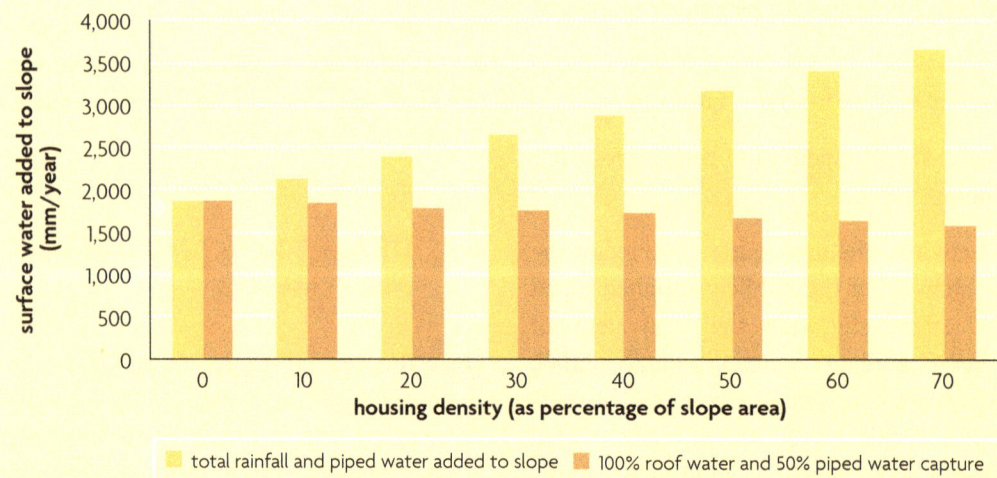

surface water added to slope (mm/year)

housing density (as percentage of slope area)

- total rainfall and piped water added to slope
- 100% roof water and 50% piped water capture

Note: See text for values of surface water inputs.

- Does the drain alignment allow households to easily connect roof water and gray water to the drain?

- Are all the proposed drains connected so as to discharge the water safely off the slope without causing flooding or instability problems elsewhere?

- Can large drainage areas be divided into subcatchments with separate drainage networks to avoid the need for very large or very deep drainage channels?

- Would the proposed alignments pose any significant construction or access challenges, such as transport of materials to site, access for excavation and disposal of debris, or close proximity to houses?

- Have the community, landowners, or individual households raised objections to drains being constructed in certain locations? Safeguards are very important; ensure that all stakeholders understand and agree to the drain alignment (figure 6.16).

FIGURE 6.17 Main cross-slope intercept drain constructed on a 35 degree slope angle

FIGURE 6.16 Drain alignment must be correctly specified in communities

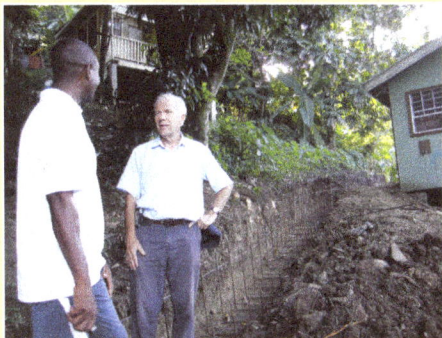

Getting the approval of residents and other stakeholders is especially important for detailed drain alignment when, as in this case, the alignment passes close to houses and may also cross informal pathways used by residents.

6.4.1 Intercept drains

Intercept, or contour, drains can play a major role in reducing landslide risk (figure 6.17). They can be very effective in preventing surface water from upper slopes reaching zones of topographic convergence and landslide hazard. More generally, intercept drains can be used to capture surface water before it infiltrates soils in the upslope areas; this water could otherwise contribute to shallow subsurface groundwater flows, serving to increase soil water pore pressures downslope. Ideally, two or more levels of surface water interception should be considered across the whole slope so that as many houses as possible are protected from uncontrolled surface water flows.

In aligning intercept drains, ask the following questions:

- Has the community mapping process identified zones of drainage convergence, increased landslide hazard, or high housing density that could be protected by an intercept drain?

- Are there zones of exposed bedrock and high surface runoff above these convergence or landslide zones? Aligning intercept drains along the interface between exposed bedrock (upslope) and soil (downslope) can be a very effective way of maximizing surface water capture as long as the upslope drain sidewall is flush with the slope surface to allow runoff to enter the drain.

- Is there potential for two or more levels of intercept drains across the hillside?

- Is there a proposed downslope drain or existing drainage channel of sufficient capacity to which to connect the intercept drains? If not, the concentrated flow of water from the intercept drain could cause problems elsewhere.

- Will the proposed alignment of an intercept drain provide a sufficient channel gradient and associated flow velocity and discharge capacity? On steep, highly vegetated slopes, it can often be difficult to establish a line of sight or identify minor topographic features that will affect the channel slope of a proposed intercept drain; it may be necessary to clear undergrowth and survey the proposed drain alignment.

6.4.2 Downslope drains

Properly aligned downslope drains can take advantage of existing natural channels or surface flow paths that are active during heavy rainfall. Capitalizing on natural channels and flow paths also enables the capture of tributary inflows that drain other areas of the slope. Thus, a single downslope drain may have a large catchment area and convey significant discharges (figure 6.18).

In aligning downslope drains, ask the following questions:

- Can major downslope drains be aligned on the hillside to take advantage of existing natural channel flows?

- Would such an alignment capture significant inflows from tributary drainage paths (including proposed new intercept drains), and can these be clearly identified?

- Can the proposed alignment help in managing water affecting zones of higher landslide hazard (such as saturated areas and areas of known instability)?

FIGURE 6.18 Poor practice: Downslope drain construction begun at top of hillside rather than base of slope

Beginning construction at the bottom of the slope and working upslope prevents concentration of flow and erosion at unconstructed sections, as is starting to occur here.

6.4.3 Footpath drains

Providing access to and within vulnerable communities is often a priority for poverty reduction and community development projects. Quite frequently, however, the focus is restricted to building footpaths or steps without considering drainage provision, which should be an integral part of good footpath or road design.

Existing or planned footpaths should be incorporated into the overall community drainage network for several reasons, including the following:

- Paths, tracks, and roads can act as preferential flow paths for surface runoff and can generate concentrated flows of water during heavy rain.

- Conversely, footpaths may have developed along minor natural drainage routes where community members have adopted these convenient, less-vegetated routes for access.

- Footpaths may follow a similar pattern to the idealized drainage pattern, with routes across the slope (along contours) and down the slope.

- The construction of a drain along an existing path may be relatively straightforward in terms of landownership issues and in getting construction materials to the site.

It is best to construct footpaths, footpath drains, and culverts simultaneously, as this enables surface water capture to be holistically designed (figure 6.19). The decoupling of access provision from surface drainage design is not uncommon, perhaps partly because drainage and access are typically provided by different development projects or agencies. If there is provision for footpath construction in conjunction with the MoSSaiC project, two drain alignment and design issues should be incorporated at this stage:

- Provision for widening and stepping down the drain at the base of a long run of footpath steps to reduce flow velocity

FIGURE 6.19 Examples of footpath and footpath drains being constructed simultaneously

- Provision for culverts where drains need to connect across footpaths.

In aligning footpath drains, ask the following questions:

- Are there existing drains along footpaths that could be used or improved as part of the overall drainage network?

  — Do they have sufficient capacity, or are they prone to blocking or overflowing? Particularly note discharge capacities adjacent to steps and through culverts.

  — Does the camber on the path direct water into the drain? If not, can a small upstand be constructed along the side of the path to redirect the water across the path into the existing drain?

  — Can the drain be connected to the wider drainage network?

  — Is there any evidence that the community can keep such drains clean on a regular basis? Footpath drains can easily become blocked with vegetation debris, garbage, soil, and stones.

- Are there footpaths that require better drainage?

  — Is there enough space to build a drain?

  — Can proposed footpath drains be linked to existing or proposed main drains?

6.4.4 Incomplete existing drainage

In vulnerable communities, there may be existing drains that are incomplete, unconnected, broken, or blocked (figure 6.20). In some cases, these drains may be contributing to landslide hazard or flooding problems by discharging water onto unstable/marginally stable slope zones. The most likely such circumstance is where a footpath or access intervention has previously been completed without an accompanying comprehensive drainage plan. The community slope feature mapping process should have identified such issues.

At this stage, revisit the existing drains to determine if they can be repaired, extended,

FIGURE 6.20 Incomplete and damaged drains

a. Poor design: a newly constructed drain has no planned outflow discharge management. The discharge can serve to increase landslide risk.

b. Old drain construction with no downslope management of the discharge.

and connected to the proposed new drains. If this is not possible, the flow entering these old drains should be captured upslope and diverted into the proposed drainage network.

In this regard, ask the following questions:

- Are there locations where incomplete drains discharge onto the slope rather than connect to existing drains?

- Are there locations where existing downslope drains discharge into broken drainage structures?

By channeling water to a specific slope location, both of these conditions can increase slope instability. They should be directly addressed as part of the intervention.

6.4.5 Drains above landslides to stabilize the slope

Areas of existing slope instability can be difficult to stabilize in certain cases and may continue to threaten surrounding houses. Areas above the active landslide zone can become unstable because of oversteepening of the slope at the crest of the slide, and house foundations may be undermined. Houses on or below the unstable area may be affected by progressive ground movement and subsidence, or endangered by further slope failure.

If water is contributing to the ongoing movement or potential reactivation of landslides in these areas, it may be possible to improve the stability of the slope using appropriate drainage (figure 6.21). In determining whether to install a drain above a landslide to stabilize the slope, ask the following questions:

- Examine how the water flow is channeled above the unstable area—does it flow onto the failed material, and does it have a clearly defined channel?

- Could the water be captured above the existing failed material and channeled across and down the slope away from the area?

- Is there stable material above the failed zone that would allow drain construction?

FIGURE 6.21 Drain construction above a
failed slope

Careful alignment can significantly reduce
water flowing to potentially unstable hillside
areas.

6.4.6 Incorporating debris traps into drain alignment

Drains are likely to become blocked with debris unless they are appropriately designed and subsequently kept clean and well maintained (figure 6.22). In heavy rainfall, a blocked drain can overflow and contribute to landslide hazard or flood houses. Debris traps are designed to collect debris (stones, garbage, and organic material such as leaves and wood) at key locations in the drain to prevent blockages. Typical locations for debris traps include points where debris is deposited due to reduced flow velocities (such as changes from steep to shallow channel slopes), or immediately upstream of culverts.

At debris trap locations, the drain design should include the following:

- Easy access to the debris trap from a path or road to allow removal of debris

- Widening of the drain section to accommodate the accumulation of debris without causing the drain to overflow.

Debris traps of varying designs are used around the world. On steep hillsides in Hong Kong SAR, China, for example, there are typically two styles of trap at the point the drain enters a culvert. Figure 6.23 shows an example where consideration has been given both to trapping debris and to ease of access for debris removal.

Good debris trap design must be accompanied by a realistic plan for drain maintenance that identifies both government and commu-

FIGURE 6.22 Postconstruction
maintenance: Keeping drains free of debris

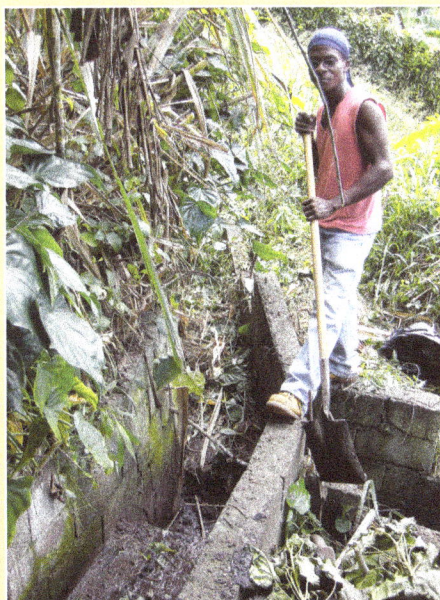

FIGURE 6.23 Debris trap in an urban area
of Hong Kong, SAR, China

nity responsibilities. A particular issue is government provision of solid waste collection from communities, since debris removed from drains and traps must be properly disposed of.

> Too often, low-income communities are expected to maintain their drainage systems with minimal assistance, either as a result of wishful thinking on the part of municipal authorities or by default, because the municipality simply does not have the resources or capacity to maintain the system it has installed. Rather, what the community needs is support to enable it to carry out its part of the work more effectively (WHO 1991, 53).

In considering the use and placement of debris traps, ask the following questions:

- Are there locations in the proposed drainage alignments, or along existing drains, that will be vulnerable to blockage by debris?

- Is there enough space to widen the drain at these locations to accommodate a debris trap?

- Are these locations easy to access for cleaning and removing debris from the community?

- Is there a realistic plan for regularly cleaning and maintaining debris traps?

6.4.7 Proposed drainage plan

Develop the first version of the final drainage plan, showing the alignments of all main intercept and downslope drains, plus smaller drains (along footpaths and connecting households). Use the on-site knowledge gained from developing the community slope feature map, the slope process zone map, and the initial drainage plan (chapter 5 and figure 6.24), and take into account the drainage alignment principles outlined in this chapter. Figure 6.25 illustrates the draft final drainage plan based on figure 6.24. Table 6.3 summarizes some of the key issues to account for in this final plan.

6.5 DRAIN CONSTRUCTION SPECIFICATIONS: MATERIALS AND DETAILS

The drainage work extent and construction specifications will be determined by the required capacity and function of each drain section, and constrained by project budget and on-site conditions. Options for drain design and construction specifications should be explained to all stakeholders to help establish reasonable expectations and avoid the need for major revisions of the drainage plan.

Factors affecting drain construction specification include the following:

- **Drain size and alignment.** The size, shape, and channel slope should be designed to give the required discharge capacity, and take into account space available for drain construction and the effect of flow velocity. Steep smooth channels with small cross-sectional areas and high flow velocities are likely to be self-cleaning (i.e., limit the deposition of debris), but may be susceptible to channel erosion and increase flooding downstream. Conversely, low-gradient wide channels can cause debris to accumulate at low flows.

- **Drain function and features.** Intercept drains will have slightly different features (such as weep holes and lower channel slopes) than downslope drains, which might need to include steps to reduce flow velocities on steep sections, and baffle walls to prevent overtopping.

- **Maintenance and safety issues.** Open drains with regular debris traps are generally easy to inspect for damage and to keep clean and free of mosquitoes. Closed drains may seem more aesthetically pleasing and take less space, but are more easily blocked, are difficult to maintain, and capture less surface runoff. Covered sections should be restricted to culverts and locations where safe access across the drain is required.

FIGURE 6.24 Example of an initial drainage plan

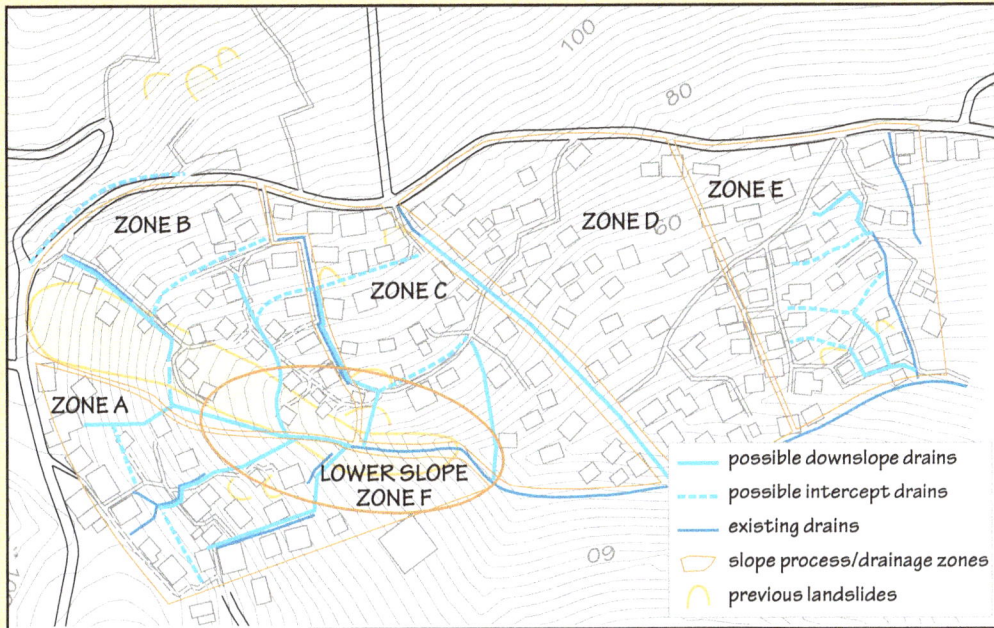

FIGURE 6.24 Example of an initial drainage plan

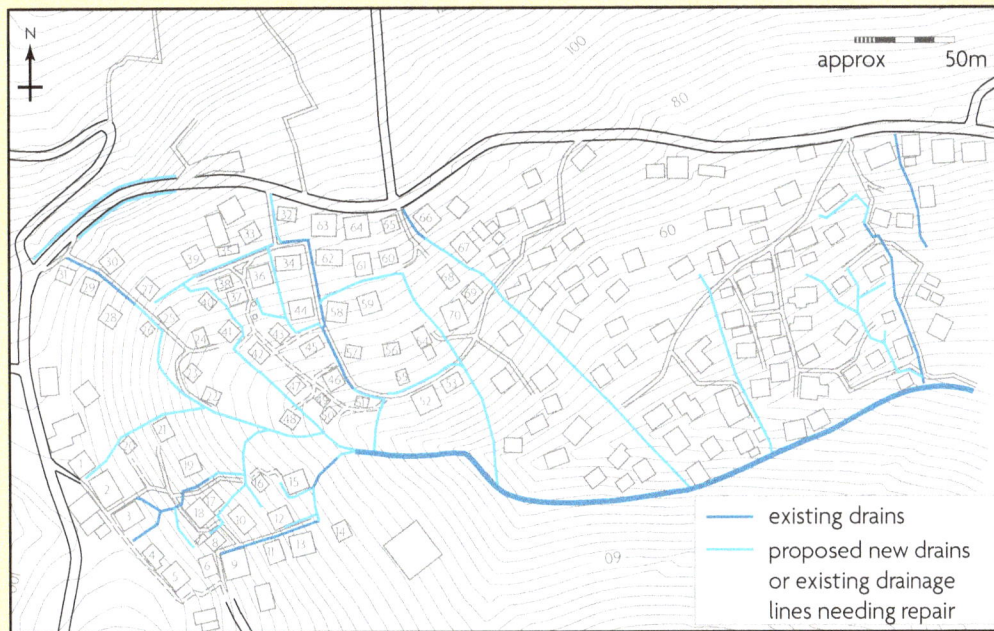

FIGURE 6.25 Example of a draft final drainage plan

- **Construction material.** For MoSSaiC projects, the purpose of surface water drains is to reduce surface water infiltration into slopes—thus, all drains should be lined and made watertight (with weep holes where necessary) using concrete (for main drains, section 6.5.1) or robust polythene sheeting (for small low-flow drains, section 6.5.2).

To optimize the project budget, it may be appropriate to include low-cost construction methods in some locations; other elements of

TABLE 6.3 Drainage alignment summary for use in developing final drainage plan

LOOK FOR	SIGNIFICANCE	ACTION: DRAINAGE ALIGNMENT DESIGN
Zones of topographic convergence	Topographic convergence concentrates water downslope and can cause slope instability	Plan an intercept drain above such zones and connect to a downslope main drain away from the area to an appropriate receiving water body.
Zones of former slope instability	Such zones imply the potential for future instability or ongoing progressive (slow-moving) failures.	Plan to capture water above such zones and route drains around unstable material.
Natural drainage channels or existing downslope drains	These channels may have a large enough capacity to remove water discharged from new drains	Map and incorporate these channels or drains into the plan if discharge capacity is sufficient. More than one downslope drain may be required in order to serve the whole community. Plan the spacing of downslope drains such that houses and intercept drains can be connected.
Existing footpath drains	Footpath drains can often intercept and convey significant surface water discharges and may be in close proximity to houses (making household water connections easy)	Map and incorporate these drains into the plan if discharge capacity is sufficient. Make adequate provision for any culverts needed to cross footpaths, as these can restrict flow and are often liable to blockage and severe flow capacity reductions.
Unconnected or damaged drains	Sections of drain that discharge concentrated, uncontrolled flows onto the slope can cause flooding, erosion, and landslide hazards	If these drains present a hazard, divert flows to other drains or incorporate into the new drainage network (indicating sections for repair).
Potential routes for intercept drain	Intercept drains are a critical element in capturing upslope water and preventing water flow into topographic convergence zones	Examine the hillside holistically—design a drainage pattern that best utilizes surface water interception routes. Note that the effect of a single cross-slope intercept drain can be achieved with several shorter intercept drains (see section 6.3.1).
Wide, smooth drainage routes	There should be enough space to construct drains with adequate capacity to accommodate the estimated discharge, without sharp bends where overtopping can occur	Estimate the surface water discharge into main drains, and calculate the required drain dimensions to accommodate the flow. Avoid aligning the drain where there is not enough space (e.g., between densely built houses). If the potential routes are too narrow, consider subdividing the catchment and building several smaller drains.
Proximity of houses to planned or existing drains	Roof water and gray water from houses can represent a significant proportion of the surface water in a community	Plan the drain alignments to optimize the number of households that can be connected to the drainage network.

the drainage design will call for more conventional construction methods. Factors such as drain size, function, and maintenance will determine which form of construction is appropriate. For example, main drains will almost certainly need to be constructed from reinforced concrete due to their high discharge and often high velocities (especially on steep slopes). Small household drains with lower flows could be constructed using precast concrete drain elements or lower-cost materials.

Use this section to identify key design elements for the two main types of drain construction used in MoSSaiC projects—concrete main drains constructed according to standard engineering specifications, and smaller low-cost drains constructed using appropriate and readily available local materials.

6.5.1 Reinforced concrete block drains

Drains that will have large discharge volumes, high flow velocities, or debris-laden flows must be robustly constructed to ensure their durability and reliability. Government engineers may be accustomed to constructing rubble wall drains for large-scale projects (figure 6.26), but these can be expensive and not

FIGURE 6.26 Rubble wall as part of drain construction

FIGURE 6.26 Rubble wall as part of drain construction

As rubble wall structures are generally expensive, it is a good practice to review alternatives such as concrete block construction carefully.

6.5.2 Low-cost, appropriate technology for drain construction

Low-cost solutions that use appropriate local materials can engage community members in contributing ideas and construction knowledge, raise awareness of good slope drainage practices, and be a valuable means of fostering project sustainability. While the advantages of reinforced concrete block drains include a durable structure and proven design protocols, low-cost approaches can be appropriate for low drain discharges and flow velocities in the following circumstances:

• For connecting small numbers of houses to main drains

• In less accessible locations, such as upper slopes, where materials for concrete drains cannot be transported or carried

always appropriate for community-based drainage projects. For MoSSaiC projects, reinforced concrete block drains (also called U-drains or open drains) are often the most suitable option for main intercept and downslope drains, footpath drains, and many of the secondary (tributary) drains.

Although there are different standard designs for reinforced concrete block drains around the world, the essential elements of excavation, a compacted base, steel reinforcement, cast concrete invert, concrete block sidewalls with weep holes, and a compacted granular backfill are likely to be similar (figure 6.27). One construction specification for MoSSaiC projects is that the tops of the drain sidewalls should be flush with the slope surface to enable surface water to flow into the drain. The design and construction of concrete drains should be carried out in conjunction with that of other structures, such as footpaths, that may be part of a MoSSaiC project.

FIGURE 6.27 Example of concrete block drain design

a. Typical section of reinforced concrete block drain

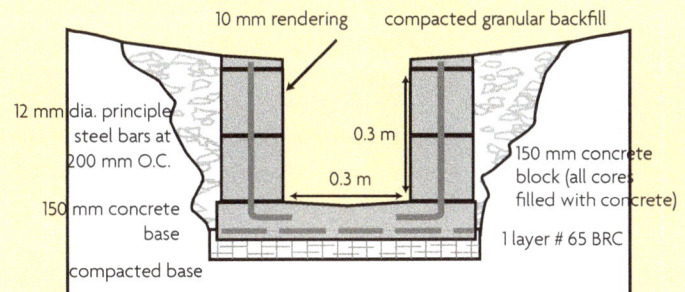

10 mm rendering   compacted granular backfill

12 mm dia. principle steel bars at 200 mm O.C.

0.3 m

0.3 m

150 mm concrete block (all cores filled with concrete)

150 mm concrete base

1 layer # 65 BRC

compacted base

b. Typical section of reinforced concrete block drain for intercepting water across a slope

specification as above (for typical block drain) plus the following design specification:

weep holes—distance to be determined on site (typically 3 m spacing)

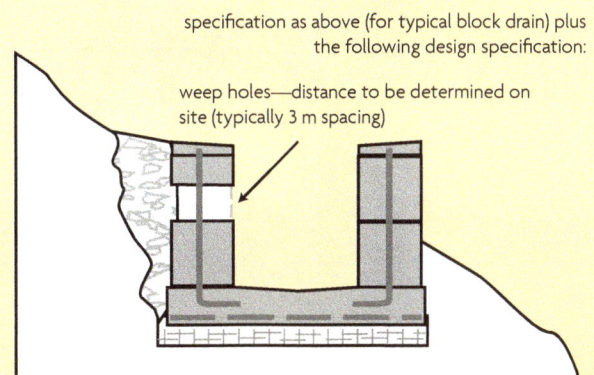

Note: Each country can be expected to have a slightly different standard design to suit local conditions and material availability.

- On unstable slope sections that need surface drainage but where slope movement may be reactivated.

A low-cost, appropriate technology drain construction method was developed by government task teams and community residents during a MoSSaiC project in St. Lucia. The drain consists of a shallow trench lined with durable polythene sheeting (typically sunlight-stable polythene) which makes the drain water tight and prevents infiltration. To keep it in place, the polythene is overlaid with a light-weight steel-wire mesh molded to the shape of the drain and anchored to the ground with U-shaped pegs made by bending lengths of reinforcing rod. These materials cost considerably less than those required for constructing a reinforced concrete block drain of equivalent size.

Beyond its cost-effectiveness, some of the advantages of this drain construction method include the following:

- **Ease of transport.** Materials can readily be carried to sites that are difficult or prohibitively expensive to transport materials to for concrete block drain construction (figure 6.28).

- **Rapid uptake.** Low cost, and the ease of transport of materials, means that such drain construction methods are more likely to be adopted as a self-help measure by individual households.

- ***Speed and flexibility of construction.*** Unlike concrete block drains, the plastic-lined drains can be quickly constructed or dismantled. New drains can be installed relatively easily to accommodate slope movement on progressive slides or the construction of new houses or paths (figure 6.29).

Certain communities in the Eastern Caribbean have been sufficiently engaged with MoSSaiC projects to use their own initiative

FIGURE 6.29 Installation of plastic-lined drain

a. Low-cost drain being installed by residents.

b. Completed drain, with household gray water connections.

FIGURE 6.28 Shipping construction material to site can be expensive

Shipping sand and cement can add significantly to the cost of conventional drain construction in more remote island locations. Here, material is being shipped some 18 miles on an inter-island ferry to reach the community.

and construct low-cost drains in appropriate locations that supplement, and connect to, the main drainage network (figure 6.30). Such initiatives are evidence of a community taking ownership of good slope management practices for landslide risk reduction.

6.5.3 Combining different drain construction approaches

It might be premature to expend funds on the construction of concrete block drains unless there is sufficient evidence that doing so will improve slope stability. Where the slope is extensive and multiple signs of instability are present, a possible solution is to use a combination of drain construction approaches:

- Construct concrete block drains upslope of unstable slope sections to intercept surface runoff and discharge water safely off the slope.

- Use low-cost or temporary drains (such as that discussed in section 6.5.2) across active areas of the landslide or previously failed material (figure 6.31).

This latter approach allows an assessment to be made of stability improvement that surface drainage affords in complex landslide zones without expending all available funds at the initial stage.

FIGURE 6.30 Community innovation and skills at work after project completion

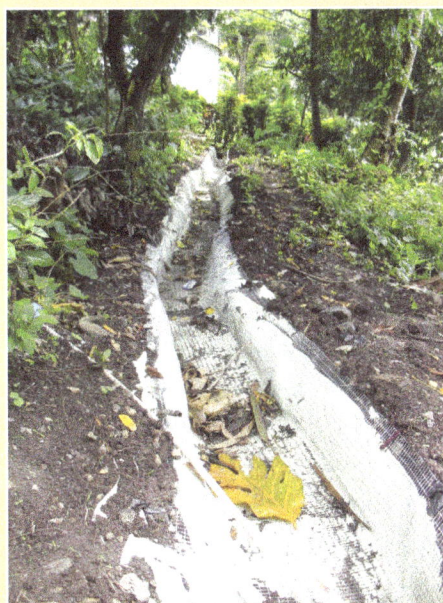

Community residents selected the location, excavated a trench, and constructed a low-cost drain to capture surface water and convey it to a main concrete drain.

FIGURE 6.31 Combination of block drain and low-cost drain

These drains were used in a former landslide area, the lower portion of which was potentially still unstable.

6.5.4 Construction design details

Define the construction specification for each drain section in the final drainage plan according to the drain alignment, size, function, and construction type. Incorporate additional drain construction design details using table 6.4 as a guide.

6.6 INCORPORATING HOUSEHOLD WATER CAPTURE INTO THE PLAN

In areas of high housing density, the capture and controlled drainage of water from houses is a vital element of the final drainage plan for landslide hazard reduction, as discussed in section 6.3.8. Household water consists of roof water (rainfall that is intercepted by roofs and runs off) and gray water (wastewater from kitchens, washing machines, washbasins, and showers—i.e., any wastewater except that from the toilet, which is termed black water or septic waste, and which should not be discharged into surface drains constructed as part of a MoSSaiC project).

Increasing the housing density and volume of publicly supplied water discharged onto a slope can result in a corresponding increase in the number of days the soil is saturated per year, if there is no drainage (figure 6.32). This level of saturation is significantly reduced by capturing roof water and gray water.

Having confirmed the alignment of drains within the community, determine which houses need to be connected to drains—prioritizing zones where household water significantly contributes to surface water infiltration and slope instability. Use the guidance in this section to identify the components that are required for each house (such as roof guttering, water tanks, gray water pipes, drain connections, and hurricane straps). This process is illustrated in figure 6.33.

Estimate the quantity and cost of materials assuming a unit cost per house for each of the prioritized houses and the approximate number of shared components, such as concrete

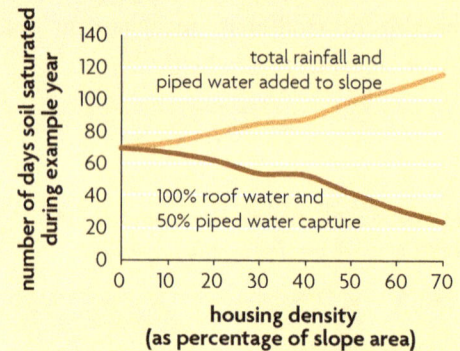

FIGURE 6.32 Number of days slope surface is saturated per year with and without household water capture

Note: Annual rainfall = 1,868 mm, slope area = 7,000 m², slope surface saturated hydraulic conductivity, K_{sat} = 1 x 10⁻⁷ m³ s⁻¹, average house footprint = 60 m², monthly average water supply per house = 2,887 gal.

chambers for connecting multiple pipes or small household drains. A detailed house-by-house survey of actual guttering lengths and parts will be undertaken during the preparation of work packages (chapter 7) after sign-off of the final drainage plan.

6.6.1 Houses requiring roof guttering

Roof guttering can be an effective way of intercepting rainwater and reducing surface water runoff in order to improve slope stability. The added benefits to the household include the opportunity to harvest rainwater for domestic use (see section 6.6.2) and a reduction in the negative effects associated with uncontrolled roof water runoff (protecting house foundations from erosion, increasing the service life of the roof and walls, and reducing problems with damp and flooding).

Identify how many houses require roof guttering as part of the project and indicate their inclusion on the final drainage plan. Use the following questions as a guide:

- Is the house in an area where surface water and household water are significantly contributing to the landslide hazard?

- Is there a problem with stagnant water or erosion of the foundations caused by water from the roof or a neighbor's roof?

TABLE 6.4 Construction design details related to aspects of drain alignment

LOOK FOR	WHERE	ACTION: DRAIN CONSTRUCTION DESIGN
Locations where drains could be overtopped	• On steep drain gradients with high flow velocities (especially where there are steps or bends in the channel) • Where drains connect (especially if the angle of the drain connection is high—e.g., a right angle) • Drains adjacent to footpath steps where the tread of the step is too low • Where debris could accumulate and block the drain	• For existing drains and footpaths, the drain depth can often be increased by building an upstand. • Baffle walls can be added where drains join to prevent any flow jumping the connection. • Make sure that bends in drains have a sufficient radius for the flow velocity, and ensure sufficient freeboard (including the use of baffle walls where necessary) to contain the superelevation of the water surface. • Avoid the use of chambers or enclosed drains where possible. • Incorporate debris traps (and widen the drain).
Locations where flow could be constricted	• Culverts • Existing drains that are under-sized	• Widen and deepen existing culverts and drains to accommodate the flow. Maintain steep drain gradient through culverts to prevent blockage. • Where drain size cannot be increased, flow should be diverted into new drains.
Locations where surface water could be prevented from entering the drain	• All drains	• Construct the top of drain sidewalls flush with the slope surface. This ensures surface water flow capture and prevents potential undermining of the sidewall by erosion. Use well-compacted fill to make up any overexcavation along channel sides. • To maximize subsurface soil water flow capture, include weep holes on the upslope channel side. This helps to ensure flow does not undermine the drain.
Locations where surface water runoff and drain flows could erode the slope or cause damage to the drain	• Bare soil on slopes adjacent to the drain • High-velocity turbulent drain flows (steep, stepped drains, especially at bends in the channel) • Natural drainage channels into which the main drains discharge and where the increased flow could erode the channel sides	• Provide a sloping apron adjacent to the channel, particularly for stepped channels, to return any out-of-channel splashing to the channels. • Include additional reinforcement in the construction design. • Steps in channels should be sloping, not horizontal. Multiple small steps should be designed, rather than a few large steps. • Rip-rap can be used to armor the sides and base of natural channels, and gabion baskets or rubble walls can be designed to protect and retain steep channel sides.
Safeguards	• Housing proximity to drains	• Ensure, where possible, that drainage channels are not placed too close to housing structures and that considerations of channel design are viewed within the context of all relevant safeguard requirements.

Source: Hui, Sun, and Ho 2007.

FIGURE 6.33 Process for incorporating household water capture into the drainage plan

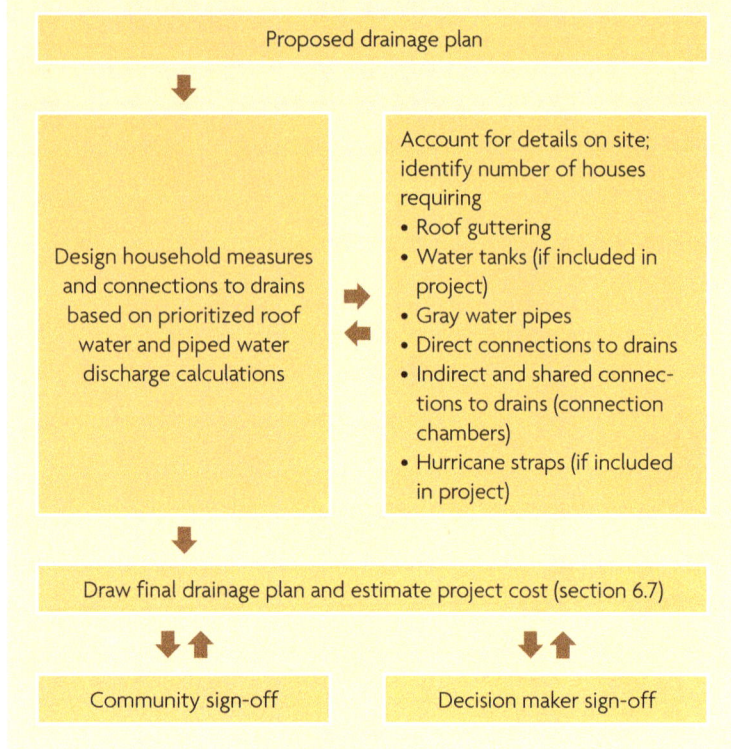

Proposed drainage plan

Design household measures and connections to drains based on prioritized roof water and piped water discharge calculations

Account for details on site; identify number of houses requiring
- Roof guttering
- Water tanks (if included in project)
- Gray water pipes
- Direct connections to drains
- Indirect and shared connections to drains (connection chambers)
- Hurricane straps (if included in project)

Draw final drainage plan and estimate project cost (section 6.7)

Community sign-off

Decision maker sign-off

FIGURE 6.34 Retrofitting roof guttering

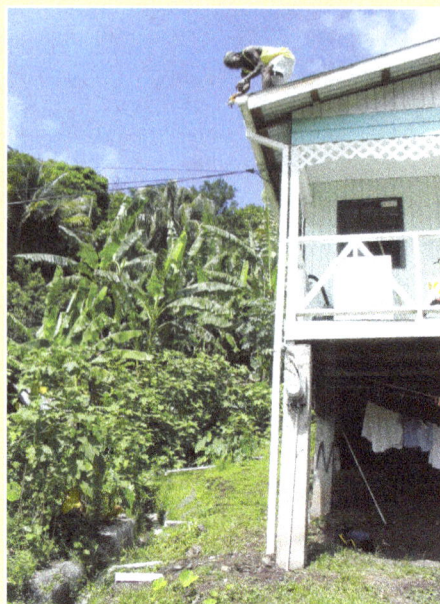

- Is there already guttering on part of the roof?

- How easy would it be to fit roof guttering (figure 6.34)?

- How will the downpipes connect to the main drainage network? Use section 6.6.4 to identify the most appropriate means of connection.

6.6.2 Rainwater harvesting

Providing water for washing and cleaning

The harvesting of rainwater captured by the roof can be a major priority for some communities if there is no public water supply, or if the supply is interrupted on a regular basis and for long periods (figure 6.35). Roof guttering is an inexpensive way of collecting significant volumes of water for household use for washing and cleaning purposes. Homeowners may already be collecting rainwater from part or all of their roof area using a drum (ideally covered with a fine mesh to prevent mosquitoes) or a modern domestic water tank.

Harvesting for drinking water

Rainwater harvesting installations that are designed to provide drinking water typically comprise the following major components: catchment area (usually a roof), guttering, prestorage filtering, storage in a tank, and poststorage treatment. Figure 6.36 illustrates typical systems for filtering and purifying roof water for human consumption.

The cost of a small water tank is typically only half that of a complete system (figure 6.37); there are additional recurrent costs to the homeowner to maintain, clean, and replace filters and other components. These set-up and maintenance costs will likely be prohibitive for MoSSaiC projects (and residents) unless the project objectives include provision of rainwater harvesting for drinking water and there is associated funding for this purpose.

Assessment of quantities

If the project provides for installing household water tanks in conjunction with roof guttering, identify which households will benefit most and determine whether to provide a standard domestic water tank or connect the roof guttering to an existing tank. For each

FIGURE 6.35 Rainwater harvesting

a. Many communities have unreliable water supplies and have to make what provision they can to harvest rainwater.

b. Providing water tanks as part of a MoSSaiC intervention to those residents most in need can be a cost-effective means of rainwater harvesting.

FIGURE 6.36 A system for filtering and purifying water for human consumption

a. Rainwater harvesting for drinking water can be a relatively expensive installation because of the filtration systems required.

b. Filtration unit running costs can generally only be justified in the most deserving of cases.

FIGURE 6.37 Cost components of small domestic rainwater harvesting system

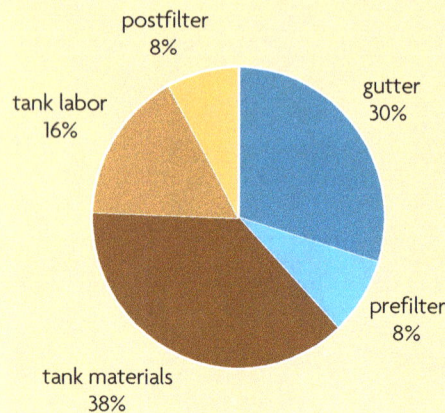

postfilter
8%

tank labor
16%

gutter
30%

prefilter
8%

tank materials
38%

Source: University of Warwick 2003.

Note: A small system is here considered to be 600 L. Costs are based on fieldwork in southern Uganda.

house identified for roof guttering provision, ask the following questions:

- If the house is already harvesting roof water:

  — Is the water being harvested from the whole roof? If not, the roof guttering will need to be configured to do so, or to deliver excess water directly to a drain.

  — Is there adequate overflow connection from the tank to a drain? If not, such a connection will need to be made (see section 7.5.6).

  — Are there sufficient measures for preventing mosquitoes breeding in the tank?

- If roof water is not currently being harvested:

  — Would the homeowner like to be able to harvest rainwater from the roof?

  — Would the homeowner be willing or able to provide a drum or tank for collecting water?

  — Would the household benefit from being provided with a water tank as part of the project? If so, is there a way of prioritizing the neediest households?

6.6.3 Gray water capture

Providing communities with a piped public water supply can mean that water from houses (a point water source, in slope hydrology terms) can be a significant source of surface runoff and infiltration into the slope if left unmanaged (figure 6.38).

Drainage design should account for household gray water by making provision for houses to be connected to the main drains wherever feasible. If homeowners are changing the layout of their home, it is important to discuss ways in which they plan to connect new bathrooms and kitchens to the drain.

FIGURE 6.38 Capturing gray water from showers and washing machines

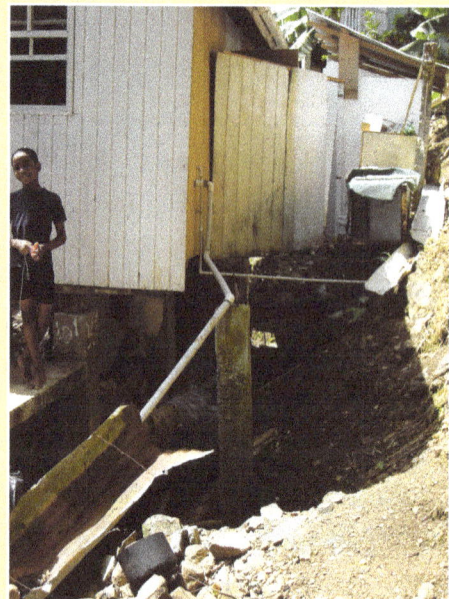

In the lower photograph, gray water discharges to a former landslide on which the house has been rebuilt.

Identify how many houses require gray water connections as part of the project and indicate their inclusion on the final plan. Use the following questions as a guide:

- Is the house in an area where surface water and household water are significantly contributing to the landslide hazard?

- Has the house already been selected for roof guttering installation? If so, it is likely to also require gray water connection to the drains.

- What form of connection is most appropriate? Use section 6.6.4 to identify the most appropriate means of connection.

6.6.4 Connection to the drainage network

Once it has been decided which houses should receive roof guttering, water tanks, and gray water connections, determine the method for connecting the downpipes, water tank overflows, and gray water pipes to the drainage network (figure 6.39). Household connection options include direct pipe connections, connection by pipe to a concrete chamber and

FIGURE 6.39 Gray water and roof water connections to block drain

then by pipe to the drain, or construction of a small drain to connect to the main drain.

If the homeowner has already made some provision for drainage (earth drains, trenches, concrete-lined drains), use the following questions to help decide how to incorporate these drains into the plan:

- Can the existing drains be connected to the proposed drains?

- Do they need to be improved to prevent leakage?

- Do they need to be extended to connect with the proposed drains?

- Is the current capacity sufficient to cope with additional flow from new roof guttering or gray water connections?

- Can a low-cost method of drain construction be used? (See section 6.5.2.)

- Are there preexisting connections to drains (roof guttering, water tank overflow, gray water)?

- Is the homeowner willing and able to make the necessary improvements? (This should be encouraged as a form of in-kind contribution to the project.)

If there are no connections:

- How far is it to the nearest existing or proposed drain?

- Can the house be connected directly to the drain?

- If it is too far or too complicated to connect pipes directly, is it appropriate to route the pipes via concrete connection chambers or a minor new drain?

Direct drain connections

Houses can be connected to existing or proposed block drains simply and inexpensively if the drain is adjacent to the house (figure 6.40a). Connections can sometimes be retrofitted to cross footpaths (figure 6.40b), but this is not ideal from either a hydraulic standpoint or in terms of residents' safety when using the foot-

FIGURE 6.40 Household connections to main drains

a. Connection of household roof water to a nearby main drain.

b. Provision should be made for household water connections before a footpath is constructed.

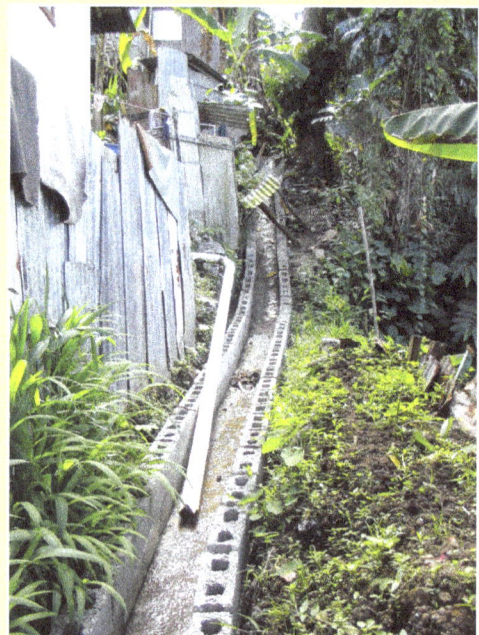

c. It is important to tidy up residents' makeshift gray water connections when drains have been built.

path. If new footpaths are to be constructed as part of the project, allow for household connections to be integrated into the design.

Pipes and connection chambers

Concrete chambers can be used to collect water from several downpipes and gray water pipes in cases where the distance between houses and drains prohibits direct connections. The water can then be routed to the main drain in a single large pipe. Concrete chambers can serve to collect water from several houses (figure 6.41), and a sequence of

chambers can be connected via pipes to a main drain.

Assessment of quantities

On the final drainage plan, indicate how roof guttering and gray water from each house will be connected to the drainage network. Estimate the costs of materials required based on approximate unit costs per length of drain or concrete chamber. A detailed quantity survey and preparation of work packages should be undertaken once the plan has been approved (chapter 7).

FIGURE 6.41 Concrete chambers connecting water from multiple houses to a single collection point with an outflow pipe to a main drain

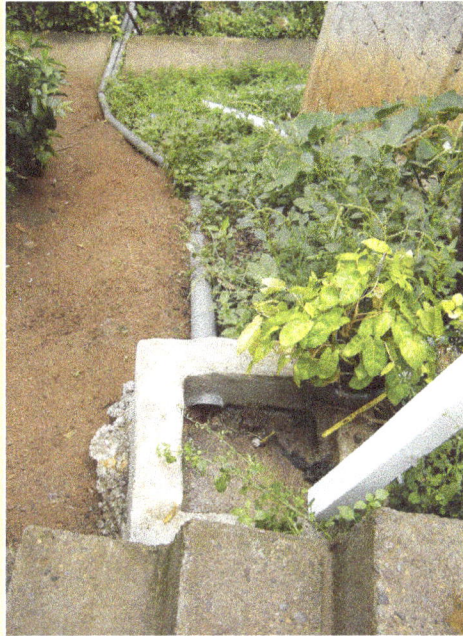

6.6.5 Hurricane strapping

Roofs are an important part of a surface water management strategy, especially in communities with high housing densities. In countries affected by tropical cyclones, the roof must be structurally sound and able to withstand not just heavy rainfall but also hurricane-force winds. Retrofitting roofs with hurricane straps should be included in the project wherever possible (figure 6.42).

Comprehensive retrofitting using a range of building ties on the structure strengthens a house's structural frame to create a continuous load path (IBHS 2002). A continuous load path is a method of construction that uses a system of wood, metal connectors, and fasteners such as nails and screws to connect the structural frame of the house together from roof to foundation (figure 6.43). The house is thus more likely to withstand a hurricane event and remain intact. Hurricane straps are the primary means of strengthening the roof of most one- or two-story structures. Although the straps are inexpensive and easy to install,

FIGURE 6.42 Fragile roof structure

Roof structures are typically relatively fragile, with galvanized sheeting nailed to joists and wall plates.

they are rarely seen as a priority in vulnerable households. Typical installations on a modest-sized house should involve the fitting of some 16–20 hurricane straps to the joists and rafters (figure 6.44). There are a variety of hurricane straps available; product selection will depend on local availability and house structural details.

FIGURE 6.43 Hurricane strapping ties

FIGURE 6.43 Hurricane strapping ties

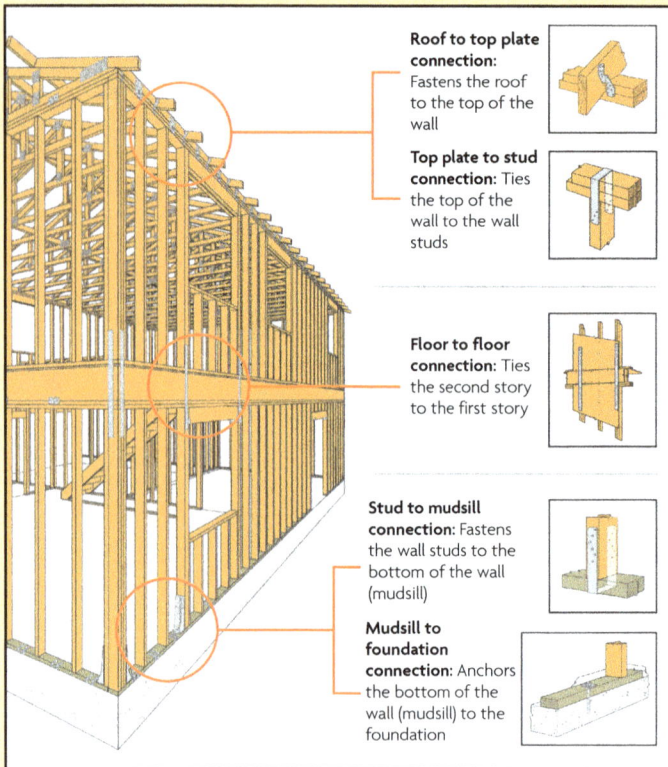

Roof to top plate connection: Fastens the roof to the top of the wall

Top plate to stud connection: Ties the top of the wall to the wall studs

Floor to floor connection: Ties the second story to the first story

Stud to mudsill connection: Fastens the wall studs to the bottom of the wall (mudsill)

Mudsill to foundation connection: Anchors the bottom of the wall (mudsill) to the foundation

Source: Image courtesy of Simpson Strong-Tie Company Inc.

FIGURE 6.44 Roof hurricane strap

6.7 SIGNING OFF ON THE FINAL DRAINAGE PLAN

The process for signing off on the final drainage plan will typically include the following steps:

- Drawing up the final drainage plan

- Estimating project costs

- Revising the plan according to the project budget

- Reviewing the plan (MCU, government task teams)

- Consulting with the community and other stakeholders, and incorporating any revisions into the plan

- Signing off on the plan with the community and decision makers.

The MCU should set a realistic schedule for this process and support the task teams in completing each step. Build in sufficient time for consultation with the community and use a variety of participatory approaches to allow different groups to contribute their opinions on the drainage plan (such as formal meetings and informal conversations). Keeping to the advertised schedule builds community trust and engagement.

6.7.1 Drawing the final drainage plan and estimating costs

The final drainage plan should include the following:

- The project name; community name; date; plan revision number; names of those involved in designing and drawing the plans; and any names or logos of funders, government ministries, and other agencies involved (according to local protocols)

- Proposed drain locations, lengths, construction types, and internal dimensions (calculated for main drains and estimated for minor drains)

- Houses with identification numbers or names to allow cross-reference to a list of households requiring roof guttering, gray water pipes, and connections to drains (and provision of water tanks and/or hurricane straps, if included in the project)

- Connection chamber locations

- Debris trap locations

- Any other relevant details for estimating project costs

- Reference to any relevant supplementary plans or documents.

Estimate the total project cost based on the proposed drain lengths, dimensions, and construction types, and the approximate quantities of each of the household drainage components. Obtain local unit costs for each component, and use these to calculate total project cost. Table 6.5 shows how a spreadsheet for calculating initial project costs could be organized. Once the proposed drainage plan and estimated costs have been approved, the cost estimates for each item will be fully specified for preparation of work packages (chapter 7).

6.7.2 Community agreement

Display the drainage plan (figure 6.45) at suitable locations within the community, such as at bars and shops (figure 6.46a). Walk through the community with the plan to obtain further feedback from community members and other stakeholders or decision makers (figure 6.46b). Members of the government and community task teams involved in community liaison, design of the drainage plan, and implementation of the proposed works should be part of this community visit, and should be prepared to answer any issues residents may wish to discuss. Convene a community meeting to discuss, refine, and agree on the plan. Government and community task team members should attend the meeting, together with members of the MCU and relevant stakeholders.

TABLE 6.5 Initial costs for drain construction and for household water connections

a. Drain construction

ITEM FOR CONSTRUCTION	CROSS-SECTION DIMENSIONS	APPROXIMATE LENGTH (m)	UNIT COST	TOTAL COST
New main concrete block drains				
New minor concrete block drains				
Existing drains to make-good				
New soft engineered drains				
Total				

b. Household water connections

ITEM FOR CONNECTION	NUMBER (n)	APPROXIMATE LENGTH (m)	UNIT COST	TOTAL COST
Roof guttering	n houses	—		
Water tanks	n houses	—		
Hurricane straps	n houses	—		
Gray water pipes	—			
Connecting pipes	—			
Connection chambers	n items	—		
Household drains	—			
Total				

FIGURE 6.45 Extracts from a final drainage plan for agreement with stakeholders and sign-off

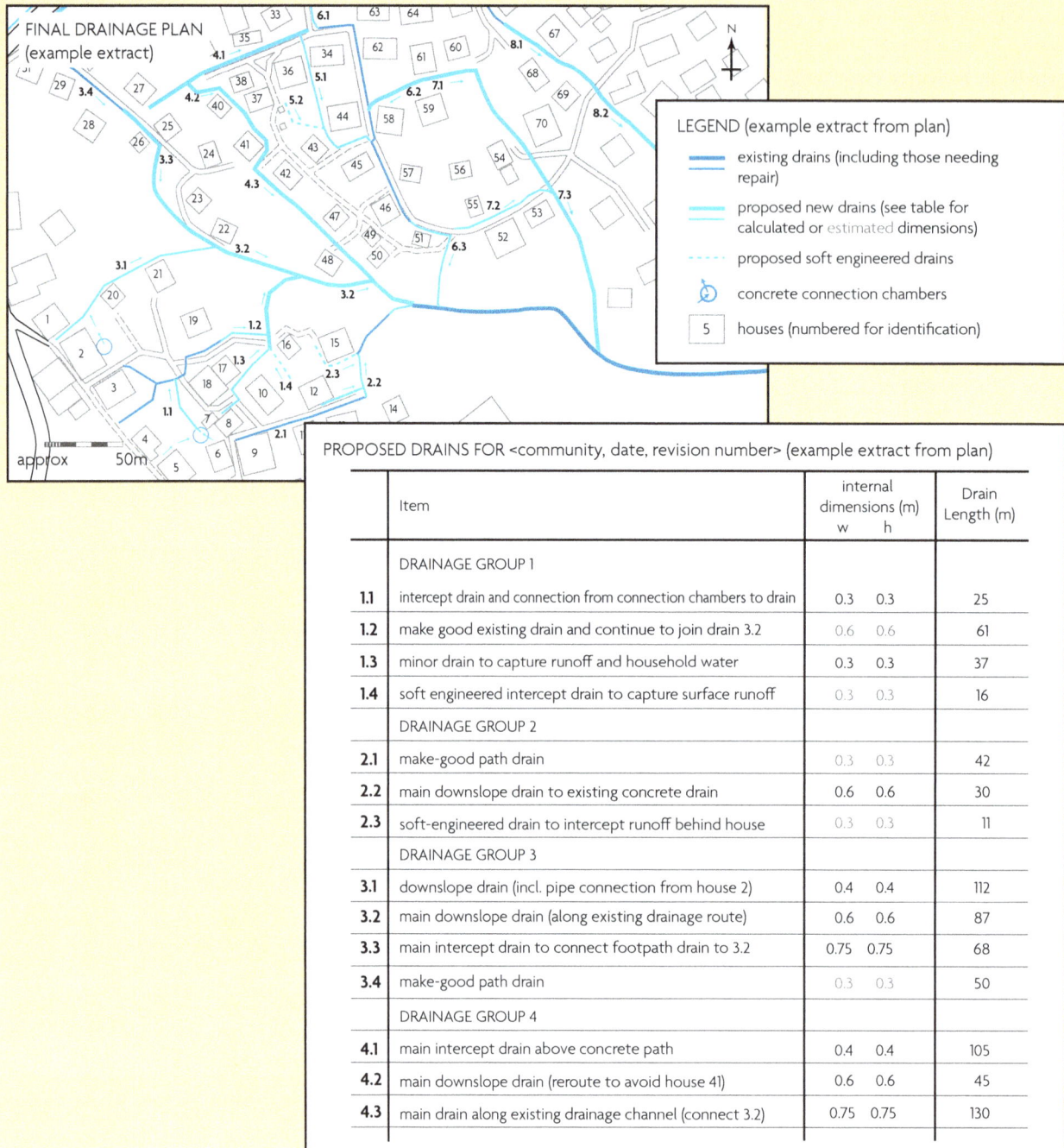

FINAL DRAINAGE PLAN
(example extract)

approx 50m

LEGEND (example extract from plan)

- existing drains (including those needing repair)
- proposed new drains (see table for calculated or estimated dimensions)
- proposed soft engineered drains
- concrete connection chambers
- 5 houses (numbered for identification)

PROPOSED DRAINS FOR <community, date, revision number> (example extract from plan)

	Item	internal dimensions (m) w h		Drain Length (m)
	DRAINAGE GROUP 1			
1.1	intercept drain and connection from connection chambers to drain	0.3	0.3	25
1.2	make good existing drain and continue to join drain 3.2	0.6	0.6	61
1.3	minor drain to capture runoff and household water	0.3	0.3	37
1.4	soft engineered intercept drain to capture surface runoff	0.3	0.3	16
	DRAINAGE GROUP 2			
2.1	make-good path drain	0.3	0.3	42
2.2	main downslope drain to existing concrete drain	0.6	0.6	30
2.3	soft-engineered drain to intercept runoff behind house	0.3	0.3	11
	DRAINAGE GROUP 3			
3.1	downslope drain (incl. pipe connection from house 2)	0.4	0.4	112
3.2	main downslope drain (along existing drainage route)	0.6	0.6	87
3.3	main intercept drain to connect footpath drain to 3.2	0.75	0.75	68
3.4	make-good path drain	0.3	0.3	50
	DRAINAGE GROUP 4			
4.1	main intercept drain above concrete path	0.4	0.4	105
4.2	main downslope drain (reroute to avoid house 41)	0.6	0.6	45
4.3	main drain along existing drainage channel (connect 3.2)	0.75	0.75	130

FIGURE 6.46 Community involvement in finalizing the drainage plan

a. Displaying the plan within the community is important.

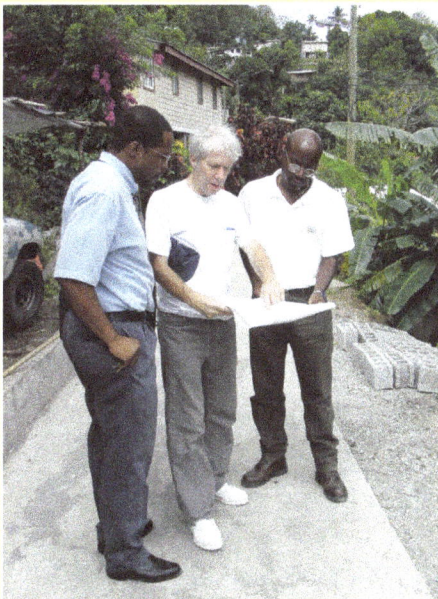

b. Walk though the community with the plan and have as many on-site discussions as possible.

6.7.3 Formal approval and next steps

Once the final community consultation process is completed, submit the plan to the relevant authorized ministry for formal approval.

In conjunction with the process for obtaining formal approval for the plan, identify issues regarding access from one property to another, landownership, the provision of pipe work requiring neighbor permissions, and so on. Review and comply with relevant safeguards and obtain residents' or landowners' agreement to relevant aspects of the proposed drain alignment or construction process.

Submit the final approved drainage plan to the landslide hazard and engineering team or other implementing agency responsible for developing work packages (chapter 7).

MILESTONE 6:
Sign-off on final drainage plan

6.8 RESOURCES

6.8.1 Who does what

TEAM	RESPONSIBILITY	ACTIONS AND HELPFUL HINTS	CHAPTER SECTION
MCU	Understand drainage alignment principles and drain types	• Review principles of drainage design for surface water capture in communities	6.3
	Ensure the final drainage plan meets required engineering design standards	• Identify local experts in drainage design for consultation and/or incorporation into the landslide assessment and engineering task team	6.2
	Ensure the community is fully consulted with on the final drainage plan	• Identify local community development experts for consultation and/or incorporation into the community liaison task team	1.3.3
	Coordinate with government task team		
Government task teams	Understand and apply methods for estimating slope surface water discharge and household water discharge Understand and apply methods to calculate drain dimensions for design discharges	• Review equations and online tools **Helpful hint:** It is useful to have one individual assigned this important task, so that his or her knowledge base is built up with regard to available estimation methods and approaches.	6.3.2–6.3.8
	Draw first version of final drainage plan to indicate drain alignment and construction details	• Confirm and refine drain locations on site • Identify both conventional and low-cost engineering construction materials and design details • Incorporate local construction practices into the design	6.4
	Optimize the number of houses that can be linked to drains	• Use the slope process zone map and calculations of household water capture to identify areas where household drainage will be most beneficial	6.6
	Develop the final drainage plan and cost estimate	• Incorporate all drain construction and household connection details into the plan • Estimate quantities and costs (drain lengths, household connection components)	6.7.1
	Discuss proposed plan with the community	• Discuss draft plan on site with residents and at a community meeting • Display the plan at a suitable location in the community	6.7.2
	Coordinate with community task teams		
	Secure approval of final drainage plan	• Secure formal stakeholder agreement and decision-maker approval **Helpful hint:** To ensure safeguard compliance, obtain any necessary written agreements from stakeholders.	6.7.3
Community task teams	Contribute local construction knowledge and practices	• Identify local slope water management and construction good practices and collaborate with government engineers to incorporate them into the drainage plan	6.5
	Contribute local knowledge to the final drainage plan	• Facilitate community feedback to the final drainage plan prior to formal sign-off	6.7
	Coordinate with government task teams		

6.8.2 Chapter checklist

CHECK THAT:	TEAM	PERSON	SIGN-OFF	CHAPTER SECTION
✓ The landslide assessment and engineering task team has sufficient capacity or support from an expert/consultant for developing the final drainage plan				6.1.3
✓ An appropriate drainage alignment pattern identified, discharge into drains estimated, and drain dimensions calculated				6.3
✓ Detailed drain alignments confirmed on site and drain dimensions revised if necessary				6.4
✓ Proposed drainage plan drawn up				6.4
✓ Drain construction types and details specified				6.5
✓ Low-cost, appropriate technology engineering approaches to drain construction considered				6.5.2
✓ Houses for roof guttering, water tanks, and hurricane straps identified, and connections to drains designed				6.6
✓ Final drainage plan prepared				6.7.1
✓ Quantities and costs estimated				6.7.1
✓ Plan discussed and revised in conjunction with community and stakeholders				6.7.2
✓ **Milestone 6**: Sign-off on final drainage plan				6.7.3
✓ All necessary safeguards complied with				1.5.3; 2.3.2

6.8.3 Local designs for concrete drains, catchpits, and baffles

This section provides examples of typical design drawings for surface water drains.

Reinforced concrete block drains are well suited to MoSSaiC projects. The materials are generally readily available and can be carried by hand over short distances, and the method of construction is familiar to local contractors. Typical drawings are shown in figure 6.27.

It is helpful to compile a set of design drawings to accompany the final drainage plan and to guide estimation of project costs. Such drawings will be required in the development of work packages for contractors (chapter 7).

First, try to identify examples of relevant drainage design drawings from other local projects that use local expert knowledge and experience, and will be familiar to community-based contractors. These could include conceptual drainage plans or detailed construction design drawings for specific drain types and components.

To supplement local designs, refer to similar types of surface water drains used in other countries. See, for example, information from the Geotechnical Engineering Office, Civil Engineering and Development Department, Hong Kong SAR, China, available online at http://www.cedd.gov.hk/eng/publications/manuals/index.htm.

Several commonly used drain types are discussed below, along with conceptual sketches and useful guidance on design issues (table 6.6). This information provides a context in which to review and refine local drain designs.

TABLE 6.6 Illustrative drawings for drain design

DRAIN TYPE/DESIGN DETAILS	FIGURE
Reinforced concrete block (downslope)	6.27
Reinforced concrete block (intercept)	6.27
U-channel	6.47
Baffle wall junction	6.48
Debris trap	6.49
Stepped channel	6.50
Catchpit junction	6.51

FIGURE 6.47 U-channel

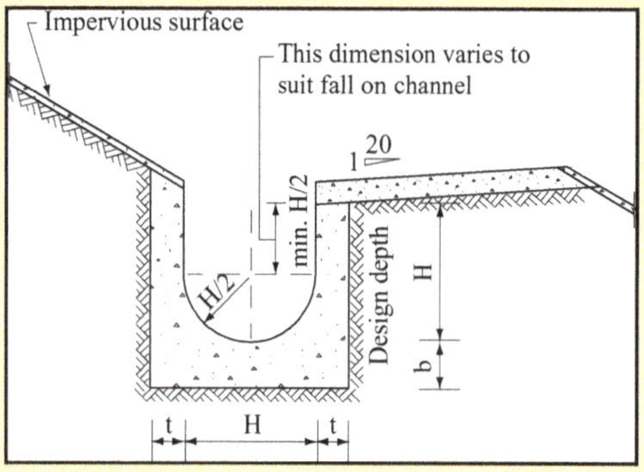

Dimensions of U-channel

Nominal size of channel H (mm)	Thickness t (mm)	Thickness b (mm)
225–600	150	150
675–1,200	175	225

Source: GCO 1984. Reproduced with permission of the Head of the Geotechnical Engineering Office and the Director of the Civil Engineering Department, Hong Kong SAR, China.

Note: U-shaped channels are used for small drains in many countries. Construction requires the casting of concrete U-shaped drain sections prior to installation. Some on-site instruction may be needed to familiarize contractors and laborers with this process (WHO 1991). The figure shows typical specifications commonly used in Hong Kong SAR, China.

FIGURE 6.48 Baffle wall junction

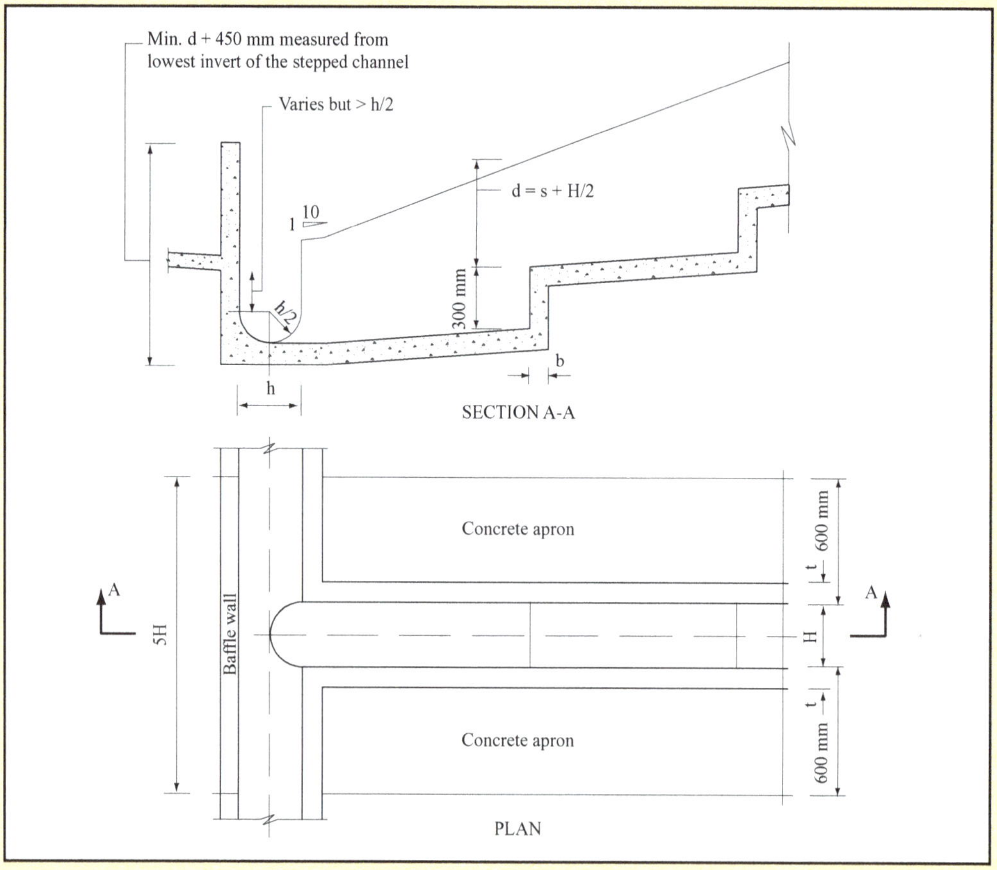

Source: GCO 1984. Reproduced with permission of the Head of the Geotechnical Engineering Office and the Director of the Civil Engineering Department, Hong Kong SAR, China.

Note: A downslope drain can be connected to a cross-slope drain at the base of a slope by using (1) a baffle wall at the downslope side to prevent overtopping and (2) a concrete apron on the immediate upslope section of the downslope drain to contain and divert any splash back into the drain.

FIGURE 6.49 Typical debris/sand trap

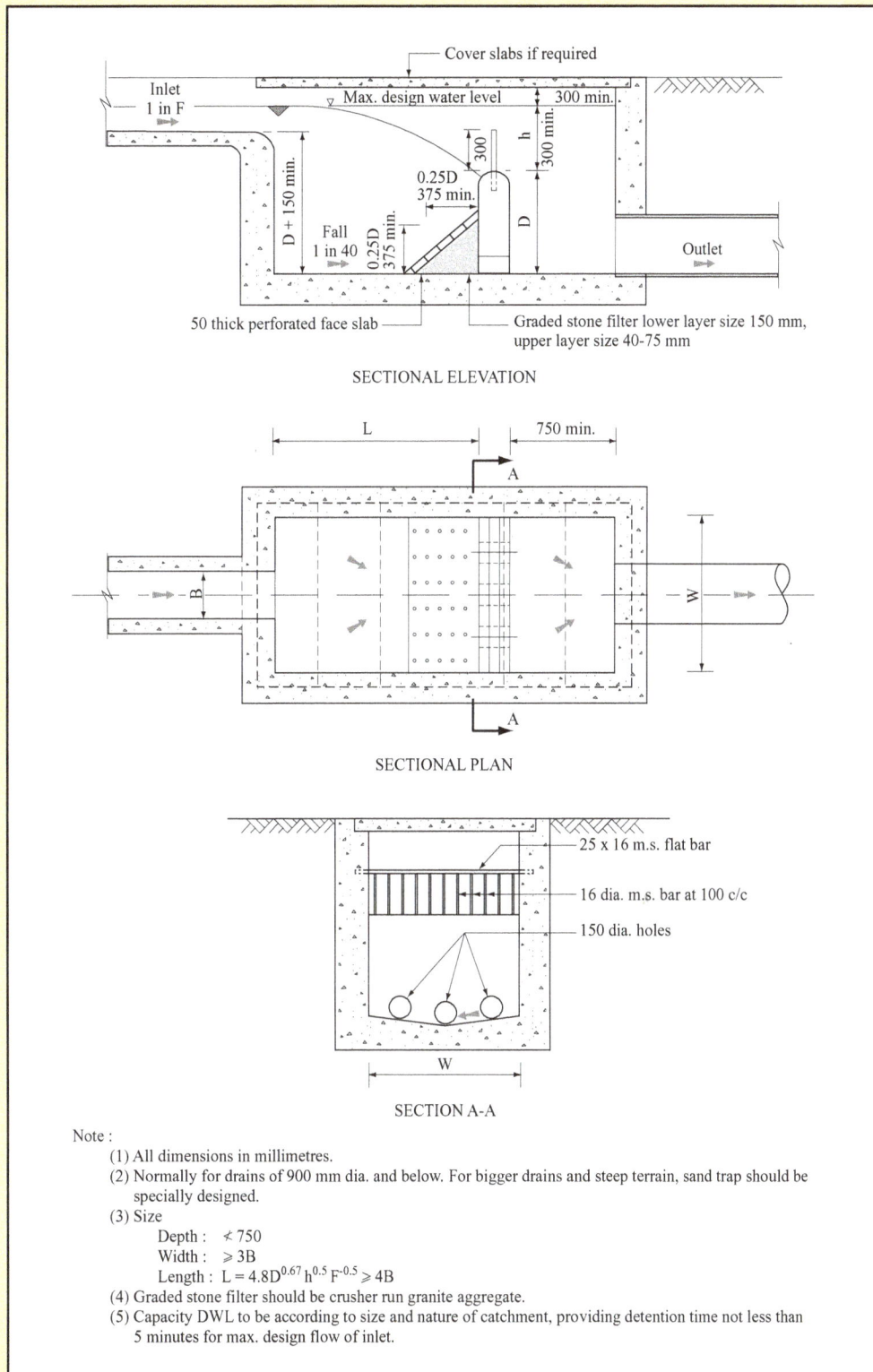

SECTIONAL ELEVATION

SECTIONAL PLAN

SECTION A-A

Note :
    (1) All dimensions in millimetres.
    (2) Normally for drains of 900 mm dia. and below. For bigger drains and steep terrain, sand trap should be
        specially designed.
    (3) Size
        Depth :   ≮ 750
        Width :   ⩾ 3B
        Length : $L = 4.8D^{0.67} h^{0.5} F^{-0.5} \geqslant 4B$
    (4) Graded stone filter should be crusher run granite aggregate.
    (5) Capacity DWL to be according to size and nature of catchment, providing detention time not less than
        5 minutes for max. design flow of inlet.

Source: GCO 1984. Reproduced with permission of the Head of the Geotechnical Engineering Office and the Director of the Civil Engineering Department, Hong Kong SAR, China.

Note: Debris traps can be combined with a catchpit and sand/sediment trap.

FIGURE 6.50 Stepped channel

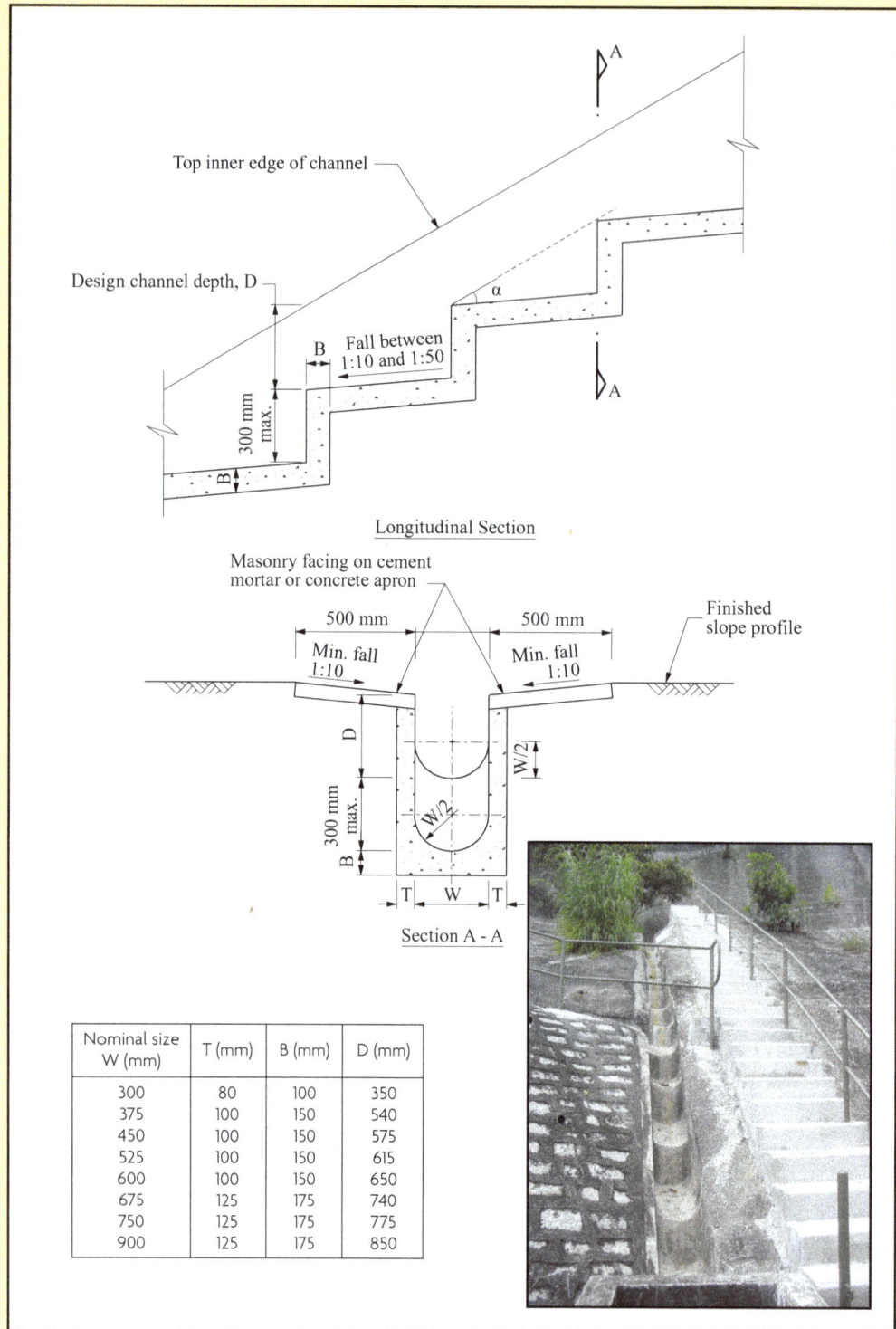

Top inner edge of channel

Design channel depth, D

Fall between 1:10 and 1:50

300 mm max.

α

B

B

Longitudinal Section

Masonry facing on cement mortar or concrete apron

500 mm

500 mm

Finished slope profile

Min. fall 1:10

Min. fall 1:10

D

W/2

300 mm max.

W/2

B

T   W   T

Section A - A

Nominal size W (mm)	T (mm)	B (mm)	D (mm)
300	80	100	350
375	100	150	540
450	100	150	575
525	100	150	615
600	100	150	650
675	125	175	740
750	125	175	775
900	125	175	850

Source: GCO 1984. Reproduced with permission of the Head of the Geotechnical Engineering Office and the Director of the Civil Engineering Department, Hong Kong SAR, China.

Note: Stepped channels are used to reduce flow velocity, especially in downslope drains. The example in the photo is in Hong Kong SAR, China.

FIGURE 6.51 Catchpit junction

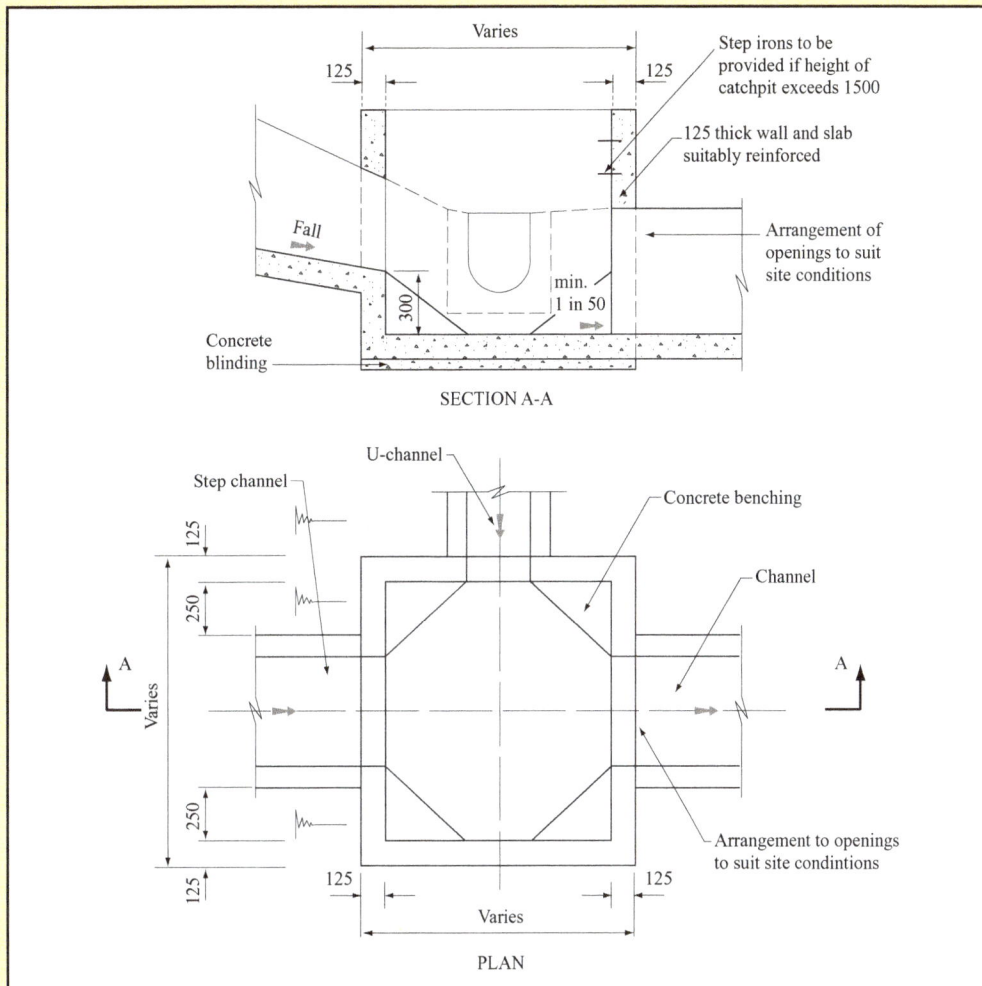

SECTION A-A

- Varies
- 125 ... 125
- Step irons to be provided if height of catchpit exceeds 1500
- 125 thick wall and slab suitably reinforced
- Arrangement of openings to suit site conditions
- *Fall*
- min. 1 in 50
- 300
- Concrete blinding

PLAN

- U-channel
- Step channel
- Concrete benching
- 125
- 250
- Channel
- A
- A
- Varies
- 250
- 125
- 125 ... 125
- Arrangement to openings to suit site conditions
- Varies

Source: GCO 1984. Reproduced with permission of the Head of the Geotechnical Engineering Office and the Director of the Civil Engineering Department, Hong Kong SAR, China.

Note: Catchpits can be used to connect downslope and intercept drains.

6.8.4 References

GCO (Geotechnical Control Office). 1984. *Geotechnical Manual for Slopes.* 2nd ed. Hong Kong Government.

Hui, T. H. H., H. W. Sun, and K. K. S. Ho. 2007. "Review of Slope Surface Drainage with Reference to Landslide Studies and Current Practice." GEO Report 210, Geotechnical Engineering Office, Government of Hong Kong Special Administrative Region.

IBHS (Institute for Business & Home Safety). 2002. *Is Your Home Protected From Hurricane Disaster? A Homeowner's Guide to Hurricane Retrofit.* Tampa: IBHS.

Premchitt, J., H. F. Lam, and J. M. Shen. 1986. "Rainstorm Runoff on Slopes." Special Projects Division Report SPR 5/8699, Geotechnical Control Office, Hong Kong Government.

University of Warwick. 2003. "Roofwater Harvesting for Poorer Households in the Tropics. Inception Report. Domestic Roofwater Harvesting Research Programme R7833." School of Engineering, University of Warwick, Warwick, UK.

Wamsler, C. 2006. "Mainstreaming Risk Reduction in Urban Planning and Housing: A Challenge for International Aid Organizations." *Disaster* 30: 151–77.

WHO (World Health Organization). 1991. *Surface Water Drainage for Low Income Communities.* Geneva: WHO.

"The quality of site supervision has a major influence on the overall performance and efficiency of construction projects. Inadequate supervision is believed to be one of the major causes of rework."

—S. Alwi, K. Hampson, and S. Mohamed,
"Investigation into the Relationship between Rework and Site Supervision in High Rise
Building Construction in Indonesia" (1999, 1)

CHAPTER 7

Implementing the Planned Works

7.1 KEY CHAPTER ELEMENTS

7.1.1 Coverage

This chapter provides guidance on contracting and constructing MoSSaiC (Management of Slope Stability in Communities) drainage works in communities to improve slope stability.

Emphasis is placed on the critical role of site supervisors, working in partnership with community contractors. The listed groups should read the indicated chapter sections.

AUDIENCE				LEARNING	CHAPTER SECTION
F	M	G	C		
✓		✓		How to prepare work packages	7.3
	✓	✓	✓	Importance of site supervision during construction	7.5.1
		✓	✓	Good practices in construction	7.6
		✓	✓	Practices to be avoided in construction	7.7
	✓	✓	✓	Ensuring works are completed to the required standard	7.8

F = funders and policy makers   **M** = MoSSaiC core unit: government project managers and experts   **G** = government task teams: experts and practitioners   **C** = community task teams: residents, leaders, contractors

7.1.2 Documents

DOCUMENT TO BE PRODUCED	CHAPTER SECTION
Bill of quantities	7.3.1
Work packages	7.3.2
Materials procurement plan	7.3.3
Schedules of construction defects and outstanding works	7.8

7.1.3 Steps and outputs

STEP	OUTPUT
1. Prepare work package and request for tender documentation • Prepare a bill of quantities for the planned works • Incorporate appropriate contingency and any double-handling costs (i.e., where material has to be delivered to sites where access is difficult and requires the establishment of a storage site between delivery and construction site locations) • Decide on work package size that maximizes community engagement and meets procurement requirements • Prepare design drawings and plans to accompany each work package • Identify an appropriate plan for procuring materials depending on the community contracting approach, community capacity, and project procurement requirements	Work packages for implementation of drainage intervention to reduce landslide hazard
2. Conduct the agreed-upon community contracting tendering process • Identify potential contractors from the community and provide briefing on proposed works and work packages, emphasizing the need for good construction practice • Invite tenders from contractors, providing assistance or training on how to submit a tender document • Evaluate tenders, award contracts, and brief contractors on safeguards	Briefing meeting for contractors held; community contracts awarded
3. Implement construction • Select experienced site supervisors • Authorize start of construction and meet with the community to discuss the construction process and introduce site supervisors • Closely supervise the works to ensure good construction practices; clear communication among contractors, supervisors, community, and the MoSSaiC core unit; and timely disbursement of funds for procurement of materials and payment of contractors/laborers	Briefing meeting for community held; construction under way
4. Sign off on completed construction • Identify outstanding works • Arrange for any necessary repairs or minor modifications • Sign off on completed construction and pay withholding payments to contractors	Construction completed and signed off on

7.1.4 Community-based aspects

The chapter involves the selection and supervision of contractors from within a community to construct the planned drainage works and improve slope stability.

7.2 GETTING STARTED

7.2.1 Briefing note

Drainage construction for landslide hazard reduction

Poor drainage is a common issue for vulnerable urban communities where the provision of basic drainage infrastructure has not kept pace with rapid unauthorized housing construction. Community-based development projects often include drain construction to address flooding and environmental health problems. MoSSaiC has much in common with such projects (e.g., taking a community-based approach, using appropriate construction methods, and building local capacity) but with the vital additional requirement that the drains reduce the landslide hazard. There are thus two key ingredients for effective implementation of MoSSaiC drainage works: high-quality construction that adheres to the design specification and a community-based approach to engaging and working with contractors from the community.

MoSSaiC drainage works are based on a formally agreed-upon drainage plan that specifies drain alignments, designs, and construction details (chapter 6). This plan is designed to address local landslide mechanisms, specifically, the infiltration of rainfall and household water into the slope material (chapters 3 and 5). Implementing the planned works requires technical understanding of the rationale for the drain alignment and design, and skill in constructing drains and installing household connections that function as intended—alleviating the landslide hazard without creating additional hazards or drainage problems.

MoSSaiC drainage works should be implemented using an appropriate form of community contracting to engage contractors and laborers from within the community to implement the drainage works. Community contracting can be broadly defined as "procurement by or on behalf of a community" (de Silva 2000, 2). During this stage of the project, site supervisors play a vital role in both delivering high-quality construction and encouraging community engagement. Hands-on site supervision allows contractors to contribute their detailed knowledge of the hillside and local construction practices, while providing instruction on detailed construction issues and good construction practices. There should be clear processes for evaluating the works and disbursing contractor payments to ensure that design and construction specifications are met.

Implementation processes and good practices

Using a community-based approach to deliver good-quality drainage works in vulnerable urban communities requires coordination among government and community task teams. Government engineers and site supervisors may not be used to working with informal contractors in unauthorized communities and will need to adapt to this environment. Similarly, contractors and laborers in communities may be unfamiliar with formal construction sector processes and practices. The MoSSaiC core unit (MCU) should therefore establish a process for implementing the

works that allows the community contractors and the government task teams to work together effectively (figure 7.1).

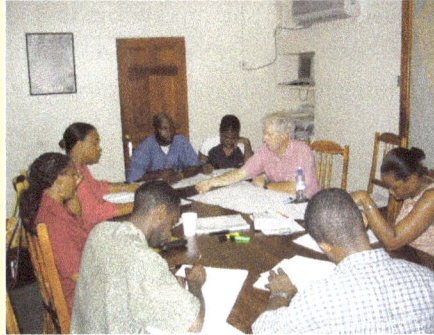

FIGURE 7.1 MCU meeting to agree on responsibilities during construction process

The process for delivering effective drainage for landslide hazard reduction should facilitate the following:

- Construction procurement using an appropriate form of community contracting—developing work packages from the drainage plan, preparing a bill of quantities, running a tendering process, and awarding contracts to contractors from the community

- Clear communication and feedback among government engineers, site supervisors, contractors, and community residents—explaining the procurement and contracting processes to all stakeholders, providing training for community task teams (depending on the forms of construction procurement and community contracting selected), and providing formal and informal ways for community residents to participate

- High-quality, hands-on supervision by experienced technicians and/or engineers—briefing contractors on drainage design and construction specifications, setting out drain alignments on site, day-to-day site supervision during construction to ensure specifications are met and problems resolved, reporting to the MCU on progress, and signing off on completed works to allow contractors to be paid.

A good site supervisor–contractor relationship is important for delivering sound construction and slope stability management practices. Knowledge of such practices can come from traditional classroom training, but is more likely to be developed on site during construction through practical experience and knowledge sharing. Site supervisors should be familiar with good construction practices, help contractors achieve high-quality construction, contribute to the learning experience of contractors and laborers, and minimize any points of potential disagreement between residents and contractors during construction. In this regard, site meetings with contractors (figure 7.2) are vital in setting out the works, reinforcing good practices, and building contractor confidence.

Community contracting

A key element of the MoSSaiC approach is contracting works out to community-based contractors and laborers. This chapter introduces the concept of community contracting for construction works, but does not cover different procurement approaches and processes.

Community contracting can take many forms, depending on community organiza-

FIGURE 7.2 Contractor site meeting

tional capacity and project funding and procurement requirements, but the following general characteristics and goals can be recognized (de Silva 2000, 3):

- Community members are involved in identifying needs and selecting a project.

- Community participation is encouraged throughout project identification, preparation, implementation, operations and maintenance, and is usually done through an elected community project management committee.

- Communities provide contributions in the form of labor, cash and/or materials. Their contributions promote community ownership and hopefully eventual subproject sustainability.

MoSSaiC projects share these broad characteristics and goals in that they promote community participation and ownership throughout the mapping and drainage design stages (to which community members contribute time and knowledge), and maintenance of completed works (also involving some form of community contribution). A distinction of MoSSaiC is that communities are not necessarily required to contribute labor, cash, or materials for construction.

For MoSSaiC projects, skilled contractors and laborers from within the community are contracted and remunerated for delivering good-quality drainage works that meet the required design and construction specifications for reducing landslide hazard. This ensures that a substantial portion of external funding is retained in the community, and the self-esteem of contractors is built through the experience of completing formally contracted works. Community members not directly involved in construction can make in-kind contributions (e.g., by providing secure storage for materials, water, and access across properties to the construction site).

An extensive study of 800 urban infrastructure projects in India, Pakistan, and Sri Lanka in which the construction component was contracted to the community found that their overall performance was comparable to, or better than, conventional microcontracts awarded to external contractors using a traditional bid evaluation process (Sohail and Baldwin 2004). Additionally,

> the performance of these [community partnered] projects in terms of socioeconomic elements was likely to far exceed that of conventional microprojects. For example, the number of community labor days generated by microcontracts injects significant money into the local economy (Sohail and Baldwin 2004, 201).

Table 7.1 shows the rank ordering of a number of performance indicators and their associated yardsticks from the Sohail and Baldwin study. This information can provide the MCU with initial guidance on which project delivery components are most important to monitor and keep on track during implementation.

7.2.2 Guiding principles

The following guiding principles apply in implementing planned works:

- Ensure that roles and responsibilities are agreed on, well defined, communicated, and acted on.

- Operate a transparent process for community contracting that builds confidence and capacity for all involved.

- Continue to communicate the purpose of the drainage intervention (to capture surface and household water to reduce landslide hazard) as the basis for the drain alignment and construction design. This understanding is especially important for contractors and supervisors, as it will help guard against deviations from drain designs and construction specifications, or poor construction practices that may make drains ineffective.

- Stress the importance of supervision as a critical component in achieving a high-quality drainage intervention and in maintaining community engagement during construction.

- Ensure that all relevant safeguards are addressed with both landowners and community residents, especially those regarding drain alignments.

7.2.3 Risks and challenges

Project interruptions

Interruptions to projects because of protracted institutional procedures or cash flow problems can be very damaging to morale. The MCU and government task teams should be proactive in preventing potential delays and offsetting their impact by making clear to the communities and contractors

TABLE 7.1 Yardsticks for selected community-based performance measures

PERFORMANCE INDICATOR	YARDSTICK
Accuracy of preliminary technical estimates	± 5%
Cost growth (final contract cost/initial contract cost)	± 9%
Proximity of engineers' estimated cost and initial contract cost	± 12%
Time growth (final contract duration/initial contract duration)	± 20%
Lead time (time required to commence works/contract duration)	± 20%
Proximity of engineers' estimated cost and final contract cost	± 25%
Time between tender invitation and start of contract	20 days
Time from approval stage to tender inviting (or equivalent) stage	50 days
Time to start operation and maintenance after the contract is completed	65 days

Source: Sohail and Baldwin 2004; data are from a survey of 800 community-based microprojects.

Note: Shaded items indicate the components that are potentially most important for the MCU to monitor during implementation.

- the time frame relating to the availability of funds,

- the specific purpose of funds, and

- the precise point at which works can be allowed to proceed.

Setting realistic expectations and following through with project delivery during the mapping and drainage design phases (chapters 5 and 6) will reassure the community that the works will actually be undertaken if they are appropriate. Provision of mobilization funds for all contractors is likely to be an important prerequisite to a successful and timely project start.

Inadequate contractor briefing

Ensuring that community contractors are adequately briefed and supervised is one of the most critical elements of a MoSSaiC project.

Community-based contractors will ideally put together teams of laborers and skilled workers from within the community. The success in reducing landslide hazard rests on the quality of the construction that they deliver. Initially, however, these teams may not have a clear understanding of the project rationale. It is vital that contractors and their teams be briefed on the overall drainage plan, the purpose of the work package they are contracted to deliver, and the reasons for specific design requirements and details in that package. If possible, contractors should be shown examples of good and bad construction practices in other communities and locations.

Poor supervision and rushed work

Good design can be diluted by poor site supervision and by contractors wishing to speed up construction times to be paid sooner. Contractors should be made aware that completed works will be evaluated for construction quality before payments are made.

Contractors' desire to speed completion can be moderated by adequate (and often close) supervision of works to ensure that enthusiasm to complete the work program is accompanied by an appreciation of good con-

struction practices. For their part, site supervisors also have a pay incentive to see works completed quickly. It is therefore important to stress the critical nature of design details and good practice to all parties.

Questionable practices

It is well known that any form of construction can be associated with questionable or corrupt practices associated with project planning and prebid stages, contract award and project implementation, and monitoring of the works. The World Bank (2010) details a number of such activities and practices (listed in section 7.10.4) that the MCU should be mindful of during implementation of the drainage works.

7.2.4 Adapting the chapter blueprint to existing capacity

The effectiveness of a MoSSaiC project in reducing landslide hazard ultimately rests in what is delivered on the ground. Use the matrix opposite to assess the capacity of the MCU and the government and community task teams for implementing the planned drainage works.

1. Assign a capacity score from 1 to 3 (low to high) to reflect the existing capacity for each of the elements in the matrix's left-hand column.

2. Identify the most common capacity score as an indicator of the overall capacity level.

3. Adapt the blueprint in this chapter in accordance with the overall capacity level (see guide at the bottom of the opposite page).

7.3 PREPARING WORK PACKAGES

In preparation for tendering and construction, the drainage plan (chapter 6) should be broken down into itemized components (materials, parts, and labor, and their associated costs—a bill of quantities), and manageable units of work (work packages) to be undertaken by contractors.

CAPACITY ELEMENT	EXISTING CAPACITY		
	1 = LOW	2 = MODERATE	3 = HIGH
Government/community experience and organizational base for contracting construction works to community-based contractors	No previous experience with community contracting	Some experience with community contracting, but not related to construction	Existing proven capacity in community contracting of construction
Site supervision of construction works in vulnerable communities	No experienced site supervisors for community-based construction	Experienced site supervisors for drain construction, but no experience of community-based construction	Availability of experienced supervisors for community-based drain construction
Local construction practice guidelines and documents	Few (or no) construction good practice documents	Construction guidelines available, but no distinction between good and poor construction practices	Existing documents showing local good construction practice
Audit and accounting process	Relatively immature accounting and auditing process for community contracting	Experience with accounting and auditing for community contracting, but no processes for encouraging good construction practice	Transparent accounting and auditing processes that encourage good construction practice (e.g., linking disbursements to contractors to approval of completed works)
Project safeguards	Documented safeguards need to be located; no previous experience in interpreting and operating safeguard policies	Documents exist for some safeguards	Documented safeguards available from all relevant agencies

CAPACITY LEVEL	HOW TO ADAPT THE BLUEPRINT
1: Use this chapter in depth and as a catalyst to secure support from other agencies as appropriate	The MCU needs to strengthen its resources prior to allowing construction to proceed. This might involve the following: • Hiring experienced site supervisors from the commercial sector • Using best practice documentation in this book to supplement available information that might be available regionally • Developing a suitable accounting and auditing policy, including a payment schedule, that is sufficiently resolved to the community contractor level rewards good practice • Approaching all relevant agencies to acquire their safeguard documents and distill them into a coherent working document for community-based contracting and construction
2: Some elements of this chapter will reflect current practice; read the remaining elements in depth and use them to further strengthen capacity	The MCU has strength in some areas, but not all. Elements that are perceived to be Level 1 need to be addressed as above. Elements that are Level 2 will need to be strengthened, such as the following: • If there is limited supervision experience, a senior supervisor could be recruited • If relevant safeguard documents are available but not collated, the MCU should systematically integrate them into the implementation process • If the local audit process is insufficiently resolved, the process should be refined to incorporate features such as contractor final withholding payments to encourage quality construction
3: Use this chapter as a checklist	The MCU is likely to be able to proceed using existing proven capacity. It would be good practice, nonetheless for the MCU to document relevant prior experience in community-based construction and related safeguards.

A work package should have the following characteristics (based on Wideman 2012):

- Have a defined size and duration, limited to relatively short periods of time

- Be able to be realistically estimated in terms of quantities and costs of works

- Produce measurable outputs (deliverables)

- Entail a large enough scope of work that could be competitively bid for and contracted for by itself (the test of reasonableness)

- Be distinguishable from, but integrate with, other work packages.

Work packages should be prepared by an engineer or quantity surveyor who is part of the landslide assessment and engineering or technical task team, or who has been appointed by the MCU for this task.

The engineer or quantity surveyor should use this section to guide the preparation of work packages and request for tender (RFT) documents—preparing a bill of quantities, identifying work packages, and preparing detailed construction design requirements for each work package. This process should be undertaken in accordance with the chosen form of construction procurement and community contracting for the project, which affects the size (value) of contracts; the tendering process; and roles/responsibilities of the government, community, and contractors.

7.3.1 Prepare a bill of quantities

The bill of quantities is a document containing an itemized breakdown of the quantity and costs of materials, parts, and labor required for a construction project. Costs are estimated based on approximate local costs for delivering a unit of a certain type of work, such as constructing a meter of reinforced concrete block drain.

The bill of quantities serves two purposes— it provides a detailed breakdown of project costs for the MCU (against which the project budget and progress can be managed), and forms the basis for the specification of the works in the work package RFT documents and contracts.

To create work package RFT documents, the information from a bill of quantities is combined with detailed construction specifications (a specified bill of quantities), and terms and conditions for construction. Contractors use these specified quantity estimates and associated construction activities to price the work for which they are bidding.

Estimate quantities

The final drainage plan includes an estimate of the total project cost based on approximate drain lengths and the number of houses for roof water and gray water capture (chapter 6). To create a detailed bill of quantities, the drainage plan needs to be further broken down into appropriate component parts (units) for construction.

Measure and record the lengths of each type of new drain section, culvert, and repairs to existing drains (distinguished by drain size, design, and construction specifications), and itemize drain components such as debris traps.

To obtain a bill of quantities for the capture of household roof and gray water, complete a detailed survey of each house selected in the drainage design phase (section 6.6). This task should be performed by a surveyor or someone familiar with the MoSSaiC methodology to ensure that proper connections are made between houses and existing or proposed drains. Table 7.2 lists the main items to include in the survey of each house. Ideally, the surveyor should also sketch a plan view of each house and mark details such as where the roof might need preparation for the works (figure 7.3); the length of guttering; and the locations of downpipes, water tanks, and drain connections.

Obtain accurate estimates of all the components needed for roof water management, including brackets, connectors, and other fixings (figures 7.4 and 7.5). Underestimation of quantities can result in work delays and loss of project momentum (figure 7.6).

TABLE 7.2 Items to include when surveying houses identified for household water capture

COMPONENT	ITEM	DISCUSS WITH HOUSEHOLD, MEASURE, AND RECORD
Preparation of roof	Galvanized roofing	Time allowances for trimming irregular galvanized roofing
	Replacement joists	Lengths of joists to be repaired or replaced to allow fitting of facia boards and guttering
	Facia boards	Lengths of facia board to be repaired or replaced prior to affixing roof guttering
Roof water capture	Guttering and downpipes	• Lengths required • Estimated number of connectors and brackets to support gutters and downpipes during heavy rainfall events. • Where downpipes will be located in order to connect with water-tanks and drains • Connections to existing rainwater drums or tanks, and make the necessary provision for overflow into the nearest drain
	Water tanks (if allocated to this house)	• Water tank locations • Connections to downpipes • How overflows will be connected to drains
Gray water capture	Pipes from kitchen and bathroom	Length of piping required to capture gray water from kitchen sinks, washing machines, bathroom washbasins, and showers
Drain connections	Pipes and connection chambers or small drains	Confirm form of connection, quantity of parts, and location (ensure that connections are of sufficient gradient to maximize flow rates)
Hurricane strapping	Roof to top plate connections	Ideally, enough straps should be included to allow the roofing material to be attached at every joist

FIGURE 7.3 Modifications to roof structure for roof guttering installation

Develop a spreadsheet with a page for every house to detail the quantities of each item required (figure 7.7); include a master sheet that sums the quantities for all the houses. Add a contingency (usually 10 percent) to allow for unforeseen additional works or costs.

FIGURE 7.4 Downpipe installation detail

FIGURE 7.5 Roof guttering and downpipe components

FIGURE 7.6 Connection of downpipe to drain awaits purchase of a connecting section

FIGURE 7.7 Spreadsheet to assist in developing bills of quantities

Household name

Household number

Fill in cells colored blue

Task	Item	Item cost	Quantity	No.lengths	Remainder	Total Cost
Fascia board replacement	1"x8"x12' fascia board		ft	0	0 ft	0.00
	2"x6"x14' rafter		ft	0	0 ft	0.00
	2"x6"x16' rafter		ft	0	0 ft	0.00
	2"x6"x18' rafter		ft	0	0 ft	0.00
	2"x6"x20' rafter		ft	0	0 ft	0.00
	hurricane strap		items	-	-	0.00
Install guttering	6"x13' guttering		ft	0	0 ft	0.00
	support bracket		items	-	-	0.00
	joint bracket		items	-	-	0.00
	stop end		items	-	-	0.00
	angle (D/M & PF angle)		items	-	-	0.00
Connect guttering to downpipe	running outlet		items	-	-	0.00
	112° bend		items	-	-	0.00
	92° bend		items	-	-	0.00
	6"x13' down pipe		ft	0	0 ft	0.00
	down pipe clips		items	-	-	0.00
	down pipe connector		items	-	-	0.00
	shoe		items	-	-	0.00
Connect downpipe to drain	connection pipes		ft	0	0 ft	0.00
Connect wastewater to drain	1.5" elbow connector		items	-	-	0.00
General	1lb bag screws		items	-	-	0.00
	rawl plugs		items	-	-	0.00
Total						0.00

Confirm quantities and update the plan

The detailed drain alignments, the houses to be connected, and the location of pipes and connection chambers should be confirmed with householders and all other relevant stakeholders (figure 7.8). Update the approved drainage plan with these details. The inventory of items needed to connect each house should be appended to the plan as a separate document. The combined document, consisting of the approved plan and the complete quantity schedule, is the definitive working document to use in generating work packages.

Use realistic unit costs

Government ministries that regularly undertake or contract out construction works will often have a standard list of unit costs. The unit costs selected by the engineer or quantity surveyor for a MoSSaiC project should be adjusted appropriately to account for anticipated fluctuations in the cost of construction materials and on-site conditions (such as poor access by road), and to ensure that there is profit for the community contractor.

Particular unit costs relevant to MoSSaiC interventions may include the following:

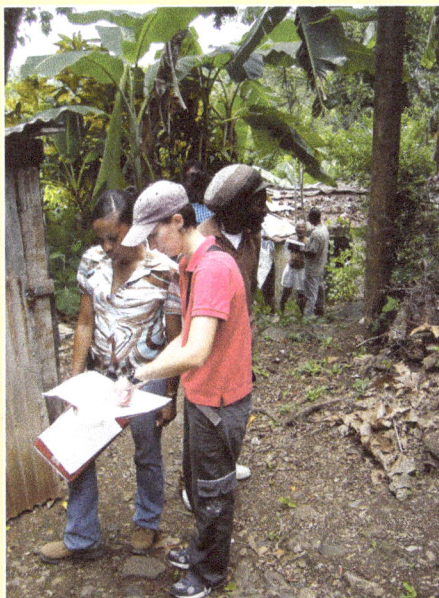

FIGURE 7.8 **Confirming with residents connection of households to drains**

- Cost of materials per meter of drain (consider relevant construction methods, materials, and drain dimensions)

- Cost of roof guttering, pipes, water tanks, and hurricane straps (include all fittings, screws, nails, etc., and materials such as facia boards for repairing roofs)

- Cost of transporting materials to the site (if there is no access by road, materials may need to be double handled—carried to a storage point and then again to the site)

- Cost of labor

7.3.2 Define work packages

The MCU should determine the most appropriate contract size and structure for the chosen community contracting process. In some cases, work packages can be relatively small so that as many community-based contractors as possible can be awarded contracts for the works. For typical interventions in the Eastern Caribbean, contracts have been let for construction of approximately 100 m of reinforced concrete block drains. Similarly, the installation of household roof water and gray water connections and related items may be split into work packages involving approximately 20–30 houses.

Creating a large number of small work packages can maximize the number of community residents (serving as contractors and laborers) benefiting from the short-term employment opportunity, but this approach creates a higher administrative and supervisory burden than if a smaller number of higher-value contracts were awarded.

Balancing the larger number/lower-value work package option against smaller number/higher-value work packages needs careful evaluation. In the former case, the provision of adequate on-site supervision for a large number of contractors, perhaps all starting on the same day, poses a major demand on supervisory staff. However, engaging larger numbers of community contractors can help create a very positive atmosphere that encourages postproject maintenance and behavioral changes with regard to surface water management at the household scale.

Comply with relevant government or funding agency regulations regarding the value and issuance of contracts. In certain circumstances, regulations may permit contracts below a certain value to be fast tracked through the tendering process. Designing work packages that fall below that value maximizes the number of contracts to be awarded (if this is considered manageable and appropriate) and minimizes project lead times—an important performance indicator for community-based construction projects (table 7.1).

7.3.3 Prepare a plan for procurement of materials

The project engineer or quantity surveyor should develop a plan for procuring materials for construction based on the bill of quantities and the form of community contracting being used. This plan should include the following information:

- For project management and RFT documents:

  - Required standards for products and services

  - Approved local suppliers

  - Purchasing procedures and responsibilities

- For project management and discussion with contractors once contracts are awarded:

  - Recommended unit costs

  - Anticipated transportation and storage costs and requirements

  - Recommended schedules for delivery (just in time/daily/weekly)

  - Monitoring and security of materials on site

Depending on community capacity and project procurement requirements, the responsibility for procurement of materials may lie with a government task team member, an implement-ing agency, or individual appointed by the MCU; a construction committee formed by the community; or individual contractors from within the community. In the latter two cases, the MCU may have oversight of procurement through the approval of contractors' accounts and verification on the ground of both material delivery and construction.

It is important that the process for procuring materials meets project funder requirements while remaining community based. It should balance the need for upward accountability to donors and downward accountability to those for whom the project is intended.

7.3.4 Prepare detailed construction specifications

For each work package, list the relevant construction specifications and include any appropriate design drawings. Use table 7.3 as a guide for preparing construction specifications for typical drainage components and refer to the examples of drain design drawings in section 6.8.3.

These specifications should be used to inform potential contractors of the details of the construction work required, and thus guide the bids they submit; they should also form part of the terms of reference for work package contracts.

7.3.5 Compile documents for each work package

The following documents should be prepared and included in the RFT for each work package; upon award, these documents will be issued to the contractors as part of their contracts:

- Description of the scope of work required and contract duration

- Quantity estimates and a detailed description of associated construction activities (based on the specified bill of quantities, section 7.3.1); note that cost estimates should not be provided to potential contractors

- The final drainage plan and the location of the work package (section 7.3.2)

TABLE 7.3 Requirements and specifications to be developed for work packages

CONSTRUCTION COMPONENT	SPECIFICATION	RATIONALE
Reinforced concrete block drains	Dimensions	Correct drain capacity, sidewalls flush with slope surface to allow inflow of surface water
	Depth of excavation	Strong foundations and prevention of undermining
	Reinforcement spacing	Strength of structure, preventing leaks and maximizing drain lifetime
	Cement mix	
	Finishing	
Downslope drains	Locations and design of stepped sections	Correct flow velocity (therefore correct capacity), prevention of stagnant water
	Location and height of upstands (raised drain walls)	Prevent overflow
Intercept drains	Gradient	Sufficient to ensure flow and prevent stagnant water
	Weep holes on upslope wall of drain	Allow inflow to drain
All drains	Debris trap locations	Prevent blockage
	Covered sections and grills	Allow pedestrian access to houses
	Culvert design and gradient	Sufficient gradient/capacity, self-cleaning to prevent blockage
	Location of connections	Allow drains/pipes to connect
Concrete connection chambers	Dimensions	Sufficient capacity and gradient for flow to drain
	Inflow and outflow pipes	
	Covering/debris traps	Prevent blockage
Ancillary retaining structures	Design of minor soil retaining structures	Appropriate additional protection of slopes, drains, and ravines from erosion or landslides
	Design of gabions	
	Design of rip-rap in natural channels	
Roof guttering	Access to roofs	Allow safe access for installation
Safeguards	Specification of how all required safeguards are of be met	Provide assurance that safeguards are complied with, and thus that proposed design/construction can proceed

- Requirements for procurement of materials, parts, and labor (section 7.3.3); note that depending on the form of community contracting, contractors may not be responsible for procuring materials

- Construction specifications and design drawings (section 7.3.4)

- Annexes to the terms of the contract relating to the financing schedule (advances/mobilization sum, contingencies, final payment upon satisfactory completion, or withholding of payment until poor work is corrected)

- Annexes to the terms of the contract relating to safeguards (such as procurement procedures, environmental requirements for soil disposal, landownership issues, etc.)

- Guidance relating to good and bad construction practices (sections 7.5, 7.6, and 7.7)

- Instructions to bidders on how to submit a tender

7.4 THE TENDERING PROCESS

A typical community contracting tendering process involves three main activities: soliciting potential contractors and requesting that they tender for the works, providing guidance on how to submit tenders, and evaluating tenders and awarding contracts. This process, and the roles and responsibilities of those evaluating and awarding contracts, must be clearly defined, publicly transparent, and fair.

7.4.1 Identifying contractors from the community

It is important to have a clear, comprehensive, well-advertised, and transparent process for soliciting potential community contractors and inviting them to tender.

Sources of names of potential contractors include the following:

- Residents approaching government task teams for work during mapping and drainage design stages

- Word of mouth within the community

- Community meetings

- Lists of community contractors previously engaged by government agencies.

7.4.2 Briefing potential contractors

Invite potential contractors to a project briefing led by the person or team that drew up the work packages and the person in charge of the tendering process. There could be several components to the briefing:

- On-site briefing—a comprehensive walk-through of the proposed works on site in the community (figure 7.9)

- Detailed briefing—explaining the specific terms of the RFT documents and contracts, the process by which tenders will be evaluated and contracts awarded, and how contracts will be managed

- Assistance and guidance—given to contractors wishing to submit bids but unfamiliar

FIGURE 7.9 On-site meetings with potential community contractors

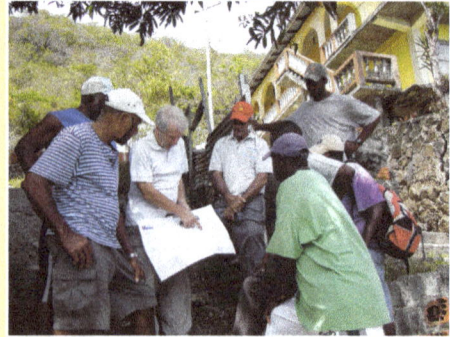

On-site meetings with potential community contractors can help convey good practice, encourage inexperienced contractors to participate, and share local knowledge relevant to construction practice or site details.

with formal bidding processes and requirements.

On-site briefing

For each work package, potential contractors should be shown the following on site:

- Where proposed drains start and finish, drain dimensions and form of construction, how they will connect to other drains, the specific construction requirements (excavation issues, weep holes, stepped falls, culverts, access to properties, etc.)

- Which houses are to have roof water and gray water connections to main drains, how they are to be connected, and any ancillary construction requirements (e.g., hurricane straps, water tanks, water tank overflow pipes).

While on site, encourage potential contractors to consider the following:

- How materials will be transported to the site and where they will be delivered (figure 7.10a)

- If double handling of materials will be necessary

- Where materials will be stored (on site and off site if necessary)

- Where cement will be mixed and water obtained (figure 7.10b); this location should provide access to an adequate water supply, storage space, and reasonable proximity to both material delivery and construction sites, while not interrupting preexisting pathways residents would be expected to use regularly

- Where fabrication of construction components will take place (shaping of reinforcement, construction of formwork, etc.)

FIGURE 7.10 Some issues to address during on-site briefing

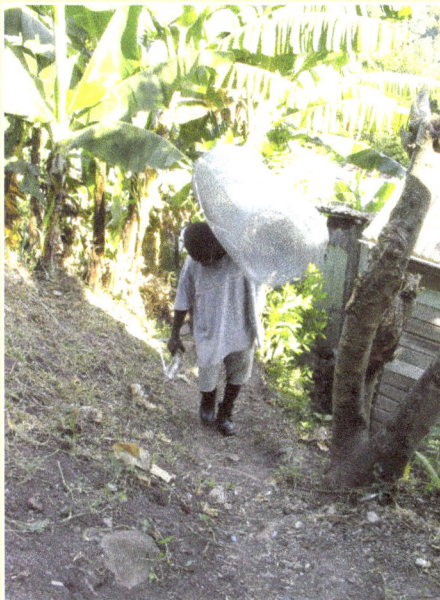

a. Consider how materials will be transported on site.

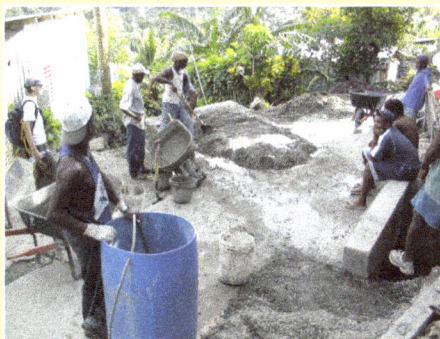

b. Plan where cement mixing can take place.

- Where soil from excavation will be taken

- How roofs will be accessed for installation of guttering

- Any issues that might have been overlooked in the work package specifications

- Any local best practices and experience that could be incorporated into the work package specifications.

Detailed briefing

Inform contractors of the following:

- The process by which tenders should be submitted, and how contracts will be awarded

- The form of contract that will be issued

- The inclusion of a contingency sum (often 10 percent), against which authorization for expenditure would be given separately in a written variation order

- The procedure for materials procurement

- The terms for final payment and requirement for completion of works to a satisfactory standard

- The withholding of payments if works are unsatisfactory

- Any other contract terms specific to government practice or funding agency requirements; for instance, if double handling and storage of materials are required, conditions relating to agreed-on procedures for storage site selection may need to be included in the contracts (figure 7.11)

Assistance and guidance

Attempt to gauge the level of support needed to enable contractors to submit bids. Support may be necessary when contractors

- have limited experience with formal contracting,

- are unfamiliar with the relevant terminology,

FIGURE 7.11 Double handling of materials can require temporary storage

- need help in completing the required tender documents,

- require assistance in interpreting an awarded contract, or

- are not able to read or write.

Assess the level of assistance needed during the contractor briefing process. The process of offering assistance and guidance should be transparent, open to all potential contractors, and without breaching any contracting and procurement protocols. The process should avoid the perception that one contractor is being favored over another.

While there can be many benefits in using small-scale community-based contractors, small contracting enterprises have certain limitations such as their ability to obtain credit and financial resources (Larcher 1999). In many cases, a contractor's size and turnover may be below the level required for achieving a credit rating, thus preventing access to loans for construction mobilization (i.e., procuring materials and employing laborers at the start of construction, before receiving any payments for completed works). This is often compounded by the fact that the institutional framework that supports the construction industry in the majority of developing countries is very weak and underdeveloped.

For the above reasons, the project procurement plan may allow the disbursement of start-up (mobilization) funds to contractors. Additionally, contractors may wish to assist each other by pooling resources for common tasks such as purchasing materials and paying for laborers to manually transport materials on site. Contractor collaboration is a potentially powerful process in facilitating capacity building among community members in project initiation, delivery, and implementation.

If the procurement of materials is to be the responsibility of the contractors (rather than an agency or individual appointed by the MCU, or a community construction committee) guidance should be provided on cost and price structures. In preparing tenders, potential contractors will need to consider the price they are likely to pay for materials and therefore likely costs for construction work (Ogunlana and Butt 2000). Cost estimates should also account for potential fluctuations in material prices due to factors such as material shortages, charges for transportation to the site, or changes in supplier (typically, some 60 percent of construction materials are imported in the developing world—Nordberg 1999) Ideally, the contractor needs to have an integrated view of the relationship between estimating, tendering, budgeting, and cost control.

7.4.3 Evaluating tenders and awarding contracts

The process for evaluating tenders and awarding contracts will vary from project to project depending on government and funding agency requirements, the form of community contracting chosen, and the value (or size) of the contracts. In most cases, submitted tenders will be evaluated by a tenders board on the basis of proposed costs and the technical skill or expertise of the contractors. The evaluation may also take into account wider project objectives such as building local capacity and providing short-term employment. For small projects or urgent works, contracts can often be awarded to nominated contractors as single-source (no bid) contracts, providing approval is received from the funding agency.

7.4.4 Contractors and safeguard policies

Throughout the processes leading to contract award (figure 7.12), the MCU and all the associated MoSSaiC teams should be aware of all relevant safeguards, including those detailed in table 7.4 (see also 1.5.3 and 7.10.4). These safeguards are included for guidance only; different countries, funding agencies, and legal systems can be expected to have other or differing requirements. The MCU should agree on a mechanism for communicating safeguards to contractors, which should be reinforced by the site supervisor.

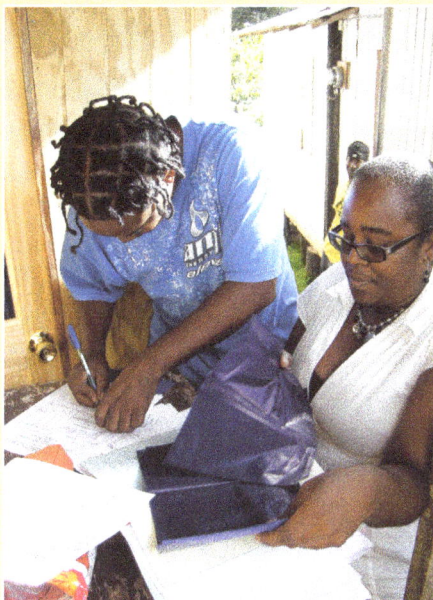

FIGURE 7.12 Contractor signing on site with implementing agency representative

TABLE 7.4 Illustrative safeguard checklist for contractors

SAFEGUARD	ILLUSTRATIVE TRIGGER	WHAT CONTRACTOR SHOULD DO
Natural habitats	• Is there the potential to cause significant conversion (loss) or degradation of natural habitats?	Alert the site supervisor
Disputed areas	• Is the project situated in a disputed area? • Has landownership been established and permission granted in writing if required?	Seek assurance from the government task team

Involuntary resettlement	• Are the works likely to lead not only to physical relocation, but to any loss of land or other assets resulting in the following:
	  • Relocation or loss of shelter
	  • Loss of assets or access to assets
	  • Loss of income sources or means of livelihood, regardless of whether affected people must move to another location
		Avoid these issues during construction

Questionable (corrupt) practices	• Contractor's claim for costs beyond the common labor cost raise and inflation rates • Materials and equipment used and workmanship not as specified; paperwork not consistent with items delivered • Contractors providing false information to project inspectors on progress of work or inspectors being coerced to approve progress payments or certify conformance with building permits • Inaccurate as-built drawings being presented or accepted	Ensure honest submissions are always made

Source: http://go.worldbank.org/WTA1ODE7T0.

7.5 IMPLEMENTING THE WORKS: ON-SITE REQUIREMENTS

7.5.1 Importance of site supervision

Experienced, trained site supervisors should oversee implementation of the works, providing technical advice for contractors, interpreting the construction design specifications on site, and ensuring good-quality construction. Good supervisors can help identify and address problems such as a lack of skills among contractors and laborers, unclear construction design specifications, incorrect choice of construction methods and equipment, and difficult site conditions.

> The quality of site supervision has a major influence on the overall performance and efficiency of construction projects. Inadequate supervision is believed to be one of the major causes of rework. Therefore, experienced and well-trained supervisors have an important role in minimising the amount of rework due to construction defects (Alwi, Hampson, and Mohamed 1999, 1).

Data on the inverse relationship between the costs of poor-quality construction (rework) and funds spent on training (percentage of total project cost) demonstrate that training of site supervisors and contractors is cost-effective (figure 7.13).

Trained site supervisors should be used for community-based construction projects such as MoSSaiC in which

- contractors are unlikely to have been in regular work and may need technical assistance and advice from site supervisors,

- laborers are likely to have been unemployed for a considerable time or may only have limited construction experience,

- a large number of people are likely to be employed simultaneously as work commences, and

- residents often request additional works to be undertaken once works have commenced.

Use the following sections as a prompt for training site supervisors for MoSSaiC projects and as a guide to implementing the drainage works.

Selecting the site supervisor

The site supervisor should be experienced in the technical aspects of drainage construction and the supervision of small contracts. If possible, he or she will also have worked with informal contractors in vulnerable urban communities.

Ideally, the supervisor will have been involved in the community-based mapping and drainage design process. This involvement will help ensure that the supervisor is conversant with the rationale for the landslide hazard reduction and drainage plan, which is useful for two reasons:

- Adjustments or adaptations of construction details are likely to be required during the course of construction (figure 7.14), and these will need to take into account the slope processes and contribute to reducing the landslide hazard.

- During construction, the supervisor will probably be the most regular point of contact between the community and government task teams and the MCU. The supervisor should be willing and able to answer residents' questions and resolve minor issues related to the works (such as ensuring access to houses during construction).

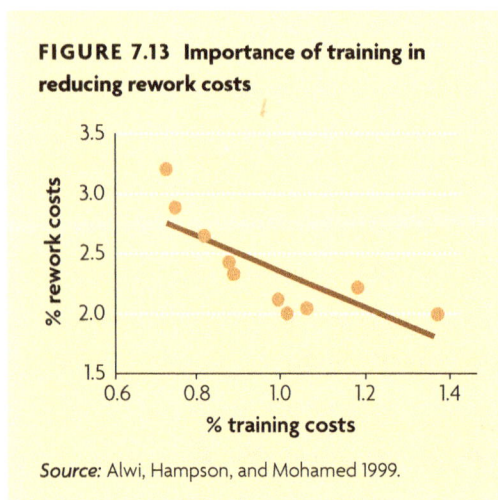

FIGURE 7.13 Importance of training in reducing rework costs

Source: Alwi, Hampson, and Mohamed 1999.

FIGURE 7.14 Clear markings help remove issues of ambiguity for site supervisor

Spraying paint marker positions on the ground helps ensures clarity of alignment details.

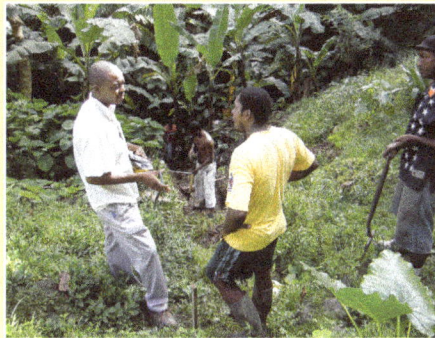

FIGURE 7.15 Site supervisor is critical to project success and to ensuring good construction practice

Meeting with the community before the start of construction

From their involvement in the slope feature mapping and discussions concerning the draft and final drainage plans, the community should already be aware of the timetable for commencement of the drainage works. Once a site supervisor has been appointed, it is good practice for that individual to meet on site with community residents in both formal and informal contexts. The supervisor can explain details of the timing of the construction and other issues that may concern residents, such as materials storage and temporary access to properties during construction.

The MCU should make known to community residents who the primary point of contact will be during construction—often this will be the site supervisor. Supervisor-community contact is an important element in securing continued, positive community engagement (figure 7.15).

Supervising construction start

The contractors should be informed of the proposed site supervision program: who the supervisor will be, how to contact the supervisor, and how often the supervisor will be on site. It should be stressed to the contractors and supervisor that construction quality is critical to the overall performance of the intervention in reducing landslide hazard.

The site supervisor should make daily visits to the site during the initial stages of construction to address the following:

- Resolve any ambiguity contractors may have in establishing drain alignments

- Resolve any unforeseen issues with residents

- Demonstrate a hands-on approach, which will help build trust among contractors and community residents alike

- Set a standard of engagement for those working for the contractors, who are likely to have been unemployed for some time and in need of clear guidance

- Be alerted early on to any potential contingency drawdown

- Ensure that contractors only employ the number of laborers required; the project's start-up might attract a large number of residents, some of whom are not employed on the project but might wish to be so (figure 7.16).

7.5.2 Beginning construction: Excavation and alignment requirements

During the initial phase of drain excavation and construction, the following design and construction details will need to be determined on site in the context of the work package contract and the ground conditions.

FIGURE 7.16 Supervision issue: Large numbers of residents engaging with contractors

Construction commencement location

Construction of a drain should typically commence at the planned furthermost downslope location of the drain. Starting excavation and construction at the highest elevation of a drain may concentrate and direct water to those areas of the hillside lacking drains, thus increasing the potential for soil erosion and landslides. Heavy rainfall can also overdeepen the already excavated drain routes, resulting in the need for more materials (to construct larger drains commensurate in size with the newly eroded and overdeepened trench), or excessive backfilling of completed drains (which can create preferential subsurface flow paths and erosion alongside the drains).

Detailed alignment issues

Supervisors and contractors will likely have to make minor adjustments to drain alignments, excavation, and preparation of reinforcement or formwork according to detailed site and ground conditions.

Minor on-site adjustments to the drainage design may involve the following:

- Removing or avoiding obstacles to drain excavation, such as tree roots and boulders

- Adjusting the alignment according to minor topographic variations that would otherwise affect drain gradient and flow capacity; this is especially relevant with intercept drains designed to run cross-slope

- Smoothing the alignment of bends or junctions in the drain; these should not be sharply angled or water will overshoot or damage the drain, and there should be sufficient depth and width to accommodate increased flows

- Incorporating asymmetry of the ground slope conditions in drain cross-sections; reinforcement and drain side walls will need to be adapted (for example, figure 7.17 shows higher reinforcement on the upslope side of the intercept drain)

FIGURE 7.17 Example of detailed alignment issue encountered at construction start

Channel gradient issues

In the context of the work package specifications and the above issues related to drain alignment, the supervisor and contractors will need to make on-site judgments as to the appropriate depth and gradient of excavation, and the detailed locations of any required drain steps. Drain channel gradients should ensure sufficient flow velocity, especially through culverts, and limit the build-up of debris; but should not be so steep as to cause overtopping, erosion of the drain, and flooding further downslope.

Specific on-site requirements relating to drain channel gradient include the following:

- Creating steps in the drains with steep channel gradients to slow flow velocity especially where the drain changes direction or where two drains join (steps reduce the risk of overtopping due to excess flow velocity)

- Making intercept and downslope drains self-cleaning by establishing drain channel gradients that maintain adequate flow velocity and thus reduce the deposition of debris (figure 7.18)

- Ensuring that finished invert levels will prevent standing water or an incorrect flow direction

7.5.3 Ensure that water can enter drains

Casting of the base of the drains and construction of block work side walls is a critical phase of drain construction. If construction is too hasty or poorly supervised, the result can be an ineffective drain that fails to capture surface runoff—and therefore to reduce landslide hazard. Ineffective drain construction can be avoided by the contractor adhering to the following construction guidance.

Drain wall

Construct the top of drain side walls flush with the ground surface (on both sides of downslope drains and on the upslope side of intercept drains) (figure 7.19). This construction detail needs to be stressed to residents and contractors. Where there is inadequate design and site supervision, it is not uncommon for sidewalls to be constructed above ground level, thereby preventing surface water from entering the drain.

Incorporate weep holes

Weep holes allow water to enter drains by capturing subsurface (infiltrated) water from the uppermost soil horizons. Weep holes on the upslope sidewall of an intercept drain are especially important. If they are excluded, subsurface flow may, as a consequence, pass under the drain base and erode drain foundations on the downslope side.

Discuss weep hole provision with the contractor since the spacing of vertical reinforcement rods needs to be accommodated at the start of drain construction.

Weep holes can be formed in several ways, the most common of which are by leaving gaps in block construction (figure 7.20a), using a

FIGURE 7.18 Self-cleaning stepped drains

Ensuring stepped drains that self-clean is a vital element of good practice and needs to be carefully supervised on site because ground conditions may not always make that easy to achieve.

FIGURE 7.19 Finished drain wall height same as adjoining ground surface

When the finished drain height is the same as that of the adjoining ground surface, water can enter the drain from the side slopes. Here, the drain walls are the correct height, and surface water will be able to enter the drain once the backfill has been added and compacted. Inexperienced contractors often construct drain side walls to a finished level above that of the ground surface.

FIGURE 7.21 Drain construction providing for eventual connection with gray water pipes

half block (figure 7.20b), and inserting plastic piping (figure 7.20c).

Construct drains before installing roof guttering and house connections

If household water (gray water and roof water) is to be connected to the drain via pipes or minor household drains, make provision for these connections during construction (figure 7.21).

Install roof guttering after drains are completed. Installation prior to drain construction can result in concentrated discharge from unconnected downpipes, kitchens, and bathrooms, eroding the soil, damaging unfinished drains, and potentially increasing local flooding or landslide hazards.

7.5.4 Capture household roof water

Prepare and repair roofs

A careful and comprehensive survey of any required roof work should have been undertaken during preparation of the bill of quanti-

FIGURE 7.20 Weep hole formation

a. Weep holes should be incorporated in concrete block drain construction on the upslope side, to allow the capture of subsurface flow.

b. Weep hole formed by a half block laid orthogonal to the drain wall.

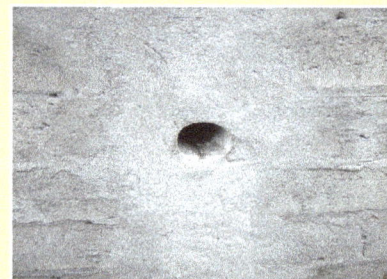

c. Weep hole formed by small plastic pipe.

ties and the work packages (sections 7.3.1 and 7.3.2). Omission of these details from the schedule of works can result in cost overruns, potential difficulty in acquiring additional materials, and delays in completion of the works.

Carry out minor roof repairs and preparations (figure 7.22a and b) such as the following:

- Repairing or replacing facia boards and the ends of joists

- Trimming galvanized roof sheets to ensure that the roof guttering is able to capture all the roof water

- Reattaching galvanized sheeting to joists where fixings have been lost.

It may be decided that it is impractical or uneconomical to repair certain roof structures within the constraints of the project budget (figure 7.22c). If such a decision is reached, the reasons for not installing roof guttering need to be discussed with the resident(s) concerned and with the community more widely, in the context of the agreed project and budget priorities.

Install roof guttering

Attach roof guttering to sound facia boards. Identify downpipe locations that allow con-

nection to water tanks, drains, or concrete chambers with piped connections to drains.

Once the downpipe locations have been determined, install the roof guttering so that water will flow along the guttering to the downpipes with sufficient velocity to prevent overtopping during major rainfall events. Brackets and other fittings should be aligned to ensure flow in the correct direction (figure 7.23).

FIGURE 7.23 Newly installed roof guttering

Roof guttering may require the reversal of existing guttering to create flow directions that are efficient for downpipe and main drain connections.

FIGURE 7.22 Issues involved in roof repair

c. Some roof structures may require complete replacement. The decision to undertake such extensive works needs to be carefully assessed in terms of community and government expectations regarding levels of household support being provided.

a and b. Make minor roof repairs to allow the installation of guttering, downpipes, and hurricane straps.

7.5.5 Connect household water to drains

Each house receiving roof guttering and gray water connections must be connected to the drainage network. Potential connection options should have been identified during the drainage design process (section 6.6.4) such as direct pipe connections, connection by pipe to a concrete chamber and then by pipe to the drain, or construction of a small drain to connect to the main drain.

All household guttering and piped connections to drains need to be watertight. Supervisors should inspect roof guttering, downpipes, and all other pipes during and after rainfall to ensure that they are performing properly and are securely fitted. It is not usually difficult to remedy small problems. If left untreated, however, loose connections can leak, damage walls and foundations, and result in erosion and flooding.

Direct connections

In some cases, downpipes and gray water pipes can be connected directly to drains (figure 7.24). It is good practice to do the following:

- Bury connection pipes wherever possible to prevent damage.

- Securely attach connection pipes to the drain wall at the pipe discharge point to prevent potential disconnection during times of high flow rates.

Construct concrete chambers for connecting drainage pipes

Concrete connection chambers should be constructed when the roof guttering is installed to ensure that the planned locations are viable with respect to the final location of downpipes.

Connection chamber location, design, and construction should

- ensure a sufficient gradient on the pipe outfall to the drain for self-cleaning;

- incorporate as large an outflow pipe as possible, or use two smaller pipes to ensure sufficient capacity;

FIGURE 7.24 Household roof water connections to main drains

Care needs to be taken to ensure that household roof water connections to main drains are sufficiently rigid and deliver rapid flow rates to encourage self-cleaning.

- incorporate a cover or debris trap to minimize blockages and enable cleaning; and

- be carefully finished with a skim of cement to prevent leakage (figure 7.25).

Install water tank overflows

Whether the resident already collects rainwater, or a new water tank is being provided as part of the project, an overflow pipe needs to be fitted to the tank and connected to a drain (figure 7.26). The routing of the overflow can dictate tank location and therefore which downpipe is best connected to the tank.

7.6 IMPLEMENTING THE WORKS: GOOD PRACTICES

The following guidelines provide examples of good practices beyond the construction requirements previously outlined.

7.6.1 Cast concrete in good weather

The base of the drain should be cast in good weather, allowing sufficient time for the concrete to set before there is a flow in the partially constructed drain. Rainwater discharge over a drain base that has not set can easily erode the mix and waste valuable materials and construction time (figure 7.27).

- Estimate the time needed for excavation, preparation, material delivery, and carrying materials to the site.

- Use these estimates to break up the required works into tasks that can be managed realistically and completed each day, in accordance with weather conditions.

- Anticipate the possibility of overnight rainfall.

- Take high temperatures into account; concrete can set too quickly and crack if it is not properly shaded and kept damp.

FIGURE 7.25 Concrete connection chambers

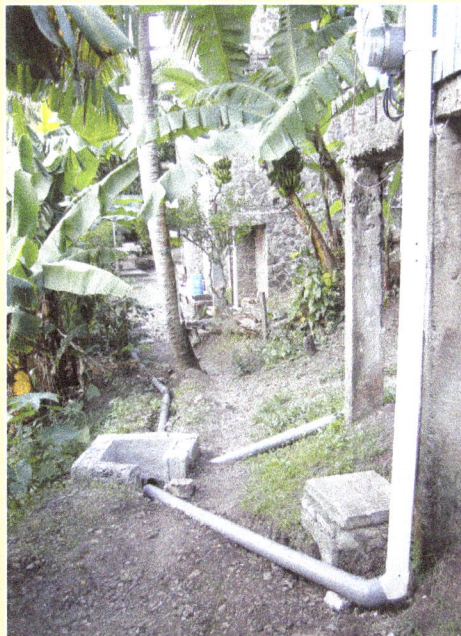

Concrete connection chambers are an efficient way of collecting roof water in high-density housing areas. When finished, pipes should be covered over to prevent them from causing an obstruction, and chambers should be fitted with a removable cover.

FIGURE 7.26 Connecting water tank overflow pipes to nearby drains

Rainwater harvesting to water tanks should be accompanied by the provision of an overflow to a nearby main drain.

FIGURE 7.27 Examples of drain bases

a. A well-constructed drain base cast in good weather conditions.

b. Erosion of a newly cast drain base: reinforcement is exposed and water may eventually break though the base.

7.6.2 Store materials securely

Identify a secure on-site location for storing materials and minimizing the risk of theft.

- Time the purchase and delivery of materials to coincide with planned construction tasks so that there is not too much material on site at any one time; be sure to take possible delays in delivery into account.

- Coordinate with residents to find a trusted individual who can store the materials securely, for example, at a shop, community center, house, or backyard.

- Use a locked container if there is no suitably secure alternative.

- Store materials in more public areas if they will be used within the working day.

7.6.3 Keep an inventory

Inventory control by those in charge of procurement and by contractors helps prevent theft, and is useful in resolving potential disputes between and among residents, laborers, and contractors regarding material usage.

- Keep records of all materials purchased, such as open bills, receipts, and delivery records.

- Ensure that material is sent from the storage location to the site only when it is needed.

- Ensure that materials released can be used within the working day; this reduces the likelihood of theft.

7.6.4 Provide access for residents

Excavation and construction of drains can lead to temporary problems with access to paths and houses. Contractors need to keep the goodwill of residents and be sensitive to any unavoidable disruption caused.

- Create temporary access for residents when drains are being constructed (figure 7.28).

- If the final design has not made provision for access across a drain, consider using contingency funds to construct a step over the drain.

- Because extensive sections of covered drain will not capture surface flows and may become blocked with debris, limit covered

FIGURE 7.28 Providing adequate temporary access to houses during construction

sections only to what is necessary for access.

7.6.5 Minimize leakage from pipes

Ensure that roof guttering, downpipes, and all piped connections to drains are watertight to avoid damaging houses and creating concentrated flows that could increase localized soil erosion, flood, or landslide hazards. Be aware of the locations of existing drainage or water supply pipes to avoid causing damage during construction.

- Ensure drainage pipe connections are watertight (figure 7.29).

- Check for leaks in existing water supply and gray water pipes and household stop taps.

- Ensure that excavation and construction do not cause new leaks in existing pipes.

- Ask the water company to reroute pipes that cross the proposed alignment of new drains.

FIGURE 7.29 Using sleeving to join drainage pipe sections

7.7 IMPLEMENTING THE WORKS: PRACTICES TO BE AVOIDED

The desire for community workers to be paid quickly, together with poor site supervision, can sometimes lead to poor construction. Steps should be taken at the outset to avoid such circumstances. Since poor construction can be difficult to rectify (both politically and financially), this section identifies drainage design details and related construction practices that should be avoided.

Getting drainage design and construction details correct helps prevent unnecessary additional construction costs due to wasted materials or the need for rework, ensures that drains function as intended, and can improve the physical environment for residents (e.g., by reducing localized flooding, deposition of eroded materials and debris, standing water, and waterlogged soils). Site inspections in Hong Kong SAR, China (reported by Hui, Sun, and Ho 2007), highlight some examples of inadequate attention given to surface drainage design and construction details construction details (table 7.5). Figure 7.30 illustrates several such drainage problems commonly found in unauthorized communities

7.7.1 Wasted materials and no surface water capture

Contractors may perceive drain sidewall construction design to be similar to that of small soil-retaining structures, thus incorrectly building above the level of the slope surface and preventing surface water runoff from entering the drain. Stress to contractors that drain sidewalls must be flush with ground level to capture hillslope surface flow along its length.

Contractors should avoid building drain block work above ground level since this

- wastes materials;

- renders the drain largely ineffective in capturing surface water; and

- can result in flow occurring along the outside of the drain, causing flooding downslope while potentially undermining the drain (figure 7.31).

7.7.2 Restricted capacity of footpath drains

The flow capacity of drains adjacent to steps in a footpath is determined by the point of minimum drain depth in line with the back of the

TABLE 7.5 Examples of frequently overlooked drainage design and construction details

DETAIL	DESCRIPTION
Sharp bends	Presence of sharp bends in drainage channels with no baffle walls provided to control potential splashing
Inadequate capacity	Inadequate capacity of downstream drainage provisions to cater to discharge from the slope (e.g., large channels discharging into smaller-sized channels), hence resulting in overflow
Wrong fall	Drainage channels with an as-built fall in a direction opposite design intent
Obstructions in drain	Presence of obstructions in drainage channels leading to reduction in drainage capacity
Sidewalls too high	Inadequate construction of drainage channels with the tops of sidewalls being above the adjacent ground level, leading to erosion along the side of the channel
Lack of upstands	Lack of upstands at the downhill side of road/pavement to minimize the chance of uncontrolled discharge of surface runoff to the downhill slope at low points or vulnerable locations
Lack of intersecting drains	Lack of intersecting drains along a long sloping road/pavement, which may act as a conduit to reduce accumulated discharge at certain points down the road/pavement and avoid surface erosion or flooding
Channels constructed close to mature trees	Drainage channels constructed close to mature trees necessitate removal of some tree roots, with the attendant risk of adverse impact on tree health as well as possible damage to the channels by tree root action in due course
Undersized drainage channels	Undersized drainage channels that can lead to splashing, overflow, and hence erosion of the slope surface alongside the drainage channels
No debris/silt traps	Absence of trash grill or debris/silt traps at inlets to main culverts/drainage channels, making them vulnerable to blockage, especially where the site setting involves major surface runoff during heavy rainfall leading to scouring and washout debris in the upstream/uphill area
Poor debris/silt trap design	Inappropriate detailing of trash grill/debris screens at drainage inlets, which are liable to lead to turbulent flow and splashing
Inadequate protection of cross road culverts headwalls	Inadequate protection of headwalls at inlets to cross-road culverts against water ingress into the road embankment leading to wetting of the ground and potential subsurface erosion and ground movement (hence possible cracking of the culverts and consequential leakage which can affect the downhill slope)
Insufficient downslope drainage points	Inadequate number of drainage discharge points provided
Undersized connection chambers	Undersized drain connection chambers can be prone to blockage
Poor footpath/drain design	Presence of a concrete stairway adjoining drainage channel that is liable to act as an interceptor and prevent surface runoff from getting into the channel
Poor connecting drain design	Poor detailing at the connection between existing drainage provision and the new slope drainage systems
Absence of intercept drains	Absence of intercept drains or inadequate sizing of intercept drains for slopes with sizeable surface catchments

Source: Hui, Sun, and Ho 2007.

FIGURE 7.30 Illustrations of frequently overlooked drainage design and construction details

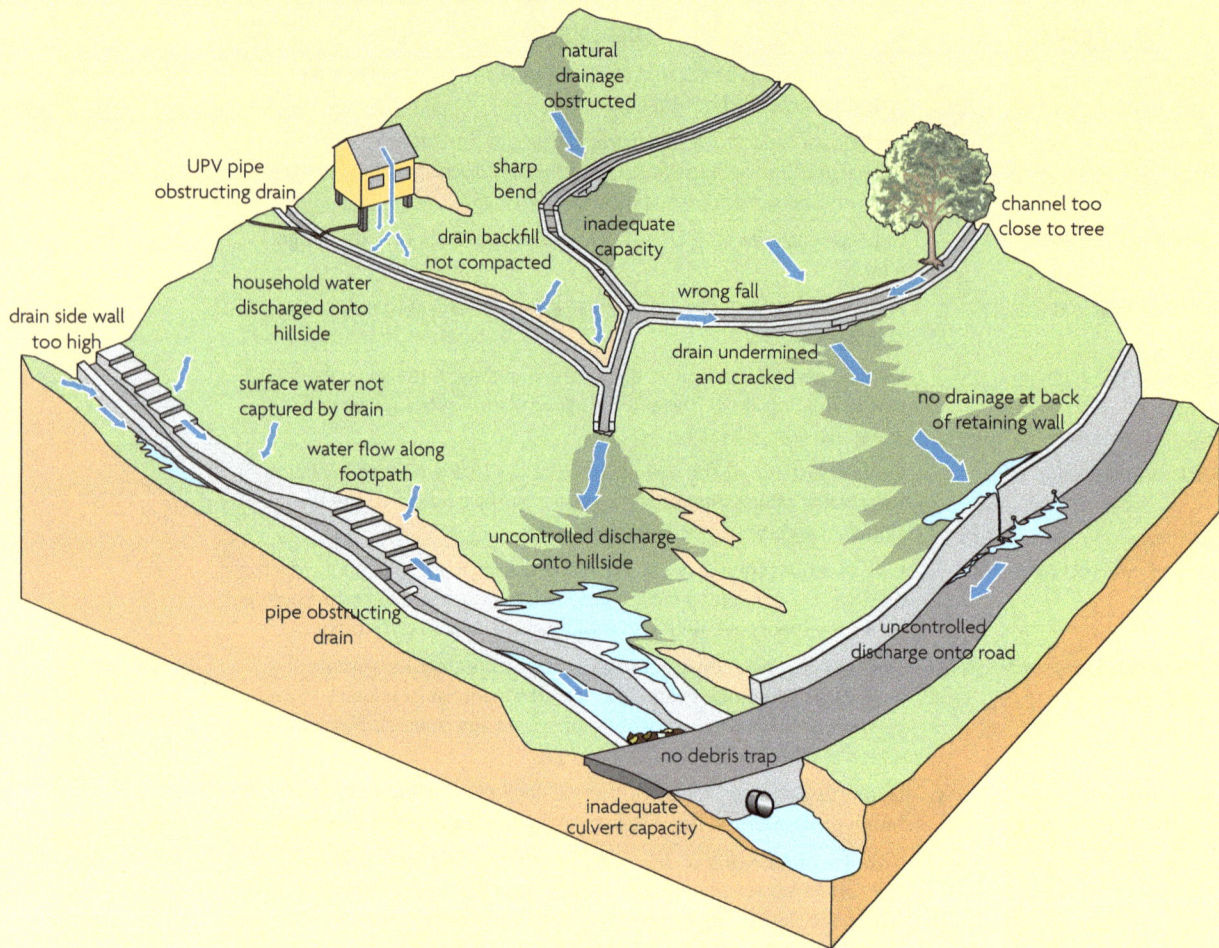

natural drainage obstructed

UPV pipe obstructing drain

sharp bend

channel too close to tree

drain backfill not compacted

inadequate capacity

wrong fall

drain side wall too high

household water discharged onto hillside

drain undermined and cracked

no drainage at back of retaining wall

surface water not captured by drain

water flow along footpath

pipe obstructing drain

uncontrolled discharge onto hillside

uncontrolled discharge onto road

no debris trap

inadequate culvert capacity

Source: Hui, Sun, and Ho 2007. Reproduced with permission of the Head of the Geotechnical Engineering Office and the Director of the Civil Engineering Department, Hong Kong SAR, China.

FIGURE 7.31 Drain built with inappropriately high sidewalls

High sidewalls prevent inflow and encourage flow alongside and under the drain. Drain finished height should be in line with that of the adjacent ground surface.

footpath tread. Once this flow depth is exceeded, water will flow onto the steps and down the footpath. Typically, footpath drain capacity is less than 50 percent of perceived capacity (figure 7.32).

Footpath drains should be designed and constructed to account for the tread depth of footpath steps where this is feasible; otherwise, depth compensation must be made such that the minimum drain depth is considered adequate.

This design detail is significant in heavy rainfall, and can make the difference between a safe footpath and one swamped with so much water it is too hazardous to use.

FIGURE 7.32 Identify maximum drain capacity adjacent to footpath steps

This capacity may be less than it first appears and result in water overtopping the drain and flowing down footpath steps.

7.7.3 Hazardous access for residents

During and after drain construction, residents may be affected by access issues where new drains cross footpaths. Although it is good practice to provide steps or grills over drains, these should be carefully designed so as not to cause a further hazard:

- Grills where a path passes over a drain can be a hazard to young children unless the spacing of the bars is sufficiently small (figure 7.33).

- Where concrete slabs are used to bridge drains for access, they should be textured to prevent the surface from becoming slippery during heavy rain.

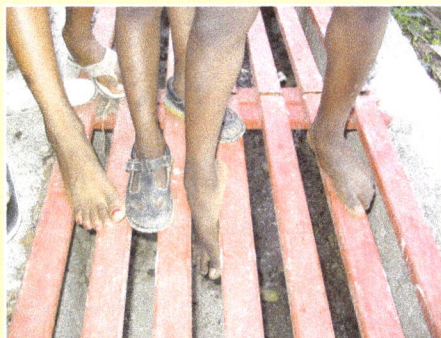

FIGURE 7.33 Some construction practices can pose dangers to small children

7.7.4 Construction detailing notes

Site supervision and final construction detailing are important in achieving landslide hazard reduction. The MCU should consider providing contractors and supervisors with copies of sections 7.6 and 7.7, incorporating additional local good practices as applicable.

7.8 SIGNING OFF ON THE COMPLETED WORKS

The landslide assessment and engineering task team and/or engineer appointed by the MCU should ensure that each work package is completed satisfactorily before works are signed off on and final payments made to contractors. This process involves confirming that there are no works outstanding from the contract and there are no construction defects. Minor additional works may also be identified beyond the scope of the original contract.

Construction defects could include the following:

- Unauthorized deviations from the design or construction specification

- Use of substandard materials

- Poor workmanship

- Problems with the original design and specification of the works.

Site supervisors should advise the engineer of any issues during construction such as the need for minor changes in drain alignment or design due to conditions on site. Community residents should also be given the opportunity to comment on the works and suggest small additions that may reasonably be required, such as access across drains.

Outstanding works and defects due to contractor error should be corrected before final payment. However, contractors should not be penalized for deficiencies in the original design and construction specification. Rather, additional works required due to redesign or unforeseen works should be agreed upon with contractors and paid for using the contingency sum, or a further single-source contract issued.

The engineer and site supervisor should prepare a schedule of construction defects and outstanding works for each work package and identify remedial actions required for completion; table 7.6 provides an example template. Additional works may also be specified and a payment schedule agreed upon. Discuss this schedule on site with contractors and agree on a time frame for completion. Provide copies of the this schedule to the contractor, site supervisor, engineer, and community leaders.

Once the works are completed, the construction is signed off on by the authorized engineer, and final payments are released to contractors.

> **MILESTONE 7:**
>
> **Sign-off on completed construction**

7.9 POSTCONSTRUCTION BIOENGINEERING

Although MoSSaiC is focused on appropriate surface water drainage to reduce landslide hazard, other related interventions and practices such as bioengineering can potentially add value (Anderson 1983; Florineth, Rauch, and Staffler 2002; Howell 1999a; Lewis, Salisbury, and Hagen 2001; Stokes et al. 2007). While specific plants can sometimes increase the strength of slope materials, a particular benefit of bioengineering is in reducing slope erosion. Erosion is the detachment and transport of material particles by rainfall and flowing water (or other agents), and involves a different set of physical processes from those associated with slope stability (as defined in chapter 3). In some communities, residents erroneously regard erosion as synonymous with landslides. It can be appropriate to discuss these two slope processes with residents,

TABLE 7.6 Example of an informal schedule of construction defects and outstanding works

CONSTRUCTION DEFECTS, OUTSTANDING WORKS, AND REQUIRED REMEDIAL WORKS			
COMMUNITY:			
DATE:			
REPORTING TECHNICIAN/ENGINEER:			
CONTRACTOR:			
LOCATION (NUMBER ON PLAN)	**DESCRIPTION OF PROBLEM AND REFERENCE NUMBER OF PHOTO**	**RATIONALE AND PRIORITY**	**DESIGN DRAWING**
12	Complete connection of main drain to footpath drain above bakery	Prevention of flooding of existing landslide area	i
18	Complete drain by House 15: link drains above and below already constructed; 30 m reinforced concrete block drain required	Essential to avoid flooding of Property 16	ii
23	Install house downpipe connections to main drains	Essential to prevent erosion of path	iii
27	Realign drain to ensure reverse flow of drain into existing ravine	Site instructions given May 21	iv
30	Install concrete slab over drain to provide access to Houses 2 and 7	Additional works identified by community and approved by authorized project engineer	v

and explain that appropriate slope vegetation management can help reduce both erosion and landslide hazard. Reducing soil erosion can also assist in reducing the amount of debris deposited in drains during heavy rainfall events.

This section provides a short introduction to bioengineering and how it can be part of good slope management practice in communities. A discussion with a local plant or forestry specialist would assist the landslide assessment and engineering task team in reviewing the potential for supplementing the drainage intervention with bioengineering where housing density permits.

7.9.1   What is bioengineering?

Bioengineering is commonly defined as the use of any form of vegetation as an engineering material (i.e., one that has quantifiable characteristics and behavior). Bioengineering measures use two distinct components: living components (live species), and nonliving or structural components such as dead stakes, cribwalls, and timber. These two component types may be used alone or in combination (Campbell et al. 2008).

Soil bioengineering applications require careful planning, since both engineering practices and ecological principles need to be applied. Most natural plant communities do not have the desired engineering properties for slope stabilization or surface erosion protection because species have not evolved specifically for those purposes (Howell 1999a); this underscores the importance of careful planning. An ideal plant community configuration has to be both engineered and maintained as the vegetation grows (figure 7.34).

7.9.2   The effect vegetation on slope stability

Some plants can have a significant role in stabilizing and protecting slopes. Plant roots can reinforce the slope by adding tensile strength and anchoring slope materials (figure 7.35). In terms of slope hydrology, there are three main positive hydrological effects:

FIGURE 7.34 Typical development of plant communities under a bioengineering and maintenance program

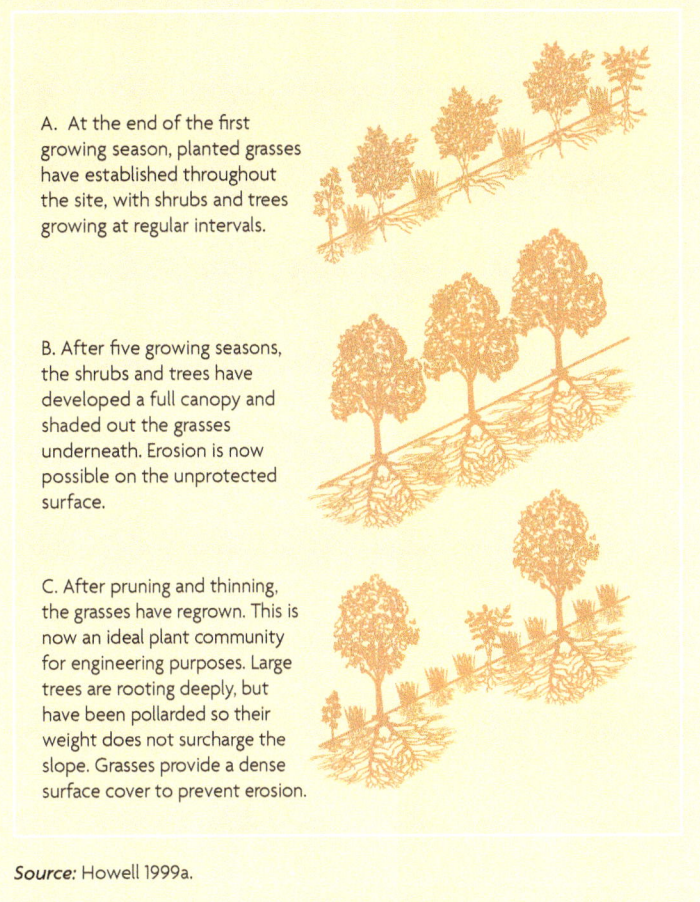

A. At the end of the first growing season, planted grasses have established throughout the site, with shrubs and trees growing at regular intervals.

B. After five growing seasons, the shrubs and trees have developed a full canopy and shaded out the grasses underneath. Erosion is now possible on the unprotected surface.

C. After pruning and thinning, the grasses have regrown. This is now an ideal plant community for engineering purposes. Large trees are rooting deeply, but have been pollarded so their weight does not surcharge the slope. Grasses provide a dense surface cover to prevent erosion.

Source: Howell 1999a.

- Uptake of soil water by roots reduces the water content of the slope material and therefore reduces pore water pressures.

- Vegetation intercepts rainfall, thus reducing surface water infiltration.

- By intercepting rainfall and reducing surface water runoff, vegetation can reduce soil erosion.

In some cases, vegetation can act to reduce the stability of a slope by the following mechanisms:

- Large trees increase slope loading.

- Trees are subject to "wind throw," which exerts a force on the slope during high winds.

- Stem flow and live or decaying roots can generate preferential flow paths into and

FIGURE 7.35 Lateral root spread

The extent of lateral root spread in this red cedar can help reinforce upper soil layers; species with a larger tap root would reinforce the slope at depth.

within slope material (macropores), increasing the concentration of water in certain locations.

- Some cultivated species, such as banana and plantain, contribute to slope loading while developing only very limited root systems.

There are acknowledged limitations to bioengineering. Campbell et al. (2008, 13) summarize these: "although the benefits of vegetation to prevent soil erosion are well established, its ability to stabilise slopes subject to shallow failures is less well proven, and certainly less well quantified."

7.9.3 Vegetation and urban slope management

In areas of unauthorized housing, vegetation is commonly removed for house construction, potentially increasing landslide hazard and soil erosion. The slope may subsequently be kept clear of vegetation or planted with crops that do not provide adequate stabilization or surface protection.

When considering bioengineering to supplement a MoSSaiC drainage intervention, talk to community residents about local vegetation management practices, the removal of vegetation from slopes, whether they grow subsistence crops or crops to sell, and the benefits and disadvantages of different planting schemes. Involve local plant experts and engineers in identifying plants that have a positive effect on slope stability and provide protection from soil erosion.

Refer to studies and guidance notes on bioengineering to inform the discussion on the most appropriate planting scheme for the community. Comprehensive processes for selecting bioengineering approaches are given by Howell (1999b; see table 7.7) and Campbell et al. (2008); major reviews of bioengineering practice can be found in Barker (1995), Campbell et al. (2008), Coppin and Richards (1990), and Gray and Sotir (1996); Wilkinson et al. (2002) provide modeling evidence of slope types for which vegetation increases or decreases landslide risk. It is beyond the scope of this book to provide species information or specific planting guidance, as local climatic conditions will play a significant role in this regard.

In many cases, grasses and shrubs may provide a good bioengineering solution for communities. Some grass species, such as vetiver, have extensive root networks and can provide both soil strength and surface protection. They can also trap loose slope material and reduce sedimentation in surface drains. Grasses need significant sunlight to become established and will not easily survive in a community of other plants, so any shrubs and trees should be kept thinned and pruned for the grasses to continue to thrive. Because long grass can provide an ideal environment for insects, rats, and other pests in urban areas, due care and consideration are needed in planning their use in any community bioengineering intervention.

Figure 7.36 illustrates different vegetation covers for four slopes. Vegetation manage-

TABLE 7.7 Decision aid for choosing a bioengineering technique

START SLOPE ANGLE	SLOPE LENGTH	MATERIAL DRAINAGE	SITE MOISTURE	PREVIOUS/ POTENTIAL PROBLEM	FUNCTION REQUIRED	TECHNIQUE
> 45°	> 15 m	Good	Damp	Erosion, slumping	Armor, reinforce, drain	**Diagonal grass lines**
			Dry	Erosion	Armor, reinforce	**Contour grass lines**
		Poor	Damp	Slumping, erosion	Drain, armor, reinforce	**1. Downslope grass lines & vegetated stone pitched rills** or 2. Chevron grass lines and vegetated stone pitched rills
			Dry	Erosion, slumping	Armor, reinforce, drain	**Diagonal grass lines**
	< 15 m	Good	Any	Erosion	Armor, reinforce	**1. Diagonal grass lines** or 2. Jute netting and randomly planted grass
		Poor	Damp	Slumping, erosion	Drain, armor, reinforce	**1. Downslope grass lines** or 2. Diagonal grass lines
			Dry	Erosion, slumping	Armor, reinforce, drain	**1. Jute netting and randomly planted grass** or 2. Contour grass lines or 3. Diagonal grass lines
30°–45°	> 15 m	Good	Any	Erosion	Armor, reinforce, catch	**1. Horizontal bolster cylinders & shrub/tree planting** or 2. Downslope grass lines & vegetated stone pitched rills or 3. Site grass seeding, mulch & wide mesh jute netting
		Poor	Any	Slumping, erosion	Drain, armor, reinforce	**1. Herringbone bolster cylinder & shrub/tree planting** or 2. Another drainage system and shrub/tree planting
	< 15 m	Good	Any	Erosion	Armor, reinforce, catch	**1. Brush layers of woody cuttings** or 2. Contour grass lines or 3. Contour fascines or 4. Palisades of woody cuttings or 5. Site grass seeding, mulch & wide mesh jute netting
		Poor	Any	Slumping, erosion	Drain, armor, reinforce	**1. Diagonal grass lines** or 2. Diagonal brush layers or 3. Herringbone fascines and shrub/tree planting or 4. Herringbone bolster cylinders & shrub/tree planting or 5. Another drainage system and shrub/tree planting
< 30°	Any	Good	Any	Erosion	Armor, catch	**1. Site seeding of grass and shrub/tree planting** or 2. Shrub/tree planting
		Poor	Any	Slumping, erosion	Drain, armor, catch	**1. Diagonal lines of grass and shrubs/trees** or 2. Shrub/tree planting
	< 15 m	Any		Erosion	Armor, catch	**Turfing and shrub/tree planting**
	Base of any slope			Planar sliding or shear failure	Support, anchor, catch	**1. Large bamboo planting** or 2. Large tree planting
SPECIAL CONDITIONS						
Any[a]	Any[a]	Any[a]	Any[a]	Planar sliding, shear failure	Reinforce, anchor	**Site seeding of shrubs/small trees**[b]
> 30°	Any	Any rocky material		Debris fall	Reinforce, anchor	**Site seeding of shrubs/small trees**
Any loose sand		Good	Any	Erosion	Armor	**Jute netting and randomly planted grass**
Any rato mato		Poor	Any	Erosion, slumping	Armor, drain	**Diagonal lines of grass and shrubs/trees**
Gullies ≤ 45°		Any gully		Erosion (major)	Armor, reinforce, catch	**1. Large bamboo planting** or 2. Live check dams or 3. Vegetated stone pitching

Source: Howell 1999b.

Note: "Any rocky material" is defined as material into which rooted plants cannot be planted, but seeds can be inserted in holes made with a steel bar. "Any loose sand" is defined as any slope in a weak, unconsolidated sandy material. Such materials are normally river deposits of recent geological origin. "Any rato mato" is defined as a red soil with a high clay content. It is normally of clay loam texture, and formed from prolonged weathering. It can be considered semilateritic. Techniques in **bold type** are preferred.

a. Possible overlap with parameters described in the rows above.

b. May be required in combination with other techniques listed in the rows above.

FIGURE 7.36 Four vegetation covers typically found on hillsides housing vulnerable communities

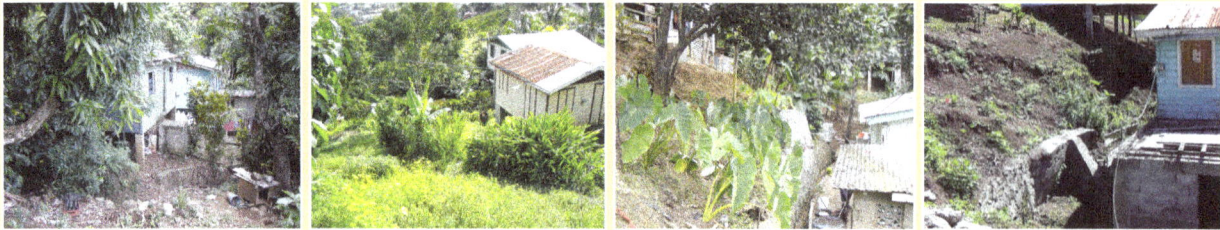

Slopes with acceptable vegetation cover from a slope stability perspective

a. Low-density housing with minimum disturbance to the slope. Care needs to be taken to ensure maintenance of this mixed cover, should other houses be built.

b. Vegetation comprising mostly grasses and medium shrubs on a shallow slope with minor slope failures.

Slopes for which bioengineering improvements could be considered in order to reduce landslide risk

c. Natural vegetation cleared and crops grown on a previously failed slope (dasheen, indicating damp conditions). Care needs to be taken that more mature vegetation is not removed, drainage is adequate, and surface cover is maintained.

d. Marginally stable slope with essentially no vegetation. This slope would benefit from grass and shrub planting to assist landslide risk reduction.

ment, especially on slopes similar to those shown in c and d of figure 7.36, can help limit the amount of rain and surface water infiltrating the hillslope, thereby reducing landslide risk. Figure 7.37 illustrates sound bioengineering practice on a steep slope in the absence of housing structures; the grasses exhibit an excellent water shedding quality, which helps maintain slope stability.

FIGURE 7.37 Bioengineered slope in Hong Kong SAR, China

7.10 RESOURCES

7.10.1 Who does what

TEAM	RESPONSIBILITY	ACTIONS AND HELPFUL HINTS	CHAPTER SECTION
MCU	Confirm community contracting approach for implementation of the drainage works	• Define and facilitate an appropriate contracting approach in accordance with funder/government procurement requirements and government/community capacity	7.2
	Ensure that processes for procurement of works and materials and standards for construction meet funder/government requirements	• Define and facilitate the tendering process • Identify appropriate work package size (value) • Authorize an engineer and/or quantity surveyor to prepare work package specifications and be responsible for signing off on completed works	7.3; 7.4; 7.8
	Ensure that adequate site supervision processes are in place	• Select a committed site supervisor **Helpful hint:** This is a pivotal role in construction quality, so choose a committed person is likely to be respected by contractors and community/government task team members.	7.5.1
	Coordinate with government task teams		
Government task teams	Prepare work packages	• Prepare a specified bill of quantities for the planned works and a plan for procurement of materials • Identify work packages according to contract size and number agreed with the MCU • Create RFT documents	7.3
	Issue RFTs and brief potential contractors on required works, good practices, and safeguards	• Hold briefing meeting with potential contractors and provide guidance and assistance with tendering process	7.4.1; 7.4.2
	Facilitate the tender evaluation and contract award in accordance with selected community contracting approach	• Adhere to tendering procedures, ensuring transparency **Helpful hint:** Typically, more contractors will want work than can be employed. Try to ensure that the contracting process is as positive as possible for all potential contractors.	7.4.3
	Facilitate site supervision and communication among community residents, contractors, and government task teams	• Provide training for site supervisors • Ensure day-to-day presence of supervisor on site to deliver good-quality works	7.5; 7.6; 7.7
	Coordinate with community task teams		
	Sign off on completed construction	• Ensure comprehensive snagging is recorded and completed prior to sign-off **Helpful hint:** Spend time on site with government task team members and key residents to ensure, as far as possible, that all snagging is identified and competed. Once the project has been closed, contractor remobilization even for small tasks can be time consuming.	7.8
Community task teams	Coordinate with the MCU and government task teams on the community contracting process	• Participate in agreed-upon community contracting process	7.2
	Understand the planned works, good construction practices, appropriate safeguards, and tender for works	• Attend briefing by government task teams on scope of work packages, good construction practices, and safeguards • Submit tenders for work packages	7.4
	Implement contracted works	• Construct drains and install household roof water and gray water connections • Adhere to site supervision and good practice guidelines **Helpful hint:** Avoid material waste (and consequent income loss) by following design specifications and not overconstructing—seek advice from the site supervisor on details that require on-site design decisions.	7.5; 7.6; 7.7
	Complete construction to required specifications	• Address construction defects and complete any outstanding works to the satisfaction of the authorized project engineer	7.8
	Coordinate with government task teams		

7.10.2 Chapter checklist

CHECK THAT:	TEAM	PERSON	SIGN-OFF	CHAPTER SECTION
✓ A specified bill of quantities and a plan for procurement of materials have been completed				7.2; 7.3.3
✓ A specified bill of quantities and a plan for procurement of materials have been completed				7.3
✓ Work packages and request for tender documents have been drawn up and potential contractors briefed on how to tender				7.3.5; 7.4
✓ Contract details include construction specifications and design drawings, and adequate provision for mobilization and contingencies				7.3
✓ A site supervisor has been selected and trained, and contractors briefed on good construction practice				7.5; 7.6; 7.7
✓ A schedule of construction defects and outstanding works has been drawn up and acted on				7.8
✓ **Milestone 7**: Sign-off on completed construction				7.8
✓ All necessary safeguards complied with				1.5.3; 2.3.2, 7.10.4

7.10.3 Low-cost appropriate construction methods

Debris trap construction

The following method can be used to construct a low-cost debris trap suitable for installation in modest-sized, well-maintained drains in vulnerable communities.

1. Choose a location for the debris trap that can be easily accessed for debris removal (figure 7.38).

2. Acquire reinforcing rods, an angle iron, and all necessary welding equipment.

3. Mark the location and angle of the trap against the drain side walls; measure and cut the angle iron on which the trap grill will rest.

4. Drill holes in the drain sidewalls to place reinforcing rods that will support the angle iron.

5. Cut the reinforcing rods to fit the depth of the holes and the angle iron width. Cut vertical and horizontal reinforcement bars to length.

FIGURE 7.38 Choosing a debris trap location

6. Position all vertical reinforcement bars and weld in position (figure 7.39). Weld the handle so the finished trap can be easily removed by sliding up the angle iron; this will make it easier to maintain the drain not just upstream of the trap, but also in the culvert under the footpath as necessary.

FIGURE 7.39 Welding in-situ and completion of debris trap

How to construct a low-cost drain

Installing low-cost drains that use appropriate local materials can engage the community in developing good slope management practices and provide hands-on training for supervisors, contractors, and laborers.

Contractors and residents can use the following method (figure 7.40) to construct a simple low-cost drain in locations with low drain discharges and flow velocities, such as in the following circumstances:

- For connecting small numbers of houses to main drains

- In less accessible locations, such as upper slopes, where materials for concrete drains cannot be transported or carried

- On unstable slope sections that need surface drainage, but where slope movement may be reactivated

1. Assemble materials and tools:

   - Pickaxes, shovels, and a wheelbarrow for excavating the drain trench

   - Scissors to cut polythene

   - Wire cutters to cut mesh

   - 16-gauge mesh (the drain shoulder should be approximately 50 cm wide)

   - Sunlight-stable polythene (200 micron or equivalent; allow for sufficient overlap of sheets)

   - 10 m measuring tape

   - Sand for sand blinding (if necessary)

   - Galvanized wire to tie mesh sections together

   - Reinforcing rods to create U-shaped clamps

2. Excavate drain trench and shoulders.

3. Where the base of the drain is on a combination of stony material and soil, sand blind the drain base.

4. Estimate the length and width of plastic and mesh required.

5. Sand blind the drain shoulder where necessary.

6. Cut the mesh to the overall drain width.

7. Starting at the downslope end of the drain and working upslope, position and mold the mesh to the drain and then remove.

8. Lay plastic lining in the drain starting at the lowest elevation and working upslope (so sheets overlap and shed water without leaking) (figure 7.40b).

9. Overlay the plastic with the mesh (figure 7.40c).

10. Anchor the plastic and the mesh on the drain shoulders with appropriate nails (e.g., ~30 cm long U-shaped clamps made from reinforcing rods).

11. Tie the mesh sections together with galvanized wire (figure 7.40d).

12. Make steps in the drain where appropriate (figure 7.40e).

13. Connect house waste pipes to the finished drain.

FIGURE 7.40 Construction of low-cost drain

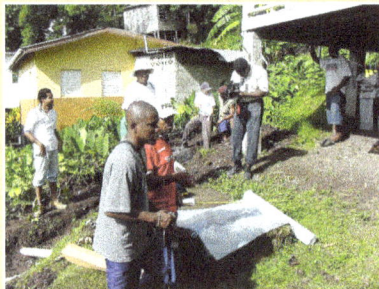

a. Community leaders, residents, local contractors, and site supervisors assemble on site to begin construction of a low-cost drain.

b. Laying plastic lining on sand blinded base.

c. Overlaying with galvanized mesh.

d. Tying mesh lengths with galvanized wire.

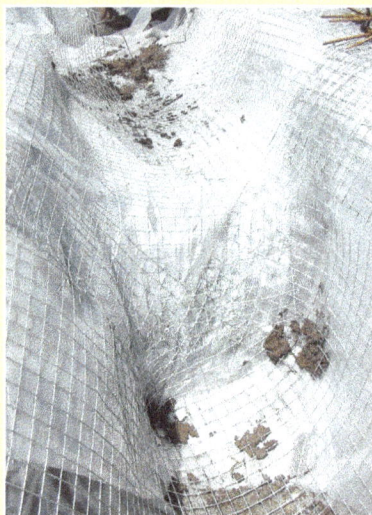

e. Forming a step down in the drain.

f. Finishing the drain with a cement skim on the drain base.

14. Modify the drain design as required or as materials allow; this might include lining the drain with a skim of cement (figure 7.40f).

7.10.4 Questionable or corrupt practices in construction

The MCU, and all stakeholders involved in construction, should apply relevant project safeguards (such as those in section 1.5.3), and avoid questionable or corrupt practices including the following (World Bank 2010).

Planning and prebid

- Inflated cost estimates, including for land purchases

- Information leaked to a private owner or buyer about land needed for a public project

- Projects approved without proper permits or designs

- Projects prepared for bidding without comment by the public or responsible local officials

- Project specifications that limit the number of bidders

- Deviation from standard bidding documents

- Direct contracting of bids without proper justification

- Restricted advertising, insufficient notice, and/or inadequate time for preparing bids

- Advance release of bid information to one bidder

- Bids accepted after the submission deadline

Contract award and project implementation

- Bid evaluation committee has conflict-of-interest ties with bidders

- Amending evaluation criteria after receipt of bids

- Company presenting competing bids

- Government allowing bid evaluation report to be revised or reissued

- Government imposing subcontracting requirements on prime contractor

- Staff members involved in contract award participating in contract supervision

- Contract variations and change orders approved without proper verification

- Contractor claims for costs beyond the common labor cost raise and inflation rates

- Materials and equipment used and workmanship not as specified; paperwork not consistent with items delivered

- Contractors providing false information to project inspectors on progress of work, or inspectors coerced to approve progress payments or certify compliance with building permits

- Inaccurate as-built drawings presented or accepted

Monitoring

- Staff responsible for oversight have conflicts of interest

- Control systems are inadequate, unreliable, or inconsistently applied

- No follow-up undertaken regarding indications, suspicion, or accusations of corruption

- Lack of confidentiality on accusations of corruption

- Delayed or superficial evaluation; delayed publication of evaluation report

- Failure to disqualify companies impugned in evaluation reports

7.10.5 References

Alwi, S., K. Hampson, and S. Mohamed. 1999. "Investigation into the Relationship between Rework and Site Supervision in High Rise Building Construction in Indonesia." In *Proceedings of the 2nd International Conference on Construction Process Reengineering*, 189–95. July, Sydney. http://eprints.qut.edu.au/4161/1/4161_1.pdf.

Anderson, M. G. 1983. "The Prediction of Soil Suction for Slopes in Hong Kong." CE3/81, Geotechnical Control Office, Hong Kong Government.

Barker, D. H., ed. 1995. *Vegetation and Slopes: Stabilisation, Protection and Ecology*. London: Thomas Telford Publishing.

Campbell, S. D. G., R. Shaw, R. J. Sewell, and J. C. F. Wong. 2008. "Guidelines for Soil Bioengineering Applications on Natural Terrain Landslide Scars." GEO Report 227, Geotechnical Engineering Office, Government of Hong Kong Special Administrative Region.

Coppin, N. J., and I. G. Richards. 1990. *Use of Vegetation in Civil Engineering*. London: CIRIA/ Butterworths.

de Silva, S., 2000. *Community-Based Contracting: A Review of Stakeholder Experience*. Washington, DC: World Bank.

Florineth, F., H. P. Rauch, and H. P. Staffler. 2002. "Stabilization of Landslides with Bio-Engineering Measures in South Tyrol/Italy and Thankot/Nepal." In *INTERPRAEVENT 2002 in the Pacific Rim, 2002, Matsumoto/Japan*, vol. 2, 827–37. Matsumoto, Japan.

Gray, D. H., and R. B. Sotir. 1996. *Biotechnical and Bioengineering Slope Stabilisation: A Practical Guide for Erosion Control*. New York: Wiley.

Howell, J. 1999a. "Roadside Bio-Engineering— Reference Manual." Department of Roads, Government of Nepal.

Howell, J. 1999b. "Roadside Bio-Engineering—Site Handbook." Department of Roads, Government of Nepal.

Hui, T. H. H., H. W. Sun, and K. K. S. Ho. 2007. "Review of Slope Surface Drainage with

Reference to Landslide Studies and Current Practice." GEO Report 210, Geotechnical Engineering Office, Government of Hong Kong Special Administrative Region.

Larcher, P. 1999. "Construction: Is There a Place for Small-Scale Contracting Enterprises?" *Urban Forum* 10: 75–89.

Lewis, L., S. L. Salisbury, and S. Hagen. 2001. "Soil Bioengineering for Upland Slope Stabilization." Washington State Transportation Center, University of Washington. http://www.wsdot.wa.gov/eesc/cae/design/roadside/rm.htm.

Nordberg, R. 1999. "Building Sustainable Cities." International Union for Housing Finance. http://www.housingfinance.org/publications/others-publications.

Ogunlana, S. O., and K. Butt. 2000. "Construction Project Cost Feedback in Developing Economies: The Case of Pakistan." http://www.irb.fraunhofer.de/CIBlibrary/search-quick-result-list.jsp?A&idSuche=CIB+DC8938.

Sohail, M., and A. N. Baldwin. 2004. "Community-Partnered Contracts in Developing Countries." *Proceedings of the Institution of Civil Engineers—Engineering Sustainability* 157(4): 193 –201.

Stokes, A., J. Spanos, J. E. Norris, and E. Cammeratt, eds. 2007. *Eco- and Ground Bio-Engineering: The Use of Vegetation to Improve Slope Stability. Proceedings of the First International Conference on Eco-Engineering.* Developments in Plant and Soil Science vol. 103. Dordrecht, the Netherlands: Springer. http://www.springerlink.com/content/978-1-4020-5592-8/#section=291629&page=1.

Wideman, M. 2012. "Project Management of Capital Projects—An Overview." http://www.maxwideman.com/papers/capitalprojects/breakdown.htm.

Wilkinson, P. L., M. G. Anderson, D. M. Lloyd, and J. P. Renaud. 2002. "Landslide Hazard and Bioengineering: Towards Providing Improved Decision Support through Integrated Model Development." *Environmental Modelling and Software* 7: 333–44.

World Bank. 2010. *Safer Homes, Stronger Communities. A Handbook for Reconstructing after Natural Disasters.* Washington, DC: World Bank.

"...people are generally not well prepared to interpret low probabilities when reaching decisions about unlikely events... People underestimate both the probability of a disaster and the accompanying losses."

—H. Kunreuther and M. Useem,
"Principles and Challenges for Reducing Risks from Disasters" (2010, 6–7)

CHAPTER 8

Encouraging Behavioral Change

8.1 KEY CHAPTER ELEMENTS

8.1.1 Coverage

This chapter presents communication and capacity-building strategies for achieving behavioral change in MoSSaiC (Management of Slope Stability in Communities) landslide hazard reduction practice and policy. The listed groups should read the indicated chapter sections.

AUDIENCE				LEARNING	CHAPTER SECTION
F	M	G	C		
	✓	✓		Steps involved in behavioral change	8.3
	✓	✓		How learning by doing can build capacity	8.3
	✓	✓	✓	Ways to communicate	8.4; 8.5
	✓	✓	✓	Ways of building local capacity	8.6
	✓	✓	✓	Postproject maintenance options	8.7.1
✓	✓	✓	✓	Mapping the behavioral change strategy	8.7.2

F = funders and policy makers   **M** = MoSSaiC core unit: government project managers and experts   **G** = government task teams: experts and practitioners   **C** = community task teams: residents, leaders, contractors

8.1.2 Documents

DOCUMENT TO BE PRODUCED	CHAPTER SECTION
Communication strategy	8.5
Capacity-building strategy	8.6
Behavioral change strategy	8.7.2

8.1.3 Steps and outputs

STEP	OUTPUT
1. Understand how new practices are adopted • Use the steps in the ladder of adoption and behavioral change model to identify communication and capacity-building needs in each community and in government • Understand stakeholder perceptions and the role of community participation	Assessment of aspects of behavioral change to be addressed by communication and capacity-building activities
2. Design a communication strategy • Review existing resources and methodologies for designing a communication strategy • Identify communication purposes and audiences • Select forms of communication and design messages	Communication strategy
3. Design a capacity-building strategy • Review knowledge into action approaches • Identify levels of capacity, capacity requirements, and activities for building capacity	Capacity-building strategy
4. Plan for postproject maintenance • Understand the need for incorporating maintenance into drain design and project planning	Project maintenance options
5. Map out the complete behavioral change strategy • Map the agreed-upon behavioral change strategies and associated actions	Map of capacity-building strategies

8.1.4 Community-based aspects

The chapter outlines the process by which communities adopt new risk reduction behavior. It develops communication and capacity-building strategies to encourage behavioral change with respect to landslide hazard management practices in vulnerable urban communities.

The chapter also describes how MoSSaiC's community-based approach encourages behavioral change in government task teams, the MoSSaiC core unit (MCU), and decision makers as they gain new knowledge, build their capacity, and change practices and policies.

8.2 GETTING STARTED

8.2.1 Briefing note

A fundamental medium-term objective of MoSSaiC is to change urban landslide risk management perceptions, practices, and poli-

cies. To achieve such behavioral change, MoSSaiC projects deliver landslide hazard mitigation measures that are scientifically based, grounded in community participation, and supported by ex ante landslide mitigation policies.

During project implementation, two complementary mechanisms can encourage communities and governments to adopt effective landslide risk reduction practices and policies: the development of a clear and comprehensive communication strategy, and the building of local capacity. These mechanisms target behavioral changes, and should be developed and applied from the start of a MoSSaiC project.

Communication strategy

A communication strategy is a well-planned series of actions aimed at achieving certain objectives through the use of communication methods, techniques, and approaches (FAO 2004). Developing a communication strategy entails clearly identifying (and segmenting) audiences, defining messages, determining the means of communication best suited to the local context, and integrating the strategy into the process of project implementation.

Communication strategies for disaster risk reduction (DRR) may explicitly address risk perception and understanding in order to encourage a change in risk reduction behavior. However, "concern does not mean understanding, and understanding does not necessarily lead to action" (World Bank 2010). Communication strategies should thus be developed and applied in conjunction with other behavioral change strategies such as community participation and empowerment (Paton 2003). In community participatory projects such as MoSSaiC, the communication strategy facilitates interaction among stakeholders and provides the common ground by which project objectives can be achieved (Bessette 2004).

Building capacity

DRR capacity building refers to actions that develop the skills and societal infrastructures within communities or organizations to reduce the level of disaster risk. These actions include training and education, public information, transferring technology or technical expertise, strengthening infrastructure, and enhancing organizational abilities (UNISDR 2004).

Capacity building and communication overlap in their aim to increase knowledge and change behavior. However, as already noted, DRR knowledge and technology do not automatically translate into action or increased capacity (Paton 2003). Capacity building should go beyond traditional approaches that emphasize education and training in the classroom, and include on-the-job learning and informal knowledge sharing (CADRI 2011).

MoSSaiC encourages a learning-by-doing approach to build the capacity of individuals, communities, and governments to understand and address rainfall-triggered landslide hazards. Learning by doing enables community and government teams to develop new knowledge, skills, and expertise as they implement the project.

8.2.2 Guiding principles

The following guiding principles apply in encouraging behavioral change:

- Recognize that it takes time and strategic implementation of MoSSaiC projects to start to change the landslide risk reduction behavior of communities and governments. Behavioral change involves changing perceptions, motivations, capabilities, and actions to enable new practices to be adopted. Communication and capacity-building strategies are an important part of the behavioral change process.

- Clearly communicate project messages to set expectations about the project scope, process, and outputs. These messages should be backed up by timely project delivery to maintain trust among project stakeholders.

- Incorporate the communication strategy into the community participation process. The MCU and the government task teams should be aware of local social and cultural conditions and how their interactions with the community will be interpreted.

- Plan capacity-building activities that both translate new knowledge into action and action into new knowledge (learning by doing). This second, less formal, aspect of capacity building is a key part of MoSSaiC projects for communities and government teams.

- Project messages and new capabilities for landslide risk reduction can be lost with government staff turnover. The MCU should develop communication and capacity-building strategies for government task teams (as well as communities) to avoid project disruption due to staff turnover and to sustain new capacities over the long term.

- Policy champions are important in keeping landslide hazard mitigation on the government agenda. This support can provide a policy and funding environment for longer-term project continuity and behavioral change at both the community and government levels.

8.2.3 Risks and challenges

Risk perception

People generally underestimate the probability of disasters, the associated risks, and the accompanying losses. They also have a tendency to estimate risks based on their own experience rather than on information conveyed by experts. One outcome is an overinvestment in prevention after a disaster has occurred—prevention is then undertaken too late (Kunreuther and Useem 2010). Defining a sound communication strategy therefore requires an understanding of people's perceptions and behavioral biases.

Clear project messages

Having a clear set of project messages for stakeholders is essential. Community residents, government task teams, decision makers, funders, and the wider public will need to know about the MoSSaiC approach and project implementation process (such as project steps, time frames, roles and responsibilities, procurement, training, and maintenance) in varying levels of detail.

Messages for each audience need to be developed and delivered ahead of the time they will be needed so that they influence, rather than simply record, events. A lack of harmonized and clear communication may mean projects exhibit poor coordination, insufficient lesson learning, high rates of duplication, and poor integration with related projects in communities.

Timing of media reports

The local media can want a project news item before there is anything of substance to report. Additionally, unless there is clear communication, expectations among those who pick up on project news items could run ahead of project delivery. It is critical to ensure that reported timelines are as accurate as possible when communicating with the media; correctly

answering such questions as "When is the project going to start?" is key.

Relevant forms of communication and capacity building

In reaching community residents and the wider public with project messages,

> project managers should be wary of "one-size-fits-all" solutions that appear to solve all problems by using media products. Past experience indicates that unless such instruments are used in connection with other approaches and based on proper research, they seldom deliver the intended results (Mefalopulos 2008, 20).

Media such as TV, radio, newspaper articles, and static forms of awareness raising (posters, leaflets, and displays) should thus be combined with personal contact and community participation in a way that is locally appropriate.

Similarly, DRR capacity-building activities should be case specific and adapted to local conditions at three interrelated levels: individual, organizational, and institutional/societal (the enabling environment) (CADRI 2011). For MoSSaiC projects, a combination of formal and informal activities should be designed to equip individuals, communities, government task teams, and the MCU to deliver landslide hazard reduction measures. At the level of the societal/institutional enabling environment, the aim should be to show that such measures both work and pay so as to provide an evidence base for changing broader landslide risk reduction practices and policies.

High staff turnover

While the MCU may interface with key government officials and elected officials at the time of project initiation, there is every prospect that, through the project period, there could be significant turnover among the staff responsible for project delivery and those supporting the project indirectly. Personnel changes can result in loss of project ownership, understanding, and capacity as well as potentially delaying project delivery. The MCU should develop clear project messages and mechanisms for bringing new staff onboard and up to speed.

8.2.4 Adapting the chapter blueprint to existing capacity

Successful communication and capacity-building strategies for landslide hazard reduction do not follow an easily specified formula but should be developed according to local conditions. Use the capacity guides from previous chapters (each relating to a MoSSaiC project step) to identify the following:

- Critical points for communication among stakeholders during project implementation

- Areas that need capacity building in order to deliver effective landslide hazard reduction measures.

Use the matrix on the next page to assess existing capacity for delivering the necessary communication and capacity-building activities.

1. Assign a capacity score from 1 to 3 (low to high) to reflect the existing capacity for each of the elements in the matrix's left-hand column.

2. Identify the most common capacity score as an indicator of the overall capacity level.

3. Adapt the blueprint in this chapter in accordance with the overall capacity level (see guide on page 311).

8.3 ADOPTION OF CHANGE: FROM RISK PERCEPTION TO BEHAVIORAL CHANGE

MoSSaiC uses a combination of community and government teamwork, scientific methods, and the delivery of hazard reduction measures on the ground to reduce urban landslide risk (chapters 2–7). If it is to be sustainable, landslide risk reduction needs to be embedded in urban slope management practice and policy by communities and governments. The

outcome should be reduced landslide hazard (physical mitigation measures) and increased resilience to landslide risk (awareness and avoidance, or mitigation, of future landslide hazards). Some specific aspects of behavior change associated with MoSSaiC follow.

- *At the household level.* Residents have greater confidence in adapting how they build on, drain, bioengineer, and maintain their part of the hillside, dedicating money and time to appropriate landslide mitigation measures and slope management.

- *At the community level.* Communities recognize the importance of drain maintenance in reducing landslide risk, and act on that recognition by advocating for, and becoming involved in, a postproject maintenance strategy (section 8.7.1).

- *At the government level.* Practitioners and policy makers have a greater ability to address small-scale everyday landslide hazards, which reflect an accumulation of disaster risk, and anticipate the capacity to deal with medium- and large-scale landslide events (Bull-Kamanga et al. 2003).

Use this section to understand how people adopt new risk reduction behavior and how two crosscutting issues—risk perception and the knowledge into action learning process—affect communication and capacity-building strategies for behavioral change.

8.3.1 The behavioral change process

UNICEF (2008, 1) notes

> The global experience of the development community has demonstrated that Community-based Disaster Risk Reduction (CBDRR) efforts approached from a social and behaviour change perspective ensure that the poorest, most vulnerable and marginalised communities understand the simple and practical actions required to protect lives and personal assets in the case of natural disasters.

The process of adopting innovation (behavioral change) can be seen as a series of steps in a "ladder of adoption" (Mefalopulos and Kam-

CAPACITY ELEMENT	EXISTING CAPACITY		
	1 = LOW	2 = MODERATE	3 = HIGH
MCU and government understanding of the behavioral change process with respect to DRR in communities	Behavioral change strategies not considered in previous community-based DRR projects	Some success in behavioral change by raising disaster risk awareness through media campaigns and formal classroom training courses	Experience with successful DRR behavioral change using a range of formal and informal communication and capacity-building activities
MCU and government experience with community-based DRR awareness campaigns	Little experience with community-based DRR awareness campaigns on which to build	Small number of ad hoc community campaigns undertaken by different government agencies	Previous successful high-profile campaigns led by an experienced government agency or specialized team
Community interaction with the media—persons willing and able to communicate disaster risk problems and solutions to the wider public	Little evidence of community interaction with the media	Community residents willing to talk to the media but with little prior experience	Community residents available who may have participated in other community programs and would be willing to articulate the project vision
Media relationship with government	No substantive media production houses; media functions on an ad hoc basis	Government has previously outsourced a limited number of media campaigns	Government uses professional media outlets that are respected by the general public
MCU and government experience in using different forms of communication as part of the community participation process	No experience with community participation and associated forms of communication	Some experience with formal and informal communications with communities	Effective use of a range of appropriate formal and informal communications as an integral part of community participation projects
MCU and government experience in delivering formal capacity-building training courses (classroom-based education, training workshops, and conferences)	No local venues suitable for training government or community teams; very limited MCU experience in course management and delivery	Some MCU members have participated in courses at different venues; limited MCU experience in course management	Well-frequented conference venue for training that is known to the MCU and community residents alike; MCU members have previously run and attended training courses
MCU and community experience of, and openness to, informal capacity-building activities (on-the-job training, learning by doing) for DRR	DRR capacity-building activities perceived to be based on formal knowledge transfer (classroom-based education and training)	Some experience of, and openness to, delivering and participating in informal DRR capacity-building activities	Experience with successful informal capacity-building approaches that have helped changed DRR perceptions, practices, and policies
Engagement of policy champions for advocating community-based DRR policies	Senior government officials have an administrative rather than advocacy approach to community projects	A senior government official has offered to support community projects, but perhaps not in an advocacy sense	One or more senior government officials are active advocates of the MoSSaiC approach and support DRR policy change
Project safeguards	Documented safeguards need to be located; no previous experience in interpreting and operating safeguard policies	Documents exist for some safeguards	Documented safeguards available from all relevant agencies

longera 2004; World Bank 2011). These generic steps, and the associated MoSSaiC context, are outlined in table 8.1.

Movement from awareness to adoption is often explained in terms of factors affecting how people are motivated, form intentions, and then act to reduce the risk. These three classes of behavior change factors are outlined in table 8.2. This model can be used to understand capacities and gaps in the process of adoption of MoSSaiC by individuals, communities, government teams, and decision makers. For example, a small number of successfully implemented MoSSaiC projects can encourage decision makers to commit resources to more projects and increase the outcome expectancy

CAPACITY LEVEL	HOW TO ADAPT THE BLUEPRINT
1: Use this chapter in depth and as a catalyst to secure support from other agencies as appropriate	The MCU needs to strengthen its capacity in order to deliver strategies that encourage behavioral change. This might involve the following: • Spending considerable time in a community to find champions for the vision • Advocating to the government and identifying a policy champion • Seeking advice from government public information agencies, local media consultants, and local nongovernmental organizations (NGOs) on effective forms of communication • Seeking advice from donors, NGOs, and government agencies on appropriate capacity-building strategies for both communities and government practitioners • Using MoSSaiC resources as a training platform adapted to local conditions
2: Some elements of this chapter will reflect current practice; read the remaining elements in depth and use them to further strengthen capacity	The MCU has strength in some areas, but not all. Those elements that are perceived to be Level 1 need to be addressed (as above). Elements that are Level 2 will require strengthening, such as the following: • Where there is limited experience of different forms of communication appropriate for community-based DRR, seek advice from local media, NGOs, and relevant government agencies to identify culturally relevant, acceptable, and effective forms of communication • Where there is limited experience of DRR capacity building within communities and government, assemble examples of, and resources for, delivering both formal and informal activities
3: Use this chapter as a checklist	The MCU is likely to be able to proceed using existing proven capacity. It would be good practice nonetheless for the MCU to document relevant prior experience in communications and capacity building for community-based DRR.

of government teams and other communities; while visits to finished projects and on-the-job training can increase self-efficacy.

A combination of behavioral change strategies is needed to facilitate change in all of these factors and encourage effective landslide risk reduction. Communication and provision of information can help change risk perceptions

and outcome expectancy; community participation and capacity-building activities may be more effective in changing self-efficacy, problem-focused coping, or trust (Paton 2003).

The MCU should use the ladder of adoption and behavior change model to identify strengths and gaps in the process of behavior change for each MoSSaiC stakeholder group.

TABLE 8.1 Steps in the ladder of adoption and associated MoSSaiC context

STEP IN THE LADDER OF ADOPTION	MoSSaiC CONTEXT
1. Awareness of the problem	• Risk perception and critical awareness of local landslide hazards, risks, and drivers
2. Interest in the specific problem	• Personal interest in the idea that urban landslide hazard can often be reduced
3. Knowledge/comprehension of how to change the situation	• Understanding of the MoSSaiC vision, science, and project process for urban landslide hazard reduction
4. Attitude affecting tendency to accept and adopt an innovation	• Acceptance at the community level • Decision to accept, fund, and initiate the MoSSaiC approach in a particular country
5. Legitimization within local norms and context	• Adaptation of MoSSaiC at the community level (bottom up) as well as by funders and within government (top down)
6. Practice putting knowledge into action before adopting	• Delivery of landslide hazard reduction measures on the ground in communities
7. Adoption of new approach—behavioral change	• Improved landslide hazard reduction and slope management practices within communities and government

Source: Mefalopulos and Kamlongera 2004.

TABLE 8.2 Behavior change factors: From motivation to action

PHASE	FACTOR
1. Motivating factors (often collectively referred to as risk perception)	**Risk perception:** What is the hazard, and does it pose a threat?
	Critical awareness of hazard: How much do I think/talk about the hazard compared with other hazards?
	Hazard anxiety: How much destruction and death can the hazard cause? (This can also be a demotivating factor, as people seek to reduce anxiety by ignoring the hazard.)
2. Intention formation factors or beliefs	**Outcome expectancy:** Will my actions be effective in reducing the problem?
	Self-efficacy: Do I have the capacity to act effectively?
	Problem-focused coping: Will I try to confront this problem?
	Response efficacy: Are there enough resources (technical, financial, physical, social, and political) to allow me to confront this problem?
3. Moderating factors affecting conversion of intentions into actions	**Timing of hazard activity:** What is the frequency/predictability/interval since the last event?
	Sense of community; perceived responsibility: What are people's attachments to places and other people?
	Response efficacy: What is the actual availability of resources?
	Normative beliefs within a community: What are the community experiences, perceptions, beliefs, trust in authorities, degree of participation/empowerment?

Source: Paton 2003.

8.3.2 Understanding stakeholder perceptions

The first steps in the ladder of adoption (table 8.1) and behavior change motivation factors (table 8.2) deal directly with risk perception. Risk perception is commonly thought of as a combination of what people know about a risk and how they feel about it. Communication and capacity-building strategies should account for both dimensions of risk perception, as well as how different stakeholders perceive the project as a whole.

This subsection explains that perceptions of different stakeholder groups will differ, and that vulnerability and uncertainty can play a role in shaping these perceptions. Make sure different stakeholder perceptions of risk—and of the project—are recognized before developing appropriate communication and capacity-building strategies (sections 8.4–8.6).

Windows of perception

Different stakeholders are likely to perceive landslide risk and MoSSaiC projects differ-

ently: "What counts is not what it is, but what people perceive it to be" (FAO 2004, 15). One way of understanding stakeholder perceptions is to identify common ground, blind spots, and knowledge that is hidden to one or another of the parties.

The ***Johari Window*** is a tool that enables these aspects of perception to be explored through dialogue and knowledge exchange (figure 8.1). Use the four windows of perception to identify potentially differing perceptions held by communities, government officials, funding agencies, and other relevant stakeholders. Consider perceptions relating to motivations to reduce landslide risk, intentions to act, the translation of intentions into behavior, and factors that modify these intentions (as discussed in section 8.3.1). Be aware of differences in community and government or funder perceptions of urban landslide risk and the project scope and benefits.

Develop the communication and capacity-building strategies in such a way as to increase open knowledge areas (table 8.2) and positively influence people's motivations, inten-

FIGURE 8.1 The Johari Window for increasing common ground and knowledge among stakeholders

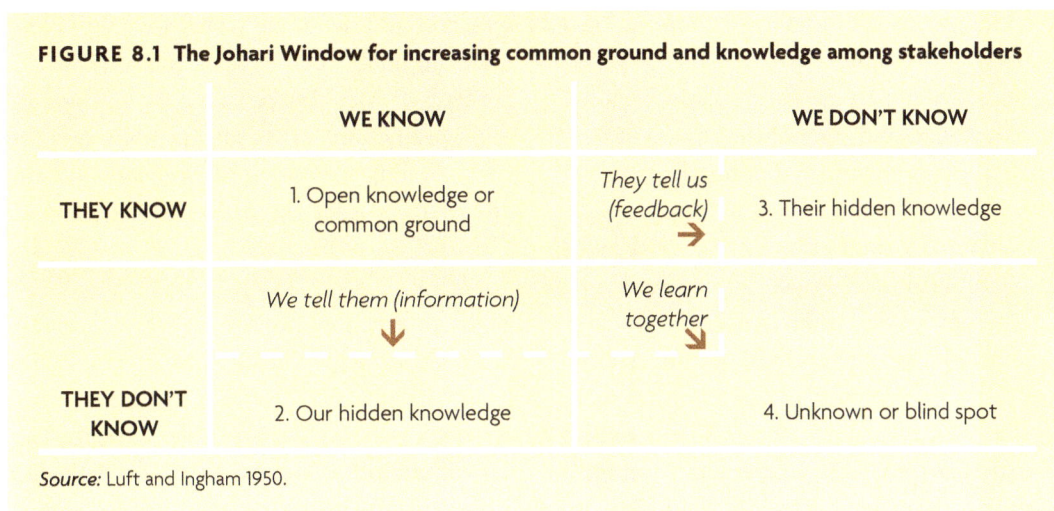

	WE KNOW		WE DON'T KNOW
THEY KNOW	1. Open knowledge or common ground	*They tell us (feedback)* →	3. Their hidden knowledge
	We tell them (information) ↓	*We learn together* ↘	
THEY DON'T KNOW	2. Our hidden knowledge		4. Unknown or blind spot

Source: Luft and Ingham 1950.

tions, and behavior regarding landslide risk reduction.

Vulnerability and risk perception

Vulnerability is related to the capacity to anticipate a hazard, cope with it, resist it, and recover from its impact. It is determined by a mix of physical, environmental, social, economic, political, cultural, and institutional factors (Benson and Twigg 2007). Although MoSSaiC is primarily concerned with reducing landslide hazards in vulnerable communities, there is a need to account for the influence of vulnerability on risk perception and the adoption of new slope management practices:

> The poorer people become, the more their vulnerability to a variety of hazards increases and the more difficult it becomes to play one off against another to achieve security. People have to balance extremely limited resources to deal with threats like homelessness, landlessness, illness, and unemployment. In general, people are unlikely to change or adapt their living patterns and activities to reduce their vulnerability to natural hazard, if it increases their vulnerability to other more pressing threats (Maskrey 1992, 2).

The effects of vulnerability on risk perception and the motivation to reduce landslide risk can include the following behavioral biases (FM Global 2010):

- **Deniability.** Deniability is the belief that bad things will not happen:

  — The bad thing is not going to happen.

  — If the bad thing does occur, it will affect others and not me.

  — If the bad thing does affect me, the effects will be minimal (FM Global 2010, 7).

- **Procrastination.** Procrastination is the tendency to postpone taking actions that require investment of time and money.

- **Short-term focus.** This is the difficulty of computing benefit-cost trade-offs.

- **Hyperbolic discounting.** Hyperbolic discounting is putting too much weight on immediate considerations rather than on the long-term benefits of investing in mitigation.

The MCU and government task teams should be aware of the potential effects of vulnerability on community perceptions of landslide risk and the project. Communication and capacity-building strategies should be developed that address these risk perceptions and demonstrate that landslide hazard can often be reduced. Thus, a secondary benefit of MoSSaiC can be increased community resilience (reduced vulnerability) stemming from a greater capacity to understand, anticipate, and mitigate landslide hazards.

Uncertainty and risk perception

Risk perception and risk reduction behavior are affected by how experts, decision makers, and those at risk (in this case, communities) interpret uncertainty about that risk. A growing source of uncertainty is arguably a shared, common uncertainty about the results of hazard and risk modeling predictions, leading to a hesitation to invest in ex ante DRR.

Increasingly complex hazard and risk models, combined with uncertainty in model parameters, have resulted in disaster risk predictions with greater and greater uncertainty bounds. A consequence is that decision makers and the public may learn from one expert that there is little to be concerned about for a particular risk, and from another that the very same risk is of major significance (Kunreuther and Useem 2010). Seemingly conflicting messages are compounded by the fact that

> the concepts, nature and implications of scientific uncertainty are not well understood by policymakers and/or society... This causes confusion when it comes to confidence in the work that physical scientists produce (Malamud and Petley 2009, 167)

and further uncertainty when deciding how to act.

These messages and associated uncertainties will be processed in different ways by each stakeholder—ignoring the message, trying to find more information to reduce their uncertainty, or accepting the message that is most compatible with existing risk perceptions or biases.

For example, among decision makers and politicians, uncertainty can generate a falsely optimistic (biased) confidence that a catastrophic event will "not happen in my term of office" (Kunreuther and Useem 2010). Vulnerable communities may discount messages about uncertain disaster risks in light of their experience of more pressing threats such as unemployment or illness (Maskrey 1992). Such interpretations of risk are perhaps most important for low-probability uncertain events because, unlike high-probability events, personal experience is likely to be absent (McNabb and Pearson 2010).

The MCU and government task teams should be aware of uncertainties in model predictions and how these uncertainties might be interpreted. Encourage transparency in communication between experts and other stakeholders so that the possibilities of over- or underprediction of landslide risk can be accounted for in community selection and the design of landslide mitigation measures.

8.3.3 Combining knowledge and action

Traditional risk communication and capacity-building strategies both tend to emphasize transfer of knowledge from experts or decision makers to laypeople. However, as the ladder of adoption (steps 3–6) and behavior change factors in section 8.3.1 indicate, knowledge must be combined with action in order to change stakeholder perceptions and practices. It is now well known that traditional knowledge transfer approaches can be ineffective unless balanced by other forms of communication and capacity-building activities (CADRI 2011; World Bank 2010). Dialogue-based communication and learning by doing or action learning are thus a fundamental part of community participatory approaches such as MoSSaiC.

Use this subsection to understand how knowledge and action can be combined to encourage behavioral change and to guide the inclusion of learning by doing in project communication and capacity-building strategies.

Conventional knowledge transfer and disaster risk reduction

Gaillard and Mercer (2012, 2) note that "the field of DRR is a battlefield of knowledge and action, which often results in poor outcomes in terms of actual reduction of disaster risk for those most vulnerable." Conventional Western-style education emphasizes written knowledge as the precursor and only effective basis for action (Crookall and Thorngate 2009). The one-way transfer of knowledge is evident in top-down DRR policies that focus on classroom-based training, education, and public awareness campaigns to increase knowledge and encourage behavioral change. Yet it is understandably difficult for local decision makers, practitioners, and community residents to turn scientific knowledge into hazard reduction actions (GNDR 2011). The knowledge and practices identified at international and national scales are simply not trickling down fast enough to achieve DRR on the ground (Wisner 2009).

Community-based DRR has, in part, emerged as a response to conventional top-down approaches—focusing on vulnerability rather than hazard reduction and emphasizing community participation, local knowledge, appropriate technologies, and practical actions. This approach addresses many of the limitations of top-down national DRR policies, but usually cannot address the hazard component of landslide risk. Even at the local government level, "the knowledge base required to identify landslide prone areas is often either nonexistent or fragmentary" (UNU 2006).

Given the limitations of either purely top-down or bottom-up approaches in addressing urban landslide risk, it is now recognized that a combination of these approaches is required. Landslide risk reduction necessitates the integration of different disciplines so that scientific knowledge of the hazard is combined with local knowledge and appropriate actions (Malamud and Petley 2009); "we must avoid romanticising indigenous knowledge, and combine it with scientific knowledge" (Pelling 2007, 16). Similarly, conventional top-down communication and capacity development methods should be balanced by more informal dialogue and participatory-based methods.

Learning by doing

"Knowledge and action are closely intertwined," note Crookall and Thorngate (2009, 17), and the process of adopting new DRR behavior requires both to be present. Learning by doing integrates learning, action, and reflection; and is carried out during, rather than prior to, project implementation (IFRC 2008). Learning by doing goes beyond conventional classroom-based knowledge into action activities and public awareness education by emphasizing action as a means for learning and generating new knowledge.

MoSSaiC projects involve learning by doing: combining local and scientific knowledge about slope stability; encouraging funders, governments, and communities to develop and apply MoSSaiC in the context of local expertise, practices, and policies; and generating new knowledge through the process of putting MoSSaiC into action (table 8.3).

MoSSaiC communication and capacity-building strategies should include activities designed to enable or encourage participants to do the following (Crookall and Thorngate 2009, 19):

- "[A]pply new knowledge to a practical situation" (knowledge into action)

- "[G]enerate understanding, learn new skills, and gain new knowledge from a concrete experience" (action into knowledge)

- "[M]ake connections between actions and related knowledge" (integrating action and knowledge).

Use table 8.3 as a guide to review for each stakeholder group what works locally in terms of knowledge into action and action into knowledge activities. Use this review to inform the development of communication and capacity-building strategies.

8.4 COMMUNICATION PURPOSE AND AUDIENCE

A communication strategy is typically developed by defining the purpose of communication and identifying audiences, messages, and appropriate forms of communication.

Designing the strategy is an art, not a science, and there are many ways of approaching the task. Table 8.4 presents five questions that can help the MCU and communications task team in organizing the necessary information and developing a strategy.

Use this section to identify the purposes and key audiences of the communication strategy; use section 8.5 to help identify specific communication tools and messages.

TABLE 8.3 Knowledge and action as part of the adoption of the MoSSaiC process

STAKEHOLDER	KNOWLEDGE INTO ACTION	ACTION INTO KNOWLEDGE
Community task teams—residents, leaders, and local contractors	• Detailed knowledge of slope history and features (drainage, cuts/fills, soil depth, signs of instability) contributes to mapping and landslide hazard reduction design process • New information about slope stability is provided by government • Contractors from within the community are engaged and apply existing skills	• Residents involved in the process see the direct results of good slope management practices and simple measures in their own households • Good construction practices and new skills are generated and shared among site supervisors, engineers, and contractors
MCU and government task teams—engineering and science practitioners	• Engineering and technical knowledge is increased and applied to design of landslide hazard reduction measures • Site supervisors are briefed and oversee delivery of physical mitigation works	• Government team members develop new local knowledge and practices while working on site and with local contractors in the communities
MCU and government task teams—community development practitioners	• Knowledge of community context and dynamics is applied to enable community participation in the project	• Learning the science from other team members and integrating community mobilization skills with hazard reduction agenda
MCU, politicians, and funding agencies	• Decision makers, funders, and MCU briefed on MoSSaiC vision and the science of landslide hazard reduction • Existing project management skills employed in new ways	• Project reports provide new evidence base for policy change and innovation for adopting the approach more widely
Academic researchers and private sector consultants	• Application and development of landslide theory in the field	• Refinement of approach to landslide research—experience of working with end users results in new priorities, scientific methods, and ways of communicating

TABLE 8.4 Questions to guide the design of a MoSSaiC communication strategy

QUESTION	ACTION
Are there resources already available for communication?	Review existing methods and toolkits for communication in a development, DRR, or community participation context (e.g., IFRC 2010; Mefalopulos 2008; UNICEF 2008)
What are the purposes or functions of the communication strategy?	Review the MoSSaiC vision and foundations (chapter 1) and behavior change process (section 8.3.1), and identify communication requirements (see section 8.4.1)
Who are the audiences and messengers?	Identify MoSSaiC stakeholders (table 1.16 and chapter 2); identify communication requirements and strength, frequency, and directions of communication flows (see section 8.4.2)
How and when can these audiences be best engaged?	Based on communication purposes and audiences, identify appropriate modes (written/verbal/visual, and one-/two-way), channels (face to face or mediated), tools, and timing (see section 8.5)
What are the key messages for each audience?	Based on communication purposes and audiences, design messages with appropriate content, language, and presentation style (see section 8.5).

8.4.1 Defining communication purposes and functions

For MoSSaiC projects, the communication strategy serves the following purposes:

- Raising awareness and changing perceptions about urban landslide hazard risk

- Facilitating community participation, understanding, interaction, and trust among stakeholders

- Providing information and managing expectations about project implementation and outcomes

- Generating new knowledge as part of a learning-by-doing approach

- Encouraging the adoption of new landslide risk management behavior.

  As the World Bank (2010, 327) notes,

  Well-designed communication campaigns that address individuals as members of a local community—and not as powerless members of an unmanageably large group—can empower them to act. This treatment can help make a global phenomenon personally relevant and immediate, and accentuate the local and individual ownership of the solutions.

The MCU should review the purposes that communication will serve and use these purposes to guide the development of the communication strategy.

8.4.2 Identifying audiences

MoSSaiC stakeholders include the following:

- Project funders

- Politicians and government decision makers

- MCU and government task teams

- Community task teams (including individual residents)

- Landowners.

  Additional audiences may include the general public, regional MoSSaiC user groups, and the scientific community.

Each stakeholder can act as a messenger or audience (or both) in a communication network with information flowing in one or many directions at different times during the project. The characteristics of each audience should determine the form of communication selected to suit the purpose of that communication:

> The importance of defining your target groups cannot be overstated. Knowledge, beliefs, and customs often vary widely from one group to another and the ways in which knowledge is acquired are not the same in each community. Even within a given target group, it's important to learn how to segment (IDRC 2012, 2).

The MCU should compile a list or communication network diagram of audiences and messengers. For each audience, consider perceptions, motivations, and intentions regarding landslide risk and the potential for adopting new risk reduction behavior (section 8.3.1); the cultural, political, and social context; and local factors that might affect communication and limit behavior change (table 8.5). Use tools like the Johari Window (figure 8.1) and baseline studies to help understand stakeholder (audience and messenger) perceptions. This analysis will help identify communication requirements in terms of appropriate forms of communication and messages (section 8.5).

8.5 FORMS OF COMMUNICATION AND PROJECT MESSAGES

Forms of communication can be classified in terms of modes, channels, and tools:

- The basic modes of communication are written, verbal, and visual; and one way (information transfer) or two way (consultation or dialogue).

- Communication channels are either face-to-face (direct) or mediated (indirect), and either target specific individuals or groups, or diffuse audiences.

TABLE 8.5 Examples of local factors affecting communication

FACTOR	EFFECT ON COMMUNICATION
Community perceptions	• There may be views regarding who should have assistance that are embedded within social groups and not in accord with likely project recommendations • Perceptions regarding landslide risk and mitigation measures may vary from one community to another, thus requiring different messages • Government agencies and staff may not initially be seen as trustworthy
Social behavior	• Where a community is highly polarized by criminality or other factors; this situation could make project acceptance difficult to achieve
Perceptions of timing	• Cultural differences in the perception of time could affect project time frames (e.g., where a laissez faire attitude is prevalent)
Government messages	• Different parts of established government bureaucracies may send different messages regarding DRR priorities and practices
Political agendas	• Communities might move faster than government in recognizing the need for DRR • DRR may be low on the current government agenda, but high on that of the political opposition parties
History	• Project fatigue among residents may mean that motivational messages need to be stronger than simply justifying the science of the intervention
Gender	• Women may be the day-to-day decision makers in the household, but have less exposure to certain communication methods
Landownership	• Project messages need to take into account local landownership protocols
Meetings	• Views expressed in meetings may reflect dominant rather than majority views and could reflect special, undeclared, interests
Stakeholder availability	• Critical stakeholders may not be reached by some forms of communication (e.g., landlord residing overseas)

• Different communication tools are appropriate for different modes and channels of communication as illustrated in table 8.6.

MoSSaiC projects need to use a wide range of communication modes, channels, and tools to achieve project objectives and encourage behavioral change. Communication tools should be used as part of the overall project process rather than as stand-alone outputs (e.g., landslide maps, posters, leaflets, or a TV documentary).

TABLE 8.6 Examples of communication tools by mode, channel, and purpose

MODE, CHANNEL, PURPOSE	TOOL
One-way communication to provide information indirectly with no feedback mechanism	• Leaflets, posters, information packs • Newsletters, project updates • Reports, documents, protocols • Exhibitions, demonstration of technologies • Mass media (TV, radio, newspapers)
Two-way communication to seek information and feedback indirectly or face to face	• Site visits • Consultation documents, surveys • Formal public meetings, presentations
Two-way communication and dialogue to facilitate mutual exchange, understanding, and stakeholder participation	• Interactive mapping, workshops, and training activities • Consensus-building meetings, mediation • Various community participatory tools

Source: Burgess and Chilvers 2006.

Direct two-way communication (consultation and dialogue) is particularly important for community participation and learning by doing during community selection and mapping, drainage design and construction, and postproject maintenance. These forms of communication are summarized in section 8.5.1 with respect to project audiences.

Selected examples of indirect forms of communication, using written and visual materials and the media (TV and radio), are introduced in sections 8.5.2–8.5.5. These forms can be used to support community participation and learning by doing, and are the primary means of providing information to a wider and more dispersed audience.

Use table 8.7 to assist in deciding what forms of communication are best suited to each stakeholder audience and purpose, after reviewing sections 8.5.1–8.5.5. Determine

TABLE 8.7 Deciding which forms of communication to use for each stakeholder audience

WHO (AUDIENCE)	WHEN AND WHY (PURPOSE)	HOW (FORM)
Funders	Throughout project: • Fulfill formal reporting requirements • Raise awareness • Advocate for policy change	• Project proposals and reports • Invited site visits • Informal briefings on project impact
Politicians and government decision makers	Especially at key project milestones: • Fulfill formal reporting requirements • Raise awareness • Seek public endorsement • Advocate for policy change	• Site visits by government officials recorded and reported by the media • Briefings to elected community constituency representatives • Cabinet briefings
MCU, government task teams	Especially at early project stages: • Create familiarity with MoSSaiC approach • Provide technical information • Generate new knowledge • Facilitate engagement with community • Change DRR practice	• Training materials for formal classroom-based and on-site training • Formal and informal interaction with community teams and residents • Practical experience and dialogue with community
Community task teams, community residents, landowners	Throughout project: • Raise awareness • Provide technical and project information • Facilitate participation in project • Generate new knowledge • Change DRR behavior	• Community meetings • Demonstration homes • Posters and leaflets • TV, newspaper, and radio coverage • MoSSaiC certification of key community contractors • Knowledge transfer among communities
General public	Throughout project, especially at construction/completion phases: • Provide information • Raise awareness	• TV, newspaper, and radio coverage • Leaflets available on request
Regional MoSSaiC user groups and regional stakeholders	At project completion: • Provide information • Facilitate knowledge sharing	• Workshops • Conferences • Short write-ups of case studies • Internet community of practitioners
Academic and professional community (science, engineering, social science)	Throughout project: • Peer review and dissemination of science, methods, and project outcomes	• Publication of research papers in academic and professional journals • Presentation at academic conferences • Collaborative research

whether these forms of communication will be considered appropriate and trustworthy by their audiences. Identify key messages for each audience and which forms of communication will convey those messages most effectively (section 8.5.6).

8.5.1 Direct communication, consultation, and dialogue

Direct two-way communication encourages behavioral change by allowing stakeholders to understand one another's perceptions, collaborate on project activities, and learn from each other (see table 8.8 for examples). Boham (1996, 2) notes that "In a dialogue, nobody is trying to win. Everybody wins if anybody wins... In a dialogue, there is no attempt to gain points, or to make your particular view prevail."

Specific tools for this form of communication include the following:

- Consultation documents, surveys, site visits

- Formal meetings, presentations

- Interactive mapping, workshops, and training activities

- Consensus-building meetings, mediation

- Community participation tools such as collective mapping, priority ranking, and observation walks

TABLE 8.8 Examples of direct two-way communication tools for use throughout the MoSSaiC project process

MoSSaiC PROJECT ACTIVITY	TOOL
Building the MCU government task teams (chapter 2)	• Formal meetings to present the project concept to government decision makers and agencies and to consult on the selection of MCU and government task team members • Consensus-building and planning meetings within the MCU and the government task teams to agree on project steps
Understanding landslides (chapter 3)	• Education/training on landslide risk for landslide assessment and engineering task team • Presentation of landslide information by experts to all stakeholders throughout the project
Selecting communities (chapter 4)	• Consultation among the MCU, government task teams, local government agencies, and communities to collect basic landslide risk information • Site visits and consensus-building meetings to agree on community selection
Community-based mapping (chapter 5)	• Formal meetings and presentations to raise community awareness of landslide risk and MoSSaiC project • Consultation with community to identify representatives • Community participation tools (observation walks, mapping, and priority ranking) to identify landslide hazards and solutions • Informal (on-site) training of government task teams
Drainage design (chapter 6)	• Education/training on drainage design for landslide assessment and engineering task team • Consensus-building meetings and focus groups to agree on a drainage plan with government decision makers and the community • Formal meeting/presentation of drainage design to community and government decision makers
Implementation of works (chapter 7)	• Formal (classroom-based) and informal (on-site) training for local contractors and site supervisors and (if relevant) community teams involved in procurement • Mediation between residents and those working on site • Invited site visits for government decision makers and funders
Postproject maintenance and evaluation (chapter 9)	• Consultation and consensus building on approach to maintenance • Formal project completion ceremony for all project stakeholders • Site visits, focus group meetings, and consultation with all stakeholders to determine project impact and lessons learned

Using direct two-way communication for MoSSaiC projects

These communication tools are used throughout the MoSSaiC project to facilitate collaboration among key government and community stakeholders. To understand and apply these tools, the MCU and government task teams should review their use in the context of their specific purpose for MoSSaiC; see table 8.8 as a guide.

Delivering project messages

The approach that the MCU and the government task teams adopt for communicating with communities will determine the extent to which they are accepted and trusted by them and how effective project messages will be in encouraging behavioral change:

> Any strategy intended to effect change in a community should be discussed with, understood and agreed upon by the community, since the primary decision-makers about what and how to change are the very people who are going to be affected by the change (FAO 2004, B1).

Consider local customs, norms, and resources that will guide the approach to two-way communication in communities. Take guidance from the community liaison task team and community representatives to identify ground rules for government task teams engaging with communities. In this regard, note the following (IFRC 2008 and Mefalopulos 2008):

- Agree on the timing, location, and purpose of meetings and site visits with community representatives beforehand

- Chose meeting venues that are accessible to the community

- Start and finish meetings and site visits promptly

- Respect cultural formalities and language in addressing individuals and groups

- Be aware of unspoken messages conveyed by body language and conduct

- Turn off mobile phones and stay present throughout meetings

- Respect opinions and include all participants

- Remember that active listening can be as important as speaking

- Be frank and answer questions honestly

- Keep explanations brief and easy to understand

- Provide practical guidance on community actions

- Use flipcharts, maps, leaflets, and other visual interactive tools as a means of sharing information.

Identify the best means of notifying communities about project meetings and site visits—e.g., word of mouth, communication via a community leader or representative or by an individual who is paid to make community announcements.

8.5.2 Community demonstration sites and show homes

In many vulnerable communities, the best form of communication is highly visual and based on demonstration. Visits to sites of past hazard events and demonstration of successful hazard mitigation measures is a powerful way of changing perceptions about how to tackle hazards effectively. Demonstration sites, example infrastructure, and show homes in communities provide tangible evidence that can help governments and communities envisage what they might have the capacity to do in similar situations (self-efficacy). Combining demonstration sites with information materials and training allows people to understand and adopt risk reduction behavior.

MoSSaiC demonstration sites and show homes

Completed MoSSaiC projects provide the context for demonstrating urban landslide hazard solutions such as surface water drainage networks, houses with roof guttering, rainwater tanks, and gray water connections to drains. When viewed in the context of past landslides at similar sites, demonstration sites enable community residents and invited visitors to see practical examples of how landslide hazard can be reduced by households.

During the community mapping and drainage design phases, and guided by the government task teams, community residents should select a potential show home by agreement with the owner. Ensure that the householder has a genuine commitment to the concept and to the exposure within the community it could bring. Equip the show home with the following drainage features as an integral part of the wider community drainage intervention (figure 8.2):

- Guttering and downpipes to drain the roof

- Collection of gray water from kitchens and bathrooms

- Connection of all household water into lined drains

- Use of low-cost drain construction where appropriate

- Monitoring of groundwater levels, if appropriate (see chapter 9)

- Monitoring of any cracks in the house (see chapter 9).

Use table 8.9 to help identify the use of demonstration sites and show homes as part of the project communication strategy.

Delivering project messages

Demonstration sites and show homes can change the perceptions and motivations of

FIGURE 8.2 Show homes

a. Show home located prominently within a community; note gray water pipes connected to a new drain.

b. Signage posted on the show home's property helps reinforce the message of good surface water management.

c. Show home erected by a commercial company is in a prominent roadside location for maximum impact.

TABLE 8.9 Example uses of demonstration sites and show homes during the MoSSaiC project process

MoSSaiC PROJECT ACTIVITY	LOCATION	PURPOSE (AND KEY AUDIENCE)
Understanding landslides	Sites of previous landslides	• Raise awareness of MoSSaiC approach and good/poor landslide hazard reduction practices (government stakeholders and community representatives)
Selecting communities	Drains and show homes in communities with completed MoSSaiC projects	
Community-based mapping		
Drainage design		• Provide context for training (site supervisors and contractors)
Implementation of works	New drains and show homes in current MoSSaiC project	• Raise awareness of good landslide hazard reduction practices (community residents)
Postproject maintenance and evaluation		

communities by demonstrating that households have the capacity to manage roof and gray water effectively and contribute to landslide mitigation. Such example infrastructure can also change perceptions of contractors and government stakeholders about the impact and effectiveness of relatively low-cost, simple measures for mitigating landslide hazards.

The visibility of the house and the accompanying drainage and pipework is vital for this to be an effective communication tool. A drawing of the house could subsequently be incorporated into posters, which may then be used by the media for further promotion.

Some commercial housing providers exhibit show homes (figure 8.2c). With government support, encourage local commercial firms to partner with the project so that MoSSaiC drainage interventions can be given additional visibility. This measure could also help in advocating the inclusion of sound household-scale slope drainage practices in building codes. The frequent absence of legally binding building codes and mandatory construction standards means show homes have a potentially highly influential role to play in the communication strategy for landslide hazard reduction.

8.5.3 Written and visual materials for communities

Materials that provide information in a combined written and visual format can be a powerful way of communicating. Communication tools such as photographs, maps, graphs, diagrams, and cartoons can help audiences understand risks and risk reduction behavior in the following ways identified by Lundgren and McMakin 2009:

- Providing information in a memorable way

- Clarifying abstract or complicated concepts

- Revealing patterns and trends that would otherwise be hidden

- Encouraging comprehension and problem solving

- Transmitting information more rapidly, realistically, and accurately than verbal messages

MoSSaiC information materials

Appropriate written and visual information materials should accompany and support other forms of communication to project stakeholders, especially communities. The community slope feature map and drainage plans are central to the project and can be a helpful visual tool for communicating slope processes, hazardous locations, the rationale for drainage routes, and the construction process. Written and visual tools should also be used in explaining urban slope stability processes, what the MoSSaiC project process is, how slope drainage and good slope management practices can help, and why and how drains should be maintained. Such tools should allow an appreciation of the communitywide approach to slope stability as well as personal actions and responsibilities.

Use table 8.10 as a guide in using written and visual tools in communities throughout the project.

Delivering project messages

The local cultural and educational context will determine the relative efficacy of different written and illustrated media in vulnerable communities. The MCU should determine whether written media such as maps, posters, cartoons, and leaflets are likely to be effective. Consider levels of literacy, formality/informality of language used, and the balance of written and visual material. Where appropriate, use images or illustrations of familiar locations in the community to show relevance and encourage ownership. Pretest materials with community representatives to ensure they are culturally relevant and appropriate.

Communication tools should be matched to message and purpose, as these examples illustrate:

- Fliers and meeting invitations should be personal and to-the-point to generate inter-

TABLE 8.10 Examples of written/visual materials to be used during the MoSSaiC project process

MoSSaiC PROJECT ACTIVITY	MATERIAL	PURPOSE FOR COMMUNITIES
Community-based mapping	Posters/leaflets on MoSSaiC project and slope stability	Raise community awareness of MoSSaiC and of urban landslide causes and solutions
	Community plans for use during mapping process	Provide opportunity for residents to contribute knowledge to and participate in project
Drainage design	Poster-size plan of drain locations displayed at meetings and in prominent community location	Provide information and opportunity for community involvement in design of planned works
Implementation of works	Leaflets on slope drainage, slope management, and drain maintenance practices	Raise community awareness of good practices for landslide risk reduction
Postproject maintenance and evaluation		

est in the project and provide at-a-glance information about how to participate.

- Leaflets and fact sheets can be used to provide detailed information that can be read and reread by people at home.

- Maps can either be stylized to convey simple project concepts, or accurate and realistic to convey exact spatial scale and co-location of features.

- Posters should be designed to attract audience attention and convey one or two messages simply and legibly from a minimum distance of 1 meter away.

Use these materials to reinforce other forms of communication during the project:

- Distributing fliers or meeting invitations provides the opportunity for residents to ask questions and engage with the project, regardless of whether the leaflet is actually read or not (figure 8.3).

- Leaflets and small versions of posters can be used during house-to-house conversations and on-site training to help explain the science and to show good construction and slope management practices (figure 8.4).

- Obtain permission to display posters in prominent locations such as shops and bars, community centers, or other natural gathering points. Posters can provide a focal point for meetings, training, TV reports, and endorsement and advocacy of the project by policy champions (figure 8.5).

8.5.4 TV, radio, and newspaper coverage

Local and national TV, radio, and newspapers can be used to disseminate risk information and messages to project stakeholders and the wider public. The content, messages, and effect of media coverage depend on who sets the agenda. For example, official government messages may focus on mitigation and reassurance, while media outlets can be drawn to disaster impacts and drama (Höppner et al. 2010).

News coverage will often tend to be event based and may be initiated by the media or by government risk managers. Governments may commission risk communication campaigns with sustained media coverage using a variety of formats (such as news items, discussion forums, documentaries, and human interest stories) to generate interest, influence perceptions, and change behavior.

MoSSaiC media coverage

Media coverage can be appropriate for MoSSaiC projects as a way of communicating information about the project itself and about urban landslide risk reduction. Ensure that there is a member of the MCU or communica-

FIGURE 8.3 Meeting invitation and project flier given to community residents at project start

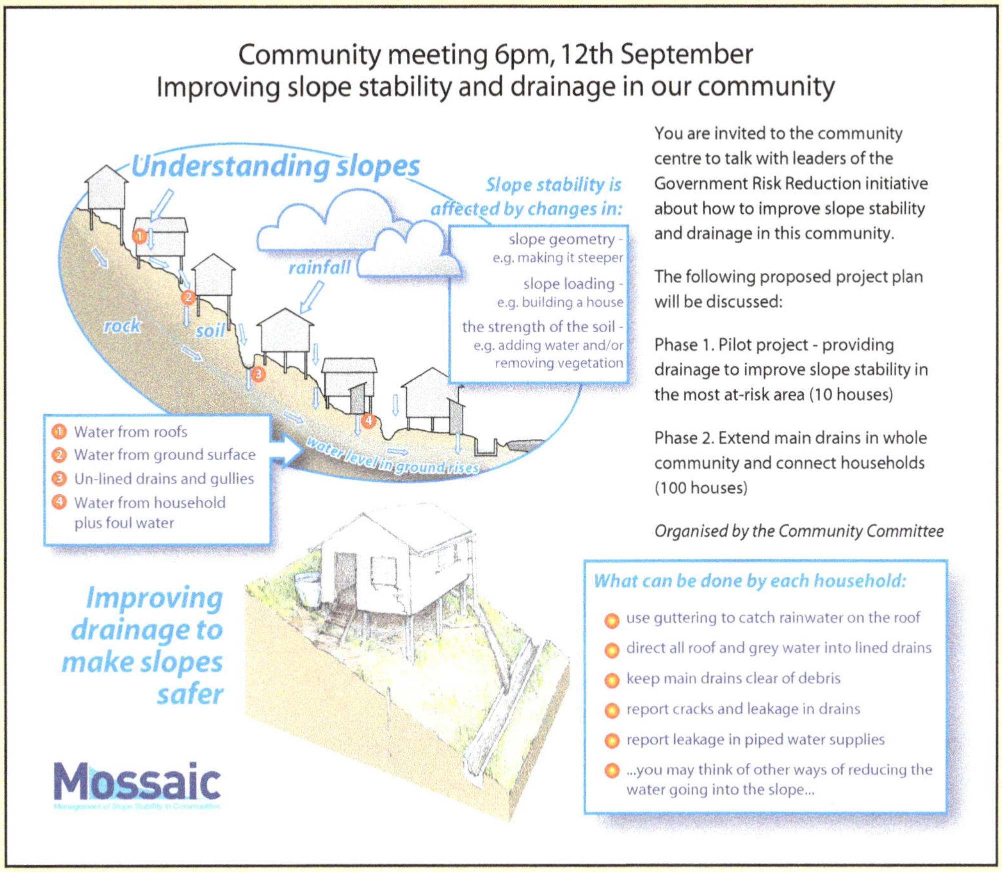

Community meeting 6pm, 12th September
Improving slope stability and drainage in our community

Understanding slopes

Slope stability is affected by changes in:

slope geometry - e.g. making it steeper

slope loading - e.g. building a house

the strength of the soil - e.g. adding water and/or removing vegetation

rainfall

rock   soil

water level in ground rises

❶ Water from roofs
❷ Water from ground surface
❸ Un-lined drains and gullies
❹ Water from household plus foul water

Improving drainage to make slopes safer

Mossaic
Management of Slope Stability in Communities

You are invited to the community centre to talk with leaders of the Government Risk Reduction initiative about how to improve slope stability and drainage in this community.

The following proposed project plan will be discussed:

Phase 1. Pilot project - providing drainage to improve slope stability in the most at-risk area (10 houses)

Phase 2. Extend main drains in whole community and connect households (100 houses)

Organised by the Community Committee

What can be done by each household:

● use guttering to catch rainwater on the roof
● direct all roof and grey water into lined drains
● keep main drains clear of debris
● report cracks and leakage in drains
● report leakage in piped water supplies
● ...you may think of other ways of reducing the water going into the slope...

FIGURE 8.4 Example of a leaflet or small poster to use in informal conversations with residents

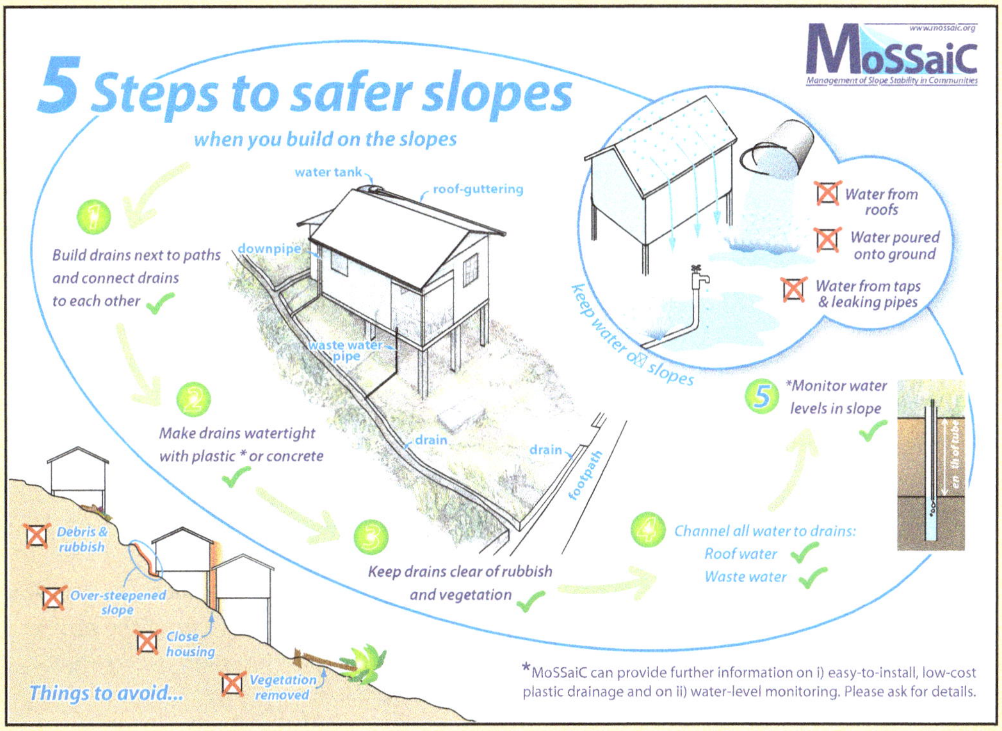

MoSSaiC
www.unmossaic.org
Management of Slope Stability in Communities

5 Steps to safer slopes
when you build on the slopes

water tank   roof-guttering

downpipe

waste water pipe

drain   drain   footpath

keep water off slopes

❶ Build drains next to paths and connect drains to each other ✓

❷ Make drains watertight with plastic * or concrete ✓

❸ Keep drains clear of rubbish and vegetation ✓

❹ Channel all water to drains:
Roof water ✓
Waste water ✓

❺ *Monitor water levels in slope ✓

⊠ Water from roofs
⊠ Water poured onto ground
⊠ Water from taps & leaking pipes

Things to avoid...
⊠ Debris & rubbish
⊠ Over-steepened slope
⊠ Close housing
⊠ Vegetation removed

*MoSSaiC can provide further information on i) easy-to-install, low-cost plastic drainage and on ii) water-level monitoring. Please ask for details.

FIGURE 8.5 Using posters to convey project messages

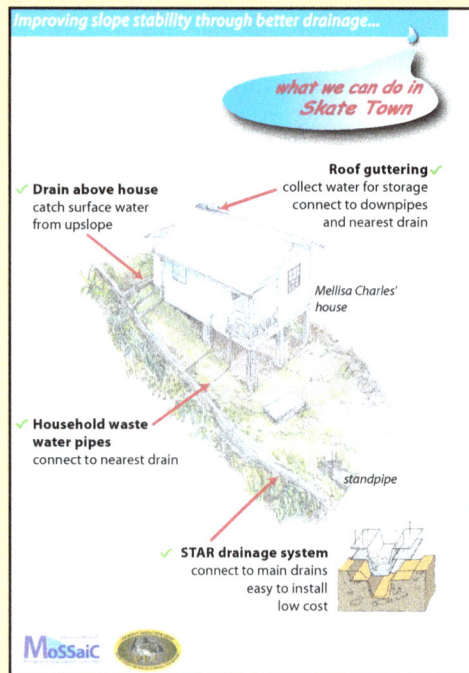

a. Design a poster illustrating good slope drainage practice.

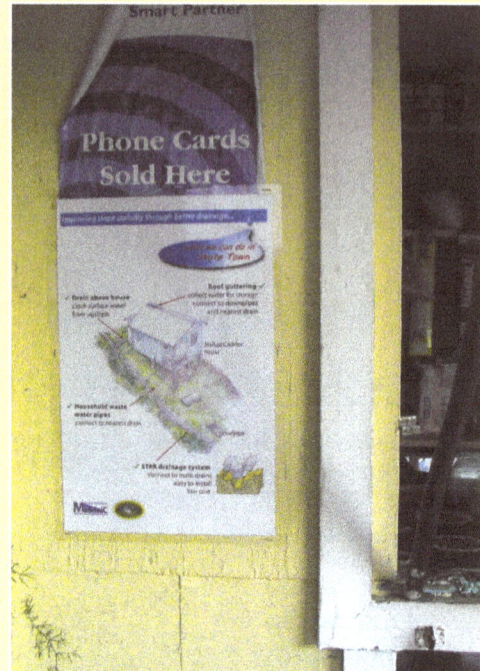

b. Display the poster prominently on the wall of a community shop, bar, or meeting place.

c. The displayed poster is here filmed for inclusion in a TV documentary on MoSSaiC.

d. A senior government official uses the poster to explain the intervention during a training course for government staff.

tions task team who is experienced in working with the media, or seek assistance from another government agency or approved media outlet.

Identify windows of opportunity in the project process (meetings or milestones) and activities such as mapping and construction and human interest stories that will lend themselves to media coverage. Consult with government task teams and community representatives to agree on the message, scope, and content of coverage before inviting the media. Use table 8.11 to guide the use of media coverage during the project.

Delivering project messages

Radio and TV interviews are likely to be requested by the media at initial project stages, including the decision to fund the project and the selection of communities. At these early stages, it is important to manage expectations by giving clear information about what the

TABLE 8.11 Examples of media coverage during the MoSSaiC project process

MoSSaiC PROJECT ACTIVITY	TV, RADIO, AND NEWSPAPER COVERAGE	PURPOSE FOR WIDER AUDIENCE
Selecting communities	Press release to announce MoSSaiC project in selected communities	Information and transparency, and to raise awareness of the MoSSaiC approach
Community-based mapping	Tell community and science stories	Raise awareness of local landslide causes and solutions
Drainage design		
Implementation of works		
Postproject maintenance and evaluation	Recap community and science stories and show evidence of effectiveness	Change perceptions of, and motivations for, urban landslide risk reduction

project is designed to achieve and how communities will be selected.

Arrange for media presence during construction and interview leading community figures who are actively engaged in the project (figure 8.6). Media presence within a community adds momentum to a project and builds a sense of ownership among community residents. For live interviews especially (which do not allow for subsequent editing), have a clear message—say who the project participants are and what the project is doing to reduce the landslide hazard.

TV documentaries can be used by governments to raise awareness of and report on project outcomes (figure 8.7). Ensure that there is footage of community engagement, particularly during mapping and construction.

FIGURE 8.7 Opening frame of a MoSSaiC TV documentary

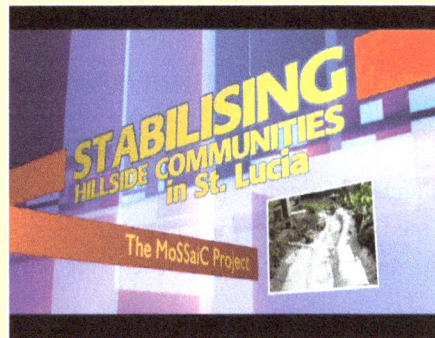

A documentary focusing on the project can be a powerful means of raising public awareness, and of giving a strong sense of ownership to the community and to those engaged in supervising and managing the project.

Source: Government of St. Lucia.

FIGURE 8.6 Media filming during construction

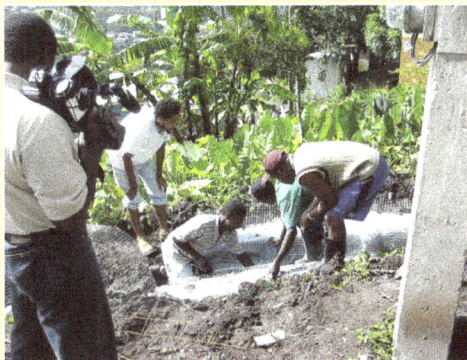

a. Filming community contractors during low-cost drain construction. Media presence in such circumstances is usually positively received by vulnerable communities.

b. A community resident (also a contractor) explains the project to a local TV station. Having community members tell the story can be more powerful than project managers doing so.

The TV program can be repeated when subsequent MoSSaiC projects start in new communities. The advantages and associated risks of this programming style should be reviewed before a program is commissioned (table 8.12). General guidelines for imparting messages to the media include the following:

- Keep it simple; use words people understand.

- Be clear and avoid detailed explanations.

- Describe, simply, what the project does, not how it works.

- Describe the differences the project will make to the local community.

- Give a human story—explain what the project will do for an individual.

Many organizations provide comprehensive media guidelines for community development and DRR projects—see, e.g., UNDP (2012)

8.5.5 Scientific and professional publications

There is a gap between DRR knowledge and action—and between researchers, policy makers, different academic disciplines, and related professions such as engineering (Gaillard and Mercer 2012). Efforts are being made to address the communication gaps between these various actors. Potential solutions include adopting new paradigms to combine hazard and vulnerability reduction approaches and developing new knowledge exchange mechanisms, ways of communicating scientific information and uncertainty, multidisciplinary collaborations, and action-research approaches (Malamud and Petley 2009).

MoSSaiC takes a multidisciplinary approach to delivering community-based, science-based, and evidence-based landslide risk reduction measures. This specific collaboration of DRR researchers, practitioners, and policy makers lends itself to dissemination of project research and results in professional and academic circles.

Publishing an article in a local professional magazine or academic journal, with key project participants as coauthors, can be a good communication channel for the following reasons:

- Academic journals require papers to be peer reviewed, thus providing feedback and critical evaluation of the project, opportunities to learn, and subsequent credibility once accepted for publication.

- Articles in local publications will be read by colleagues in government and private companies who may be participants in decisions relating to MoSSaiC.

TABLE 8.12 Factors for the MCU to consider when commissioning a TV documentary

ADVANTAGE	RISK
• Very much a "gold standard" as far as media recognition is concerned	• Another organization may be in charge of the overall message sent
• Likely to have a long shelf life	• There is no guarantee that all elements of MoSSaiC will be covered
• Professionally produced	• Production costs for a professional media house can be high
• By being filmed in a familiar location/context, a locally produced documentary can raise awareness that landslide hazard can be addressed in similar communities	• It may not be possible to capture the full impact of the intervention, e.g., drains flowing during major storm events
• Could attract the attention and endorsement of a prominent and respected person	• Dominant, rather than representative, views may be expressed by those community residents who volunteer to participate
• Can be used in subsequent team training	

- Articles may reach a different audience than those for TV and radio programs.

- Any article will have a reasonably long shelf life, and thus be an accessible resource for a period of time likely exceeding that of a radio interview, for example.

- Other construction initiatives are typically showcased in local professional magazines—an article on MoSSaiC would raise awareness of the relationship between construction and landslide hazard.

- Having a tangible item (an article reprint) means copies can be shared with community residents; this may be the first time they have seen their community featured in such a key way. This will add to residents' feeling of being valued, which is so important in a community-based project.

8.5.6 Finalizing project messages

The communication strategy is finalized by designing messages for the various stakeholders. In this regard, "[k]eep in mind your message should—inform the head, impact the heart and move feet into action!" (IFRC 2010, 47).

Design messages that persuade stakeholders to support a community-based approach to landslide risk reduction. The messages should explain

- *one main point:* community-based landslide mitigation works and pays, in many cases;

- *what is being proposed:* management of surface water in the community;

- *why it is worth doing:* to achieve a reduction in landslide hazard;

- *the actions required by the community:* active participation throughout the project, especially regarding community mobilization and construction;

- *the logic and research upon which it is based:* evidence that the intervention should work, including slope stability pre-

dictions and the performance of previous interventions; and

- *an example of risk reduction community action:* a real-life example involving community residents.

8.6 WAYS OF BUILDING LOCAL CAPACITY

Capacity building for changing landslide risk reduction behavior involves more than just the transfer of new knowledge about how to understand and reduce landslide hazards in communities. MoSSaiC projects should build and develop "the abilities, relationships and values" of governments and communities (UNEP 2002). Developing landslide risk reduction abilities requires a combination of activities that put knowledge into action and generate new knowledge through action (learning by doing). These abilities, or technical capacities, must be supported by the development of functional capacities—funding and policies, collaboration among government agencies, and community participation.

In behavior change terms, capacity-building activities can influence risk perceptions, belief in the ability to address the risk (effectiveness of actions, availability of resources, and expectation of positive outcomes), sense of responsibility, and empowerment. Table 8.13 identifies the capacity requirements for MoSSaiC projects to influence landslide risk reduction behavior at the individual, organizational/group, and institutional levels.

Similar principles underpin MoSSaiC capacity-building and communication strategies. Both should involve a balance of one-way (information and knowledge transfer) and two-way (dialogue and interactive learning by doing) and formal and informal activities. Examples of capacity-building approaches and tools are presented in table 8.14.

The MCU should use the capacity guides from the previous chapters to identify specific technical and functional capacities that need building or developing. Engage relevant stake-

TABLE 8.13 MoSSaiC capacity requirements at individual, organizational, and institutional levels

LEVEL	WHO IS INVOLVED	CAPACITY REQUIREMENT
Individual	• Community residents and contractors • Government task team members • MCU	• Scientific and local knowledge on landslide hazard causes and solutions • Experience in how to reduce landslide hazards • Confidence in ability to act effectively
Organizational	• Community leaders; community as a whole • MCU • Government decision makers • Regional user groups	• Sense of shared responsibility and project ownership • Processes and protocols to enable multidisciplinary/agency approach • Experience in working as a team to deliver solutions on the ground • Community of practitioners
Institutional/societal (enabling environment)	• Government decision makers • Funders • DRR researchers	• Evidence for investing in ex ante landslide hazard reduction • Policy processes for enabling MoSSaiC projects and sustaining project outcomes • Research informed by policy and practitioner needs

TABLE 8.14 Examples of capacity-building tools by learning mode

MODE	TOOL
Knowledge transfer (knowledge into action)	• Formal classroom-based workshops and training • Presentations • One-way communication
Learning by doing (action learning, or action into knowledge)	• Interactive mapping, workshops, and training activities conducted on site during project implementation • Various community participatory tools
Knowledge exchange and mutual learning	• Conferences • Peer-to-peer learning, mentoring, and coaching • Communities of practitioners

holders in assessing these requirements, and use this section to identify appropriate capacity-building activities for individuals, teams, and decision makers.

8.6.1 For individuals

Recognize and engage the expertise and skills individuals already have by inviting their participation and assigning appropriate roles and responsibilities. Provide training in a group setting (see section 8.6.2) to enable the development of new skills, knowledge, and confidence and to allow individuals to take on new responsibilities.

For many MoSSaiC project roles, it is important to both develop an individual's capacity and provide mechanisms for accountability as they carry out their responsibilities. Supervision, coaching, mentoring, and accountability to peers can help fulfill these two requirements. For example, site supervisors should provide impromptu training and instruction to contractors and workers during construction; engineers can mentor technical staff or trainees; and members of the MCU should support the government task team members.

Acknowledge the achievements of individuals who have completed high-quality work, attained new skills or knowledge, or played an important role in the project. One way to do this is to devise a formal recognition (certification) process for individuals (section 8.8.3). The MCU should have the certification process formally approved by the government or an appropriate body, since the legal and administrative basis for awarding certificates or for formal recognition can differ from country to country.

Certification should be formally recorded for the individual. This builds self-esteem among those in vulnerable communities and of government task team members, and provides a tangible form of recognition that should help in medium-term capacity building (figure 8.8).

8.6.2 For teams

Create training courses for the MCU and for the government and community task teams. This training is best achieved through a combination of classroom-based and on-site instruction (figure 8.9). Where feasible, course instructors should include community residents and contractors who have received formal recognition for their skills and knowledge.

Make site visits an integral part of training. Include active participation by attendees in exercises that relate to the preparation of the community slope feature map, slope process zoning map, and each stage in the development of the final drainage plan (figures 8.10 and 8.11).

FIGURE 8.9 MoSSaiC training in the Eastern Caribbean

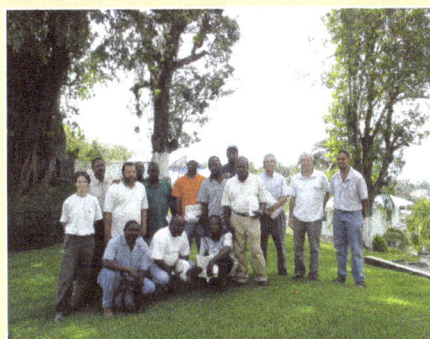

The MCU-led training comprised both in-class and on-site sessions.

8.6.3 For politicians

Politicians need information. They need facts about a project to understand the rationale and to be able to convey this information to the media (figure 8.12a) and to government and community groups, as opportunities arise. Demonstrate evidence of project effectiveness by organizing site visits where politicians can

FIGURE 8.8 Community surveyor and contractor receive MoSSaiC certification

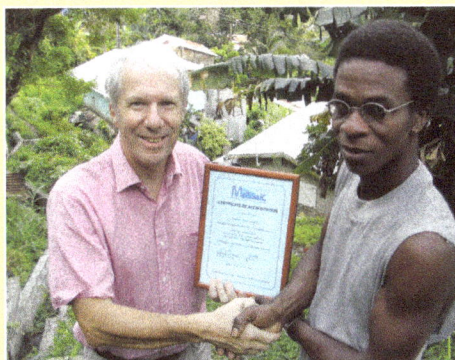

FIGURE 8.10 Building team capacity

Government technical personnel work together to produce community slope feature maps and review completed construction.

FIGURE 8.11 Combined slope process zone map and initial drainage plan

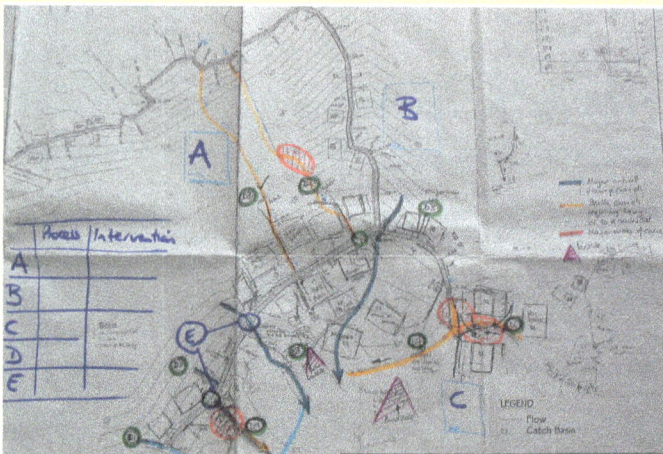

FIGURE 8.12 Building political capacity

a. Ensuring a media presence when politicians and community members talk about the intervention on site is helpful in promoting the vision of community-based interventions more widely.

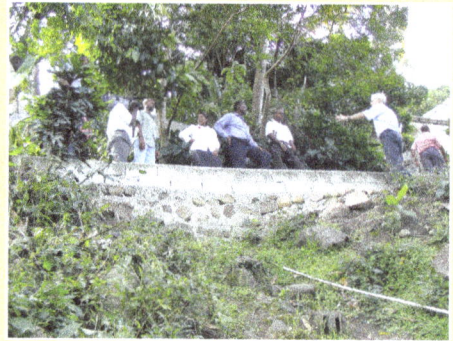

b. Showing politicians a completed intervention on site helps build potential political champions.

see results for themselves (figure 8.12b). The added benefits of site visits are that politicians see structures in place and talk with community residents, who may then take the opportunity of reinforcing messages on related community needs.

Site visits with politicians build capacity by fostering interaction among the core stakeholders (government staff and community residents), and often stimulate immediate follow-on actions such as cabinet briefings and advocacy, instigated by the participating politicians.

8.6.4 For communities

Community participation is the main mechanism for building DRR capacity in communities. Chapter 5 introduces some general community participation principles and identifies specific principles and practices related to MoSSaiC. The MCU should also review guidelines on community participation for development and DRR from international development agencies and practitioners (see, e.g., ALNAP 2003; Mansuri and Rao 2003; Maskrey 1992; World Bank 2010).

Consider how the approach to community participation is related to capacity for behavior change—from awareness, interest, knowledge, and attitudes, to legitimization, practice, and adoption of new landslide hazard reduction behavior. Identify the balance needed between providing information and formal training and empowering the community to take part in identifying, designing, implementing, and maintaining landslide mitigation measures.

Dialogue and exposition of landslide hazard mitigation measures and project processes can build trust between community and government. Government task teams should spend a significant proportion of their time in communities to build local capacity during the mapping, design, and construction phases of the project. Specific capacity-building activities to be engaged in include the following:

- Learn from the community and gain local knowledge.

- Share the science and rationale for the intervention (figure 8.13a).

- Discuss the prioritization of certain areas and the location of drains.

- Encourage the community to participate in decision making.

- Provide supervision and on-the-job training for contractors.

- Create opportunities through site visits and local media for community residents to be heard by politicians, decision makers, and the wider public.

- Award certificates to residents and contractors.

- Get community residents to assist in the training of government staff and members of other communities for subsequent projects (figure 8.13b).

8.6.5 For all user groups

Organize a stakeholder conference to share best practices after several MoSSaiC interventions have been undertaken. Report on issues that might have arisen during the project, and receive community residents' reactions to the process. Such a meeting should build trust

FIGURE 8.13 Building community capacity

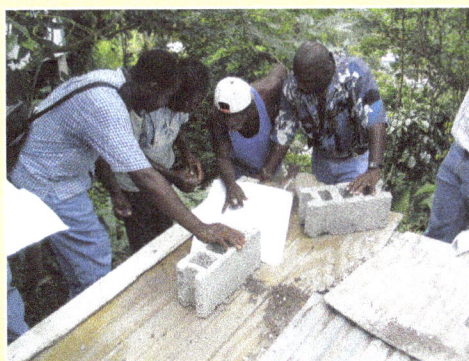

a. During implementation is one of the best times to engage with community residents and for them to engage with each other as they discuss project progress and assist in minor elements of redesign as the construction takes place.

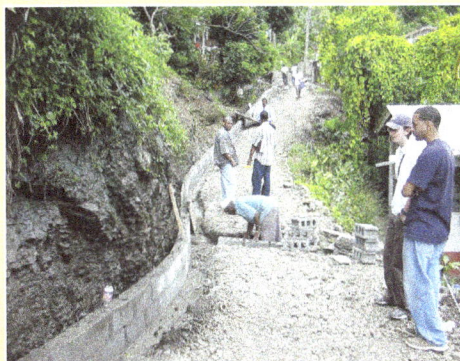

b. Community members who have also been community contractors on MoSSaiC projects should be used wherever possible to provide on-site instruction to help build capacity and further develop individual self-esteem.

across a wide constituency and thus be a significant capacity-building exercise. For some residents, it will be the first time they have attended a conference or workshop, giving them increased levels of self-esteem.

Hold discussions on site as well as in a conference environment (figure 8.14), as informal dialogue captures valuable insights into how project delivery might be improved.

FIGURE 8.14 Building regional capacity: In conferences and on site

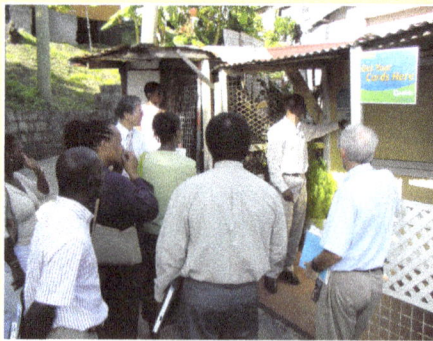

8.7 FINALIZING THE INTEGRATED BEHAVIORAL CHANGE STRATEGY

Both communities and governments need to adopt new practices and policies if urban landslide hazards are to be tackled effectively and sustainably. Integrating communication and capacity-building strategies into the MoSSaiC project process can help change people's perceptions, awareness, and knowledge, as well as their motivations and capacity to act.

The final step in the ladder of adoption is for stakeholders to continue to use the prac-

tices learned during project implementation and to embed these in their everyday activities. This includes maintaining the infrastructure provided during the project as well as initiating new projects.

Postproject maintenance of the drainage infrastructure is critical to the success of the MoSSaiC intervention. Maintenance allows infrastructure to function according to the purpose for which it was designed and constructed. Many studies have shown that timely maintenance delivers cost-effective benefits (World Bank 1994), and disregarding maintenance "can cause larger expenditures in the future, it can also impose an additional, immediate, cost to users" (Rioja 2003, 2282).

Use this section to develop a plan for maintaining drainage infrastructure as part of the overall strategy for behavioral change. Finally, integrate the communication and capacity-building strategies into the project plan and identify key outcomes for evaluating the level of behavioral change.

8.7.1 Encouraging adoption of good drain maintenance practices

Three strategies for postproject maintenance can contribute to the overall behavioral change strategy: designing and constructing drains with ease of maintenance in mind, assigning maintenance responsibilities, and involving the community.

Promote good drain design and construction supervision

Drains can be designed and constructed so that maintenance is made easier—e.g., by reducing the likelihood of siltation or blockage by debris, creating access points for drain cleaning, restricting access where drains go through people's properties (to prevent trespassers), and controlling flow velocities to limit erosion or scouring of the drain or overtopping in high flows.

Modest structural design details can result in significant maintenance savings. Small drains flowing under paths should be designed to increase flow velocity and be self-cleaning by having smooth alignments and increased gradient. Conversely, baffle walls, steps, and rip-rap should be used to reduce flow velocities on steep sections of the drain and prevent damage. Debris and silt traps should be incorporated into the drain design at locations where the flow gradient or velocity changes, resulting in sediment or debris being deposited, such as prior to vulnerable culverts, and in locations that are easy to access for cleaning and debris removal.

To ensure that maintenance features are correctly implemented, site supervision should be sufficiently rigorous in monitoring construction details. For example, a contractor may decide to change the designed drain alignment to work around problems on site. This can have the effect of rendering a drain or culvert more prone to blockage, uncontrolled flows, or damage postproject.

Be aware of negative behavior that could result from the construction of new drains or affect their functioning. For example, without adequate access to waste disposal facilities, residents may use new drains to dump their garbage (figure 8.15a). Consider the effect of

creating new drains across the hillside that could provide access routes for criminals and create new insecurities for residents (figure 8.15b). Such incidents cannot necessarily be eliminated, but can be moderated by incorporating suitable design details such as new fences to prevent unauthorized access to sections of drain that cross people's properties.

However, incorporating drain design features that limit the need for maintenance is not sufficient in itself. The rapid construction of new houses after a project (figure 8.16a) and without attention to building controls, drainage, or good slope management practices also can limit the effectiveness of MoSSaiC project drains. It is not always possible to ensure that adequate household drainage connections are planned for or made in such cases. This is equally true when houses are rebuilt in unsuitable locations, such as on former or existing landslide areas (figure 8.16b).

Assign maintenance responsibility

In some cases, maintenance issues may not be effectively addressed at the project conceptu-

---

FIGURE 8.15 Unintended consequences of drainage interventions

a. Roadside and hillside drains can become the location of choice for dumping garbage.

b. This intercept drain, when completed, was regularly used by criminal groups for rapid access to and escape from adjoining properties.

FIGURE 8.16 Absence of building controls can lead to inappropriate construction

a. In unauthorized communities, a house can be built in a few days; overall housing density can increase significantly in a relatively short time period.

b. Repair on a house built on a landslide site experiencing subsidence.

alization stage. Part of the reason may lie in information given to different stakeholder groups, which can result in ambiguity as to where responsibility for maintenance lies:

- **Communities.** Residents may be told maintenance will be their responsibility postproject, but are not given a framework in which to mobilize the community (and secure real commitment) for such activity.

- **Government.** Staff rarely include a maintenance strategy in project proposals, since

this would inevitably take the project beyond the standard donor funding time frame.

- **Institutional donors.** Donor project audits repeatedly indicate the necessity of maintenance, but consider it the responsibility of the funding recipient to "own" the issue.

As a consequence of this ambiguity, the responsibility for postproject maintenance of infrastructure in communities often remains ill defined (ILO 2005). This lack of ownership has an adverse effect on the medium- and long-term effectiveness of such projects. MoSSaiC projects should therefore review practical ways for maintenance responsibilities to be assigned, which may include the following:

- Residents maintain roof guttering and household connections, clean drains adjacent to their property, and report any damage to the implementing agency.

- A community resident takes on the role of cleaning principle drains.

- The government contracts with a community member to clean drains and inspect for damage.

- The government contracts with a local company for drain cleaning.

- The government contracts with the public works agency to inspect drains for damage and make repairs.

Encourage structural inspections and community clean-up days

Undertaking structural maintenance helps maximize construction design life. The structural integrity of drains, roof guttering, and household connections should be regularly inspected by residents to identify—and report—cracks, leaks, general degradation, or damage that could compromise the effectiveness of the drainage in reducing landslide hazard (figure 8.17).

If drains are not designed for easy maintenance (figure 8.18a) or maintenance responsi-

FIGURE 8.17 Importance of promoting community clean-up days

Without regular cleaning, this drain became blocked only six months after it was built.

bilities are not clearly agreed upon (figure 8.18b), drains can become blocked.

Encourage residents to be proactive in organizing community clean-up days. These events can be reasonably effective, but are rarely comprehensive; moreover, the social dynamic can be negative if they are not well supported by the community. This latter risk may be mitigated to some degree by encouraging leading community residents (including MoSSaiC certified contractors) to take responsibility for the events (figure 8.19).

FIGURE 8.18 Debris traps should be installed and cleared regularly

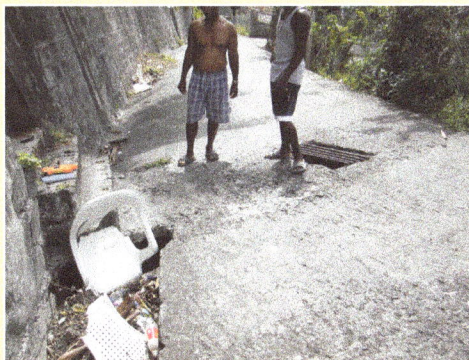

a. Debris blocking a drain that feeds a culvert under the road. When it rains heavily, the blocked culvert causes the drain to overflow, and the steep road becomes unsafe for pedestrians. A debris trap would prevent the culvert from becoming blocked.

b. Debris trap installed by a community during a MoSSaiC project. Installed correctly, such traps prevent drain blockage further downslope, but a process for maintenance must be agreed upon.

FIGURE 8.19 Debris collection and disposal

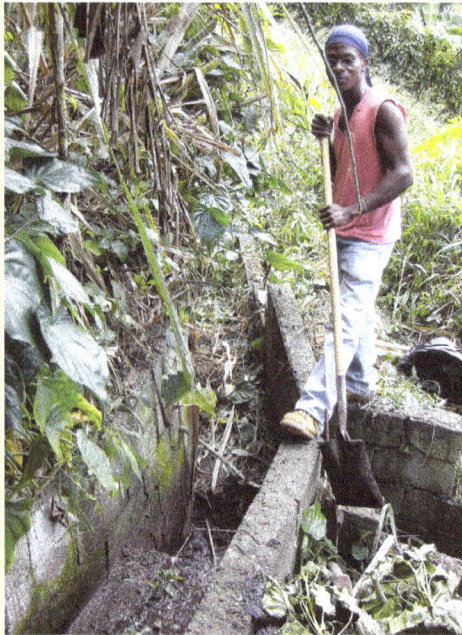

a. MoSSaiC certified contractor takes the lead in organizing and participating in a community clean-up day.

b. Removing vegetation that may block the drain.

8.7.2 The integrated behavior change strategy

Outcome mapping can be used to plan, monitor, and evaluate behavior change initiatives by focusing on (1) the perceptions and motivations of specific actors (individuals, groups, and organizations), and (2) the environments that enable two-way learning, participation, and accountability. Outcome mapping can overcome some of the issues of planning and measuring the effectiveness of behavior change strategies (Twigg 2007). It is applied best in projects where the following pertains (Jones and Hearn 2009):

• Stakeholders are working in partnership

• Capacity building is an important aspect of the project

• Understanding of social factors is critical

• Knowledge needs to be promoted and policy influenced

• Complex or multidisciplinary problems need to be tackled

• Problem solving requires reflection, dialogue, communication, and teamwork.

Outcome mapping uses a matrix to identify the integrated strategy for achieving a specific project outcome—in this case, landslide risk reduction behavior change. Strategies designed to achieve this outcome are divided into those targeted at specific individuals, groups, or organizations and those focused on the environment in which these stakeholders operate. Strategies are then subdivided as to whether they cause change directly, persuade people, or provide support to achieve the outcome. (See Earl, Carden, and Smutylo 2001 for detailed guidelines.)

Outcome mapping is a helpful tool for integrating communication and capacity-building strategies for encouraging behavioral change. The distinction between stakeholders and environments is similar to the three capacity levels (individual, organizational, and institutional/societal). The classification of strategies as causal, persuasive, or supportive approximately mirrors the distinctions between various communication tools (one-way information sharing and two-way consultation and dialogue) and between capacity-building tools (knowledge transfer, learning by doing, and learning networks).

Use table 8.15 as a guide for summarizing and integrating communication and capacity-building strategies. Use the resulting matrix as a means for monitoring and evaluating behavioral change outcomes.

> **MILESTONE 8:**
> **Communication and capacity-building strategies agreed upon and implemented**

TABLE 8.15 Mapping the integrated behavioral change strategy

FOCUS	EFFECT	MoSSaiC EXAMPLE
Individuals, groups, or organizations	**Causal** • Cause a direct effect • Produce an output	• Initiate/fund MoSSaiC project • Select MCU, government, and community task teams • Select communities • Prepare maps, studies, and reports
	Persuasive • Increase knowledge • Transfer technology/skills • Expert driven and single purpose • Change perceptions and intentions	• Communication: dissemination of information, consultation, demonstration sites • Capacity building: formal training and workshops, on-the-job training
	Supportive • Sustained/frequent involvement that encourages learning/skill development • Based on support from instructors, supervisors, mentors, and peers • Produce self-sufficiency	• Communication: community participation, dialogue • Capacity building: participation, learning by doing, certification
Stakeholder environment	**Causal** • Change the physical or policy environment • Incentives and rules	• Agree on project steps, protocols, and collaborations among government ministries • Implement physical works for landslide mitigation in communities
	Persuasive • Disseminate information • Change perceptions of wider public and decision makers	• Evidence for community-based landslide risk reduction • Communication: mass media, advocacy, site visits • Capacity building: government task team interaction with community to build trust and empowerment
	Supportive • Develop collaborations and networks for user groups	• Community of practitioners • South-South collaboration, knowledge transfer, and support

Source: Earl, Carden, and Smutylo 2001.

8.8 RESOURCES

8.8.1 Who does what

TEAM	RESPONSIBILITY	ACTIONS AND HELPFUL HINTS	CHAPTER SECTION
Funders and policy makers	Promote behavioral change	• Use evidence of completed interventions to promote landslide risk mitigation	8.4; 8.6.3
	Coordinate with the MCU		
MCU	Clear communication to all stakeholders and to the wider public via appropriate media	• Understand risk perceptions • Develop a communication strategy • Develop a clear message on the purpose of the intervention, how it is to be undertaken, how community engagement will occur, and realistic timelines **Helpful hint:** If project timelines are given, ensure they are met; failure to meet stated delivery times can lead to a lack of project support within the community.	8.3; 8.4; 8.6
	Ensure that all stakeholders have the opportunity to build capacity	• Identify on-site learning opportunities • Recognize and give responsibilities to those who adopt the project and add value to it	8.6
	Postproject maintenance strategy	• Develop a postproject maintenance strategy	8.7.1
	Develop behavioral change strategy	• Map the behavioral change strategy and associated actions	8.7.2
	Coordinate with government task teams		
Government task teams	Community awareness	• Hold community meetings to sensitize residents	8.5.1
	Consider establishing a show home	• Discuss the show home concept within the community and seek to identify a home that could be used	8.5.2
	Develop project promotional material	• Create posters and similar materials to raise awareness	8.5.3
	Develop project media message	• Engage the media, along with key community members	8.5.4
	Capacity building	• Take opportunities to learn and apply new knowledge and skills on site • Consider certification for key community individuals	8.6
	Communication with government	• Deliver facts to policy makers relating to the interventions that can be used to promote behavioral change	8.6.3
	Postproject maintenance	• Seek to implement the postproject plan developed by the MCU	8.7.1
Community task teams	Awareness of risk perceptions	• With government task teams, discuss risk perceptions, project expectations, and factors that could moderate project uptake	8.3.2
	Involvement in two-way communication process	• Provide guidance on appropriate communication tools • Engage in dialogue with government task teams and other community residents, and attend meetings • Help select demonstration sites and show homes within the community	8.5
	Adopt new practices for landslide risk reduction	• Participate in certification process and training courses where appropriate	8.6.1
		• Follow guidelines on household drainage and drain maintenance	8.7.1

8.8.2 Chapter checklist

CHECK THAT:	TEAM	PERSON	SIGN-OFF	CHAPTER SECTION
✓ Stakeholder perceptions and communication and capacity needs understood				8.4.2; 8.5
✓ Community representatives consulted about proposed communication and capacity-building activities				8.5; 8.6
✓ House suitable as a community show home identified, if relevant				8.5.2
✓ Posters explaining project's science created, if relevant				8.5.3
✓ Opportunity created for TV/radio interview at project start, if relevant				8.5.4
✓ Funds available to produce a short project documentary, if relevant				8.5.4
✓ Placing an article about the project in a local professional journal considered, if relevant				8.5.5
✓ Communication strategy finalized				8.4; 8.5
✓ Capacity-building strategy developed				8.6
✓ Postproject maintenance strategy created				8.7.1
✓ Integrated behavioral change strategy reviewed by the MCU				8.7.2
✓ **Milestone 8:** Communication and capacity-building strategies agreed upon and implemented				8.7.2

8.8.3 MoSSaiC certification

The following provides guidelines for a MoSSaiC certification process that could be adapted to suit local conditions.

Basis of the certification program

Certification entails evaluation of work performed by a given individual on a MoSSaiC intervention. Consideration of an individual for MoSSaiC certification is generally based on a recommendation from an MCU member, a community member, or some other person with sufficient knowledge of the role the individual has played in the MoSSaiC project.

Objectives of certification

Certification of an individual associated with MoSSaiC-related activities is an important element in assuring quality and the maintenance of standards. Certification helps stakeholders, professional societies, and potential employers identify specific individuals who meet the minimum criteria.

The primary objectives of the certification process are as follows:

- Recognition of individuals who have demonstrated a consistently high standard of contribution to a MoSSaiC project

- Promotion and dissemination of best practices

- Stimulation of innovation and diversity in MoSSaiC-related activities

Benefits of certification

By providing a standard for judgment of an individual engaged in a MoSSaiC project, the certification process publicly assures the competence of the individual and provides a reference of standing independent of educational provider or employer.

Assessment

To become certified, an individual must be assessed on his or her demonstration of the following:

- ***Effective communication with all relevant stakeholders.*** Stakeholders may include, but not be limited to, community members, government officials, MoSSaiC team personnel, and others engaged in the project in an official capacity.

- *Understanding of the impact of low-cost community-based landslide risk reduction within his or her particular specialty.* Examples of such specialties are low-cost drain construction, site survey work, site construction, and supervision.

- *Delivery of high-quality work.*

- *Taking the initiative in his or her area of specialization.*

- *Consistency of performance and commitment throughout the project.*

The above generic attributes recognize the broad nature of the potential skills an individual may possess and practice on a MoSSaiC activity.

8.8.4 References

ALNAP (Active Learning Network for Accountability and Performance in Humanitarian Action). 2003. *Participation by Crisis-Affected Populations in Humanitarian Actions—A Handbook for Practitioners*. London: Overseas Development Institution. http://www.alnap.org/publications/gs_handbook/gs_handbook.pdf.

Benson, C., and J. Twigg. 2007. "Tools for Mainstreaming Disaster Risk Reduction: Guidance Notes for Development Organisations." ProVention Consortium, Geneva.

Bessette, G. 2004. "Involving the Community: A Guide to Participatory Development Communication." Southbound in association with the International Development Research Centre, Penang, Malaysia.

Bohm, D. 1996. "On Dialogue." Schouten & Nelissen, Zaltbommel, the Netherlands. http://sprott.physics.wisc.edu/chaos-complexity...../dialogue.pdf.

Bull-Kamanga, L., K. Diagne, A. Lavell, E. Leon, F. Lerise, H. MacGregor, A. Maskrey, M. Meshack, M. Pelling, H. Reid, D. Satterthwaite, J. Songsore, K. Westgate, and A. Yitambe. 2003. "From Everyday Hazards to Disasters: The Accumulation of Risk in Urban Areas." *Environment and Urbanization* 15 (1): 193–203.

Burgess, J., and J. Chilvers. 2006. "Upping the Ante: A Conceptual Framework for Designing and Evaluating Participatory Technology Assessments." *Science and Public Policy* 33 (10): 713–28.

CADRI (Capacity for Disaster Reduction Initiative). 2011. "Basics of Capacity Development for Disaster Risk Reduction." United Nations, Geneva.

Crookall, D., and W. Thorngate. 2009. "Acting, Knowing, Learning, Simulating, Gaming." *Simulation Gaming* 40: 8–26.

Earl, S., F. Carden, and T. Smutylo. 2001. *Outcome Mapping: Building Learning and Reflection into Development Programs*. Ottawa: International Development Research Centre. http://web.idrc.ca/openebooks/959-3/.

FAO (Food and Agriculture Organization of the United Nations). 2004. "Participatory Communication Strategy Design." Document ID 188865. http://www.fao.org/docrep/008/y5794e/y5794e00.htm.

FM Global. 2010. "Flirting with Disasters: Why Companies Risk It All." http://www.fmglobal.com/assets/pdf/P10168.pdf.

Gaillard, J. C., and J. Mercer. 2012. "From Knowledge to Action: Bridging Gaps in Disaster Risk Reduction." *Progress in Human Geography* doi:10.1177/0309132512446717.

GNDR (Global Network of Civil Society Organizations for Disaster Reduction). 2011. *If We Do Not Join Hands: Views from the Frontline—Local Reports of Progress on Implementing the Hyogo Framework for Action, with Strategic Recommendations for More Effective Implementation*. Teddington, UK: GNDR.

Höppner, C., M. Buchecker, and M. Bründl. 2010. "Risk Communication and Natural Hazards." Cap Haz-Net. WP5 Report, Berne, Switzerland.

IDRC (International Development Research Centre). 2012. "Developing a Communications Strategy." http://web.idrc.ca/uploads/user-S/11606746331Sheet01_CommStrategy.pdf.

IFRC (International Federation of Red Cross and Red Crescent Societies). 2008. "VCA Training Guide: Classroom Training and Learning-by-Doing." IFRC, Geneva.

——. 2010. *Advocacy for Disaster Risk Reduction Training Course: Facilitator's Guide*. http://drrinsouthasia.net/downloads/Publications_Case_Studies/IFRC/Advocacy%20for%20DRR%20Trg.%20Kit/Facilitators%20Guide%20Advocacy%20Trg.%20Kit.pdf.

ILO (International Labour Organization). 2005 "Community Contracting and Organisational Practices in Rural Areas: A Case Study of Malawi." http://www.ilo.org/wcmsp5/groups/public/@ed_emp/@emp_policy/@invest/documents/publication/wcms_asist_8030.pdf.

Jones, H., and S. Hearn. 2009. "Outcome Mapping: A Realistic Alternative for Planning, Monitoring and Evaluation." Overseas Development Institute, UK. http://www.odi.org.uk/resources/docs/5058.pdf.

Kunreuther, H., and M. Useem. 2010. "Principles and Challenges for Reducing Risks from Disasters." In *Learning from Catastrophes*, ed. H. Kunreuther and M. Useem. Upper Saddle River, NJ: Wharton School Publishing.

Luft, J., and H. Ingham. 1950. "The Johari Window, a Graphic Model of Interpersonal Awareness." In *Proceedings of the Western Training Laboratory in Group Development*. Los Angeles.

Lundgren, R. E., and A. H. McMakin. 2009. *Risk Communication—A Handbook for Communicating Environmental, Safety, and Health Risks*. Hoboken, NJ: Wiley.

Malamud, B. D., and D. Petley. 2009. "Lost in Translation." *Public Service Review: Science and Technology* 2: 164–67.

Mansuri, G., and V. Rao. 2003. *Evaluating Community-Based and Community-Driven Development: A Critical Review of the Evidence*. Development Research Group. Washington, DC: World Bank.

Maskrey, A. 1992. "Defining the Community's Role in Disaster Mitigation." *Appropriate Technology Magazine* 19 (3). http://practicalaction.org/practicalanswers/product_info.php?products_id=214.

McNabb, M., and K. Pearson. 2010. "Can Poor Countries Afford to Prepare for Low-Probability Events?" In *Learning from Catastrophes*, ed. H. Kunreuther and M. Useem. Upper Saddle River, NJ: Wharton School Publishing.

Mefalopulos, P. 2008. *Development Communication Sourcebook—Broadening the Boundaries of Communication*. Washington, DC: World Bank.

Mefalopulos, P., and C. Kamlongera. 2004. *Participatory Communication Strategy Design: A Handbook*. Southern African Development Community, Centre of Communication for Development. Rome: Food and Agriculture Organization of the United Nations.

Paton, D. 2003. "Disaster Preparedness: A Social-Cognitive Perspective." *Disaster Prevention and Management* 12: 210–16.

Rioja, F. K. 2003. "Filling Potholes: Macroeconomic Effects of Maintenance versus New Investments in Public Infrastructure." *Journal of Public Economics* 87 (9–10): 2281–304.

Twigg, J. 2007. "Characteristics of a Disaster Resilient Community: A Guidance Note." https://practicalaction.org/docs/ia1/community-characteristics-en-lowres.pdf.

UNU (United Nations University). 2006. "Landslides. Asia Has the Most; Americas, the Deadliest; Europe, the Costliest; Experts Seek Ways to Mitigate Landslide Losses; Danger Said Growing Due To Climate Change, Other Causes." News Release MR/E01/06/rev1.

UNDP (United Nations Development Programme). 2012. *Communicating for Results: Reaching the Outside World*. http://web.undp.org/comtoolkit/reaching-the-outside-world/outside-world-tools.shtml.

UNEP (United Nations Environment Programme). 2002. *Capacity Building for Sustainable Development: An Overview of UNEP Environmental Capacity Development Activities*. www.unep.org/Pdf/Capacity_building.pdf.

UNICEF. 2008. "Conference on Community-based Disaster Risk Reduction." November 26–28, Kolkata. www.unicef.org/india/Conference CommunitybasedDisasterRiskReductionreport.pdf.

UNISDR (United Nations Office for Disaster Risk Reduction). 2004. "Hyogo Framework for Action 2005–2015: Building the Resilience of Nations and Communities to Disasters." UNISDR, Geneva. http://www.unisdr.org/wcdr.

Wisner, B. 2009. "Local Knowledge and Disaster Risk Reduction." Keynote presentation at the Side Meeting on Indigenous Knowledge, "Global Platform for Disaster Reduction," Geneva, June 17.

World Bank. 2010. *Development and Climate Change*. World Development Report. Washington, DC: World Bank.

——. 2011. "Mainstreaming Adaptation to Climate Change in Agriculture and Natural Resources Management Projects. Engaging Local Communities and Increasing Adaptive Capacity." Guidance Note 2 http://siteresources.worldbank.org/EXTTOOLKIT3/Resources/3646250-1250715327143/GN2.pdf.

"'What gets measured is what counts.' This focus on outcomes helps policymakers choose the best options for serving poor people. It helps the providers know when they are doing a good job. And it helps clients judge the performance of both."

—World Bank, *Making Services Work for Poor People* (2004, 108)

CHAPTER 9

Project Evaluation

9.1 KEY CHAPTER ELEMENTS

9.1.1 Coverage

This chapter provides a framework for MoSSaiC (Management of Slope Stability in Communities) project evaluation and highlights the need for an evidence base for ex ante landslide risk reduction. The listed groups should read the indicated chapter sections.

AUDIENCE				LEARNING	CHAPTER SECTION
F	M	G	C		
✓	✓	✓		Importance of project evaluation	9.2
	✓	✓		Development of key performance indicators	9.4–9.5

F = funders and policy makers   **M** = MoSSaiC core unit: government project managers and experts   **G** = government task teams: experts and practitioners   **C** = community task teams: residents, leaders, contractors

9.1.2 Documents

DOCUMENT TO BE PRODUCED	CHAPTER SECTION
Key performance indicator list for immediate project outputs	9.4
Key performance indicator list for medium-term project outcomes	9.5
An agreed-upon evaluation framework	9.4, 9.5

9.1.3 Steps and outputs

STEP	OUTPUT
1. Agree on key performance indicators (KPIs) for immediate project outputs • Develop and agree on a list of KPIs that comply with donor/government needs and MoSSaiC output measures	List of project output KPIs for evaluation
2. Agree on KPIs for medium-term project outcomes • Develop and agree on a list of project outcome measures that allow evaluation of landslide hazard reduction, project costs, and behavioral change	List of project outcome KPIs for evaluation
3. Undertake project evaluation • Agree on responsibilities for short- and medium-term data collection and the project evaluation process • Carry out the evaluation	Project evaluation report

9.1.4 Community-based aspects

The chapter outlines how community members can contribute to postproject evaluation and the evidence base for community-based landslide hazard reduction.

9.2 GETTING STARTED

9.2.1 Briefing note

Evaluation aims

Project evaluation aims to "determine the relevance and fulfillment of objectives, development efficiency, effectiveness, impact and sustainability" (OECD 2002, 21). Evaluation is carried out both during and after projects (formatively and summatively, respectively) as follows (World Bank 2007):

- Formative evaluations focus on project implementation and improvements, regardless of whether the assumed operational logic corresponds to actual operations and what immediate consequences each implementation stage produces.

- Summative evaluations focus on outcomes and impacts at the end of the project (or after a particular project stage) to determine the extent to which anticipated outcomes were produced (the consequences and results of the project)—enabling an assessment of the creation,

continuation, or scaling-up of a given project or policy.

Evaluation of a MoSSaiC project provides the evidence base for ex ante landslide risk reduction (which is one of the three foundations of MoSSaiC) by demonstrating whether community-based landslide risk reduction works and pays, and what the most appropriate practices and policies are. This evidence base comprises three levels and time frames of project evaluation information:

- ***Standard key performance indicators (KPIs).*** Have the requirements of the funders and other stakeholders been met?

- ***Short-term MoSSaiC outputs and KPIs.*** Have MoSSaiC milestones been met using appropriate community- and science-based methods?

- ***Medium- and longer-term MoSSaiC outcomes.*** Are there continuing benefits from the project in terms of reduced landslide hazard and adoption of effective urban landslide risk reduction practices and policies by communities and government (i.e., behavioral change)?

In addition to these three levels or time frames, MoSSaiC project evaluations should consider three categories of effectiveness—technical and physical (reducing the hazard), cost, and behavioral change (including risk reduction awareness and capacity).

Evaluation is of interest to the intended beneficiaries in communities; government and community task teams participating in the project; the MoSSaiC core unit (MCU) and the agency with a contractual or legal responsibility to report on results to the funding source; development funders, policy makers, and practitioners; and scientific researchers.

Designing the evaluation process

Project managers frequently view audits as complex, time consuming, expensive, and not always focused on answering the right questions (Baker 2000). In this regard, Easterly (2002, 53) notes that

> ...vast sums of money and unbelievable levels of technical complexity have been expended to make Monitoring and Evaluation...into a functional tool... Moreover, bureaucracies can manipulate quantitative indicators of performance to achieve "success" without real quality improvements. (This is different from evaluation for the sake of learning lessons for future practice.)

This form of project evaluation tends to lead to a short-term view of project success based on technical efficiency (inputs, activities, and immediate outputs). Medium- and long-term outcome and impact evaluation is seldom built into risk reduction projects (World Bank 2003); and, in many cases, adequate baseline data are not collected. This situation has two consequences: first, it is difficult to find adequate measures of success on which a project may be evaluated after just two or three years following completion. Second, longer-term project impact evaluations are rarely, if ever, instigated (Benson and Twigg 2004).

Project evaluation design should be driven by project objectives in order to determine whether short-term outputs are effective in generating medium-/long-term outcomes, and whether those outcomes are consistent with stakeholder needs and project objectives (McDavid and Hawthorn 2005) (figure 9.1).

The MoSSaiC evaluation process is of greatest potential benefit if, as with the project delivery mechanism, its scope is locally formulated. It should be designed with objectives, outputs, and outcomes in mind and to enable lessons to be learned for future practice (East-

FIGURE 9.1 Links between project objectives and overall project success

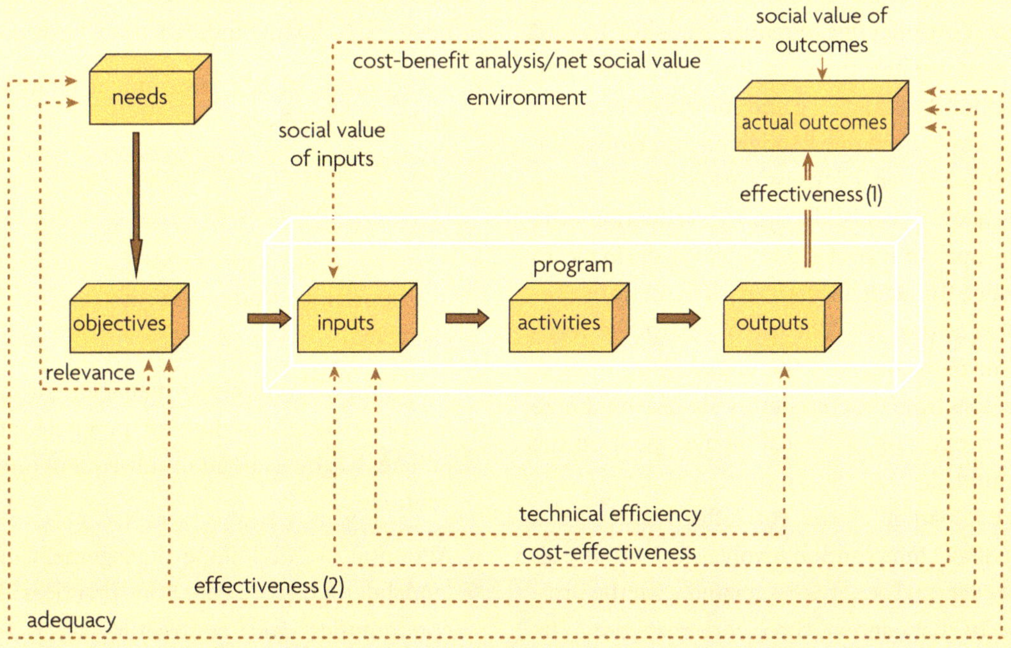

Source: McDavid and Hawthorn 2005.

erly 2002). This evidence base is important if the perceptions of individuals, governments, and major international funding agencies are to be changed regarding community-based landslide risk reduction.

Evaluating technical and physical effectiveness (landslide hazard reduction)

MoSSaiC employs scientific methods to assess landslide hazard and drainage issues affecting communities and to determine if improved drainage will increase slope stability. Drainage interventions are then designed on this basis. An evaluation of a MoSSaiC intervention should demonstrate the level to which landslide hazard has potentially been reduced. Hazard reduction can be determined through

- the use of slope stability calculations and models,

- observations relating to rainfall events and the effectiveness of drains,

- observations relating to subsequent slope stability, and

- comments from residents.

Evaluating cost-effectiveness

A central premise of MoSSaiC is that it is often more cost-effective to reduce landslide hazard in communities than it is for a government to respond to a landslide and for the community to recover from one (Anderson and Holcombe 2006). This cost-effectiveness extends to the method of landslide hazard reduction—the appropriate use of slope surface drainage to reduce the landslide hazard for as many households as possible. The use of existing government personnel and the engagement of contractors from the community should maximize the proportion of project money spent on the ground.

Evaluation of the cost-effectiveness of a MoSSaiC intervention involves monetizing all the costs and benefits associated with the project. In that context, three core costs are to be determined:

- Costs incurred in reducing the landslide hazard (in conjunction with the outcomes of the technical/physical evaluation)

- Costs of not undertaking the intervention (potential cost of a landslide)

- Proportion of project money spent on construction materials and labor.

Evaluation of capacity-building, awareness, and behavioral change

The emphasis on community engagement and the development of a government team to design and implement landslide risk reduction means that MoSSaiC can build capacity. This capacity building may occur through hands-on experience, the use and development of existing skills, or some form of training. Additionally, the project may employ (or attract) the media and demonstrate good slope management practices to the wider public. The aim is to generate a culture of awareness of landslide causes and of appropriate measures that can reduce this hazard. Over time, with the ongoing implementation of projects in different communities, a degree of behavioral change will become embedded in the approach to landslide risk.

To evaluate the capacity-building and behavioral change achievements of a MoSSaiC project, the following indicators are relevant:

- Involvement of key government technical and managerial staff

- Involvement of community contractors, residents, and leaders

- Training of government staff, contractors, or community leaders on site and in the classroom

- Adoption of good slope management and landslide hazard reduction practices and policies by government in subsequent interventions

- Adoption of good slope management and landslide hazard reduction practices by communities and contractors after the project is completed

- Media uptake and presentation of the approach

- Comments from project participants.

9.2.2 Guiding principles

The following guiding principles apply in project evaluation:

- Agree on MoSSaiC project evaluation objectives with stakeholders at the start of the project. Make sure KPIs directly relate to these objectives over short, medium, and longer time frames.

- Where possible, integrate the collection of project performance data into the project process rather than creating separate (or duplicate) activities. For example, data collected during community selection, detailed community mapping, landslide hazard assessment, and drainage design (landslide hazard, exposure, and vulnerability) can also be used as baseline data for evaluating postproject changes in landslide risk and surface water flows. Similarly, capacity assessments, studies of risk perception, and the behavior change strategy map (discussed in chapter 8) can be revisited after the project to evaluate changes.

- Establish responsibilities for project evaluation both during and after the project. The responsibility for medium- and long-term postproject evaluation (or monitoring) may need to reside with a local agency that already has a mandate or research program for disaster risk assessment and management.

- Ensure the collection and evaluation of project performance data are transparent and open to independent or external auditing. Adhere to funder and government safeguards for evaluation and monitoring. Invite independent review of the project evidence base to establish credibility and learn lessons for future practice.

9.2.3 Risks and challenges

Evaluation seen as low priority

Project evaluation is rarely seen as a priority during project implementation, and record-keeping for KPIs or evaluation purposes frequently takes a backseat to more immediate and pressing issues. But without project evaluation, performance and progress cannot be measured; data collection to this end is vital. A member of the government task teams must be given responsibility for coordinating project evaluation in terms of securing agreement on KPIs, developing a template for recording relevant data, and recording the data in a timely manner.

Sustaining project data capture over the medium term is another challenging issue, and must be addressed so that the true project impact can be demonstrated. It may be appropriate to initiate a formal assessment of ongoing impact on government capacity and the extent of behavioral change. Other data relating to the physical effectiveness of the mitigation measures should be collected as and when major rainfall events occur months—or even years—after project completion.

Responsibility for acquiring and maintaining postproject evaluation data might best be given to and overseen by an agency with an existing mandate for disaster risk management, community vulnerability reduction, or geological and geotechnical surveys, or with a local university research program.

Top-down evaluation

Development and disaster risk reduction (DRR) project evaluations remain predominantly top down, designed to provide information to headquarters staff and donors. What is certain is that

> evaluations need to go far beyond "bureaucratic" reports presenting financial accounts and "physical" achievements of projects, such as those required by many funding organizations. In fact, this kind of reporting tends to encourage and allow precisely the dis-

torted presentations of achievements that emphasize successes and minimize failures (Platteau 2004, 243).

Impediments to data collection

The time and resources allocated to project evaluations are usually very limited, leading to overemphasis on selective field evidence. Data can be further skewed by the methods used and perceptions of those involved in both acquiring and providing the data. For example, "agency evaluation teams dominated by external specialists—often men—appear to be common" (Benson and Twigg 2004, 115).

Organizations may not want to provide information that shows that a program was ineffective. Nonetheless, the MCU should promote the importance of evaluation regardless of potential outcome; as the World Bank (2004, 106) notes:

> There are impediments to collecting such information [data and information to facilitate the evaluation]. Provider organizations often do not want to acknowledge their lack of impact (even if it does not affect their pay directly), but knowing when things are not working is essential for improvements. Further, it is necessary to know not just what works but also why—to replicate the program and increase the scale of coverage.

9.2.4 Adapting the chapter blueprint to existing capacity

Use the capacity scoring matrix opposite to assess the capacity of the MCU and government task teams to carry out evaluation during and immediately after the project. Identify potential capacity for medium- to long-term postproject evaluation of outcomes.

1. Assign a capacity score from 1 to 3 (low to high) to reflect existing capacity for each of the elements in the matrix's left-hand column.

2. Identify the most common capacity score as the overall capacity level.

3. Adapt the chapter blueprint in accordance with this overall capacity level (see guide at the bottom of the opposite page).

9.3 DATA REQUIREMENTS FOR PROJECT EVALUATION

KPIs are metrics, or data, used for project evaluation that relate project objectives and inputs to the resulting outputs and outcomes.

- **Inputs.** Inputs are the funds, time, and resources required for the project.

- **Outputs.** Outputs are the immediate results of project implementation such as number of persons employed, meters of drain constructed, or number of houses with roof guttering installed.

- **Outcomes.** Outcomes are the longer-term results of the project such as reduction in landslide probability, reduced cost of landslides, or improvements in slope management practice.

9.3.1 MoSSaiC project evaluation data

To achieve a holistic evaluation of the MoSSaiC program, the MCU should develop a plan for acquiring KPI data and evidence relating to three categories—technical/physical effectiveness, cost-effectiveness, and behavioral change (including risk reduction awareness and capacity)—over two postproject time frames:

- At project completion (outputs)

- Over the medium term—three to five years after project completion (outcomes).

Data within these categories (table 9.1) facilitate construction of three KPI clusters, introduced in sections 9.4 and 9.5:

- **Typical donor-focused KPIs.** The MCU should ascertain if there are any donor KPI requirements for the MoSSaiC project (table 9.2).

- **Detailed MoSSaiC KPIs for project outputs.** The MCU should create an agreed-upon list of output KPIs relevant to the specific project (table 9.3).

- **KPIs for MoSSaiC project outcomes.** The MCU should create a list of outcome KPIs

CAPACITY ELEMENT	EXISTING CAPACITY SCORE		
	1 = LOW	2 = MODERATE	3 = HIGH
Experience of project evaluation in previous DRR or community-based projects	Limited awareness of project evaluation requirements and methods	Project evaluation not routinely undertaken, but some experience in requirements and methods	Value of project evaluation well recognized and undertaken on a routine basis
Level of community participation and ownership of project	Low level of community engagement; little apparent interest in evaluation	Good level of community engagement and some interest in taking part in project output evaluation	High level of community engagement; willingness to evaluate and monitor project outputs and outcomes
Existing precedent within government for postproject evaluation	No precedent within government for postproject evaluation	Postproject evaluations undertaken on ad hoc basis	Government agency or unit responsible for evaluation and monitoring of DRR projects
Culture of data acquisition for project evaluation	No culture of data acquisition for project evaluation	Occasional attempts at systematic data acquisition but no coordinating agency	Relevant databases systematically maintained; consultants engaged to report on impact of major projects
Experience with cost-effectiveness and cost-benefit analyses for DRR and community-based projects	No previous relevant experience in undertaking cost-effectiveness or cost-benefit analyses	Some examples of cost-effectiveness analysis but not in the context of community-based or DRR projects	Previous experience undertaking both cost-effectiveness and cost-benefit analyses relevant to MoSSaiC
Project safeguards	Documented safeguards need to be located; no previous experience in interpreting and operating safeguard policies	Documents exist for some safeguards	Availability of documented safeguards from all relevant agencies

CAPACITY LEVEL	HOW TO ADAPT THE CHAPTER BLUEPRINT
1: Use this chapter in depth and as a catalyst to secure support from other agencies as appropriate	The MCU needs to strengthen its resources prior to designing and implementing the project evaluation. This might involve the following: • Using this book to develop a brief training course for MCU and government task team members on the rationale for MoSSaiC project evaluation • Integrating project evaluation data acquisition into the community participation process • Searching within government for expertise and data collection processes relevant to MoSSaiC project evaluation • Developing a suitable cost-effectiveness evaluation method
2: Some elements of this chapter will reflect current practice; read the remaining elements in depth and use them to further strengthen capacity	The MCU has strength in some areas, but not all. Those elements that are perceived to be Level 1 need to be addressed (as above). Elements that are Level 2 will require strengthening, such as the following: • Negotiating the collection of relevant data from other government departments • Discussing project outputs and outcomes at community meetings and establishing a postproject evaluation plan • Confirming where responsibility for postproject evaluation lies within the government and how it will be undertaken
3: Use this chapter as a checklist	The MCU is likely to be able to proceed using existing proven capacity. It would be good practice nonetheless for the MCU to document relevant experience with project evaluation and related safeguards.

TABLE 9.1 Data needed to evaluate outputs and outcomes by category of evaluation

EVALUATION CATEGORY	FOR PROJECT COMPLETION OUTPUTS	FOR MEDIUM-TERM OUTCOMES AND IMPACT
Technical/ physical	Community slope feature map, slope process zone map, prioritization matrix, and final drainage plan	Not applicable
	Hazard assessment (rainfall recurrence intervals, slope stability analysis simulations)	Slope stability performance (slope monitoring, landslide inventory, rainfall data)
	Drainage design and construction	Drain performance and maintenance (observed)
	Improved community environment, environmental health, and other physical benefits (resident feedback)	
Cost	Total cost of intervention	Actual or potential cost of landslide (for use in cost-benefit analysis)
	Budget spent on the ground	Ongoing use of local personnel for design and construction (observed)
	Other benefits to community (capable of being monetized), both short and long term (for use in cost-benefit analysis)	
Capacity, awareness, and behavioral change	Government personnel involved/trained	Ongoing use and adoption of experience, good practice, and skills (observed/ stakeholder feedback)
	Contractors involved	
	Community residents involved	
	Media uptake	Peer-reviewed professional papers written on projects

and associated mechanisms for data collection and analysis (table 9.4).

9.3.2 Community knowledge and project evaluation data

Communities can provide valuable information for all three categories of MoSSaiC project evaluation:

- Contributing local knowledge of slope features before the intervention (chapter 5)

- Monitoring structural cracks, water table levels, and drain performance after the intervention (sections 9.5.3, 9.5.4, and 9.5.5)

- Observing and commenting on conditions in the community before and after an intervention (sections 9.5.6 and 9.5.7).

These and similar observations are a major contribution to evaluation and performance measures, and community engagement is a prerequisite to determining the project's holistic benefits.

Before the project

During the community mapping process (chapter 5), the government task teams should have recorded indications given by residents on the maximum water levels experienced during times of heavy rainfall, areas of stagnant water, flooding of property, previous landslide impact on property, and other issues to be addressed in designing interventions (figure 9.2).

After the project

After the project, first-hand comments and observations should be sought from residents on the impact of interventions to supplement other evidence of project outcomes (section 9.5). Of particular value is information on the depth of flow in the constructed drains following heavy rainfall (figure 9.3).

Seek and record residents' views, such as the following, that reflect their post-intervention experiences:

FIGURE 9.2 Residents showing issues to be addressed by MoSSaiC interventions

a. Resident indicating maximum observed flood levels prior to intervention.

b. Resident in area of slope instability adjacent to his home prior to a MoSSaiC intervention.

c. Resident indicating occurrence of stagnant water before intervention.

- "If it were not for the MoSSaiC drains, people would have perished" (government official)

- "The drains worked perfectly and there were no landslides" (community resident)

FIGURE 9.3 Maximum observed flow level in a MoSSaiC drain during Hurricane Tomas

- "The rain was heavy, heavy but the slope held—there were no landslides at all" (community resident)

- "The health of children has improved as there is less stagnant water" (community resident).

Use pre- and postproject questionnaires to quantify or monetize benefits (and problems) resulting from the project; see section 9.7.5.

Look for evidence of increased awareness and understanding of landslide causes and solutions and changes in slope management practices; see chapter 8 and section 9.5.8.

9.4 PROJECT OUTPUTS: EVALUATING IMMEDIATE IMPACT

9.4.1 Typical key performance indicators

At the start of a project, the implementing agency, the government, and—potentially—the donor agency need to agree on a set of appropriate KPIs. KPI specification is typically a donor requirement for funds awarded and will tend to focus on immediate, easily identifiable project outputs rather than longer-term outcomes. This focus enables the progress and "success" of a project to be tracked during implementation and at completion. Table 9.2 presents a sample set of KPIs that may be selected for a MoSSaiC project.

9.4.2 Output key performance indicators for MoSSaiC projects

While typical KPIs can provide a checklist for project progress and completion, it is important to recognize what is actually happening on the ground. Standard outputs such as those listed in table 9.2—a map, a report, the number of personnel involved—do not tell the full story. Indicators need to be adopted that allow evaluation of MoSSaiC's effectiveness in using science- and community-based methods (outputs) to reduce landslide hazard in the most vulnerable communities (outcomes):

> Good evaluation is the research necessary to assign causality between program inputs and real outcomes. It should be directed at the full impact of programs—not just the direct outputs of specific projects. But few evaluations have been done well, even though most

major donors (including the World Bank) have always made provisions for them (World Bank 2004, 106).

The MCU should assemble a list of MoSSaiC-specific project outputs to be reported on at the completion of an intervention (table 9.3). These outputs will probably be more comprehensive than the potential KPIs requested by donors.

9.5 PROJECT OUTCOMES: EVALUATING MEDIUM-TERM PERFORMANCE

Measures beyond the immediate project completion benefits (outputs) need to be considered in order to achieve a holistic picture of project performance. Possible indicators of benefits accruing over one to five years after project completion (outcomes) are given in table 9.4.

TABLE 9.2 Typical donor-focused key performance indicators for project outputs

EVALUATION CATEGORY	TYPICAL KPI	OUTPUT
For each community		
Technical/ physical	Community-based mapping of slope features relating to landslides and slope processes	Community slope feature map
	Assessment of landslide hazard processes	Slope process zone map, prioritization matrix, scientific report
	Design of an appropriate drainage intervention	Final drainage plan
	Generation of work packages and contracts for community-based contractors and laborers	Contracts
	Construction of drains	Drains
	Installation of household gray water and roof water connections	Roof guttering, etc.
For the project		
Cost	Cost of construction materials and labor	Monetary value
	Cost of other items in project budget	Monetary value
Capacity, awareness, and behavioral change	Government personnel able to implement landslide hazard reduction in communities	Number of personnel in teams
	Contractors from communities employed in construction of drains for landslide hazard reduction	Number of contractors and laborers
	Community residents aware of good slope management practices	Days spent in community, number of meetings

TABLE 9.3 Detailed MoSSaiC key performance indicators for project outputs

EVALUATION CATEGORY	MoSSaiC KPI	OUTPUT
Technical/ physical	Use of scientific methods for assessing landslide hazard	Scientific rationale and model results
	Use of appropriate engineering methods for designing drains	Design drawings and calculations
	Drain construction and supervision of works to an acceptable standard	Good construction practices, good-quality drains—e.g., no leaks or uncontrolled flows
	Acceptable standard of connection of households to drains	
	Improvement of drainage and slope stability issues for whole community (not just a few houses)	Number of houses/people benefiting directly and indirectly
	Improvement in water supply to most vulnerable households	Number of water tanks installed
Cost	Benefit to community in terms of employment	Number of person/weeks of employment
	Proportion of budget spent on construction materials and labor	Percentage of budget
	Final project costs in relation to original budget	Percentage of budget
	Comparison of project cost with potential community relocation costs	Project cost as percentage of potential community relocation cost
Capacity, awareness, and behavioral change	Government personnel, contractors, or community members receiving certification for involvement and skills	Number receiving certification
	Evidence of residents providing free project input in terms of design, construction, and materials	In-kind contribution
	Evidence of uptake of good slope management practices and self-help in communities	Independent and appropriate installation of drains/gutters, etc.
	Evidence of media interest and promotion	Number of interviews, posters, news items, etc.

9.5.1 Observed slope stability

MoSSaiC interventions are designed to reduce the risk of rainfall-triggered landslides. However, it is difficult to establish what would have happened to a particular slope if a drainage intervention had not been carried out; this is the counterfactual problem in arguing for risk reduction.

Because such interventions cannot completely eliminate landslide hazard, there is the residual likelihood of instability on such slopes that may be triggered by

- more extreme rainfall events,
- poor drain maintenance (blocked, overflowing, or broken drains),

- poor maintenance or disconnection of household roof guttering and gray water pipes, and
- construction of new houses with no connection to drains.

Therefore, evidence of postproject slope stability must be collected, particularly in relation to high levels of rainfall, but also with a view to other causes as an indication of the effectiveness (or limitation) of each intervention.

Landslides in adjoining areas

Areas immediately adjacent to intervention areas can serve as a control group of slopes,

TABLE 9.4 MoSSaiC key performance indicators for project outcomes

EVALUATION CATEGORY	MoSSaiC KPI	OUTCOME (EVIDENCE BASE)
Technical/ physical	Slope stability during and after high rainfall events	• Observed slope stability (section 9.5.1) • Rainfall data and landslide inventory (section 9.5.2) • Household crack monitoring (section 9.5.3) • Water table monitoring (sections 9.5.2 and 9.5.4)
	Drain performance	• Recorded drain flows (section 9.5.5)
	Benefits to the community in terms of improved community environment	• Observations, community feedback, formal survey (section 9.5.6)
Cost	Actual or potential costs of a landslide	• Cost-benefit analysis (section 9.5.7)
	Benefits to the community in terms of employment, improved access, reduced damage to houses	
Capacity, awareness, and behavioral change	Ongoing use of local personnel for design and construction	• Observed good/bad slope management practices
	Ongoing use and adoption of experience, good practice, and skills	• Stakeholder feedback • Formal survey (section 9.5.8)

used to infer what might have happened if an intervention had not been undertaken. For example, following heavy rainfall, an area in which a MoSSaiC intervention had been completed remained stable; in contrast, the adjoining hillside area 50 m away experienced a major landslide, resulting in the loss of houses and relocation of families (figure 9.4).

Evidence base

The following information should be recorded over a one- to five-year period after the project ends:

• The observed stability of the drainage intervention area (the community), during and after rainfall events that would have been

FIGURE 9.4 Landslide in an area immediately adjacent to a slope successfully stabilized by a MoSSaiC intervention

expected to (or actually did) trigger landslides in the region/country

- The effect of such rainfall events on the surrounding/adjacent hillside

- Any other evidence of slope stability/instability within the drainage intervention area and the surrounding/adjacent hillside that may be the result of physical or human factors other than rainfall.

Sources of information include the following:

- *Government.* Agencies will typically be contacted by communities when landslides occur and will send engineers or technicians to inspect or remedy the damage.

- *Meteorological agencies.* These can provide rainfall data and associated recurrence interval estimates.

- *Communities.* Residents usually have a sound and detailed knowledge of the effects of rainfall events.

- *Photographs and measurements of the physical disturbance.* These should be taken as close to the time of the event as possible, before vegetation growth masks the landslide, or residents begin to reconstruct houses on the failed material.

9.5.2 Rainfall and slope stability information

The following information should be obtained over a one- to five-year time frame:

- Rainfall intensities, volumes, and durations for events that would be expected to (or actually) trigger landslides in the region/ country

- Rainfall intensities, volumes, and durations for hurricanes and tropical storms or events that have > 1-in-1-year return periods

Calculate rainfall magnitude and frequency

Detailed rainfall intensities, volumes, and durations for major storms are needed to estimate the return period of an event. If a slope has proved stable for a particular rainfall

event, this demonstrates the degree of protection provided by the drainage intervention.

Figure 9.5 illustrates the return periods for different cumulative rainfalls for a location in St. Lucia in October 2008. As the table shows, while the 24-hour rainfall on October 11 had a low return period, the 15-day cumulative rainfalls for each of the days in the period October 10–21 amounted to a > 1-in-50-year event. The figure plots the accumulated rainfall totals to obtain a clear idea of the respective return periods. A number of landslides were triggered in the period when the cumulative 15-day rainfalls exceeded the 1-in-50-year event; notably, no landslides were triggered on hillsides where drainage interventions had been completed.

Estimate before and after recurrence interval

Using data related to specific return period rainfall events gives an indication of intervention performance (table 9.5).

A slope stability back-calculation can be used to estimate what the effect of the rainfall event would have been in the absence of drain construction. The results can also be compared to any calculations undertaken prior to the drainage intervention as part of the landslide hazard assessment (chapter 6).

Additional rainfall information

Satellite imagery relating to major rainfall events such as hurricanes is a useful data source to accompany quantitative rainfall data, especially if there are associated calculations of rainfall intensity (figure 9.6). Hurricanes can cause substantial long-term damage to infrastructure and set economies back many years, particularly those of small island developing states. Associating hurricane tracks and rainfall intensities with the effectiveness of implemented project elements, such as hurricane strapping and drainage, is useful for benchmarking medium-term outcomes.

Evidence base

Collect the following data to assess the effectiveness of landslide hazard mitigation proj-

FIGURE 9.5 Daily and cumulative rainfall with associated return periods for a location in St. Lucia, October 2008

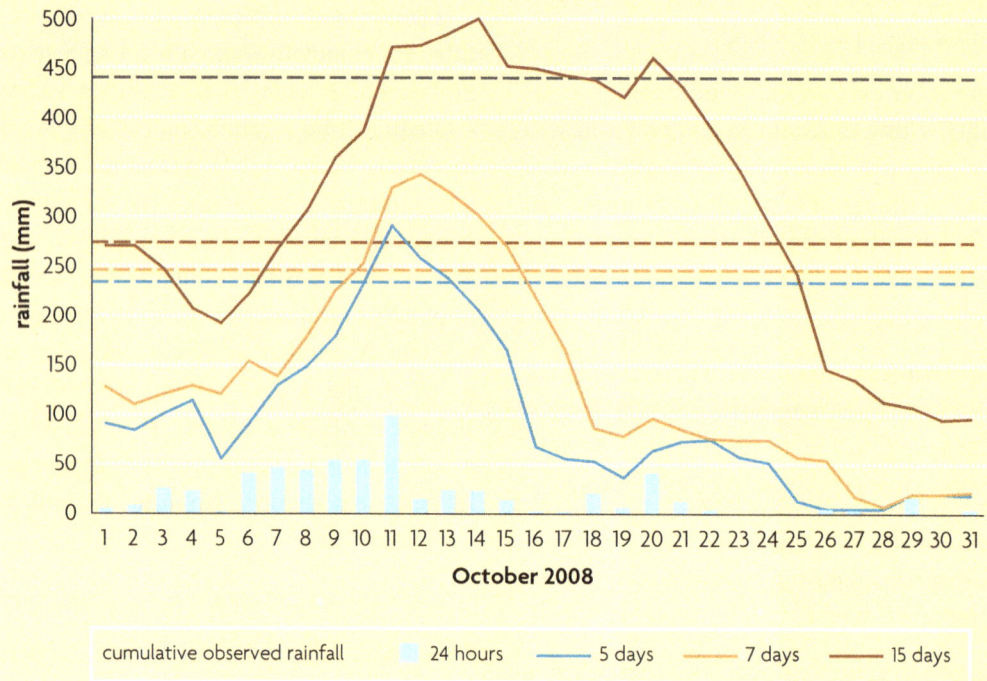

RAINFALL EVENT THRESHOLDS	DATES WHEN CUMULATIVE OBSERVED RAINFALL > THRESHOLD EVENT
- - - 1-in-5-year 5-day event	each day: October 10–13
- - - 1-in-5-year 7-day event	each day: October 10–15
- - - 1-in-5-year 15-day event	each day: October 7–24
- - - 1-in-50-year 15-day event	each day: October 11–21 except October 19

ects for major storm events affecting countries or whole regions:

- Rainfall data and recurrence interval rainfall event data from the relevant meteorological office

- Remote sensing imagery and rainfall intensity calculations associated with major storm events (from the National Oceanic and Atmospheric Administration, National Hurricane Center, or similar agency)

- Consultant reports containing rainfall event data (intensity, duration, and frequency)

9.5.3 Cracks in houses

Cracks in concrete structures can provide useful clues to the stability of a slope. They are all too common in vulnerable communities with unauthorized housing, as residents construct homes in conditions of marginal slope stability, using limited technical equipment, no specific design criteria, and no reference to a building code (if available):

> Failure to comply with codes is a major cause of vulnerability in buildings. Often perverse incentives make it more attractive for administrators, architects, builders, contractors and even homeowners to circumvent construction standards (UN-Habitat 2009, 3).

A consequence is that, in vulnerable communities, residents do not always appreciate the impact of poor construction on the movement of structures.

TABLE 9.5 Landslides reported pre- and post-project with respect to major rainfall events in the Eastern Caribbean

COMMUNITY	NUMBER OF HOUSEHOLDS	Pre-MoSSaiC	RAINFALL IMPACT			
			Post-MoSSaiC			
			2006 111 mm, 1-in-4-year 24-hour event	2007 132 mm, 1-in-5-year 24-hour event	2008 340 mm, 1-in-100-year 15-day event	2010 533 mm, > 1-in-500-year 24-hour event
St. Lucia 1	55	Major slides at low rainfall rates	None reported; landslide in adjoining area	None reported	None reported; reactivation of landslide in adjoining area	None reported
St. Lucia 2	428	Major slide and evacuation of 100 homes in adjoining area		None reported	Minor slide within community	Minor slide within community
St. Lucia 3		Major slide		None reported	None reported	None reported
St. Lucia 4		Modest slides affecting properties		None reported	None reported	None reported
St. Lucia 5	20	Retaining wall failures and significant slides			None reported	None reported
St. Lucia 6	60	Major previous slide with several lost houses; subsequent minor landslides				None reported
St. Lucia 7	30	Landslide potentially threatening highway				None reported
St. Lucia 8	40	Landslides with two houses lost				None reported
St. Lucia 9	21	Landslide with one house lost				None reported
St. Lucia 10	20	Landslide and collapsed retaining wall				None reported
Dominica 1	72	Major slides		None reported	None reported	n.a.

Note: n.a. = not applicable. Blank cells indicate that the project had not been implemented at the time of the rainfall event. Major rainfall events that triggered landslides in St. Lucia and/or Dominica were as follows:':
- 2006: September 2–3
- 2007: Hurricane Dean, August 16–18
- 2008: October 9–24
- 2010: Hurricane Tomas, October 30 (rainfall data for Castries, St. Lucia)

Although structural cracks may be the first indication of slope movement, there are a variety of reasons for cracks:

- Shallow foundations in deep residual soils can move when soil water conditions change;

residents often inappropriately attribute these changing conditions to slope instability.

- Too little cement in the mix, insufficient reinforcement, poor design, and other ele-

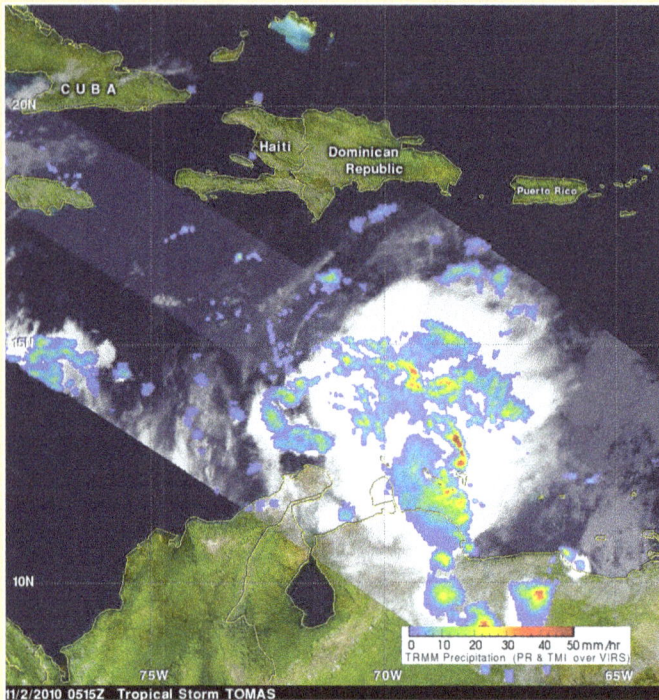

FIGURE 9.6 Benchmarking major rainstorms with satellite imagery

Source: Image courtesy of National Aeronautics and Space Administration.

ments of poor construction can result in inappropriate or uneven loading on a structure.

- Most buildings experience cracking naturally at some point during their service life.

It is important to attempt to distinguish between cracks in buildings caused by land movement, poor construction, or a combination of both. Building cracks are frequently a cause of concern to residents, but are rarely investigated in a systematic manner that fosters risk reduction or reassures residents.

Evidence base

Monitoring the changes in structural crack width helps determine the cause of cracking and the remedial work that should be specified. Because crack monitoring takes time, it is essential to begin at the earliest opportunity and continue throughout the period of inspection and investigation.

Cracks in structures can be monitored simply and inexpensively using crack monitoring gauges (see section 9.5.3) in order to distinguish types of crack behavior and causes:

- **Static:** not increasing in width, and hence not a cause for concern

- **Cyclic:** the crack opens and then partially closes, following a cyclic pattern, likely due to shrinking and swelling of the soil caused by seasonal changes in soil water conditions on the slope

- **Progressive:** a steady increase in width over time, which may suggest that there is ground movement (slope instability) and that the foundations are inadequate to protect the structure (figure 9.7).

9.5.4 Surface and subsurface water

MoSSaiC drainage interventions are designed to capture surface water and reduce infiltration into slope materials in order to improve slope stability. The twofold effect on slope hydrological processes should be a reduction in both unmanaged surface water runoff and the moisture content of slope materials in landslide-prone locations. Changes in surface water flows and saturated soils can be observed by residents, and subsurface water levels can be monitored with simple methods.

Interpreting the causes of erosion and saturation

Residents are often concerned about surface water flows or the emergence of groundwater around their house causing soil erosion and affecting house foundations (figure 9.8a). Although erosion is not a landslide process, it can indicate inadequate surface water management and lead to oversteepening at the base of slopes. Saturated conditions can be caused by a shallow (near-surface) water table emerging locally at the soil surface as return flow, and can potentially lead to soil erosion and undermining of foundations (figure 9.8b).

Evidence base

Use the slope process map (chapter 5) to identify the locations of surface water flows and saturation prior to the project. Revisit these

FIGURE 9.7 Assessing and monitoring structural cracks

a. Cracks in structure attributable to poor construction (insufficient pile depth).

b and c. Worsening of cracks attributable to a progressive landslide which continued to move over a four-year period, finally resulted in a complete loss of property.

a. Surface water.

b. Subsurface water.

locations after project completion to determine if the slope hydrology has changed. Indi-cate postproject slope hydrology conditions on a plan of the implemented drainage works.

Consider monitoring water tables close to properties in the following locations:

- Where saturated soils occur
- In areas prone to instability
- Downslope of intercept drains.

For example, figure 9.9 shows a 20 degree slope, upslope of which is a zone of significant topographic convergence. Despite the shallow nature of the topography, the water table is close to the soil surface and is the cause of instability. Note the presence of dasheen, a potential indicator of near-surface saturated

FIGURE 9.9 Convergence of water upslope results in slope instability and property destruction on shallow slope

FIGURE 9.10 Drain performance

a. Discharge in a stepped drain during a major storm event indicates adequate capacity.

b. Resident notes maximum depth of observed flow in a recently constructed drain during a storm event.

soil water conditions (see section 3.5.5). The water table depths in such an area could be monitored to ascertain whether, over time, an upslope drainage intervention has had a beneficial effect in lowering the water table.

Water tables can be monitored simply, efficiently, and inexpensively using low-tech piezometer systems (section 9.7.4). These simple piezometers take the place of costly automated monitoring and data-logging devices. Where community participation in the project has been high, residents may carry out monitoring themselves after some basic instruction.

9.5.5 Drain performance

Drain performance should be carefully monitored after project completion. Government engineers and community task teams should organize site visits during major storm events to check drain capacity (figure 9.10a). Additionally, residents can be asked to indicate, record, or recollect observed maximum flow depths in drains relating to the project (figure 9.10b).

The following comprises the evidence base for drain performance:

- Depth of flow during and after heavy rainfall

- Rainfall data (intensity, volume, and duration) for extreme events

- Evidence of blockages or overflowing

- Evidence of cracks and leaks

9.5.6 Environmental health benefits

In poorly drained areas with inadequate sanitation, urban runoff mixes with excreta, spreading pathogens around communities and increasing health risks from various waterborne diseases (Parkinson 2003) (figure 9.11). These circumstances allow the transmission of a number of significant diseases, including diarrheal diseases and malaria (table 9.6).

Stagnant water also provides a breeding ground for the *Aedes aegypti* and *Aedes albopictus* mosquitoes that spread dengue fever. Dengue fever is endemic to most tropical countries, and cases have increased in many regions in recent years. Similarly, there has also been an increase in the number of cases of the more severe dengue hemorraghic fever in Latin America and the Caribbean (figure 9.12).

The primary method of controlling *Aedes aegypti* is by eliminating breeding habitats (figure 9.13). This may be achieved by effective drainage, emptying containers of water, or adding insecticides or biological control agents to these areas. Reducing areas of stagnant water is the preferred method of control, given the potential negative health effects of insecticides.

Residents in some communities with MoSSaiC interventions have noted that their children's health has improved due to less stagnant water and that the number of mosquitoes has been reduced. By improving surface water drainage and reducing stagnant water, it is possible that MoSSaiC projects can reduce the number of suitable habitats for the mosquitoes that spread dengue fever. Evidence of the effect of MoSSaiC on environ-

FIGURE 9.11 Stagnant water and disease transmission: The health consequences of poor drainage

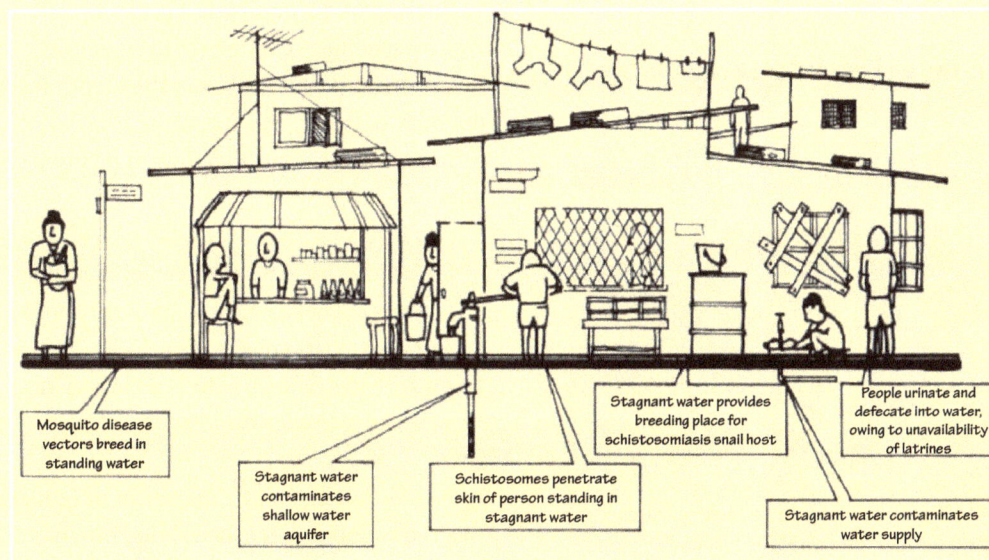

Source: Cairncross and Ouano 1991.

TABLE 9.6 Transmission routes of water-related diseases

CLASSIFICATION	TRANSMISSION ROUTE	EXAMPLE OF DISEASE TRANSMITTED
Waterborne	Through ingestion of pathogens in drinking water	• Diarrheal diseases • Enteric fevers, such as typhoid • Hepatitis A
Water washed	Through incidental ingestion of pathogens in the course of other activities; results from having insufficient water for bathing and hygiene	• Diarrheal diseases • Trachoma • Scabies
Water based	Through an aquatic invertebrate host; results from repeated physical contact with contaminated water	• Guinea worm • Schistosomiasis
Water-related insect vector	Through an insect vector that breeds in or near water	• Malaria (parasite) and yellow fever (virus)

Source: Zwane and Kremer 2007.

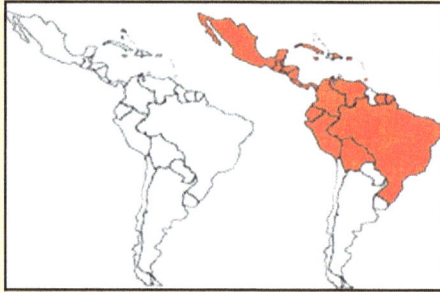

FIGURE 9.12 Laboratory-confirmed dengue hemorraghic fever in the Americas prior to 1981 and 1981–2003

Source: Centers for Disease Control and Prevention, http://www.cdc.gov/Dengue/epidemiology/index.html.

FIGURE 9.13 MoSSaiC and mosquito breeding habitats

a. MoSSaiC interventions can help control mosquito habitats by removing areas of stagnant water drainage.

b. A discarded old freezer is a perfect habitat for mosquito breeding.

mental health issues is currently anecdotal, but could be investigated further.

9.5.7 Economic appraisal: Project value for money

Economic appraisal refers to various analytic methods that investigate whether projects and programs deliver value for money. The scope of an economic appraisal can range from calculation of simple measures of the economy, efficiency, and effectiveness of a project to analysis of the costs and benefits of that project over its lifetime. Ideally, an economic appraisal should be carried out both during the project planning phase and as part of the evaluation of the completed project.

A particular challenge in assessing the direct benefits of DRR lies in the fact that such benefits occur in the future as avoided costs rather than as a continual flow of positive benefits:

> the benefits are not tangible; they are...disasters that did not happen. So we should not be surprised that preventive policies receive support that is more often rhetorical than substantive (Annan 1999, 3).

It is vital that economic appraisal of landslide risk reduction projects be carried out, not only as a means of ensuring accountability, but in order to build the evidence base for ex ante landslide mitigation.

Economic appraisal of MoSSaiC projects

Economic appraisal of MoSSaiC projects must consider whether the project budget has been spent in the right way and on the right things—whether the project has been efficient and effective. For example, a particular MoSSaiC project may use resources very economically and efficiently and build a substantial network of well-constructed drains in a community. However, if the drains are in the wrong location or are unnecessary (not an appropriate solution to the landslide hazard), then the project will not have met its objective of reducing landslide risk and will not be cost-effective or physically effective. Another project may be very effective in reducing the physical landslide hazard, but in an inefficient way by overspending on materials and other inputs. This would lead to the conclusion that the project has been effective in meeting a key outcome, but not in a cost-effective manner.

This subsection outlines two possible approaches to the economic appraisal of completed MoSSaiC projects:

- Simple measures of project value for money based on the monetary costs of producing the desired number of units of project outputs and/or outcomes in order to meet the project objectives

- Cost-benefit analysis, which seeks to quantify all of the costs and benefits of the project in monetary terms, including items for which the market does not provide a satisfactory measure of economic value

Simple measures of project value for money

The MCU should use the generic questions on project economy, efficiency, and effectiveness in table 9.7 to create a list of questions directly related to MoSSaiC project evaluation (measured in terms of inputs, expenditure, outputs, and outcomes).

This approach to appraising project value for money is straightforward to understand and use. It works well where there are a small number of clearly defined and measurable inputs, outputs, outcomes, and objectives, and where these measures are the same for multiple projects. The value for money of each project is demonstrated in relation to comparable projects. This approach is not appropriate for assessing complex projects with multiple interrelated objectives, or for interproject comparisons where the performance metrics are different for each project.

Cost-benefit analysis

Governments and donors might agree that mitigation is a good idea, but to answer the question "will it pay?" requires evidence of the likely returns on investment made in the project. Cost-benefit analysis provides a framework for monetizing the present and future costs and benefits associated with different projects—either at the project appraisal stage or as an ex post assessment. While the simple cost-efficiency and cost-effectiveness questions described above consider projects in relation to each other, cost-benefit analysis allows the absolute value of projects to be quantified.

Cost-benefit analysis of specific DRR projects has consistently found that mitigation pays. In general, for every $1 invested, between $2 and $4 are returned in terms of avoided or reduced disaster impacts (Mechler 2005; Moench, Mechler, and Stapleton 2007). Although such statements can make a con-

TABLE 9.7 Simple questions to help measure MoSSaiC project value for money

MEASURE OF VALUE	GENERIC QUESTION	MoSSaiC PROJECT EVALUATION EXAMPLE
Economy	Have project resources been used carefully to minimize expenditure, time, or effort?	Has the method of procurement of materials (sand, cement, reinforcement, etc.) enabled the selection of the cheapest supplier? (The cheapest supplier is not necessarily the best supplier.)
Efficiency	Has the project delivered the required outputs for a minimum input of cost, time, or effort; or obtained maximum benefit from a given level of input?	How many dollars (input) did it cost to construct a meter of drain (output), and is this unit cost higher or lower than it should have been (given environmental factors such as the need to carry materials to the site)?
Effectiveness	Have the project outputs and outcomes enabled project objectives to be met as fully as possible?	Are the new drains and roof gutters capturing the anticipated proportion of rainwater and surface water runoff? Has slope stability been improved?

vincing case for risk reduction, they should be treated with caution (Twigg 2004), as studies are few and far between—at least in the published literature—and are usually presented as statements of fact without explaining how the calculations were made. As Twigg (2004, 358) notes, "The readiness with which publications on disasters repeat such assertions should perhaps be worrying, as it suggests that little substantiated data is available."

Because such studies are relatively scarce, especially in developing countries and with respect to landslide risk reduction, investment in DRR remains low in the face of numerous competing development opportunities (Benson and Twigg 2004).

Use the following steps as a guide in undertaking a cost-benefit analysis of a MoSSaiC project.

1. ***Monetize the costs and benefits of the project.*** If these are given in physical or welfare terms, different methods can be used to convert them to monetary values. For DRR projects, the main physical benefits are the avoided future disaster costs (rebuilding, relocating, and replacing possessions). Thus, the cost of landslides with and without the project, and the difference between the two scenarios, should be calculated. To determine these costs, the nature of the anticipated landslide hazard (type and magnitude) needs to be known at a spatial scale relating to the landslide hazard reduction project. This allows identification of elements exposed to the hazard (such as houses) and estimation of the likely damage caused (the landslide cost). There may also be less tangible environmental, welfare, and social benefits to the community. In some analyses, a value of life assumption is made to account for potential loss of life; assigning such values can be controversial, and they are generally utilized in wide-area studies where multiple hazards and risk reduction projects are being compared.

2. ***Estimate the probability of landslide costs occurring in the future.*** In the case

of landslide hazard reduction, this requires calculation of the probability of landslide occurrence with and without intervention. These calculations can be made using a physically based slope stability model to determine the rainfall return frequency required to trigger a landslide.

3. ***Discount all expected future landslide costs into present values according to how far into the future they are expected to occur.*** The present value depends on the discount rate and project lifetime specified (i.e., how long the project infrastructure will continue to provide a reduction in landslide hazard).

4. ***Use cost-benefit analysis decision criteria to determine project value for money.*** Standard criteria include the benefit-cost ratio, the net expected present value of the project, and the internal rate of return. The benefit-cost ratio of a landslide risk reduction project is the ratio of the cost of the initial investment in hazard reduction to the difference in the net expected value of landslide costs before and after the project (the benefit in terms of avoided costs). The net expected present value is simply the project benefits minus the costs. It is positive where the project results in a reduction in future landslide costs (and potential additional benefits to the community) that outweigh the cost of the intervention. Conversely, the net expected present value could be negative if the project has the effect of increasing the landslide hazard or if a landslide destroys part of the project.

An example of a MoSSaiC project cost-benefit analysis is given in section 9.7.5. A helpful review of general cost-benefit analysis tools and resources can be found at the ProVention Consortium website (http://www.preventionweb.net/files/8088_WP1highres1.pdf).

The results of cost-benefit analysis should be used in the context of other project information when evaluating the project as a whole:

The question often left for us to ponder when reviewing Cost-benefit Analysis (CBA) on a particular hazard mitigation project is not what values we place on the moneterized impacts but rather how large or small are these compared to the "value" of the non-monetized impacts. CBA alone cannot answer this question, but human experience and reflection can (Ganderton 2005).

9.5.8 Adoption of good landslide risk reduction practices

One of the key objectives of MoSSaiC is to encourage individuals, communities, and governments to adopt practices that reduce urban landslide hazards. Chapter 8 outlined the process of behavioral change in terms of a ladder of adoption (from perception and awareness, to knowledge and action, and finally to adoption of MoSSaiC), factors affecting motivations and intentions to act, and strategies for communicating and capacity building. The resulting behavioral change strategy was summarized in the form of an outcome map (section 8.7.2).

Use this outcome map to evaluate whether the planned outputs (communication, capacity-building activities) have been delivered. To evaluate the effectiveness of the behavioral change strategy, look for evidence of adoption of good landslide risk reduction practices (discussed in this section) and policies (section 9.5.9) during and after the project.

Community evidence

Evidence of communities adopting good landslide risk reduction practices might typically involve the following:

- Installation of drains around houses using the residents' own resources

- Installation of roof guttering and adoption of roof water harvesting by residents

- Reduction in the dumping of garbage in drains

- Maintenance and cleaning of drains around homes and, more widely, during commu-

nity-organized events to clear the drainage network and debris traps

- Fewer cut slopes excavated at the rear of properties

- An increased general awareness among the majority of residents of the need for good drainage practices, such as the prompt reporting of leaking water supply pipes to the water company

Government evidence

At the government level, decision makers should seek to embed the above practices into larger-scale infrastructure and community development projects. Evidence of adoption can include the following:

- Using appropriate scientific methods for assessing slope stability prior to construction on landslide-prone slopes

- Including the provision of adequate drainage in road and footpath construction projects on slopes

- Including specific contractual requirements for drain cleaning and maintenance when new infrastructure is constructed

- Incorporating slope stability assessment and drainage standards into planning protocols and other policy instruments

- Generating awareness and providing training for government practitioners involved in activities that may affect slope stability.

9.5.9 Development of new landslide risk reduction policies

Evidence-based policy making is becoming more central to development funding and policies. Policy makers are increasingly asked "to explain not just what policy options they propose, and why they consider them appropriate, but also their understanding of their likely effectiveness" (Segone 2008, 28). This approach requires a move from opinions (which rely on ideals, speculation, or the selective use of evidence) to evidence from project evaluations, academic research, and experience (figure 9.14).

FIGURE 9.14 Dynamics of policy making

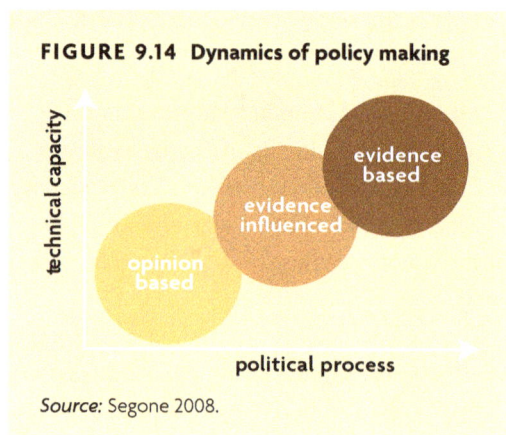

Source: Segone 2008.

The move from opinion to evidence, and the adoption of new evidence-based policies, tends to be both strategic and incremental. The evidence base is developed through a cycle of pilot projects, project evaluation, recognition of project performance and value by policy makers and funders, increased policy commitment to the initiative, and the resourcing of similar initiatives. This strategic incremental approach can create favorable conditions for reform over the longer run, thus enabling behavioral change in the institutional and policy environment (Lavergne 2004, 2005; World Bank 2004). In contrast, incremental but nonstrategic temporary work-arounds cannot create conditions for policy change. The objective has to be that of striking a sensible trade-off between comprehensive and incremental reforms—seeking early wins for stakeholders and supporting policy champions and cross-agency teams that can bring along others of like mind (World Bank 2004).

MoSSaiC projects and evidence-based policy

MoSSaiC projects provide policy makers with both the scientific basis for landslide hazard reduction in communities and the evidence of effective solutions delivered on the ground:

> To change the perceptions of individuals, as well of those of Governments regarding the most cost-effective way of reducing risk, is best achieved when there is clear evidence of

interventions having actually worked (World Bank 2003, 212).

The cycle of interactions among government, communities, and international agencies can be used as a platform for behavioral change, as shown in figure 9.15, which depicts six steps from the formation of the MCU (step 1) through the recognition of on-the-ground projects by agencies (step 4) and the move to a wider acceptance of preventative policies and implementation (step 6). This cycle is reflected in the project sequence and structure of this book: starting with establishing government teams (chapter 2), moving to understanding and implementing landslide hazard reduction measures through community participation (chapters 3–8), and ending with the development of the evidence base through project evaluation (chapter 9).

The MCU, project decision makers, and funders should use this subsection to identify how MoSSaiC can provide an evidence base for ex ante landslide risk reduction and to evaluate how effective the project has been in influencing policy.

The MCU should present MoSSaiC project progress, outputs, and outcomes to policy makers in a way that answers their questions and enables them to make evidence-based decisions. Specific actions that can help support evidence-based policy are listed in table 9.8.

Evaluating MoSSaiC influence on policy

Evidence that could be recorded as policy uptake might include the following:

- Inclusion of MoSSaiC in government disaster risk management planning documents (e.g., Government of St. Lucia 2006, 26–27) and promotion in regional disaster risk management forums

- Community-to-community knowledge transfer (figure 9.15, step 3)

- Interest, visits, and support from new donors (step 4)

FIGURE 9.15 Process of strategic incrementalism

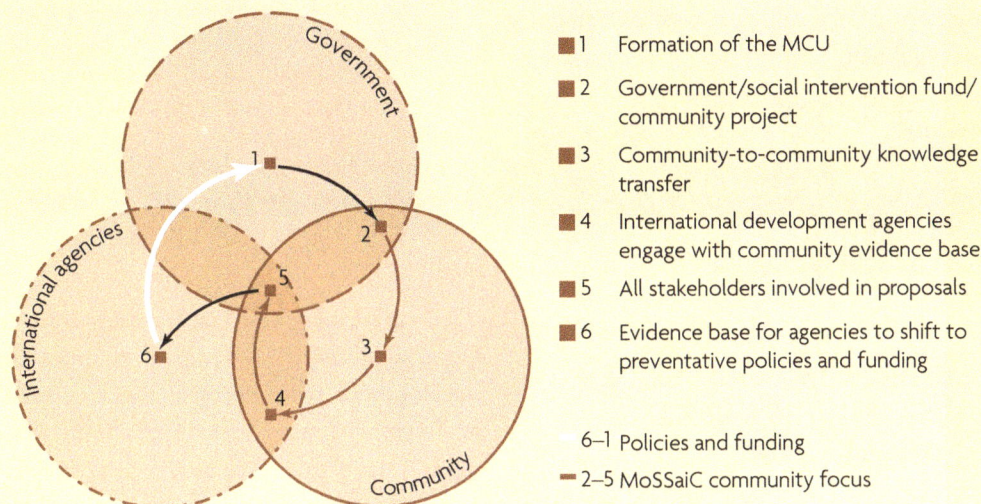

1 Formation of the MCU

2 Government/social intervention fund/
   community project

3 Community-to-community knowledge
   transfer

4 International development agencies
   engage with community evidence base

5 All stakeholders involved in proposals

6 Evidence base for agencies to shift to
   preventative policies and funding

6–1 Policies and funding
2–5 MoSSaiC community focus

Source: Anderson at al. 2010, based on Segone 2008.

TABLE 9.8 Requirements for achieving evidence-based policy in ex ante disaster risk reduction

CATEGORY	GENERIC REQUIREMENT	MoSSaiC REQUIREMENT
Evidence-based policy require-ments	Require the publication of the evidence base for policy decisions	Provide project outputs from community selection, mapping, hazard assessment, and drainage design (chapters 4–6)
	Require departmental spending bids to provide a supporting evidence base	Provide supporting evidence from previous MoSSaiC interventions, including evidence of value for money and results of cost-benefit analysis (chapter 9)
	Provide open access to information leading to more informed citizens and interest groups	Communicate project information through community participation and mass media, and encourage empowerment of stake-holders (chapters 5 and 8)
Facilitating better evidence use	Encourage better collaboration across internal services	Encourage collaboration of the MCU and government task team members (chapter 2)
	Cast external researchers more as partners than as contractors	Encourage inclusion of academics and researchers in the MCU or government task teams (chapter 2)
	Integrate analytical staff at all stages of the policy development process	Provide opportunities for the MCU and government task teams to present the project to decision makers (chapter 2)

Source: Nutley, Davies, and Walter 2002.

- An enlarged group of stakeholders (government, donors, social funds) working together and submitting a new proposal for MoSSaiC interventions (step 5)

- Evidence of donors themselves promoting and proposing MoSSaiC interventions (step 6).

9.5.10 Finalizing the project evaluation process

The MCU should decide with government decision makers and funders who will be responsible for project evaluation both during and after the project. The responsibility for medium- and long-term postproject evaluation (or monitoring) may need to reside with a local agency that already has a mandate, or research program, for disaster risk assessment and management.

MILESTONE 9:
Evaluation framework agreed upon and implemented

9.6 ADDRESSING LANDSLIDE RISK DRIVERS OVER THE LONGER TERM

The drivers of landslide risk relate to the hazard (the landslide event) and the vulnerability of exposed elements (such as people, communities, and infrastructure) to damage by that hazard event. Since the primary aim of MoSSaiC is to identify and reduce physical landslide hazard drivers affecting the most vulnerable urban communities, the evaluation process (sections 9.3–9.5) is concerned with project effectiveness in reducing landslide hazard and improving slope management practices over short- and medium-scale time frames.

This section considers MoSSaiC as a potential contributor to holistic policy responses to landslide risk and trends in landslide risk drivers (both physical and societal) over longer time scales:

- DRR under present and future climate scenarios

- Risk transfer through insurance at individual and national scales

- "No regrets" landslide risk management given uncertain trends in risk drivers.

9.6.1 Disaster risk reduction and climate proofing

DRR and climate change adaptation policies are, to some extent, complementary even though they have been evolving independently until recently:

DRR can deal with current climate variability and be the first line defence against climate change, being therefore an essential part of adaptation. Conversely, for DRR to be successful, account needs to be taken of the shifting risks associated with climate change, and ensure that measures do not increase vulnerability to climate change in the medium to long-term (Mitchell and van Aalst 2008, 1).

"Climate proofing" is shorthand for the identification and reduction of risks posed to development projects by climate variability and change. Today the need for climate proofing is greater than ever as risk drivers change (see section 9.6.3) and increase the hazard, exposure, and vulnerability of communities and regions to climate-related disasters.

Climate proofing in the most vulnerable communities requires urgent attention because the destruction of, or damage to, unauthorized housing is one of the most common and serious impacts of many extreme-weather events (Parry et al. 2009). Unauthorized housing is often not constructed to withstand such events even under current climatic conditions:

> ...property is built at a substandard level and does not conform even to minimal building codes and standards. This widespread failure to build enough weather resistance into existing and expanding human settlements is the main reason for the existence of an adaptation deficit... The evidence suggests strongly that the adaptation deficit continues to increase because losses from extreme events continue to increase. In other words, societies are becoming less well adapted to current climate. Such a process of development has been called "maladaptation" (UNFCCC 2007, 99).

MoSSaiC can contribute to a planned harmonization and alignment of incentives of climate change adaptation in developing countries. Table 9.9 sets out key elements of MoSSaiC that can be regarded as contributing to climate proofing in vulnerable communities.

TABLE 9.9 Summary of MoSSaiC elements contributing to climate proofing

CURRENT ISSUE RELATING TO LANDSLIDES IN VULNERABLE COMMUNITIES	ELEMENT OF MoSSaiC METHODOLOGY THAT COULD CONTRIBUTE TO WIDER CLIMATE-PROOFING AGENDA
Rainfall-triggered landslide hazard	
Frequent landslides triggered by low-intensity or low-duration rainfalls; potential for major landslide events with high-intensity/-duration, low-frequency rainfall events	Rainfall-triggered landslide hazard reduced through surface water management in vulnerable communities
Surface water management issues on slopes	
Absence of roof water capture and surface water drainage leading to rapid rainfall runoff, surface water infiltration, saturated soils, and localized flooding	Household roof and gray water capture and surface water management, reducing landslide hazard and potentially improving environmental health issues by reducing stagnant water
Water supply issues	
Piped water supply issues, but limited capture of rainwater	Integrated rainwater harvesting and storage for use by households provides reliable supply for washing/cleaning when piped water is unavailable
Damage to houses by extreme rainfall events (e.g., hurricanes)	
Roof and house structures vulnerable to damage by strong winds	Retrofitting of hurricane straps increases the likelihood of roofs staying intact in storm events, ensuring continued rainwater capture
Public awareness of landslide hazard causes and solutions	
Need for awareness of good slope management practices and how to reduce landslide hazards at the community scale	Community engagement throughout the MoSSaiC project helps deliver better understanding of landslide risk and good slope management and construction practices
Landslide risk reduction policy	
Lack of policy regarding landslide risk reduction in vulnerable communities	MoSSaiC methodology discussed by international agencies in the context of contributing to climate proofing (World Bank 2010a) encourages governments to consider community-based policies and approaches to landslide risk reduction

9.6.2 Connecting hazard reduction and insurance

The aim of a holistic landslide risk reduction strategy should be to reduce the degree to which vulnerable communities and governments have to bear, or cope with, the impact of landslides; since "what cannot be prevented or insured, has to be borne" (World Bank 2010b, 154). Landslide hazard, exposure and vulnerability reduction, and risk transfer strategies can each contribute to a reduction in the level of risk carried by communities and governments. Some of these preventative, insurance, and coping mechanisms are highlighted in table 9.10.

Despite recognition of the importance of risk prevention, there is still comparatively little practical implementation of risk reduction measures on the ground in developing countries (Wamsler 2006). Successful MoSSaiC projects thus represent a significant opportunity to reduce overall landslide risk and the risk burden on communities and governments.

This section considers how hazard reduction initiatives such as MoSSaiC might be connected to risk insurance for households in vulnerable communities, and how ex ante government investment in risk reduction might reduce the resource gap for ex post disaster risk financing (figure 9.16).

TABLE 9.10 Holistic context of prevention, insurance, and coping strategies of individuals, communities, and governments

RISK REDUCTION MEASURE	INDIVIDUAL/HOUSEHOLD	COMMUNITY	GOVERNMENT
Prevention	Investment to protect assets	Community training programs and participation in risk mitigation construction	Public works in support of mitigation measures
Self-insurance	Owning financial and nonfinancial assets	Local borrowing	Adequate physical and social infrastructure
Market insurance	Property and catastrophe insurance	Microfinance	Sovereign budget insurance and catastrophe bonds
Coping	Running down stocks of human and physical resources	Interhousehold transfers and private remittances	Disaster aid funds, social investment projects by social funds, and other cash-based safety nets

Source: World Bank 2010b.

Note: MoSSaiC is focused on preventative measures (highlighted).

FIGURE 9.16 Generalized impact of MoSSaiC interventions on reducing the burden of coping

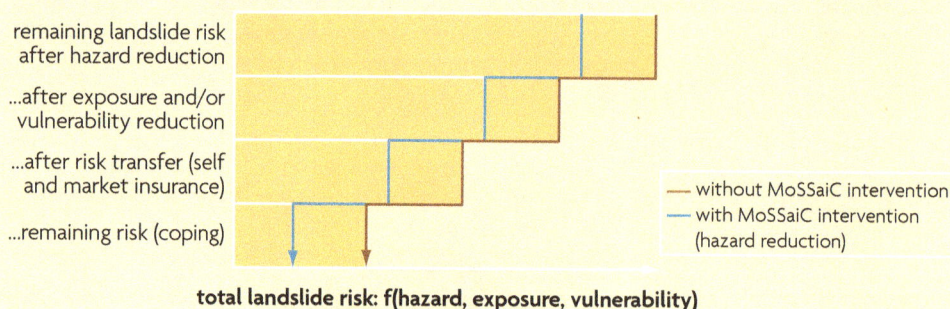

Challenges of insuring households in vulnerable communities

Household risk from disasters, including landslides, can theoretically be transferred through the insurance market. However, increasing the disaster resilience of vulnerable households through schemes that aim to spread risks faces major constraints:

- The most socioeconomically vulnerable households have income profiles that are far below minimum acceptable thresholds and virtually no capacity to save.

- The budgets of these most vulnerable households clearly have many demands that are more pressing than insurance, whose costs are up front and payoffs far off.

- The most vulnerable require direct and immediate assistance after a disaster—schemes that pool losses will not suffice.

Table 9.11 summarizes these constraints from the standpoints of government, insurers, and households.

Insurance solutions can only support effective adaptation where they are implemented alongside measures to reduce disaster risk and increase societal resilience. If not embedded in a comprehensive risk reduction strategy, insurance may actually encourage risk-taking behavior, potentially leading to greater fatalities and damage.

TABLE 9.11 Design issues and challenges for linking risk reduction and insurance

CHALLENGE	GOVERNMENT	INSURANCE	HOUSEHOLD
Generic (apply to all)	• Commit to cover upfront program development costs • Manage perception of risk and benefits (long term) versus costs • Coordinate with postdisaster assistance to avoid disincentives • Build institutional capacity	• Commit to engage in dialogue about risk reduction • Design innovative longer-term insurance tools applicable in developing country context • Design tools to address moral hazard	• Upfront costs/affordability • Perception of risk • Perception of benefit (particularly given time scales of benefit) • Availability of postdisaster assistance
Awareness raising and risk information	• Develop appropriate dissemination channels for risk information	• Develop appropriate dissemination channels for risk information	• Engage in insurance literacy programs • Need tools to build ability to understand risk information
Risk pricing (i.e., a price signal to incentivize risk reduction)	• Address equity issues to ensure affordability of and access to insurance for vulnerable/poorer communities in high-risk areas	• Need high-resolution risk analysis • Lower transaction costs (expense and time for verification of risk and loss in developing countries)	• Upfront costs of risk reduction versus relatively small potential premium adjustment
Enabling conditions and regulation	• Governance • Legal frameworks • Monitoring and enforcement	• Potential limits to competitiveness and implications for actuarial soundness of insurance	• Understanding of DRR and insurance • Availability of technical assistance programs (adaptation support)
Financing risk reduction	• Establish funds or invest in ex ante risk reduction measures that are independent of election cycles or other political considerations (to overcome barriers, i.e., no reward for catastrophe avoided)	• Upfront costs • Need close collaboration with public sector to coordinate risk reduction compatible with insurance programs, risk information • "Who pays versus who benefits"; insurer may see little direct benefit from investment	• Potential of risk reduction for insurance coverage (exchange of work time devoted to risk reduction measures for insurance coverage)
Risk reduction as a prerequisite for insurance	• Voluntary participation in insurance programs with prerequisite of ongoing DRR	• Competitive market conditions may work against incentives if not coordinated with public sector	• Need knowledge of appropriate risk reduction techniques and options

Source: Adapted from UNFCCC 2009.

Linking climate proofing and household insurance

A major challenge for disaster-prone low-income countries is to develop instruments with adequate incentives (inevitably entailing subsidies) that will make it possible for the poor to participate in disaster risk mitigation programs such as climate proofing and insurance.

It is worth noting the experience of an insurance program that ran in St. Lucia for six years (OAS 2003). The National Research and Development Foundation in St. Lucia offered a hurricane-resistant home improvement program for low-income earners. The program trained local builders in safer construction, offered small loans to families wishing to upgrade their homes, and provided the services of a trained building inspector who approved materials to be purchased and verified that minimum standards were met. Low-income homeowners who strengthened their homes through the program could obtain property insurance underwritten by a regional subsidiary of a U.K.–based insurance company and established through a local broker. The insurance plan covered major natural disasters. Figure 9.17 shows the management structure of the loan process and associated insurance scheme.

The insurance scheme was mandatory for recipients of the home improvement loans. Full coverage with a 2 percent deductible was specified in the policies. Premium rates ranged from 0.60 percent for concrete block homes to 1.05 percent for homes made of timber. Between 1996 and November 2002, 345 loans were disbursed within this program, with an average loan size of approximately $4,100 (in 2002 dollars) (OAS 2003).

The program is noteworthy because it is a rare example of targeting insurance to the most vulnerable households, coupling home improvement for natural hazard mitigation with property insurance cover. The home improvement conditionality of the scheme offset the reported "catch-22" insurance position for natural hazard cover alone—namely, that natural hazard insurance premiums are usually very high, as only those likely to make frequent claims consider insuring themselves against them. High premiums associated with hazard cover alone lead to one of two possibilities: the customer decides that the insurance is too expensive and does not insure the property, or the insurance companies decide there will be no profit in underwriting hurricane damage at a premium customers are willing to pay and decline to offer the business.

Being mindful of the possible constraints mentioned above, funders and governments could consider combining an insurance scheme with MoSSaiC projects to create a comprehensive landslide risk management plan in which

- preventative measures are provided (or encouraged) through MoSSaiC projects;

- insurance is available for participating households, assuming a model analogous to that outlined in figure 9.17; and

- should a landslide occur, the government would manage a damage repair program.

Landslide risk reduction and macrofinancing disasters

Insurance is just one of several financial instruments used by governments to fund disaster relief and recovery. Table 9.12 lists a variety of other ex ante and postdisaster financing instruments available to governments. Disaster financing is especially demanding for developing countries because there can be a shortfall, known as a resource gap, between the disaster costs and the funds available to the government to rebuild and provide relief and assistance with the recovery efforts (Mechler et al. 2010). These resource gaps are often greatest immediately after a disaster when funding needs are urgent and high, but funds and financial assistance have not yet been mobilized (Ghesquiere and Mahul 2007).

A country's resource gap is calculated by identifying the probability (or annual recurrence interval) of a disaster event in which net losses exceed all available financial resources (figure 9.18). For some developing countries, a resource gap can be created by a disaster event with as high a probability of occurrence as 1 in 15 years (Mechler et al. 2010).

The frequency and impact of disaster events determine whether it is more effective for governments to invest in risk reduction or risk financing. Generally, risk prevention is more cost-effective for high-probability events with low to medium-size losses, while risk financing targets less frequent, higher-impact events (Mechler et al. 2010). For countries prone to rainfall-triggered landslides and where high-frequency events can trigger a resource gap, it is conceivable that a national program on MoSSaiC projects could contribute to disaster resilience at a national scale.

9.6.3 Anticipating future disaster risk scenarios

In chapter 1, a number of policy issues and trends were identified that affect urban landslide risk in developing countries, including the speed of conventional DRR uptake, the rate of societal change and urbanization, and

FIGURE 9.17 Model used in St. Lucia for hurricane-resistant home improvement program for low-income earners

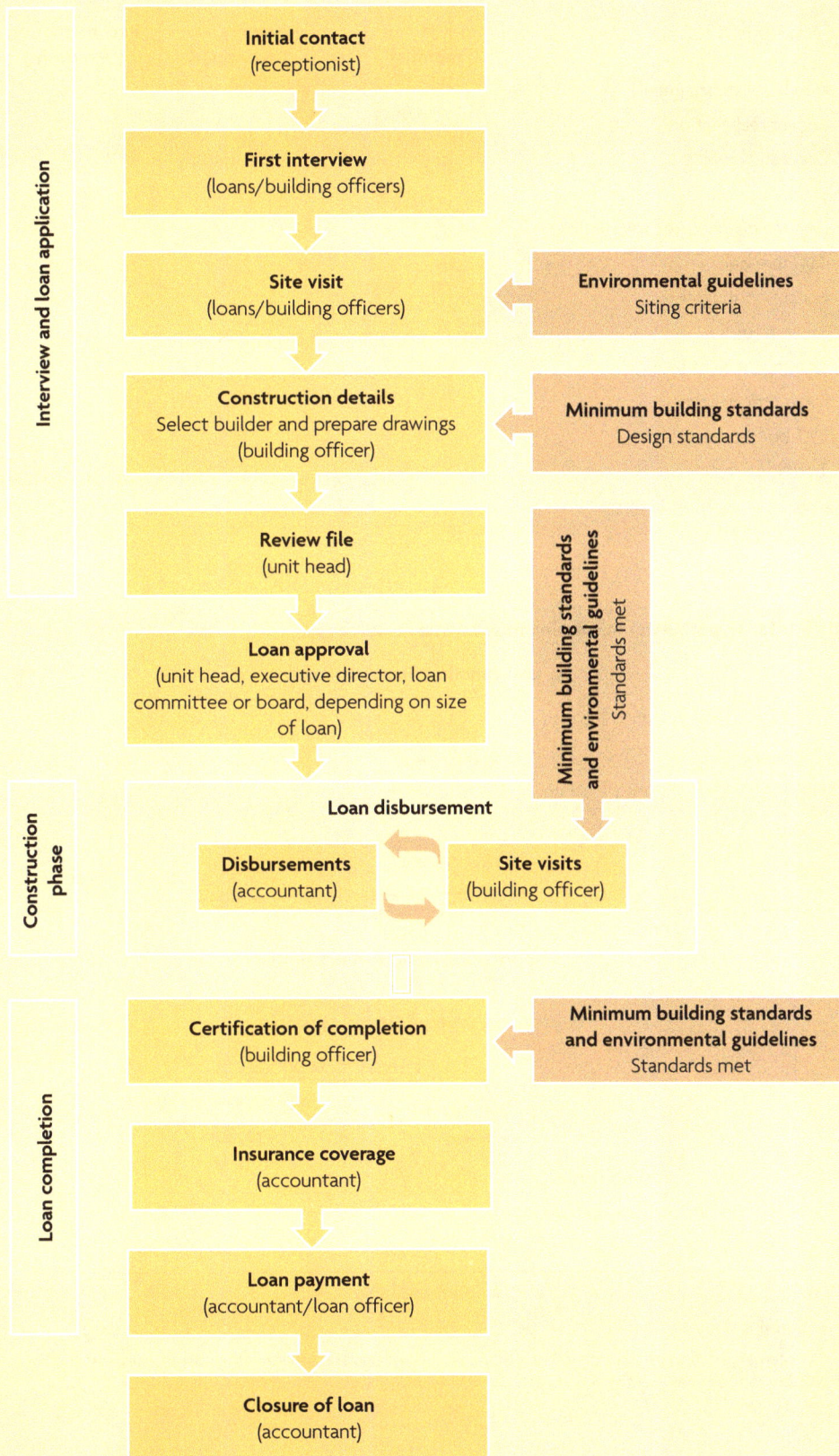

Interview and loan application

- **Initial contact**
  (receptionist)
- **First interview**
  (loans/building officers)
- **Site visit**
  (loans/building officers) ← **Environmental guidelines** Siting criteria
- **Construction details**
  Select builder and prepare drawings
  (building officer) ← **Minimum building standards** Design standards
- **Review file**
  (unit head)
- **Loan approval**
  (unit head, executive director, loan committee or board, depending on size of loan)

Minimum building standards and environmental guidelines Standards met

Construction phase

- **Loan disbursement**
  - **Disbursements** (accountant) ⇄ **Site visits** (building officer)

Loan completion

- **Certification of completion**
  (building officer) ← **Minimum building standards and environmental guidelines** Standards met
- **Insurance coverage**
  (accountant)
- **Loan payment**
  (accountant/loan officer)
- **Closure of loan**
  (accountant)

Source: OAS 2003; reproduced with permission of the OAS General Secretariat.

TABLE 9.12 Sources of postdisaster financing

		Relief (1–3 months)			Recovery (3–9 months)		Reconstruction (+9 months)		
Postdisaster financing	Donor assistance (relief)	▓	▓	▓	▓	▓			
	Budget reallocation		▓	▓	▓	▓	▓		
	Domestic credit				▓	▓	▓	▓	▓
	External credit				▓	▓	▓	▓	▓
	Donor assistance (reconstruction)						▓	▓	▓
	Tax increase							▓	▓
Ex ante financing	Budget contingencies	▓	▓	▓	▓				
	Reserve fund	▓	▓	▓	▓	▓			
	Contingent debt facility	▓	▓	▓	▓	▓	▓	▓	▓
	Parametric insurance	▓	▓	▓	▓	▓	▓	▓	▓
	CAT bonds	▓	▓	▓	▓	▓	▓	▓	▓
	Traditional insurance		▓	▓	▓	▓	▓	▓	▓

Source: Ghesquiere and Mahul 2007.

FIGURE 9.18 Hypothetical calculation base for the resource gap

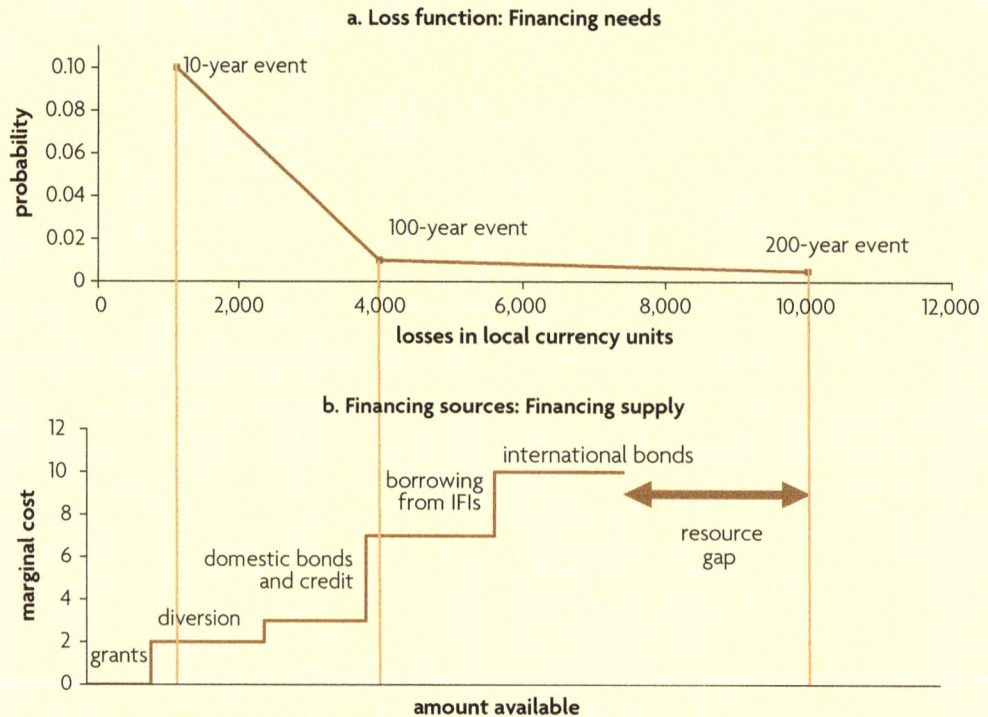

a. Loss function: Financing needs

b. Financing sources: Financing supply

Source: Mechler et al. 2010.

Note: IFI = international finance institution. The resource gap is the shortfall between the cost of a disaster and the funds available to the government to rebuild and provide relief and assistance with the recovery efforts.

possible trends in other human or physical landslide risk drivers. A society may be changing more quickly than DRR policies can be adopted—e.g., in terms of rapid urbanization and a consequent growth in slum populations, leading to the development of communities on landslide-prone slopes, all of which are powerful drivers in a cycle of risk accumulation. Because property on landslide-prone slopes is cheaper to rent, the most vulnerable live in these areas. Further, because unauthorized houses can be built in a matter of days, people can move to urban areas faster than planning authorities can respond.

DRR policies need to take different risk scenarios into account. Scenarios are "plausible descriptions of possible future states of the world...not a forecast; rather each scenario is one alternative image of how the future can unfold" (IPCC 2011). Identifying future disaster risk scenarios involves thinking about and creatively exploring what is happening now (trends that make headlines—figure 9.19) and projecting what the future holds (Rayner and Malone 1997). However, "in creating scenarios, researchers often extrapolate from the present to posit a future that is 'more of the same'" (Rayner and Malone 1997, 332). The future world of many current DRR approaches is essentially today's world but more so: more mainstreaming, more knowledge transfer, more technology (largely of the same sort), more integration of multihazard mapping. History suggests that such an approach might be unrealistic. Mahmoud et al. (2009, 800) note that

> the simplest baseline future is that of an "official future," a "business as usual" scenario of a widely accepted future state of the world. Most decision makers will not accept future alternatives unless the official future is questioned.

With respect to urban landslide risk, it is possible to define a set of different but plausible alternative future scenarios (figure 9.20) relating to possible trends in human and physical landslide risk drivers. The following two scenarios—which are physically, socially, and politically plausible—illustrate possible opposite extremes of a set of scenarios:

FIGURE 9.19 Media recognition of the world's urban population crossing the 50 percent mark

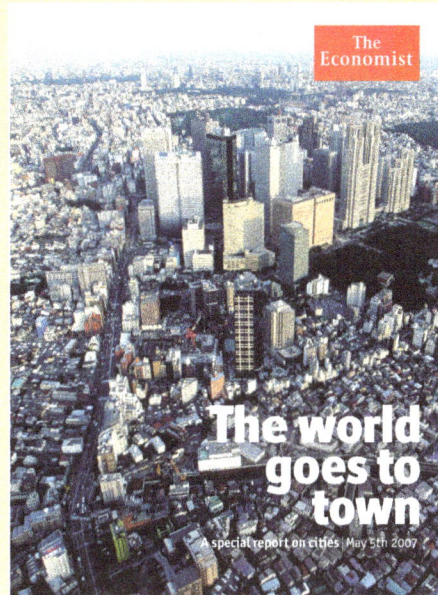

Source: The Economist May 5, 2007.

- **Maximum increase in landslide risk drivers.** This scenario entails an increased number of high-intensity landslide-triggering rainfall events driven by climate change, more high-density vulnerable housing created by urban population growth, and

FIGURE 9.20 Conceptual diagram of a scenario funnel

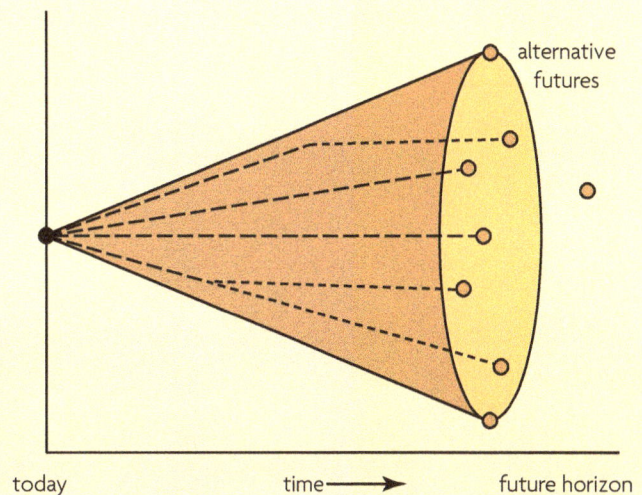

Source: Mahmoud et al. 2009.

absence of planning and construction regulation and enforcement (all of which could be expected to further increase the currently observed landslide risk accumulation).

- *Minimal increase, or even a decrease, in landslide risk drivers.* This scenario assumes no change (or a reduction) in the number of high-intensity landslide-triggering rainfall events, housing density limits enforced on landslide-prone slopes, and implementation of physical and socio-economic measures to improve household resilience (limiting the currently observed landslide risk accumulation).

Between these two extremes, various scenarios for landslide risk drivers could be envisaged, modeled, and analyzed to identify different strategies to address future risk. MoSSaiC contributes to those strategies by addressing current landslide hazard drivers and offsetting potential future increases in those drivers, and provides governments and communities with the science, community, and evidence bases for effective landslide risk reduction over the long term.

9.7 RESOURCES

9.7.1 Who does what

TEAM	RESPONSIBILITY	ACTIONS AND HELPFUL HINTS	CHAPTER SECTION
Funders and policy makers	Awareness of the importance of project evaluation	• Familiarity with the need to have measures of both project outputs and project outcomes	9.2.1
MCU	Establish project KPIs	• Agree on KPIs for both project outputs and outcomes	9.4
	Agree upon an agency to review project outcomes	**Helpful hint:** Talk to other agencies and government departments to see if project evaluation is already being carried out. There could be an opportunity to collaborate, or for an existing arrangement to incorporate MoSSaiC evaluation needs.	9.2.4
	Develop project outcome schedule	• Discuss feasible arrangements with relevant agencies to ensure a project outcome schedule can be created and a body made responsible for a medium-term evaluation	9.5
	Arrange for a cost-benefit analysis to be undertaken	**Helpful hint:** A specialist group (perhaps a college research group, or an appropriate branch of government) may be willing to undertake this task.	9.5.7
Government task teams	Develop database system for recording project outcomes	• Observe changes in slope stability • Acquire rainfall information associated with major storms to show stability (or otherwise) of interventions	9.5.1; 9.5.2
	Coordinate with community task teams		
Community task teams	Community residents contribute to project evaluation	• Provide commentary on drain performance during rainfall • Monitor cracks in structures and water table levels • Describe conditions before and after the intervention	9.3.2
	Coordinate with government task teams		

9.7.2 Chapter checklist

CHECK THAT:	TEAM	PERSON	SIGN-OFF	CHAPTER SECTION
✓ KPIs for short-term project outputs identified and agreed upon				9.4
✓ KPIs for medium-term project outcomes identified and agreed upon				9.5
✓ Data collection roles and responsibilities agreed upon for all KPIs				9.4; 9.5
✓ **Milestone 9: Evaluation framework agreed upon and implemented**				9.5.10
✓ Policy for addressing landslide risk drivers over the longer term reviewed				9.6
✓ All necessary safeguards complied with				1.5.3; 2.3.2

9.7.3 Installing crack monitors

Most masonry and concrete buildings crack at some time during their service life. The appearance of a crack is a symptom of distress within the fabric of the building. Often the cracking is of little consequence, but it could be the first sign of a serious defect affecting the building's serviceability or structural stability. Monitoring changes in crack width over time will establish if the crack is static, progressively opening, or opening and closing following a cyclic pattern of movement. This information is essential in diagnosing the cause of the crack.

Simple gauges (figure 9.21a) allow monitoring of horizontal and vertical movement across a crack on a flat surface using two partially overlapping plates. The bottom plate is calibrated in millimeters; the top plate is transparent and marked with a hairline cross-shaped cursor. The gauge is preset at zero with four pegs. The pegs are removed after the gauge is fixed across the crack. As the crack opens, or if vertical movement occurs, the cursor moves relative to the calibration scale.

Ideally, the gauge should be fixed with screws or rawl plugs and adhesive, as there is the risk of tampering if screws alone are used. On some surfaces, only adhesive can be used; the adhesive must fully cure before the four plugs are removed.

Once the gauge is set in place, the crack's opening or closing can be monitored, and results recorded on a crack record sheet (figure 9.21b).

9.7.4 Installing and using simple piezometers

A simple piezometer can be used to measure the depth of the free water table below the ground surface. The device consists of a tube with holes in it, placed in a narrow borehole. Water enters the piezometer until it reaches the same level as that in the soil.

To install a piezometer, perform the following steps:

1. Drill a hole in the soil 1–3 m deep, using a power soil auger (figure 9.22a). A hand-held power auger may be sufficient to insert a piezometer to a depth of 1–2 m in residual soils. In heavy clay soils, a more powerful auger may be required.

2. Put a plastic piezometer tube in the bore hole; 2 inch plastic tubing can be used for the piezometer. Drill holes, typically toward the lower third of the tube at 10 cm spacing, to allow water to flow into the tube. The holes can be drilled on site (figure 9.22b).

3. Cover the top of the piezometer to prevent rain from infiltrating.

FIGURE 9.21 Crack monitoring gauge and crack record charts

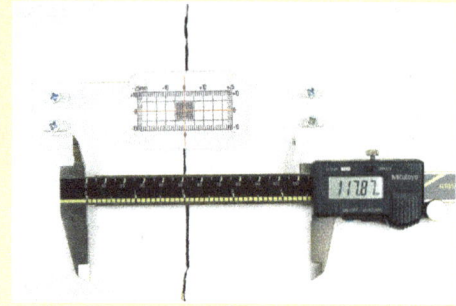

a. Callipers are used with the crack monitoring gauge to increase measurement resolution.

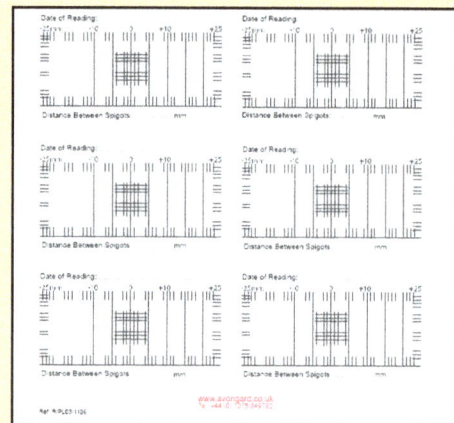

b. Crack record charts.

Source: Avongard, www.avongard.co.uk.

Installing piezometers in an array may allow determination of a groundwater surface (figure 9.22c).

To read the piezometer, perform the following:

• Lower a piece of tubing into the piezometer and blow into it until bubbling is heard; this indicates the water level in the piezometer.

• Record the length of tubing used (remember to subtract the above-ground distance); this is the depth of the water table.

Take and record regular readings from the piezometer over a period of months, particularly over the wet season. The readings can be used to ascertain any apparent reduction in water levels that could be attributed to surface drainage works undertaken upslope.

FIGURE 9.22 Installing piezometers

a. Drilling for a piezometer installation.

b. Drilling holes in piezometer tube.

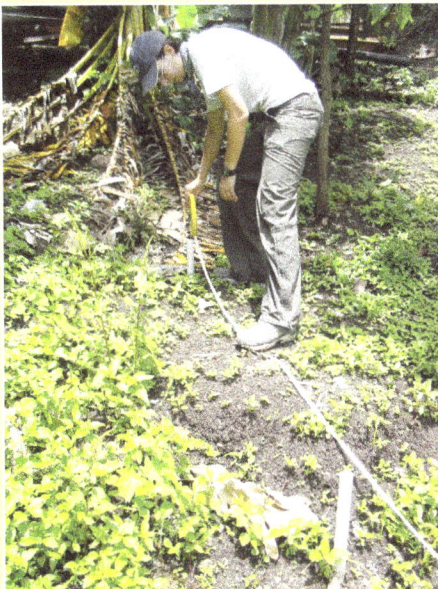

c. Setting out piezometer array.

9.7.5 Cost-benefit analysis

The components of the integrated model of landslide risk assessment, risk reduction, and cost-benefit analysis used in a MoSSaiC intervention are shown in figure 9.23. This cost-benefit analysis approach is illustrated using the example of Holcombe et al. (2011), the slope stability analysis for which can be found in section 5.6.3.

Landslide hazard and drainage scenarios

Two landslide scenarios were tested using CHASM (Combined Hydrology and Slope Stability Model) (see figures 5.25 and 5.26):

- Failure of the entire slope (cross-section X_1-X_2)

- Failure of multiple small cut slopes (cross-section Y_1-Y_2) (Holcombe et al. 2011).

Prior to the construction of new drains, a rainfall event with a probability of 1 in 10 years was predicted to cause landslides along section X_1-X_2 which would affect a large part of the slope (figure 5.27), while a 1-in-5-year event was predicted to trigger smaller slides in multiple cut slopes along section Y_1-Y_2.

After constructing new drains and capturing household water, less water was available for infiltration into the slope. Thirty-five percent of rainfall was known to be intercepted by roofs and conveyed to new drains, while approximately 50 percent of the remaining rainfall was estimated to be removed from the slope in the form of surface water runoff intercepted by drains. This was reflected in the slope stability simulations by reducing the water added to the slope, and an improvement in slope stability was demonstrated (figure 5.28). The predicted probability of the two landslide scenarios was reduced to 1 in 100 years for the entire slope (cross-section X_1-X_2) and 1 in 50 years for smaller failures in cut slopes (cross-section Y_1-Y_2).

FIGURE 9.23 Components of an integrated model of landslide hazard and risk assessment

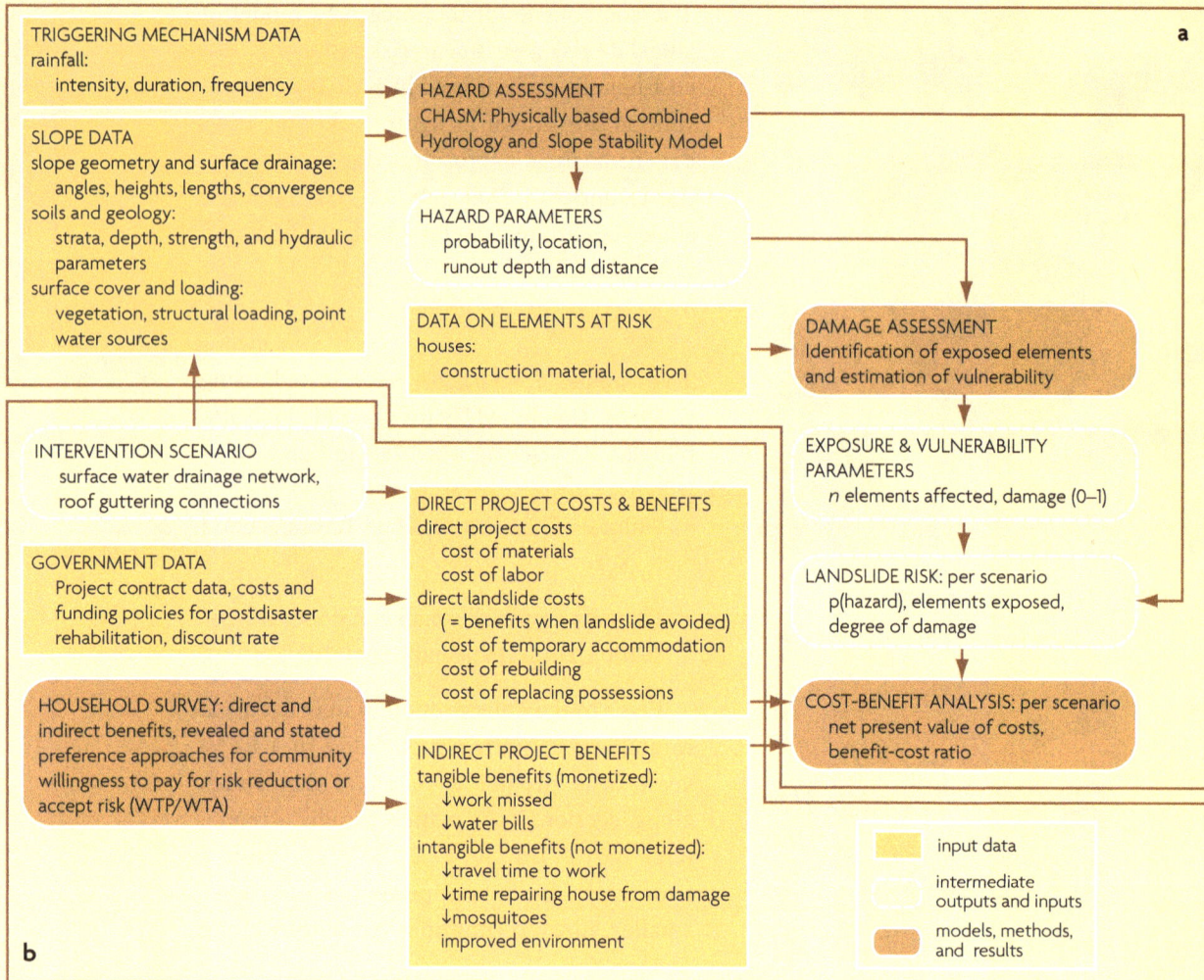

Source: Holcombe et al. 2011.

Note: (a) Landslide risk assessment and cost-benefit analysis of risk reduction, (b) monetization of project costs and benefits.

Monetizing project costs and benefits to the community

The expected damage to houses of different construction types was calculated from predicted magnitude and location of landslides. The direct benefits of the landslide mitigation project were calculated from the probability of avoided future costs, expressed in today's values using a process of discounting and a discount rate of 12 percent.

Indirect benefits to the community, relating to improved drainage and installation of roof guttering, included improved access (less flooding and fewer debris-blocked paths), shorter travel times to work, reduction in minor damage to homes from flooding and

debris, and savings in water bills through harvesting of rainfall from roofs. The value of indirect benefits was assessed using stated and revealed preference methods (via a household questionnaire) to determine willingness to pay for benefits and willingness to accept compensation for landslides. These benefits comprise a substantial part of the overall project benefit.

To determine costs and benefits, information was collected from the community regarding direct and indirect costs and benefits associated with the intervention. This information was gathered using a questionnaire designed with the help of residents from another community who were knowledgeable about MoSSaiC—and who distributed the questionnaires and helped residents to complete them.

A sample questionnaire that may be adapted can be found in Holcombe et al. (2011). The specific information that needs to be captured by the questionnaire will depend on the cost-benefit analysis method used. Seek expert guidance from those knowledgeable in this field to guide the design of a cost-benefit model appropriate to the local circumstances and likely data availability. It is outside the scope of this book to provide guidance beyond illustrating the potential outcomes of a cost-benefit analysis (section 9.5.7); for more information on a MoSSaiC application of cost-benefit analysis, see Holcombe et al. (2011).

Results and discussion

The resulting benefit-cost ratio of the landslide hazard reduction project was estimated to be 1.7:1 without drain maintenance (assuming a seven-year drain design life), rising to 2.7:1 with proper maintenance (conservatively assuming a 20-year design life).

The findings of this study should be taken only as a basis for encouraging further design of appropriate cost-benefit analysis models for this type of project, and not as a general confirmation of any specific form of intervention. The findings are based on a study undertaken in a small community of 25 houses in the Eastern Caribbean. The hope is that by illustrating these results from a single small-scale prototype cost-benefit analysis, the MCU is encouraged to consider cost-benefit analysis of further MoSSaiC projects.

9.7.6 References

Anderson, M. G., and E. A. Holcombe. 2006. "Sustainable Landslide Risk Reduction in Poorer Countries." *Proceedings of the Institution of Civil Engineers—Engineering Sustainability* 159: 23–30.

Annan, K. A. 1999. "UN Report of the Secretary-General on the Work of the Organization General." Assembly Official Records Fifty-Fourth Session Supplement No. 1 (A/54/1). http://www.un.org/Docs/SG/Report99/intro99.htm.

Baker, J. L. 2000. *Evaluating the Impact of Development Projects on Poverty: A Handbook for Practitioners.* Washington, DC: World Bank. http://siteresources.worldbank.org/INTISPMA/Resources/Impact-Evaluation-Handbook--English-/impact1.pdf.

Benson, C., and J. Twigg. 2004. "Measuring Mitigation Methodologies for Assessing Natural Hazard Risks and the Net Benefits of Mitigation—A Scoping Study." ProVention Consortium, Geneva.

Cairncross, S., and E. A. R. Ouano. 1991. *Surface Water Drainage for Low-income Communities.* Geneva: World Health Organization and United Nations Environment Programme. Cited in Parkinson 2003.

Easterly, W. 2002. "The Cartel of Good Intentions: The Problem of Bureaucracy in Foreign Aid Cartel of Good intentions." Working Paper 4, Center for Global Development, Washington, DC. http://papers.ssrn.com/sol3/papers.cfm?abstract_id=999981.

Ganderton, P. 2005. "Benefit–Cost Analysis of Disaster Mitigation: Application as a Policy and Decision-Making Tool." *Mitigation and Adaptation Strategies for Global Change* 10: 445–65.

Ghesquiere, F., and O. Mahul. 2007. "Sovereign Natural Disaster Insurance for Developing Countries: A Paradigm Shift in Catastrophe Risk Financing." Policy Research Working Paper 4345. World Bank, Washington, DC.

Government of St. Lucia. 2006. "Landslide Response Plan." http://web.stlucia.gov.lc/nemp/plans/LandslidePlan.pdf.

Holcombe, E. A., S. Smith, E. Wright, and M. G. Anderson. 2011. "An Integrated Approach for Evaluating the Effectiveness of Landslide Hazard Reduction in Vulnerable Communities in the Caribbean." *Natural Hazards.* doi:10.1007/s11069-011-9920-7.

IPCC (Intergovernmental Panel on Climate Change). 2011. "Definition of Terms Used within the DDC Pages." http://www.ipcc-data.org/ddc_definitions.html.

Lavergne, R. 2004. "Debrief—Tokyo Symposium on Capacity Development, February 4–6, 2004." Presentation prepared for Canadian International Development Agency staff.

——. 2005. "Capacity Development under Program-Based Approaches: Results from the LENPA Forum of April 2005."

Mahmoud, M., Y. Liu, H. Hartmann, S. Stewart, T. Wagener, D. Semmens, R. Stewart, H. Gupta, D. Dominguez, F. Dominguez, D. Hulse, R. Letcher, B. Rashleigh, C. Smith, R. Street, J. Ticehurs, M. Twery, H. van Delden, R. Waldick, D. White, and L. Winter. 2009. "A Formal Framework for Scenario Development in Support of Environmental Decision-Making." *Environmental Modelling and Software* 24: 798–808.

McDavid, J. C., and L. R. L. Hawthorn. 2005. *Program Evaluation Performance Measurement: An Introduction to Practice.* Thousand Oaks, CA: Sage Publications.

Mechler, R. 2005. *Cost-Benefit Analysis of Natural Disaster Risk Management in Developing Countries: Manual.* Bonn: Deutsche Gesellschaft fuer Technische Zusammenarbeit (GTZ) GmbH.

Mechler, R., S. Hochrainer, G. Pflug, A. Lotsch, and K. Williges. 2010. "Assessing the Financial Vulnerability to Climate-Related Natural Hazards: Background Paper for the World Development Report 2010 'Development and Climate Change.'" Policy Research Working Paper 5232, World Bank, Washington, DC.

Mitchell, T., and M. van Aalst. 2008. "Convergence of Disaster Risk Reduction and Climate Change Adaptation: A Review Paper for DFID." UK Department for International Development, London. http://www.preventionweb.net/files/7853_ConvergenceofDRRandCCA1.pdf.

Moench, M., R. Mechler, and S. Stapleton. 2007. "Guidance Note on the Costs and Benefits of Disaster Risk Reduction." Prepared for UNISDR Global Platform on Disaster Risk Reduction High Level Dialogue, June 4–7.

Nutley, S., H. Davies, and I. Walter. 2002. "Evidence Based Policy and Practice: Cross Sector Lessons from the UK." Working Paper 9, Economic and Social Research Council, UK Centre for Evidence Based Policy.

OAS (Organization of American States). 2003. "Safer and Environmentally Sustainable Low-Income Housing in the OECS through Property Insurance and Home Retrofit Programs." World Bank Contract #7122427, OAS, Washington, DC.

OECD (Organisation for Economic Co-operation and Development). 2002. Glossary of Key Terms in Evaluation and Results Based Management. Paris: OECD.

Parkinson, J. 2003. "Drainage and Stormwater Management Strategies for Low-Income Urban Communities." *Environment and Urbanization* 15: 115.

Parry, M., N. Arnell, P. Berry, D. Dodman, S. Fankhauser, C. Hope, S. Kovats, R. Nicholls, D. Satterthwaite, R. Tiffin, and T. Wheeler. 2009. *Assessing the Costs of Adaptation to Climate Change: A Review of the UNFCCC and Other Recent Estimates.* London: International Institute for Environment and Development and Grantham Institute for Climate Change.

Platteau, J.-P. 2004. "Monitoring Elite Capture in Community Driven Development." *Development and Change* 35: 223–46.

Rayner, S., and E. L. Malone. 1997. "Zen and the Art of Climate Maintenance." *Nature* 390: 332–34

Segone, M. 2008. "Evidence-Based Policy Making and the Role of Monitoring and Evaluation within the New Aid Environment." In *Bridging the Gap: The Role of Monitoring and Evaluation in Evidence-Based Policy Making,* ed. M. Segone, 16–45. UNICEF. http://www.unicef.org/ceecis/evidence_based_policy_making.pdf.

Twigg, J. 2004. "Disaster Risk Reduction: Mitigation and Preparedness." *Development and Emergency Programming Good Practice Review* 9.

UNFCCC (United Nations Framework Convention on Climate Change). 2007. "Investment and Financial Flows to Address Climate Change." http://unfccc.int/resource/docs/publications/financial_flows.pdf.

———. 2009. "Adaptation to Climate Change: Linking Disaster Risk Reduction and Insurance." Paper submitted to the UNFCCC for the 6th Session of the Ad Hoc Working Group on Long-Term Cooperative Action under the Convention, Bonn, June 1–12. http://unfccc.int/resource/docs/2009/smsn/ngo/163.pdf.

UN-Habitat. 2009. *Planning Sustainable Cites: Global Report on Human Settlements 2009.* http://www.unhabitat.org/documents/GRHS09/FS5.pdf.

Wamsler, C. 2006. "Mainstreaming Risk Reduction in Urban Planning and Housing: A Challenge for International Aid Organizations." *Disaster* 30: 151–77.

World Bank. 2003. *Strategic Communication for Development Projects: A Toolkit for Task Team Leaders.* http://siteresources.worldbank.org/EXTDEVCOMMENG/Resources/toolkitwebjan2004.pdf.

———. 2004. *Making Services Work for Poor People. World Development Report.* Washington, DC: World Bank.

———. 2007. *Introduction to Development Evaluation.* International Program for Development Evaluation Training. http://www.worldbank.org/oed/ipdet/modules/M_01-na.pdf.

———. 2010a. *Natural Hazards Unnatural Disasters: The Economics of Effective Prevention.* Washington, DC: World Bank.

———. 2010b. *Safer Homes, Stronger Communities. A Handbook for Reconstructing after Natural Disasters.* Washington, DC: World Bank.

Zwane, A. P., and M. Kremer. 2007. "What Works in Fighting Diarrheal Diseases in Developing Countries? A Critical Review." *World Bank Research Observer* 22 (1): 1–24.

Glossary

Abney level. A low-cost instrument used in topographic surveying to measure slope angle in degrees and percentage of grade. The instrument consists of a fixed sighting tube, a movable spirit level connected to a pointing arm, and a protractor scale.

Acceptable risk. The level of risk loss a society or community considers acceptable given existing social, economic, political, cultural, technical, and environmental conditions.

Anisotropy. Variation of a physical property depending on the direction in which it is measured.

As Low As Reasonably Practicable (ALARP). ALARP risks are those in which the cost of further risk reduction measures would be grossly disproportionate to the benefits they would deliver.

Baffle. An upstand in the drain intended to reduce flow velocity and water surface super-elevation on drain bends (likely overtopping).

Behavioral change. A change in attitudes and practices of individuals and groups (in the case of MoSSaiC, the desired behavioral change is the adoption of good slope management practices and policies by communities and governments alike).

Bill of quantities. Document containing an itemized breakdown of the works to be carried out in a unit price contract, indicating a quantity for each item and the corresponding unit price.

Building code. A set of standards that specify the minimum acceptable level of safety for buildings or structures.

Capacity building. A complex concept that conveys the process by which individuals, groups, and organizations build their knowledge, abilities, relationships, and values in order to solve problems and achieve development objectives. The impact of capacity building may thus be seen at different scales—in individuals, households, communities, and governments.

Catchpit. A structure linking inflow and outflow drains (similar to connection chambers).

Catalytic people. In the context of MoSSaiC, existing staff working in government or relevant local agencies who understand the MoSSaiC vision and show an aptitude and a willingness to participate in its delivery.

Certification. The achievement by an individual against a previously agreed schedule of performance, signed off on by government representatives. The term may be varied in different countries for legal or other reasons.

Community. A group of households that identify themselves in some way as having a common interest or needs as well as physical space. A social group that resides in a specific locality.

Community engagement. Informing, collaborating with, involving, consulting, and empowering community members.

Community meeting. Meeting of community residents to discuss any aspect relating to a project. Such meetings can be formal or informal, depending on the nature of the community and what works best for the residents in terms of timing and venue.

Community contracting. Procurement by or on behalf of a community. While there are many different models of community contracting, a common feature is that they seek to give the community varying degrees of control over investment and implementation, which it is hoped will encourage ownership and sustainability.

Connection chamber. A reinforced concrete vault (with height, width, and depth of between 300–500 mm each) allowing inflow from one or more pipes carrying household gray water and roof water, and outflow via a single pipe to a nearby main drain or another connection chamber. The top of the chamber is usually flush with the ground surface and covered with a concrete slab that can be removed to allow access for maintenance and cleaning.

Consequences. The outcome of an event such as a landslide hazard occurring. Dependent on the exposure and vulnerability of the elements at risk (e.g., people, houses, infrastructure).

Convergence (of a slope). When viewed in plan, orthogonals to the ground contours converge in the downslope direction. This situation is conducive to the concentration of sub-surface and surface water, and thus to higher downslope pore water pressures.

Cost-benefit analysis. A systematic calculation of project cost-effectiveness in terms of the balance between the net present value of project costs and project benefits (discounted over the project lifetime). Project costs and benefits must be "monetized" (assigned a monetary value) for inclusion in the calculation.

Direct shear test. A widely used method for determining the shear strength of soils (in terms of cohesion and angle of internal friction), first used by Coulomb in 1776.

Disaster risk management. An understanding of what processes and factors contribute to risk, sufficient that management of the risks can be undertaken.

Divergence (of a slope). When viewed in plan, orthogonals to the ground contours diverge in the downslope direction. This situation is conducive to the divergence of subsurface and surface water, and thus to lower downslope pore water pressures.

Double-handling costs. Additional costs incurred when construction materials cannot be delivered directly to site due to limited access. The material is instead manually transported between the point of delivery, an intermediate storage site, and the construction site.

Elements at risk. Such as people, communities, agricultural areas, roads, facilities (e.g., hospitals, schools), utilities (e.g., water mains, power lines, power stations), economic/industrial infrastructure (factories, mines).

Erosion (soil). The gradual wearing away of soil by an agent such as water or wind, and its loss, particle by particle.

Evidence-based policy. A policy process that helps make better-informed decisions by putting the best available evidence at the center of the policy process.

Exposure. The location of elements at risk with respect to a specific hazard.

Ex ante measures. Measures taken before a disaster in the expectation that they will either prevent, or significantly reduce the impact of, a possible disaster.

Ex post measures. Measures taken after a disaster has occurred to seek to make good all related damage caused by the disaster.

Factor of safety. The ratio of shear strength (acting so as to resist slope failure) of a soil to the shearing force (tending to induce slope failure) experienced by slope material. A factor of safety < 1 indicates potential slope instability.

Focus group. A small number (typically around 10) of individuals who provide information during a directed and moderated interactive group discussion. The purpose is to subject ideas to review by the group in order to determine the viability of those ideas.

Geographic information system (GIS). Any system that captures, stores, analyzes, manages, and presents data that are linked to their geographical location.

Gray water. Gray water is all nonseptic waste from houses, typically including water from washing machines, showers, and kitchen sinks.

Hazard. A process that has the potential to cause damage (e.g., landslide).

Hazard map. A map showing areas affected by a particular hazard, such as landslides.

Herringbone drainage. A drainage pattern that is frequently used to drain hillsides, most commonly for cut-slopes in highways. It comprises a central downslope drain with feeder intercept drains running to either side.

Heterogeneity. Exhibiting diverse (non-homogeneous) properties.

Hurricane strapping. Typically, galvanized strapping bars of various shapes to affix roof timbers to wall plates to ensure the stability of the entire roof structure during high winds.

Intercept drain. A drain running almost parallel to slope contours (but with a slight downslope gradient) to capture water flowing down the slope.

Key performance indicators (KPIs). Quantitative and qualitative measures of project outputs and outcomes used to evaluate the progress of success of the project.

Landowners. Those who "own" the land upon which MoSSaiC project construction takes place. Note that landownership may be difficult to establish, landowners may not reside within country, and landownership may be disputed—refer to any relevant safeguards.

Landslide hazard. The probability of occurrence of a landslide of a specific type and magnitude in a particular location.

Landslide risk. A function of landslide hazard, exposure, and vulnerability—communities with relatively high landslide risk will be those where high landslide hazard coincides with high-level exposure (e.g., dense housing) and high socioeconomic vulnerability.

Landslide susceptibility. The propensity of an area to experience landslides—the inherent instability of a slope.

Low-cost drain. Non–concrete block drains constructed using polythene and galvanized mesh for lining an excavated drain trench. Especially useful for small drains conveying low-volume or low-velocity flows, and where the delivery of cement and blocks may be difficult.

MoSSaiC core unit (MCU). The main management coordinating body for MoSSaiC interventions, comprising within-country "catalytic" individuals from different government ministries, agencies, and related bodies.

Mitigation. The lessening of the adverse impact of hazards or disasters.

Point sources. Sources of water that have a specific point of discharge onto a hillslope, such as gray water discharge from a house or an unlined drain.

Preparatory factors. Factors that can have a potential role in slope instability.

Project outcomes. Medium-term, post-implementation results of a project.

Project outputs. Results of a project that are measurable at the immediate point of project completion.

Project step template. The document that sets out the initial project steps for a MoSSaiC intervention and which the MCU has the responsibility of refining to suit local conditions.

Rainfall threshold. A threshold measure of rainfall (typically duration and depth or intensity) that, if exceeded, has been shown empirically to be associated with the occurrence of landslides.

Rational method. A widely used equation to estimate water discharge, being a product of rainfall intensity, hillslope contributing area, and a runoff coefficient.

Recurrence interval. Time between hazard events of similar size in a given location based on the probability that the event will be equaled or exceeded in a given period (typically a year). Thus a 30-year event is one that is likely to occur once every 30 years.

Reporting lines. The way people participating in a project are organized. Individuals responsible for a specific aspect of project delivery should be assigned to a supervisor or line manager to ensure that they are fully supported (technically and operationally) and accountable in their role. Clear reporting lines are particularly important for community-based projects. Community residents will interact with different government team members over the course of a MoSSaiC project and should be able to identify "who is responsible for whom about what."

Resilience. The ability of a community or society potentially exposed to hazards to resist, absorb, adapt to, and recover from the stresses of the hazard event. Often referred to as the converse of vulnerability.

Resistance envelope. A means of assessing the threshold soil water conditions for stability, typically used to determine whether the maintenance of negative pore pressures is required for a slope to remain stable. This technique also enables the likely slope failure depth to be identified.

Resolution. The accuracy at which a given map scale can depict the location and shape of map features; the larger the map scale, the higher the possible resolution. As map scale decreases, resolution diminishes and feature boundaries must be smoothed, simplified, or not shown at all. It is the size of the smallest feature that can be represented in a surface. For example, small areas may have to be represented as points.

Retrofitting. Reinforcement or upgrading of existing structures to make them more resistant and resilient to hazards.

Risk. With respect to disasters, a function of the hazard, exposure, and vulnerability. A measure of the likelihood of damage.

Risk analysis. The process of hazard, exposure, and vulnerability identification and risk estimation. This may be qualitative—landslide probability, exposure, and vulnerability of exposed elements expressed in relative terms; semi-quantitative—indicative probability or relative vulnerability; or quantitative—numerical probability and loss measures.

Risk drivers. Factors that serve to promote a potential increase in the level of risk (e.g., rainfall, discharge of water onto hillslopes).

Scale (of maps and plans). The scale of a map or plan is defined as the ratio of a distance on the map to the corresponding distance on the ground. Scales are often qualified as small scale, typically for large regional maps, or large scale, typically for county maps or town plans.

Safeguards. Requirements, protocols, guidance notes, etc., from funding agencies, governments, and other such bodies that define ways of working that the MCU, and all concerned with a MoSSaiC intervention, should both take note of and adhere to wherever they are deemed or shown to be relevant.

Shear strength. The resistance to deformation by continuous shear displacement of soil particles along a surface of rupture.

Show home. A home within a community in which drainage provision is configured to provide an example of good practice to the rest of the community.

Squatter housing. Housing occupying land illegally.

Stakeholders. Groups who have any direct or indirect interest in the MoSSaiC intervention, or who can affect or be affected by the implementation and outcomes, including such groups as those undertaking, managing, reporting on, affected by, promoting, and funding the interventions.

Strategic incrementalism. An approach to changing practice and policy that is incremental.

Tolerable risk. A risk that society is willing to live with so as to secure certain benefits in the confidence that it is being properly controlled, kept under review, and further reduced as and when possible.

Triggering event. A natural (e.g., rainfall, seismic, volcanic) or human-induced (e.g. slope loading, slope cutting) event that results in the occurrence of a landslide.

Unacceptable risk. The level of risk that society is not prepared to accept.

Unauthorized housing. Housing not in compliance with current regulations concerning landownership, land-use and planning zones, or construction.

Vulnerability. The potential degree of damage or loss experienced by the exposed elements for a given landslide event, usually expressed on a scale of 0–1 (no damage to total loss). With respect to urban landslides, damage can be thought of as direct or indirect, physical (loss of life, homes, or property), or socioeconomic (loss of livelihoods, loss of assets).

Vulnerable community. With respect to MoSSaiC, a community that can be considered likely to be significantly physically and socio-economically damaged by a landslide. It will have low resilience to such an event and will find it difficult to recover. Poverty may be used as an indicator of vulnerability and resilience. Different countries will be expected to apply different measures to assess vulnerability to identify and prioritize communities for MoSSaiC projects.

Weathering. The physical and chemical alteration of minerals into other minerals by the action of heat, water, and air.

Weathering grades. A scale describing the level of weathering of a rock mass, typically divided into six classes (fresh rock being grade I; fully weathered soil being grade VI).

Work package. The complete specification of works to be completed by a contractor. This should specify the detailed nature of the works to be undertaken with clear indication of extent marked on the ground on site, as well as on the drainage plan. Design drawings and similar specifications should be included as part of the package.

Index

Bishop, A. W., 101, 114, 116
Bishop method, 100
Bishop stability equation, 120
black water. *See* septic waste
Blake, J. R., 122
Brooks, S. M., 114
Buchanan, J. M., 61
budget constraints, 7
building code, 227, 323, 370, 387

C

Campbell, S., 294
capacity building. *See also* adapting the MoSSaiC
        blueprint to existing capacity
    defined, 387
    government capacity, 34
    local capacity, 309, 329-34
Caracas, República Bolivariana de Venezuela,
        unauthorized housing in, 25
Caribbean. *See* Latin America and the Caribbean
Caribbean Catastrophe Risk Insurance Facility, 19
catalytic people, xxv, 4, 43, 387
catchpits, 255, 255-59f, 387
categories of disasters, 9, 9t
certification process for MoSSaiC, 341-42, 387
CHASM (Combined Hydrology and Slope
        Stability Model), 113-15, 114-16f, 120,
        121t, 134, 194, 196, 201, 201f
Chowdhury, F., 146
clean-up days, 336-37, 337f
climate change, 23
climate proofing, 370, 371t, 373
cohesion, 99-100, 105, 117, 120-23, 195t. *See also*
        shear strength
communication
    briefing key leaders about MoSSaiC, 47
    clear project messages for stakeholders, 308
    community demonstration sites and show
        homes, 321-23, 322f, 322t, 391
    community involvement methods, 174-75
    defining communication purposes and
        functions, 317
    delivering project messages, 322-24, 325f
    direct communications, 320-21, 320t
    examples of communication mode, channel,
        and purpose, 318t
    finalizing project messages, 329
    focus groups, 177, 177f, 389
    forms and project messages, 317-29
    in government-community partnerships, 34
    identifying audiences, 317, 318t, 319t
    meetings. *See* community meetings
    MoSSaiC information materials, 323
    relevance, 308
    scientific and professional publications, 328-
        29
    timing of media reports, 308
    TV, radio, and newspaper coverage, 324-28,
        327-28t, 327f
    written and visual materials for communities,
        323-24, 324t, 326f
communications task team, 69, 70f
communities at risk, prioritizing of, 2, 3f, 129-63

    adapting the MoSSaiC blueprint to existing
        capacity, 132, 133
    base map preparation for detailed community
        mapping, 159-60, 160f
    briefing note, 130-31
    combining hazard and vulnerability
        information, 157
    community-based aspects, 130
    confirming selection, 156-58, 157t
    guiding principles, 131
    interpreting landslide hazard maps, 132
    key elements, 129-30
    landslide susceptibility and hazard
        assessment methods, 140-51, 142t
        deterministic methods, 150-51
        field reconnaissance and hazard ranking
            methods, 141-46, 143f, 144-45t
        GIS-based qualitative landslide
            susceptibility mapping, 146-49,
            155-56
        probabilistic approaches, 149
        semi-quantitative and quantitative, 149-51
        statistical methods, 149-50
    psychological barriers of, 6-7
    risks and challenges, 131-32
    selection process, xxvi, xxix, 44-45, 132-40,
        135t
        bivariate and multivariate statistical
            approaches, 134
        choice of risk comparison approach, 135-
            36
        comparison of risk at multiple locations,
            134-36
        data and analysis methods for, 137-38, 138t
        deterministic spatially distributed
            modeling, 134
        digital data and GIS analysis, 132, 134
        field reconnaissance and risk ranking, 134
        heuristic methods, 134
        MCU agreement to, 138-39
        methods for, 136-39, 137f
        probabilistic methods, 134
    short-term planning of, 7
    situational barriers of, 6-7
    size of cities and, xxiii
    vulnerability assessment, 151-56, 152t
        defined, 12
        exposure, 151
        field reconnaissance and vulnerability
            ranking methods, 153-54, 154-
            55t
        GIS-based mapping for, 155-56
    who does what, 161
community-based approach, 3, 4f, 26t, 29-34. *See
        also* community engagement; *specific
        topics*
    behavioral change, 306
    communities at risk, prioritizing of, 130
    community-based mapping, 166, 169-70
    coping mechanisms, 30, 31t
    definition of community, xxiii, 388
    drainage design and good practice, 214
    government-community partnerships, 34

implementation of planned works, 262
landslides as community issue, 4, 23
mapping. *See* community-based mapping
MoSSaiC's approach to, 5–6, 32–33
teams. *See* community task teams
community-based mapping, xxvi–xxvii, 165–210,
204*f*
adapting the MoSSaiC blueprint to existing
capacity, 170, 171
base map preparation for detailed mapping,
159–60
briefing note, 167–68
community-based aspects, 166, 169–70. *See
also* community engagement
community knowledge and gaining
acceptance, 176–78
connecting with key community members,
169, 175
defined, 167
guiding principles, 168–69
identification of landslide hazard zones, 189–
91, 192*f*, 193*t*
information to be included, 168
key elements, 165–66
physically based landslide hazard assessment,
191–93, 194*t*, 202*t*
pore water pressure, 88, 99-101, 105-108, 114-
20, 198
purpose of, 167, 168
qualitative landslide hazard assessment, 188–
91, 190*f*
repeating survey, 188
risks and challenges, 169–70
scientifically based justification, 189
slope features, 178–88, 187*f*
accuracy of map, 187–88
alterations to natural drainage, 181–82, 182*f*
evidence of slope movement, 185–87, 186*f*
hillside scale, 178–82, 179*f*, 183*t*
household drainage, 184–85, 184–85*f*
household-scale contributors, 182–85,
185*t*, 187*f*
local knowledge of past landslides, 185
local slope geometry and material, 183–84,
183*f*
seepage zones, 181, 181*f*
slope angle. *See* slope angle
slope stability issues, 185–87, 187*t*
slope stability models, 194–98, 195–98*f*,
195*t*. *See also* CHASM
(Combined Hydrology and
Slope Stability Model)
topography and natural drainage, 169, 179,
179–80*f*
timing of visits and meetings with residents,
169, 188
topographic features to be identified at
necessary resolution, 169
zones for drainage interventions, 203
community clean-up days, 336–37, 337*f*
community contracting, 264–65, 264*f*, 265*t*, 388
community engagement
benefits of, xxi–xxii, 2, 4, 4*f*, 32–34, 33*t*

collaborative approaches, 170, 172
community-based mapping requiring, 166,
169–70
defined, 388
how to work within a community, 170–78
avoiding bias and considering interests of
all groups, 175–76
community leaders' involvement, 47, 175
culture and diversity, 172–73
formal meetings, 177–78, 178*f*
gender relations, 173–74, 173*f*, 174*t*
house-by-house discussions, 176–77, 177*f*
informal focus groups, 177, 177*f*
interactive process, 176
listening to residents, 175
practices and communication methods,
174–75
types of participation, 170, 172, 172*t*
instrumental approaches, 170
mapping. *See* community-based mapping
practices, 174–76
principles, 170–74
selection of community. *See* communities at
risk, prioritizing of
stakeholders, 44, 44*t*
supportive approaches, 172
community leaders' involvement, 47, 175
community liaison task team, 67, 68*f*, 140, 174
community meetings, 177–78, 178*f*, 388
community task teams, xxx–xxxi, 5*t*, 43, 71–74, 75*f*
concave downslope profile, 179, 180*f*
concrete drains. *See* drainage design and good
practice
connection chambers, 248, 249*f*, 284, 285*f*, 388
consequences, 388. *See also* cost-benefit analysis;
fatalities and losses
damages exceeding 1 percent of GDP, 41*f*
outputs and outcomes as evidence of
effectiveness, 34, 35*t*, 390
unintended, 335, 335*f*
construction task team, 73, 73–74*f*
contracts, tendering process, 276–77
convergence zones, 179–80, 180*f*, 388
Coppin, N. J., 294
corruption, 300–301
cost-benefit analysis, 18–19, 18–19*f*, 365–67, 381–83,
382*f*, 388
Craig, R. F., 122
Crozier, M. J., 21
Cruden, D. M., 91
Cuba's National Landslide Risk Assessment
Project, 148–49, 149*f*
cultural differences, 172–73

D
debris traps, 235–36, 235*f*, 335
clearing, 336–37, 337–38*f*
construction, 298–99, 298–300*f*
demonstration sites and show homes, 321–23,
322*f*, 322*t*, 391
Department for International Development (UK),
128
de Regt, J. P., 42

desk studies, 194
Dietrich, W. E., 150
disaster risk, 7–25
    "acceptable risk," 13–14, 15*f*
    categories of disasters, 9, 9*t*
    definition of risk, 11–14
    future scenarios 374, 376-78, 377*f*
    increases in costs of, 8, 8–9*f*
    increases in number of, 7–8, 8*f*
    insurance, 19–20, 19*f*
    landslide risk, 9–10. *See also* landslide hazards
    management. *See* disaster risk management
        (DRM)
    records of disasters, 9
disaster risk management (DRM), 11–14, 14*f*
    assessment, 12. *See also* science-based approach
    benefits of, xxi, 2, 18
    catastrophe risk models, 18
    definition of, 11–12, 388
    disaster risk insurance, 19–20, 19*f*
    evidence of project's effectiveness. *See*
        evidence base of effectiveness
    exposure, defined, 12
    hazard, defined, 11–12
    influences on, 14–23
        international advocacy groups, 15*f*
        national and local studies, 21
        social funds, 21–23, 22*f*
        UN disaster response organizational
            framework, 16*f*
    process and steps involved, 12–13, 13*t*
    recent influences on, 14–23
    reduction (DRR), 13, 307. *See also* disaster risk
        mitigation
        top-down evaluation, 349–50
    science-based approach. *See* science-based
        approach
    shift from ex post to ex ante policies, 14–17
    vulnerability, defined, 12
disaster risk mitigation
    benefits of, 2, 3*f*, 18–19, 18–19*f*
    definition of mitigation, 390
    need for evidence of benefits of, 17–19. *See also*
        evidence base of effectiveness
    psychological barriers to, 6–7
    scope of, 13
    situational barriers to, 6–7
divergence of a slope, 388. *See also* slope angle
Dominica, impacts of community-based risk
    reduction program in, 34, 35*t*
double-handling costs, 226, 271, 274, 275, 388
double or triple wedge analysis, 100
downslope
    concave downslope profile, 179, 180*f*
    drains, 232, 232*f*
drainage design and good practice, xxvii, 213–59
    adapting the MoSSaiC blueprint to existing
        capacity, 216–17
    alignment of drains, 217–29, 219*f*
        calculation of drain flow and dimensions,
            222, 223*f*, 224*t*
        complex topography and difficult access,
            220, 221*f*

        currently active landslide sites, 221–22,
            222*f*
        currently inactive landslide sites, 220–21,
            222*f*
        estimation of house discharge, 226–29
        estimation of main drain dimensions, 227
        estimation of surface water discharge,
            223–26, 225*t*
        idealized alignment, 219–20, 220*f*
        impact of household water, 229, 230*f*
        intercept drain effectiveness, 227–29,
            228–29*f*
        linear drain alignment and easy access,
            220, 220*f*
        patterns and principles, 218–22
    alterations to natural drainage, 181–82, 182*f*
    assignment of maintenance responsibility,
        335–36, 336*f*
    briefing note, 214–15
    capacity, 218
    channel slope, 218
    community-based aspects, 214
    community slope feature map as part of, 167
    connectivity, 218
    drain specifications, 236–42, 240–42*f*, 243*t*
    drain performance, 362, 362*f*
    drain types, 229–36, 231*f*
        downslope drains, 232, 232*f*
        footpath drains, 232–33, 233*f*
        incomplete existing drains, 233–34, 234*f*
        incorporating debris traps, 235–36, 235*f*
        intercept drains, 227–29, 228–29*f*, 231–32,
            231*f*, 389
        placement above landslides to stabilize
            slope, 234, 235*f*
    easy drain maintenance, 215–16, 334–35
    effectiveness of drains, xxv
    gray water management, 216, 246–47, 246*f*.
        See also gray water management
    guiding principles, 215
    household water capture, 218, 242–50, 282–84
        connection to drainage network, 247–48,
            247–49*f*
        hurricane strapping, 249, 250*f*, 389
        rainwater harvesting, 244–47, 245–46*f*
        roof guttering, 242, 244, 244*f*, 282, 283*f*
    importance of good design, 215
    key elements, 213–14
    local designs for concrete drains, catchpits,
        and baffles, 255, 255–59*f*
    locations chosen to reduce landslide hazard, 216
    low-cost drains, 298–301, 389
    proposed drainage plan, 236, 237*f*, 238*t*
    reinforced concrete block drains, 238–39, 239*f*
    risks and challenges, 215–16
    signing off on final drainage plan, 250-51
        community agreement, 251, 252–53*f*
        formal approval, 253
    slope stability and, 107–8
    who does what, 254
    zones for interventions, 203–7
        assigning intervention to each zone, 203,
            205

impact of household water, 229, 230*f*
unauthorized housing, 10, 24, 25*t*, 28, 108, 109*f*, 391
Howell, J., 294
Human Development Index (HDI), 155
hurricanes. *See also* disaster risk
    Hurricane Allen's impact on St. Lucia economy, 40, 41*f. See also* St. Lucia
    Hurricane Mitch debris flows, 151
    Hurricane Tomas over Eastern Caribbean, 103*f*
    risk management components of, 18–19, 18–19*f*
hurricane strapping, 249, 250*f*, 389
hydraulic conductivity, 102, 106, 115, 195*t*
hyperbolic discounting of risk, 7, 313

I
implementation of planned works, xxvii–xxviii, 261–302
    adapting the MoSSaiC blueprint to existing capacity, 266, 267
    briefing note, 262–65
    community-based aspects, 262
    community contracting, 264–65, 264*f*, 265*t*, 388
    debris trap construction, 298–99, 298–300*f*
    drainage construction, 262–63
    good practices, 285–88
        access for residents, 287, 287*f*
        casting concrete in good weather, 285, 286*f*
        inventory control, 287
        reduced leakage from pipes, 288, 288*f*, 289*t*
        secure storage of materials, 287
    guiding principles, 265
    inadequate contractor briefing, 266
    key elements, 261–62
    low-cost appropriate construction methods, 298–301
    on-site requirements, 278–85
        capture of household roof water, 282–84
        channel gradient issues, 280–81, 281*f*
        connection of household water to drains, 284–85, 284–85*f*
        drain effectiveness, 281–82
        drain walls, 281, 282*f*
        excavation and alignment requirements, 279–81, 280*f*
        roof guttering, 282, 283*f*
        site supervision, 278–79, 278–79*f*
        water tank overflows, 285, 286*f*
        weep holes, 281–82, 282*f*
    poor supervision and rushed work, 266
    postconstruction bioengineering, 292–96
        decision aid for choosing technique, 295*t*
        definition of bioengineering, 293, 293*f*
        vegetation's effect on slope stability, 293–94, 294*f*
    practices to be avoided, 288–91, 290*f*, 292*t*
        hazardous access for residents, 291, 291*f*
        questionable or corrupt practices, 300–301
        restricted capacity of footpath drains, 289–90, 291*f*

wasted materials and no surface water capture, 288, 290*f*
    preparation of work packages, 266–73, 391
        bill of quantities, 268–69, 269–70*f*, 269*t*, 387
        compilation of documents, 272–73
        defining work packages, 271–72
        detailed construction specifications, 272, 273*t*
        procurement plan, 272
    processes and good practices, 263–64, 263*f*
    project interruptions, 265–66
    questionable practices, 266
    risks and challenges, 265–66
    signing off on completed works, 291–92
    tendering process, 274–77
        briefing potential contractors, 274–76, 274–76*f*
        evaluating tenders and awarding contracts, 276–77
        identifying contractors, 274
        questionable or corrupt practices, 300–301
        safeguard policies, 277, 277*f*, 277*t*
    who does what, 297
India
    potential applicability of MoSSaiC principles and methods to, 41, 41*f*
    urban infrastructure projects in, 264–65
inspections
    site inspections finding inadequate drainage, 288, 290*f*
    structural inspections and community clean-up days, 336–37, 337*f*
insurance
    Caribbean Catastrophe Risk Insurance Facility, 19
    connecting hazard reduction and, 371–74, 372–73*t*, 372*f*, 376*t*
    disaster risk, 19–20, 19*f*
insured losses, 8*f*, 9*t*,
intercept drains, 227–29, 228–29*f*, 231–32, 231*f*, 389
International Union of Geological Sciences Working Group on Landslides, 13
Italian Istituto di Ricerca per la Protezione Idrogeologica (IRPI), 120
Italy, direct landslide mapping in, 97, 98*f*

J
Janbu, N., 101, 114
Johari Window, 312–13, 313*f*, 317

K
Keefer, D. K., 90
key performance indicators (KPIs), 346, 350, 351, 354, 354–56*t*, 389
Knutson, T. R., 23
Ko Ko, C., 146
Konietzky, H., 106
Kosugi, K., 106
Kunreuther, H., 304

L

laboratory and field measurements, 194
land-locked developing countries, 40
landowners, 73–74, 389
landslide assessment and engineering task team, 68, 68f, 140, 201–2, 202f, 203, 291
landslide hazards, xxv–xxvi, 81–127, 141
  accumulation of risk, 10
  adapting the MoSSaiC blueprint to existing capacity, 85, 86t
  aggravating factors, 93, 94t
  assessment of, xxvi
    community-based mapping for. See community-based mapping
    scientific methods for, 112–18
  briefing note, 82–83
  community-based aspects, 82
  as community issue, 4. See also communities at risk, prioritizing of; community-based approach
  as component of landslide risk, 83
  construction on former landslide zones, 111, 113f
  coupled dynamic hydrology and slope stability models, 113–15
    dynamic hydrology component, 114
    interpreting simulation results, 115
    model configuration, 114
    slope stability component, 114
  defined, 389
  direct landslide mapping, 97–98
  empirical rainfall threshold modeling, 98–99, 99f
  fatalities and losses associated with, 9–10, 10–11f, 23, 83, 87–91, 120, 167–68
  geometry and features of landslides, 87, 88f
  GIS-based susceptibility mapping, 95–96, 97f, 132, 134
  guiding principles, 83–84
  holistic awareness of slope processes, 84–85
  identifying, xxvi, 10–11, 84–85
  instability and. See slope stability
  key elements, 81–82
  lack of awareness of risk, 7
  as management issue, 4
  mapping of. See community-based mapping; mapping
  physically based slope stability modeling, 99–101
  preparatory factors and triggering mechanisms, 87–91, 93, 94t, 102f, 390
  probability, 95
  rainfall and earthquakes, 87–91
  reduction practices, 367–69
  regional policies and, 84
  risks and challenges, 84–85
  science-based approach, 20, 83, 84t, 112–18. See also CHASM (Combined Hydrology and Slope Stability Model)
    resistance envelope method for determining suction control, 116–17, 117f

  small retaining walls, inadequacy of, 117–18, 118f, 122–23, 122f
  seismic events, 89–91, 91f
  slope movement and landslide material, 85–87
  slope stability and. See slope stability
  susceptibility, 95, 96t, 140, 141
  types of landslides, 85–92. See also rotational slides; translational slides
  understanding landslide processes, 82–83
  who does what, 119
landslide risk drivers
  definition of landslide risk, 389
  Eastern Caribbean, 35–36, 40f
  longer term, 370–78
  MoSSaiC targeting, 23–25, 40f
  physical, 22, 26-27
  science-based approach, 28
  urbanization, 2, 10, 23-25, 89, 108, 374
  vulnerability and, 22
Latin America and the Caribbean. See also specific countries
  Caribbean Catastrophe Risk Insurance Facility, 19
  Caribbean regions vulnerable to natural disasters, 36, 41f
  Eastern Caribbean typical communities and risk drivers, 35–36, 40f
  housing density in, 29
  La Red studies of disasters, 9
  MoSSaiC development in, 10–11
    pilots, 35–41, 40t
  rainfall-triggered landslide risk in, 9
learning by doing, xxiii, 169, 307, 314-17, 319, 329, 330t, 339t
lessons learned
  in disaster risk management, xxv
  failure to apply from past disasters, 7
  from World Bank natural disaster projects, 17–18, 17t
limit equilibrium method, 99–101
loading and slope stability, 111–12, 112f
logframe format, 45, 47t
Londell, M. K., 61
low-cost drains, 298–301, 389
Lundgren, R. E., 323

M

macrofinancing disasters, 374, 376f
Mahmoud, M., 377
Malone, E. L., 30
management issue, landslide hazards as, 4. See also government expertise, engaging in risk reduction measures
mapping
  community-based. See community-based mapping
  direct landslide mapping, 97–98
  GIS-based landslide susceptibility mapping, 95–96, 97f, 132, 134, 146–49
  landslide hazard map, 147, 389
  national risk maps, 21
  resolution of maps, 21, 67, 132, 149, 169, 390
  task team, 67, 67f, 140, 159, 178

R

rainfall
    slope stability and, 101–2, 357–58
        assessment of rainfall events, 102
        empirical rainfall threshold modeling. *See*
            rainfall threshold
        triggering landslide disasters and fatalities,
            9–10, 10–11*f*, 23, 83, 87–91, 120, 167–
            68
rainfall threshold, 95, 98–99, 120, 390
rainwater harvesting, 244–47, 245–46*f*
Random Hacks of Kindness event (Washington,
    D.C.), 115
rational method, 223, 224, 225*t*, 227, 228, 390
Rayner, S., 30
records of disasters, 9
regression methods, 96
reporting lines, 74, 75*f*, 390
resilience of structures, 153, 153*f*, 390
resistance envelope method, 116–17, 117*f*, 198, 390
resolution of maps, 21, 67, 132, 149, 169, 390
resource gap, 371. 374, 376*f*
retaining walls, 117–18, 118*f*, 122–23, 122*f*
retrofitting, 244*f*, 247, 249, 390
Richards, I. G., 294
risk, definition of, 11–14, 390
risk drivers. *See* landslide risk drivers
risk management. *See* disaster risk management
    (DRM)
roof guttering, 242, 244, 244*f*, 282, 283*f*
root reinforcement equation, 122
rotational slides, 27, 84*t*, 85, 87, 87*f*, 87*t*, 90*f*, 91, 92,
    108*f*, 100, 108, 137*t*, 158*t*, 190*t*, 204*t*

S

safeguards, 45, 46*t*, 64-5, 73, 74, 136, 205, 215, 231,
    243t, 273t, 277, 300, 391
St. Lucia
    drain construction method in, 240–41, 240–
        41*f*
    economic losses from disasters in, 40
    hurricane damage in, 18–19, 18–19*f*, 40, 41*f*
    hurricane-resistant home improvement
        program, 373, 375*f*
    impacts of community-based risk reduction
        program in, 34, 35*t*
    progressive slides in, 92*f*
    rotational slides in, 90*f*
    translational slides in, 90*f*
"Samaritan's dilemma," 7, 61, 61*t*
Samoa, economic losses in disasters in, 40
San Salvador and coping with disasters, 29–30
scale of maps and plans, 391. *See also* community-
    based mapping
science-based landslide risk assessment, xxi, 4*f*,
    20–21, 26–29, 26*t*, 27*f*
    anthropogenic contributors to risk, 27–28, 28*f*
    landslide hazard, 112–18
    in landslide risk management, 20, 83, 84*t*
    local risk drivers, 28
    mapping for. *See* community-based mapping
scientific and professional publications, 328–29

seepage zones, 181, 181*f*
seismic events, 89–91, 91*f*
septic waste, 182, 226, 242
Shakoor, A., 95
shallow landsliding model (SHALSTAB), 150
Sharma, R. H., 106
shear box, 94*t*, 106*f* 107, 194, 195, 199
shear strength, 99–100, 114, 120, 391
shear surface. *See* slip surface
show homes, 321–23, 322*f*, 322*t*
site supervision, 278–79, 278–79*f*, 291
situational factors
    as barriers to landslide mitigation measures,
        6–7
    as determinants of vulnerability, 12
slip surface, 99
slope angle, 103–4, 104*f*, 144*t*, 181
slope drainage. *See* drainage design and good
    practice
slope hydrology, 88–89, 107–8
slope instability classification, 87*t*
slope stability
    calculations, 100, 100*f*
    CHASM. *See* CHASM (Combined Hydrology
        and Slope Stability Model)
    community-based mapping, 178–88. *See also*
        community-based mapping
    continuum and discrete element models, 101
    direct landslide mapping, 97–98
    GIS-based landslide susceptibility mapping,
        95–96, 97*f*, 132, 134, 146–49
    loading, 111–12, 112*f*
    material types and properties, 104-7
        hydrological properties, 105–7, 106*f*
        geotechnical properties, 99-101, 105. 117,
            120
        soil formation, 104, 105*f*
        weathering and strength, 104–5, 106*f*
    medium-term performance, 355–57
    models, 134, 194–98, 195*t*
    observed slope stability, 355–57, 356*f*, 356*t*
    over time, 91–92, 92*t*
    overview of assessment methods, 93–95, 94*t*
    physically based modeling, 99–101
    postfailure, 92, 93*f*
    processes and their assessment, 93–101, 94*t*
    project evaluation, 357–58
    rainfall and, 101–2
        empirical rainfall threshold modeling,
            98–99
    slope angle and, 103–4, 104*f*, 144*t*, 181
    slope hydrology and drainage, 100–101, 107–8,
        107–8*f*
    urban slope drainage, 108
    variables, 101–12
    vegetation and, 108–11, 110*f*, 110*t*, 114–15
slums. *See* urbanization
small island developing states (SIDS), 8, 36, 40
social funds, role of, 21–23, 22*f*
socioeconomic vulnerability, 12, 151–52, 155–56,
    156*t*
soil parameters. *See also* cohesion; angle of
    internal friction.

Mohr-Coulomb equation for soil shear
strength, 114, 120
slope stability, 104, 105*f*
uncertainty in, 199–200, 200*f*
Sotir, R. B., 294
Southeast Asia, rainfall-triggered landslide risk
in, 9
Spector, S., 42
squatter housing, 391
Sri Lanka, urban infrastructure projects in,
264–65
Stability Index Mapping (SINMAP) model, 150
stakeholders, 44, 44*t*, 308, 312–14, 391. *See
also* communication; community
engagement
statistical methods, 149–50
strategic incrementalism, 368-69, 369*f*, 391
supervision. *See* site supervision
surface and subsurface water, 29, 89*f*, 360–62. *See
also* drainage design and good practice;
gray water management
estimation of surface water discharge, 223–26
susceptibility, 95, 96*t*, 140–51, 142*t*
defined, 389
GIS-based landslide susceptibility mapping,
95–96, 97*f*, 98*f*, 132, 134, 146–49
hazard assessment methods, 140–51, 142*t*
sustainability of MoSSaiC projects, xxii–xxiii, 64
Svekla, W., 29

T
Tarboton, D. G., 150
Task teams. *See* advocacy task team;
communications task team; community
liaison task team; community task teams;
government task teams; landslide assessment
and engineering task team;
mapping team; technical support task team
technical support task team, 69, 69*f*, 140
Tegucigalpa, Honduras, debris flow hazard in,
150–51, 150*f*
temporal vulnerability, 12
threshold modeling, 98–99, 99*f*
tolerable risk, 391
top-down approach, 25
balancing with bottom-up approach, 61–62
negative aspects of, 17
topography
alignment of drains in complex topography,
220, 221*f*
convergence zones, 179-80*f*
mapping features, 169, 179, 179–80*f*
slope reconnaissance form, 144*t*
translational slides, 27, 84*t*, 85–86, 87*f*, 87*t*, 90*f*,
100, 132, 137*t*, 158*t*, 190*t*, 204*t*
triggering events, 135*t*, 391. *See also* rainfall
Twigg, J., 21, 366

U
"unacceptable risk," 391. *See also* "acceptable risk"
unauthorized housing. *See* housing
uncertainty

in model formulation, 200–201
in physically based landslide hazard
assessment, 199–200
in soil parameters, 199–200, 200*f*
risk perception and, 313–14
United Nations
capacity assessment methodologies of UNDP,
60
on culture and community interests as
elements of project success, 172
disaster response organizational framework,
16*f*
Economic and Social Council's definition of
gender mainstreaming, 173
"Global Assessment Report on Disaster Risk
Reduction," 80
Human Development Index (HDI), 155
International Strategy for Disaster Reduction,
23
risk assessment recommendations from,
20–21
UNICEF on behavioral change process in
Community-based Disaster Risk
Reduction, 309
on vulnerability of Eastern Caribbean, 36, 40
University of Wollongong, Australia, example of
field reconnaissance and hazard ranking
methods, 145–46
urbanization, 23–25, 24*f*, 374
slope drainage and, 108, 109*f*
vegetation and slope management, 294–96,
296*f*
U.S. Federal Highway Administration, example of
field reconnaissance and hazard ranking
methods, 146
Useem, M., 304
user groups, 75–76, 75*f*, 333–34, 334*f*

V
Varnes, D. J., 85, 91
value for money, in projects. *See* project evaluation
vegetation
restricting alignment of drains, 220, 221*f*
slope stability and, 108–11, 110–11*f*, 110*t*, 114–15,
144*t*, 293–94, 294*f*
urban slope management and, 294–96, 296*f*
Venture Philanthropy Partners, 60
Victoria, Lorna P., 164
vulnerability
of community to landslides, 151–56, 391.
See also communities at risk,
prioritizing of
defined, 12, 83, 391
drivers of landslide risk, 22
unauthorized housing, 24, 25*t*

W
Wamsler, C., 16, 212
weathering features, 104–5, 106*f*, 179–80, 180*f*, 391
Wharton School of the University of
Pennsylvania, 18
wide-area landslide hazard mapping, 21, 167

Wilkinson, P. L., 114, 120, 294
women. *See* gender relations
work packages. *See* preparation of work packages
World Bank
    assessment of economic impact of natural
        disasters, 36
    on communication campaigns, 317
    on housing tenure in low-income countries, 24

Making Services Work for Poor People, 344
natural disaster projects, 17, 17*t*
Safeguard Policies, 45
World Development Report's overview of
    MoSSaiC, 25–26

Y

Yunus, M., xxix

www.ingramcontent.com/pod-product-compliance
Lightning Source LLC
Chambersburg PA
CBHW080409270326
41929CB00018B/2963

* 9 7 8 0 8 2 1 3 9 4 5 6 4 *